T0371593

JAN TINBERGEN (1903-1994) AND THE RISE
OF ECONOMIC EXPERTISE

Jan Tinbergen was the first Nobel Prize Winner in Economics and one of the most influential economists of the 20th century. This book argues that his crucial contribution is his theory of economic policy and the legitimation of economic expertise in service of the state. It traces his youthful socialist ideals, which found political direction in the Plan-socialist movement of the 1930s, new economic models to combat the Great Depression. After World War II he was able to synthesize that work into a theory of economic policy which not only provided a lasting framework for economic policy around the world, but also secured a permanent place for economic experts close to government. The book then turns to an examination of his attempt to repeat this achievement in the development projects in the Global South and at the international level for the United Nations.

Erwin Dekker is Assistant Professor of Cultural Economics at Erasmus University Rotterdam. He is the author of *The Viennese Students of Civilization* (Cambridge University Press, 2016), which won the award for Best Book in Austrian Economics.

HISTORICAL PERSPECTIVES ON MODERN ECONOMICS

Series Editor: Professor Harro Maas, Walras-Pareto Centre for the History of Economic and Political Thought, University of Lausanne

This series contains original works that challenge and enlighten historians of economics. For the profession as a whole, it promotes better understanding of the origin and content of modern economics

Other books in the series:

Jeff E. Biddle, *Progression through Regression* (2020)

Erwin Dekker, *The Viennese Students of Civilization* (2016)

Steven G. Medema, Anthony M.C. Waterman (eds.), *Paul Samuelson on the History of Economic Analysis: Selected Essays* (2014)

Floris Heukelom, *Behavioral Economics: A History* (2014)

Roger E. Backhouse, Mauro Boianovsky, *Transforming Modern Macroeconomics: Exploring Disequilibrium Microfoundations, 1956–2003* (2013)

Susan Howson, *Lionel Robbins* (2012)

Robert Van Horn, Philip Mirowski, Thomas A. Stapleford (eds.), *Building Chicago Economics: New Perspectives on the History of America's Most Powerful Economics Program* (2012)

Arie Arnon, *Monetary Theory and Policy from Hume and Smith to Wicksell: Money, Credit, and the Economy* (2011)

Malcolm Rutherford, *The Institutionalist Movement in American Economics, 1918–1947: Science and Social Control* (2011)

Samuel Hollander, *Friedrich Engels and Marxian Political Economy* (2011)

Robert Leonard, *Von Neumann, Morgenstern, and the Creation of Game Theory: From Chess to Social Science, 1900–1960* (2010)

Simon J. Cook, *The Intellectual Foundations of Alfred Marshall's Economic Science: A Rounded Globe of Knowledge* (2009)

Continued after the Index

Jan Tinbergen (1903–1994) and the Rise of Economic Expertise

ERWIN DEKKER

Erasmus University Rotterdam

CAMBRIDGE
UNIVERSITY PRESS

University Printing House, Cambridge CB2 8BS, United Kingdom

One Liberty Plaza, 20th Floor, New York, NY 10006, USA

477 Williamstown Road, Port Melbourne, VIC 3207, Australia

314–321, 3rd Floor, Plot 3, Splendor Forum, Jasola District Centre, New Delhi – 110025, India

103 Penang Road, #05-06/07, Visioncrest Commercial, Singapore 238467

Cambridge University Press is part of the University of Cambridge.

It furthers the University's mission by disseminating knowledge in the pursuit of education, learning, and research at the highest international levels of excellence.

www.cambridge.org
Information on this title: www.cambridge.org/9781108495998
DOI: 10.1017/9781108856546

© Erwin Dekker 2021

First published 2021

Printed in the United Kingdom by TJ Books Limited, Padstow Cornwall

A catalogue record for this publication is available from the British Library.

Library of Congress Cataloging-in-Publication Data
Names: Dekker, Erwin, 1984– author.
Title: Jan Tinbergen (1903–1994) and the rise of economic expertise / Erwin Dekker, Erasmus University Rotterdam.
Description: New York : Cambridge University Press, 2021. | Series: Historical perspectives on modern economics | Includes bibliographical references and index.
Identifiers: LCCN 2021012013 (print) | LCCN 2021012014 (ebook) | ISBN 9781108495998 (hardback) | ISBN 9781108811385 (paperback) | ISBN 9781108856546 (epub)
Subjects: LCSH: Tinbergen, Jan, 1903-1994. | Economists–Netherlands–Biography. | Economic history–1945- | BISAC: BUSINESS & ECONOMICS / Economics / General | BUSINESS & ECONOMICS / Economics / General
Classification: LCC HC322.5.J36 D45 2021 (print) | LCC HC322.5.J36 (ebook) | DDC 330.092 [B]–dc23
LC record available at https://lccn.loc.gov/2021012013
LC ebook record available at https://lccn.loc.gov/2021012014

ISBN 978-1-108-49599-8 Hardback

Ja, mach nur einen Plan
Sei nur ein großes Licht!
Und mach dann noch'nen zweiten Plan
Geh'n tun sie beide nicht.
Denn für dieses Leben
Ist der Mensch nicht schlau genug,
Doch sein höhres Streben
Ist ein schöner Zug.

—Bertolt Brecht

No act of man can claim to be more than an attempt, not even science.

—Karl Barth

Contents

List of Figures/Tables

Figures

Tables

Preface

Economists are, in our day and age, best known as policy experts. This book is about one of them, Jan Tinbergen. He paved the way for this new type of economist. The economic expert is a government functionary, who works in service of the economic and social goals of government. The rise of the economic expert was intimately connected with a change in what was considered the most valuable sort of economic knowledge. For the expert, an economy is not a natural system he studies as a physicist would, but a system that he can steer – and improve. The rise of expertise also gave birth to new types of institutions: business-cycle institutes, planning offices, forecasting bureaus, and international organizations of economic expertise.

Economists have, of course, always been concerned with policy. From (free) trade regimes, the best way to manage the currency, and the role of the state in the provision of public goods, policy questions have never been far from the minds of economists. But they typically did so in their roles as professors and public intellectuals. Economists since Adam Smith, and undoubtedly before him, have played an important role in shaping the thought of both politicians and the public about markets and trade, and the proper functions of the state. They often also had the ear of those in charge. The most famous economist of the past century, John Maynard Keynes, had the ear of the politicians in Britain of his age, and his ideas had influence across the world. And it is often recounted how important the ideas of Friedrich Hayek were for Margaret Thatcher, who carried his book in her hand bag. But the authority of both Keynes and Hayek was based on their personal standing, their personal reputation, not because of the techniques they mastered or their official government position. That is different for Tinbergen, who will not be remembered for his contributions to economic theory, proper. But he should be remembered for designing the way that economic policy is done. Keynes and Hayek will be remembered for their economic ideas; Tinbergen should be remembered as the most important economic "bureaucrat" of the twentieth century.

That might sound boring: Who wants to read a book about a bureaucrat? Ideas have more charm, but ideas go in and out of fashion. What has remained far more stable since the middle of the twentieth century is the position of economic experts, and more generally the position of expertise in the modern state. If we want to understand this rise of the expert, we should be willing to look beyond the originators of economic ideas, and to economist experts and policymakers like Jan Tinbergen.

He in fact stands in a longer tradition: economists have more often worked quite directly for those in power. François Quesnay, one of the important economists before Adam Smith, worked at the Court of Louis XV. In Germany, there is a famous intellectual tradition in which economics is part of a broader field of knowledge known as *Kameralwissenschaften*. The *Kameralwissenschaften* were defined as those parts of science that were required to work at the court. Around 1900 that term had changed to *Staatswissenschaften*, but the idea remained similar: the knowledge relevant to govern the state. It is in this tradition that Tinbergen worked. From his earliest work on business-cycle statistics to his work on econometric models, and then on development planning, he was concerned with questions of governance. One of his later books was called *Can We Govern the Planet?*, a question with a philosophical connotation, but for Tinbergen it was a question about governance. Can we design our global governance institutions so that those in power can *govern* the planet and its climate?

If we are willing to look beyond the ideas, we discover that from central banks to the IMF, and from government advisory boards to antitrust agencies, economic experts are very prominent. Occasionally, the experts even come into power, then we call it a technocracy. But the ideal position of the expert is not on the throne, but right next to it. Not as visible to the public, and unlikely to be the subject of political controversy, but no less influential because of it. The proper position of the expert was in fact one of the major concerns of Tinbergen. He was active in the design of expert institutes on economic policy, and their proper position in relation to government, parliament, and the public. In his home country, the Netherlands, he quite literally created a position for the economic expert. But his aspirations were global, as was expressed in one of his most famous reports, *Reshaping the International Order*. Much of that reshaping was about creating better institutions for governance and an improved position for expertise at the international level.

Underlying Tinbergen's work on governance is a more fundamental, hopeful idea that we, as humans, can direct our own fate. He scoffed at the idea that we could predict the future using economic forecasting tools. We had to take the reins and direct the economy in the desired direction. Planning, for him, above all else, meant setting goals and finding rational means to reach those goals. The Dutch and German languages have a beautiful word to describe that perspective, *Machbarkeit* or *Maakbaarheid*: the ability to construct or shape the social world. Modern economic expertise is built on this foundational belief, that with rational policy instruments we can achieve our goals. It was Tinbergen who gave us the language of policy instruments and targets.

Perhaps the most surprising part of the story of Jan Tinbergen is that these goals were pursued by one of the greatest idealists the economics profession has ever known. He was a pacifist, an internationalist socialist, co-founder of Novib (later part of OXFAM-Novib), lifelong party member, and admirer of Gandhi, who until late in life addressed his friends as "comrade" (*partijgenoot*). His work in service of many national governments around the world, and international organizations like the League of Nations and the United Nations, had to lead to serious tensions, and it did.

A biographical approach has the virtue of making us aware of the contingencies and failed ambitions. Tinbergen's own ideals extended far beyond the foundation of economic expertise, to economic justice, global equality, and most of all social peace. His religious background and socialist youth instilled an appreciation for culture in him and made him suspicious of materialism, a curiosity for an economist pursuing growth goals in much of his work. He grew up in The Hague not far from the Peace Palace and from a young age was a pacifist, but his economic work for governments brought him in contact with General de Gaulle (France), General Franco (Spain), and the German occupiers during WWII; in Turkey and Indonesia, he even secured his advisory position in the aftermath of a military coup. At other times, science could not quite deliver what he hoped for. His lifelong search for the definition and measurement of economic justice never succeeded. His famous models never brought the certainty and rigor that he sought but were successful pragmatic tools. This book is about the deep tensions between the three elements that made up Tinbergen's life: the pursuit of scientific economics, the transformation of economic knowledge into expertise to improve governance both nationally and internationally, and his pursuit of social and global peace.

Acknowledgments

Only a few months after I started my research into Jan Tinbergen, I joined a wonderful course by Hans Renders at his Biography Institute in Groningen, whose guidance helped me in connecting person and work. My own approach has been the other way around, to connect the work of Tinbergen to his personal beliefs, ideals, and lifestyle. Economics is a discipline about human beings by human beings, "humanomics," as Deirdre McCloskey never tires of stressing. I see this biography as a contribution to that project.

The conversations with Tinbergen's daughter Els Barendrecht and her late husband Maurits revealed much about him as a family man. I will never forget the warmth with which Hanneke and Els touched the bust of Tinbergen when it was revealed at the celebration of the fiftieth anniversary of his Nobel Prize in Economics. They could touch his hair, once more. I hope this book reveals a bit more about what their father was doing when he was away from home. Wilfred van Peski inspired and connected. Caecilia van Peski encouraged and intrigued. Peter Cornelisse, one of his more critical *and* loyal students, was an amazing support throughout the process. His patience and trust generated insight and gave me the courage to develop a more critical perspective.

Marcel Boumans, Roger Backhouse, and Mary Morgan formed the dream team of historians of economics who oversaw the project from a distance. They corrected me where needed, but most of all encouraged me to write my own story about Tinbergen, however different that would be from theirs. Marcel, to my surpise, endorsed the epigraph of Bertolt Brecht. Arjo Klamer's official role as supervisor is over, but he was still close, and his influence is visible throughout. Jack Vromen, Conrad Heilmann, and the other colleagues at EIPE provided a stimulating and hospitable academic home and have already ensured that the Tinbergen project will continue.

Philip Hans Franses and Ronald Groot at the Erasmus School of Economics made the project possible and showed me what academic professionalism is. All of them together, joined by Ivan Boldyrev and Peter Rodenburg, created an unforgettable academic memory when we discussed the first half of my manuscript in February 2019.

Pete Boettke had the wisdom to advise me to take up the project, even when it meant less time for Austrian economics. But I am sure he will find many unexpected connections in this book. Stefan Kolev was there all along as friend. Our endless conversations about ordo-liberalism and thinking-in-orders shaped this book and my interpretation of Tinbergen. Not econometrics, but economic order is Tinbergen's major field. Because of him, Max Weber is in the final paragraph. Pavel Kuchař, Carolina Dalla Chiesa, Blaž Remic, and Julien Gradoz made sure I also kept writing, and talking, about things other than Tinbergen. That was important.

Emre Demirkiran and Ali Somel made the chapter about Tinbergen in Turkey possible with extreme generosity. Max Ehrenfreund saved me a trip to Geneva by his immaculate work in the League of Nations archive and was a great sparring partner for the correct interpretation of Tinbergen's work there. Bernard van Praag and Thomas Cool provided important context and material for the chapter on measurement. Karthik Raghavan read the whole manuscript and provided invaluable editing suggestions. *Vasudhaiva Kutumbakam.*

Tinbergen's former students were invariably helpful in providing help and sharing stories. Jasper Lukkezen made sure that Tinbergen's legacy would be passed on to the next generation of Dutch economists. His efforts and the Tinbergen events at the SER, CPB, the Dutch Central Bank, and the Ministry of Economic Affairs demonstrated to me what parts of his legacy were still alive, and which parts were in need of renewed attention. My work was greatly helped by the near-complete bibliography that Kees van Opijnen and Jacob Kol prepared in 2003. Pieter van Leeuwen provided the best access possible, under the circumstances, to Tinbergen's archives.

The community of historians of economics and science was a kind and helpful audience for the many, many draft chapters I presented. There are too many to name them all, but I must mention some: Ariane Dupont-Kieffer, Juan Acosta, Erich Pinzón-Fuchs, Hans-Michael Trautwein, Kevin Hoover, Beatrice Cherrier, Andrej Svorenčík, James Morrison, Quinn Slobodian, Henk Don, Bert Tieben, Raphaël Fèvre, and Harald Hagemann. Harro Maas dared to ask for more, when that was most needed.

But this book was made possible, first and foremost, by the support and sacrifice of those closest to me. Katinka recognized my passion and made space for it. Eline is now taking over her role in making sure daddy spends enough time away from work. Madee is already showing signs of my absentmindedness, or, should we say, "concentration." Harm passed away, but we will make sure the book will be added to his library. Ruben joined the family right in the middle of the writing process. They will forever be connected to it.

PART I

BECOMING AN ECONOMIC EXPERT

1

The Construction of Peace

> In the final analysis, our world is ruled by ideas – rational and ethical – and not
> by vested interests. The power of the idea, the particular weapon of scientists,
> moralists and concerned citizens, must prove of decisive importance in
> constructing a fairer and more peaceful world.[1]
> —Jan Tinbergen

If every thinker is ultimately a local thinker, our Tinbergen story must start in The Hague. It was in April 1903, the month of Jan Tinbergen's birth, that Andrew Carnegie ordered his banker to send the sum of $1.5 million to a representative of the Dutch government. It was a gift intended for the construction of a Peace Palace, or in Dutch, the Vredespaleis. The Peace Palace was only a small walk across the park from Tinbergen's parental home. The Palace opened the year that Jan turned ten, 1913. Its construction had taken seven long years (Figure 1.1). But it turned The Hague into "the capital of the United States of the World," as one, perhaps overly enthusiastic, commentator wrote.

1.1 High Hopes

The Vredespaleis was the crowning achievement of a series of events in The Hague that slowly transformed it into a center of global affairs, something it remains to this day. Currently, the city is home to the International Court of Justice, as well as the International Criminal Court and a host of other international legal organizations and United Nations offices. This history of The Hague as an international city starts in the late nineteenth century, when after a successful international

[1] Tinbergen, *Reshaping the International Order: A Report to the Club of Rome*, 107, 1976.

Figure 1.1 The Peace Palace under construction in The Hague, 1911.

conference on private law in 1893, The Hague was chosen as the location
of the first Peace Conference in 1899. The initiative for this new type of
international conference was taken by one of the least likely candidates,
a representative of the final generation of imperialists, Tsar Nicolas II of
Russia. He had extended invitations to all European countries, the United
States, and Mexico as well as four Asian countries: Japan, Siam, Persia, and
China. To everyone's surprise, all countries accepted.

The 1899 conference lasted two whole months, was held in the royal
Huis ten Bosch, and was presided over by the Dutch Queen, Wilhelmina.

The imperial leaders of Germany and the United Kingdom were skeptical of the whole undertaking and suspicious about the true political goals of the Tsar. But the burgeoning pacifist movement saw the conference and its official aims as an enormous opportunity. Under the spiritual guidance of Bertha von Suttner, whose novel *Lay Down Your Arms* of 1889 marked an important milestone in the pacifist movement, they put serious pressure on the gathered officials. Diplomatically, the conference proved a great success and resulted in the first multilateral agreement of its kind, an agreement that included the founding of the International Court of Arbitrage, which for the first decade of its existence was housed in the city center of The Hague. This supranational court could arbitrate in international conflicts through binding rulings, although the involved countries had to accept that the case be brought before the Court. But the pacifist movement was deeply disappointed that the first conference made no significant steps in the direction of its most important aim: disarmament.

Another, unintended, consequence was that the 1899 conference brought many social organizations, intellectuals, and journalists of a pacifist bent from all over the world to The Hague.[2] The delegates of various countries, some of them idealistic politicians, were quite willing to listen to the peace activists gathered in the city. In particular, the American delegates were impressed with the spirit surrounding the conference. Two among them, Frederic W. Holls and Andrew White, would encourage their friend Andrew Carnegie in the following years to support the cause of international peace. Carnegie, who had a particular fondness for libraries, of which he funded no fewer than 3,000 in his life, was soon convinced that he could help finance a comprehensive library on international law. But Holls and White were out for more than just a library, and in the end persuaded Carnegie that something bigger than a library was possible. This resulted in the plan to build a center that would house both the library and the international court. It was for this purpose that Carnegie transferred the $1.5 million in 1903. After much deliberation, an architectural design was agreed on in 1907, the same year that the second international Peace Conference was held, this time in the geographical heart of Dutch politics and the seat of the Dutch parliament, the Binnenhof. During this four-month conference there was a ceremony for the official laying of the first stone.[3]

---

[2] Sluga, *Internationalism in the Age of Nationalism*, 2013.
[3] Eyffinger and Hengst, *Het Vredespaleis*, 1988.

It would take another six years before the Vredespaleis was officially opened. On the opening of the Vredespaleis, the Dutch society "Peace through Law" (Vrede door Recht) described the Peace Palace as "the symbol of the near future, in which international law rules, and thereby simultaneously serves the interests of all peoples."[4] The German legal professor Walter Schücking described it as "a new age in world history, *the age of the organization of the World*."[5] They were lofty words written in an age in which violent international conflict was the norm, and in all honesty that would remain so for the next few decades. Yet in the eyes of many of the age, the Vredespaleis was a symbol not just of the increased economic integration of the world in the years leading up to World War I – what has been called the first wave of globalization – but also of the growing sense that the twentieth century required a different world order than the nineteenth-century empires. For the enthusiasts, the Peace Temple, as they sometimes called it, symbolized the increased rationality in international politics that would one day lead to a world without war.

1.2 Naïve Utopianism

The Vredespaleis came about as a combination of state initiative, private philanthropy, and civil society activism; Tsar Nicolas II, the most old-fashioned Imperial leader, had brought the states together; Andrew Carnegie, the steel magnate, had donated the money; and its realization reflected both the emergence and the activism of an international civil society.

It is hard, however, to look at this new spirt of international collaboration without a healthy dose of skepticism. Just after the 1899 conference concluded, the second Boer War broke out in South Africa, a typical imperial conflict. And over the coming decade a variety of international conflicts continued to plague both Europe and Asia. The new International Court of Arbitrage handled four cases during the period between the first and the second Peace Conference, and eight more before World War I broke out. It was a mere fraction of the number of international conflicts of the period. It did not take long after the opening before satirical postcards appeared that declared the bankruptcy of the Vredespaleis and offered it to the highest bidder (Figure 1.2). The postcards were inspired by

[4] Algemeene Nederlandsche Bond "Vrede door Recht," *Het Vredespaleis Gedenkboek: Ten dage van de Plechtige Opening op 28 Augustus 1913*, v, 1913.
[5] Algemeene Nederlandsche Bond "Vrede door Recht," 62. Emphasis in original.

's Gravenhage   Vredespaleis
Te huur of te koop
wegens faillissement
Geschikt voor Kazerne of Bios-
coop. Van alle gemakken voorzien
Electrisch licht, Waterleiding enz.
Brieven onder letter C
aan den Vredesengel.

Figure 1.2 Satirical postcard that suggested the Peace Palace was bankrupt, and could be repurposed as cinema. Interested bidders could address their letters to the Angel of Peace, C. (for Carnegie).

a short play written by the Herman Heijermans in which the main character was an auctioneer who tries to sell this "gentleman's home," but to no avail: "[N]obody wants it, so now we're stuck with it."

Politically too, there were disappointments. Attempts at the Second Conference to make the use of the International Court of Arbitrage obligatory in the case of an international conflict failed because it was opposed by some of the imperial powers. The conferences certainly had not measured up to the expectations of those in the pacifist movement. But this did not prevent the movement from gaining more momentum. Bertha von Suttner had been in contact with Alfred Nobel, and that might have been one of the reasons why the Nobel Prizes included one for peace. She was the first female laureate in 1905.

Even so, peace movement did not find widespread acceptance. From the socialist side many mocking voices could be heard about the Peace Conference between the imperial powers, and the hopes for peace under imperial capitalism more generally. For them it was clear that only a more fundamental overhaul of the capitalist system with its imperialist tendencies could bring about peace. It was thus not hard to simply dismiss the Vredespaleis as at best a naïve Utopian project, and perhaps nothing more than a plaything of the rich and powerful. Even its opening had missed much of the international allure of the previous conferences: Andrew Carnegie and the Dutch Royal Family were present, as were a host of international law professors, but few foreign governments had sent a delegation.[6] It seemed that The Hague was indeed stuck with the Vredespaleis.

If a skeptic wanted any evidence that the Vredespaleis project was little more than a cover-up for imperialist aspirations, they only had to point to its design. Andrew Carnegie had requested that the architectural design contest should be open, but the committee that oversaw the competition consisted of relatively conservative architectural experts who insisted that designs be solicited from a list of renowned architects (who also would receive a higher fee if their design won). When the jury announced the winner, Louis Cordonnier, an able but conservative architect who had submitted an almost baroque proposal, there was a general outcry in the press. The general opinion was that the Vredespaleis deserved an architectural design that fitted its aspirational, forward-looking spirit.

There had been several progressive submissions, such as those of Otto Wagner, the Viennese avant-garde architect, and the even more daring futuristic design of Eero Saarinen, a Finnish architect, which enjoyed the admiration of a few jury members. Instead, the winning design was by an architect of one of the imperial powers on the world stage, in a style that reflected Old World grandeur. It symbolized the tension at the heart of the whole endeavor: Were the old imperial powers trying to accommodate some of the social pressure through this whole project, or did they really aspire to the construction of a new type of world order?

It was a question that could also be asked about the Peace Conferences themselves. Were they not merely a continuation by the Great Powers to maintain and strengthen existing power positions? Or did they reflect the start of a new era in international politics? Were the peace conferences merely a modern version of an old tune, the final symphonies of the Concert of Europe? Or did they represent a new type of music altogether?

1.3 Tinbergen's The Hague

To many the answer was clear as day: of course, this building and not just its architecture was nothing more than a façade. But it is unlikely that

---

[6] Joor, "The Way of the Law above the Way of Violence," 2013.

Tinbergen would have seen it like that. Tinbergen worked in the realm of possibilities. To him, though the peace palace did not lead to disarmament or world peace, it still embodied a vision, a hope for a better future. Although it might not have been the bringer of peace, it was certainly a model of what the world could become. It was this perspective that would become central in Tinbergen's work. His perspective was idealistic and often ignored whether something was politically feasible in the short run. He preferred to offer a vision that could guide present efforts and give a sense of direction. Even his famous mathematical models of the economy, which were designed to be practically useful, offered not primarily a description of what the world already was, or what it would become if current trends persisted, but rather what the world could become. The Peace Palace, if anything, symbolized possibilities, not realities.

And in its favor, the location was not badly chosen at all. After all, The Hague is the seat of the government of the Netherlands, a small open country that owes its existence to successful (and peaceful) relations with its much bigger neighbors. It is now considered a natural home for international institutions. Much like Geneva in Switzerland or Brussels in Belgium, it is a medium-sized city in a small country, which is acutely aware of the dangers and costs of international conflict. As centers of governance of small nations, they have much to gain from international cooperation, if only because much of what they seek to realize cannot happen without the cooperation of other nations. Or to put that sentiment into the language of power politics, it is unlikely that the Netherlands, Belgium, and Switzerland could ever exert much direct influence over its large neighbors. Economically, too, these cities and their host countries are completely dependent on trade with the rest of the world, and trade requires friendly relationships and preferably open trading routes. It was no coincidence that Hugo Grotius, the great legal scholar of international maritime law, was a Dutchman.

Cities like The Hague, and countries like the Netherlands, Switzerland, and Belgium often present themselves as neutral places that can act as arbiters in the international context. The three countries all have a long history of political neutrality. The Hague, moreover, is located close to the sea and is hence well connected to the rest of the world. As if to symbolize this connection, the Vredespaleis was built on the Scheveningsestraat, a street originally designed by Christiaan Huygens, the seventeenth-century natural scientist. It connects The Hague to Scheveningen, a small fishing and beach town, and the connection of The Hague to the sea and the rest of the world.

What is more, the Netherlands shares with Switzerland an interesting history of decentralization of power within a common structure, a history that in the Netherlands goes back to the days of the Dutch Republic of the Seven Provinces, founded in 1579. It is this type of federalism, decentralization within a common overarching structure, which was held up by the peace movement of 1900 as a model for world governance. It was not a world government that was their goal, but instead a shared legal (infra) structure, within which nation-states could retain (most of) their sovereignty. It was intent not on breaking the power of the nation-state, or even that of the Empires, but on the creation of a small set of shared rules for international security. It was a similar model that Tinbergen would uphold in 1945, and the same model that inspired the World Federalist Movement of which he was an active member until his death in 1994. It is not a federalism in which all local sovereignty is lost, and the world becomes one, but instead a decentralized form of governance within a federalist structure. That structure would provide a set of general rules to which all countries were bound.

For the pacifists of 1900 it was believed that the law, or rather, international law, could provide this kind of ordering, and to this day The Hague is known as the city of international law. Their slogan was "Peace through Law." The intellectual symbol for this Dutch tradition is Hugo de Groot, or Grotius. His seventeenth-century works were some of the first that considered the possibility of international law, especially international law at sea, efforts in which he was joined by Cornelis van Bijnkershoek (who died in The Hague). A statue of Grotius was installed in the Vredespaleis to mark that this endeavor was to be a continuation of his project of international law. The Hague, not otherwise known as a great intellectual center (it is the largest city in the Netherlands without a university), was enriched by the library of international law. It is this tradition that was continued in the International Institute of Social Studies in The Hague, aimed at international cooperation and founded in 1952; from its start Tinbergen was deeply engaged with it.

Jan Tinbergen is now often remembered for his work in econometrics and as a pioneer in the practice of modeling in economics. But that is to miss the greater significance of his work, and most importantly his own aspirations. It is remarkable how many of the features that characterize The Hague – the internationalism and the focus on legal order as well as governance – are central to Tinbergen's work and life. For starters, he was a lifelong proponent of international organizations and he worked for many of them, including the League of Nations and the United Nations. And although it is undeniable that he was a quantitative economist who lived by Kelvin's dictum that "if one cannot measure something, our knowledge of it is only meagre and unsatisfactory," it is surprising how much of his work is about institutional and policy design. His deep institutional awareness stands out in the modern discipline of economics, which has typically treated them as background material. The idea that in order for an economy to function it has to be ordered is central to Tinbergen's work but strangely absent from most reflections on his work.

This omission has also meant that the literature on Tinbergen has too easily accepted the idea that took firm root after he won the first Nobel Prize in Economics, that he was one of the founders of the field. It is undeniable that he was one of the pioneers of econometrics, the combination of measurement, modeling, and economic theory that is the foundation of macroeconomic models to this day. But Tinbergen continued a nineteenth-century tradition of economics, which believed that it was one of the sciences in service of the state. This was directly at odds with the dominant trend of the time, which had started with the marginal revolution, which sought to turn economics into an autonomous scientific discipline, modeled after physics.

Not only did Tinbergen work in service of the state at the bureau of statistics, the planning bureau, and at various international political organizations. He also made sure that the knowledge he produced could be used by the modern state, in particular, in expert organizations that advised governments. His approach is far more deeply rooted in the nineteenth century and the German tradition of *Kameralwissenschaften* and *Staatswissenschaften* than is often acknowledged. And it was therefore no coincidence that during his long career he was often caught between his own ideals and the political goals of the governments he was serving. He hoped that the modern scientific methods he promoted for the design of policy represented a way to rationalize politics, and the state more generally. But there was always the danger that these same methods were used for quite different purposes: the continuation of conflict and imperialism as it had been practiced in the nineteenth century. This was perhaps nowhere more evident than in his work on development economics where he was constantly caught between international power politics and his own efforts to improve the economic situation in the underdeveloped parts of the world.

1.4 The Organization of Peace and Economic Prosperity

Tinbergen's work points the way forward to modern economics in which both model-building and quantitative economics in the form of econometrics are central, but it also represents an older legal understanding of the economy. In that legal understanding the crucial distinction is not between equilibrium and disequilibrium or growth and a recession as it is in economics, but rather between social order and disorder or conflict. In his perspective the threat of war was never far away. Peace, both internal peace between social classes and external peace organized through international law and organizations, was a precondition for economic prosperity. Tinbergen more than many of his fellow economists has been concerned with issues of international governance and security. After his retirement he wrote extensively on these subjects, for example, in *Welfare and Warfare*. But he was intimately concerned with them as early as 1945[7] and was one of the first economists to explore the consequences of economic integration, in the context of the emergence of the European Union and other such organizations in his work of the 1940s and 1950s. His convergence theory explores how the institutional orders of the East (under socialism) and the West (under capitalism) are slowly growing toward each other.

In his work, this institutional and legal focus takes the form not of legal analysis directly, but rather of the institutional design of the economy. The fact that he worked *through* so many organizations, from the League of Nations to the UN, the Central Planning Bureau, and the Social-Economic Council in the Netherlands, is no coincidence but central to his understanding of how a peaceful, that is, stable economy can be ordered and constructed.

This project started with the 1930s' attempts to stabilize the Dutch economy in the midst of the Great Depression, and remained with him until his very last work on the "optimal economic order." As such, Tinbergen's work was rooted in an older historical and legal approach, characteristic of the nineteenth century. And at the same time his constructivist vision of the economy (the belief in *Machbarkeit*) and his preference for mathematical and quantitative models were unquestionably modern. Most secondary accounts about Tinbergen have emphasized the modern nature of his economics. But his contributions literally mark the break between the nineteenth century and the twentieth century, much like the period leading up to World War I, in which the Vredespaleis was constructed, represented the break between the imperial nineteenth-century international order and the nationalist and internationalist order

---

[7] Tinbergen, *International Economic Co-operation*, 1945.

of the twentieth century. Together with Ragnar Frisch, the Norwegian econometrician with whom he shared the Nobel Prize, he is presented as the father of econometrics and macroeconomic modeling and a pioneer in development economics. But that obscures that Tinbergen's thought was far broader, and crucially shaped by his thinking in terms of legal and institutional orders that support the economy. He used that insight to modernize the economy, but the insight itself was *historical and institutional*. It belonged to an older, nineteenth-century approach to economics that emphasized law and historical development.

That tension is visible in other aspects of his work. Although he was in contact with the leading physicists of the age, including Albert Einstein, he remained wedded to a nineteenth-century belief in determinism – not completely unlike Einstein himself. But it is mostly the optimism of his work that is also thoroughly of the nineteenth century, for Tinbergen the line of history is upward. The path toward modernity that the West has traveled has to be perfected in a mature socialism, free of dogma, he argued.[8] And this ideal was universal and should be expanded to the rest of the world. Tinbergen was a pacifist and weary of imperialism, much like the pacifists who invigorated the internationalist spirit of the Vredespaleis. But their vision was still wedded to a modernist perspective that took the expansion of Western civilization across the planet as the natural and ultimate goal. The means of doing so could no longer be imperial, but the fundamental goal had not changed. In Tinbergen's work the means become development economics; his goals remained modernist and universalist.

I will argue that Tinbergen's greatest contribution to this project is not a particular theory that explains or helps us understand the world, but instead is a theory and technique of governance. The core of his work is a technique for policymaking and an institutional design through which that technique could be effective. Tinbergen is never primarily concerned with how to explain the world; the goal is always to improve it. His theory of governance connects what we know about the dynamics of the economy to the theory of how we would like the world to be. If science is about what the world is, and politics about what the world could be, then we should situate Tinbergen's most important contribution precisely at the intersection. It shows the politicians how they can achieve what they hope to achieve, and it shows the scientists how their knowledge can be put to use. It was, so to speak, the institutional legwork that allowed the knowledge of

---

[8] Tinbergen, "Some Thoughts on Mature Socialism," 1973.

the library of the Peace Palace to be put to practical use. If politics is the art of the possible, then Tinbergen's economics is the exploration of the possible.

More than once his work has been called naïve or overly optimistic, charges that anyone associated with the Vredespaleis will instantly recognize. But they will also realize that such charges are at least partly off the mark – nobody had ever suggested that international peace was easy or even attainable within a generation. Tinbergen himself would, late in his life, capture it clearly – he was not optimistic, but he was *hopeful*.

The deep tension between the lofty ideals embodied by the Vredespaleis and the political reality of its time is mirrored in the life of Tinbergen. In his oeuvre we find plenty of these lofty ideals: a more integrated and peaceful economy, the convergence between the East and the West, the economic development of the Global South, and a more just and equal economic order in the West. But his work spans the turbulent political-economic reality of the twentieth century. It involves many compromises on his side. This is all too apparent as he moves from the idealistic cultural socialism of his youth to the polarized political reality of the 1930s and the mostly failed attempts to do something about the Great Depression; as he attempts to navigate the Central Bureau of Statistics through World War II without getting in trouble with the German occupiers, and without helping them too much; as he attempts to set up neutral economic expertise institutions in the Netherlands, which rise above party lines, at the expense of his own political-economic ideals; as he attempts to plan economic development of the newly sovereign countries around the world such as India or Turkey, where he has to cope with the military generals and internal political conflicts; as he attempts to argue for convergence of the East and the West amid the hardening of the Cold War; as he attempts to convince governments around the world of their global responsibilities, while national interests seem to trump more idealistic goals time and again; and as he attempts to put on the agenda the environmental threats facing humanity late in his career.

The balancing act he faced is not merely one between ideals and political realities. It is also a human tension. Tinbergen's most successful political student, Jan Pronk, minister of development aid and adjunct-secretary at the United Nations Conference on Trade and Development (UNCTAD), once said that God is required, humanism is not enough. Ultimately, the Heidelberger Catechism, one of the foundational documents of German and Dutch Protestantism, is correct: "Man is ultimately flawed, that is the decisive human condition."[9] He and Tinbergen shared this particular Protestant view, and drew from it the conclusion that rules were required. In the form of law and institutions, but also in the form of cultural norms. The *Ordnung*[10] Tinbergen sought to create both nationally and internationally was meant to prevent the worst from happening. Models of how the world might be were necessary to provide hope and guidance. But it was a second-best option; perfection is not attainable for humans.[11]

His economics thus comes about as a response to the conflict and instability in the world. His macroeconometric model, the first one in the world, is primarily an outcome of the efforts to present a way out of the crisis not tainted by ideological dogma. His theory of economic policy is an outcome of his activities at the Central Planning Bureau, a new organization of economic expertise that becomes an important part of economic policymaking in the Netherlands. His theory of planning in stages is developed in his efforts to boost economic growth in India, Turkey, and elsewhere. His convergence theory cannot be disconnected from his attempts to maintain a dialogue across the Iron Curtain. His work in international trade and order is often written as a direct response to real-world developments in those areas and his activities at the United Nations. The measurement of human welfare he tries to develop is intimately tied up in his efforts to provide a scientific definition of equality.

His efforts are frequently frustrated and fruitless, as such efforts often are. World War I broke out only one year after the Vredespaleis opened. But then again, just a few years before his death in 1994, the Iron Curtain came down and Michael Gorbachev, Prime Minister of Russia, paid him a personal visit to thank him for his hopeful work on the convergence of the East and the West. Planning, perhaps the central word in Tinbergen's vocabulary, had little do with the downfall of communism. Nonetheless, he had worked toward it, he had hoped for it, he had believed it was possible. His final manuscript dealt with the subject of an optimal world order. No, the Vredespaleis did not bring peace, but it believed in it.

---

[9] Brandsma, *Jan Pronk: Rebel met een Missie*, 28, 1996.

[10] Throughout the book the German word *Ordnung*, a term that has no close equivalent in English, will be used for the institutional ordering of the economy through laws and organizations. The German word is more widely known, and very close to the Dutch *Ordening*. We will discuss *Ordnung* in more detail in several chapters, particularly Chapter 5.

[11] For an idiosyncratic reading of Tinbergen along these lines, see Rugina, "The Unending Search for Universal and Lasting Peace, from Leon Walras to Jan Tinbergen and Beyond," 1988.

The text of the guided tour written in 1914 by the civil engineer J. A. G. van der Steur, who oversaw the construction of the Vredespaleis, concluded that this building is "Special, for from it one can hear a calling from the future; a calling easily mocked in this era of war and violence, but one that manages to rise above the mockery, when one realizes that the Vredespaleis is not a palace *of* the Peace, ready to provide a home for it, as if Peace had already conquered the world, it is a palace *for* the Peace, ready to symbolize all of the power which emanates just from her spirit alone."[12] Tinbergen's work is not a palace where a just economy is realized, where the blueprint for a stable international economy can be found, but it is a palace *for* an economy realizing socialist ideals, a palace *for* the construction of an international order. That project would take him to Leiden where he became a scientist; to Geneva where he contributed to the League of Nations;, to Ankara, New Delhi, Jakarta, Cairo, and other capitals of the new world where he shaped development economics in practice; to New York for the United Nations headquarters and the agenda of Development Decade II (1970–80); to Rome where he sought to continue the work of the people behind the famous environmental Club of Rome report; to Stockholm where he was awarded the first Nobel Prize in Economics; and to the Soviet Union where he sought to create a dialogue between East and West. But the project was fundamentally shaped in outlook and ideals in his place of birth The Hague; for Tinbergen, home was the ultimate place of peace.

---

[12] Steur, *Beschrijving, behoorende bij het Vredespaleis*, 29, 1914. In Dutch: "Bijzonder, omdat er van dit gebouw eene roeping der toekomst uitgaat; roeping, die te bespotten schijnt in dezen tijd van strijd en geweld, maar die uitsteekt boven alle spotternij, wanneer men slecths bedenkt, dat het Vredespaleis niet is een paleis *van* den Vrede, gereed als 't ware dezen te huisvesten, als had hij de wereld reeds verwonnen, maar *voor* den Vrede, gereed dus wel om in zijn hulsel te symboliseeren geheel de macht, die van zijne gedachten alleen reeds uitgaat."

2

A Progressive Education

The greatest difficulty of our age is the distance between children and their
parents which has come about by the collapse of the world from before 1914.
—Dirk Cornelis Tinbergen (Jan's father)[1]

2.1 The Tinbergen Household

In the summer of 1902, Dirk Cornelis Tinbergen and Jeanette van Eek
married in The Hague. She was a teacher and so was he. Together they
would raise five children. Two of them would go on to win Nobel Prizes:
Jan in economics, Niko in physiology. A unique achievement, if one can
credit the parents, or a household, with something like that. At the very
least, it makes one wonder if there was anything special about this household. The family lived in a bourgeois neighborhood in The Hague on the
Bentinckstraat (although for the first eight years of Jan's life, they occupied
a smaller apartment in the Van Bylandtstraat). The street was lined with
identical connected three-story houses, without a front yard, but with a
small balcony facing the street (Figure 2.1). The family home was closer to
the harbor than to the city center, and only a twenty-minute walk from the
beach. A walk of about the same length in the other direction led to
Zorgvliet, where a stately home once housed the poet Jan Cats, and one
could enjoy a large park known as the Scheveningse Bosjes, which was
developed in the late nineteenth century as a public employment program.
Adjacent to this green area was the Peace Palace, which the family would
inevitably pass on their way to the city center.

The family was part of the upper bourgeois in the city, although they
were not rich by contemporary standards. Both Dirk Cornelis and Jeanette

---

[1] D. C. Tinbergen, "De Toekomst onzer Kinderen," *Haagsch Weekblad*, 1928.

17

Figure 2.1 The parental home of Jan Tinbergen in the Bentinckstraat, The Hague.

would take additional teaching jobs when they could get them. It was a highly cultural family, firmly wedded to the ideals of a *Bildungsbürgertum*: the ideals of humanism and education that grew out of enlightenment ideals. The pater familias Dirk Cornelis had earned his PhD (cum laude) in Dutch medieval literature, based on a study of Jan van Brederode's *Des Coninx Summe*. Van Brederode's work was a high point in early Dutch literature and originated as a translation and adaptation of *La Somme le Roi* – a work written for the children of Philip II of France in the thirteenth century – which contrasted vice and virtue through a series of parables. Dirk Cornelis's edited version of the book came out in 1907. During his studies he learned a wide variety of European languages. He not only mastered old French to study *La Somme le Roi* but also read Dante's thirteenth-century *Divine Comedy* in the original Italian version, and Beowulf, an epic from about the year 1000 in the original Old English version. He completed his PhD alongside C. G. N. de Vooys, a future professor of Dutch literature, who similarly specialized in medieval literature. Dirk Cornelis had been a temporary teacher in Schiedam and was hired in The Hague as a teacher at the local Hogere Burgerschool (HBS) in September 1900, a position that became permanent a year later. But both graduates, Tinbergen and De Vooys, would spend most of their career teaching Dutch literature at a gymnasium, a prestigious school that prepared its students for university education and included instruction in Latin and ancient Greek. They would later jointly publish a textbook of Dutch literature for this level of education.[2]

Despite his training in classical European languages and his position at the classical humanist gymnasium, Tinbergen's father was not a very conservative man. In fact, Dirk Cornelis and his good friend De Vooys shared a progressive vision for the education of the youth. They were inspired by the work of Maria Montessori and Rudolf Steiner to integrate play and children's own curiosity into the curriculum. De Vooys published an article on the development of children's language illustrated with many examples.[3] It was an empirical approach to the development of language, which was novel and pathbreaking, and part of an attempt to better connect learning methods to the way in which children acquired language. A year later in 1917 inspired by De Vooys's study, Van Ginneken published

---

[2] De Vooys, Van den Bosch, and Tinbergen, *Letterkundig Leesboek voor Hoogere Burgerscholen, Gymnasia en Kweekscholen,* 1919.
[3] De Vooys, "Iets over Woordvorming en Woordbetekenis in Kindertaal," 1916.

The Novel of a Toddler,[4] in which through various phases, the toddler becomes aware of the world and develops language to make sense of it. These new approaches prompted Jan Tinbergen's father to observe closely the development of language of his third son Luuk. It resulted in a wonderful article, *Toddler-Talk* (*Kinderpraat*), in which Dirk Cornelis illustrated in elaborate detail how sounds developed, how brief sentences were formed, and how through language Luuk became aware of his surroundings.[5] Barely three years old, Luuk started to correct his own use of language: "I have do it. No, done it, Jan says so." As his father remarked, he looked up to his older brother Jan, whose corrections he started to pick up.

De Vooys and Dirk Cornelis Tinbergen together actively supported a movement to simplify spelling in order to make it more "logical" and to facilitate the ease of learning among pupils. The fight over the appropriate spelling of Dutch was part of a wider movement to modernize education and to make it more accessible to those from lower classes. The so-called Kollewijn Spelling (named after R. A. Kollewijn) sought to simplify Dutch spelling rules and to bring them more in line with phonetics. De Vooys spearheaded the movement in the magazine he edited, *De Nieuwe Taalgids*, to which Dirk Cornelis regularly contributed.[6] His oldest son, Jan Tinbergen, would use this same spelling in his first publication. The families remained in contact and Tinbergen would later work with the son of De Vooys at the Central Bureau of Statistics. In a curious coincidence, Jan Tinbergen would be part of a committee with De Vooys on the correct pronunciation and spelling of numbers and fractions many years later.[7]

In this family of devoted linguists, a high point of every year was the St. Nicolas celebration on December 5, when according to Dutch tradition the gifts are accompanied by little teasing rhymes. Very old ones have not been preserved, although one of his nieces remembers that Tinbergen was from a young age busy with words, languages, and rhymes, through which he taught her naughty words.[8] The rhymes of the 1928 celebrations, when Jan was already twenty-five years old, give a flavor of what such occasions were like. The rhymes tease Jan about his precision, his stubbornness, and his failure to listen to the advice of his mother and doctors when he fell ill.

---

[4] Van Ginneken, *De Roman van een Kleuter*, 1917.   [5] Tinbergen, "Kinderpraat," 1919.
[6] See, for instance, *De Nieuwe Taalgids*, vols. 8 and 9, in which various articles from De Vooys and D. C. Tinbergen argued for the adoption of the new spelling.
[7] See the correspondence between Tinbergen, De Vooys, Kloeke, and Haeringen in 1950 and 1951, TL.
[8] Hupkes in Jolink and Barendrecht-Tinbergen, *Gedeelde Herinneringen*, 1993.

They make fun of his constant talk of trams and his forgetfulness when he is at work (he was so deeply engaged in work that he even missed the honking vegetable truck which came by with deliveries). In another rhyme, fun is made of Tine, Jan's girlfriend and later wife, feeling cold all the time and the enormous fires in their fireplace:

> A thermometer was bought
> And this rhyme was wrought
> And of Tine it is asked
> To not worry too much about the draft
> Sint advises Jan, (oh yes he is quite bright):
> Install the gift at a warm site
> Pete[9] believes this trick might fail
> In that case Jan should adjust the scale
> He might lead her astray at last
> The thing is twenty degrees fast.[10]

The rhymes that year also teased him with his, even by the family standards, Spartan work habits and his fascination for progressive Scandinavia. The St. Nicolas family tradition of corrective rhymes, which exists to this day, provided a way of keeping everyone grounded, since the rhymes were all written in the (semi)-anonymous voice of Saint Nicolas, the all-knowing observer. Jan and Tine received a full twenty-one pages of rhymes that year. Creativity with language was highly valued in the family, and Jan Tinbergen developed a lifelong fascination for differences between languages and always tried to learn a few words of the local language, wherever he was.

His father Dirk Cornelis also pursued poetry more seriously and even wrote in Old Dutch.[11] He stayed in touch with various other educated families in The Hague and was keenly interested in new developments in the humanities. These included various movements of the time to reform education that typically emphasized more freedom for young children. In a small article on the raising of children, he strongly rejected the idea that parents should raise their children based on authority and suggested that they should instead rely on softness and lead by example. He even

---

[9] A reference to St. Nicolas's assistant.

[10] Available in TL, 5 December 1928. In Dutch: "Een thermometer werd gekocht / En dit gedicht erbij gewrocht / En aan Tine werd verzocht / Niet al te bang te zijn voor tocht / Sint raadt Jan (Sint is ook niet gek): / Hang hem op een warme plek / Piet denkt dat grapje heeft ze door / Hij maakt een hogere schaal ervoor / Leidt zo Tine op een dwaalspoor / Het ding loopt twintig graden vóór!"

[11] Kruuk, *Niko's Nature*, 16, 2003.

suggested that raising children was for the parent about raising oneself, so that they could imitate. In another short article on the future of "our children" he explored the new (socialist) spirit among the youth, which was more communal, less individualistic, and less focused on money. This posed new challenges for the parents, who had to practice more than ever a "hands-off approach." This new pedagogic spirt was embodied, for Dirk Cornelis, by Krishnamurti, a spiritual teacher from India. Krishnamurti led by example and urged others not to follow him, but instead to seek liberation. He was associated with the theosophical movement of the 1920s, which in turn was closely related to the anthroposophical movement of Rudolf Steiner. Spirituality was a recurring theme in Dirk Cornelis's writings for *Het Haagse Weekblad* (The Hague Weekly).[12] Dirk Cornelis wrote on immortality, mysticism and its dangers, the hyper-ethics of Coudenhove-Kalergi (the proponent of Pan-Europeanism), karma, and astrology, alongside other subjects such as free will, vegetarianism (which he rejected), and the relationship between the individual and mass society. This mixture of humanism and spirituality was quite common in the first decades of the twentieth century in the Netherlands and Germany and continued through the socialist youth movements that would influence Jan Tinbergen deeply. In these progressive circles there was a fascination with the East, with the novelists from Russia and the philosophies of China and India.[13] Dirk Cornelis and his contemporaries combined spiritual teaching with progressive views and reflections on modern society. Although Jan Tinbergen would never be comfortable writing about spiritual themes, it nonetheless left a deep imprint on him; he would later send his daughters to anthroposophical schools, a family tradition that continues. And science never became merely an instrumental endeavor for him; it was also supposed to bring moral guidance, and if that proved impossible it was at the very least important to integrate scientific insights into a broader worldview. That integration was known at the time as a synthesis.

The progressive character of the perspective of Jan's father and those close to him was more personal and spiritual than social and political. They believed that the rise of modern society would bring about a fundamental shift in the way human beings relate to one another, but they did not draw

---

[12] For a year he contributed articles to *Haagsch Weekblad*, a magazine that existed for only a small number of years in the late 1920s, available at Haags Gemeentearchief.

[13] Brolsma, "'Het Humanitaire Moment.' Nederlandse Intellectuelen, de Eerste Wereldoorlog en de Crisis van de Europese Beschaving (1914–1930)," 2015.

direct political conclusions from this. Dirk Cornelis instead preferred to reflect on what this change meant for the personal sphere. He reflected on what the rise of modern society would mean for the relation between parents and children, or teachers and pupils, and he wrote about the new relationship between husband and wife. A modern relationship between husband and wife, he argued, should be based on camaraderie rather than difference. And although such a new relationship would still require a division of tasks, it would allow man and woman to understand one another better and treat one another more like equals.

Dirk Cornelis wife Jeanette was more mathematically inclined and less high-minded than her husband. In contrast to her idealistic husband, the man of books and philosophy, she had a hands-on approach. Jeanette was interested in social questions, but from a more practical perspective. On her urging Tinbergen sought contact with the fishers of the fishing town Scheveningen. She hoped that in this way he would get a better understanding of the working and living conditions of the proletariat. Jeanette quit her job when the children were born and spent most of her time with them. There is some temptation to think that Jan was inspired by his father to pursue an intellectual career and that his social concerns were inspired by his mother. But any such simple linear relationships from his family to his career run up against the fact that his siblings pursued rather different paths than their older brother.

2.2 Luuk and Niko

Jan (born in 1903) was the first-born son of the family; his brother Niko (Nikolaas, 1908) was five years his junior, and his brother Luuk (Lukas, 1915) twelve years his junior. Between Jan and Niko, the only daughter Jacomien (1905) was born. She taught German at a high school in Eindhoven and Delft. Jacomien was an important point of connection for the brothers and the wider family and shared the humanism and thrift of many other family members.[14] Between Niko and Luuk, the fourth son Dik (1909) was born. He studied engineering in Delft and worked, among other places, at the energy company of the city of The Hague. He was the least intellectual of the family and often felt somewhat inferior for it.[15]

Jan's two younger brothers would develop their scientific interests in a radically different direction than Jan. Whereas Jan was attracted to the

---

[14] A brief obituary of her appeared in the magazine *Elsevier*, 25 March 2006.
[15] Kruuk, *Niko's Nature*, 21, 2003.

exact sciences and how these could be employed to improve society, his two brothers both pursued biology, with special interest in the behavior of birds. These differences were evident from an early age, when his brothers were attracted to long hikes in the dunes near The Hague where they would go birdwatching, while Jan was more interested in trams. The love for nature was cultivated on a yearly holiday to the countryside where the family rented a cottage at Hulshorst, a small village located next to the biggest national park of the Netherlands, Hoge Veluwe, which provided more opportunity for the exploration of nature.

But it was not just hiking and enjoying the beauties of nature; their father also encouraged them to draw whatever they had seen in nature. Dirk Cornelis, a fine artist himself, would teach them to draw, for which they all, Jan included, developed great skill.[16] But whereas Jan's drawings where at least as often of urban settings, in particular of trains and trams, Niko and Luuk preferred to draw birds, and they became very good at it (Figure 2.2). It was probably Niko who teased Jan and his younger brother Dik for their fascination with trams in one of the St. Nicolas rhymes:

> Then suddenly, Dik pricks his ears
> Jan immediately puts his pen down
> Gloriously they look each other in the eyes
> There is one-sixteen from town
> And yes, he is pulling a little carriage
> Yes, yes, it is one-nineteen
> A beautiful tram with a cage like that
> Ah, I can barely watch it
> They cozily chat for an hour
> Then Jan says, well I have to stop
> I have to get back to my formulas
> Oh geez, where did I leave off.[17]

In the humanistic and nature-minded, if not outright romanticist family, Jan and Dik stood out with their interests in engineering and technology. Niko and Luuk, on the other hand, were naturally at home. Luuk would

---

[16] Hupkes in Jolink and Barendrecht-Tinbergen, *Gedeelde Herinneringen*, 1993.
[17] Available in TL, 5 December 1928. In Dutch: "Daar plots, zie Dikkie spitst de oren / Jan legt gelijk de vulpen neer / Verheerlijkt zien ze elkaar in de ogen / Daar heb je honderzestien weer / Ja, hoor je wel hij sleept een bakkie / Ja, ja, dat is honderdnegentien / Zo'n mooie wagen met zo'n kooitje / 't Is werkelijk niet om aan te zien / Gezellig kout men zo een uurtje / Dan roept Jan: Nou ik houd eens op, / Ik ga weer gauw aan mijn formules / O, jee, wat heb ik daar een ... op."

Figure 2.2 Tinbergen was taught drawing from his father. He proudly noted that this tram was drawn from memory.

publish his first articles, which featured his own drawings at age eighteen, and his first book on waterbirds only a year later.

The 1920s were a period with new chances for the youth of the middle classes in the Netherlands. Several youth organizations of a recreational and more idealistic nature sprung up, typically with strong pedagogical goals. Jan Tinbergen joined the socialist youth movement, which would have an important influence on him. Luuk and Niko, on the other hand, both joined the Dutch Youth League for the Study of Nature (NJN). The NJN was founded as a response to the increasing urbanization, and it sought to familiarize the urban youth with nature by organizing trips into the outdoors. Outdoor activities were believed to be healthy for body and soul, and the NJN actively encouraged the study of nature and thus formed an important impetus for later natural conservation movements. The NJN drew inspiration from two widely popular naturalists in the Netherlands, Eli Heijmans and Jac. P. Thijsse, whose books adorned most family living rooms and were still around when I grew up in the 1980s. The NJN also drew inspiration from the more explicitly romantic *Wandervögel* movement in Germany, which is somewhat notorious for its later links to Nazism. The NJN, and similar groups, fostered camaraderie between its members and hence also sought to contribute to the "new" social relationships.

The difference between Niko and Jan was perhaps the strongest. Niko enjoyed nothing more than the outside life and excelled at sport; Jan was studious and at ease in his home. Luuk combined a bit of both. He was drawn to the study of nature, but could equally often be found behind his desk, and his PhD drew on some of the statistics that his oldest brother Jan had taught him. Both Luuk and Niko specialized in ecology, the study concerned with the relation between the organisms and their environment, a field pioneered by Charles Darwin. Niko would later extend this field and pioneer a wholly new field of inquiry: ethology, the study of the (social) behavior of animals. Ethology is a field of research that combines experimental methods with intensive fieldwork. The experiments are virtually always done in the natural habitat of the animals. Its method, especially in the early days, depended on intuitive observation and a keen eye for patterns. It favored insight and intuition over systematization. In a telling anecdote, Niko is discussing quantification with his (later) fellow Nobel Laureate Konrad Lorenz; the question is how often a behavior must be observed before it can be said that it is characteristic of the species. Konrad said that he never made such a claim unless he had seen the behavior at least five times. Niko laughed, patted him on the back and said: "Don't be silly Konrad, you know you often said it when you have seen it only once."[18]

Jan Tinbergen would become famous for the introduction of quantitative models into economics; their methods could hardly have been more different. Niko's method was based on close observation and inference from just a few instances, Jan's method on the aggregation of lots of data,

---

[18] Kruuk, *Niko's Nature*, 128, 2003.

and the systematic analysis of them. These differences were reflected in their personalities, Jan with his love of tram schedules and patterns, Niko with his adventurous nature and frivolity. Their father's up-close observation of the development of language in young children is certainly much closer to Niko's approach in ethology. The studies in language development of father Tinbergen had great similarity with the way that Niko would extract typical, characteristic, or exemplary cases from his observations of animal behavior. It was an approach in which the anecdotal was, if not the preferred method, at least important enough to illustrate the essence of something.

Jan, to the contrary, was a strong adherent to the idea that to know something one has to be able to quantify it and infer from many cases, while Niko's approach in ethology was rooted in the idea that in order to know something one has to observe closely and interpret accordingly. The contrast was not merely in the method: Jan's approach was rooted in the natural sciences and based on mechanistic explanations, Niko's approach was a combination of sociology and biology and based on evolutionary explanations. Although Niko himself was strongly behaviorist and not prone to psychologize animals, his approach does humanize the species he studied, and later work in the field has often toggled back and forth between social behavior found among humans and that among animals. Niko, too, later in his life, more frequently engaged in debates about similarities in behavior between animals and humans. Jan's more mechanistic approach to economics, arguably, took some of the humanity out of humans, while Niko's ethology put some humanity into animals.

Such differences also seem to be reflected in their personalities. Niko was never one to sit still and was not much of a perfectionist; he got by in school, but certainly did not perform on par with the exacting Tinbergen family standards. Jan, on the other hand, was patient and loved to be indoors more than outdoors, and although his work never exhibited great perfectionism, his work habits were indeed Spartan. Niko excelled in sports and even made it to the national field hockey team, while Jan shied away from sports. When their father wrote that one should teach the youth soberness and to achieve as healthy and a fit body as possible, it was as if Jan had absorbed only the former and Niko only the latter.

But we should not lose ourselves in too many easy generalizations. Jan, as we will see below, was not quite the rationalist calculator that he is sometimes made out to be, and Niko dismissed any notion that we could know the emotions of animals, if they even had them. It was Niko Tinbergen more than Konrad Lorenz who did much to systematize the study of ethology, not in the least by inspiring a younger generation to follow in his footsteps. Both Niko and Jan can claim to have formed their own approach and school of thought in their respective disciplines.[19] The two brothers grew closer in their worries about the nuclear threat and environmental problems during the 1970s. Niko might not have been directly involved in the improvement of society, but the sense of responsibility that characterized many in the Tinbergen family never left him. Niko's career knew enormous successes, but he always combined it with more popular illustrated books and films for the broader public. He did not construct a great scheme to improve the economy, but his work was equally meant to lift people up. Emancipation through knowledge remained close to both their hearts. And if both Niko and Jan picked up anything from their father the linguist, it was an ability and ease of writing.

2.3 Growing Up

Jan completed elementary school in a nearby "Burgerschool" in the Van Merlenstraat, just across the canal which connected The Hague to the sea. Afterward he did not go to one of the gymnasia, the type of school where his father worked. Instead, Jan attended an HBS. These schools were founded in the middle of the nineteenth century with the goal of providing a broad and relevant education for the bourgeois youth. Although technically a level lower than the gymnasia, they also represented a more modern type of education. Not Greek and Latin but modern subjects such as engineering were part of the curriculum. A few years before Tinbergen completed the HBS, the five-year variant of this HBS was also officially recognized as a sufficient preparation for the exact sciences at university. Earlier it provided entrance to the universities of applied science, such as the school of engineering in Delft (now the University of Delft), which his brother Dik attended, and the school of economics in Rotterdam (now the Erasmus University in Rotterdam).

Jan attended the second municipal HBS in The Hague at the Stadhouderslaan, not far from his parental home. While the rest of Europe was waging World War I, the Netherlands remained neutral. At the HBS he met his later wife Tine. Her family had just returned from the "East," as colonial Indonesia was called in the Netherlands, where her father had served as an officer in the army. The progressive and

---

[19] Jan's school is well documented in Van Dalen and Klamer, *De Telgen van Tinbergen* (*The Descendants of Tinbergen*), 1996.

Figure 2.3 Wedding picture of Jan and Tine with Jan's parents on the left, and Tine's parents on the right, 1929.

particularly socialist views Tine was developing during the 1920s were met with a lot of resistance; her father was sure that all "reds" were wrong, period.[20] But her brother recounted that at least relatively speaking, their father was progressive; he had an eye for the poverty in the world and had always attempted to treat the servants in Indonesia humanely (Figure 2.3).

At the HBS, Jan excelled in the natural sciences; his teacher Taverne would lovingly recount his achievements in chemistry classes. His love for physics and mathematics was sparked by Teunis van Lohuizen (born 1883). Van Lohuizen had graduated in 1912 in Amsterdam under the supervision of the famous physics professor and Nobel Laureate Pieter Zeeman, after whom the Zeeman effect is named, describing a particular effect of magnetic fields on light rays. It was in this same line of research that Van Lohuizen had written his dissertation. It was also Van Lohuizen who brought Tinbergen in contact with his eventual PhD advisor Paul Ehrenfest.[21]

---

[20] De Wit in Jolink and Barendrecht-Tinbergen, *Gedeelde Herinneringen*, 6, 1993.
[21] Van Lohuizen presented a joint paper with Paul Ehrenfest, in 1917. See *Het Atoommodel van Rutherford-Bohr*, T. van Lohuizen, L. S. Ornstein en E. H. Büchner, Natuur- en Geneeskundig Congres, gehouden op 12, 13 en 14 april 1917 te 's-Gravenhage.

It was common for teachers at the HBS to have a university degree, but Van Lohuizen's status must have been somewhat extraordinary. School pictures[22] show him repeatedly in his own classrooms surrounded by experimental equipment. In the 1920s, he was part of a committee for the modernization of the teaching of physics at the HBS. An important criterion for these reforms was that education had to make visible and tangible the principles that were being taught. This was done by introducing posters and maps into the classroom, or by taking the students outside to learn in nature. Learning was no longer believed to be a process of hierarchical instruction, but rather a process of participation. Tinbergen benefited from this hands-on education and enjoyed it greatly: he drew a map of Africa in class that was so well done that it was still used by his teacher ten years later.[23] Tinbergen, an eager pupil, also edited the school paper, which he typeset all by himself.

For Van Lohuizen, "making visible" meant engaging his pupils through experiments that would quite literally make visible the effects and mechanisms they read about in their books.[24] Tinbergen was so taken by his classes that he held on to his notebook on conic sections including applications in engineering for the rest of his life. The notebooks also bear witness to the precise drawing skills and the faultless handwriting that would remain with him until old age.

Van Lohuizen became a mentor of sorts to Tinbergen and was instrumental in motivating Jan to pursue studies in the natural sciences. When Tinbergen later decided to pursue a career in economics rather than physics, he wrote a letter to Van Lohuizen to seek his approval or at least understanding for this choice. Van Lohuizen was more than understanding and even encouraged Tinbergen to pursue this progressive career choice:

[In mathematical economics] you can solve problems with the help of your scientific knowledge, from which an economist without mathematical training will shrink back. So, there is a field where you can work for the betterment of humankind. And there is a great need for such works, since love for humankind alone is not enough to bring about progress in the world. In the circles in which

[22] A number of them are available at the Haagse Beeldbank, www.haagsgemeentearchief.nl/mediabank/beeldcollectie/.

[23] Van Sprancken to JT, 15 March 1929, TL. In the digital archive there is a mistake since the letter is from M. Van Spronsen.

[24] Reindersma and Van Lohuizen, *Nieuw Leerboek der Natuurkunde: Voor Hoogere Burgerscholen met 5-Jarigen Cursus, Lycea en Gymnasia*, 1930; Tompitak and Beckers, "Solide en Gedegen Onderwijs. Wiskunde en Natuurkunde Onderwijsdiscussies in de Jaren 1920 als Monitor voor Disciplinevorming," 2015.

you work there is a great need for good leaders. And it is therefore that I am not primarily disappointed by your decision. Perhaps you do not know, that in religious and economic thinking and feeling I am much closer to you than you might think, that our spirits are more related than you perhaps think.... So never consider the years of study in the natural sciences as wasted time. Your perspective on the problems and the skills in solving problems has become much broader and deeper because of them.[25]

It speaks to the progressive nature of much of the physics milieu of the time, which sought to improve society and believed that a natural science approach had much to contribute to a coming "synthesis"[26] and to a better society in general.

Tinbergen's father was similarly convinced that learning was best done through experience and seeing and took Jan frequently on long cycle trips. During the summer of 1919, he and his father went on a cycling trip through the Achterhoek, a rural region near the German border, where they would cycle about fifty to sixty kilometers per day and stay at local hotels. On their trip they would repeatedly be stopped by soldiers who were still patrolling the border area, just one year after the end of World War I. In a diary of the trip, Tinbergen described in detail the varied scenery and wrote about his enjoyment of being outdoors. His father took him to a neighborhood built by a local industrialist (Stork) to provide proper housing for his staff in Tuindorp Lansink near Hengelo. They both admired the living and working conditions in this progressive industrial village. And during the hours on the bike, there was time for conversation about other matters, for example, about the "Men of the Eighties" (a progressive group of poets from the 1880s, a few of whom were not "men"). Some snobbery in cultural taste was not alien to Tinbergen; in his diary he commented wittily on one of the local hotels: "The music was not as good as the potatoes." In the evening he and his father would invariably take a walk through the local village where they spent the night.

That same year Tinbergen joined a youth camp close to the Hoge Veluwe National Park. Here he spent time camping, cooking, and cycling from one campsite to the next with his friends. When they had some spare time at a campsite, they took out the drawing pads and made detailed pictures of the nature around them. Tinbergen sometimes copied the local map in detail in his little travelogue. The youths spent most of the

---

[25] Teunis van Lohuizen to JT, 5 April 1927, TL.
[26] Baneke, *Synthetisch Denken: Natuurwetenschappers over hun Rol in een Moderne Maatschappij 1900–1940*, 2008.

noncycling days roaming the woods or having a Codd neck bottle at the local café. But occasionally they expressed some more cultural interests; at an otherwise nonexceptional statue of Jesus, Tinbergen took notice of the inscription that read "Pax vobis" (May peace be with you). It is clear that Tinbergen felt at home on his bicycle, because on the final day of the camp he woke up at four, announced to his friends that he would leave in an hour and set off from Leuvenum to his parental home in The Hague, a trip of about 125 kilometers. He arrived around six in the evening, proud of the guilders he had saved by not taking the train.

His decision to leave his friends behind and return home by himself illustrates well his steadfastness and somewhat solitary nature. And it also nicely symbolizes his longing for home. For a man who would achieve his level of international fame he spent surprisingly little time abroad. After his long trip of 125 kilometers it is not surprising that a feeling of relief fell over him the moment he saw the Haagse tower in the distance, as he described in his travel diary. He, however, also left early because of a desire to be back home. The next year he left summer camp after just two days because he felt homesick. He described his decision to return early as a mixture of a desire to be alone in peace and quiet and a deep sense of responsibility that did not allow him to enjoy the idleness of a trip with his friends. About another trip home with his father on a Sunday, when most others were in church, he wrote:

The road was completely abandoned, not a living soul in sight, quiet between the beautiful pine trees. It gives one the sense of something that continues endlessly, as well as that of a blissful ease. In a moment I will be in Utrecht again, tonight in The Hague. It is seemingly contradictory to the calm, peaceful silence on the Woudenbergschen Straatweg. But we must go on, further, everything fits together, including the delights; we have no more time to lose, we have to continue. Off the hill. Then a beautiful cycling path from the Pyramid of Austerlitz to Zeist, silent too, calm, peaceful. Delicious scent of the pine trees. Fortunately, it was a long path. Finally, we were forced to take the main busy road to get home. In the evening we took the train to The Hague, and now the 6th of September, back to work. To work hard is good.

His family remembered with much joy the vacations on which Jan and his wife Tine would later take their children and grandchildren. They were unique moments in which some idleness and some luxuries were allowed that were otherwise out of the question. But even these vacations would be interspersed with work. It was this dedication and seriousness that found a direction in Leiden, where he went to study after the HBS.

3

The Bourgeois Socialist

For the improvement of society we need to study, for the improvement of man
  we need the youth.
                              —Jan Tinbergen[1]

3.1 In between Classes

In 1926 Jan Tinbergen reviewed a novel, the only time he did so to my
knowledge – he later frequently remarked that he left the arts to his wife
Tine. The novel, Leonhard Frank's *De Burger*, which originally appeared in
German, details the internal struggles of Jurgen, a bourgeois son who is
destined to succeed his father in business and become a respectable
"burgher." But during his years at the gymnasium Jurgen feels that he does
not fit into the expectations of his family and social surroundings. After
repeated conflicts he decides to break with his family and move in with
Catharina. She comes, like him, from a bourgeois background but has left
her parents behind and now lives in a small one-room apartment amid the
workers. For years Jurgen works hard for the socialist cause but grows
frustrated with both the futility of his efforts and the crudeness of the
workers around him. Over time he realizes he fits in as poorly among the
working class as he believed he did in his family. A girl lures him back to
the bourgeois world of his youth and Jurgen finally fulfills his destiny,
becoming the director of the family firm as his family had always desired of
him. He leaves Catharina behind, pregnant with their first child.

   From that moment on he lives a life plagued with anxieties. Much of the
power of the novel is derived from a Dostoyevskean description of these
anxieties, which increasingly intertwine with the descriptions of his day-to-

---

[1] Quoted in "Jeugdbond voor Socialistische Studie," *Het Volk*, 11 November 1929.

day life. And they torment Jurgen so much that he finally returns to look for Catharina, finding his son handing out leaflets for a rally at which she will be speaking. It feels to Jurgen like coming home. But by then it is too late; Jurgen's life is over and he has failed to act on his calling.

The novel is a psychological exploration of socialist consciousness among the bourgeois, and it promotes the idea that this consciousness is present in every human being, not just in members of the working class. The message is that anyone who is willing to listen to this inner socialist consciousness can become a true socialist. In his teenage years Jurgen awakens and his first act of resistance to the complacency of his times is his refusal to accept that a poor, but gifted, classmate is sent away from school. Some years later, he defies the career path laid out for him and starts to work for the socialist press. This awakening, as depicted in the novel, is primarily an individual process, in which the bourgeois son can equally be called on to serve the socialist cause as the worker can. In fact, the book suggests that the real hope lies with the bourgeoisie acting on this calling. In one of the key scenes in the novel, Jurgen does answer this calling and becomes one with the workers: "[T]he hate of these five-thousand people was *his* hate, their hope, their goal, was *his* hope, *his* goal."[2]

There is a hopeful message in the book. It suggests that most people ignore their inner calling; certainly, the majority of the bourgeoisie does. But once Jurgen has started to listen to this inner sense of justice he can ignore it only at the cost of great inner conflict. Jurgen's fate is to remain a tormented soul for the rest of his life. The genie cannot be put back into the bottle, despite Jurgen's wish, later in life, to do so. In this perspective, typical for the 1920s, socialism was less a social philosophy and more a personal conviction and outlook.[3] What the novel suggests is that anyone can come to socialism, if only one follows one's inner consciousness. This "calling to socialism" was a third way of conversion. Before the 1920s either one had this socialist consciousness as a member of the proletariat or it was arrived at through the rationalist acceptance of Marxist analysis. Now one could also become a socialist by answering one's inner calling, and one's feelings: "[T]he feeling came first, was forever there." In the novel it is represented by Jurgen's love for Catharina, with whom he becomes one for a moment. And when he leaves her, he also leaves behind the socialist cause.

---

[2] Frank, *De Burger*, 1925.

[3] This was part of more general trend in the 1920s and 1930s during which, for example, French personalism as exemplified by the thought of Emmanuel Mounier became influential.

It is perhaps only natural to expect that Jan Tinbergen read this novel and empathized with Jurgen. Even though Tinbergen was not quite the son of an industrialist, he did come from a bourgeois background and understood he was anything but socialist by class credentials.[4] And he never accepted the traditional social and economic analysis of Marxism. In his review, however, he turned Catharina into the "real" hero of the story, the one who demonstrated what true commitment was, and who was willing to accept the personal costs which came with this. Jurgen's love for socialism seems to have much to do with his fascination for Catharina; it is she who remained committed to the cause. Even when Jurgen left, she did not hesitate for a moment. For Tinbergen it is Catharina who feels the real weight of the injustice and misdeeds that her class has imposed upon the workers for so many generations. Jurgen, on the other hand, was ultimately unwilling to sacrifice his material needs and his spiritual needs and egoistic need for self-development.[5]

The anti-individualistic interpretation of Catharina's character is also present in another publication of that same year in which Tinbergen set out what social-democratic students should do. He praised his fellow socialist students for limiting their material consumption, but he argued that most of them are still stuck in a spiritual egoism that leads them astray. It makes them hold on to individual opinions and unwilling to sacrifice some of their individuality for the greater good of the community. He urged them to search for a spiritual altruism to create a new balance between the development of an individual character and unity within the movement. But most of all, he expressed that their full energy and commitment should be to socialism. One cannot serve two lords. Liberalism must not only be overcome as a political program, but we should also overcome that other remnant of liberalism: the cult of the individual and their spiritual needs. Jurgen, in other words, failed not because he still longed for luxury, but because he was still stuck psychologically in the bourgeois frame of mind.

It was much more radical than the progressive reflections on individuality in modern society that his father wrote around the same time. But the questions that occupied Jan and his father were quite similar: how to think about personal responsibility and morality in modern society. But whereas his father argued for a liberal gradualism, Tinbergen was attracted to the dichotomous worldview of Leonhard Frank's novel:

---

[4] Tinbergen, "A.J.C.-er en Student," 1928.
[5] Tinbergen, "Boekbespreking van L. Frank's De Burger," 1926.

Jurgen is either part of the bourgeois or he is a socialist; there is no room for compromise, no middle ground.[6] It is around 1925 that Tinbergen is going through his most radical phase. He faulted the religious socialists for living in their minds and dreamt-up utopias, faulted his fellow students for their bourgeois individualism, and accused a recent party report on employment of being bourgeois and not providing any truly socialist solutions.[7]

His radicalism extended beyond words, and, indeed, Tinbergen sought to commit himself fully to socialism. Although he did not quite end up living among the poor, he did start to visit them frequently. In Leiden, where he had moved for his studies in physics, he was in regular contact with a mailman who showed him the inner parts of the city and introduced him to some proletarian families. It strengthened his resolve to switch from physics to economics.[8] It also resulted in a series of articles for the social-democratic newspaper *Het Volk* (*The People*) in which he vividly described the hardships of the poorest workers and the unemployed in Leiden. The first one is entitled "Our Duty,"[9] followed by "Desperate Poverty,"[10] "The 'Blessing' of a Big Family,"[11] "One Who Needs Some Peace,"[12] "The Privilege of Being a Party-Member,"[13] and "Disgrace!"[14] and ends with "A 'Typical' Case."[15] All of them detailed the daily struggles of particular families, their lack of proper clothing if they had any at all, their repeated rejection by employers, the constant insecurity in which they lived, and the abysmal conditions in which their children grew up without any cultural stimulation and just one broken toy. It is a tone and style that Tinbergen would never return to, and given this deviation it is quite possible that these articles have been edited substantially. But the articles nonetheless demonstrated the deep way in which he was affected by his engagement with the poor in Leiden.

The fact that he had to deliberately seek contact with the poor first in Scheveningen and then in Leiden is, however, also indicative of the separate

[6] Tinbergen, "Wat we Doen Moeten," 1926.
[7] Tinbergen, "Wetenschappelijk Sosialisties Werk," 1927.
[8] Tinbergen, "Solving the Most Urgent Problems First," 1992.
[9] "Het Leven van Werklozen: Onze Plicht," 1925.
[10] "Het Leven van Werklozen: Gruwelike Armoe," 1925.
[11] "Het Leven van Werklozen: De 'Zegen' van een Groot Gezin," 1925.
[12] "Het Leven van Werklozen: Van een Die Rust Nodig Heeft," 1925.
[13] "Het Leven van Werklozen: 'De Luxe S.D.A.P.-er te Zijn,'" 1926.
[14] "Het Leven van Werklozen: Schande!," 1926.
[15] "Het Leven van Werklozen: Een 'Gewoon' Geval," 1926.

worlds in which the bourgeois and the proletariat still lived during the 1920s. It is telling that Tinbergen highlighted party membership as a privilege that some of the poor could not even afford. The social-democratic party, of which he had already become a member, was mostly a middle- and upper-class organization. A recurring theme in the descriptions is whether the poverty is in any way deserved: "Let this man be a little less strong, a little less practical than most others, do he and his family have to be punished for this with such a life?"[16] It is clear that for Tinbergen the matter is not merely social; it is personal, too. In the first article he wondered: "Does our solidarity demand perhaps not more than party membership and party work? What can we do personally, without erecting new organizations and clubs, purely as fellow human beings – and how many of us do what is really demanded?"[17] The question is personal, and it is again Catharina that is the exemplar of the true socialist, since she was not merely working out ideals, was not merely a party intellectual, but willing to give up her individuality and personal aspirations.

But whereas the novel tends toward a romantic vision of the working class if not of the life of its individual members, Tinbergen moved in a different direction. The hardship and impoverishment he described in his articles could lead only to cultural *degeneration*.[18] The revolutionary spirit was seeping away from the poor and the unemployed. Unemployment did not automatically lead to resistance against capitalism among the poor; it was more likely to lead to moral and cultural degeneration. It was up to the social-democratic students for whom Tinbergen wrote the review to iden-tify with their lot, and to seek to improve it. Tinbergen felt this special personal responsibility deeply, and it made him critical of Jurgen. For it was Jurgen who failed to shoulder this responsibility, who ultimately opted out despite having seen the fate of the poor, despite having realized his own role and that of his family in the process. But the path that Jan set out for himself was not that of Catharina, his stay with the poor in Leiden was temporary. Instead, he sought a path through which he could lift the workers, from above, out of their spiritual and cultural degeneration.

3.2 The Social-Democratic Student Club of Leiden

In 1921 Tinbergen started his physics studies in Leiden. This relieved him, at least temporarily, from his military duties. He lived in the heart of town

---

[16] Ibid.   [17] Tinbergen, "Het Leven van Werklozen: Onze Plicht," 1925.
[18] Tinbergen, "Uit een andere Wereld," 1926.

in the Kloksteeg, in a small student room whose floor was so slanted he had to tilt his chair to sit straight. In Leiden he soon joined the Social-Democratic Labor Party (SDAP) as a youth member. And in 1922 and 1923 he took part in the initiative to set up the Leiden branch of the newly founded social-democratic student club (SDSC). This association of student clubs in different cities was a progressive response to the traditional elitist fraternities that, particularly in Leiden, were a rite of passage for young men entering the upper echelons of society.

The social-democratic student clubs drew from the many new students who entered the university in the 1920s from middle-class backgrounds, whose parents had never attended university. His friend from that period, Marnius van der Goes van Naters, described Jan's zeal in these early years: "[1923] was the year of the big textile industry strike, and poverty was visible on every street corner in Leiden, which was dependent on textile. Belligerently Tinbergen went from door to door to collect money for the strikers."[19]

The founding of the alternative student clubs across the country was perceived as a threat by the more traditional fraternities, who in 1924 proclaimed through its president that "the class struggle has now entered academia."[20] The SDSC was, however, was not particularly engaged in an active class struggle, but sought to end "the splendid isolation" of the student world. It was an association for students by students and hoped to forge a bridge between the studies and the social problems of the day. It was not so much that socialist ideals had never been entertained in student circles; in fact, they had always enjoyed some fascination among intellectuals. But the prevailing view was that the student days were for the free exploration of different positions and the development of oneself, meaning socialism could be freely entertained by the elite, but only as a theoretical possibility and not as a firm commitment, let alone as part of one's identity.[21] The new social-democratic clubs sought to change this; they wanted the students to be serious about socialism. There were similar attempts from idealistic Christian clubs, who were in close contact with the social-democratic clubs. These new societies sought to create a more

[19] "Tinbergen 90 jaar; Onverwoestbaar gelovige in een betere Wereld," *NRC Handelsblad*, 3 April 1993.
[20] Hakker and Tijn, "Kentering," 1924.
[21] Knegtmans, "Voor Wetenschap en Maatschappij. Het Zelfbeeld van Studenten in de Sociaal-Democratische Studentenclubs," 40–44, 2008.

socially engaged student body, but over time they also hoped to help transform the university into a more socially useful institution.

One of the first initiatives was the founding of a publication, the magazine *Kentering (Turn)*. The early issues of the magazine reflect well the main issues of concern for the students. The memory of World War I was fresh, and there was lots of attention to the peace movement and the newly founded League of Nations. The other major concern was how the working classes could be culturally emancipated. To these first-generation students one of the major concerns was how they could spread their knowledge and cultural appreciation with the workers. The SDSC was certainly not Marxist, but instead took much of its direction from the social-democratic reformer in Amsterdam, Floor Wibaut (1859–1936). He was one of the most prominent social-democratic politicians, famous for his social housing projects in Amsterdam and his progressive way of life; he and his wife had an open marriage. In 1924, Wibaut was one of the invited speakers at the Leiden branch of the SDSC where Tinbergen, in all likelihood, first met him.

Tinbergen was a national board member of the SDSC in the academic year of 1925–26. There were about seventy-five members at that point in various cities.[22] Part of his responsibility as a board member was to be on the second editorial board of *Kentering*. His first contribution to that journal was likely his first published piece of writing.[23] His article was a report of his visit to a Practical Idealists Association pioneer camp, one of the related Christian-socialist youth clubs. Tinbergen reported on a talk he delivered at this gathering, in which he argued that "the struggle" will, in the future, require science. Others responded that it was primarily a matter of spirit, hope, and love rather than science. This almost spiritual socialism of the mind, often based on Christian virtues, was characteristic of the circles in which Tinbergen moved in those years.

In these circles, Tinbergen's emphasis on technical knowledge and science struck a somewhat different chord. In the same article, *Intellect or Feeling*, he argued for the necessity of technical knowledge for the future leaders of socialist businesses. The socialist managers of the future must be schooled in management and economics, he argued, and capable of using statistics. They will have to limit or even shut down luxury industries, improve living conditions, and generally possess a broad economic understanding. Broad, because it required more "than the admiration and

[22] "Het Congres van de Soc. Dem. Studentenclubs," *Voorwaarts*, 20 May 1925, p. 9.
[23] Tinbergen, "Verstand of Gevoel?," 1924.

reiteration of Marx' theories – for they only provide us with the tragic downfall of capitalism." Therefore, "science will have to be our sword." The "sword" metaphor, and the invocation of the "struggle" is more combative than his later writings, but he would never abandon his early belief that socialism had to build on modern science and progress beyond Marx.

That conviction is on full display in what should be considered Tinbergen's first scientific (economic) publication, "Mathematics – Marginal Value – Marx,"[24] again in *Kentering*. In this little article he argued that simple mathematics in the form of geometry – the world of cones and parallelepipeds as it was taught to him in high school[25] – was indeed not applicable to economics. But mathematics, Tinbergen argued, was not static. And the new mathematics in which quantities were often left unspecified could be more useful for economics. This higher form of mathematics has three functions: (1) it acts as an archive of logic and helps one work out all the logical implications of a hypothesis; (2) it provides an easier way of organizing data; and (3) mathematical formulas are easier to combine than verbal chains of reasoning. It is particularly the third function, he argued, that is of significance, since in the economy many factors influence each other.

Tinbergen was not merely arguing for the use of mathematics in economics. He also suggested, in line with mathematical economists of the age such as Vilfredo Pareto, that a mathematical formulation of two competing theories will help us draw out all their implications and consequently allow us to determine which of them is correct. That argument was modern, but quite widely accepted at the time. The same could not be said for the next step in his argument. Theories, Tinbergen suggested, are sometimes used not because they are correct – he referred to Newton's theory – but rather because they provide good approximations. That view was near the cutting-edge of the scientific philosophy of the time, and most certainly novel in economics. It is precisely in this direction that he developed his argument. He argued that the marginal value theory, in which valuation is based on the preferences of consumer, is probably more correct, but also more complicated and less determinate than the classical view of Marx. Marx's theory of value, based on the costs of production, is much simpler and a good approximation. In other words, the marginal theory of value is the equivalent in economics of relativity theory in physics, that is, an

[24] Tinbergen, "Wiskunde – Grenswaarde – Marx," 1925.
[25] See Tinbergen's notebook "Wis- en Natuurkunde: Kegelsneden en Simplices," in possession of the author.

abstract theory that might provide a full picture but is sometimes indeterminate. The Marxist theory, on the other hand, is the equivalent in economics of Newton's theory, false in some respects, but useful as a first approximation. Or as Tinbergen put it: "[T]he marginal value theoretician will deal with the case as a special instance of a more general phenomenon and formulate his answer; the Marxist just knows the answer for this particular instance; in their formulation they are not at all alike, in their answer they are often very close together."[26] The marginal theory of value was at the time most closely associated with the liberal Austrian school of economics.[27] The reconciliation of opposing views between the capitalists and the socialists would become a true Tinbergen specialty.

If science was the sword in the fight for socialism, then we should use the very best science that is out there. And Tinbergen showed himself perfectly open to the suggestion that this might be the theory of marginal value, especially if it would prove more accurate in other fields. Economic science, for him, can certainly be different from the theories proposed by Marx.[28] So, in his very early work he was able to demonstrate that he was conversant in three fields of economics, physics, and mathematics; aware of the complex relationship between theories and the real world; and willing to revise his political views based on the newest scientific insights. It has been suggested that Tinbergen was trained as a natural scientist and transitioned after his dissertation into an economist. But his mentor, Paul Ehrenfest, whom we will discuss in detail in the next chapter, trained him in both physics and economics. And even though he studied physics at the university, the discussions and literature he encountered in the socialist movement were all about economics. If anything, it is perhaps better to think of Tinbergen during these years as being in a *superposition*; just as a particle in quantum mechanics can be both positive and negative at the same time before an experimental intervention is made, so too Tinbergen was still physicist and economist at the same time, before the Great Depression would intervene and turn him into an economist.

---

[26] Tinbergen, "Wiskunde – Grenswaarde – Marx," 1925.

[27] This was certainly true for Tinbergen, who based his treatment of marginalism on the work of Böhm-Bawerk, the leading theoretician of the Austrian school, but it was not necessarily the case. One of the marginalist pioneers, Leon Walras, was a socialist, and later socialist theories would use marginalism to argue for the possibility of central planning the economy.

[28] This early attempt to bridge Marxist and neoclassical theories followed the example set by his mentor in physics, Paul Ehrenfest, who had pursued a similar project.

The SDSC was certainly not the environment in which Tinbergen's socialism developed most deeply. But it was the place that allowed him to combine his scientific studies with his political convictions, a combination that would shape his work deeply. And the SDSC was also the place where he met what would become a new generation of social democrats in the Netherlands, and where he thus developed connections to some of the political leaders of the future. This included Marinus van der Goes van Naters, nicknamed the "Red Esquire" for his aristocratic descent, a law student in Leiden who would later lead the social-democratic party in parliament;[29] Wiardi (Stuuf) Beckman, a history student in Leiden and later a great reformer within the social-democratic party in the 1930s, who did not survive World War II; and Hein Vos, a student in Delft who would later be the driving force along with Tinbergen behind the Plan of Labor – a socialist plan to get out of the Great Depression of the early 1930s.

Among these later prominent social democrats, there were quite a few who combined their membership of the SDSC with that of the traditional "corps," the elite fraternity. In Jan's eyes they were having their cake and eating it too, by joining both the elite and socialism at the same time. Much like the fictional Jurgen, they remained on the fence about their commitments. Tinbergen, on the other hand, never became a member of one of the traditional fraternities. Instead, he combined his SDSC membership with that of the socialist youth movement (AJC), which included many with a working-class background. This demonstrated his commitment to the broader socialist movement, something that he occasionally found missing at the SDSC, as he complained to Wiardi Beckman. He believed the club was too "voluntaristic," and its members were not sufficiently "submerged" in the new socialism.[30]

Tinbergen identified more with those in the social-democratic student clubs who thought of the new students as intellectual *workers*, who included, among others, Hilda-Verwey Jonker.[31] This was to some extent merely a symbolic distinction, but Tinbergen did attempt to develop what it might mean to be an intellectual worker. For him that certainly implied that the intellectual work should, first and foremost, serve the cause of socialism. He suggested that overcoming bourgeois individualism as

[29] For an excellent biography, see Mrijen, *De Rode Jonker: De Eeuw van Marinus van Goes van Naters (1900–2005),* 2015.

[30] Wiardi Beckman to JT, 5 May 1927, TL.

[31] Knegtmans, "Voor Wetenschap en Maatschappij. Het Zelfbeeld van Studenten in de Sociaal-Democratische Studentenclubs," 45–47, 2008.

personified by Jurgen in the novel *De Burger* required giving up the "bourgeois illusion" of individual creativity. Or, worse yet, the idea that science existed only for the sake of science. Such luxuries could not be afforded in the struggle for social change. Instead, intellectual workers should organize themselves to solve social problems or strengthen the socialist cause. Too much science takes place because it is interesting to the individual scientist and not because it is socially relevant, he argued.[32]

The years in the mid-1920s were the most radical of his life. Tinbergen never came close to communism, but his articles on the organization and planning of science shared important similarities with the organization of science in the Soviet Union. In the same set of articles, he labeled one of the recent reports on unemployment from the SDAP "bourgeois" and suggested that once in power the party should have a blueprint for how to solve the unemployment problem. The idea of a blueprint for a new and better society, too, was close to the ideals of the communists. It was kindly pointed out to him in the next issue of *Kentering* that for the solution of the unemployment problem, the socialists would need the cooperation of the bourgeois, and that name-calling others "bourgeois" would be of little help in that process. Nor would it be of much help to organize research along the lines Tinbergen suggested, since all it would do was raise suspicion that the conclusions were predetermined.[33] The planning of science and the restrictions on the freedom of individual inquiry that Tinbergen had proposed went too far for his fellow SDSC members.

It was around this same period that Tinbergen was considering whether he would continue his studies in physics or whether he should shift to something of more direct use for the working classes. In 1926 he wrote to Floor Wibaut – the éminence grise of social-democratic party and well known for his progressive, although not necessarily Marxist ideals – whether economics is a subject worth pursuing: "I have completed my studies in mathematics and physics, but I don't believe I can serve the socialist cause much with these subjects. Since my professor [Ehrenfest] strongly believes I should continue my studies, I have started with statistics and economics."[34] Wibaut responded with some ambivalence. Although statistical-economic expertise will eventually be of great value at the municipal level and in the management of (socialist) firms, he said he was uncertain whether there would be a demand for this type of skill by the

[32] Tinbergen, "Wetenschappelijk Sosialisties Werk," 1927.
[33] Mok, "Slechte Voorlichting," 1927.
[34] JT to Wibaut, 14 September 1926, IISG, nr. ARCH01630, folder 86.

time that Tinbergen would finish his studies. It demonstrates that even a social reformer such as Wibaut who had been city governor and a major socialist intellectual could not yet quite see how economics could be turned into a socially useful science in the short run.

At that point Tinbergen decided not to switch disciplines yet. And he and Paul Ehrenfest, his dissertation advisor, decided on the subject of his dissertation in December 1927 and January of the next year.[35] But the idea of eventually transitioning to economics remained on both their minds, as is evident from their correspondence.

Despite all the radicalism of these years, he did not switch studies and neither did he cut ties with his bourgeois family. In fact, in one of the most significant episodes of his early career, his father helped him get a job at the Central Bureau of Statistics instead of the penitentiary institution where he was fulfilling his social work obligations as a conscientious objector to the draft. But as we will see, Tinbergen did break with a number of "bourgeois" habits of life.

3.3 The AJC in Leiden

The SDSC was the place for the socialist intellect, but it was in the socialist youth movement of the AJC that Tinbergen *became* a socialist. In the SDSC Tinbergen suggested that the intellect was more important than the emotions for the socialist, but in his writings for the AJC he reversed that order: socialism was first and foremost a feeling, and a calling.

In 1923, Tinbergen and his wife Tine joined the Leiden branch of the AJC. This would become a formative organization in their life. It was an organization in which they met, as they later described it, people from a different, more proletarian, background than themselves. The AJC, however, was not a simple youth organization for the children of workers. It sought to be a kind of cultural avant-garde of the workers' movement, and therefore was particularly appealing to youths with some cultural interests, who typically had educated parents. As a youth organization, the AJC was deeply formative for many of its members, including Jan and Tine. At the AJC Jan and Tine developed a lifelong spirited socialism, which included both a set of ideals – guiding principles of what socialism entailed politically – and a personal vision, a way of life. Even when interviewed about it

[35] The letter in which the proposed subject by Ehrenfest is mentioned has faded, but the first part of the title is still legible: "Studien über Minimalprincipien und Reciprozitätsbeziehungen in der Physis ..." (Studies on Minimum Problems and Reciprocal Relations in Physics ...). It is therefore unclear whether they also sought to explore these problems in economics, as Tinbergen ended up doing; see Paul Ehrenfest to JT, 25 December 1927, BA: EC.

more than sixty years later, Tinbergen would still emphasize the "Geist" of socialism present in the AJC.[36]

A variety of socialist youth programs were started around the time of World War I all across Europe, in Austria, Germany, Belgium, and the Netherlands. The Dutch branch, the AJC, was founded in 1918 by the SDAP and the National League of Unions (NVV). Initially, it was little more than a means to keep the children off the street. This changed when it came under the direction of Koos Vorrink. He was a highly idealistic man who was particularly concerned about alcohol abuse among workers and the youth of his day, and who more generally felt that moral standards were in steady decline, not least among the proletariat.

Under his leadership, the AJC was transformed into a youth movement that, although it never grew beyond a few thousand members, had great cultural impact in the larger Dutch socialist movement. And it would become the breeding ground for the mid-twentieth-century leaders of the social-democratic party in the Netherlands. Vorrink had from the start important intellectual and financial support from Floor Wibaut. Wibaut is perhaps best described as a Dutch Walther Rathenau. He was a free-spirited and progressive entrepreneur, who not only had behind him a successful career in business but was also publishing a steady stream of intellectual reflections on socialism, and around the time was busy realizing, as alderman, the social housing projects in Amsterdam. The housing projects, considered a great success to this day, combined avant-garde architecture from the designers of the Amsterdam school with social idealism aimed at improving or uplifting the lifestyle of the working classes. They reflected well the combination of economic and moral improvement that was pursued; the housing projects sought not merely to raise living standards but also to alter the lifestyles of the proletariat by preventing alcohol abuse and providing access to modern communication through post offices.

This moral elevation of the working classes (*verheffing*) was also the central goal within the AJC. Vorrink thought it could become an elite movement that would provide a moral exemplar for the rest of the working classes. And thus, this new lifestyle had to be on display prominently. In 1922, Koos Vorrink and the other pioneers of the AJC had realized "De Paasheuvel," an outdoor campsite in the Hoge Veluwe National Park. There they would jointly build a major clubhouse, which would be their refuge away from the city. It was there that they would pioneer a new

---

[36] IISG, nr. BG GC10/140, interview with Bep en Jan van der Feer, 18 February 1988.

socialist lifestyle around folk dances and music, a close study of nature, long hikes, the recital of uplifting poetry, and amateur theater. It was a serious lifestyle in which there were plenty of restrictions, or forms of "self-control," as the members called it. The consumption of alcohol, smoking, sweets, and luxuries were not allowed. The fashion had to be plain but not proletarian; one had to avoid both the vulgar and the bourgeois in speech. In writing one should use the new plain Kollewijn Spelling, in which words were written as they were pronounced. And there was a distinct list of movies and books one was supposed to enjoy. On the grounds of the Paasheuvel there was an open-air theater, in which various progressive plays were staged that conformed to the nonvulgar, nonbourgeois, authentic aesthetic of the organization. Its aesthetic had something in common with folk, without any of the hedonistic elements.

In hindsight it seems restrictive and rather extreme. But by most of its members it was experienced as liberating. The first reason for this was that it liberated the children from their mostly urban surroundings and their parents. The AJC allowed for the development of a youth culture, some decades before this became more widespread in society with the counterculture of the 1960s. And although Vorrink was a strong leader in the movement, he was still relatively young – twelve years senior to Tinbergen – and many of the other leaders were drawn from the more senior members. As such there was a strong feeling that the AJC was a self-governing organization; this was particularly true at the local level. This was further enhanced by the fact that although it received some financial support from the social-democratic party, most of its activities were self-organized and self-funded. The Paasheuvel club building was funded through donations from the members, who were stimulated in a variety of smart ways to save up money throughout the year.

In terms of organization it therefore resembled the Protestant churches in the Netherlands. It was a horizontal organization, with lots of local autonomy, and strongly dependent for funding on the contributions of its members. That resemblance went further than organizational structure. The AJC provided a year-long program which was clearly inspired by the religious calendar. And in fact, many of the major events were similar. Easter was celebrated in the spring, but even more significant were the Pentecost celebrations, which were the most important gatherings of the year. The descent of the Holy Spirit was celebrated and interpreted as an encouragement to spread the socialist gospel. This was done through public marches, events, and gatherings, in which clashes with local Christian clubs were not unusual. The Pentecost event also included

Figure 3.1 Celebration of Pentecost at an AJC camp, 1924.

dances around the maypole, an event at which many members got married (Figure 3.1). The year ended like the Christian year with Christmas, in which the spirit of charity was interpreted as the spirit of solidarity.

Jan Tinbergen and his wife Tine became deeply involved in the activities of the AJC. Tine frequently wrote poetry for the magazines of the organization, in the style of Henriette Roland Holst, the most famous Dutch socialist poet. These poems described the process of the spiritual awakening of socialism and professed hopeful images of the future. In one of them Tine described the past struggles of the working class and the better future that lies ahead:

> They still carried the light like a hidden dream
> Suspicion accompanied their heart like a stern guard
> What bound them were the old silent worries
> When they spoke it was soft and in fear
>
> The heart had forgotten its own strength
> Fruitless doubt kept the will in chains
> But in us lives the blessed and joyous Knowing
> Light, like a wonder it has blossomed.[37]

---

[37] In Dutch: "Zij droegen het licht nog als een droom verborgen / Argwaan hield naast hun hart een starre wacht / Hen bonden nog de oude stille zorgen / En als zij spraken was 't

This blend of spiritual awakening and socialist struggle was typical for the contributions to the AJC magazine *Het Jonge Volk* (*The Young People*, after the socialist newspaper *The People*), which presented socialism as a promised land that could be reached through suffering and determination. Inspired by a woodcut with the engraving "In the dark alleys of our cities a bright call awakens," Jan Tinbergen wrote a short story for *Het Jonge Volk*. His contribution tells of a troop of AJC members who invited local children to their cultural evening, but the poor children were reluctant and somewhat afraid. "They watch from a distance, they want to sing along, but don't know the words. But after one has joined, others follow. How much can we achieve if we are just open to others?" Tinbergen asked rhetorically. "Once inside the venue the fear is shaken off, everybody joins into the chorus, and dances along. Now we felt stronger, we knew that we had really lived our ideal, we had shown them that life could be different," he concluded.[38]

This mixture of spiritual, if not Christian, upliftment was promoted by Koos Vorrink, who thought of socialism as an open ideal, rather than a blueprint for society. In one of his Pentecost speeches, he argued that socialism was not an ossified formula or a complete theory, nor was it the socialist party. Instead, Vorrink argued, it was the thirst for justice and the never-ending fight against injustice. Socialism is service to the community and is to be found in human connections.[39] In the AJC, socialism thus moved away from the struggle of the workers' movement and instead became a movement of ideals. It was also drawn away from materialist concerns and toward immaterial goals. Justice was important, but for the AJC members, socialism was in particular to be found in a new and more meaningful lifestyle. It was from this concern that the life rules emerged. The AJC sought to be a vanguard in the exploration of a lifestyle that would be attainable for everyone in the socialist society of the future. But for the vanguard it was a matter of will and determination; they could realize socialism if they willed it enough, even when the rest of society was still capitalist. According to Marxist doctrine this was a naïve "utopian" socialist idea, a variety of prescientific socialism, and the AJC was often

bevreesd en zacht / Het hart was lang de eigen kracht vergeten / Vrucht'loze twijfel hield de wil geboeid / Maar in ons woont het hoge blijde Weten / Licht, tot een wonder is het opgebloeid."

[38] Tinbergen, "In der Steden Donk're Stegen is een Lichte Roep Ontwaakt ...," 1928.
[39] Van der Louw, *Rood als je Hart: Geschiedenis van de AJC*, 37, 1974.

Figure 3.2 Jan on the left sitting in his AJC clothes in the fields near Ermelo, 1928.

mocked for it, not in the least by the older generations within the social-democratic party.

But if anything, that only seemed to harden the determination within the AJC. The movement was known for a severe, almost Spartan discipline, somewhat ironic given its pacifist ideals. The same discipline and unity made the organization incredibly effective even though it remained relatively small. The radicalness of their alternative lifestyle, including a typical style of dress and their own symbols and signs, made them very visible to the outside world. This was promoted further with marches and public rallies and events. At later reunions the members could rejoice in the songs and dances that had been engraved in their memory, and frequently the members retained the strict living habits for the rest of their lives. Jan Tinbergen would never drink in his life, never own a car, and he never got rid of the typical haircut which was fashionable during those days, a haircut that a barber in New York once described as the semi-crewcut (Figure 3.2).[40]

It was thus literally true that in the AJC one became a socialist. One made new friends, adopted a different style of clothing and new habits, and

[40] "Ontwikkelingslanden op de been Helpen," *Het Parool*, 27 June 1964, 7.

engaged in spreading the "gospel." In this way socialism was much more than a set of political ideals, but became a way of life, sometimes even at the expense of political ideals. Contemporary observers and social-democratic party members were often critical of this socialist pathos, of style only. But that is selling the movement considerably short; many of the members combined it with an honest inner conviction that a better way of living was possible. More importantly, it provided a sense of direction for a young generation, which at least in the case of Tinbergen stayed with him for the rest of his life. In fact, the way in which socialism was realized in this movement became for him a model for how socialism could be attained more broadly in society.

The youth movement was important for one other reason. Although its ethos was elitist, its membership came from various backgrounds, and, as such, it represented on a small scale the ideal of an integrated and harmonious society. It attracted children from the working classes, but also those of the middle classes, and some from the upper middle class such as Tinbergen. This was different from many of the other youth movements of the time, which remained tied to religious or class background. Within the broader social-democratic party the integration of workers and intellectuals remained problematic. There had always been prominent upperclass members of the SDAP, such as Floor Wibaut, who were attracted to its progressive nature, but individuals like him and particularly the older Marxist ideologues of the movement did not always mix well with the workers in the party. It was in societies like the AJC that classes could integrate, and this was meant to be facilitated by the unique simple, but never vulgar, dress style, and the curious combination of bourgeois and folk culture.

Tinbergen reflected on this goal of integration in a brief article on the place of the student in the AJC.[41] He detailed his ambiguous feelings about, on the one hand, turning his back to his own class and, on the other hand, not being able to identify with some of the prominent lines in the AJC songs: "We have felt it ourselves / the poignant pain of work."[42] But it was in the AJC that he felt that class differences were overcome. It was where, at least for the time being, social background did not matter, and everybody could treat each other as equals. For Tinbergen this was the most

---

[41] Tinbergen, "A.J.C.-er en Student," 1928.
[42] His good friend Marinus van der Goes van Naters remembered that emotion seventy years later; see "Tinbergen 90 jaar; Onverwoestbaar gelovige in een betere Wereld," *NRC Handelsblad*, 3 April 1993.

important cultural achievement of the AJC. It is this same sentiment that would underlie his later attempts to create a socialist party for everyone, not just for workers, of which the Plan movement of the 1930s was one of the most visible outcomes[43] and which motivated the postwar "Doorbraak" (Breakthrough) movement of the 1950s.

Tinbergen was more drawn to the small-scale events at the AJC, than the large-scale gatherings and manifestations. In 1924 Tinbergen had formed a small study club in Leiden within the AJC, where in the winter they discussed macro-economics, or *Staatshuishoudkunde*, as it was then called in Dutch.[44] During these years, not only Jan, but also his fiancée Tine was actively involved; she talked, for example, about the history of the youth movement[45] and wrote frequently in the AJC periodical about the social outdoor activities. In 1925 Tinbergen had to move to Rotterdam to fulfill the duties resulting from his objection to the military draft, and there too he was an active member of the AJC (Figure 3.3). He gave talks on astronomy on the club nights and tried to act as a mediator in an enduring conflict within the local Rotterdam branch.[46] When he started working in The Hague at the Central Bureau of Statistics in 1927, he remained involved with the AJC, this time as group leader of the local branch. This long involvement was more typical, and it was only in their late twenties that members typically left the AJC for other organizations within or associated with the social-democratic party.

In the same year that he became group leader, Tinbergen contributed a small article to the Christmas edition of *Het Jonge Volk* that talks of a small social miracle in which some working girls in Scheveningen who had first been hooting at the AJC group along with the other local youth had now joined the AJC group and were singing along with the members. They hiked along, back to the clubhouse, and Tinbergen concluded hopefully: "We have a chance, to make things better . . . it is growing! Everywhere!"[47]

The SDSC allowed him to combine his studies and his idealism, but his socialist awakening happened in the AJC, a movement that turned socialism into a cultural program. It was the shared outdoor activities that formed the heart of the organization, the hikes with the accompanying songs, the cultural events involving folk dancing and amateur theater. This

---

[43] Tinbergen, "A.J.C.-er en Student," 1928.
[44] See report "Leiden," *Het Jonge Volk*, vol. 11, no. 26, 26 December 1924.
[45] See report "Leiden," *Het Jonge Volk*, vol. 14, no. 19, 16 September 1927.
[46] Wim Booij to JT, 12 August 1927, TL.
[47] Tinbergen, "Gewonnen," 1927. Tinbergen was writing here in a typical style, characteristic of the articles in *Het Jonge Volk*, and his writing appears to have been quite heavily edited; see Klaas (Toornstra) to JT, 16 December 1927, TL.

Figure 3.3 Tine and Jan visiting Jo and Emilien, friends from the AJC in Rotterdam, ca. 1926.

culminated in the celebration of Pentecost in the spring, when the budding flowers were compared to the budding spirt of socialism. It was this mixture of progressive Christian humanism and socialist ideals that would remain characteristic for Tinbergen's socialist ideals.

3.4 Pacifism

The pacifist movement in the Netherlands, which we already encountered in the building of the Peace Palace in The Hague, was another important formative influence. The Netherlands pursued a strategy of neutrality, which it successfully maintained during World War I. This neutrality meant that the country did not take sides during the war, but also meant that it did not engage in the building of military alliances during peacetime. As a small trading nation with global connections, the position of neutrality was not primarily idealistic, but reflected the self-interest of the Netherlands. The pacifism that inspired Tinbergen was certainly not unrelated to the ideal of neutrality, but it had additional Christian and socialist roots.[48]

---

[48] Van den Boomen, *Honderd Jaar Vredesbeweging in Nederland*, 14, 1983.

Much of the particular pacifism that influenced him can be traced back to Ferdinand Domela Nieuwenhuis, a progressive Christian minister who embraced socialism, translated Marx into Dutch, and was in parliament for the SDAP from 1888 to 1891, where he consistently argued for the reduction of money spent on war and the navy. In 1904 he founded the International Antimilitaristic Association, which drew in fellow-travelers from various European countries, but remained primarily a Dutch organization. In fact, one of his most important targets was the militaristic German social-democratic party under August Bebel. Domela Nieuwenhuis became famous with his slogan "No man and no penny for militarism," which was frequently proposed as a party motto within the SDAP, although never officially adopted.[49] It reflected a combination of the reduction of military spending with opposition to the military draft.

Although for Domela Nieuwenhuis socialism meant the rejection of Christianity, there was also a strand of Christian-socialists which sought to combine pacifism and the Christian faith. This movement found its origins in the years leading up to World War I and resulted in the Federation for Christian-Socialists, which was the driving force behind the "conscientious objection manifesto" of 1915, a manifesto that was signed by progressive Christians, left-wing SDAP members, and communists.[50] The cause of pacifism was thus able to unite people with different ideological convictions, but the manifesto itself did not have great success. The signatories were arrested and sued; it was a minor victory for the pacifist cause that they won their appeal. Several progressive ministers were part of this movement, including J. B. Th. Hugenholtz, Bart de Ligt, and the remonstrant minister from Leiden, G. J. Heering.[51] Tinbergen had connections to some of them. With Hugenholtz he would later help establish the NOVIB, the organization for international aid. And Tinbergen knew Heering from his time in Leiden when he attended his church meetings; the two remained in contact afterward.[52] Tinbergen hardly ever spoke about his religious convictions but was lifelong member of the Remonstrant Brotherhood. The Remonstrants are a Protestant community with links to the humanism of Desiderius Erasmus, the early modern philosopher. They pursue a liberal Christianity that is undogmatic in its Christianity, but strongly idealistic. Tinbergen never regularly attended

---

[49] Ibid., 16–25.   [50] Bijnsdorp, Ermers, and Kenkhuis, *De Wapens Neder*, 1985.
[51] Noordergraaf, *Niet met de Wapenen der Barbaren: Het Christen-Socialisme van Bart de Ligt*, 189ff., 1994.
[52] Their correspondence is available in TL.

their meetings, but this was not wholly uncharacteristic since the Remonstrants believed that Christianity was primarily personal. In that sense it had some similarities to the type of socialism pursued in the AJC.

Unlike pacifism, the ideals of peace and international order enjoyed more than fringe support among Protestants in the Netherlands. The Society for the League of Nations and Peace was led by two prominent Protestant lawyers, Anne Anema and Victor Henri Rutgers.[53] Another strand of this Christian-socialism was present in the work of Henriette Roland Holst, the Dutch poet, who in 1912 left the SDAP to establish an organization radically dedicated to internationalism. Her poetry was the defining style for the literary work in the AJC (and inspired Tine). Roland Holst's socialism was voluntarist, personal, and active, much like that of the AJC. Her strongly antimilitaristic stance, which she shared with some other poets, had a strong influence on the contents of the periodical *De Jonge Gids*, which promoted pacifism among socialist youth. That periodical was later succeeded by *Fundament*, to which Tinbergen would contribute as both author and editor.[54] Within socialist circles the notion of peace had a double connotation. On the one hand, it referred to the absence of war between nations, but, on the other hand, it was also the goal to arrive at social peace within society, to end the class war. For these socialists the goal was not to triumph over the capitalists, as it was for the communists, but to overcome the class struggle. They believed the socialist spirit could be awakened in anyone, and once this succeeded, a harmonious society was possible.

While Henriette Roland Holst and her followers differed in terms of strategy from the communists, they shared the internationalism promoted by that group. To understand Tinbergen's later work, it is crucial to understand this somewhat curious combination of peaceful methods and internationalist ideals. Socialists such as Henriette Roland Holst were more radical in political ideals than the social-democratic parties of Europe, and hence they often felt drawn to the communists – and their critics often dismissed them as such. But in political methods, they were less conflict-prone than even the social-democratic parties and the often-combative

[53] Reinders, "Macht in Dienst van Recht. Gereformeerden over Oorlog en Vrede in de Periode 1918–1940," 248–49, 1987.

[54] Kröger, "Vervolging, Verbanning en het Nazi-Regime in het Tijdschrift 'Het Fundament,'" n. 9, 1999; Bijnsdorp, Ermers, and Kenkhuis, *De Wapens Neder*, 325–29, 1985.

unions. They thus combined radicalism in ideas with moderation in political means.

Although disarmament was an important goal, it was clear to the Dutch pacifist movement that this was not enough. What was required was international law and governance. This type of internationalist thinking that stressed the potential of global harmony and later global organization deeply influenced Tinbergen and his later students such as Jan Pronk. They believed that truly global organizations such as the United Nations are the embodiment of this universalist position, and they always harbored a suspicion toward regional blocs such as NATO and to some extent the European Union. The idealists within these organizations sought an international order, not the stability of power between regional blocs. It was therefore natural for the Dutch pacifists to oppose colonialism, although they certainly did not seek to promote a revolutionary spirit in the colonies. Instead, it was hoped that much like the class conflict at home, a new mode of harmonious coexistence could be found between oppressor and oppressed. The anticolonialism of the pacifists was shared by most in the Dutch social-democratic party, but the party leaders ultimately had to make important concessions on this point – precisely because the political reality was that the Netherlands still had significant colonial possessions in both the East (Indonesia) and the West (Surinam and several islands in the Caribbean).

Tinbergen's internationalism would leave an important mark on his professional career. And he frequently wore his "broken rifle" lapel pin – the symbol of pacifism. But toward the end of his undergraduate studies in physics, when he was in his early twenties, he was faced with a much more direct and personal choice: Would he join the military draft? He received his first call for military service late in 1922, not long after he had started his studies in physics in Leiden. It was around the same time that a military issue came to dominate Dutch politics. In 1923 the Dutch government proposed to expand the naval presence in the Dutch Indies (what is now Indonesia) at a cost of 300 million guilders in total (the total government budget in 1923 was about 800 million). The proposed Naval Act (Vlootwet) generated widespread opposition from the public, especially the unions and the social-democratic party that mounted a campaign against it. The heart of this campaign was a petition against the law, which was signed by 1,132,228 voters, nearly one-sixth of the total population.[55]

[55] For the historical data, see Centraal Bureau voor Statistiek, *Tweehonderd Jaar Statistiek in Tijdreeksen 1800–1999*, 2001.

With the support of the petition, various members of parties belonging to the government voted down the Naval Act, with a crucial one-vote difference, and consequently the government fell. Despite this initial success, an identical law was accepted by the next government.

Part of the same society-wide debate was also the right to be a "conscientious objector" or, more precisely, the right to substitute one's military service for social service. This right was finally granted in the same summer of 1923 when the Naval Act was first rejected. This was just in time for Tinbergen, who was first drafted in 1922, but twice got a deferment of one year in order to be able to complete his studies in physics. In fact, he had seriously considered to not even ask for a deferment, but to object to the draft in 1923, which would have meant he had to serve a jail sentence: "Refusing the draft was my own idea. Wars were typically nationalistic back then – pursued by nationalists and militarists.... There is almost nothing worse than nationalism."[56] Only a few years earlier J. P. Berlage Jr., son of the famous architect and similarly a student of physics in Leiden, had refused and was sentenced to jail. His courage was much admired by Tinbergen.[57]

But his friends managed to talk Tinbergen out of the idea of not asking for a deferment since change was on the horizon.[58] He heeded their advice and decided to request social service as replacement for military service. It was a small compromise; some of the most radical opponents of the draft also refused this social service and still ended up serving time in jail. The compromise Tinbergen chose was advocated in particular by the newly founded organization Kerk en Vrede (Church and Peace), in which minister Heering, who Tinbergen knew well, was of particular importance.[59]

Tinbergen's request to be considered for social service was granted, upon which he had to explain his moral objections to the military draft in front of a military committee in September 1925.[60] Permission was more easily granted for those who objected on religious grounds, but Tinbergen stubbornly argued his case on political grounds. But much to his frustration, the committee was more interested in the personal side of the question than the political side of the matter.[61] It was finally decided in April 1926 that he would have to do a full two years, instead of his requested

---

[56] Tinbergen, "Ik heb Geluk Gehad . . .," 1984.
[57] Boumans, "Jan Tinbergen," 2003; Tinbergen, "Ik heb Geluk Gehad . . .," 1984.
[58] Archived in TL as NL-RtEUR_TBCOR01_001D007, January 1925.
[59] Schöll, *Dienstweigering in Nederland Voor de Tweede Wereldoorlog*, 73–78, 1981.
[60] Archived in TL NL-RtEUR_TBCOR01_001D008, 10 September 1925.
[61] Tinbergen, "Ik heb Geluk Gehad . . .," 1984.

period of one and a half years, of social service. And it was thus that Tinbergen did end up in jail after all, not as a convict serving time but as an administrative clerk. In 1925 he moved to Rotterdam, where he started his social service in the penitentiary institution in the northern part of town.

The job was repetitive and unstimulating, although it seems that even here, he found opportunities to engage with his superiors about the future of penitentiary institutions and the importance of crime prevention.[62] It was a great relief when his father arranged through Henri Methorst, then director of the Central Bureau of Statistics (CBS), for Tinbergen to complete his social service at the statistical institute. His request to do so was granted, and he was awarded the sum of seventy cents for traveling expenses. In August 1927 he worked his final day in Rotterdam and started at the CBS in The Hague the following Monday. His journey into business cycle statistics and econometrics began there, largely unintentionally. In some sense it was Tinbergen's return to his father, much like Jurgen had done, because it was his father, through his connections, who had secured the alternative position at the CBS. It also meant that he returned to The Hague after his time in Leiden and Rotterdam. But at that point the job in statistics still seemed like a temporary engagement, after which he would return to Paul Ehrenfest and his studies in physics and mathematical economics. Nobody could have predicted at that point that it would be the combination of statistics and mathematics that would make him into one of the most influential economists of the 1930s.

***

The question we should ask is whether Tinbergen succeeded in living up to Catharina's high standards. Did he live up to her standards of not merely dedicating one's life to the cause of the working classes but also becoming part of the working classes? On some basic level the answer to that can only be negative. He tried to make contact with the working classes repeatedly, but was never at home among them. Tinbergen had attempted to justify intellectual pursuits as a kind of intellectual labor, but by his own admission the jobs in academia came with many privileges and an unjustly high wage.[63]

---

[62] A. K. Hardenberg to JT, 29 November 1928, TL.
[63] Tinbergen, "Socialisten en Hoge Inkomens," 1930; Tinbergen, "Socialisten en Hoge Inkomens: Een Antwoord," 1930.

His deep engagement with the AJC came closest to the immersion in the working class that Tinbergen praised in Catharina. But even the AJC, although its members were primarily proletarian, was an elite organization, elevated above the proletariat, and designed to lead it. Especially for members from a bourgeois background, it was ambiguous what the organization truly was. In a letter written in 1928 when both Tinbergen and his wife Tine were leaving the AJC, their fellow member and friend from Leiden, Jan van der Moolen, wrote Tinbergen a letter in which he questioned how much of the AJC spirit will last beyond the years of actual membership.

Van der Moolen, who came from a working-class family and had always had a manufacturing job, complained that when he encountered his old friends from the AJC and the SDSC on the streets of Leiden they pretended to not know him anymore. Even Tine had now walked past him without acknowledging him, and she no longer attended socialist meetings. It seemed that the social integration of the AJC was only temporary, Van der Moolen suggested. He concluded that it was finally becoming clear to him after thirty years in the socialist movement that socialism is ultimately a movement *for* the working class and not *of* the working class.[64] He appealed to Tinbergen to not fall into this trap, and to remain true to the cause and particularly loyal to his friends.

It is unlikely that it was Van der Moolen who shaped Jan and Tine's decision of where to live in the Hague. But perhaps it was a similar sentiment to the one he expressed that motivated them to choose the Tesselsestraat in Scheveningen, only a stone's throw away from the dunes. The street was part of Duindorp, a social housing project for families of fishermen. It was erected between 1915 and 1930. As many of the other social housing projects of the time it was also built to generate a new sense of community, and Jan and Tine actively engaged with the community center. Van der Moolen suggested that once his old friends had decided to live in a certain bourgeois neighborhood, he knew for certain that he had lost them. Tinbergen was indeed proud that he and Tine had chosen Duindorp; it was their first home where they hoped to start a family together.[65] Later he recounted frequently that he was still proud that he reported on the working conditions of the poor in Leiden and that he moved to Scheveningen afterward. But his daughter also remembered that as soon as they had picked up "the wrong words" on the street in Scheveningen, the family quickly moved to a bourgeois neighborhood,

[64] J. M. van der Moolen to JT, 17 April 1928, TL.
[65] IISG, nr. BG GC10/140, interview with Bep en Jan van der Feer, 18 February 1988.

De Vogelwijk, in The Hague. Tinbergen certainly remained more committed to socialism than Jurgen did in the novel, but bringing up his children among the workers as Catharina did in the novel was certainly a step too far for him.

Nonetheless, Tinbergen's contact with the poor in Leiden was a formative experience that motivated his socialism, much like his visit to the slums of Calcutta in the early 1950s would motivate his turn to development economics. Tinbergen never fully integrated with the working classes, and the AJC was not a movement that could ultimately make this happen. When Van der Moolen thus wrote that (his) socialism is *for* the working classes rather than *of* the working classes, he was correct. But Tinbergen's socialism was not a socialism merely borne out of intellectual curiosity or youthful rebellion against his bourgeois background; instead, it was one borne out of an awareness of social differences and an emotional commitment to eradicate such differences.

4

From Ehrenfest to the Econometric Society

Einstein, my upset stomach hates your theory – it almost hates you yourself!
How am I to provide for my students? What am I to answer to the
philosophers?
—Paul Ehrenfest in a letter to Einstein, 1919

The most important intellectual influence on the young Jan Tinbergen was
his PhD supervisor Paul Ehrenfest. In many ways this is surprising:
Ehrenfest was not a socialist, he was not an economist, and he committed
suicide before Tinbergen's career as an economist really started. Still, there
are few parts of Tinbergen's work that are not inspired by Ehrenfest. He
was the guiding figure in Tinbergen's career choice, took him under his
wing, and in many ways Ehrenfest became a father figure for Tinbergen.
Their relationship was intimate, intense even, as is evidenced by their
frequent and personal correspondence. And yet, for all the inspiration
and guidance that Ehrenfest provided, the men could hardly have been
more different. Ehrenfest was jovial, open, witty, and forthright. Tinbergen
was somewhat shy, solitary, serious, and rather private. Ehrenfest was often
insecure about himself, most effective as a critic of others' work, and went
for long periods without publishing anything. He pondered fundamental
principles and relied on his intuitions, reasoned by analogy. Tinbergen had
darker periods, but outwardly always showed great confidence in his work,
and was at his best when he pioneered new approaches and fields. He
published nearly anything he wrote, however incomplete or tentative. He
was little interested in fundamental principles, but preferred to focus on
what worked, relying on data to evaluate the quantitative effects. Tinbergen
was weary of unproductive theoretical disputes, which he often dismissed
as dogmatic. And yet the two found in one another much to admire, and
Ehrenfest's outlook would remain the foundation for Tinbergen's
own work.

Ehrenfest, who had studied with Ludwig Boltzmann in his native Vienna, arrived in Leiden in 1912 to succeed the world-renowned Nobel Prize laureate Hendrik Antoon Lorentz as the chair in theoretical physics. The physics department in Leiden at the time towered above other universities in the Netherlands and could be measured against the premier departments for physics in the world, such as at Göttingen and Vienna. The Dutch physicist Heike Kamerlingh Onnes won the Nobel Prize in 1913 for his experimental work in physics, just one year after the arrival of Ehrenfest. And although Ehrenfest would never achieve a similar status, he was both locally and internationally a central node in the network of superstar physicists of the age, the men who revolutionized our perspective on the universe through relativity theory and on the world of atoms and subatomic particles through quantum mechanics. Individuals like Albert Einstein, Max Planck, Erwin Schrödinger and Niels Bohr.

Ehrenfest brought most of them to Leiden. He was particularly well acquainted with Albert Einstein, who came over regularly. On one of those visits he even spent some time at the summer lodge of the Tinbergen family, in Hulshorst in the Veluwe. Ehrenfest also arranged for his best students to study abroad at other premier physics departments in Europe: Tinbergen went briefly to Göttingen in 1923.[1] Ehrenfest was also a modernizer of the way in which physics was taught and, perhaps even more importantly, the way students and professors interacted.

His impact on both the intellectual and personal development of Jan Tinbergen is hard to overestimate. Tinbergen did not move away from physics and Ehrenfest after his graduate studies, as is sometimes suggested; rather, Ehrenfest and Tinbergen jointly explored economics and the possibilities for the application of tools and insights from physics to economics. In fact, Ehrenfest started exploring analogies between the two fields before Tinbergen became his student around 1920, and Tinbergen's desire to study economics was much stimulated by Ehrenfest. It was therefore an enormous tragedy for Tinbergen when Ehrenfest took his own life only weeks before the meetings of the Econometric Society took place in Leiden in 1933. The conference hosted by Tinbergen included a scheduled keynote lecture from Ehrenfest. It would have been the crowning achievement of their collaboration and exploration of economics and the budding field of econometrics. But before we reach those events, let us start with Ehrenfest's educational and academic reforms in Leiden.

---

[1] JTC: Klein over Ehrenfest manuscript.

4.1 The Socrates of Leiden

The arrival of Ehrenfest in Leiden was described by one student as "a bolt of lightning."[2] Ehrenfest broke with much of the formality and stiffness of his predecessors to create a lively academic community. It meant convincing the students that he wanted to see their eyes when he lectured, not their heads as they were busy jotting down notes. More important than the lectures should be the conversations afterward and especially the discussions during seminars. He wanted to break down the barrier created by the hierarchy between professor and student, so that they could engage in conversation, rather than instruction.[3]

Ehrenfest's students all remember how he achieved most of these things through example: he kept asking questions. His inaugural lecture in Leiden is a case in point, it provided an overview of the field, but ended with a set of open questions on which he hoped others would work. Whether his students or one of the great physicists of the era gave a talk, Ehrenfest would always keep asking questions to elicit clearer and more basic explanations of the phenomenon or principle under discussion. Not infrequently, he got up from his chair and took over the chalk and the presentation and attempted to present the idea with more clarity. Einstein said he could "strip a theory of its mathematical accouterments until the simple basic idea emerged with clarity. This capacity made him a peerless teacher."[4] In order to arrive at these basic understandings, Ehrenfest believed that active engagement and discussion was essential; it was only through interrogation and further questions that we could arrive at a more fundamental understanding. Understanding meant being able to explain a phenomenon in the most basic terms.

Ehrenfest's inquisitive style was very direct, and, not infrequently, guest speakers were taken aback by the probing questions of the short, spectacled, and energetic professor (Figure 4.1). Some of his students, especially the talented ones, were attracted to it, while for those lacking such special gifts Ehrenfest's approach was less appealing. In an academic culture that was still very hierarchical and quite formal, Ehrenfest broke with many norms and developed very personal relationships with his students. They came to his house, where Tatyana Afanasyeva, Ehrenfest's wife, was an integral part of the intellectual community. Ehrenfest mentored his

[2] Klein, *Paul Ehrenfest: The Making of a Theoretical Physicist*, 1985.   [3] Ibid., chapter 1.
[4] Ehrenfest quoted in Klein, "Not by Discoveries Alone: The Centennial of Paul Ehrenfest," 1981.

Figure 4.1 Paul Ehrenfest performing a classroom experiment, with his students including Tinbergen, Sam Goudsmit, and Eliza Wiersma in attendance, ca. 1924.

students intensely and did not refrain from offering solicited and unsolicited advice about their personal life, health, and even their partner choice.[5] The flip side to this meddling was that he also supported his students' nonacademic pursuits. He helped one of Tinbergen's friends, Wim Planjer, with the creation of an idealistic business venture in city gardening, even though he rightly saw from the start that Planjer was, as the Dutch put it, a man of twelve trades and thirteen mistakes.

Ehrenfest put great effort into creating an informal atmosphere. He once decried that "physics picnics are so much more productive than physics lectures."[6] He was deeply devoted to natural science and saw the single-minded pursuit of knowledge as a central goal. Ehrenfest expected little less than total devotion from his students, which at least for some was a little too much to bear. This vision of the pursuit of knowledge as a process of interaction was reflected in the way that Ehrenfest managed to transform the practice of physics in Leiden. The first of his academic reforms was the

---

[5] Casimir, *Haphazard Reality: Half a Century of Science*, 64, 1983.
[6] Ehrenfest quoted in Hollestelle, *Paul Ehrenfest: Worstelingen met de Moderne Wetenschap, 1912–1933*, 59, 2011.

creation of a reading room in the physics lab. The main function of the Bosscha reading room was not the availability of books, which were already available in the university library. Instead, Ehrenfest had seen in Göttingen that such a reading room could have an important social function as a meeting place for students and staff and, most importantly, as a place where students and professors would run into one another for more casual conversation. In order to facilitate this meeting place function, books could not be taken out of the reading room. One of his students remembered how Ehrenfest would close the reading room for days when he found that one of the volumes had gone missing.[7]

The second innovation was that Ehrenfest tried to spot talented students. At the time studies were divided into two parts: the "*kandidaats*" (BA) and the "*doctoraal*" (MA/PhD) phase, both consisting of two years. The first two years consisted of virtually only lectures, and there was little to no interaction between students and professors. To change this, in 1923 Ehrenfest founded the "Leidsche Flesch" (Leiden Jar, named after the first capacitor, invented in 1746 by Pieter van Musschenbroeck). It was a place for talks and discussions specifically aimed at *kandidaats* students. In this way young students were already familiarized with the practice of science, rather than just the acquisition of knowledge. Ehrenfest encouraged his graduate students to tell them if there was a younger student with talent whom he should get to know better. For those who had proceeded to the final two years, he revived the previously dormant Christiaan Huygens society. The purpose of this restricted society was not specialized discussions about physics, but rather general discussions about science and society, on topics introduced by the various (student) members. Ehrenfest, like other educational reformers of the age, believed that there should be an intimate connection between modern science and society.

His most important initiative, however, was the Wednesday evening colloquium. It was intended for his PhD students (although not completely restricted to them). Ehrenfest soon reformed this traditional colloquium when he arrived in Leiden. He hoped to transform it from a formal lecture by a guest speaker to a lively, if not heated, forum for discussion. The Wednesday Colloquium was the central meeting point for students and professors, and it was the place where new research and recent developments in physics were discussed, preferably introduced by one of the

---

[7] Casimir, *Haphazard Reality: Half a Century of Science*, 76, 1983.

leading European physicists or, alternatively, by one of the PhD students. The meetings were certainly no mere picnics. He treated his renowned guests with the same lack of regard for status or titles as he hoped the students would treat him. Ehrenfest often dominated discussions and was a demanding host to his speakers, who not infrequently grew frustrated with his incessant probing. He demanded regular attendance from the students he invited and excluded them in the case of unjustified absences. The informality of the sessions and his skill for thorough inquiry made the colloquium meetings of great value for his students. He would not let the speaker get away with any sleight of hand or gap in the argument, but would probe and probe again to identify the core of the problem. By doing so he forced the speakers to explain their work in the simplest terms. In this critical attitude it was a modern seminar that did away with much of the decorum that had dominated before he arrived. It generated inter-actions that were highly rewarding for those who could keep up. But it was also a daunting stage, where even many of Ehrenfest's peers did not feel safe.

Ehrenfest's probing was based on his firm conviction that one of the fundamental skills for physicists was to develop a physical intuition, which could help them grasp the fundamental truths about nature. The development of this intuition would help his students to work on a wider range of problems than just their dissertation topics. Ehrenfest loved to draw analogies between different, seemingly disconnected, fields within physics. It was a habit that probably owed much to his study with Boltzmann in Vienna[8] and embodied a belief in a kind of unity in the principles underlying the workings of the (natural) world.

The lively colloquium, as well as the other social institutions, did indeed manage to create a sense of community and an idea among his students that they were contributing to something special.[9] The group of students shared ideas and was in intense contact with one another under the leadership of their witty and energetic mentor. The community, Ehrenfest hoped, would be so lively and immersive that they could replace the traditional student community of the fraternities: "with their noses high and their pockets full of guilders."[10] It expressed the same sentiment

---

[8] Klein, *Paul Ehrenfest: The Making of a Theoretical Physicist*, 36–38, 1985.
[9] Alberts, "On Connecting Socialism and Mathematics: Dirk Struik, Jan Burgers, and Jan Tinbergen," 1994.
[10] Ehrenfest quoted in Klein, *Paul Ehrenfest: The Making of a Theoretical Physicist*, 8, 1985.

Figure 4.2 Paul Ehrenfest (with glasses) surrounded by his students. From left to right: Gerhard Heinrich Dieke, Samuel Goudsmit, Jan Tinbergen, Ralph Kronig, and fellow physicist Enrico Fermi, ca. 1924.

that Tinbergen and his fellow SDSC members had felt toward the old fraternities.

During Tinbergen's work on his dissertation, there were five other PhD students around: George Uhlenbeck and Sam Goudsmit[11] (together they introduced the concept of spin in quantum mechanics), Arend Rutgers (later professor in physical chemistry), Hendrik Casimir (known for his work on superconductors, the Casimir effect and the Casimir operator in quantum mechanics, he headed the Philips laboratory for many years), and Roelf Krans (mostly known for his work in physics education at the high-school level) (Figure 4.2).[12] That was sufficient to create a lively and engaging community around Ehrenfest. Not infrequently, the community was further expanded by students from abroad who spent a few weeks

[11] Goudsmit had attended the same HBS as Tinbergen in The Hague and was, like Tinbergen, inspired by science teacher Teunis van Lohuizen to study physics.

[12] For a discussion of their respective doctoral work and careers, see Hollestelle, *Paul Ehrenfest: Worstelingen met de Moderne Wetenschap, 1912–1933*, 71–86, 2011.

of a semester in Leiden. Ehrenfest was very demanding of those in the community, but also developed his own work in dialogue with his students. It was for this reason that he became known as the Socrates of Leiden, who learned in dialogue and by admission of his own ignorance. When asked why he had such good students, Ehrenfest replied characteristically: "because I am so stupid."[13]

4.2 The Essential Problems in Science

Tinbergen followed the colloquium from October 1923 onward,[14] when he had just entered his third year of studies. He was clearly one of the bright young students who had been noticed by Ehrenfest and given additional support and opportunities. Eagerly he made detailed notes of the proceedings of the colloquium. The notes provide a sense of the lively discussions that were going on and the long interventions by Ehrenfest. The notes also attest to the international allure of the speakers. Ehrenfest was at the heart of the network of European physicists of the period, and therefore the students in Leiden encountered many of the period's greats who were presenting the most recent developments in the field: Max Planck, Max Born, Niels Bohr, Wolfgang Pauli, Lisa Meitner, and Otto Hahn. The material included relativity theory and quantum mechanisms, both of which were cutting-edge research fields at the time. In the foreword to his dissertation from 1929, Tinbergen would recount:

> It is difficult to express how intense and how many-sided the influence of the daily guidance of Prof. Ehrenfest has been. His stimulating lectures, the really lively discussions at the colloquium and elsewhere – in particular the hospitable home of Mrs. and Prof. Ehrenfest – the international atmosphere, all had a powerful effect on me, and they taught me above all how necessary it is always to seek out what is essential in problems.[15]

When Tinbergen was later hired at the Central Bureau of Statistics, his first job after obtaining his PhD, he quickly adopted many of the modern scientific practices he had learned from Ehrenfest. He convinced his supervisor to subscribe to the relevant international journals, sought to integrate the Dutch CBS into the European network of statistical bureaus, and set up a new journal *The Dutch Business Cycle* (*De Nederlandse Conjunctuur*). It took a while before he assembled a group of like-minded

---

[13] Ibid., 72–76.   [14] Tinbergen Colloquium Notebook, in possession of the author.
[15] The foreword was printed on a separate inlay and is reprinted in Alberts and Weeder, *Distantie en Engagement: Jan Tinbergen Autobiografisch*, 1988.

researchers working in the same field; for many years, more than half of the articles in the journal were written by Tinbergen. As if that was a little embarrassing, many of them simply appeared without an author, as output of the statistical bureau.

By the early 1930s he had gathered a group of like-minded researchers around him at the CBS and through his other networks. It became a distinguishing feature of Tinbergen's scientific practice that he performed his work in teams, at bureaus, institutes, and even in committees. He was not the social community-builder that Ehrenfest was; nonetheless, he was impressed by how physics was organized in laboratories and research teams. The social sciences lagged behind this development and were too often still practiced by individuals, he believed.

Scientific practice, more generally, provided an exemplary way for how people should engage and interact with one another. This was particularly true of the internationalist spirit in science.[16] Ehrenfest believed that science should embody the practices of internationalism. It was a conviction that was strengthened by the havoc that World War I had wrought, especially in Germany, on the international cooperation among physicists.[17] Not only did Ehrenfest's network extend across Europe and the United States, but he was also politically engaged and in favor of increasing international cooperation politically to overcome nationalist conflict. He was not quite the pacifist that his close friend Einstein was, but Ehrenfest did believe that more international integration between nations was desirable, even if this came at the expense of national differences. This was different from his predecessor Lorentz, for whom national traditions and identities formed the basis of his internationalism, and to whom any kind of universalism was unacceptable.[18] Ehrenfest remained skeptical of Marxist theories, but like his student Tinbergen, believed in many socialist ideals. These included the idea that the future would benefit from more planning and international cooperation. Science, for Ehrenfest and Tinbergen, could lead the way; it was already universalist in aspiration and practice.

But if we look closer it is not hard to see that there really are two competing models at work. The Ehrenfest model of collaborative science seeks to bring the minds of the different outstanding individuals in contact

---

[16] JT archive: "Klein over Ehrenfest", three-page manuscript.
[17] Klein, *Paul Ehrenfest: The Making of a Theoretical Physicist*, 299–301, 1985.
[18] Van Lunteren, "Wissenschaft internationalisieren: Hendrik Antoon Lorentz, Paul Ehrenfest und ihre Arbeit für die internationale Wissenschafts-Community," 2006.

with each other. It is the interaction that will further sharpen their minds, and lead to deeper understanding. But the individuals remain completely free, idiosyncratic also. They preferably have quite different skills and backgrounds, but enough overlap to stimulate and challenge one another. The Tinbergen model of collaborative science organizes research labs, teams, and projects. Within those teams there is a clearly defined division of tasks, and typically also a hierarchy. It is a more bureaucratic model, and it was this mode of organizing research that would characterize much of Tinbergen's work. And although that was still far away in the future, he already developed ideas on planning and organization in science. He compared the waste inherent in the competitive market system with the waste being generated by competition between different scientists. He suggested that the SDAP might be the institution that young, ambitious scientists might turn to for advice on the subjects to be studied.[19] When he sent his proposal to the intellectual leader of the party, Floor Wibaut, however, it was met with little enthusiasm.[20] In the proposal he sketched, a dream that he would partially realize later at the Central Planning Bureau (CPB, the policy institute of which he was director from 1945 to 1954), he wrote: "I deeply hope that we will play an active role, and will turn into an active community of socialist social-engineers. Socialist in both thought and action!"[21]

Such plans were for later; for now, he was in the most classic academic relationship of them all: that between professor and student, between master and apprentice. Tinbergen's first publication in a scientific journal, and his only one in physics, came about as a result of Ehrenfest setting a problem, and Tinbergen solving it.[22] He learned a great deal about the practice and purpose of science from his professor. Ehrenfest was weary of the use of heavy "mathematical artillery" before a problem was understood in all its essentials. Mathematical proofs were at best of secondary importance to Ehrenfest.[23] Although Tinbergen was more concerned with what works in his economics than Ehrenfest, he too believed that the most important part of the scientific process was understanding the problem at hand. Both master and pupil would also develop a habit of letting others work out the finer details or even the solution to a problem. Their great

[19] Tinbergen, "Wetenschappelijk Sosialisties Werk," 1927.
[20] Floor Wibaut to JT, 13 January 1928, TL.
[21] Tinbergen, "Wetenschappelijk Sosialisties Werk," 9, 1927.
[22] Tinbergen, "Faze- en Energieverandering van een Slinger en een Snaar gedurende hun Brown'se Beweging," 1925.
[23] Klein, "Physics in the Making in Leiden: Paul Ehrenfest as Teacher," 1989.

skill was in laying out the problem as clearly as possible. It allowed both Ehrenfest and Tinbergen to reduce complex problems to a basic structure. A model, sometimes almost a caricature, that represented the fundamental issue.

Yet Tinbergen certainly never became the Socrates of economics. In fact, Tinbergen's style in scientific interactions could hardly have been more different. He was modest to the point of shy, and intervened only when he believed it was appropriate. Although his moral presence could feel equally as demanding as Ehrenfest's meddling could, the two were completely different in the way they dealt with others. Ehrenfest would probe and was not afraid to get under the skin of others. Tinbergen kept a distance from his students and peers, and above all attempted to preserve the peace in social relations. Nonetheless, both Ehrenfest and Tinbergen would build "schools" of students. And those students praised them in similar terms, for their clarity and ability to make difficult problems simple.

4.3 A PhD in Physics, and a Start in Economics

It is tempting to assume that Tinbergen first completed his PhD in physics and afterward decided that economics was more promising. But that is a serious misconception. Not only did his dissertation, on which he started working in 1927, contain a chapter that drew an analogy between the two fields, but Ehrenfest actively encouraged him to pursue problems in economics during his studies in physics. In 1923, Tinbergen presented his ideas on mathematical economics to the Christiaan Huygens society, and as early as 1924, Ehrenfest showed Tinbergen some of his own work on problems of oligopolistic competition.[24] In the following years, Ehrenfest introduced him to the work of Arthur Bowley, Knut Wicksell, Vilfredo Pareto, Francis Edgeworth, Enrico Barone, and Charles Roos, all pioneers in the use of mathematics in economics. And when Karl Menger, the Viennese pioneer in mathematical economics, visited the Netherlands in 1925, Tinbergen used the opportunity to discuss the latest developments with him. Menger, who had recently spent time in Sweden with Wicksell and others urged Tinbergen to also get in contact with Wicksell.[25]

[24] Tinbergen, "Antwoord Prof. Tinbergen op Erepromotie," 1954; Hollestelle, *Paul Ehrenfest: Worstelingen met de Moderne Wetenschap, 1912–1933*, 211, 2011.
[25] Scheall and Schumacher, "Karl Menger as Son of Carl Menger," 2018; JT to Knut Wicksell, 23 June 1925, TL.

Given that Tinbergen was a member of the SDAP since 1922 and active in the socialist youth movement in Leiden from 1923 onward, economic and social problems were always close to his heart. In 1924, there was a note in the AJC magazine that a small study club in Leiden was forming, devoted to public finance (*Staatshuishoudkunde*);[26] Tinbergen was in all likelihood the initiator of this study group.[27] An interest in economics was common among the socialists, and in his early publications in the socialist youth magazines he engaged with the literature of the time. He wrote a belated review of the Marxist classic *Das Finanzkapital* by Rudolf Hilferding,[28] considered the reflections of Henry Ford,[29] and started to develop some ideas on the persistent unemployment of the 1920s, which especially in Germany was a serious problem.[30]

Given the strong Marxist influence on the socialist movement, most intellectually minded party members were familiar with the classic works in the Marxist tradition, and therefore knowledgeable about (aspects of) economic theory. In 1925 Tinbergen published his first short article on the labor theory of value in the social-democratic student magazine *Kentering*. He was already critical of Marxist dogmas, but content-wise he was less concerned with the economic implications of the labor theory of value and more with its social significance: the idea that labor is the source of all value.[31] But despite the fact that Tinbergen did not write directly about economics, he already confidently referred to the Austrian approach, as well as the system of competitive markets in the work of mathematical economist Leon Walras. In the summer of 1925 Tinbergen was already conversant in the field of economics, and not just the Marxist stream. And as early as 1927, two years before the completion of his dissertation with Ehrenfest, Tinbergen published a scholarly article that sets out the path that he would pursue for the next ten years. It was published in the most important Dutch economics journal, *De Economist*, and was entitled "About the Mathematical-Statistical Methods for Business-Cycle Research."[32]

---

[26] *Staatshuishoudkunde* later took on a more general meaning, equivalent to macro-economics, but that concept did not yet exist in the 1920s.

[27] In *Het Jonge Volk*, December 1924, vol. 11, no. 26.

[28] Tinbergen, "Boekbespreking van R. Hilferding's Das Finanzkapital," 1926.

[29] Tinbergen, "Boekbespreking van H. Ford's Productie en Welvaart," 1926.

[30] Tinbergen, "Tewerkstelling-Premie," 1927; Tinbergen, "Werkloosheidsproblemen," 1927.

[31] Tinbergen, "Opmerkingen over de Arbeidswaardeleer," 1925.

[32] Tinbergen, "Over de Mathematies-Statistiese Methoden voor Konjunktuuronderzoek,"1927.

But what is remarkable is that the article is hardly connected at all to the work that Ehrenfest suggested to him. It does not use mathematical models and approaches to analyze markets, but rather statistical data to empirically analyze the movement of the economy. The article was the first result from the more applied work at the Central Bureau of Statistics, which he pursued as part of his obligatory social service. At the CBS Tinbergen had found fertile ground for his development of economic statistics.

H. W. Methorst, the director of the bureau, was a member of an international committee on economic barometers for the League of Nations. In 1927 he had sent his right-hand man, M. J. de Bosch Kemper, trained as an engineer, to the international conference in Paris on the collection of business-cycle data. The conference was also attended by Corrado Gini (Italy), Bowley (from England), and the German expert Ernst Wagemann. The most important subject for discussion was the development of an economic barometer. The first economic barometer was developed at Harvard and showed, in the language of the time, the development of horizontal markets. Different trend lines in crucial markets were presented next to one another, and together they "measured" the current "pressure" of the economy.

The barometer was an important milestone in the measurement of the economy, but its deficiencies were already recognized at the time. At the international conference of the Economic Division of the League of Nations, a desire was expressed to present vertical markets.[33] Such vertical markets were not merely correlated as in the Harvard barometer but were causally related to one another. The difference is easy to explain in an analogy with the weather. Measuring the air pressure is helpful in telling the current weather situation, although it provides an incomplete picture. The weather consists of more than just the air pressure, but includes the level of humidity, as well as wind level and weather conditions (sun, rain, etc.). The Harvard barometer gave the air pressure in a few key markets, but a barometer by itself does not tell anything about what causes the current weather conditions, or even about the correlations between the different measured elements. Consequently, the Harvard economic barometer told nothing about what caused the current levels of economic activity in the various measured markets.

So, researchers from various countries were attempting to develop approaches to determine the correlation between the different A, B, and

---

[33] Boumans, *A Case of Limited Physics Transfer: Jan Tinbergen's Resources for Re-shaping Economics*, 1992.

C lines in the Harvard barometer (see Figure 4.3). And the even more ambitious goal was to arrive at a causal explanation of the movements in the different lines. One step in that direction was to attempt to separate out the different causes for the movement of these variables. And that was the approach that Tinbergen took. He suggested that the movement in the lines consisted of three distinct types of movement: seasonal variations, the structural trend (growth), and the business cycle proper. It was his goal to explain the business cycle proper.

He suggested that in order to do so, it was important to analyze a specific type of economic variable, the cumulative variable.[34] The level of inventory is such a cumulative variable, which results from the excess production of the previous periods. Tinbergen argued that cumulative variables are quite common, and of particular importance in business cycle research. During a slump, stocks will build up; inventory levels will rise because sales are going down; and unemployment (another cumulative variable) will rise for similar reasons. These stocks might thus have an important role to play in the explanation of the cyclical movements. The notion of cumulative variables was also used in physics, and so there was a clear influence from the Ehrenfest approach in the article. But its focus, the empirical measurement and determination of the cycle, was quite alien to Ehrenfest's way of approaching problems. Many other economists at the time were attempting to formulate theories of the cycle that identified the ultimate cause of the boom and bust cycle; for this they relied on economic theory and fundamental principles. That was much closer to Ehrenfest's approach in physics, which was also rooted in the search for underlying principles and the fundamental understanding of a phenomenon. Tinbergen, instead, approached the business cycle problem from the movements that could be observed, and then sought "proximate" causes to explain those movements.

That difference in approach and subject matter, however, did not mean that Ehrenfest attempted to steer Tinbergen in a different direction. It has occasionally been suggested that Ehrenfest wanted to retain Tinbergen's talents for physics and perhaps even actively discouraged Tinbergen from pursuing economics further. But things could not be further from the truth. Ehrenfest's response to Tinbergen's first published article is

---

[34] The idea of cumulative variables was based on work by Karl G. Karsten and judged sufficiently similar to it that the editors of *Journal of the American Statistical Association* rejected Tinbergen's article; see Boumans, *A Case of Limited Physics Transfer: Jan Tinbergen's Resources for Re-shaping Economics*, 1992.

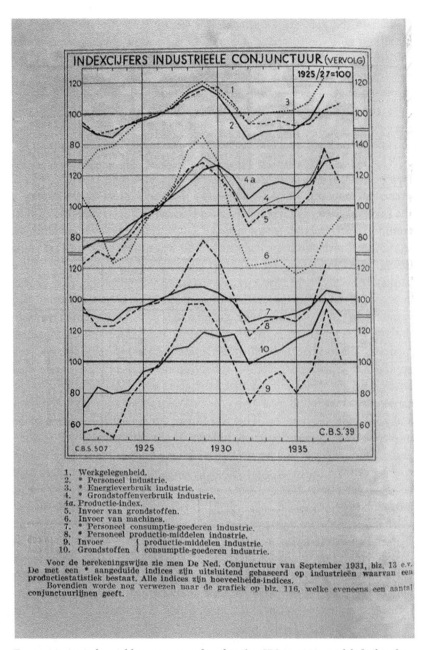

Figure 4.3 An industrial barometer produced at the CBS in 1939, modeled after the Havard barometer of the 1920s. The lines track industrial production, employment, usage of inputs, and the import of inputs and machines.

encouraging if not ecstatic: "You should proceed more and more in economic training. This will lead to something very good." He goes on to praise Tinbergen's way of distinguishing between accumulating and non-accumulating economic variables and compared it to related phenomena in physics: "volume, electric tension vs. pressure, potential and entropy versus temperature."[35] In the same letter, Ehrenfest hints that Tinbergen might pursue his doctoral work elsewhere, but expresses his hope that Tinbergen still has enough to learn in physics so that they can explore more analogies between physics and economics. In 1927, Tinbergen was already at a crossroads: Would he pursue economics or continue in physics?

This leaves open the question of whether Tinbergen perhaps believed that his own talents were more suited for economics than physics, that perhaps he believed he was talented enough to be an economist, but not to be a physicist. It is certain that except for one small publication, Tinbergen did not make any contributions in physics.[36] And later in life he would recount how he failed to arrive at a solution to another problem suggested by Ehrenfest.[37] On the other hand, there is an editorial from the 1950s by a fellow student from his Leiden period which recounts the following: "During my student years in Leiden it was said with the false modesty and local chauvinism, which are a natural part of university youth, that there were only two people who understood Einstein. One was professor Ehrenfest, the other was his student Jan Tinbergen. Both were, of course, locals."[38] And at her parental home, Tine bragged about Jan's knowledge of general relativity theory. Tine's brother recounted: "We were not aware of the significance of it; we barely knew the name Einstein, but it was told in such a manner that we couldn't help but be impressed."[39]

But most likely it is the wrong question to ask. It was not a question of ability for Tinbergen, but rather where he could make the biggest difference. By the late 1920s that was crystal-clear for Tinbergen: it was through the study of economics that he could contribute most to the improvement

---

[35] Paul Ehrenfest to JT, 29 November 1927, BA: EC.
[36] Tinbergen, "Faze- en Energieverandering van een Slinger en een Snaar gedurende hun Brown'se Beweging," 1925. His fellow PhD student H. B. G. Casimir, who did continue in physics, contextualizes the article in his reminiscences and makes clear that although it points in the direction of later developments, Tinbergen's article is itself of limited value. See Casimir in Jolink and Barendrecht-Tinbergen, *Gedeelde Herinneringen*, 13–14.
[37] IISG, nr. BG GC10/141, interview "Een Leven Lang," 14 February 1992.
[38] Wigbold, "Alles is Maar Betrekkelijk!," 1955.
[39] De Wit in Jolink and Barendrecht-Tinbergen, *Gedeelde Herinneringen*, 1993.

of society. There is, however, a genuine surprise in Tinbergen's development, something that could not have been foreseen by either Tinbergen or
Ehrenfest in 1927. And that surprise is the type of economics that
Tinbergen would develop. When Ehrenfest himself explored economics
during the years in which he felt uncertain about his progress in physics
just following World War I, it was of a theoretical kind: both Marxist
theories and the marginalism of the Austrian school. He had been in
contact with Joseph Schumpeter, one of the prominent Austrian economists, during that period.[40] The purpose of his work at the time was to
draw analogies between thermodynamics and economics in what he called
"*Öko-dynamik*" in his notebooks.[41] That theoretical bent was also evident
in his work in physics, which was virtually completely theoretical. The
analogies Tinbergen and Ehrenfest explored were along the lines of
Ehrenfest's specialty: theory and causal mechanisms. And although the
analogy was also supposed to pertain to the underlying mathematical
structure of the phenomenon, it was primarily in seeking an analogy
between different types of mechanisms and ways of framing a problem
that Tinbergen and Ehrenfest worked during their time together. The
search for analogies between economics and physics is modeled after
Ehrenfest's own work in physics, where he tried to seek analogies between
seemingly disparate physical phenomena. There are such examples in
Tinbergen's early work, such as a 1928 article on the theory of exchange
that draws an analogy to principles of energy conservation in physics[42] and
an article that seeks to explore dynamic optimization of demand and
supply,[43] and he utilizes the adiabatic method[44] developed by Ehrenfest
in his article on the ship-building cycle.[45] In his dissertation an analogy is
drawn between certain minimum problems in physics and in different
market structures in economics.[46]

[40] Paul Ehrenfest to Joseph Schumpeter, 3 May 1918, and further correspondence, BA: EC.
[41] Boumans, *A Case of Limited Physics Transfer: Jan Tinbergen's Resources for Re-shaping Economics*, 1992.
[42] Tinbergen, "Opmerkingen over Ruiltheorie," 1928; Tinbergen, "Opmerkingen over Ruiltheorie II," 1928.
[43] Tinbergen, "Bestimmung und Deutung von Angebotskurven ein Beispiel," 1930.
[44] It was a method that allowed one to treat slowly moving variables, such as trend variables, as constant.
[45] Tinbergen, "Ein Schiffbauzyklus?," 1931.
[46] Tinbergen, "Minimumproblemen in de Natuurkunde en de Ekonomie," 1929; Boumans, *A Case of Limited Physics Transfer: Jan Tinbergen's Resources for Re-shaping Economics*, 1992.

But such work was the exception and not the rule in Tinbergen's work, even in his early work from around 1930. Tinbergen did not pursue analogies between physics and economics for long. In fact, only a few years later, in a letter to Ragnar Frisch, editor of *Econometrica*, he expressed his deep skepticism about the usefulness of analogies between the two fields.[47] His interests developed increasingly in the direction of statistics and their use for research into business cycles and, ultimately, stabilization policies. While he would continue to rely on various mathematical analogies to describe the dynamics of the cycle, the concern with policy and business cycles meant he had to engage with empirical material in nearly all his work. Measurement is secondary in the physics of Ehrenfest and his friend Einstein. For them, the primary test is whether something accords with their "physical intuition."[48] Measurement is primary in Tinbergen's economic and statistical work, in particular, in his work on the business cycle, the subject that dominates his work from the 1930s.

4.4 Useful Education and Science

But let us not get ahead of ourselves and return to the years of Tinbergen's dissertation. In 1928, the prospects for Tinbergen were uncertain. Although it was clear he was a brilliant student with many talents, and Ehrenfest treated him as such, there was no clear career path. Both economics journals in the Netherlands had already rejected articles by Tinbergen for being too technical, a clear sign that he did not fit in among the economists, either. Although there was some interest in mathematical economics among a selected few in Dutch academia, it was not clear that a position in the subject would become available. The Central Bureau of Statistics repeatedly made Tinbergen temporary offers, but he was paid very little, if anything at all, for these assignments. The temporary jobs at the CBS were attractive because they provided access to high-quality statistical material but provided no clear career prospects. Ehrenfest, however, had important connections at Philips, the leading (Dutch) electrical engineering company of the age. At Philips he ran a seminar for the

---

[47] JT to Ragnar Frisch, 26 September 1934, NLN: FC.
[48] JTC, "Klein over Ehrenfest" manuscript. It is notable that in the review of Tinbergen's dissertation, Hamburger emphasized, with a nod to John Maynard Keynes, that intuition is of supreme importance in economics too; mathematics can only be of help. Hamburger, "Boekbespreking van J. Tinbergen's Minimumproblemen in de Natuurkunde en de Ekonomie," 1929.

research staff that was meant to introduce scientific insights to the product developers.[49]

It is difficult to imagine that some of the top physicists of the age spoke at a seminar at a private company. That is, unless one imagines Philips as a kind of Google of its age, at which research was an essential part of the business model.[50] Philips was a company founded in the late nineteenth century that originally sold mostly filament lamps, but in the 1920s introduced innovative products such as vacuum tubes and shortwave radios. Their research lab was headed by Jan Goudriaan, an engineer with broad scientific interests and a committed socialist, who would remain an important influence on Tinbergen throughout the 1930s. In late 1928 Philips considered hiring Tinbergen, but in the end the offer was withdrawn. Then in 1929 they made a similar offer and chances seemed high that Tinbergen would indeed become an engineer at Philips.

In March 1929, matters came to a head. Ehrenfest and Tinbergen were planning something big; in particular, Ehrenfest believed that it would be possible to set up a new program in economics in Leiden, which combined mathematics, statistics, and economics. He believed that within the next two to three years they would certainly be able to identify and "raise" half a dozen excellent people to start a new program.[51] These had to be "fine people, with both a deep sense of responsibility and social concerns, who were mathematically gifted and had a clear awareness of the new training and goals." Ehrenfest, ever-enthusiastic, tried to convince Tinbergen: "[I]magine how many of these individuals are lost every year to this 'Tinbergen goal.' And how the world needs such people. Even Bowley is rather limited, what is required are Keynes types."[52]

---

[49] Hollestelle, *Paul Ehrenfest: Worstelingen met de Moderne Wetenschap, 1912–1933*, 185–89, 2011.

[50] For a historical analysis of the way in which science and technology provided an important basis for modern business, see Noble, *America by Design: Science, Technology and the Rise of Corporate Capitalism*, 1977.

[51] Hollestelle refers to 500 prospective students, but this is based on an inaccurate translation of the German word *Dutzend* as thousand rather than the correct "dozen."

[52] Paul Ehrenfest to JT, 20 March 1929, BA: EC. Their image of Keynes diverges substantially from the Bloomsbury Keynes, who felt that he was above social norms. But it was his integrated vision and internationalist outlook of *The Economic Consequences of the Peace* that they admired. It is unclear whether Ehrenfest and Tinbergen were aware that Keynes had also been commissioned to write reports for Philips about the state of the economy after the outbreak of the economic depression of 1929; see Backhouse and Bateman, *Capitalist Revolutionary: John Maynard Keynes*, 129; Dimand and Bateman, *John Maynard Keynes Narrates the Great Depression: His Reports to the Philips Electronics Firm*.

In the meantime, the three (or four) senior figures of Tinbergen's (potential) professional career were all in contact with one another. Ehrenfest contacted Bosch Kemper and Methorst, his superiors at the CBS, while Goudriaan at Philips was in touch with Methorst. It was Goudriaan who suggested after his consultation with Methorst that Tinbergen might be better off at the CBS. He believed Tinbergen to be more suited to government work than to work in a private company, which was likely to disappoint him.[53]

Tinbergen, in the meantime, outlined the pros and cons of the different options open to him; after all, economists prefer making rational decisions. Philips will offer him plenty of opportunity to learn. At the Bureau of Statistics such opportunities are perhaps more limited, since Tinbergen will be the most advanced economic statistician. But on the pro side, he wanted to consider that if business cycle research was not professionalized quickly at the CBS, it might be done by private parties and a unique opportunity would be lost.[54] And then finally Tinbergen wrote that he did not want to base his choice on the "crude principle of competition alone" but on a moral and organizational principle. Competition was a euphemism for the lower pay he would receive at the CBS.[55] "I have eliminated all other motives, as being of secondary importance." He made his choice in favor of the CBS, and from then onward Tinbergen's research project for the coming year was set: business cycles (Figure 4.4). It would turn out beneficial for his career that only a few months earlier the most serious economic downturn during his lifetime had started to set in. In 1929, the signs were clear that another downturn was under way, but the general sense was still that it would be a regular downturn in line with the theory of the recurring business cycle. Not much later, it would become clear that this "Great Depression" was quite a different beast, and managing the business cycle would soon become *the* central problem in economics. Tinbergen would later always urge to work on the most urgent problems first, but this time it was the urgency that found him, rather than the other way around.

---

[53] Goudriaan to Ehrenfest, 27 March 1929, BA: EC.

[54] In Germany there was a more explicit struggle over the ownership and access to official statistics; see Tooze, *Statistics and the German State, 1900-1945: The Making of Modern Economic Knowledge*, 2001.

[55] In 1933 he reports to Ehrenfest that his salary will double to 4,600 guilders per year (with four weeks of paid leave), which indicates that in 1930 his salary was around 2,300 guilders, which would have been similar to the income of a civil servant at the local level in 1930 (CBS data: www.historisch.cbs.nl/detail.php?id=117382485).

Figure 4.4 An early picture of the team at the CBS, on the right Jan Tinbergen, next to him M. Eisma and A. L. G. H. Rombouts, man on the left unidentified, ca. 1929.

Ehrenfest's enthusiasm for Tinbergen keeping his position at the CBS in large part derived from his vision to set up a new program in modern economics with Tinbergen. In order to be able to do this, Tinbergen had to remain close, and the CBS in The Hague, about fifteen kilometers from Leiden, provided that opportunity. Although the plan to start a new university program never materialized, Tinbergen and Ehrenfest did continue to work on a joint program that was rooted in the progressive vision of education they shared. This new type of education should enable scientific knowledge to be useful for society at large. Ehrenfest worked in and was trained in an environment of pure science, where applied science was looked down on.[56] But there was a curious development in the Dutch physics community around the 1920s. A number of physics professors became interested in the budding field of pedagogy, and the first two professors in the Netherlands in this new field of study had a background

---

[56] Van Lunteren and Hollestelle, "Paul Ehrenfest and the Dilemmas of Modernity," 535, 2013.

in physics: Rommert Casimir[57] and Philipp Kohnstamm.[58] These professors had an interest in modernizing education, starting with primary education. Most of them, including Paul Ehrenfest and his wife Tatyana, were interested in the Montessori movement, which was taking off around this time in the Netherlands. Tinbergen was, of course, familiar with these progressive views on education from his father. These schools sought to provide an integrated vision of the modern world, based not on a knowledge of fact, but rather on a comprehensive worldview that would strengthen the character of the kids. Children were, moreover, expected to learn far more independently than in the old educational system. Notable around the same time was the rise of primary schools based on the philosophy of Rudolf Steiner, known as Waldorf schools and the so-called Free Schools (Vrije Scholen).

Montessori schools were an expression of what at the time was called the search for synthesis. It is an idea that is quite alien to our modern idea of science as consisting of specialized fields and a strong division of intellectual labor. Those seeking synthesis were instead looking for a new coherent worldview that integrated modern science, philosophy, and a political worldview,[59] and could hence replace religion as a guide in life. The best expression of this ideal in the Netherlands was the *Encyclopedic Handbook of Modern Thought*, compiled by the Woodbrookers, a Dutch variant of the Quaker movement. Tinbergen contributed several entries to this encyclopedia. The religious socialism of the editors of the Woodbrooker handbook had plenty of similarities with the progressive educational ideas of Montessori and Steiner. Encyclopedias of this kind were popular among those who felt they were living through a second Enlightenment. The most well known is the modern encyclopedia project by the Vienna Circle. These philosophers had laid out what their own goals were in their synthetic manifesto *The Scientific Worldview*.[60] The ideal outcome of such a progressive synthetic education was someone with a strong moral character, intellectual power, and social responsibility. It was a new kind of

[57] Rommert Casimir was the father of Tinbergen's fellow PhD student Hendrik Casimir.
[58] Klomp, *De Relativiteitstheorie in Nederland: Breekijzer voor Democratisering in het Interbellum*, 1997; Hollestelle, *Paul Ehrenfest: Worstelingen met de Moderne Wetenschap, 1912–1933*, 2011.
[59] Baneke, *Synthetisch Denken: Natuurwetenschappers over hun Rol in een Moderne Maatschappij 1900–1940*, 2008.
[60] Hahn, Neurath, and Carnap, "Wissenschaftliche Weltauffassung: Der Wiener Kreis," 1979.

humanist ideal, and the same ideal that Ehrenfest had described and ascribed to Tinbergen in his letters.

This broadly humanist synthetic thinking was important in shaping the pedagogical ideal of the interwar progressive educators. But we should not underestimate the role that the progress in engineering played in the optimism of Ehrenfest about the potential of knowledge to improve society. The Philips laboratory was of great significance to the physicists of his age. Philips was one of the biggest industrial firms of the time, with cutting-edge R&D. Early on, the lab recognized the importance of connecting pure science with technology and sought to hire some of the talents from Leiden. It was here that Ehrenfest saw the practical value that pure science could have. It was a curious moment in time, for it was precisely major scientific breakthroughs that had practical value; this undercut the old notion that engineering was secondary to pure science.[61]

Firms like Philips were significant for another reason; they pioneered new industrial planning and management techniques. Under the general banner of rationalization, new strategies were developed that greatly impressed those in Ehrenfest's circle. The innovations of Walther Rathenau, Henry Ford, and Frederick Taylor had shown what modern business could look like and how it could be combined with a new social ideal of better working and living conditions. There was a general sense that a similar revolution in planning and management had to happen in modern state organizations. While the private sector was modernizing fast, the administrative techniques and structure of the state were still stuck in the nineteenth century, and that included, sadly, the state's warmongering ambitions. Tinbergen and Ehrenfest believed that institutions like the CBS could rationalize the way the state designed policies. It is in this sense that one can begin to comprehend why the choice for Tinbergen was such a difficult one, and why both the CBS and Philips looked like attractive options. He was faced with the question of whether he should learn about this rationalization from the inside, at Philips, or implement it at the CBS. It was not the last time for Tinbergen that an admiration of modern business practices went hand in hand with a belief that state governance could be improved. In his vision, the state and business were more often partners in the modernization of society rather than opposing poles.

---

[61] Hollestelle, *Paul Ehrenfest: Worstelingen met de Moderne Wetenschap, 1912–1933*, chapter 5, 2011.

That impression was reinforced by some major state projects that had been undertaken around the same time. In the previous chapter we already briefly encountered the social housing projects that replaced the traditional slums in various cities around Europe, most notably, in Amsterdam and Vienna. In the Netherlands, another major public engineering project was under way, the closing off of the Zuiderzee, a shallow bay off the North Sea. The project was based on the plans of engineer Cornelis Lely, but the committee that calculated the effects of the project was headed by Hendrik Antoon Lorentz, Ehrenfest's predecessor in Leiden.[62] It was a project with great prestige and symbolic value in a country that prides itself as a nation united in its fight against the sea.

The blend of private and public modernizing forces, with the aid of science, was also visible in the business cycle institutes of the age. Some were for-profit economic consultancy firms that sought to sell relevant data about the state of the economy and primary markets to major firms, in particular, banks and insurance companies. An example of such a firm was the Institute for Applied Economics (later Econometric Institute), founded by Charles Roos.[63] His institute provided broad forecasts about the economy, which it sold in the form of reports to firms like General Motors. But it also produced books that demonstrated how quantitative techniques could be used in business planning: *Charting the Course of Your Business*.[64] Charles Roos was, however, anything but a mere private consultant; he was also a premier economist.

Other business cycle institutes around Europe were heavily supported by the Rockefeller Foundation. In Rotterdam, a research institute in economics, the Netherlands Economics Institute (NEI), was founded in 1929 by the same group of entrepreneurs who had founded the Netherlands School of Economics in 1913 where Tinbergen would work most of his career. It was hoped that it would be an "economic laboratory" that would be of direct help to business. It was founded as a nonprofit, but nonetheless with the goal of obtaining research assignments from third parties in the future. Initially, this was not successful, but over time the NEI succeeded and the institute became internationally renowned for its economic

---

[62] Schils, "Hendrik Antoon Lorentz," 2012.

[63] Dimand and Veloce, "Charles F. Roos, Harold T. Davis and the Quantitative Approach to Business Cycle Analysis at the Cowles Commission in the 1930s and Early 1940s," 2007.

[64] Roos, *Charting the Course of Your Business: Measuring the Effects of External Influences*, 1948; many of the early econometricians combined scientific explorations with attempts to predict and beat the stock market. Friedman, *Fortune Tellers: The Story of America's First Economic Forecasters*, 2013.

consultancy work, later even in development economics.[65] To some extent there was thus competition between the public and the private sector to develop better economic statistics and forecasts about the future. Tinbergen could join the "public party" at the CBS and ensure that economic statistics would be publicly available and not merely to paying clients. Or he could join the "private party" and help rationalize business planning methods at Philips. But it was not the private/public distinction that was the most relevant, but modern or old, rational or old-fashioned, or, in the language of the 1930s, planning or chaos. That public or private was not the defining factor is clear from the fact that Tinbergen also joined the NEI just a few years later.

Wibaut had still expressed doubts about the practical value of a training in mathematics and economics. But the options that Tinbergen had in front of him reflected the fact that there was an increasing demand for those who were able to apply science to social and business problems. And to meet that demand Tinbergen now urged Ehrenfest to take up the plan for a new educational program once more. The new program should contain (1) theoretical mathematical economics, (2) probability theory and correlations, (3) literary economics, including business cycle theory, and (4) quantitative research methods based on books of Wesley Clair Mitchell and Ernst Wagemann. Tinbergen suggested that they could jointly teach mathematical economics; Ehrenfest could teach statistics; Tinbergen could take care of business cycle theory; and for quantitative methods they might draw on an existing course of Professor Durk van Blom, who taught public finance at the University of Leiden to law students. Tinbergen was excited that this program could be jointly organized by the university and the CBS, like a statistical program in Paris.[66] Ehrenfest responded enthusiastically, but he also complained that he lacked energy and was increasingly feeling depressed and unsure whether he had it in him to start anew.[67] The can-do attitude and confidence that characterized Ehrenfest during his good periods had infected Tinbergen, but it was now fading in his mentor.

4.5 The Econometric Society in Leiden

As early as 1929 Tinbergen was contributing to a community of statistical economists. In June he visited Lucien March, who was working at the

---

[65] For some historical reflections on the NEI, see *Economisch-Statistische Berichten*, no. 2704, 1969.
[66] JT to Paul Ehrenfest, 16 February 1930, BA: EC.
[67] Hollestelle, *Paul Ehrenfest: Worstelingen met de Moderne Wetenschap, 1912–1933*, 227, 2011.

Institut de Statistique de l'Université de Paris. That meeting led to an invitation for a meeting in July with Bowley, Wagemann, March, and Methorst, four leading figures at their respective national statistical institutes.[68] In the fall of 1929, he visited Wagemann again at the German Institut für Konjunkturforschung (IfK) in Berlin where he met some of the premier business cycle researchers in Germany, among them Wagemann, Otto Nathan, Carl Ruberg, and Anton Reithinger. The IfK was founded in 1925 under the directorship of Wagemann, and in the words of the historian of the institute: "[T]he innovations of the years after 1925 marked a fundamental break with the past. Economic expertise entered into a new relationship with political power."[69] The IfK was a combination of public initiative and private interests, with relations not just to the state but also to the major industrial organizations and prominent unions. In July 1930, Tinbergen was invited to the joint meeting of the different European business cycle institutes. To Ehrenfest he reported: "It was exceptionally nice and interesting. It was a conference of about 20 people, of which five were of the old guard, five middle-aged, while the other 10 were just a few years older than I was. We formed a very nice group of the young ones, who promised to keep in close contact with one another.... I knew those from Berlin from last year, the Austrians [among them, Morgenstern], a Belgian [most likely, Bernard Chait] and a Hungarian were new." This period coincided with the attempts of Ragnar Frisch to establish an econometric society, which would organize its first meetings in 1931 in Lausanne, France. Econometrics in the vision of Frisch was the combination of economic theory with statistics and mathematics.

Although Tinbergen was not one of the founders of the Econometric Society, he did become one of its charter members, and he attended the first meeting. Financially, it was a struggle to get there, as he was dependent on the hustling qualities of Ehrenfest, who supported him with some money from a fund that he managed on behalf of Albert Einstein. (When Tinbergen wanted to express his thanks to Einstein, Ehrenfest urged him not to do so since the fund was meant for other purposes.)[70] The conference brought together about twenty researchers from somewhat disparate fields: statistics, mathematics, and economics. Tinbergen wrote that he met a few very good people, but one of them was head and shoulders above the others: Ragnar Frisch. From the very first moment,

---

[68] JT to Paul Ehrenfest 22 June 1929, BA: EC.
[69] Tooze, *Statistics and the German State, 1900–1945: The Making of Modern Economic Knowledge*, 2001.
[70] Paul Ehrenfest to JT, 18 September 1931, BA: EC.

Tinbergen recognized in him the leader of the new field of research, econometrics. And for their pioneering efforts in that field Tinbergen and Frisch would share the first Nobel Prize in Economics in 1969.

By 1931, Tinbergen's professional position had become more stable. In July his temporary position at the CBS became permanent.[71] A few months later, he accepted an offer as *Privatdozent* (lecturer) at the University of Amsterdam, at the invitation of Professor Théodore Limperg. His job was to teach mathematics and statistics for business. Two years later, in 1933, he became extraordinary professor at the Netherlands School of Economics in Rotterdam.

From the engagements with the budding community of econometricians, a few important developments started to take shape in his own work. A theoretical picture of the business cycle as an endogenous phenomenon began to emerge; this meant that this cycle was internal to the economy and not caused by external factors (as some others had suggested). The endogenous mechanism that he was attempting to identify should be able to explain all of the cycle: its length, its intensity, and both of the turning points, from downswing back up, and from upswing back down. Such a theory, which explained the cycle as an endogenous phenomenon, could be called truly dynamic.[72]

If we now think of the economic cycle, we instantly think of a macro-economic phenomenon, that is, the dynamics of the whole economy. But Tinbergen and his contemporaries typically studied particular markets; early examples were drawn from the pig and shipbuilding markets. But Tinbergen also explored the macro-dynamics of the economy.[73] It was clear from the outset that for Tinbergen, the way to progress is not to be found merely in collecting more data or better data. He did not become fully inductivist. Instead, he started exploring, and here his training in physics served him well, the various types of dynamics that are possible and theorized by the "verbal economists."[74] It was an approach in which

[71] "Dr. J. Tinbergen," *Het Volk*, 17 July 1931, p. 2.
[72] Tinbergen, "Ein Problem der Dynamik," 1932; Tinbergen, "The Notions of Horizon and Expectancy in Dynamic Economics," 1933.
[73] Tinbergen, "Konjunkturforschung und Variationsrechnung," 1929; Tinbergen, "Kapitaalvorming en Conjunctuur in Nederland 1880–1930," 1932; Tinbergen, "Prijsvorming op de Aandelenmarkt," 1932.
[74] Tinbergen, "L'Utilisation des Équations fonctionnelles et des Nombres complexes dans les Recherches économiques," 1933; Tinbergen, *De Konjunktuur*, 1933. Mathematical economists would later frequently refer to the verbal economists in a derogatory manner, where "verbal" was a synonym for vague, convoluted, and backward. Tinbergen used this phrase very early because it was also used by the small group of physicists who studied in

the Ehrenfest strategy of simplicity in both exposition and understanding was of great help.

Even during this formative period in his economics research, questions of policy and the stabilization of the cycle were never far away. There was no period in his career when Tinbergen explored theory and data for their own sake. Tinbergen's work was from the start to the end a blend of political ideals and goals, and scientific means. Often this is even evident from his scholarly publications, but it is a lot clearer when those are read alongside his more popular and political publications (often in party magazines). Then the true interaction becomes clear, including the underlying motivation for studying business cycle dynamics. His inaugural lecture in Rotterdam from 1933 was entitled "Statistics and Mathematics *in Service of* Business Cycle Research" (emphasis added).[75] In the lecture he developed a typology of different types of economic dynamics, but it was clear that the main purpose was stabilization. For this he already offered some tentative suggestions, but more important is what he offered as a vision. Statistics and mathematics are instrumental to the study of the cycle. He was making clear to his fellow economists that they could no longer rely merely on theoretical analysis. Business cycle research in turn was instrumental to the real goal: stabilization of the economy. The language of his inaugural address, however, was formal and somewhat cautious.

That caution is absent in his more popular book, entitled *De Konjunktuur* (*The Business Cycle*),[76] written that same year. The way forward is through reform: a change in the property rights and the decision structure of the economy and more planning. And, more importantly, he conceived of it as "his task" to fight unemployment and to keep on reforming capitalism. But the book was not simple party rhetoric; to the contrary, after a combative introduction most of the book is curiously apolitical. Ideology was completely absent, and when he discussed the vision of the liberals and the socialists regarding the current crisis, he focused on what they shared, not what differentiated them. Science was not merely a means for solving social problems, but also a way to overcome ideological differences. If liberals and socialists shared the goal of reducing unemployment, then they could jointly, aided by modern science, find out

Leiden to refer to all the other students, since Leiden was traditionally a bulwark of the humanities.
[75] Tinbergen, *Statistiek en Wiskunde in Dienst van het Konjunktuuronderzoek*, 1933.
[76] Tinbergen, *De Konjunktuur*, 1933.

the most effective way for doing so. This allowed Tinbergen to propose what he regarded as nonpartisan solutions to the problem of business cycles, although at that point in time most of his fellow party members were skeptical of his econometric approach.[77] And the more liberal-minded economists were skeptical of his proposed reforms.

It was ironically this instrumentalization of science for practical purposes that had worried Ehrenfest deeply. Although he was a proponent of many of the modern theories in physics, he was weary of the overall development in his field. The tendency of theories to become more mathematical with an unclear relationship to physical reality worried him. Moreover, he remained a classical physicist for whom randomness was not an acceptable feature of physical reality; as Einstein famously proclaimed, "God does not play dice with the universe." It was an attitude that Tinbergen inherited; for him, too, randomness was merely that part of the phenomenon that was not yet explained. Ehrenfest was more generally dismissive of the fragmentation and mathematization of physics that was occurring during the 1920s. More and more physicists with a mathematical bent were satisfied with an accurate mathematical description of a phenomenon rather than with a theoretical and ultimately intuitive understanding of the underlying phenomenon.[78]

For Ehrenfest the goal remained a unified physics based on a set of universal underlying principles that could be understood preferably by a single individual such as himself. But that was increasingly difficult not merely because mathematical formalism was developing at a high speed during these years, but also because theoretically physics was fragmenting with the development of quantum theory, relativity theory, and thermodynamics. Ehrenfest repeatedly expressed his concern with this "degeneration" of physics. And although, following his important mentor Boltzmann, Ehrenfest believed that models had an important heuristic function in facilitating understanding, he was worried that mathematical models increasingly became little more than shorthand descriptions, and not stepping-stones toward deeper understanding.

The tension regarding modern developments ran deeper. Although Ehrenfest was excited about research labs like those at Philips, he worried at the same time about the development of large research labs at universities, which he regarded as exemplifying little more than the introduction

[77] S. de Wolff, "Dit Boek is Tinbergen ten Top," *Het Volk*, 26 March 1934, Wetenschappelijk Bijvoegsel.
[78] Van Lunteren and Hollestelle, "Paul Ehrenfest and the Dilemmas of Modernity," 2013.

of the logic of modern industry into the university. The division of labor that such large laboratories fostered would lead only to a further fragmentation of knowledge, which would hamper real understanding.[79] Ehrenfest would have no planning in science of the kind that Tinbergen had proposed. It is evidence of the elitist bend in Ehrenfest's thought: scientific physics should not become an industrial endeavor full of specialists working in a system of division of labor but ought to remain the domain of a smaller elite who could oversee the field. That elitism was not restricted to science but extended to a skepticism toward democratic developments in society.[80] That skepticism could lead to technocracy, and indeed Ehrenfest was attracted to a more rational form of governance, but perhaps more dominant was his emphasis on a nineteenth-century ideal of *Bildung*, the educational ideal which integrated moral and cultural development. Education was ultimately a goal and a means toward self-realization. The American pragmatic tradition, which emphasized practical and factual knowledge over understanding, was frequently the object of his scorn. To Robert Oppenheimer, who to Ehrenfest embodied many of the dangerous tendencies in modern physics, he wrote: "If you want to spend at least your first few months patiently, comfortably, and joyfully in discussions that keep coming back to the same few points, chatting about a few basic questions with me and our young people – and without thinking much about publishing (!!!) – why then I welcome you with open arms."[81]

The pursuit of pure knowledge was important to him because it was able to foster critical thinking, open-mindedness, and rationality, and not primarily because the knowledge was directly useful. And one's primary obligation was to the scientific field, not toward society, and certainly not toward one's own ambitions. It was this vision of knowledge that was also promoted in the various pamphlets about mathematics education written by his wife Tatyana.[82] It was first and foremost an individualistic goal of emancipation through knowledge, and not much of a political program. In

[79] Ibid., 523.
[80] Hollestelle, *Paul Ehrenfest: Worstelingen met de Moderne Wetenschap, 1912-1933*, 229–34, 2011. It is an elitism also present in his theory of justice, which Tinbergen develops and we will discuss in Chapter 17.
[81] Ehrenfest quoted in Klein, "Not by Discoveries Alone: The Centennial of Paul Ehrenfest," 1981.
[82] Ehrenfest-Afanassjewa, *Wat Kan en Moet het Meetkunde-Onderwijs aan een Niet-Wiskundige Geven?*, 1924; Ehrenfest-Afanassjewa and Freudenthal, *Kan het Wiskundeonderwijs tot Opvoeding van het Denkvermogen Bijdragen?*, 1951; Ehrenfest-Afanassjewa, *Didactische Opstellen Wiskunde*, 1960.

that sense it connected well with the cultural socialism Tinbergen knew from the AJC. But by the 1930s, Jan was starting to move beyond this cultural socialism toward political Plan socialism, as we will see in the next chapter. Part of that transformation meant a far more instrumental view of scientific knowledge, which had to be socially useful, but most of all should serve certain political goals. Tinbergen moved away from the vision of his mentor at a rapid pace, and his view that economic theories primarily have to "work," that is, make a difference in society, was the precise embodiment of the American pragmatist vision that Ehrenfest scorned. Tinbergen's suggestion that science could facilitate a more rational discussion, on the other hand, was much more in line with the emancipatory view of science that Ehrenfest held.

Ehrenfest, however, would not live to see the further development of these aspects in Tinbergen's work. He had suffered from bouts of depression before, which he blamed in his own letters on his lack of progress on the scientific front. During the early 1930s he felt increasingly out of touch with recent developments in physics, but he also expressed to Tinbergen that he was not sure whether he had the strength to start anew in economics. There was enough energy left, however, to offer his institute in Leiden as the place where the Econometric Society meetings of 1933 could take place. On September 24, a week before the meetings would start, Tinbergen confirmed the subject of the keynote lecture that Ehrenfest would give at those meetings: an introduction to harmonic oscillations.[83] It is the end of their correspondence. A day later, Ehrenfest shot himself and his young son Wassik, who was born with Down syndrome.

Reading through the correspondence of the final year, it is hard not to come away with the impression that Ehrenfest had considered suicide for some time by then. In a letter of April 1933, Ehrenfest expressed his pride of Tinbergen, but urged him to be more careful with how he used his energy, because he would need it for a long time to come: "[T]he young'ns will need you more and more the coming twenty to twenty-five years, unfortunately there is no surplus of people of your kind." It is the advice of somebody who is saying goodbye, a sense that is only reinforced because Ehrenfest asked for a good picture of Tinbergen in the same letter, as if he were collecting the memories of his life.[84] The goodbye note of Ehrenfest to Tinbergen is a curious mixture of deeply personal remarks and business as usual. He apologized for being unable to give his talk at the conference and

---

[83] JT to Paul Ehrenfest, 24 September 1933, BA: EC.
[84] Paul Ehrenfest to JT, 15 April 1933, BA: EC.

advised on an alternative speaker from Amsterdam who could fill his slot. Then he wrote: "Remain for Galinka and Pawlik [his son and daughter] the loyal, humane and rare advisor, you have always been to them." Then he urged Tinbergen to introduce the son of a minister Ehrenfest had recently met to Jan's brothers Luuk and Niko, who were studying biology. And then he concluded with personal advice: "Live well with your loved ones – don't overwork yourself!!! Let the following be known for coming periods of doubt: the very rare combination of intellectual and human qualities which are united in you, make you into a person with a wonderful beneficial impact!"

Ehrenfest also wrote a joint goodbye letter to his former and current PhD students: "Each of you has been to me like a child of myself for a period. And some of you have felt that as well." In the letter he also explained why he felt he had to kill himself: "I lost contact with physics and mathematics of the highest worth, THAT is the core of my collapse, my 'Lebens-Müdigkeit.'" And continued: "Forgive me. Forgive me first and foremost, that I did not have the power to die earlier." His dedication to physics was so deep that Ehrenfest wrote that he was happy that the Leiden chair was now finally vacant again. The burden of this responsibility, the chair of Lorentz, had always worn heavy on him. Just months after his appointment, he wrote to Lorentz that he was unsure whether he would be able to fill the big shoes and that he regarded his first two or three years as no more than a probation period.[85] It speaks volumes to the standards Ehrenfest held himself to. It was an intense form of intellectual noblesse oblige. When he failed to make significant progress, Ehrenfest felt he had let down not only himself, but also those around him, and his greatest love, physics. Or as Tinbergen put it: "[H]e felt deeply unhappy about the fact that physics was becoming more abstract, about things being 'wave and particle at the same time' . . . he felt a need for things to be vivid and clear (*anschaulich*), to the extent that his tragic death was in part due to it."[86]

It was not the only time that such feelings of personal failure would be expressed in the milieu of Tinbergen, and it was not the only time that they would lead to suicide. Although Jan Tinbergen was not given to such deep personal doubts in his correspondence, he shared the sense of personal responsibility. He repeatedly expressed this with references to the biblical story about talents, from Matthew 25:14–30:

[85] Klein, *Paul Ehrenfest: The Making of a Theoretical Physicist*, 14, 1985.
[86] JTC, "Klein over Ehrenfest" manuscript.

For the kingdom of heaven is like a man traveling to a far country, who called his own servants and delivered his goods to them. And to one he gave five talents, to another two, and to another one, to each according to his own ability; and immediately he went on a journey. Then he who had received the five talents went and traded with them, and made another five talents. And likewise he who had received two gained two more also. But he who had received one went and dug in the ground, and hid his lord's money. After a long time the lord of those servants came and settled accounts with them.

The men who were given five and two talents both return to the Lord with double the talents they had originally been given. But the man who was given only one talent did not return with any profit and is scorned by the Lord for it. His talent is given to the man who started out with five and now has ten talents.

For to everyone who has, more will be given, and he will have abundance; but from him who does not have, even what he has will be taken away.

It is an unlikely parable for a socialist, as it speaks of an almost aristocratic notion of the differences between individuals. Those who have a lot, and use it wisely, deserve more. And, indeed, the moral Tinbergen draws from it has nothing to do with equality, and all the more with the greater responsibility of those who were given more talents. Everyone has the duty to put his talents to the best use, and that duty was heavier for those who had been given more. In practice it meant for Ehrenfest and Tinbergen that not a moment could be wasted. Since they mirrored themselves to the man who had been given five talents, they had all the more responsibility in the world.

Tinbergen wrote in the foreword to his dissertation that it would be hard to exaggerate the joy in work (*Arbeitsfreude*) in the circle around Ehrenfest. But it is hard not to think that there was also something toxic about the intense dedication to work that prevailed. It is in that light that we should read Ehrenfest's recommendation to Tinbergen to spend his energy wisely, since he has been given the ability to lead others, and they will depend on him:[87] "Prevent any waste of those talents." Tinbergen's own complete dedication to his work was certainly fostered by Ehrenfest; perhaps, it was also the thing that attracted the two men so deeply to each other. It was only in such an environment that a lack of success in science could be so intimately tied up with personal and moral failure. At his inaugural lecture,

---

[87] See also the description of this environment in Klein, "Not by Discoveries Alone: The Centennial of Paul Ehrenfest," in particular, 11–12.

Ehrenfest concluded with a promise to his students, as was customary at such lectures: "I understand my *duties* to you in the following way: to the best of my knowledge and ability I shall help each of you to find, with the least possible damage, the way which corresponds to the very essence of your *talents*."[88] And it was in this respect, and this respect only, that Ehrenfest felt he was doing wrong by committing suicide. He had forsaken his duty to do this for his own remaining children. And therefore, he asked his students one favor, and one favor only: to make the most of their talents. He had lost the right to live otherwise, since he had been unable to put his talents to the best use, or so he felt.

The meetings of the Econometric Society in Leiden the next week took place as planned. Ehrenfest would have wanted it no other way.

---

[88] Ehrenfest quoted in Klein, "Ehrenfest Comes to Leiden," 1958.

5

Hendrik de Man and Jan Tinbergen

The Plan is our symbol of vigor, and an emblem of self-confidence, strength
and knowledge. It replaces the mythos of the dictator with clarity,
intelligibility, and will-power.

—M. Sluyser, 1934

In 1935, Jan Tinbergen and Hein Vos published the Plan of Labor (Plan
van de Arbeid). It was their plan to get the Netherlands out of the Great
Depression.[1] It followed the model of the 1934 Plan de Man of Hendrik de
Man in Belgium. In both countries, these plans were launched along with
extensive propaganda campaigns including pamphlets, brochures, songs,
flags, demonstrations, and marches. The goal was to propose a way out of
the crisis that could garner broad social support across party lines. The
Plan's combination of high-flown idealism and pragmatic solutions was

---

[1] The precise contributions of the different authors of the plan has never become clear, but
most sources work from the assumption that Hein Vos and Tinbergen were behind most
of it. But it was presented as the work of a larger committee consisting of the staff of the
newly founded scientific bureau of the SDAP: Hein Vos (director), G. van den Bergh
(chairman and legal scholar), J. van Gelderen (economist and author of chapter on
Indonesia), Jan Tinbergen, and Th. Van der Waerden (engineer and economist).
A contemporary banner singled out these men, and, in addition, A. W. IJzerman, as
"those who created the plan." Vos, "Naar Een Structuurplan," 52–53. The Plan committee
consisted of additional party members and union representatives: J. W. Albarda (party
leader SDAP), H. J. van Braambeek (transport specialist and union head), J. Brautigam
(alderman for the SDAP), W. Drees (later prime minister and party leader), E. Kupers
(union leader in the textile industry), J. W. Matthijsen (politician in Amsterdam for
SDAP), F. van Meurs (alderman for SDAP and union leader for public servants), and
Koos Vorrink (AJC leader and religious socialist). On all of them there are more extensive
entries in the *Biografisch Woordenboek van het Socialisme en de Arbeidersbeweging in
Nederland* (https://socialhistory.org/bwsa/). See Abma, "Het Plan van de Arbeid En
de SDAP."

the social-democratic answer to the threat of fascism, the perceived failure of liberal democracy, and the failure of the social-democratic movement to come up with good plans to combat the crisis. The Plan socialists felt that the social-democratic parties and their intellectuals had responded with too much complacency to the Great Depression, thinking of it as merely a symptom of a fundamentally sick social system that would sooner or later be overthrown. The chairman of the SDAP looked upon the crisis with a mixture of "Schadenfreude and bitterness"; the crisis was the fault of the capitalists, so the workers should not be called upon for the solution.[2] The proponents of the plan found that an unacceptable and decadent position; that type of complacency was a luxury that neither the workers nor the socialist cause could afford. The Plan, they hoped, would bring new élan and spirit to the social-democratic cause.

The Plan movement was a crucial episode for Tinbergen because it was an important step forward in the development of modern economic policy based on science. It was an opportunity to improve the here and now, rather than to wait for some socialist society to come in the distant future. The Plan popularized the notion of public works and unemployment policies along the lines of the New Deal: "What Roosevelt's New Deal meant pragmatically in America, de Man's Plan of Labor represented ideologically in Europe."[3] And it also made clear what a mixed economy would look like: the nationalization of certain sectors and the introduction of more coordination and planning in others. The Dutch Plan of Labor, moreover, created an institutional position for economic expertise, which would supplement if not replace parliament in matters of economic policy. The Plan of Labor was also a stepping-stone toward Tinbergen's macro-econometric model of the Dutch economy, the main reason he is now regarded as the pioneer of econometrics. The Plans of Labor in Belgium and the Netherlands have had a great impact on the way in which modern economic policy is formulated, operationalized, and executed. Most importantly for Tinbergen, it marked his transition or maturation, if you will, from an idealistic cultural socialist to an idealistic socialist with a pragmatic view of how to achieve his ideals using modern economic science. But the episode also demonstrated the extent to which his own intellectual development and the thought of the time was tied to social-democratic thought in general and the SDAP in particular. Not primarily a

---

[2] Jansen van Galen, "Doorbraak: Het Plan in de Herinnering van Tijdgenoten," 160–61, 1985.
[3] Dodge, *Hendrik de Man, Socialist Critic of Marxism*, 290, 1979.

scientist, Tinbergen was a socialist intellectual, locked in arms with (future) political leaders.

The Plans of Labor are also interesting, because they represent a rather radical break with the way in which social-democratic parties in Europe thought about policy and more generally about socialism.[4] They represented a break in the economic thinking within the social-democratic movement that had been in the making throughout the 1920s, when slowly but surely Marxist theory came under attack from within. With the development of the Plan of Labor, socialist goals became detached from socialist means. No longer was the socialization of the means of production believed to be necessary to realize the goals of socialism. A space for a new scientific socialism was created by this decoupling, because now the socialist goals could be realized while adopting the (new) methods of science. And although the plans were self-consciously crisis plans they nonetheless formed a crucial step on the path toward gradualism and reform-oriented social democracy. More important than those changes still, was the fact that the Plans sought to appeal to idealists of all parties. The cultural socialism of the 1920s had paved the way for the idea that socialist ideals could be held by all members of society and not just the workers. Plan socialism took the next step and suggested that socialist political goals should be attractive to progressives in all parties.[5] For Tinbergen the social-democratic party should no longer be a party of the workers, but of constructive, progressive individuals from all backgrounds. The Plan was to appeal not to the special interests of the workers but to the general *national* interest instead. The social theory underlying these plans was one not of class struggle but of shared problems and goals. These common, national goals could be achieved with a combination of political will and rational decision-making. It was a direct response to the fascist politics of the will of the people, which did not reject the idea of politics in name of the people, but sought to combine it with expertise.

So much for the lofty goals and long-term impact; in the short run the Plans of Labor failed to overcome party lines, but instead hardened them. In the Netherlands, unlike in Belgium, the Plan was also not successful in changing the course of economic policy before the outbreak of war. Within the SDAP it created tensions between the older socialist guard and the new

[4] Van Wijk, "Plan-Politiek en Plan-Socialisme," 1935. This issue also contains a bibliography of the contemporary Plan socialist literature of the period spanning all major European countries.

[5] Sterk, "Van Jeugdbeweging naar Socialisme," 10, 1937.

reformers, and between the more national-oriented and the more internationally oriented sides. And despite the technocratic character of the
Dutch Plan, Tinbergen had to make important compromises between
what he believed scientifically to be most effective and what was
politically feasible.

5.1 Hendrik de Man and Cultural Socialism

In our treatment of the AJC in Chapter 3 we neglected the most important
intellectual influence on the movement: Hendrik de Man. The AJC, as you
will remember, liked to see itself as a vanguard that would explore *and*
demonstrate what socialist culture could be, in contrast to the dominant
capitalist culture. More importantly, it presented itself as a kind of socialist
reformation, which sought to purify socialist ideals. Its primary purpose, at
least during the 1920s, was not to reform the political-economic program
of the party, but instead to demonstrate the superiority of the socialist
lifestyle and socialist culture. For that reason, it was often called cultural
socialism.

The enlightened elite created in this youth movement would help
prepare the workers culturally for socialism, especially since capitalism
degraded culture. Cultural socialism was an early counter-cultural movement that celebrated authentic folk and outdoor culture, over the latest
capitalist fads. It sought an idealistic if not spiritual renewal of socialism.
The socialist culture as lived in the AJC was thus a means to show that
socialism could, at least partly, be realized by a mere act of will: the level of
discipline, and self-discipline in these movements, is the stuff of legends.
This was also the reason that they felt close affinities with the (American)
Quakers, who had similarly realized their ideals and communities in a
hostile environment.

It is hard to overestimate the importance of Hendrik de Man on the
socialist youth movement. He was one of its international pioneers, as one
of the founding members of the socialist youth international. His book *On
the Psychology of Socialism*[6] was perhaps the best expression of the ethos of
the movement. Before he wrote this book, De Man had an active career
behind him. He had accompanied Jean Jaurès, one of the leading French
socialists and pacifists, in the negotiations between French and German

---

[6] De Man, *Zur Pscyhologie des Sozialismus*, 1927. De Man wrote primarily in German,
although also in Dutch and occasionally in French.

socialists to prevent the outbreak World War I.[7] He had been sent on behalf of the Allied Forces to the Soviet Union to convince the communists to remain in the World War, and he had visited the United States for prolonged periods of time motivated to witness firsthand the innovations of Taylorism and alternative forms of firm governance by workers. His book on socialism, although never translated into English, had an incredible reach on the continent. It was translated into fourteen languages, shortly after the original German publication. As his biographer Peter Dodge notes, it was hailed as the most important book since Marx's *Capital* by its enthusiastic defenders, and even its critics acknowledged that it was by far the most serious critique of Marxism of the decade.[8]

De Man's main target was the materialistic and deterministic nature of Marxism. De Man sought to demonstrate that the impoverishment thesis (*Verelendungsthese*), the thesis that the proletariat would be increasingly impoverished, was empirically false. And even the adjusted idea that this impoverishment increased in relative terms was contradicted by developments within capitalism. The same thesis also failed to account for the actual heterogeneity under modern capitalism, such as the development of groups of white-collar workers, and more generally broad social stratification, and not just a growing proletariat. De Man – who sought to differentiate Marx from Marxism in order to provide a renewal of original Marxism, a return to the origins – argued that Marx had correctly seen that the great power of capitalism was its ability to increase productivity, through which the economic fate of all would improve.

De Man's rejection of the *Verelendungsthese* was of great significance for the social theory of Marxism. For if the proletariat did not grow and did not become increasingly poor under capitalism, there was no reason to believe that socialism would be the natural outcome of history. If an increasing (lower) middle class developed material interests that were closely tied up with the current capitalist system and the proletariat did not grow into a majority, there was no longer any reason to believe that capitalism would be overthrown. If one stuck to the social analysis of Marxist theory under these conditions, then socialism would come only if it was supported by classes other than just the proletariat. But, argued De Man, within traditional Marxist theory this was inconceivable, since every class merely pursued its material self-interest.

---

[7] Jaurès was assassinated in July 1914 for his efforts to prevent a war, by a young French nationalist who desired war with the Germans.

[8] Dodge, *Hendrik de Man, Socialist Critic of Marxism*, 68, 1979.

But De Man's work was not pessimistic; he was hopeful about the prospects of socialism. The theory of the pursuit of material self-interest had always been misguided, he argued. In fact, the great blind spot of the Marxist theory had been that it had had no eye for the spiritual and moral aspects of capitalism, especially the cultural degradation that took place under it. The real impoverishment was not material, but cultural, argued De Man: "The farmer's son may be boorish, and the cottager's daughter uncouth, but as soon as they become factory-hands, their rusticity turns into vulgarity."[9] A culturally and morally impoverished, if not degraded, proletariat could not possibly form the solid basis for a new society. Worse yet, the socialist movement had done nothing to prevent this, and many of its current demands and strategies were purely motivated by material gain. In one of his harshest critiques he accused his fellow socialists of having fallen prey to capitalist materialism. The current demands of the socialist parties were not at all the consequence of the high-minded ideals of socialism and certainly did not represent a call for true justice. What was needed, therefore, was a reorientation along the lines of the original socialist ideals.

From that criticism, De Man took a few crucial steps that were of fundamental importance for Tinbergen's intellectual development and for the later emergence of Plan socialism. We will identify three here. The first was that De Man attempted to turn socialism into a set of universal values that ought to be attractive to (potentially) anyone. The second was his argument that current society is a mixture of positive developments, which tend toward socialism, and negative developments, which move society away from socialism. A political program should therefore aim, primarily, to support the positive developments. Third, De Man reversed the typical Marxist order in which social change comes about: he argued that the realization of socialism requires socialist people whose every act helps realize socialism. Or, in short, socialism would grow gradually from within capitalism, but only if a socialist vanguard had a set of clear socialist goals and the will to bring it about.

Building on the earlier work of his mentor Jaurès, Hendrik de Man argued that socialism was not a specific theory of social development and history, but rather a set of universal values.[10] And these universal values were part of a much longer Western tradition that could be traced back to

---

[9] De Man quoted in Dodge, *Hendrik de Man, Socialist Critic of Marxism*, 98.
[10] Van Peski, *Hendrik de Man*, 1969.

the rise of the bourgeoisie in the high middle ages.[11] They were the Western values that were also embodied in the Christian tradition of freedom, equality, and justice. Socialism should seek not to break with these universal values but to realize them more completely, and for all classes. Culturally, there would thus have to be great continuity between the coming socialism and the historical development of the West in the past millennium. A similar argument was made by the religious socialists in the Netherlands who found their most prominent voice in the poet Henriette Roland Holst and in the leader of the AJC, Koos Vorrink.[12]

Following this line of reasoning, Hendrik de Man depicted a socialism that would not be a rupture with current society but would instead grow out of the current capitalist system. This system, as he emphasized time and again, had already been fundamentally altered through the political action of the labor movement. But the contributions of the labor movement had as often been in the wrong direction as they had been in the right direction. Although the labor movement had contributed significantly in bringing about social legislation and redistribution, and had redrawn the power balance in society, by now it actually alienated workers from socialism by fostering and playing up materialist demands among the working classes, De Man argued.

For De Man the task of socialist youth movements like the AJC was to embody the moral and cultural values of the coming society. The AJC was frequently met with the charge that it was too independent and in fact alienated from the worker's movement, but in a paradoxical manner this was precisely what Hendrik de Man was looking for. The socialist culture that he favored differed radically from the current capitalist materialist culture, and hence the culture within the socialist movement should be radically different from the existing culture. De Man frequently compared the socialists to the Quakers, a group we will meet again below, whose puritan pioneers willed and embodied their new culture in America when they first settled there. In this way socialism could be realized even without socialist economic institutions, that is, without a socialist organization of the economy. The socialist youth movement was therefore an almost paradoxical combination of deep idealism and a rejection of politics. The AJC expected its members to accept the party line in political matters, but better yet to focus purely on the realization of its ideals. The AJC as avant-

---

[11] Dodge, *Hendrik de Man, Socialist Critic of Marxism*, 91, 1979.
[12] Verwey-Jonker, "Vijf en Twintig Jaar Socialistische Theorie," 336, 1938.

garde group should lead society into socialism by example, not political persuasion.

In 1927, within a year after the publication of his groundbreaking criticism, Hendrik de Man spoke at the Paasheuvel, the headquarters of the AJC.[13] His book was also soon translated into Dutch and widely advertised and discussed in the AJC magazines. The connection between De Man and Tinbergen is interesting for more than just the intellectual influence De Man had on him. It should come as no surprise that De Man faced strong criticisms, and the type of criticisms he received would later often be leveled against Tinbergen. The first of these criticisms was that he was promoting an elite socialism, if not in fact a misguided bourgeois illusion. Although the AJC drew members from all social classes, it was particularly attractive to the more intellectually and culturally minded among them. The dislike of proletarian culture in the AJC, as well as strict ideas about which parts of bourgeois culture were valuable, made them elitist in the eyes of many of the older elites in the social-democratic movement.[14] De Man made no secret of the fact that he believed that the real carrier of socialism was not the proletariat, but instead a socialist elite drawn from the enlightened bourgeois.

Second, De Man was criticized for being naïve about the causes of social change. A central belief among Marxists was that society would not change before economic institutions changed. Yet in De Man's alternative vision, socialism became a matter of the will and did not require different political institutions, only the good will of people. His critics suggested that without a changed property structure in society, the socialist movement would be without an economic base. Without economic power, political power would be unattainable. Even within his own intellectual circles of idealistic socialists, De Man received fierce criticism for his socialism of the will. In a debate set up with religious scholars not long after the publication of his book, he was heavily criticized by Karl Barth, one of the foremost Protestant theologians of the age, that his socialism was not sufficiently rooted in social developments and other institutions.[15]

We saw that in Leiden, Tinbergen was actively engaged with this change in socialism, away from a socioeconomic structure and toward a socialism

---

[13] Anonymous, "Een Gesprek met Hendrik de Man, de Eerste Sekretaris Der Sosialistiese Jeugdinternationale," 1927.

[14] Hartmans, "Van 'wetenschappelijk Socialisme' naar Wetenschap en Socialisme. De Ideologische Heroriëntering van de SDAP in de Jaren Dertig," 1991.

[15] Van Peski, *Hendrik de Man*, 1969.

of fellow-feeling and ideals. In a small polemic Tinbergen was also accused of being pre-Marxist, that is, naïve about how social change could be brought about. The discussion was about the high wages of (socialist) professors. Tinbergen argued that high wages for professors were not justified and in part represented an "unearned" or "laborless" income. In fact, because of their privileged work conditions they should earn less than other workers who worked the same number of hours.[16] The accusation of being pre-Marxist was leveled at him by a prominent member of the older guard within the SDAP, Jacob van der Wijk. Tinbergen naïvely held that socialist ideals could exist as islands within an ocean of capitalism, according to Van der Wijk. But Tinbergen's response demonstrated that the primary mode of analysis for this group of cultural socialists was no longer institutional, but moral. It was a matter of personal integrity, Tinbergen argued, that socialist leaders already lived according to socialist standards.[17]

But there is also a far more personal tension in the work of De Man, one that deserves to be explored more deeply precisely because Jan Tinbergen experienced that same tension. At one level, the rethinking of socialism and the position of the intellectual in the socialist movement was praiseworthy for its honesty. De Man brings out clearly that the bourgeois intellectual who is attracted to socialism need not be ashamed of his background or even of his bourgeois culture. Yes, his class is to be blamed for economic exploitation, but someone from a bourgeois background can also legitimately hold socialist ideals. But De Man quickly moved from that, by then, widely accepted point to the idea that those from a bourgeois background are actually in a superior position to lead the workers, because they have more cultural education. The intellectual socialist of the De Man type recognizes, and even is proud of, his own bourgeois roots. So, De Man, and those like him, could now have their cake and eat it too. He was no longer forced to choose between the bourgeoisie and socialism; he could now have both. The dilemma that was explored in the novel about Jurgen and Catherina has disappeared: the bourgeois son can be a socialist and elevated above the workers. There is not even the need for active participation in the class struggle; what is required is "merely" a change in lifestyle. As Van der Louw, the historian of the AJC, described, societal change starts to fade to the background while improving one's own life moves to the front.

[16] Tinbergen, "Socialisten en Hoge Inkomens," 1930.
[17] Tinbergen, "Vóór-Marxistisch?," 1930.

It was for a reason that both De Man and Tinbergen were attracted to the Quakers, the puritan pioneers. They hoped to realize for socialism a purification, a kind of socialist reformation if you like. Socialism had to return to the original ideals, since the means by which these were now pursued, the materialist worker movement, had been corrupted. And as the Quakers had demonstrated, this could be done in closed groups. So, the youth movement or other types of socialist elites could realize it amongst themselves. This strategy, however, was not without dangers. It could quickly lead to intolerance between these communities and the outside world; the AJC certainly met with frequent hostility.[18] And it was a completely apolitical strategy whose success entirely depended on the voluntary adoption of these ideals by others.

We have discussed the thought of Hendrik de Man, and the associated youth movement quite extensively, which is required to understand the transformation that Plan socialism entailed. Plan socialism, as it was known on the Continent, of the 1930s was a direct reaction against the apolitical nature of the cultural socialism of the 1920s. This means that it represented a personal challenge for the more cautious and idealistic members within the youth movement. They were now forced to commit to a political program and engage directly with politics and the organization of society. They had to leave the safe confines of youth behind them, as well as the safe community of the AJC. That transition was easy for De Man, who had known politics since his involvement in World War I, and had always been more at home on the barricades than in his private study. Tinbergen did not have De Man's political experience or savvy but had already been thinking about the way in which he could make science more useful in society. The transition did not come natural to him but did fit his aspirations. But many of his closest friends were reluctant to give up the more cultural aims of individual emancipation in favor of a program of socioeconomic reforms. Tinbergen would struggle all his life with the tension between the cultural ideals of the AJC and the socioeconomic goals that he could pursue through economics and politics. His whole upbringing, including the linguistics of his father, the intellectual goals of Ehrenfest, and the cultural socialism of the AJC, had instilled in him a deep respect for culture, personal morality, and a way of life devoted to higher ideals. And yet in his work in economics and later as policymaker he would nearly completely limit his efforts to material improvements

---

[18] Van der Louw, *Rood als je Hart: Geschiedenis van de AJC*, 211–41, 1974.

rather than to cultural or moral improvement. In fact, he would frequently distinguish in his work between that which can be measured and the so-called imponderables. From the distinction itself it was clear that science by necessity was limited to the analysis of the former, and hence could not help that it neglected the imponderable.[19]

5.2 From Cultural Socialism to the Plan Movement

The Plan movement in Belgium really came into its own during 1933 and cannot be detached from the sudden rise of fascism across the Continent, in Germany and Italy, in particular.[20] The seizure of power by Hitler in that year added a new urgency. But before we analyze this movement it is important to take a brief detour to a book by a good friend of Jan Tinbergen, Jan Goudriaan. Goudriaan's book, like none other, provided the bridge between the cultural socialism of the 1920s and the Plan socialism of the 1930s. Like Tinbergen, Goudriaan had been trained in the natural sciences, and during the early 1930s he worked at the Philips research lab NatLab, the same lab where Ehrenfest ran the seminars and that made Tinbergen a job offer in 1929.

Like Wibaut, De Man, Taylor, Rathenau, Neurath, and so many others of the age, Goudriaan was a believer that the rationalization of society was taking place in many different sectors of society. The concept of rationalization originated in the work of Max Weber, who had argued that in all spheres of modern society rational procedures and reason would come to occupy a more central place. Goudriaan specialized in the rationalization of business, which was particularly associated with modern management and planning techniques. To promote the dissemination of these techniques he was the earliest promoter of the new academic field of business studies in the Netherlands. For Goudriaan it was only a small step to argue that the rationalization that was already happening in business should also take place at within the state.

In his book *Socialism without Dogmas*,[21] Goudriaan suggested specific steps for the rationalization of economy and state, but it is primarily the

---

[19] Tinbergen, *Econometrics*, 51, 1951.

[20] Sluyser, *Planmatige Socialistische Politiek*, 1934.

[21] Dogmas are also associated with a more legal form of reasoning, and it was the achievement of Goudriaan and Tinbergen to steer economics in the Netherlands away from legal traditions and toward engineering traditions. As such it thus also implies a triumph of measurement over principles. See Goudriaan, *Socialisme zonder Dogma's*, 1933.

first half of the book that is of interest to us here. In the first half Goudriaan sought to move beyond the cultural socialism of the 1920s and toward a renewed political socialism for the 1930s. Goudriaan shared De Man's criticism of Marxism and argued that Marxism had been dominated by three dogmas that must be left behind: the means (socialization of production), the strategy (class struggle), and the scientific determinism of the nineteenth century (the iron laws of history and capitalism). What would be left after those three dogmas were discarded was a socialism of ideals: peace, freedom, and prosperity.[22] It is the faith – again the religious language is very present – in this ideal that stands above scrutiny and is the essence of socialism, argued Goudriaan. But moving beyond De Man's work of the 1920s, he suggested that science is the best and most undogmatic guide to figure out how these ideals can be realized.

Socialism in Goudriaan's view is no longer the outcome of a historical process, but instead a historical task: "[T]he world will become what we make of it."[23] Such ideas were at least latently present in De Man's thought. But Goudriaan added to them that a critique of existing society was no longer enough; neither was fear-mongering about war or fascism good enough. Such defensive strategies were characteristic of the bourgeoisie protecting its own narrow interests and fearful of what the future might bring. Socialists, instead, needed a Plan that appealed to the courage of the workers, to positive ideals, to the hope for a better future. And this plan ought to appeal to people of all classes and confessions, not just to workers and certainly not only to members of the SDAP.

Goudriaan added one more strategic point, one that would rear its (ugly) head at several points in the future. His book opened with a quote from Hendrik de Man's book *Masses and Leaders*:[24] "that is why the leader should serve not the masses, but the truth. That and nothing else is the duty of the intellectuals, independent of whether he practices astronomy or politics." At that point the idealistic cultural socialism of the 1920s had become the political Plan socialism of the 1930s. It was here that the cultural vanguard was transformed into a political vanguard.

Various later commentators have argued that engineers like Goudriaan and Tinbergen had a kind of technocracy in mind.[25] It is a term that is

---

[22] Ibid., 14.   [23] Ibid., 21.   [24] De Man, *Massen und Führer*, 1932.
[25] Hollestelle, *Paul Ehrenfest: Worstelingen met de Moderne Wetenschap, 1912–1933*, 2011; Baneke, *Synthetisch Denken: Natuurwetenschappers over hun Rol in een Moderne Maatschappij 1900–1940*, 2008; Nekkers, "Een Ingenieur in de Politiek: Hein Vos en het Plan van de Arbeid," 1985.

more often associated with Tinbergen, who is typically seen as an exemplary social engineer. We are now in a good position to correct that view. What sets the elite, the leaders, apart from the masses for Goudriaan (and Tinbergen) is primarily a set of ideals and their knowledge of socialism, not their technical knowledge. The leaders of the past who Goudriaan cited as exemplars, from Robert Owen to Henry Ford, were certainly not technocrats. Instead, they were industrial leaders who stand out mostly because of their social vision, which they managed to combine with technical know-how and managerial skill. Tinbergen would later cite a similar list and include Floor Wibaut, who used his entrepreneurial skills to realize social goals. These men were able to combine moral leadership with action, and it was that combination that Goudriaan and Tinbergen admired.

This is not to deny that there are clear technocratic elements in their work. Hendrik de Man, for example, drew on the work of the Norwegian American critical economist Thorstein Veblen in his work to distinguish between the engineers who cared about maximizing production, as opposed to the financiers who cared about profit.[26] And part of Goudriaan's plans was a set of rather technocratic solutions, the most famous of which he proposed was an international commodity standard to replace the gold standard. But for all the technocratic influences, the main virtues of the Plan of Labor remained for De Man, Goudriaan, and Tinbergen its hopeful idealism combined with the fact that it that it provided a clear path toward their realization. As De Man had argued some years before: "The correct solution is to reintegrate the utopian element into socialism, but in a manner that one may recognize the utopia as the point of departure, instead of as the ultimate goal, as contemporary psychological reality instead of a future foundation for society."[27] It was a utopia that was not necessarily attainable but that provided a sense of direction.

It is therefore moral leadership that is of great importance in the work of Goudriaan and De Man around this period, a moral leadership that Ehrenfest associated with Keynes and praised in Tinbergen. This moral leadership now extended beyond the socialist lifestyle of the AJC and related socialist movements and became political. It was no longer just the ideal community that the AJC sought to exemplify, but it now included a practical plan on how a more just society could be realized. This plan

[26] Pels, "Hendrik de Man en de Ideologie van het Planisme," 1985.
[27] Hendrik de Man quoted in Horn, *European Socialists Respond to Fascism: Ideology, Activism and Contingency in the 1930s*, 85, 1996.

derived much of its urgency from the fact that many workers and especially the middle classes were turning away from social democracy and liberalism. The future promised by the fascists was a romantic one that appealed to the instincts; it was one that used the insights of psychology and the sentiments present in society, argued De Man. It was high time for socialism to do the same: to use psychology, not to inspire fear but to inspire hope.[28]

The older guard of cultural socialists, such as the longtime leader of the AJC, Koos Vorrink, were nonetheless worried that the economic would come to dominate in Plan socialism. He appealed to Tinbergen to consider not merely the economic side of the current problems. In a letter he suggested that while industrial leaders like Philips in the Netherlands did much to improve the material welfare of the workers, it is unclear whether they were sufficiently attuned to the broader well-being of their workers. And the same might be true for the Plan socialists, he argued: "[P]roduction is made into the measuring rod of all values . . . it is typical that the man at Philips who is the driving force behind this development is a party-comrade, Goudriaan."[29]

The Dutch Plan is mostly remembered for the investment plans and public works it proposed, but as Tinbergen remembered in 1985: "The Plan is what brought back a certain hope. This hope was more important in those years than the details of the Plan."[30] In fact, those very details were not quite clear; the word "planning" was used by many but defined by few.

5.3 What Planning?

In August 1931 there was a major week-long conference that brought together hundreds of experts on planning from all over the world together in Amsterdam. The conference was called "World Social Economic Planning" and was organized by two American emigrants, Mary Fleddérus and Mary van Kleeck. The opening speech was held by Floor Wibaut and the purpose was to arrive at a joint program along the lines of which the world economy could be planned. The lineup of speakers was impressive and the crowd truly international, with Asian participants, Soviets who had prepared a special booklet to inform the world about their progress in planning, economists from virtually every European

---

[28] Goudriaan, *Socialisme zonder Dogma's*, 10–12, 1933.
[29] Koos Vorrink to JT, 14 April 1930, TL.
[30] Jansen van Galen, "Doorbraak: Het Plan in de Herinnering van Tijdgenoten," 156, 1985.

country, and dozens of American economists.[31] But the conference was not the big success for which its organizers had hoped. Ed van Cleeff, a good friend of Jan Tinbergen, summarized the conference as follows: "There was a will, but no way."[32] Another observer from the AJC, looking back on that period, remembered the impotence, despite all the plans and the good intentions.[33]

Here, it is worth examining briefly the different strands of planning that come together at this juncture, and on which the Plan socialism movement built.[34] These different strands of thought hardly converged. On one extreme there was Soviet planning, which was met with very little enthusiasm at the congress, since many of the other participants were progressive liberals or socialists who wanted to differentiate themselves from communism.

These liberal and democratic planners promoted, for example, Taylorism, which was represented strongly at the congress, not in the least because the conference was organized by the International Industrial Relations Institute. Taylorism, or scientific management, originated in a new style of management that emphasized labor discipline, incentive systems, and, more generally, efficiency. But Taylorism promised not just a superior management technique, but also a change in attitudes away from the division of the surplus to an increase of the size of the surplus so that there would be ample room to increase wages. This social idealism was even more pronounced in what became Fordism.[35] In this model there was also attention to the explicit cooperation between workers and employers, which would give rise to new labor relations. Hendrik de Man had been influenced by these developments when he wrote an early book about joy in work.[36]

And although it appealed greatly to Europeans who saw these new management techniques as one of the major achievements of American

---

[31] Fleddérus and Van Kleeck, *World Social Economic Planning: The Necessity for Planned Adjustment of Productive Capacity and Standards of Living*, 1931.

[32] Van Cleeff, "Het Sociaal-Ekonomies Wereldkongres," 308, 1931; Horn, *European Socialists Respond to Fascism: Ideology, Activism and Contingency in the 1930s*, 1996.

[33] Sterk, "Van Jeugdbeweging naar Socialisme," 7, 1937.

[34] For a slightly different typology of the different types of planning, see Balisciano, "Hope for America: American Notions of Economic Planning between Pluralism and Neoclassicism, 1930–1950," 1998.

[35] Maier, "Between Taylorism and Technocracy: European Ideologies and the Vision of Industrial Productivity in the 1920s," 1970.

[36] De Man, *Die Kampf um die Arbeitsfreude*, translated as "Joy in Work."

capitalism, by the 1930s they had also run into serious criticism. Critics were worried that the unemployment of the period was in part caused by these new management techniques and the labor-saving machinery. Not infrequently, the Great Depression was blamed on excessive economic rationalization.[37] Tinbergen around this time, for example, was highly critical of rationalization as a strategy for the future. As early as 1928 he had started to point out that economic rationalization was not feasible given the current unemployment levels.[38]

From Germany there were advocates of the idea of "Planwirtschaft,"[39] which originated in the work of Walther Rathenau, the German industrialist who had overseen economic planning during World War I.[40] Otto Neurath, present at the conference, was one of the proponents of this model of planning, which at least in his conception was built on *in-kind calculation*, which did away with the (alleged) distortive measure of money. Behind this preference for in-kind calculation was a more widely shared conception that profitability and productivity were at odds with one another.[41] One of the economic consequences of the Great Depression was the fact that many firms were no longer using all their productive capacity, because it would hurt their profitability. This gave rise to what was known at the time as "poverty amid plenty," that is, widespread economic misery in an economy producing far below its full capacity. Neurath's proposals for a Planwirtschaft did not seek to do away with private initiative, but instead sought to better coordinate between (industrial) production and the needs and wants of individuals. This was also reflected in the subtitle of the congress: "adjustment of productive capacity and standards of living." Wibaut was clear in his opening address that the main challenge was "conducting

---

[37] The ideas behind economic rationalization are discussed extensively in the next chapter; the simplest characterization is that workers are replaced by machines or made redundant because of higher efficiency in production through the introduction of superior management techniques.
[38] Tinbergen, "Oorzaken en Bestrijding der Werkloosheid," 1931; Tinbergen, "Eenmanswagens," 1928; Tinbergen, "De Landbouwkrisis: Praeadvies Uitgebracht Voor de Socialistiese Vereniging ter Bevordering van de Studie van Maatschappelijke Vraagstukken," 1931.
[39] This idea is singled out as one of the formative influences on Plan socialism in De Jong, "Naar een Socialistisch Plan," 1961.
[40] Polak, "De Problematiek der Welvaartsplanning en haar Ontwikkeling in de Buitenlandse Literatuur," 1948.
[41] This idea is present in Tinbergen's defense of the Plan of Labor; see Tinbergen, "De Positie van het Plan van de Arbeid," 5, 1936.

world   production   with   the   sole   object   of   *general   welfare*"[42]
(emphasis added).

At the conference a third strand of planning was promoted by adherents
of the cooperative movement, but for our purposes that movement is of
less significance. A fourth type of planning was less rooted in theoretical
ideas and more in practice, let's call this strand "policy experimentation."
Although it would be wrong to say that Taylorism and the Planwirtschaft
had not been born out of practical applications, these systems were promoted as a kind of integrated solution, as systems that could be universally
implemented. That was different from the attempts at planning that were
reluctantly pursued by different governments at the time, most notably in
Sweden, but also in the United States as part of the New Deal.[43] Although
theoretically the policy experiments typically had some abstract justification in economic theory (e.g., an early version of the multiplier theory of
state spending), they were primarily practical experiments aimed at solving
urgent problems. They were born out of necessity, more than idealism.
And it was this type of experimentation that was crucial for the Plan
socialism movement. The experiments demonstrated a new kind of courage on the side of the state, which Fleddérus, one of the organizers,
embraced as "laboratories of planning."[44]

Tinbergen, for example, kept a keen eye on Sweden ever since he taught
himself some Swedish in order to speak to Scandinavian youths at an early
youth international meeting near Amsterdam in the 1920s.[45] And it was in
Sweden that early experiments with public works to boost employment
were tried. In 1932 Tinbergen also conducted an extensive study of the so-
called coffee valorization in Brazil, a new experiment in which the public
authorities attempted to limit price fluctuations of coffee by buying up
excess supplies of coffee in the good years, and selling those stocks in years
with meagre harvests.[46] Though this system was far from perfect, as
Tinbergen readily admitted, it demonstrated the possibilities and the need
to try similar things. These were experiments that occurred within the

[42] Fleddérus and Van Kleeck, *World Social Economic Planning: The Necessity for Planned Adjustment of Productive Capacity and Standards of Living*, 1931.
[43] These successes are also emphasized in the Dutch Plan of Labor Commissie uit N.V.V. en S.D.A.P., "Het Plan van de Arbeid," 1936.
[44] Fleddérus and Van Kleeck, *World Social Economic Planning: The Necessity for Planned Adjustment of Productive Capacity and Standards of Living*, 69, 1931.
[45] Tinbergen, "Buitenland. Zweden," 1925; Tinbergen, "De Economische Zijde van het Ordeningsvraagstuk," 1935; Tinbergen, "De Conjunctuurpolitiek in Zweden," 1936.
[46] Van Luytelaer and Tinbergen, "De Koffievalorisaties: Geschiedenis en Resultaten," 1932.

capitalist economy, and it was precisely this that made them so valuable to him. They showed that real and significant change was possible, if one would go about matters rationally. Again, Weber's rationalization thesis was looming large: the world was slowly becoming more rational. And although Weber had used the ambivalent term "iron cage" to describe the process, the social-democratic reformers embraced the introduction of more rationality into economic planning. It was also the aspiration of Neurath, the proponent of the Planwirtschaft.[47] Such proposals were even more attractive because they were consistent with De Man's belief that socialism could gradually grow out of capitalism.

But the way in which planning was to be done was not clearly defined, neither at the conference nor in in the Plans of Labor. To understand the attraction of the planning ideal we must recognize what it was opposed to. Ragnar Frisch, Tinbergen's favorite econometrician, summed that up quite well in a newspaper feature of 1931, "Planning or Chaos."[48] There was a widespread sense that the economic system had to be made stable and, even more importantly, given a clear direction, a goal. And planning first and foremost referred to this idea: we must to organize the economy in such a way that it could be steered in the desired direction. If it was still unclear how that could be done, that was a pity, but at the very least one should try. That spirit is reflected clearly in Plan socialism, which was first and foremost a political movement, rather than an economic program. Looking back, one might say that it was perhaps a remnant of cultural socialism, which was sometimes described as a socialism of the will. The Plan movement expressed the willingness to plan, and the desire to plan, more than how planning could be done. Given the dire circumstances of the Great Depression, which only worsened after 1932, planning *had* to be done. Experiments were risky, but if there ever was a time, now was the time to carry them out.

This means that Plan socialism is better understood as a program of action and experimentation than a technocratic blueprint, although certainly technocrats felt attracted to it. The technocrats were trying to engineer an economy that functioned better than crisis-prone capitalism, but the form of Plan socialism had just as much to do with the fact that the socialists needed a powerful political answer to fascism. It is unlikely that the Plans of Labor in Belgium or in the Netherlands would have been

---

[47] Neurath, *Was bedeutet rationale Wirtschaftsbetrachtung*, 1935; Tinbergen, "Review of Otto Neurath's Was Bedeutet Rationale Wirtschaftsbetragtung," 1936.

[48] Frisch, "Plan eller Kaos," 1931.

nearly as popular within the social-democratic movement if the fascist threat had not been so urgent. This also allowed De Man, Tinbergen, Hein Vos, and others of their generation to rise to prominence in their respective parties at a speed that would have been unthinkable without this imminent danger.

5.4 The Plans of Labor

In 1934 The Belgian Plan of Labor was published, and soon become known as the Plan De Man (Figure 5.1). It argued for the introduction of a mixed economy with some nationalized sectors, the organization of the economy for the general interest and the eradication of unemployment, and finally the reform of the state and the parliamentary system to arrive at a true economic and social democracy. The Plan, in other words, was both economic and political. De Man was clear that the economy had to be brought under greater control. This greater degree of control would also create decision power over the course of the economy and would thus, according to De Man, lead to more democracy. It is striking, however, that this was not to be done through more democratic checks but rather through a special Economic Council that would get an important advisory role to government. De Man made it clear that he wanted to transform democracy, not overthrow it, and to continue to rely on constitutional freedoms. The transformation of democracy he proposed was far-reaching: he wanted to abolish the Senate to move to a purely parliamentary system whose proceedings would have to be streamlined and supported by expert bodies. He acknowledged the dangers of "Etatism," but suggested that these could be prevented by creating executive bodies in charge of running the economy, necessary "for the unity of action and the concentration of responsibility."[49] De Man was clearly ceding ground to the antidemocrats, such as the fascists, who had critiqued the parliamentary system for ineffectiveness and inefficiency. But he hoped that this more efficient organization of the political system would make the state more decisive, while retaining at least the core of democracy.

The economic part of the Plan de Man, as the Belgian Plan was soon known, was little more than slogans. It promoted ill-defined goals, such as a credit policy that would allow the plan to work, or a greater satisfaction of primary needs. The one notable aspect was that it sought to combat the

---

[49] De Man, *Voor Een Plan van Actie*, 1934.

Figure 5.1 Election poster of the Belgian Socialist Party of Hendrik de Man from 1935: "He created 125,000 jobs for the unemployed."

protectionism of the 1930s, and strongly rejected any autarchic ideal. Not even ten pages long and full of slogans, the Belgian Plan stood in stark contrast with the elaborate Dutch Plan of Labor, which was finally completed in 1935. It was the result of several joint meetings and extensive discussions, as well as serious planning work for the financial sections, with no less than 300 pages. Although the goals were similar – the creation of a mixed economy, the end of unemployment, and a reordering of both politics and the economy – the Dutch Plan provided an extensive road map for how to achieve these goals. And what was more, it also sought to provide an analysis of both the political and economic crises. It contained both diagnosis of the current crises and a cure.

The first striking feature of the Dutch Plan, of which Jan Tinbergen and Hein Vos[50] are believed to be the architects, was its extensive statistical and financial underpinning. It contained extensive sections on the public works to be undertaken, the way in which rent control was to be implemented, and how industrialization was to be promoted while limiting the amount of rationalization (of which it was feared it would lead only to more unemployment). The centerpiece of the Dutch Plan was the proposal to increase employment. This was to be done through extensive public works, for the most important of which the employment effects were calculated. The employment effects were believed to have so-called multiplier effects, an idea developed by John Maynard Keynes and his student Richard Kahn.[51] The basic idea behind multiplier effects was that public investments would cause employment to rise; the resulting higher levels of income would boost consumption, and hence generate more demand including for workers, and would thus provide a virtuous circle in an economy operating far below full capacity. In this way the public investments would have a far larger positive effect than the initial stimulus and might to some extent pay for themselves.

To ensure that the gains would not end up with a small group of workers, Tinbergen pleaded for the fair distribution of work, an idea that would have a long lineage in Dutch politics.[52] This was to be achieved through the reduction of the work week to forty hours, an increase of schooling with one year so that fewer people entered the labor market,

---

[50] See note 1; it is noteworthy that the Dutch Plan never became directly associated with an individual politician, unlike the Belgian Plan "De Man."

[51] Abma, "Het Plan van de Arbeid en de SDAP," 57, 1977.

[52] There is some indication that Tinbergen pioneered the idea of a basic income for inclusion in the Plan of Labor; he discussed the idea in a letter to AJC leader Koos Vorrink: "I have recently been arguing for an idea, what I have called a basic income, an income, provided by the community to every mature citizen, whether they work or not." JT to Vorrink, 22 October 1934, TL. I thank Anton Jager for the pointer. See also Zamora and Jager, "Free from Our Labors and Joined Back to Nature: Basic Income and the Politics of Post-Work in France and the Low Countries," 2021.

and a lowering of the pension age to ensure more exit. The effects of such measures were calculated to ensure that the Plan would not create budget deficits.[53] The Dutch Plan embodied a type of economic expertise that Tinbergen favored and that would prove its most long-lasting legacy.[54] The critics wondered whether all this expertise and these calculations would be of any use without a serious political (power) strategy. De Man, the far more political leader, was at his best when strategizing for influence and adoption. But Tinbergen responded to those wishing for more emphasis on political strategy: "The authors of the Plan wish to obtain power through the economic qualities of the Plan, and in no other way."[55]

The second striking feature of the Dutch plan was an extensive reflection on *Ordnung* (*Ordening*).[56] Although the Plan contained no clear-cut definition of *Ordnung*, it was made clear through several examples of what could be understood by it: the organization and reorganization of the decision-making structure in the economy. This could be done through general laws or rules such as safety standards, which took the decision-making on these matters out of the hands of entrepreneurs. It could be done through alternative forms of organization at the industry level such as cartels, cooperatives, or nationalization of an industry. Or it could be done by changing the way that economic policy was made. *Ordnung* was

---

[53] The emphasis on the division of work should quench any doubt that that Tinbergen did not play an important role in the writing of the Plan of Labor; he was the main proponent of this idea during this period. It was summed up in one of his ex libris stamp marks, which read "Van de verdeling komt de Winst" ("From the distribution comes the gain"). This phrase is easily mistranslated since "verdeling" can also refer to income distribution. But is much better read as a social-democratic interpretation of the Smithian idea of the division of labor. Tinbergen would later continue along these lines when he argued for expanded education, so that talents would be better utilized and work (and therefore income) would be more equally distributed.

[54] This somewhat exclusive focus on the economic dimension of the solution was recognized among Tinbergen's allies, see Van Wijk, "Plan-Politiek en Plan-Socialisme," 19, 1935.

[55] Tinbergen, "De Positie van het Plan van de Arbeid," 7, 1936. In the same issue Tinbergen's economic defense is critiqued for its apolitical nature; it thus reflected his personal view rather than that of most other party members.

[56] *Ordnung* is now frequently related to the Ordo-liberals, a group of German liberal economists mostly from Freiburg. But in Germany and more broadly on the continent, there was an extensive *Ordnung* debate that discussed the optimal form of organization of the economy. Contributions came from the liberal camp, but more so from those favoring corporatist arrangements, socialists and guild socialists of various kinds, and of course those who argued for central planning. These debates concerned the institutional organization within firms, within industries, and of the economy as a whole.

associated with coordination and opposed to the uncoordinated, anarchis-
tic capitalist economy of the 1930s. The Plan argued for building on the
forms of *Ordnung* currently found in the economy, to create a more
socialist economy. This continued a trend within the social-democratic
party that was already visible in the report "New Institutions" from 1931.[57]

What *Ordnung* would mean in practice was best illustrated by a diagram
in an accompanying brochure (see Figure 5.2). In the diagram the sphere of
the state and democratic politics was still placed on top. But the economic
sphere was marked off from it with a thick line and was to be governed by a
general economic council. This council would be supported by several expert
institutions such as a technology institute, an import and export organization,
and a business-cycle institute (on the right). It would also govern the newly
nationalized central bank (on the left), which would be supervising the
commercial and private banks. At the industry level the Dutch Plan also
proposed a new *Ordnung* of the economy. Industries would be organized into
industry organizations that would facilitate a more orderly form of competition, to get rid of the so-called cutthroat competition of the crisis years.

The simplest way of summing up what the Dutch Plan proposed was more
expert influence at the government level and more coordination in markets. It
still left a lot to be worked out, but these were the directions in which the planners
were thinking. It was believed that many in parliament lacked the relevant
knowledge to make rational economic policy, and therefore this power had to
be handed over to an expert council, which worked directly for the government.
At the industry level the problem was not a lack of knowledge, although it was
believed that some industries could benefit from more modernization, but an
undesirable form of competition. It was believed that coordination between
firms could overcome some of the negative effects of competition.

The Belgian Plan should be located somewhere between the older Marxist
beliefs and the newer goals of planning and rationalization. It still called for
the nationalization of certain key industries, and vilified the majority of
capitalists. This was not the case for the Dutch Plan, which more clearly
represented a break with Marxism. There was no call for nationalization, nor
was it believed that capitalists were the problem. Instead, it was believed that
a superior form of organization of the economy could lead to more stable
and better outcomes. It called for a change not in the property structure of
the economy but in the decision structure. Therefore, it was of great
significance in reconceptualizing the institutional order of the economy.

---

[57] SDAP, "Nieuwe Organen," 1931.

Organization of society according to the scheme of the Plan of Labor

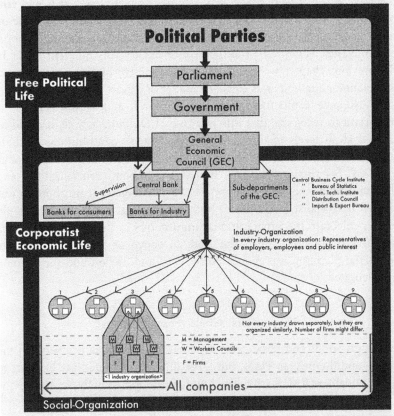

Freedom in political life and control and functional organization (Ordnung) in economic life!

Figure 5.2 Recreated from A brochure from 1936 elaborating the new political and economic order proposed by the Dutch Plan of Labor. (Adapted and translated by author)

The technocratic aspects of Tinbergen's thought and the socialist con-notations of planning have been well recognized. But both associations lead us astray easily. Planning for Tinbergen meant both the institutional reordering of the economy – that is, a change in the decision structure and the way decisions were made – as well as the planning that would take place within this institutional structure. So, planning could take place on many levels, within the firm, within the industry, and for the national economy, just as *Ordnung* could be conceived at many different levels. In the previous chapter we saw that the development of economic statistics and planning methods was equally a matter of private businesses, of banks and insurance companies, of expert institutes, and of the state. It is important to recognize that this was true of *Ordnung* as well: it could be created at all levels of the economy. Tinbergen's contributions to these matters are sometimes technical, but they are just as often institutional. One of his major postwar books was about centralization and decentralization in the economy. And Tinbergen's contribution was shaped by socialist ideals, but it built on capitalist structures. He would always celebrate the organizational innovations of private entrepreneurs and frequently even urged the state to move in the same direction. Industrial planning was pioneered by Ford and Taylor, and they should be celebrated for it.

5.5 Socialist Goals, Fascist Means?

In the proposals and the details there was a lot of difference between the Dutch and the Belgian Plans. But those differences should not blind us to their fundamental similarity. The number one goal of both was to provide a solution to the acute problem of unemployment, and both were first and foremost part of major political campaigns (Figure 5.3).

In August 1935, Ed van Cleeff sent a letter to Tinbergen in which he expressed his worries about the political if not propagandistic turn the Plan campaign was taking. Both Tinbergen and Van Cleeff had taken part in the discussions about the Plan of Labor within the SDAP. Ed van Cleeff was in many ways an equal to Tinbergen at the time. He too was involved in the youth movements of the 1920s, though not with the AJC, but in the closely related movement of Practical Idealists (PIA)[58] associated with the journal *Regeneration* (*Regeneratie*). The practical idealists were more outspokenly

---

[58] Tinbergen reported on one of the early PIA gatherings in the 1920s, at which he might have met Van Cleeff for the first time. Tinbergen, "Verstand of Gevoel?," 1924.

Figure 5.3 Iconic poster created by Harm Visser for the campaign surrounding the Dutch Plan of Labor, 1936.

religious, but equally socialist in the manner of Hendrik de Man.[59] And like Tinbergen, Van Cleeff was a member of the free-thinking Remonstrants. In the early 1930s both men had been part of a study group on modern socialism and the economy under the guidance of the religious socialist Willem Banning.[60] It was thus as a close friend that Van Cleeff could write his letter to Tinbergen, which contained serious and in Van Cleeff's eyes vital criticism of the scientific bureau of the SDAP, the bureau officially in charge of drafting the Plan of Labor for the Netherlands. Van Cleeff raised three criticisms against them, which all in important ways touched on the place of science in politics.

Van Cleeff argued that the scientific bureau had started working without first settling on a good theoretical foundation. For Van Cleeff, such a foundation meant a synthetic vision of man and society that would truly move beyond both Marxism and modern economics.[61] Such a moral and social vision was required before one could sensibly claim that one knew where one was going or had to go, he argued. Van Cleeff also suggested that the Plan, unfinished and tentative as it was, was already being used for propaganda purposes. This made it clear that the party was more interested in propaganda and saving the party than with the contents of the Plan. This was precisely the wrong way around, according to Van Cleeff. The new type of politics they pursued should appeal to ideals and reason, not to group interests or party purposes. Van Cleeff warned Tinbergen that the Plan of Labor had already become, or at least was very close to becoming, a mere tool in party politics. He knew that Tinbergen was sensitive to this type of argument, because he too believed that the economic merits of the Plan should convince the public, and not the associated propaganda.

Van Cleeff's most serious criticism hit at the heart of socialist and rationalist politics itself. He argued: "It really begins to appear somewhat like national-socialist methods:[62] first we create a sentiment, then we present people with a *fait accompli*, and finally we have them cheer at

[59] Van Cleeff, "Hendrik de Man's 'Die Intellektuellen und der Sozialismus,'" 1929.
[60] Willem Banning to JT, 11 September 1933, TL. The invitation is extended to J. S. Bartstra, Ed van Cleeff, Marinus van der Goes van Naters, J. F. de Jongh, J. P. Kruyt, P. Kuin, M. J. Langeveld, and Tinbergen.
[61] Van den Bogaard, "Economie als Wiskundige Abstractie of als Uitdrukking van Zingeving? Strijdende Visies bij het Ontstaan van het Centraal Planbureau," 2001.
[62] There is a tendency to blame the more fascist and antiparliamentary tendencies in the Plan on Hendrik de Man, who ended up supporting the fascists during World War II. Curiously, this literature tends to ignore the internal debates in the Netherlands about these dangers. See, for example, Pels, "Hendrik de Man en de Ideologie van het Planisme," 1985.

it."[63] The propaganda campaign for the Plan had already started: Hein Vos had in fact already given speeches about it to great enthusiasm from the cheering crowds, and yet the Plan was far from done. Worse yet, suggested Van Cleeff, propaganda concerns had already slipped into the actual analysis when it was decided that devaluation of the guilder would not be part of the Plan. That decision was made not because such a devaluation would not work, but rather because it was believed to generate too much opposition. Van Cleeff could have added that a consideration of budget deficits to pay for public works was ignored for the same reason.[64] Van Cleeff suggested that the SDAP was, like the fascists, distorting if not poisoning democratic debate, on the one hand, by not presenting all the options and, on the other hand, by presenting a plan that had to be accepted wholesale. He argued that the Plan could achieve its purpose only if its acceptance was based on soberness and rationality; if it was accepted for the wrong reasons, it would further contribute to the failure of democracy.

What makes Van Cleeff's critique so interesting and powerful is that it was based on values and goals that were shared by the young intellectuals within the SDAP who were supporting the Plan movement, most prominently, Hein Vos and Tinbergen. They shared Van Cleeff's commitment to sober, factual, and objective political deliberation; they shared his commitment to break open traditional ideological and political barriers and provide a plan that might appeal to everyone; and they shared his commitment to introduce scientific analysis into politics. So, it was extremely painful to Tinbergen and other scientifically minded social democrats when Van Cleeff ultimately resigned his party membership shortly after the publication of the Plan.[65] Hein Vos, seemingly replying to Van Cleeff – Tinbergen's reply to Van Cleeff is lost – argued the following about democracy: "The Plan of Labor does not aspire to form a set of dictatorial government decrees. It wants to be understood for its content and aspirations. Democracy does not merely mean influence of the people; it also means understanding by the people. For that reason, the Plan action, in all its scope and intensity, is a consequence of our democratic conviction."[66]

[63] Ed van Cleeff to JT, 24 August 1935, JT Letters.
[64] Nekkers, "Sentiment en Program," 1985.
[65] Van den Bogaard, "Economie als Wiskundige Abstractie of als Uitdrukking van Zingeving? Strijdende Visies bij het Ontstaan van het Centraal Planbureau," 228, 2001.
[66] Vos, *Waar het op Staat: Het Plan van de Arbeid Verdedigd*, 52–53, 1936.

From our current perspective that might seem to confirm Van Cleeff's worst suspicions; it is hardly a typical defense of democracy. But that is to misunderstand the context in important ways. What Vos did in his response was to cede important ground to Van Cleeff, whose religious socialism had emphasized the development of a certain awareness, a socialist spirit in the people. The concept that ideals were not always fully present but had to be developed and nurtured fitted well with Van Cleeff's progressive religious socialism, in which cultural development was essential. Vos argued not that the Plan should already find full approval of the people, but instead that such approval and support should be developed, and the propaganda campaign within and outside the party of was meant to realize this. The Plan "tries consciously to connect to that which, still partly unconsciously, moves the people."[67]

It was not that Van Cleeff disagreed with this spirit, but rather that he wanted to safeguard pluralism. Dutch society around that time was organized in different pillars along religious/political lines: Catholic, Protestant, socialist, and liberal.[68] These deep divisions were reflected in Dutch civil society, most notably the media landscape and the organization of education. What Van Cleeff feared most deeply was that "the people" were appealed to as one organic unit. Democracy, for Van Cleeff, also encompassed the recognition of pluralism. And in a Plan that was first and foremost national, it was more dangerous if "the people" were believed to possess one spirit, or one will. Vos defended the Plan by emphasizing that it recognized the need for different political parties, but Van Cleeff was uncertain whether this was enough of a safeguard. His own later work on the socioeconomic *Ordnung* of the Netherlands sought to recognize this pluralism at a deeper level, in particular, in civil society and the economy.

Van Cleeff was correct in his observation that the "popular front" movement of the time against fascism, of which Plan socialism was one expression, moved in the opposite direction of pluralism, toward unity and nationalism. It is hard not to think of the later political trajectory of De Man, who ended up collaborating with the fascists. Early in the 1930s the fundamental social distinction for De Man had already been between leaders and masses, not different societal groups (or even classes). And that was evident also in the Dutch rhetoric surrounding the Plan: "[S]ocialism can again be a vital symbol in the life of the great masses;

---

[67] Commissie uit N.V.V. en S.D.A.P., "Het Plan van de Arbeid," 1936.
[68] Lijphart, *The Politics of Accomodation: Pluralism and Democracy in the Netherlands*, 1968.

and let us hope that maybe this might happen without the formal corrosion of democratic rights."[69] But one does not have to focus on the extremes to see that Van Cleeff was highly perceptive of the trends at the time. After the war Vos and Tinbergen contributed to the so-called Breakthrough movement, which sought to break down the deep pluralism in society and move beyond the traditional pillars. Even in the 1930s, the former AJC members were already hoping to unite around ideas rather than parties.[70] That, however, could not stop the fact that the political reception of the Plan in the Netherlands was precisely as a party document. Despite support from some progressive Catholics, it failed to build any bridges across party lines.[71] In fact, the conservative and liberal parties used the Plan to warn their electoral base once more of the dangers of socialism and as evidence that the social democrats were communists after all, no matter how far off the mark that was from the intentions of those who drafted the Plan.

The critique of Van Cleeff highlighted the new relation between intellectuals, socialist goals, and the people. The vanguard role envisioned by Hendrik de Man was in the 1920s embodied in a different lifestyle in the socialist youth movement, but it turned into a political movement during the period of Plan socialism. In Vos's defense we clearly see this idea of the vanguard reflected in his claim that the Plan embodied ideals that had not yet come to fruition among the people. The extensive propaganda campaign set up for the Plan included gatherings, brochures, courses for members of the Party, flags, and, most famously, the song written by Vos:

> We want to turn the misery
> We want to liberate the time
> From the sorrow of tomorrow
> From the scourge of unemployment
> We must, we can!
> On with the Plan![72]

[69] Van Wijk, "Plan-Politiek en Plan-Socialisme," 21, 1935. In his conclusion Van Wijk emphasized that there are "objectively dangerous tendencies" in the Plan movement, so caution at any moment is required. But accepting these dangers is essential if one wants to fight fascism.
[70] Sterk, "Van Jeugdbeweging naar Socialisme," 11, 1937.
[71] For an excellent overview of the reception of the Plan of Labor in the Netherlands, see Nekkers, "Sentiment En Program," 1985.
[72] In Dutch: "Wij willen de ellende wenden / Wij willen de tijd bevrijd / Van het honende zorgen voor morgen / Van de gesel der werkloosheid / Het moet, het kan! / Op voor het plan!

Van Cleeff suggested it was unclear how we could possibly differentiate this from the propaganda of the national socialists. After all, the gatherings and marches organized to promote the Plan really did make it look like the Plan movement was taking to the streets to generate popular support reminiscent of the rise of fascism in Germany and Italy. The simple answer was that the difference was in the type of ideals that were pursued. But even that was not fully true, as some critical commentators noted that the Plan was essentially a national solution, and therefore at odds with the longer tradition of internationalism among the cultural socialists.[73]

Tinbergen was caught in the middle. He was never the political agitator that Hendrik de Man was, not even the political energizer that his friend Hein Vos was. Vos continuously lectured and defended and promoted the Plan for every imaginable group. Yet, Tinbergen unambiguously defended the Plan as a major step forward in rational politics, and it was his association that played an important role in the scientific legitimacy of the Plan. The financial and statistical appendixes in the Plan were clearly written by Tinbergen, or under his supervision, and they were used by Vos to defend the scientific merits of the Plan. More importantly, support for the Plan set Tinbergen on the pragmatist path that would mark the rest of his career. He was no longer content with statistical and theoretical studies on business cycles; he now had an opportunity to get involved in politics and do something about the instability of the current economy. Tinbergen would remain open to scientific criticism, but unlike Van Cleeff he would never let this slow down his practical and political efforts much. The urgency that was felt by Hendrik de Man, and that was represented by the Plan movement, was shared by Tinbergen. Science was a means, not the goal. As one of his ex libris stamp marks read: "Every hour counts."

When Ed van Cleeff finally completed his theoretical treatise on economic order in 1939, Tinbergen wrote a foreword with words of high praise. But Tinbergen must also have been happy that they did not wait with the Plan until this theoretical foundation was complete. That would have been scientifically correct, but politically wrong. It was a balancing act, that as we will see, Tinbergen would perform again and again.

---

[73] Nederhorst, "Vooruitzichten der Internationale Productie Ordening," 1936; Jansen van Galen, "Doorbraak: Het Plan in de Herinnering van Tijdgenoten," 171–72, 1985; Verwey-Jonker, "Plan en Internationalisme," 1936; Lieftinck, Bakker, and Van Lent, *Pieter Lieftinck, 1902–1989: Een Leven in Vogelvlucht*, 63, 1989.

6

Macro-dynamics and the Problem
of Unemployment

Our grand business undoubtedly is, not to see what lies dimly at a distance, but
to do what lies clearly at hand.
—Thomas Carlyle[1]

In 1969 Jan Tinbergen and the Norwegian Ragnar Frisch shared the first
Nobel Prize in Economics for their pioneering work in the field of
econometrics, the field at the intersection of statistics, mathematics, and
economic theory. Frisch was the technical yin to Tinbergen's practical
yang. Frisch originated many of the technical breakthroughs, which
Tinbergen put to practical use. Tinbergen's particular contribution was
the development of a complete model of the Dutch economy with a set of
equations that described the movement of the crucial macroeconomic
variables, which was fitted to historical data about the Dutch economy,
and not unimportantly used to estimate the likely effects of various policy
scenarios.

In Chapter 4 we have already witnessed the start of this field, which
originated in the development of quantitative models to study particular
markets and, in particular, production cycles on such markets. In
Tinbergen's perspective an early milestone was Hanau's analysis of the
cycle on the pig market, a pattern that Tinbergen managed to identify for
the Dutch shipbuilding industry. Perhaps equally important were the early
demand studies of Henry Schultz, who analyzed various agricultural
markets, a type of study that Tinbergen would also frequently do while
at the Bureau of Statistics (CBS). The crucial development in this field that
moved it far beyond the study of production and consumption (or supply
and demand) on specific markets was to use these and related techniques

---

[1] Carlyle is also quoted in Hendrik de Man, *Zur Pscyhologie des Sozialismus*, 1927.

to study national economies. As such, the rise of econometrics was closely intertwined with the rise of macroeconomics (the study of the economy as a whole).

The story of the rise of these fields has been told in a variety of excellent histories,[2] and I will not spend much time embedding Tinbergen's contribution to the rise of these fields extensively. Instead, the focus will be on his personal trajectory, which generates perspectives different from one that focuses on the development of these new academic fields. Most importantly, it allows us to see much better what broader purpose Tinbergen had in mind with his econometrics. It also allows us to analyze how political concerns shaped his approach to econometrics. Finally, it allows us to examine to what extent Tinbergen was able to uphold the Ehrenfest approach to science in this new field.

6.1 Unemployment and Rationalization

The 1930s were a decade of extensive unemployment. In many Western countries, over 20 percent of the working-age population was unemployed, and among young workers the situation was even worse. But unemployment had been lurking for much longer, and explaining it had been one of the theoretical challenges of economists during the 1920s. One of the dominant explanations was that of rationalization. It is a not wholly intuitive term for what today is more commonly called "technological unemployment."[3] The phenomenon caught the imagination of Tinbergen and his fellow economists with an engineering background even more, since it was the outcome of a process they generally applauded: the modernization of business and the increase of efficiency.

The problem first drew Tinbergen's attention in the context of his favorite pastime, trams.[4] In 1928, in his hometown of The Hague, the first tram operated by a single driver was introduced. This was not just a clear

---

[2] Morgan, *History of Econometric Ideas*, 1990; Hendry and Morgan, *The Foundations of Econometric Analysis*, 1995; Louçã, *The Years of High Econometrics: A Short History of the Generation That Reinvented Economics*, 2007; Boumans and Dupont-Kieffer, "A History of the Histories of Econometrics," 2011.

[3] It is the subject of a series of reviews Tinbergen writes around 1930; see Tinbergen, "Review of R. Wedemeyer's Konjunkturverslechterung durch Lohnerhöhungen," 1930; Tinbergen, "Review of J. Marschak's Die Lohndiskussion," 1931; Tinbergen, "Review of A. Ammon's Das Lohnproblem," 1932; for an overview of the debate, see Bauer, *Kapitalismus und Sozialismus nach dem Weltkrieg*, 1931.

[4] Tinbergen, "Eenmanswagens," 1928.

benefit to society, but also a clear case of rationalization; due to techno-logical improvements, two drivers were no longer required. But the prob-lem was that the second driver was now without a job, while the first one was performing a harder job. The greater productivity of the first driver could be compensated in the form of higher wages for the same number of hours, or the same total wage for fewer hours. Tinbergen suggested that the latter solution was preferable to prevent that rationalization would lead to more unemployment.[5] This suggestion for the fair distribution of work is perhaps one of his earliest constructive proposals for reform. In an inter-esting way it looks forward to John Maynard Keynes's famous prediction that the long-term effect of technological progress would be that "our grandchildren" would not need to work more than two or three days a week.[6]

His preference for the distribution of work is motivated not merely by attempts to limit unemployment but also by his skepticism toward wage increases.[7] In a review of a book detailing the achievements of trade unions over the past fifty years, he expressed skepticism that much has been achieved at all,[8] and in other articles he openly suggested that part of the high unemployment was caused by labor unions and their wage demands.[9] Such positions amounted to little less than heresy within the SDAP, and even more so in the associated unions.[10] It was not merely a peculiar political view, however. Tinbergen based his viewpoint on the economic theory of the time. In the late 1920s his economic thinking was still fully in line with the liberal Austrian school and their idea that markets should function unhampered to lead to the best results. In a seminal article, Eugen von Böhm-Bawerk, one of the leaders of the Austrian school, had argued that economic laws would in the long run be stronger than (social) legislation; all the latter could do was to lead to short-term disturbances.[11] Higher wages came at the cost of more unemployment and would in the long run be unsustainable. But more than the liberal Austrians, Tinbergen was already concerned with distributional issues, of both income and work. In 1929, shortly after the completion of his PhD, Tinbergen joined the editorial board of the *Socialist Guide (Socialistische Gids)*, the most

---

[5] Tinbergen, "Werktijdverkorting een Middel tegen Werkloosheid," 1928.
[6] Keynes, *Essays in Persuasion*, 1963.   [7] Tinbergen, "De Werkloosheid," 1930.
[8] Tinbergen, "Macht en Ekonomiese Wet," 1928.
[9] Tinbergen, "Vraagstukken van Socialistiese Ekonomie," 1929.
[10] For a characteristic response see "Smeedt het Strijdfront voor Brood en Arbeid!," *De Tribune*, 11 December 1930.
[11] Böhm-Bawerk, "Macht oder ökonomisch Gesetz," 1924.

intellectual publication of the SDAP and one of the most successful of its kind around Europe. His first major contribution immediately caused quite a stir.[12] Like his other work of the period, it denounced wage increases as only aggravating the problem of unemployment. And more importantly he argued that contrary to the popular belief among his peers, more planning in production would not resolve the unemployment issue, either. His view was a curious combination of classical economics and Marxism, which are not always that far apart. Both insist on an iron logic within capitalism, a logic that can be ignored only at one's own peril. Consequently, there was little perspective for improvements within the current economic system. And although Tinbergen was never revolutionary, he believed around 1930 that quite fundamental changes to the system were required before more just economic and social outcomes could be achieved. It is one of the many beliefs that he would shed during the crucial early 1930s.

It is around this time that Tinbergen started to rethink the basic picture of self-regulating markets. The first theoretical impetus for Tinbergen's business cycle was the discovery of the pig cycle.[13] The economist Arthur Hanau managed to demonstrate the existence of an endogenous cycle caused by the fact that pig production responded with a delay to changes in prices. One of Tinbergen's proudest moments in his early career was that he found a similar cycle for shipbuilding in the Netherlands.[14] These insights were instantly translated into policy recommendations by Tinbergen. The Netherlands has a relatively unique tradition called "pre-advices" (*prae-advies*) in which various social organizations set an extensively specified question and asked two or three experts to provide an answer, typically written out in the form of an essay or a report. In 1931, Tinbergen wrote such an advice about the agricultural crisis, which resulted from persistently low prices for agricultural products. He directly applied the theory of Hanau to argue that there are predictable cycles in agricultural markets, the knowledge of which can be used to stabilize prices. One of the problems that the Dutch agricultural sector faced, however, was that since the market dynamics were international, policy could achieve very little on the national level.

This advice was also a good example of how Tinbergen combined thinking about *Ordnung* with an analysis of the price system. He argued that there was something of a collective action problem where it was individually

[12] Tinbergen, "De Werkloosheid," 1930.
[13] Hanau, "Die Prognose der Schweinepreise," 1928.
[14] Tinbergen, "Ein Schiffbauzyklus?," 1931.

rational to expand production, but collectively rational to restrict production. This problem could be solved by reorganizing the industry in a way where the individual farmers could coordinate their production. Tinbergen was in favor of such a solution, but radically rejected any tampering with the price system. It is a practical example of his classical way of thinking about the way markets operate, while at the same time acknowledging that such markets would in the long run be replaced with, in his eyes, superior forms of organization. He still respected the fundamental price mechanism – one could not artificially raise prices – but at the same time he was exploring different institutional structures to create more stable prices. An instance of this type of institutional reorganization of a market would be studied by Tinbergen not much later: the coffee market in Brazil.[15]

Another common belief among economists of the period was that economic downturns were part of a natural cycle. A crisis, therefore, was only temporary, and recovery would commence as naturally as the downturn set in.[16] This belief was clearly shifting in 1932, when in his next pre-advice, this time for the prestigious Dutch Royal Society of Economics, he wrote about the possibility that the present downturn was not merely a "normal" downturn. It contained some remarkably cutting-edge notions floating around at the time.[17] He explored, following discussions with J. G. Koopmans,[18] the possibility of multiple equilibria. It could be, Tinbergen argued, that the economy was presently stuck in a suboptimal equilibrium, an idea that Keynes's General Theory would help popularize a number of years later. The ideas of J. G. Koopmans were inspired by his mathematical studies in which interdependent systems could have multiple solutions. In a similar way, Koopmans argued, there could be several stable economic equilibria, but only some of them would also coincide with maximum production and full employment.

---

[15] Van Luytelaer and Tinbergen, "De Kofficvalorisaties. Geschiedenis en Resultaten," 1932.

[16] Tinbergen, "Is het Einde van de Crisis in Zicht?," 1932.

[17] Tinbergen, "In Hoeverre kan het Regelen van den Omvang der Voortbrenging of van Het Aanbod van Bepaalde Goederen Door Producenten, Al Dan Niet Met Medewerking Van de Overheid, Bevorderlijk worden Geacht voor de Volkswelvaart?," 1932.

[18] Koopmans, "De Mogelijkheid van een Meervoudig Economisch Evenwicht I," 1932; Koopmans, "De Mogelijkheid van een Meervoudig Economisch Evenwicht II," 1932; Koopmans, "De Mogelijkheid van een Meervoudig Economisch Evenwicht III," 1932. This series of articles was directly sparked by Tinbergen's pre-advice of that year. J. G. Koopmans is not to be confused with Tjalling Koopmans, later collaborator of Tinbergen and winner of the Nobel Prize in Economics. There is no direct family connection between J. G. Koopmans and Tjalling Koopmans.

Koopmans also considered an idea that would prove of great importance for the further development of Tinbergen's thought: the idea that equilibria might be either stable or labile. It was long believed that the economy was a self-correcting system: if for some reason the economic equilibrium was disturbed, it would naturally (over time) return to its equilibrium state. This was a fundamental idea underlying all theories of the business cycle. As the concept of "cycle" suggests, the economy moves up and down in a cyclical manner, but it never spins out of control, or collapses.

Mathematically, it was easy to imagine systems in which this was not at all the case. There could be so-called labile systems in which, once out of equilibrium, the system would move ever further away from it.[19] And this was no mere theoretical possibility. Tinbergen suggested that this was often the case in situations of inflation: the hyperinflations in Central Europe, most notably, Germany and Austria, were fresh on his mind. And one could also think of falling prices that would lead to even more postponement of buyers, and even further falling prices. During the Great Depression, slowly but surely some economists started to wonder whether recovery would ever set in.

If natural recovery was unsure, it could be that interventions by the state might be effective. There is now a whole apparatus of economic policies and levers that are available to the state. But it is important to realize that economic policy was still very limited and underdeveloped around 1930. In 1932 Tinbergen first started to explore what the state could do. Previously, he expected very little of the state and placed all his hope in developments taking place within the industry, but he now suggested several possible functions for the state. It is a curious amalgam of measures directed at a variety of industries that retrospectively also look quite contradictory. The list consisted of six items: (1) industrial policy aimed against cartels; (2) limiting the power of brands; (3) state credits to boost lagging production and demand; (4) public works to fight unemployment; (5) rationalization of production, in particular, among small and medium-sized businesses; and (6) limiting overproduction in agriculture.

---

[19] In the economics literature an unstable equilibrium would become known as a knife-edge equilibrium, a concept often attributed to Roy Harrod, who correctly pointed out that the equilibrium on top of a shallow dome is equally unstable; see Harrod, "Harrod after Twenty-One Years: A Comment," 1970; Tinbergen, "Review of R. F. Harrod's The Trade Cycle," 1937.

It is rather contradictory, for example, to propose the breaking-up of cartels in some industries while arguing for more organization and coordination between producers in others. And rationalization, which was considered problematic in some sectors, had to be promoted in others. It is hard to find a consistent line between these proposals, except that they were all failures of the market that somehow could be corrected. They are also evidence that in the early 1930s most economic policy, and economic analysis, was still centered on particular industries, rather than the economy as a whole. The economy as a coherent system that could be manipulated had not yet been imagined, or invented, if you will.

6.2 Dynamic Steps

Even the cycle itself was believed to be a phenomenon as much of specific markets as it was of the overall economy. Although it was recognized that cycles in important primary markets and specifically in capital markets could have repercussions in other industries, there was not yet a clear idea that the business cycle was a macroeconomic phenomenon. Certainly, ever since the work of Leon Walras and Vilfredo Pareto, who were known for general equilibrium theory, there was a clear idea of the economy as an interdependent system. But an interdependent system can still consist of relatively separate individual markets. It was one of the major transformations of the 1930s that the national economy became conceived as something that could be conceptualized as a separate entity, intervened on, and studied somewhat independently from the individual markets of which it consisted. Keynes's General Theory was a hallmark achievement in this development. And that was equally true of the invention of national income accounts in various countries. The construction of these accounts allowed for the measurement of the total output of a national economy, which would become known as gross domestic product. But in the early 1930s neither Keynes general system nor national income accounts existed.

There was, however, a gradual development toward macroeconomics, especially in the German-speaking world and Scandinavia.[20] The first important contribution, one we already encountered in Chapter 4, was the collection of statistics at the national and international level. What also contributed to the development of the idea of an integrated national economy was the fact that the state increasingly sought to steer the

---

[20] For the German case, see Tooze, *Statistics and the German State, 1900–1945: The Making of Modern Economic Knowledge*, 2001.

national economy. When public works were proposed as a solution for the ongoing recession, they were naturally believed to be part of a national economic plan, and this was typically accompanied with nationalist rhetoric. The fascist parties in Germany and Italy made this perfectly clear, but the New Deal in America was based on strong nationalist sentiments, as were the various Plans of Labor from the left.

At a theoretical level, the key concept for thinking about the economy as a whole was equilibrium, which more frequently now was interpreted as a condition of the national economy, rather than of particular markets. The question was how well the adjustment process toward this general equilibrium was, and what the role of expectations was in this process.

Tinbergen's own contribution to thinking about expectations and equilibrium were two articles that are surprisingly modern even today. The first one appeared in 1932 and suggested that, previously, economic theory had been a type of comparative statics, that is, the comparison of two equilibria (before and after the analyzed change).[21] An important step forward was made by the Austrian economist Oskar Morgenstern with the explicit introduction of time into his equations. Ambitiously, Tinbergen suggested that he would now take the third step by formulating a truly dynamic theory. This dynamic theory would incorporate a new notion, what he calls the horizon (*Gesichtsfeld*) – expectations, in modern terms.

Tinbergen wondered whether expectations could be assumed to be identical between individuals but rejected this idea. Not only will plans differ between individuals, a point repeatedly emphasized in the Austrian tradition, but expectations will consider the institutional structure of markets, he argued. Tinbergen argued that expectations in different industries will be formed depending on the *Ordnung*, the institutional structure, of that particular industry. Is the market competitive or dominated by a monopolist? And what type of planning and production techniques are used in this market? It once again makes clear how much theorists still thought about particular industries rather than an overall economy in the early 1930s. Expectations were believed to be a meso-phenomenon: they were formed by producers about their own industry, and not about the state of the economy as a whole.

Tinbergen's first exploration of expectations dealt with the expectations of sellers; the second article dealt with the expectations of buyers.[22] In the former, sellers were forming expectations about the likeliest level of total

---

[21] Tinbergen, "Ein Problem der Dynamik," 1932.
[22] Tinbergen, "The Notions of Horizon and Expectancy in Dynamic Economics," 1933.

demand in the market, while in the latter, buyers were trying to buy goods, such as coffee or stocks, at the best price. Tinbergen was particularly interested in how much previous experience was used in the formation of the expectations of buyers. The way he thought about buyers was not too different from the position that the business-cycle theorists of the age were in: they knew past price movements but were unable to predict future price movements.

That analogy was further developed when he talked about the content of expectations. The assumption in his model was that consumers do the best they can and form what would later be called rational expectations.[23] But he also assumed that consumers have a specific model in mind of price movements: prices gravitate around a specific natural level, much like a ball rolling around in a fruit bowl will gravitate toward the bottom center of that bowl. This ensures a stabilizing dynamic in the model; when prices go up, buyers will respond but in a more moderate manner because they expect prices to return to long-term values over time. A similar assumption was built into many of the business-cycle theories of the age. The most famous of these theories was that of Ragnar Frisch, his so-called rocking-horse model. Economics was becoming more dynamic, but the notion of equilibrium remained important.

The work in these articles drew heavily from Tinbergen's more purely statistical analyses at the Central Bureau of Statistics (CBS) (see Figure 4.4). Much of the second "dynamic economics" article was taken from his article on price formation in the stock market.[24] The journal he founded at the CBS, *De Nederlandsche Conjunctuur*, was at this point nearly completely written by Tinbergen, sometimes with explicit attribution to himself as an author and at other times not, as if to not emphasize that it was close to being his private journal. It is at the CBS that he also started to work on statistical material relating to the national economy. In 1932 he studied capital forma-tion,[25] and in 1933 the relationship between wages and the level of employ-ment.[26] Although these were still partial analyses, in the sense that they tackled one particular segment or phenomenon in the economy, they were reliant on what are now called macroeconomic variables: data relating to the economy as a whole, such as unemployment or the price level. In the

---

[23] Keuzenkamp, "A Precursor to Muth: Tinbergen's 1932 Model of Rational Expectations," 1991.

[24] Tinbergen, "Prijsvorming op de Aandelenmarkt," 1932.

[25] Tinbergen, "Kapitaalvorming en Conjunctuur in Nederland 1880–1930," 1932.

[26] Tinbergen, "De Invloed van de Werkloosheid op het Loonpeil," 1933.

next year he expanded his analysis to the influence of the cycle on labor productivity. Such articles were heavily statistical and served the official goal of the journal to provide businessmen, bankers, insurance companies, and policymakers alike with the latest data, but for Tinbergen they served as a stepping-stone to the more theoretical issues he explored in his academic journal articles of the time. His work at the CBS was time-consuming and detracted him from systematic work on the cycle, but at the same time it brought him into close contact with the best available statistical material and experts at various other statistical institutes in Europe. His work at the bureau provided him with unique firsthand access to statistical data and, not unimportantly, some help with the calculations.

An early culmination of this theoretical work can be found in Tinbergen's survey for *Econometrica*, the new official journal of the Econometric Society. As host of the 1933 Econometric Society meetings in Leiden, he was asked to write an overall survey of significant developments in general economic theory. It was a unique opportunity for him to highlight what he believed to be important developments and how economic theory might progress. It is also his most systematic treatment of the differences between static and dynamic economics. Tinbergen followed Frisch's distinction between the two, which is peculiar in the sense that it does not argue that dynamic economics reflects an underlying dynamic economy. Instead, it suggested that a theory is dynamic if it contains variables relating to different periods, thus making 'dynamic' a purely theoretical notion.[27]

This is remarkable for the fact that Frisch and Tinbergen were already working with the modern notion of theories and models. In this modern view theories are not believed to *mirror* reality but are believed to be helpful tools for the *representation* of reality. As such, the model is an autonomous object that relates to the phenomenon it seeks to describe, and it attempts to capture something essential about it, but should not be seen as a direct reflection of it. One can thus derive, at least potentially, insight from static theories about dynamic economies and from dynamic theories about static economies. As Tinbergen put it: "[A]s in all the applied sciences, the question is how to find the happy medium between the complexity of the real world and the simplicity of an amenable theory."[28]

---

[27] Tinbergen made a small addition to Frisch's definition. Frisch considered only time derivatives of variables as dynamic elements; Tinbergen added time lags in economic relations.

[28] Tinbergen, "Annual Survey: Suggestions on Quantitative Business Cycle Theory," 243, 1935.

More importantly, this opened the possibility of thinking about models as developed for particular purposes; in this case, since their goal was the explanation of business cycles, the model developed was preferably dynamic. But if one was interested in another phenomenon, say, persistent unemployment, one might still rely on static models.

In his overview article, Tinbergen primarily treated developments in the theory of oligopoly and the investigation of supply and demand curves. Under the heading of dynamic economics, Tinbergen treated many of his own contributions, often without explicit reference. He started with the subject that he first explored, still under the direct guidance of Ehrenfest: the difference between stock and flow variables in economics. He then continued to the role of expectations in a dynamic theory. He discussed his own quantitative investigations but also embedded them in a broader discussion of the role of expectations in the economy, such as Morgenstern's analysis of the effect that forecasts will have on the economy it is seeking to describe. Morgenstern had suggested that once forecasts became public, they became part of the economic system, and hence would impact the very system they sought to describe. In this way, to take one example, a negative forecast could be a self-fulfilling prophecy through its effect on the expectations of economic actors.[29]

He also discussed lags in markets, such as that for pig production and shipbuilding, based on his own work and that of Hanau. It is a micro-analysis but the notion of the actions of different time periods affecting one another was now explicitly connected with monetary and business-cycle theory, in particular, the work on neutral and stable currencies by J. G. Koopmans and the use of lags in Hayek's theory of the cycle. He thus continued to build a bridge between the micro-dynamics in particular markets and the macro-dynamics of the economy as a whole.

6.3 Smoothing Dynamics

The early 1930s were characterized by an interesting paradox. The business-cycle scholars were attempting to make economic theory more dynamic, so that it could capture the dynamic developments in the economy. But the goal of most scholars, including Tinbergen, was to suggest how

---

[29] Morgenstern, *Wirtschaftsprognose: Eine Untersuchung ihrer Voraussetzungen und Möglichkeiten*, 1928; Tinbergen, "Boekbespreking van O. Morgenstern's Wirtschaftsprognose," 1929; Morgenstern, "Vollkommene Voraussicht und wirtschaftliches Gleichgewicht," 1935.

to make the economy more stable. Classical economic theory had taken a long-run perspective and largely neglected short-run dynamics, which was felt as inadequate by those of Tinbergen's generation. But their hope was that they could make the real economy behave more like the economies in the models of the classical economists.

Whereas Joseph Schumpeter had once championed the dynamic economy as a goal in itself, the business-cycle theorists of the 1930s were all convinced that the dynamics had to be brought under control and reduced.[30] After the war, this culminated in elusive goals such as "stable growth paths" and "balanced growth." But in the 1930s such concepts were not yet in existence, and with the continuation and worsening of the economic crisis, the urgency grew to combat this very business cycle – if indeed it was "just" a cycle, and not something worse, such as a permanent crisis or, worse yet, a sign that capitalism was coming to an end.

Hence much of the work of Tinbergen during this period was applied and driven by the most recent economic events. This is not merely to say that it was concerned with policy, which was true for nearly all his work. But during these heated economic and political years, much of the work was written in direct response to recent events. The major exception in the years leading up to the model of the Dutch economy was an article that expands upon his inaugural lecture in Rotterdam.[31] It is a piece that is quintessentially Tinbergen: it used the latest theoretical insights to formulate a theory of economic policy.

Tinbergen started by making clear the different types of movements that occur in the economy. The first relevant difference is that between exogenous and endogenous movements. Exogenous movements are caused by external factors, and the extent to which they generate economic dynamics depends on the way in which the initial shock is "absorbed." The extreme case of such quick absorption is what Tinbergen considers to be the "classical" model, in which it is assumed that all adjustments are instantaneous. The moment the economic system is hit by an exogenous shock, it will move into its new equilibrium state. As we already saw, Tinbergen and other economists at the time were more interested in endogenous movements, but it is striking that Tinbergen suggested that this was in part because policy could not be used to prevent external shocks, precisely because they came from "outside" the economy. An

[30] Weintraub, *Stabilizing Dynamics: Constructing Economic Knowledge*, 1991.
[31] Tinbergen, *Statistiek en Wiskunde in Dienst van het Konjunktuuronderzoek*, 1933; Tinbergen, "Der Einfluß der Kaufkraftregulierung auf den Konjunkturverlauf," 1934.

endogenous theory was thus not merely more theoretically satisfying (and pure), but also more helpful for informing policy.

Endogenous movements are internal to the economic system and carried through the system or even amplified by it. It is only this type of movement that can generate the dynamics associated with the cycle. This cycle was understood by Tinbergen and others at the time as roughly an eight-year period of cyclical movement that contained both an upswing and a downswing. This dynamic was believed to hold even during the Great Depression. Positive signs in 1932 and 1933 were hence interpreted as signs of the coming (and inevitable) recovery, since the downswing had begun in 1929.

Tinbergen assumed that the instrument of policy was the stabilization of purchasing power. The easiest way to imagine this type of policy is that the government makes sure that spending is at the normal level (by spending more when consumers spend less, and saving more when consumers spend more). He investigated four types of scenarios in his paper. The first one examined the dynamics resulting from different lengths of production, a scenario he had earlier investigated and that was made prominent by theorists of the Austrian school.[32] The second scenario built on this first one, but now the costs of production were also made variable. The third one also built on the first but now the possibility of speculation was introduced. And the fourth scenario investigated the influence of the fixed lifespan of machines used in production. In none of these scenarios would the cycle be eliminated by a policy that stabilized purchasing power. But under scenarios one and two, the cycle could be reduced in both amplitude and period, making it shorter and less intense. Such effects, however, were not guaranteed, as scenarios three and four demonstrated. In these scenarios there was a possibility that the stabilization of purchasing power could have pro-cyclical effects and make the cycle more intense.[33] Tinbergen was thus already experimenting with different models. This allowed him to check the robustness of his results, but it also makes clear how much importance he attributed to institutional factors in the economy. There was no reason to expect that policies that worked under some circumstances should always produce the desired effects.

---

[32] Tinbergen, "L'Utilisation des Équations fonctionnelles et des Nombres complexes dans les Recherches économiques," 1933.
[33] Tinbergen, "La Politique des Salaires, les Cycles économiques et les mathématiques," 1935.

Much like expectations depended on the market structure, so too did the effects of policy regimes depend on the structure of the national economy.

The results were of direct practical significance for Tinbergen. Although he was building a highly simplified representation of the economy, which was slowly made more realistic, he could already demonstrate that there was no simple relationship between business cycle policy and the effects on the cycle. In order to treat the patient, one first had to understand how the body functioned. And yet new medicine was being tried all the time during the 1930s. The various policy experiments in Sweden, the New Deal in America, or even the new fascist economy in Germany all provided real-time attempts to dampen the cycle.

Much of his other work in 1934 and the following years was immediately concerned with these new types of "medicine." In yet another pre-advice he wrote, this time for the National Society against Unemployment, he examined Roosevelt's policies and performed an early statistical test of their effectiveness. He was generally optimistic that public works would have the desired effects and believed that the attempts to stop the wage decrease were important. But what is remarkable is that he was also worried during the very depths of the Great Depression that the measures undertaken were insufficiently long-term, and could carry the seeds of another crisis.[34] These were traditional worries of classical economists, and they demonstrate how much of that spirit Tinbergen had absorbed in the 1920s. He would always reason, in his economics, primarily from the supply side and focus on long-term effects, not short-term treatments.

The Plan of Labor we discussed in the previous chapter was therefore even more remarkable. It was the triumph of the short run and political concerns over the long run and structural economic concerns. And thus, it entailed a compromise for Tinbergen, who saw the dangers of too much stimulus at one point in time clearly. He favored the parts of the Plan of Labor that brought structural changes to the economy, such as the institutional organization of the economy. It was one way to ensure that the changes and remedies were not merely temporary. It is, therefore, no surprise that in a more popular treatment of the New Deal measures, Tinbergen pointed to the greater significance of the shift in mindset in the United States. If even the ultimate land of free enterprise was coming to

---

[34] Tinbergen, *Praeadvies Nationale Vereeniging tegen de Werkloosheid: Is te Verwachten dat de Maatregelen van President Roosevelt zullen Bijdragen, en zo Ja in Welke Mate, tot een Blijvende Vermindering der Werkloosheid in de Verenigde Staten van Noord-Amerika*, 1934.

accept that government had a role to play in the economy, this must surely be a hopeful sign.[35]

He was even more impressed with the Swedish committee charged with the reduction of unemployment. While he was not fully convinced that the New Deal measures would turn out to be anything more than emergency aid before a return to old mistakes, he praised the Swedish vision of permanent regulation, especially admiring the list of public works that could be undertaken when the next crisis hit. He was certainly not in favor of public investment irrespective of the costs – in fact, he spent most of the article discussing the dangers of overspending on public works and how this might be prevented by a profitability test of the proposed projects. But the forward-looking mindset, the planning attitude you might say, that underlay the Swedish list was much admired by Tinbergen.

His admiration of the Swedish approach also brought out the paradox of the search for a dynamic theory. One of the recommendations in the Swedish report was more wage flexibility. What this would effectively do is remove certain "lagged" responses, and hence *make* the economy more like that described by the classical model. This meant adjustments would be instantaneous, and shocks to the economy would quickly lead to a new equilibrium, rather than a prolonged cycle. If this flexibility was absent, for example, when wages or incomes did not respond to changes in the other variables or responded with a significant delay (lag), then there was the possibility of longer cycles in the economy.

Tinbergen was critical of this "classical" recommendation of more flexible wages. In order to combat the cycle, Tinbergen suggested, we should create more stability in the economy. His proposed method of the stabilization of purchasing power, which would later be one of the central tenets of Keynesian management of the economy, would create such stability. But, curiously, it would also make the economy more rigid, that is, slower to adjust to exogenous shocks. This tension is the central problem of the era. The economists were fully aware of the virtues of a self-adjusting system, but also aware that the actual economy was not behaving anything like this ideal model. From this imperfect situation some suggested that more built-in stability would create more overall stability in the economic system; others sought to remove the barriers to quick adjustment and make the economy more flexible.

[35] Tinbergen, "De Politiek van Roosevelt," 1934; Tinbergen, "De Politiek van Roosevelt," 1935.

The tension is perhaps illustrated best with the example of wages. Classical economists were in favor of flexible wages so that in the case of a negative shock to the economy wages would adjust downward and the profitability of most firms would not be endangered. The economy would quickly find a new equilibrium at a lower wage level. The dynamic investigations of Tinbergen, Frisch, and others proved that significant lags existed in the economy. On the production side of the economy there were significant rigidities; just think of Hanau's pig cycle or Tinbergen's shipbuilding cycle. In order to counter these rigidities, they suggested that wages should not be allowed to fall, because it would merely lead to overproduction in the future. So, in order to combat one rigidity, in production, they proposed to introduce another, in wages. Therefore, the economy would be less able to respond to shocks, except with yet more management.

Tinbergen was aware of this tension, and around the same time he started to write about a new form of organization of the economy. This new organization, or *Ordnung*, was supposed to create an economic structure that maximized welfare for society as a whole and included redistribution.[36] This new *Ordnung* of the economy was supposed to bring a superior form of coordination, especially between producers. In the middle of the Great Depression it was clear for Tinbergen that the current economy was anything but optimal. The reasons why he believed so were an interesting combination of arguments that would hold even if markets operated smoothly (an unequal distribution of income, and individual entrepreneurs lacking sufficient information to plan their production), and arguments that point to areas where markets did not work optimally (the various lags in the economy, tendencies toward monopoly in some industries, as well as too much rationalization in the face of high wages, which caused overall unemployment in the economy).

Tinbergen provided few specifics on what this new *Ordnung* should be, but it is important to realize that the concern with it arises out of the tension between flexibility and stability. It moves the problem one level up, if you will. He was not suggesting particular interventions in the economy, such as higher wages now or more public spending next year. Instead, he suggested that we should search for an economic order that stabilizes that which needs stabilizing and provides flexibility to that which requires flexibility. This required a reorganization of the decision-making structure

[36] Tinbergen, "Ordening: Een Arbeidersbelang," 1935; Tinbergen, "De Economische Zijde van het Ordeningsvraagstuk," 1935.

in the economy. The scale of the small business-owner might not be the optimal scale for making decisions, nor was it desirable to have other industries being dominated by a monopolist. But the way in which economic policy had been conducted and the instruments available for government policy had been equally insufficient. The solution was thus to be found in an overall more rational economic system, although it was still unclear what that entailed.

6.4 A Model of the Dutch Economy

Amid these political discussions and a burgeoning campaign for the Plan of Labor, Tinbergen built a full model of the Dutch economy, which would be published as a pre-advice to the Royal Dutch Society for Economics in 1936. But before he reached that point, he wrote another important review article in *Econometrica*. It is an article of no less than sixty-nine pages that laid out the state of the art in business-cycle theory. It was Tinbergen's most systematic treatment of the subject, and by now he had a clear image in mind of the conditions that a complete theory of the cycle should fulfill. Most importantly, it should be able to generate an endogenous (undamped) cycle, and the system should contain no more unknowns (variables) than equations, so that a definite solution could be found and tested against the data. And finally, he suggested that lags in the economy were the most promising mechanism to explain the cycle. He was particularly interested how relatively short lags, say, a couple of months in the adjustment of wages, could give rise to longer waves (those of eight years).

The main conclusion of the article was in the negative. Tinbergen concluded that changes in the wage level did not drive the cycle, for such movements were unable to generate the "correct" dynamics. That might seem like an unimpressive result, but it was mostly through elimination that Tinbergen made progress in these years. There were many hypothetical explanations of the cycle floating around, and Tinbergen considered most of them wanting: some could not even explain a wave movement but only an upswing or a downswing; others could not explain wave movements of the "correct" length; yet others could explain only waves that would quickly dampen and hence could not give rise to recurring cycles. This series of negative results had the benefit of severely restricting the type of structure that was feasible for a model of the economy, and it was to this task that Tinbergen turned.

At the 1935 meetings of the Econometric Society in the nearby Belgian city of Namur, he presented for the first time a full model of an economic

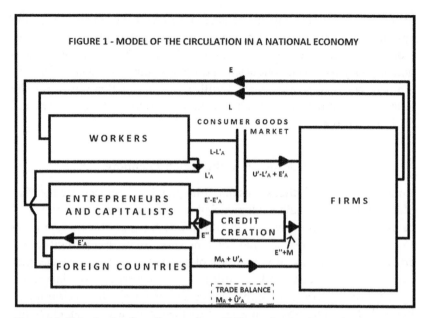

Figure 6.1 This circular-flow diagram from 1935 was the visual complement to Tinbergen's first mathematical set of equations representing an economic system. The letters (L, L'_A, etc.) refer to those used in the system of equations (adapted and translated by author).

system. It expanded on, as Tinbergen explained, the results obtained by the Dutch CBS, a euphemistic way of saying his own inquiries there. What was more prominent than before in his presentation was that he now distinguished between data and economic quantities. The data are those facts that are taken as given from the point of view of economic theory; Tinbergen singled out the natural, institutional, and technical conditions. The economic quantities are the variables that economic theory seeks to explain. This does not mean that the data are constants; indeed, they can also change, but it is not their change that the economist seeks to explain.

From this, he built a circular flow model (Figure 6.1). It is a generic structure not applied to a country or time period. The picture is best read starting with the two money flows going away from firms, which represent the wages and interest earned by workers and entrepreneurs. This is spent by workers on the market for consumption goods both domestically and abroad. And it is spent by entrepreneurs on consumption goods and saved so that it "flows" to the market for loans. This type of circular-flow diagram would become standard fare in economics; it was featured prominently in the textbook by Paul Samuelson that dominated the market for decades and had predecessors in the work of Frank Knight and others.[37] But Tinbergen's underlying set of equations was a new addition, and this was the real contribution of the paper. In eighteen equations and an equal number of variables he sought to describe the dynamics of the economic system. Tinbergen for the first time called this explicitly "a model," and he made clear that the model was a basic structure that could be further refined.

Tinbergen could build directly on the work of Ragnar Frisch, who had first suggested using a complete system of equations to describe the economy.[38] Frisch and Tinbergen shared a curious parallel path. This path would lead them to many similar themes such as econometric modeling, but also the measurement of utility, development economics, and the decision models of the 1950s.[39] The pattern for these interactions was set at the start: Frisch would develop the technical tools and Tinbergen would present them in complete form and popularize them (although, the "brand name" in the case of econometrics was coined by Frisch).

It is worth emphasizing that the goal of the business-cycle theorists of the age was to identify a mechanism that could explain the cycle. But Tinbergen was not alone in realizing that a mechanism also required a definition of what was part of the economic system and what was external to it. This delineation is one of the most significant aspects of his model: it defined the economic system as an internally functioning and autonomous system with clear boundaries. To count as an endogenous business-cycle theory, the cyclical behavior had to be explained within the boundaries of the "economic system."

As always, policy was part of the stakes involved for Tinbergen, although, in hindsight, his ideas on how such a model could be used for policy appear crude. He argued that external shocks could be mitigated by countershocks. That was a formalization of the purchasing power stabilization (through public works) argument he had made before. He also suggested that the structure of the economy could be altered but offered no clear guidance on how this could be done. And since this model was a radical simplification of the economy, in need of much refinement, it was a great leap of confidence that this could be done based on this basic model.

[37] Backhouse and Giraud, "Circular Flow Diagrams," 2010.
[38] Frisch, *Statistical Confluence Analysis by Means of Complete Regression Systems*, 1934.
[39] Dekker, "Parallel Lives: Jan Tinbergen and Ragnar Frisch," 2019.

Another element missing from this model but already on his mind was the determination of coefficients in the model. It is one thing to argue that purchasing power depends on wages, but what Tinbergen really aimed for was to determine how much a variable like purchasing power was affected by changes in wages. One way to establish such coefficients was through surveys in which one asked workers or entrepreneurs how they would respond to such changes. This survey method was often on the mind of Tinbergen and was used in similar research by Ragnar Frisch.[40] But what he came to settle on was to determine such coefficients "historically," that is, by looking at the historical relation between the two variables.

This historical method of determination was later often criticized, for good reasons. One of them is that, as Tinbergen himself observed, national economies were undergoing important institutional and policy-regime changes. The New Deal arguably set the American economy on a new course (or at least that is what Tinbergen hoped), and the Plans of Labor in Europe were meant to do the same. It was thus problematic to estimate coefficients based on historical data of the 1920s. This was well recognized by Tinbergen, who praised as one of the virtues of the "historical method" that it could take into account national differences in a way that reliance on stable psychological response functions could not. Apparently, national differences were more important to him than historical discontinuities.

This is one of the areas where there was an interesting tension between the modern notion of economics as the study of relatively abstract economic systems and mechanisms, and the older notion of economics, which emphasized historical specificity and path dependence. Tinbergen is often grouped with the economists formulating modernist economics, free of context, but his model-building was still rooted in historical notions of particular (national) economies. It is therefore an interesting question whether the "model" in the 1935 paper should be considered his first model, or whether that honor should be reserved for his "Dutch" model, in which the coefficients are estimated. There is no fully unambiguous answer to that question, and the later development of modeling in economics has used the word rather flexibly, using it for small, toy models of micro-phenomena such as the supply and demand in particular markets and full-blown quantitative estimations of the macro-economy.

---

[40] Johansen, "Establishing Preference Function for Macroeconomic Decision Models: Some Observations on Ragnar Frisch's Contributions," 1974; Bjerkholt, *Foundations of Econometrics: The Selected Essays of Ragnar Frisch*, 1995.

But given Tinbergen's own development I think the answer should be firmly that it is the specified Dutch model that should be considered the first model of an economy. His work for the League of Nations would involve him estimating a model for the American and British economy, and it was precisely their specificity that made them *useful*. The specified models are achievements whose combination of statistics, mathematical modeling, and economic theorizing is characteristic of his work during this period and the rise of econometrics more generally.

On the other hand, it is equally feasible to think of the 1935 unspecified model as the seminal contribution, not in the least because the way in which the model would have to be estimated is already laid out. For the 1936 Dutch model, Tinbergen spent a lot of time and effort to figure out the precise specification. But in his later work he was often content in laying out the basic analytical structure and providing a kind of proof of work so that others could develop his models further. Even with the national econometric model, important work was later done by others, most notably, Lawrence Klein, who won a Nobel Prize in Economics for those developments in 1980.

But from the perspective of fighting the business cycle there should absolutely be no dispute about the relative significance of the two. The specified Dutch model is far superior in that respect. The Dutch model was in fact a kind of belated appendix to the Plan of Labor. The explicit goal of the specified model was to demonstrate the effects on the Dutch economy of the various policy proposals that were circulating around the time. The scenarios sketched in the Plan were already based on a similar methodology. But the formal model was too complicated and advanced for the political purpose of the Plan and was not presented until 1936. The Dutch model contained twenty-four equations that sought to explain twenty-four different economic variables, based on yearly data. Eight of these equations were definitions; the other ten expressed behavioral relations that indicated how one variable "reacted" to another one. The model also marked his definite choice for lags as the essential cycle-generating mechanism; other candidates that he had considered, such as cumulative processes and stocks, were absent from the model.[41]

The estimation of the coefficients was based on the data that was gathered at the CBS between 1923 and 1933 for the economic barometer. The model thus also meant a definite step beyond the work of the 1920s.

---

[41] Boumans, *A Case of Limited Physics Transfer: Jan Tinbergen's Resources for Re-shaping Economics*, 1992.

The data could now be used for analysis of economic dynamics, rather than to merely "track" the economy. The barometer mindset was, however, still present in the model. The model, like the barometers, was built on the idea that macroeconomic variables fluctuated around an equilibrium value, an assumption without which the estimation of the Dutch model was not possible.

Tinbergen utilized his model to study the effects of a variety of proposed policies: the devaluation of the guilder, a reduction of wages, the Plan of Labor, public works, protection of industries, and rationalization (Figure 6.2). In other words, the model, by many considered his central achievement, was to himself primarily a tool in the evaluation of the expected effectiveness of different policies. It is once more evidence of the intimate connection between thinking about policy and the business cycle that characterized the work of Tinbergen. However, this intimate connection also involved serious trade-offs. In the pre-advice, Tinbergen explained what he altered in the equations to calculate the effects of various policy changes.[42] This was nowhere close to the sophisticated analysis of policies of income stabilization or the analysis of a change in the institutional structure of the economy that he had undertaken earlier. For the evaluated policy changes, he did little more than simple additions (or subtractions) to the basic model. They thus represented a kind of short-cut and not the type of change that Tinbergen sought to achieve in the long run, where his envisioned goal was something much closer to the stabilization of purchasing power, as he had explored in his articles of the years before. In fact, one might argue that Tinbergen modeled the various policy scenarios as external shocks, rather than structural changes, despite the fact that he was theoretically well aware that structural changes were required *and* included in the Plan of Labor.

His friend and coauthor of the Plan of Labor, Hein Vos, correctly pointed this out in his article on Tinbergen's model and an elaboration of it by Koos Polak[43] (with whom Tinbergen around the same time started working on the League of Nations model). Vos argued:

All predictions hold only to the extent that the found reactions stay valid. A deep intervention by the government, now, means certainly also a change in the reactions. Perhaps the least in the case of public works, if they remain limited in size.

[42] Tinbergen, "Kan hier te Lande, al dan Niet na Overheidsingrijpen, een Verbetering van de Binnenlandse Conjunctuur Intreden, ook zonder Verbetering van onze Exportpositie?," 102, table 6, 1936.
[43] Polak, "Publieke Werken als Vorm van Conjunctuurpolitiek," 1937.

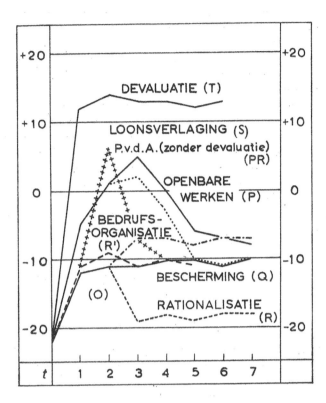

Fig. 20. Development of employment under different types of economic policy. The various policies are indicated by short and loose slogans or devices. A precise description (a definition) of these devices is given in the text (section 6) and in Table VI under the symbols indicated. Of course, the volume of the changes in employment depends upon the extent to which each of the measures adopted is applied. This is indicated and discussed in the text.

Figure 6.2 Diagram with the expected employment effects of various policy measures to combat the Great Depression, from Tinbergen's pre-advice from 1936. T, devaluation of the guilder; S, wage cut; PR, Plan of Labor without devaluation; P, public works; R', organization of industry; Q, protection; R, rationalization. This version can be found in his *Collected Papers* (1959).

But a change in Ordnung, credit control, investment policy, etc., or a shift in the power relations between the classes in social life will change the reactions, and make the predictions in the model worthless.[44]

---

[44] Vos, "Recente Literatuur over Openbare Werken en Conjunctuur," 1938.

It was a relevant critique by the more politically minded Vos, but not one without a degree of self-interest. Vos was dissatisfied with the limited effects of the Plan of Labor predicted by Tinbergen's model.

At the meeting of the Royal Society of Dutch economists, Tinbergen's model became the focal point of discussion, even though three other prominent economists had written a pre-advice (an unusually high number). Although a few economists in the room expressed their admiration for Tinbergen's model, no one embraced it wholeheartedly. G. M. Verrijn Stuart, the editor of the most important economics journal in the Netherlands and son of the classical economist C. A. Verrijn Stuart, was generally supportive of the new method but unimpressed with the very conventional results. J. G. Koopmans, who had worked with Tinbergen on ideas about equilibrium, was critical of the fact that Tinbergen had conveniently chosen certain coefficients and lags in the model, rather than basing them on statistical estimates.

Jan Goudriaan, the engineer who had worked at the Philips lab, was equally critical of Tinbergen's execution. Even more painful was that he used Ehrenfest's notion of "anschaulichkeit," the idea that a theory should be intuitively understandable, to critique Tinbergen's model. He admitted that some of the equations and coefficients had an intuitive meaning and could be easily economically understood. But other equations did not possess this "anschaulichkeit." It was harsh criticism from somebody to whom Tinbergen looked up a great deal. Goudriaan was essentially saying that Ehrenfest would have been unsatisfied with the model.

The critique extended beyond the merely technical. Koopmans was critical of the national focus of the various reports, including that of Tinbergen. He suggested that the goal of full employment could easily give rise to protectionist measures and harm the international division of labor. J. H. van Zanten, a more traditional statistical economist, suggested that Tinbergen had neglected one of the primary tasks of the economist, that is, to be able to communicate both his method and his results to a wider audience. It was a recurring problem that his technical work was not (fully) understood by others. Goudriaan drove the point home with a metaphor that would stick in the imagination about the modeling technique of Tinbergen. He compared the model to a night train, which arrived at the desired destination, but without providing any understanding of how one got there.[45] Especially before World War II there was a very small

---

[45] Kayzel, "A Night Train in Broad Daylight: Changing Economic Expertise at the Dutch Central Planning Bureau 1945–1977"; the metaphor was derived from the mathematics

Macro-dynamics and the Problem of Unemployment 149

Figure 6.3 Group picture at the CBS on the occasion of Tinbergen's departure for Geneva in 1936. Standing, left to right: A. L. G. M. Rombouts, P. de Wolff, J. B. D. Derksen, B. van der Meer, M. Eisma, and K. S. Struik. Seated, left to right: M. J. de Bosch Kemper, Tinbergen, and J. C. Witteveen.

audience, among the economists, who could follow Tinbergen's method, even when he wrote it up in a supposedly accessible manner in a report for a broader audience.[46]

But Tinbergen was busy building an audience for his new type of modeling expertise. At the CBS this process was well under way. In 1935, the bureau had submitted a proposal to the Ministry of Economic Affairs to expand the department working on business cycles (Figure 6.3). Whereas earlier the main work had been tracking the business cycle, they now wanted to expand their analysis to causal movements in the economy: "This must be done to judge the *automatic* movements of the economy as well as to create building blocks for evaluating possible economic

---

teacher of Goudriaan, who called algebraic systems of equations "the night train as opposed to the 'day train' of geometry"; see Maas, *Economic Methodology: A Historical Introduction*, 151.

[46] The full minutes of the meetings, including Tinbergen's response, are available in Tinbergen, "Kan hier te Lande, al dan Niet na Overheidsingrijpen, een Verbetering van de Binnenlandse Conjunctuur Intreden, ook zonder Verbetering van onze Exportpositie?," 1936.

policies."[47] They proposed to construct a simplified model of the economy, which was then further specified with appropriate data. Tinbergen was working on three fronts simultaneously: contributing to econometric modeling techniques (science), evaluating plans to combat the crisis (policy), and seeking funds and attracting new talent to sustain the relevant expertise (institution-building). His Dutch model was central in all three endeavors.

6.5 Tinbergen's Scientific and Econometric Vision

What has emerged by 1936 is a Tinbergen program of econometrics that would be further developed at the League of Nations and that would inspire much postwar work. But since we will not return extensively to these developments, it is good to pause for a moment and assess this program, for it tells us much about Tinbergen's scientific vision. We will highlight five elements from this program here: its dynamic nature, the combination of theory and empirics, the substantive institutional nature of the program, the optimistic constructivism of the program, and, finally, the way in which econometrics could be used to overcome differences of opinion in science and policy.

The dynamic nature of Tinbergen's business cycle theory arose from his work on cycles within markets. The idea of a lagged influence of certain variables gave rise to an endogenous movement within a market, and later within the economy as a whole. Tinbergen illustrated this nicely with diagrams, in which he showed with arrows how variables exerted influence on other variables in the next period, or even in periods further in the future.

During the 1930s he studied a variety of other mechanisms that could give rise to endogenous economic dynamics, such as the accelerator principle. The fact that he settled on the lag principle was because he found that it reflected the empirical results best and because it was the only dynamic that could reliably give rise to the eight-year cycle. This dynamic theorizing was also found in the Swedish tradition of the time, in the so-called sequence analysis as developed by Herman Wold.[48] In this approach the economy is not assumed to be moving from one equilibrium to the next, but rather fluctuating around this equilibrium. The approach of Wold and Tinbergen is frequently contrasted with the other major

---

[47] Van den Bogaard, "Past Measurements and Future Prediction," 1999.
[48] Hoover, "Lost Causes," 2004.

approach in econometrics that became popular at the Cowles Commission in Chicago after World War II. The Cowles approach was largely silent on the adjustment process and certainly from Tinbergen's perspective represented a step back from dynamic theory.[49]

The essence of Tinbergen's approach was to trace the way in which adjustments to external shocks take place within the economy. The classical assumption was that adjustment is immediate and automatic; Tinbergen suggested, instead, that there were serious lags in the adjustment process and therefore we must trace, study, and analyze the adjustment process.[50] More generally, this led to thinking about relative elasticities – an elasticity is a measure of the response in a variable to a change in another variable. The classic example of an elasticity in economics is how much the price of a good changes when the quantity demanded of it goes up (or down). Tinbergen's idea was that such elasticities differed between sectors and areas of the economy, so that some variables adjusted quickly and others with a delay (if at all). This idea was central to his work on business cycles[51] and would be the foundation for his work on international trade after the war.[52]

This reflected the fact that Tinbergen believed that the purpose of econometrics was to ask quantitative questions. His great criticism of classical theory was that it identified a logical structure, but never asked the *"how much"* question. It is one thing to prove that something matters (or, in modern terms, is statistically significant); it is quite another to say what the quantitative effect of something is (what is sometimes called the "oomph"[53]). For the determination of the *how much* question, statistical studies are required. This related directly to Tinbergen's interest in elasticities, because the size of an elasticity (the relative effect of one variable on another) is one of the premier quantitative measures developed in economics. It also pointed to the next fundamental element, the substantive institutional nature of his econometrics.

---

[49] Morgan, "The Stamping out of Process Analysis in Econometrics," 1991. The irony is that Tjalling Koopmans, a frequent collaborator of Tinbergen, although not his direct student, would do much to develop the alternative modeling approach.
[50] Tinbergen, "Conjunctuurpolitiek en Prijsstabilisatie," 1936.
[51] Tinbergen, "Critical Remarks on Some Business-Cycle Theories," 1942.
[52] Tinbergen, "Some Measurements of Elasticities of Substitution," 1946; Tinbergen, "Long-Term Foreign Trade Elasticities," 1949.
[53] Ziliak and McCloskey, *The Cult of Statistical Significance*, 2008.

After all, how much something matters is not constant. Tinbergen took the effect of the wage level during the Great Depression as an example. Its positive effect is that a relatively higher wage level will boost domestic consumption, but the negative effect of a relatively higher wage level is that it will hinder exports. His Dutch model found that wage reductions have a positive effect, because the Dutch economy is a small, open economy heavily dependent on exports. But this conclusion is not universally valid; for a more autarchic economy like that of the United States, the balance might easily shift the other way. So, while other mathematical economists and some econometricians were increasingly moving in abstract and general directions, Tinbergen's work always remained tied to a particular time and place.

This institutional sensibility developed through the analysis of particular markets. First the pig cycle, then the shipbuilding cycle, and a couple of years later the markets for meat, butter, potatoes, and so on.[54] There were certain general principles underlying models of markets, a common structure even to the equations, but the coefficients had to be estimated time and again, not in the least because the market structure, highly competitive or monopolistic, differed from market to market. And even then, the structure might change: the growing role of the government in the economy was an example of such a structural change that was certain to impact the coefficients. Policy interventions could leave most of the system intact, but if they were structural, if they meant a change in the *Ordnung* of a market or the economy, they impacted the very structure of the model. And institutions were tied to one another: in his model of the Dutch economy he gave the example of the importance of wage flexibility when a country was on the gold standard. If there was rigidity in the exchange rate, then it was important that adjustments could be made through other channels. If a country instead operated under a system of flexible exchange rates, wage flexibility was not as important.

These two elements, the iterative nature of his work and the institutional sensibility, meant that Tinbergen was skeptical of attempts to predict the course of the economy. At best a model like the one he presented in 1936 suggested some tendencies that were observed in the past. There was always the possibility that something unexpected would happen or that the structure of the economy would change through policy

---

[54] These are all markets he studied at the CBS; see *De Nederlandse Conjunctuur* (1930–1935). This focus on the institutional structure of markets is also evident in his dissertation.

measures.[55] This skepticism regarding economic prediction was a constant throughout his career.[56] And in Chapter 10 we will see how he developed this skepticism into a constructive program of task-setting, in which the goal was not the prediction of the course of the economy, but rather the steering of the economy into the desired direction.

This constructive attitude with strong pragmatist tendencies was already visible in his 1930s work. For Tinbergen the application of his theories always came first. During the 1936 meeting various commenters expressed their surprise that Tinbergen was confident in drawing quite definite conclusions from his tentative model. His response was characteristic: "One should not strive to find something that is theoretically satisfying immediately, but preferably something that is practically useful, and is approximately correct. I believe that we are on the way of finding something in that direction."[57] It was this approach and particularly the attitude that was characteristic of Tinbergen's work; it would continue to set him apart from his more technically or, should we say, scientifically oriented colleagues.

He would often leave it to others to refine a model or even an entire approach. Tinbergen tended to move on, typically because a different type of social or policy problem gained urgency and required a different approach. In hindsight some of Tinbergen's published works have a tentative character, published far before perfection was achieved. But as he later reflected, he believed this was the way to progress. He preferred to publish quickly so that his work would be discussed, and he and others could develop it further. It was through discussion and openness that one would learn. And he was often corrected, sometimes quickly and, in one instance, a full thirty years after he committed the error.[58]

Despite this pragmatic attitude when it came to theory development, Tinbergen had high hopes for the ability of science to resolve disputes. From Ehrenfest he had adopted the idea that one always should try to find

---

[55] Tinbergen, "Kan hier te Lande, al dan Niet na Overheidsingrijpen, een Verbetering van de Binnenlandse Conjunctuur Intreden, ook zonder Verbetering van onze Exportpositie?," 103, 1936.

[56] Tinbergen, "De Voorspelling en de Beïnvloeding van de Conjunctuur," 1954; Tinbergen, "Voorspellingen in Politiek, Economie en Sociologie," 1962.

[57] Tinbergen, "Kan hier te Lande, al dan Niet na Overheidsingrijpen, een Verbetering van de Binnenlandse Conjunctuur Intreden, ook zonder Verbetering van onze Exportpositie?," 112, 1936.

[58] Van Batenburg and Tinbergen, "Income Distribution: A Correction and a Generalization," 1984.

a "nobler way" of expressing disagreements than as a conflict. The simplest application of this was that when two people disagreed, one should try to reformulate it such that there is a certain domain over which A is right, while there is another domain over which B is right. Or when it came to the value of a particular coefficient or variable, one might say that when the coefficient was below a certain value, view A was correct, and when it was higher than a certain value, view B is correct: "One is led to ask what choice was best? But the question is not posed well. None is absolutely right or absolutely wrong. Progress is not to be sought through a choice but a combination."[59]

In his practice of macro-econometric modeling, this had a clear application. The model should be so general that it could contain the various variables that had been suggested as the cause of the business cycle. The model could then show the relative contribution of each of these factors to the business cycle. This was the nobler way of presenting disputes, as long as the various parties accepted the model as a kind of arbiter in the scientific dispute. As he later suggested: "Models help us order our thought. They make it possible to localize differences of opinion: to indicate the equations on which one disagrees, the term of that equation, or the term that is missing, or the variable that is missing. Finally, they make it possible to localize any errors."[60] Science could provide the neutral tools to resolve disagreements and create consensus.[61] It was for this reason that Tinbergen's work perhaps had such a long legacy in the Dutch political arena, centered on consensus. But it also has an interesting parallel in his attempts to bring about social change peacefully. Rather than seeking conflict, he sought to "pacify" scientific disputes. He believed that his models provided an ideal way of doing so, but his work in Geneva would prove that perhaps the opposite was true.

---

[59] Tinbergen, "Annual Survey: Suggestions on Quantitative Business Cycle Theory," 300, 1935.
[60] Tinbergen, "Over Modellen," 1987.
[61] Van den Bogaard, "Past Measurements and Future Prediction," 1999.

7

The Rise of the People's Party (*Volkspartei*) and the Economics of the General Interest

In 1926 Joseph Schumpeter, the Austrian economist, wrote a tribute to one of the towering figures in German economics,[1] Gustav Schmoller. Even for Schumpeter, who was known for his contrarianism, it was an unlikely tribute. The Austrian school with which Schumpeter was associated was mostly known for its opposition to the historical school of economics in Germany, the associated agenda of social reform, and Gustav Schmoller, in particular. The scientific economics that Schumpeter himself had explored in his early work did away with institutional and historical details, and strongly suggested that economics as a science should become autonomous, that is, disconnected from policy. So, it must have raised many eyebrows when Schumpeter suggested that Schmoller, who died in 1917, had been the greatest economist of his age. The tribute also came at an odd moment, just around the time that German economics seemed to break with the historical legacy.

What was even more striking was that Schumpeter did not single out Schmoller's contributions to economics, although he praised those as well. Instead, Schumpeter focused on the way in which Schmoller had sought to develop a policy perspective free from ideology, free from class interests, and free from partisanship. Schumpeter detailed, much like Schmoller had done himself,[2] how in the nineteenth century economics had been dominated by ideological approaches to economics: liberal and socialist. Schmoller famously suggested that the Historical approach had been able to overcome such ideological approaches and provide a more comprehensive analysis and policy advice based in science.

---

[1] Schumpeter, "Gustav v. Schmoller und die Probleme von Heute," 1926.
[2] Schmoller, "Wechselnde Theorien und feststehende Wahrheiten im Gebiete der Staats- und Socialwissenschaften und die heutige Deutsche Volkswirtschaftslehre," 1897.

It is safe to say that not everyone was convinced. Around 1910 an enormous debate broke out in the German academy over the feasibility and desirability of value freedom in economics. Max Weber famously denounced the socialists of the chair who had been "preaching" from their lecterns. Although Weber left ample space for political involvement of the scientist in his personal capacity, Weber believed that social science itself should be purged as much as possible from values. Schumpeter, surprisingly, did not side with Max Weber, with whom he intellectually had much in common. Instead, he suggested that Schmoller's great achievement was precisely the synthesis between science and economic policy. It had been Schmoller, in large part due to his exceptional personal qualities, who had been able to overcome partisanship and truly speak for the general interest.

Interestingly, a similar development took place in politics. During the 1920s many political parties started to reorient themselves. They typically had been founded along class lines: a liberal party for the bourgeois, a socialist party for the workers, and Christian parties of various denominations for the different Catholic and Protestant communities in Germany and continental Europe more generally. But some within the parties were starting to suggest that it was time to transform the class-based party into a *Volkspartei*, German for a People's Party. These broad people's parties would be organized around a set of ideals and a program that was (potentially) interesting for anyone in society. No longer did parties want to be restricted to a loyal base determined by class background; they wanted to attract voters from all walks of life. There was plenty of self-interest involved for the parties that started doing this. They believed they could benefit electorally from such a transformation. But the change from class-based parties to broader people's parties also reflected the fact that, increasingly, the different classes in society started to integrate, or at the very least that class divisions were becoming less pronounced. For many of the proponents of the transformation into a people's party, this social integration was an explicit goal.[3]

Tinbergen was one of them. It was integration that was crucial for him at the AJC, and it was integration that was required in society more generally. In that sense he had moved on from his position of the mid-1920s: the choice should not be between the bourgeois life of the fictional Jurgen and the proletarian life of Catharina. Instead, the goal should be the integration of the classes and ultimately a class-less society. With that change of goal

[3] Mintzel, *Die Volkspartei: Typus und Wirklichkeit*, 116, 1983.

came a change in perspective. We have already seen that Tinbergen was not much drawn to a class-based perspective, or the writing of books for the working class. Instead, he wanted to pursue what was best for all individuals, irrespective of class. In a draft pamphlet from 1936 that he wanted to publish with the other members of the Econometric Society, he stated: "[T]he task of the econometrician [is] to calculate as exactly as possible and with the utmost care, how human well-being, in the material sense of the word as well as in the spiritual sense, can be increased."[4]

Tinbergen developed his economics at a time when class-based perspectives were being replaced by a more comprehensive perspective in politics. The various parties sought to broaden their base and shed their class ideologies. Plan socialism, at least in intention, fitted right into this transformation. It sought to integrate progressive forces from various parties in a fight against reactionary fascism. Partisan perspectives became discredited, in favor of more comprehensive, integrated, or neutral perspectives. I use all different three terms – comprehensive, integrated, and neutral – because it was quite unclear what this perspective would entail, and whether it was attainable. In philosophy the search for a neutral and objective perspective has been called the "view from nowhere"[5] and has been criticized accordingly: Who could ever attain such a perspective, from nowhere?

Schumpeter had clear views on what had enabled Schmoller to achieve such a perspective: it was the combination of a historical intuition and a sense of what was practically required at different moments in time. Pragmatism will probably never be an appealing label for German intellectuals,[6] but it is hard to summarize differently what Schumpeter believed it entailed. He praised the antidogmatic pragmatism of Schmoller in his policy views, as well as the eclecticism, the willingness to look at what worked. If we extend the analogy from science to politics, it meant that this pragmatism should also be recognizable in the people's parties. They should increasingly be justifying their positions in consequentialist terms, rather than in ideological terms.

And that is, indeed, precisely what happened within the parties that sought to make this transition. In the SDAP, the social-democratic party of the Netherlands, it was first clearly visible in a 1931 report that explicitly

---

[4] JT to Ragnar Frisch, 20 March 1936, NLN: FC.
[5] Nagel, *The View from Nowhere*, 1986.
[6] Schumpeter more or less admitted this; see "Gustav v. Schmoller und die Probleme von Heute," 352.

embraced reformism. And the Plan of Labor campaign only strengthened those tendencies. It was no longer enough to condemn capitalism or to dream of socialism in the long run. It was now time to suggest pragmatic and constructive proposals in the present, proposals, moreover, that they could prove "worked." The perspective gained even more appeal due to the unemployment crisis after the Great Depression: Who could afford to worry about ideology, when unemployment was at record heights? The Dutch Plan of Labor was first and foremost a proposal to get the economy out of the crisis. But underneath those proposals was the explicit endorsement of pragmatism. Measures could no longer be condemned on ideological grounds: if they worked, they worked. This transformation of the SDAP was completed when it merged with some smaller progressive parties after World War II and renamed itself the Labor Party. The party of the workers had been transformed into a party of the people, and expertise won out over ideology.

Tinbergen felt attracted to this way of thinking from an early age. Even in his first political polemics he had no patience for a labor union protecting the workers' interests. Instead, he sought to analyze what succeeded in raising living standards, as objectively as he could. The final work that Tinbergen wrote explicitly for "the workers" was a semi-popular book in Dutch on business cycles.[7] He tried hard to demonstrate his class allegiance early in the book, by criticizing the unproductive capitalist class and by paying lip service to the idea that the working class does not get the full value of its labor. But he had to acknowledge when the analysis started properly that the book was a cool book for the head, and not a book to warm the heart. He presented objective analysis, not class perspective.

What is more, in the conclusion he explicitly sought to integrate the rival ideological perspectives on the Great Depression. The way he did so is remarkable. First, he decoupled the perspectives of left and right from their explicit class-based origins. Second, he argued that the debate should be shifted away from a qualitative discussion about the nature of the crisis and toward a quantitative discussion of unemployment levels. Whatever perspective one takes, we should be able to agree on the undesirability of the current unemployment levels, he argued. This allowed him to transform a principled discussion between liberals and socialists into a practical discussion of the unemployment problem. He did the same in his treatment of

---

[7] Tinbergen, *De Konjunktuur*, 1933.

the solutions, where he suggested that we should look at which concrete measures were effective, rather than to the question of whether these were socialist measures (or steps in the direction of socialism) or capitalist measures.

His fellow party member and Marxist Sam de Wolff wrote a perceptive review of the book in the daily newspaper of the social-democrats.[8] He argued that Tinbergen failed in his task to make the workers aware of their class position and was turning economics from a class-based science into a field of science that was merely concerned with the optimal satisfaction of needs. He took Tinbergen to task for failing to distinguish clearly between different economic systems, and merely taking from each what he found valuable. For that reason, he called Tinbergen "an eclectic." De Wolff made an even more important objection to Tinbergen. Large sections of the book could not possibly be understood by the party members. He observed correctly that Tinbergen was not at all interested in talking to the workers, let alone in raising their awareness about the economic exploitation or the ills of capitalism. Instead, he was talking to his fellow economists and other policy experts and hopefully to the government. De Wolff suggested that such a book has no place in the socialist series in which it appeared.

Indeed, Tinbergen was not at all writing to an audience of fellow socialists, and not at all to the workers. He was not seeking to emancipate them through knowledge, nor to mobilize them to action. He was writing in the tradition of Schmoller, in the genre of *Staatswissenschaften*. In that tradition the crucial questions were how to properly manage the economy and the state finances and, most importantly, how to ensure social stability. But that tradition was not static. In fact, it was undergoing an important transformation. If traditionally it had been primarily concerned with the interests of the state and its stability, it was now becoming concerned with the "general interest." That interest was different from class interests, and different from the interests of the state itself, but it appealed to the interest of all individuals in society.[9] After World War II this field of study became known as welfare economics, in which the general interest became equated with the aggregation of individual preferences. Tinbergen did not

---

[8] S. De Wolff, "Dr. J. Tinbergen's De Konjunktuur: Dit Boek is Tinbergen Op en de Op," *Het Volk*, 26 March 1934, Wetenschappelijk Bijvoegsel.

[9] Schumpeter was still unclear about the latter difference: "He [Schmoller] spoke from the standpoint of the state; or what was for him the same thing, from the standpoint of the whole, the social totality." "Gustav v. Schmoller und die Probleme von Heute," 343.

fully embrace that view in the 1950s, and it was not yet developed in the 1930s. The "general interest" was still a somewhat vague and abstract notion, but it was the way forward for Tinbergen. It was how modern science could serve society and the state.

Tinbergen did not directly cause many of these changes in science and politics. The great danger of the biographical mode of writing is that we attribute too much agency to our protagonist. These developments had been long under way in economics, and Schumpeter was completely correct to trace them back further in the past, to Schmoller. But it was in the 1930s that many political parties started making this transition, and therefore somebody *like* Tinbergen could quickly grow so influential. Because he could provide the new type of expertise, and the new type of knowledge, that was appropriate for this new type of party. The party intellectual was no longer an ideologue, but a policy expert. This new type of expertise was technical: the party intellectual now had to be a policy expert, who could evaluate the effectiveness of different policies. It was in this political context that Tinbergen's type of economics found its fertile ground.

Schumpeter's tribute to Schmoller is so surprising because the standard narrative about economics is that it became an autonomous, value-free science around 1930. The symbol for that transition is Lionel Robbins's *An Essay on the Nature and Significance of Economic Science*,[10] which defines the limits of a value-free science. But in our story, there is a direct lineage from the nineteenth-century German tradition of *Staatswissenschaften* through the work of Schmoller to the work of Tinbergen and the economists working in service of the policymakers in government. The type of expertise provided in this tradition changes over time, as does the way in which it justifies its position. For Tinbergen quantitative methods and modern economic statistics are more important than for Schmoller and the nineteenth-century economists. The appeal to the general interest by Tinbergen and later welfare economists is different from the idea of *Staatswissenschaften*. But the position of the economist and his audience is unchanged: those in charge of economic policy.

---

[10] Robbins, *An Essay on the Nature and Significance of Economic Science*, 1932.

PART II

THE YEARS OF HIGH EXPERTISE

8

From The Hague to Geneva

The World Order of the League of Nations

Let us return, however, to the League of Nations. To create an organization which is in a position to protect peace in this world of conflicting interests and egotistic wills is a frighteningly difficult task.
—Hjalmar Branting, Nobel Peace Prize winner in 1921[1]

Tinbergen's work at the League of Nations, in particular his report on business cycles, is his greatest claim to fame and, due to Keynes's harsh critique, also the most notorious part of his work. Keynes's critique has become a touchstone for many who are critical of the reliance on quantitative techniques in economics. In an anecdote often told about Tinbergen and Keynes, it is Jan who comes up to John Maynard to tell him that he has found that the value of the multiplier in his model is 2, just as Keynes had predicted.[2] Keynes was little impressed, and condescendingly congratulated Tinbergen that he finally, also had found the correct number. As Tinbergen later reflected: "He had more faith in his own intuition than in econometric studies. Perhaps rightly so." The anecdote is also telling for the barriers faced by the generation of young social engineers intent on bringing precision and scientific methods into economics. The older visionary and liberal political economists of the stature of Keynes were not going to let go easily.[3]

To add insult to injury, Tinbergen and the model-builders of his generation have also been frequently accused of having corrupted Keynes's contribution. Although Tinbergen was never a prominent Keynesian, his

---

[1] From his Nobel lecture, "Fraternity among Nations," 1922.
[2] Tinbergen, "Het Getal Twee is van Keynes," 1987.
[3] It has also been described as the clash between the dramatist (Keynes) and the scientific model-builder (Tinbergen); see Maas, *Economic Methodology: A Historical Introduction*, 2014.

followers, like Lawrence Klein, were. And the way Klein and others utilized the macroeconomic models that Tinbergen helped pioneer became the dominant way in which Keynes's own work was understood. This came at the detriment, or so argued his followers,[4] of the more subtle (psychological) insights in Keynes. There is thus more than a little irony in the fact that it was the combination of the econometric models of Tinbergen and the macroeconomic theory of Keynes that become the dominant approach to economic policy in the immediate postwar decades.

A closer look at the reception of Tinbergen's business-cycle study at the League of Nations shows that Tinbergen's study had few defenders at all. His fellow econometrician Frisch wrote an early critique of the report that deeply questioned his methodology. The League of Nations was not too satisfied with his modeling approach, which diverged in important ways from the task they had set for him: testing various business-cycle theories. And shortly after the war the Tinbergen approach was critiqued from the reinvigorated Cowles Commission as an example of "measurement without theory."[5] On top of it all there were a great number of "verbal" economists skeptical that Tinbergen had understood their theories properly. Several of the critiques packed an extra punch, because they attacked Tinbergen on the front on which Ehrenfest might have critiqued him also: Was the whole project too descriptive, and lacking good theoretical foundations? Was the theory sufficiently "anschaulich" (intuitively understandable)?

As if all that was not enough, a crucial part of Tinbergen's study was removed from the final report. For Tinbergen, who at this point was more concerned with business-cycle policy than with the mere analysis of the causes of business cycles, it might have been the most significant part of the report: the analysis of the effectiveness of the various New Deal programs. This part of the study sought to answer the question of whether government policy, and which types of government policy, made a difference in the recovery. It was too political for the economic division of the League of Nations, which officially could offer only "technical" advice. Many of his fellow party members at home found him not political and ideological

---

[4] For a characteristic statement, see Leijonhufvud, "Keynes and the Keynesians: A Suggested Interpretation," 1967.

[5] Although the critique is not directly aimed at Tinbergen but rather at the institutionalist statistical tradition at the NBER of Burns and Mitchell, a number of the criticisms leveled at them certainly implicated Tinbergen; see Koopmans, "Measurement without Theory," 1947.

enough; at the League of Nations they were worried that he was too political.

Yet his work at the League of Nations is also characteristic of Tinbergen. It offered a new approach that, however imperfect, would form the basis for much later work, not in the least by others. The work is characteristically pragmatic, working both within the institutional limitations that he faced and with the limited data and theoretical basis that he had, to produce the best possible result. And despite the fact that the final report ruffled so many feathers, it exemplified Tinbergen's goal to integrate various theories of the cycle into a coherent model. Business-cycle theory was undoubtedly the most contested field in economics. And rather than trying to resolve these disputes, Tinbergen sought to overcome them by producing a model in which the various views were all represented. As such his report represented a spirit of internationalism that was embodied by the League of Nations. His attempt to put together Austrian, French, Cambridge, Swedish, Norwegian, American, and German accounts of the cycle into one model mirrored the attempt of the League of Nations to overcome national differences and foster a spirit of cooperation. This was reflected in the team of experts who were brought in to help develop the report. It was, although formally published under Tinbergen's name, the outcome of teamwork, of a team to which he significantly contributed by bringing along two fellow countrymen, Jacques Polak (later president of the IMF) and Tjalling Koopmans, the only other Dutch economist to win the Nobel Prize in economics. The team further included important economists from nearly all major European countries.

For Tinbergen personally, the symbolism of working at the League of Nations was also immense. It was the institution that represented the political hope for a more peaceful and stable world. Now virtually forgotten, it was also engaged in active attempts to save various economies during the 1920s in Central and Eastern Europe. After the Peace Palace, the League of Nations, at the time more commonly called the Societé des Nations, was the true international institution that both had sought more coordination between countries and in the 1920s even experimented with supranational forms of governance. The League of Nations was a beacon of hope and situated just like the Peace Palace in a mid-sized city in a small country known for its neutrality. And as we will see, the League of Nations' work, especially that of the economic and financial division, would prove important in shaping postwar forms of international economic governance within the UN, the IMF, and the OECD. Much like the Peace Palace, its imposing architecture seemed to promise a better future (Figure 8.1). But it

Figure 8.1 League of Nations building at the lake of Geneva, Switzerland, ca. 1940.

was not just hope; the intellectuals who gathered in Geneva and at the League of Nations also developed a perspective in which economic stability and peaceful political relations were intimately related.[6] Tinbergen's econometric program gained a big boost from his time in Geneva, but it was even more important for his postwar work on international economic integration and order.

8.1 International Intelligence

To understand the meaning and significance of Tinbergen's study at the League of Nations we must understand the role of this international organization properly. And to understand its role we have to move beyond caricatures of it as the failed predecessor of the United Nations. This misrepresents not only what it stood for at the time, but also the extent of the continuity between the 1930s activities, especially the economic activities, at the League and the UN and the IMF.[7] This is especially the

---

[6] Clavin, *Securing the World Economy: The Reinvention of the League of Nations, 1920–1946*, 2015; Pauly, *The League of Nations and the Foreshadowing of the International Monetary Fund*, 1996; Polak, "The Contribution of the International Monetary Fund," 1997.

[7] Pauly, *The League of Nations and the Foreshadowing of the International Monetary Fund*, 1996.

case for the activities and function of the Economic and Financial Organization (EFO) within the League of Nations. The Economic and Financial Organization had always existed, but really came into its own in 1931 with the help of a big Rockefeller grant. The Peace Palace in The Hague was first proposed as a library of international law, which was then funded by a philanthropic gift from Andrew Carnegie. The situation here was eerily similar: the Rockefeller Foundation first proposed a two-million-dollar grant for a League of Nations library. But that support was soon extended to a continued commitment to fund research projects. In total the Rockefeller Foundation would donate over ten million dollars in grants to the EFO, five million of which was donated for the big research project on business cycles.[8] But if one wishes to grasp the full scope of Rockefeller support, one should certainly include its support for the entire network of business-cycle institutes around Europe, including the Netherlands Economics Institute in Rotterdam, where Tinbergen was active.[9] Not for nothing did Tinbergen quip in one of his letters that the "Societé des Nations" is the "Rockefeller des Nations."[10] As with the Peace Palace, the building of international institutions, networks, and high-quality empirical material[11] depended on private philanthropy, political will from major countries, and networks of scientific expertise.

In the case of the EFO in the 1930s, it also depended on the organizational skills of Arthur Loveday. He was a Cambridge-trained British economist who had worked for the British War Office during World War I, after which he joined the League of Nations and became director of the Financial Section of the EFO. The EFO was home to the Economic Intelligence Service, one of the various subcommittees within the intricate bureaucratic web of the League of Nations.[12] It was Loveday's spirited

[8] De Marchi, "League of Nations Economists and the Ideal of Peaceful Change in the Decade of the Thirties," 1991.

[9] Craver, "Patronage and the Directions of Research in Economics: The Rockefeller Foundation in Europe, 1924–1938," 1986. The Rockefeller Foundation also supported a Parisian institute associated with the League for the Promotion of International Intellectual Co-operation.

[10] JT to Koos Polak, 7 April 1939, LoN, Box 4540, doc. nr. 10B.12653.35838.

[11] There were some in the Rockefeller foundation who believed that an international business-cycle institute was worth pursuing, but nothing came of it. De Marchi, "League of Nations Economists and the Ideal of Peaceful Change in the Decade of the Thirties," 1991.

[12] Clavin and Wessels, "Transnationalism and the League of Nations: Understanding the Work of Its Economic and Financial Organisation," 2005.

leadership of the EFO during the 1930s which brought together many promising economists with more established voices to develop an idea of what an internationally coordinated business cycle policy might look like. An important part of that effort was dedicated to the publication of a sustained set of internationally standardized economic indicators in the *World Economic Survey* (which was later continued by the IMF as the *World Economic Outlook*). The League of Nations had been involved in similar standardization and international collection of statistics in epidemiology.[13]

And whereas the political work of the League of Nations grinded to a halt during the 1930s amid growing international tensions, the EFO really came to fruition only during the 1930s. Loveday and his colleagues sought to overcome the international differences of opinion, perhaps naïvely, through the creation of expert consensus.[14] It was a strategy that showed many similarities with the Plan socialist proposals by Tinbergen and Vos in the Netherlands. Both aimed at overcoming ideological differences through technical or expert consensus. It was hoped that this expert consensus could provide a path to coordinated policy action by the various member states of the League of Nations.

The major difference with the Plan of Labor was the international scope. The Plan of Labor had come under criticism from those otherwise sympathetic to it, for suggesting that recovery could be brought about in one country. Or as those of the far left put it: it had suggested that socialism in one country was possible. For Tinbergen the research assignment at the League of Nations thus meant an opportunity to move beyond this limited national solution, to work on an international solution.[15] He, of course, knew perfectly well that a small open economy such as that of the Netherlands could never insulate itself from international economic crises. At best the Dutch Plan of Labor was a temporary solution; it provided no true safeguards for the future.

---

[13] Tworek, "Communicable Disease: Information, Health, and Globalization in the Interwar Period," 2019.

[14] Clavin and Wessels, "Transnationalism and the League of Nations: Understanding the Work of Its Economic and Financial Organisation," 2005.

[15] Polak would later describe this logic with one of his beloved water metaphors. He suggested that they were dealing with a dual problem: the water was too low (low employment levels) and sloshing wildly (employment rates were wildly fluctuating). In that case, lifting the bucket is too risky, for one might lose all the water, so the priority is to calm the water. The Plan of Labor was intended as a measure to stop the sloshing, after which the true work of improving the fundamental economic order could begin.

The goal of international policy coordination was high on the agenda before Tinbergen arrived. Its urgency was clear to nearly everyone after the erection of tariff walls and the competitive devaluations that had been happening since 1932. In 1935, Loveday managed to draft a report that enjoyed support from the various subsections, proposing more coordination of economic policies, in the fields of trade and monetary policy. This was supposed to bring at least some relief in the trade war between Western countries that had broken out in the aftermath of the Great Depression.[16]

This and later initiatives proved unsuccessful and were hampered not in the least by the fact that the relative independence of the EFO – it consisted of "independent experts" – also made it politically weak and highly dependent on the political will of some of the key countries (France, Britain, and the United States, as well as ultimately the Axis powers, Italy and Germany). But this precise failure of coordination did prove to be an important impetus for a changing view on the international order and economic crises. If coordination of policy between countries could not be taken for granted, say, when they no longer agreed on a shared gold standard, new forms of international economic coordination and organization were required. And hence just like national economies were undergoing a reordering, so the international economy too had to be reordered. At the League of Nations "there began to emerge a sense that the world was a system in motion, with impulses to recession transmitted between nations in identifiable (and hence, in principle, controllable) ways."[17] Or as a historian of the League of Nations put it: "Stable, well-functioning markets that span discrete political jurisdictions must themselves rest on a foundation of political collaboration."[18] Koos Polak would provide an early model of this international interdependency in his *International Propagation of Business Cycles*.[19]

But before this international conception really developed, the EFO commissioned Gottfried von Haberler to inventory and, if possible, synthesize the competing theories of the business cycle. Haberler, born in 1900, was a liberal economist of the Austrian school who specialized in

[16] Clavin, *Securing the World Economy: The Reinvention of the League of Nations, 1920–1946*, 2015.
[17] De Marchi, "League of Nations Economists and the Ideal of Peaceful Change in the Decade of the Thirties," 144, 1991.
[18] Pauly, *The League of Nations and the Foreshadowing of the International Monetary Fund*, 3, 1996.
[19] Polak, "International Propagation of Business Cycles," 1939.

international trade and was at the start of a promising career. He had been given the task of providing an overview of the different theories of the cycle, which culminated in his *Prosperity and Depression*.[20] And although the book did not hide its preferences for overinvestment theories of the cycle, which were the specialty of the Austrian school of economics, Haberler shared the goal of the League of Nations and his successor Tinbergen in trying to find some common ground in the contested field of business-cycle studies. Although well received, Haberler's study was also criticized by some, notably, by Keynes, who wrote:

> My essential point is that the method you have adopted forces you to a high degree of superficiality.... I cannot believe that the solution can be reached by bringing together ... excerpts from the views of a large number of writers, each differing from the other more or less in fundamentals. The answer must lie somewhere much deeper down, yet your method tempts you to skating rather than digging.[21]

That did not prevent Haberler's final report, which went through many drafts and was widely shared among economists during the period between 1934 and 1936, from becoming a classic in the field.

The study, however, was mere theoretical synthesis and purely qualitative in nature. It brought together various possible explanations of the cycle and demonstrated which parts of the cyclical movement could *hypothetically* be explained by them. But it made no effort to quantify the influence of different factors or even to illustrate the various mechanisms with empirical material. Tinbergen was surprised that Haberler neglected quantitative questions. In his response to a draft version of the study from November 1934, he suggested to Haberler that a synthesis would in part depend on the quantitative importance of the various factors identified.

However, Haberler and Tinbergen did share the conviction that a theory of business cycles did not have to be mono-causal.[22] Haberler attempted to provide a synthesis between the various explanations offered by requiring

---

[20] Haberler, *Prosperity and Depression: A Theoretical Analysis of Cyclical Movements*, 1937.
[21] Keynes quoted in Boianovsky and Trautwein, "Haberler, the League of Nations, and the Quest for Consensus in Business Cycle Theory in the 1930s," 50, 2006. It is probably no coincidence that most critical academic responses came from Great Britain, since the British delegation was generally the most skeptical of the proposed measures to reduce tariffs and stabilize currencies as the EFO proposed; see Clavin and Wessels, "Transnationalism and the League of Nations: Understanding the Work of Its Economic and Financial Organisation," 2005.
[22] Tinbergen to Haberler, 16 November 1934, quoted in Boianovsky and Trautwein, "Haberler, the League of Nations, and the Quest for Consensus in Business Cycle Theory in the 1930s," 2006.

that a theory should be able to explain all four "phases" of the cycle: the cumulative processes of expansion ("prosperity") and contraction ("depression"), and the upper and the lower turning points ("crisis" and "revival").[23] The ultimate question was whether a theory could explain the cycle. Tinbergen made a further critical remark in his letter, one that would drive most of his own project and inform his notion of what a macro-econometric model entailed. He argued that Haberler had not sufficiently inquired whether the various authors offered a complete system, a complete picture of how the economy functioned, that was internally consistent. Both the quantitative side of the question and the notion of a complete system of the economy were at the heart of Tinbergen's survey article of the business-cycle literature in 1935.[24] What he meant by completeness had mathematical components, but it also simply meant asking whether the respective economists provided a complete picture of the dynamics in an economy or only an isolated theory of what might predict cycles within such a system.[25]

After the first draft of Haberler's report, a second draft was prepared, and Tinbergen was among those invited to Geneva in July 1936 to discuss it with a group of prominent international theorists: Dennis Robertson, Oskar Anderson, John Maurice Clark, Leon Dupriez, Alvin Hansen, Oskar Morgenstern, Bertil Ohlin, Charles Rist, Lionel Robbins, and Wilhelm Röpke.[26] What is notable is that some of those with the most skin in the game, the most established theorists, were not part of the project. Figures such as Friedrich Hayek and Ludwig Mises from Austria, John Maynard Keynes from Great Britain, Johan Åkerman and Gunnar Myrdal from Sweden, and Ernst Wagemann from Germany were all missing. Whether intentional or not, the professional consensus in Geneva was mostly one of expert observers and young talents, rather than of the big players in the cycle debate.

During this Geneva conference, nearly a full day was devoted to the discussion of the statistical testing of the business cycles that Tinbergen

---

[23] Haberler, *Prosperity and Depression: A Theoretical Analysis of Cyclical Movements*, preface, 1937.

[24] Tinbergen, "Annual Survey: Suggestions on Quantitative Business Cycle Theory," 1935.

[25] It is for that reason interesting that during his later work in the war he returned to Haberler's criteria, especially because of a growing interest in the turning points. For example, Tinbergen, "Over Verschillende Soorten Evenwicht En de Conjunctuurbeweging," 1943.

[26] Boianovsky and Trautwein, "Haberler, the League of Nations, and the Quest for Consensus in Business Cycle Theory in the 1930s," 2006.

Figure 8.2 Jan and Tine with their daughters Tineke (standing) and Els (in her father's arms) in Geneva, the family Groeneveld (on the left) was visiting, 1937.

would undertake. Much was expected of the new statistical techniques, which to most of those present were still unfamiliar.[27] Such a test, however, would never be performed. Instead, Tinbergen would formulate a model of the US economy that was supposed to capture the essential dynamics of the entire economy. The various factors identified by Haberler as potential causes would be included in this model, but the question was no longer whether they contributed or did not contribute to certain fluctuations, but rather *how much* they contributed. And the question answered by Tinbergen was not which theories of the cycle were correct, but rather which factors caused the internal dynamics of an economy. As such Tinbergen did not discriminate between theories directly, but instead combined them into an interdependent *system*.

8.2 The First Volume of Tinbergen's Study

Briefly after the July 1936 expert meeting Tinbergen inquired with Haberler what his precise task would be at the League of Nations, and whether it might include questions of economic policy (Figure 8.2). The response from Haberler was cautious: while questions of policy were not on

[27] Ibid.

principle excluded, one should proceed step by step. In September of that year Tinbergen met with various experts in Oxford including Ragnar Frisch, Colin Clark, John Hicks, Jacob Marschak, Erik Lindahl, and James Meade.[28] With them he discussed his proposed method, which at that point was a combination of his work on the statistical determination of equilibrium[29] and the model of the Dutch economy he developed earlier. In such a model, equilibrium values were calculated for various variables, and the cycle was imagined as a deviation from these equilibrium values. In the fall of that year Tinbergen started to develop his work and by early January he sent a progress report to Loveday and Haberler.

It is tempting to think of Haberler's report as the theoretical counterpart to Tinbergen's empirical approach, pitting the quantitative model-builder Tinbergen against Haberler, the promising young Austrian theorist. But matters were not as simple. Haberler was also engaged in statistical inquiries based on his work for the League of Nations.[30] Differences undoubtedly remained, but Haberler and Tinbergen shared a joint sense of purpose.

In the meantime, there was much discussion among the various economists about the appropriate approach. In a long letter, Robertson suggested to Loveday what Tinbergen could best do, and he advised that Tinbergen not be too ambitious: "I incline therefore to the view that at the present stage a succession of flank attacks on the Haberlerian citadel may really prove more fruitful than direct frontal assault."[31] The frontal assault that Robertson meant was the attempt to construct a complete model of the American economy; he suggested that Tinbergen look at individual relationships. Tinbergen had already expressed his skepticism about such partial analysis to Haberler. But in the end, he had to agree, and as a result the study consists of two volumes. The first investigates some specific relationships in the economy, and the second contains the full model of the American economy.

The first study comprised several of the flank attacks that Robertson suggested. Tinbergen sought to explain fluctuations in the level of investment, in the amount of residential (private) housing being built, and in the

---

[28] Tinbergen, "Short Report on Conversations in Oxford (26th–29th of September, 1936) in Connection with the League's Business Cycle Research," 1 October 1936, JTC.
[29] Tinbergen, "Sur la Détermination statistique de la Position d'équilibre cyclique," 1936.
[30] Gottfried Haberler to JT, 4 February 1937, TL.
[31] Robertson to Loveday, undated, Research on Business Cycles, LoN, Box 4540, doc. nr. 10B.26666.12653.

investments in railway rolling stock.[32] For this he used data from various countries, including the United Kingdom, Germany, the United States, France, and Sweden. But more than anything the volume was a kind of handbook of the new method of statistical testing with multiple correlation analysis. In particular, the housing and railway rolling-stock studies serve as illustrations more than full-blown investigations. The volume is therefore appropriately titled *A Method and Its Application to Investment Activity*.[33]

The study into the causes of the fluctuations in the level of investment was at the heart of the first volume, and soon became the center of debate among the various economists involved with the project. One dominant concern was raised by several of the experts involved: they were not convinced that Tinbergen's explanation of the fluctuations in investment had much merit. The study found that fluctuations in investment "are in the main determined by the fluctuations in profits earned in industry as a whole some months earlier."[34]

Loveday expressed the worry succinctly: "[B]ut surely both profits and investment might be the result of some common cause."[35] Tinbergen's response was both clear and puzzling: "In fact I think it is so in reality: profits as well as investment activity depend on a number of 'elementary' causes – prices, costs, volume of production of consumers' goods, rate of increase in that volume, etc. – which in principle may be combined in a *different* way for the 'explanation' of profits and for the 'explanation' of investment activity." Tinbergen then explained that these elementary causes may have only a small or partial effect on profits, and therefore are not as "complete" an explanation. But he did not make clear what it means to explain fluctuations in investment. If the underlying causes operate on profits, then surely to really *understand* fluctuations in investment one would wish to know what makes profits go up or down, rather than merely to know that once profits are high, we will see high levels of investment. It was precisely this type of argument over underlying causes that had been central to debates about the business cycle. Perhaps Tinbergen was dragging his feet a bit, and implicitly suggested that his preferred approach based on a complete model of the economy would not

---

[32] This was originally meant to include a far greater number of specific variables, including money wage-rates and the supply of investible funds; see ibid.

[33] Tinbergen, *Statistical Testing of Business-Cycle Theories: A Method and Its Application to Investment Activity*, 1939.

[34] Ibid., 49.

[35] Arthur Loveday to JT, 14 February 1938, LoN, doc. nr. 10B.26666.12653, Box 4540.

suffer from these problems. At the same time, we know from his other work during this period that he desperately wanted to move away from debates about ultimate causes. That is precisely what separated the socialists and the liberals, and he hoped that they could at least agree on what helped to stabilize the economy and restore employment.

Even if the goal was not deep understanding but was more pragmatic, say, to stabilize the level of investment, Tinbergen's results were of little use. Loveday expressed that worry clearly in a letter to Robertson, when he argued that from the point of depression policy it is of little use to know that profits cause investment, since policy is unlikely to directly affect profits. If one knew something about the effects of wages or the price of raw materials, that would be much more valuable: "I should have thought that a 50% correlation, if I may so express it, between any of these factors and investment activity might be more important than 100% correlation between profits and investment."[36] Robertson's reaction was not any more supportive: "I don't think this first report can actually be regarded as anything but an *instrument*.... I agree that more evidence should be presented about the 'rather bad' results."[37]

These issues were discussed in the fall of 1937 when an expert meeting like the one from the year before around Haberler's report was held. The most notable absentee was Ragnar Frisch, widely regarded as the premier specialist of multiple correlation analysis. But Tinbergen soon after went on a trip to Scandinavia and met with all leading economists there, including Frisch.[38] Although his report spoke of general agreement between him and Frisch about the method, it was also evident from his report that there had been quite a bit of discussion regarding the technical matters. Ragnar Frisch promised to send a written memorandum on Tinbergen's work, which as far as I have been able to ascertain was not sent until the next July and dealt primarily with the second volume (it is known as the "autonomy memorandum"[39]).

---

[36] Arthur Loveday to Dennis Robertson, 11 March 1938, LoN, Box 145, doc. nr. 18.

[37] Dennis Robertson to Arthur Loveday, 22 March 1938, LoN, Box 145, doc. nr. 18.

[38] JT note to Arthur Loveday, 22 November 1937, LoN, Box 4606, doc. nr. 10922. His note makes mention of Hammerskjöld, Helger, Johansson, Lundberg, Metelius, Kock, Myrdal, Ohlin, Svennilsson, Wigforss, Wold, Johan Åkerman, Lindahl, Gustav Åkerman, Colbjørnsen, Jahn, Frisch, Trygve Haavelmo, Pedersen, Skøvde, Vogt, Zeuthen, and, on his way back, Chait in Antwerp.

[39] Frisch, "Autonomy of Economic Relations: Statistical versus Theoretical Relations in Economic Macrodynamics," 1995.

Notably, despite the critical reception of the first part of the study it remained largely intact. The published version, like the early versions, emphasized primarily the direct relationship between profits and investment, even though nearly two years had passed between the publication of the first volume and the early draft reports that Tinbergen prepared. It would not be the last time that Tinbergen remained committed to his approach despite criticism from others. There was undoubtedly some stubbornness in this commitment, but what was also important was that others pointed mostly to the limitations of the method but were unable to suggest clear improvements. It was not that Tinbergen was wholly unresponsive to criticism: he made numerous smaller revisions and conducted additional tests to confirm his original findings and compare the robustness of his findings across different countries, but his overall approach remained unchanged.

8.3 The Second Volume of Tinbergen's Study

For the second volume Tinbergen constructed a full model of the American economy to describe its dynamics for the period of 1919–1932, along the lines of his Dutch model. The model consisted of a total of seventy variables and forty-eight equations. Tinbergen knew from the beginning of his task that his preferred method was that of the full model, something Robertson described as the frontal assault on the "citadel" of Haberler, but it required overcoming several obstacles and would not prove easy.

First, there was the problem of obtaining sufficient data. The study mentioned no fewer than twenty-seven separate sources of data, and even so it was incomplete and the values of certain variables for missing years had to be estimated (through interpolation). Second, there was the virtually endless task of the actual estimation process, which required hours and hours of endless manual calculations. It was not for nothing that Tinbergen reported back from Oslo that he was impressed with Frisch's institute, "where about five scientific assistants and five to ten calculators work"[40] – that is, human calculators, not machines.

This was the practical side of the job; the more theoretical part posed equally formidable challenges. Tinbergen complained frequently that many economists did not provide a full model of the economy, and indeed he

---

[40] JT note to Arthur Loveday, 22 November 1937, LoN, Box 4606, doc. nr. 10922.

was as much constructing as testing the theories Haberler had collected. This was even more true for the monetary side of the model, since this had not been part of his original Dutch model. That 1936 model had contained only what economists call the "real" part of the economy: the production and consumption process. It was especially the monetary side and the associated equations that were subject to endless revisions throughout 1938.[41]

But convincing his fellow economists at the League of Nations that his task was worthwhile would prove to be the hardest task. The initial response by Loveday was devastating; to Robertson he wrote: "I have just been reading, or trying to read, Tinbergen's draft second Interim Report on the United States, and I confess that I am rather aghast.... I am left with a very clear impression that his exposition is simply lamentable ... do you think he can ever do it? ... indeed what is one to do with it all?"[42] Loveday realized that his harsh critique could not be sent directly to Tinbergen and agreed to let Robertson write a response that captured their joint criticism.

Robertson came to the defense of Tinbergen, if not quite directly to his methods, then at least to the defense of Tinbergen's scientific autonomy. One of the major worries Loveday had was that it was hard to find any connection to Haberler's work in Tinbergen's study and hence that the unity of the project was lost. Robertson suggested: "I think that, in order to form a fair judgment on his method and results, it is necessary to allow him to present his results in his own order and arrangement. He has done his best in the last chapter to meet our desire that the results should be brought into relation with the propositions discussed by Haberler."[43] Robertson argued that with proper guidance and another expert conference, things should work out. Loveday was not so certain and in his letter to Tinbergen minced no words about his worries. The connection with the Haberler volume was still on his mind, as was the concern that Tinbergen was more occupied with a method than with the results.[44]

Loveday was not alone in his critique. Haberler wrote to Loveday, after repeated discussions about it with his colleagues: "It is always the same objections and the same answers to these objections that are raised. It is easy to get nonsense or spurious correlations – much easier with multiple

---

[41] See the correspondence between JT and Tjalling Koopmans from October 1938, LoN, Box 4540, doc. nr. 10B.35838.12653.

[42] Arthur Loveday to Dennis Robertson, 20 April 1938, LoN, Box 145, doc. nr. 18.

[43] Dennis Robertson to Arthur Loveday, 24 April 1938, LoN, Box 145, doc. nr. 18.

[44] Arthur Loveday to JT, 30 April 1938, LoN, Box 145, doc. nr. 18.

than with simple correlation analysis.. . . But one can guard oneself against them and I think that Tinbergen is critical enough." Haberler's letter also expressed the worry that Loveday himself raised, the idea that Tinbergen relied too much on a single method: "[S]imple methods, aided by intuition, a general knowledge of the historical background and theoretical analysis will yield quite satisfactory results."[45] Keynes, sometime before his famous published review, chimed in with the choir; he believed that Tinbergen relied on too long a period over which too many surrounding factors had changed, left out important factors, and relied on statistics that were collected at too-large intervals (most of the material was yearly). In conclusion, Keynes labeled the work of Tinbergen "obscure."[46]

In that same letter Keynes retained much praise for James Meade, one of the other promising quantitative economists of the period. Ironically, Meade himself was far more positive about Tinbergen's approach. He saw quite clearly that Tinbergen was neither "discovering" nor "proving" theories of the cycle, but only testing "their adequacy."[47] In other words, Tinbergen was analyzing the extent to which relationships suggested by business-cycle theorists were able to explain the business cycle as observed in the real world. It was not a very discriminatory method, since various explanations could be valid at the same time (to different degrees). In fact, the whole modeling approach of Tinbergen was meant to be a synthesis of different posited relationships. It was at this level, at least, that there was great consistency between Tinbergen's work and Haberler's.

Hovering over the entire discussion was Ragnar Frisch; he was not only the pioneer in economics for the analysis of complete systems,[48] but also technically the most-well versed critic of Tinbergen's work. His memorandum on the second volume is at once congratulatory and extremely critical. It praised the work as "perhaps the most important single step forward in Business Cycle Analysis of recent years." But the next sentence was crystal clear: "But I do *not* think that it can be looked upon as 'A Test of Business Cycle Theories.'"[49] The core message of the memorandum was that Tinbergen insufficiently thought about the stability, or what Frisch called

---

[45] Extract from Gottfried Haberler to Arthur Loveday, 20 April 1938, LoN, Box 145, doc. nr. 18.

[46] John Maynard Keynes to Arthur Loveday, 5 September 1938, LoN, Box 145, doc. nr. 18.

[47] James Meade to Arthur Loveday, 15 February, 1938, LoN, Box 145, doc. nr. 18.

[48] Frisch, "Statistical Confluence Analysis by Means of Complete Regression Systems"; reprinted in Hendry and Morgan, *Foundations of Econometric Analysis*, 1995.

[49] Frisch, "Autonomy of Economic Relations: Statistical versus Theoretical Relations in Economic Macrodynamics," 1995.

the autonomy, of the relationships he investigated. A relationship is more autonomous the more it remains stable while other things change. When profits are still highly correlated with investments even if profit taxes are substantially increased, then this relationship is relatively more autonomous. Frisch argued that what Tinbergen's model insufficiently did was to distinguish between contingent relationships, which just happen to hold in this particular instance, and autonomous relationships, which were likely to hold under a variety of different circumstances such as different types of policy interventions or alternative institutional arrangements. The conclusion was damning. Frisch suggested that Tinbergen had only uncovered contingent relations, because of a flawed methodology.

Tinbergen was, perhaps unsurprisingly, not deterred by the note and quickly wrote a reply, suggesting that both Frisch's memorandum and his reply be circulated to the experts who were present at the 1938 conference in Cambridge. The reception of the Frisch memorandum was mixed. Robertson wrote frankly to Loveday that he "couldn't make much of Frisch's portentous document!"[50] He went on to suggest that Frisch was merely using fancy mathematical language to make points that had also come up in their own discussions, a view that might in part reflect the fact that Frisch's note arrived shortly after the Cambridge conference on Tinbergen's second volume, from which Frisch was absent.[51] Roy Harrod, an Oxford economist, warned that the text was already quite technical and that it would be a very bad idea to add an additional even more technical chapter.[52] Haberler and Bowley agreed and suggested that many of the dangers Frisch highlighted were already understood by Tinbergen.[53]

What was at stake in the exchange was in part the very definition of clarity. Frisch's memorandum was couched in general terms, and a technical mathematical language – it spent only the final page discussing how its conclusions related to Tinbergen's work. To Tinbergen he wrote that the publication of the whole exchange might clarify matters "provided the two parties are reasonably free from muddle-headedness, which I think we may

---

[50] Dennis Robertson to Arthur Loveday, 25 August 1938, LoN, Box 4540, doc. nr. 10B.26666.12653.
[51] In attendance were Divisia, Lundberg, Marschak, Bowley, Harrod, Robertson, and Koopmans.
[52] Roy Harrod to Koos Polak, 1 September 1938, LoN, Box 4540, doc. nr. 10B.34983.12653.
[53] Tjalling Koopmans to Arthur Loveday, 11 October 1938, LoN, Box 4540, doc. nr. 10B.34983.12653.

both claim to be."[54] For Frisch certainly, and most likely for Tinbergen, the mathematical memorandum was precisely what clarity entailed. But the other economists involved were worried that the technical language would obscure the limitations of Tinbergen's approach, and desired a more applied and verbal explanation of these. There was a difference between clarity among experts and clarity between experts and their intended audience, politicians.

There was another aspect, however, that is easily missed in the contrast between Frisch and Tinbergen. Whereas Frisch was primarily concerned with formal requirements and general methodological principles, Tinbergen had his feet in the mud. His statistical testing was neither the inductive endeavor that Frisch in his memorandum implicitly suggested it to be nor the deductive formal theory testing that later became associated with econometric methods, in particular, at the Cowles Commission – where Koopmans and Trygve Haavelmo, the star pupils of Tinbergen and Frisch, were influential. Instead, it was an iterative back-and-forth process with Tinbergen constantly checking results against one another, doing informal robustness tests, and seeking plausible but contestable interpretations. Hendry and Morgan have attempted to count the various tests and arrived at the impressive number of seventeen different types of tests.[55] It was perhaps not a methodology that one could write down for others to follow, but neither was it lazy or simplistic. The economic and historical intuition that Haberler and Keynes believed was missing from the reports was at the very least replaced with a technical intuition and deep familiarity with the peculiarities of the data.

A wonderful example of this was the fact that while all of the revisions were going on, Tinbergen took it upon himself to conduct a similar study for the United Kingdom for the period 1870–1914, a more stable and "normal" period, to check the extent to which the results were comparable. It was an enormous additional task, and one that was published only much later because insufficient data were available at the time.[56] But it marked Tinbergen as a researcher who never strove for perfection but was always hopeful that improvements could be made. However, even he had to admit later that Frisch's repeated corrections were a painful and hurt his

---

[54] Ragnar Frisch to JT, September–October 1938 (undated), LoN, Box 4540, doc. nr. 10B.34983.12653.

[55] Hendry and Morgan, *The Foundations of Econometric Analysis*, 1995; Malinvaud, "About the Role, in Older Days, of Econometrics in Quantitative Economics," 2007.

[56] Tinbergen, *Business Cycles in the United Kingdom 1870–1914*, 1951.

pride.[57] But in the letters of the period, his spirit was unbroken. He optimistically kept looking for improvements; to Polak he wrote that "the discovery nevertheless brings me joy, because I always hope I can make the coefficients converge a bit more. But I am a great optimist."[58]

The compromise reached in the end was that Tinbergen would write an extended introduction to the second volume that reflected the points raised by Frisch. The resulting introduction raised many interesting issues, such as the difference between statistical and economic significance, and the importance of a priori theorizing for the construction of an econometric model. But although inspired by Frisch's criticism, the introduction clearly presented Tinbergen's views on the matter. The issues discussed in the introduction were, because of the extended internal discussion, essential, and they occupy econometricians to this day. It speaks to the unique moment at which in an international institution aimed at promoting a stable world economy, cutting-edge technical econometric issues were explored. But that very fact can equally be used to cast doubt on the whole undertaking. The EFO, part of the League of Nations, was occupied with technical econometrics in the crucial years leading up to World War II. These were the same years that Tinbergen would repeatedly add to his travel plans the letters H.D.: "Hitler dienende" (Hitler allowing). Times were increasingly tense and international contact increasingly difficult and uncertain. There was a growing disconnect between the international political reality of which the League of Nations was an integral part and the technical econometric research developed by its economic experts.

8.4 Tinbergen or Tinbergen, Polak, Koopmans, Loveday, Robertson, and Frisch

One of the remarkable features of the work at the League of Nations was its collaborative nature. This really took off with the Haberler report, which was subject to repeated rounds of expert discussions, and came together in close collaboration with the permanent staff members of the League of

---

[57] Tinbergen, "De Centrale Gedachte van de Correlatierekening," 1951. It might have been more than a little painful. In this retrospective account Tinbergen in fact tells first about the repeated reprimands Henry Schultz's demand-studies received from Frisch, to conclude that something like that might happen to all of us. He then adds that, fortunately, some are so lucky that the criticisms do not appear in print, a clear reference to the unpublished memorandum of Frisch.

[58] JT to Koos Polak, 20 November 1938, LoN, Box 4540, doc. nr. 10B.35838.12653.

Nations. In recent work this has come to be called the Haberler model.[59] This collaborative nature of the work was important for a few reasons. First, it reflected a broader shift that would take place primarily in quantitative economics, where big research teams became common in economics. Second, teamwork became a mainstay in Tinbergen's work, from the economic planning work to the development economics he would engage in later. But, most importantly, it represented the nature of institutional economic work, which was quite different from that done by the theorists of the business cycle within the university.

The last point is often overlooked; it is simply suggested that Haberler and Tinbergen were overcoming theoretical differences and that they sought to synthesize a debate on business cycles that had been raging for a couple of decades. But as Trautwein and Boianovsky claim about the Haberler report: "*Prosperity and Depression* was not a book where all rival explanations of the business cycle would find room, but primarily an expression of the League's quest for a consensus that would allow the formulation of a testable synthesis."[60] This goal of a synthesis, or, better yet, an institution-wide consensus, was an explicit goal of the Rockefeller Foundation in its funding of the research, and it also reflected the political role of the Economic and Financial Section of the League of Nations, which was supposed to provide expert advice. Tinbergen's project was therefore meant as a continuation of this institutional research project, and not as a stand-alone investigation. It should certainly not be read as his personal expert advice to the League of Nations.

This posed serious constraints on Tinbergen's research. A good example of this is the separate study he undertook for the 1932–37 period for the United States, the New Deal Period. The study was an application of the model that most directly engaged with political interventions to combat the cycle and contained a distinction between incidental and systematic policies to stabilize the business cycle. The New Deal draft was on the program for the Cambridge expert meeting in June 1938 but was ultimately not discussed there. What was instead decided at that meeting was that it would not be included in volume two of the study, because it overstepped the supposed mandate of the study. And although Tinbergen made repeated requests to publish the results separately, this was never

[59] Slobodian, *Globalists: The End of Empire and the Birth of Neoliberalism*, 2018.
[60] Boianovsky and Trautwein, "Haberler, the League of Nations, and the Quest for Consensus in Business Cycle Theory in the 1930s," 2006.

allowed.[61] The limited "ownership" of the results of the research extended more broadly. When Tinbergen wanted to give public lectures, he had to receive explicit permission from the League of Nations.[62] The sharing of statistical information with other nations through the League of Nations was a not insignificant victory for transparency; previously, it had often been claimed that such figures had to remain secret for (military) strategic reasons. But that did not mean that all the work at the League was suddenly meant to be public.

Another interesting instance of this tension is the fact that Dennis Robertson, who was the most important consultant of Loveday throughout the period on more advanced technical matters, and who was also an important guide for Tinbergen during his work, particularly on the first volume, asked for his name to be left out of the first volume. He even asked for his name to be left out of the preface as one of the consultants.[63] He had been of great help in bringing the study about but preferred not to be directly associated with it.[64]

But whereas Robertson was primarily a consultant, the fact that both Jacques Polak and Tjalling Koopmans were not mentioned as coauthors of the second volume is a lot more curious. As is evident from their correspondence during 1938, Polak was crucial in the revisions of the monetary side of the model. Tinbergen was never much of a monetary economist, and the monetary side had not been part of his model of the Dutch economy. Polak was an economist with a strong statistical training in Amsterdam. He had been hired in the fall of 1937 at the League of Nations at the recommendation of Tinbergen, and would stay at the League until 1945 (Figure 8.3). His suggestions were not merely corrective, but often constructive proposals for improvement, and at the height of the

---

[61] The results confirmed Tinbergen's earlier view that the New Deal had not been systematic and consistent enough. Tinbergen, "De Politiek van Roosevelt," 1935; Tinbergen, "De Politiek van Roosevelt," 1934.
[62] See, for example, JT to Arthur Loveday, 25 May 1937, and JT to Arthur Loveday, 18 October 1937, TL.
[63] Arthur Loveday to Dennis Robertson, 16 June 1939, LoN, Box 4540, doc. nr. 10B.33994.12653. This might have been due to the fact that he sought to avoid a conflict with Keynes and other British economists and at the time; see Clavin, *Securing the World Economy: The Reinvention of the League of Nations, 1920-1946*, 208; Weintraub, "Roy F. Harrod and the Interwar Years," 147. Another explanation might have been his more general reluctance to attach his name to projects; see Toporowski, *Michał Kalecki: An Intellectual Biography*, 114.
[64] Mizen, Moggridge, and Presley, "The Papers of Dennis Robertson: The Discovery of Unexpected Riches," 1998.

Figure 8.3 Tinbergen in his office at the League of Nations which he shared with Koos Polak, 1937.

revision process a couple of letters per week were exchanged between him and Tinbergen, who was long since back in the Netherlands. The letters they exchanged were always jointly addressed to Koopmans, who in the team was the most technical economist, their in-house Frisch.

Tinbergen had come into frequent contact with Koopmans in 1934 when they spent ample time discussing modern economics.[65] Koopmans was quickly developing into one of the most technically sophisticated economists of the age. Tinbergen had secured a position for him at the Netherlands Economics Institute where he already published cutting-edge material on the analysis of time series.[66] During World War II, Koopmans would end up doing the work that later earned him the Nobel Prize. Tinbergen urged him to join the League of Nations, which Koopmans did with some hesitation. He did not feel at ease in the bureaucratic environment. And he was worried that he, trained in physics, would be unable to develop his knowledge of economic theory much at the League.[67]

The three of them worked for a year on the revisions until finally volume two was deemed fit for publication. During this period, Polak was not only

[65] Tjalling Koopmans to Tinbergen, 19 November 1938, TL.
[66] Koopmans, *Linear Regression Analysis of Economic Time Series*, 1937.
[67] Tjalling Koopmans to JT, undated probably June 1940, archived as NL-RtEUR_TBCOR01_025Z058, TL.

the expert of the monetary side, but also managed the research, coordinating between the people at the League, the various experts, and Tinbergen. Koopmans took care of many of the calculations and more technical aspects, while Tinbergen made the final decisions on the revisions. When in the summer of 1939 he was asked to come to Geneva to talk about the final revisions, Tinbergen decided to stay home. To his two colleagues he wrote: "because I am personally sure that the two of you know more together than I do." Despite this teamwork Koopmans's name was not even mentioned in the second volume, and Polak's only in the preface.[68]

Authorship within an institution like the League of Nations was not a simple matter, and both the Tinbergen volumes and the Haberler studies are best read as collaborative efforts. In Tinbergen's case this is even more so since parts of the technical work and the calculations were done by others. But even thinking in terms of authorship is perhaps somewhat misguided. The volumes were meant to represent expert opinion, as well as a consensus view from within the League of Nations. The expert reports by Haberler and Tinbergen had a somewhat extraordinary character because their authors were brought in as outside experts. The two wartime volumes on international economic stability, which are the subject of the next section, were explicitly published as a continuation of the Haberler and Tinbergen studies, but the names of the group of authors who worked on them can be found only in the preface. It represented a further step in the idea that experts, and even expert institutions, could speak with one voice.

That idea was not merely scientific, but also political. During one of the meetings about the research at the EFO, a representative of the French government is described as arguing that "an interpretation of the facts proposed by the League of Nations would be an official international interpretation, and [the French official] knew the risks. He did not believe that any state would ever consent to the official interpretation of economic facts with which it was well acquainted."[69] In other words, as an employee of the League, Tinbergen to some extent spoke with the voice of the institution rather than as an external expert. This was reflected in the

---

[68] In another similar instance, Haberler, as editor of the *Review of Economic Studies*, assumed that the article "On the International Propagation of Business Cycles" was to appear under Tinbergen's name, and inquired whether Polak should be mentioned as co-author. Polak in fact was the sole author, and Tinbergen had merely provided comments. Matters were cleared up, however, and the article did appear under Polak's name. See JT to Koos Polak, 14 January 1939, LoN, Box 4540, doc. nr. 10B.35838.12653.

[69] Quoted in Ehrenfreund, "The World Economy as Scientific Object, 1930–1939," 34–35, 2019.

approval he had to get before he could present his findings outside official meetings and in the way the study was undertaken, including the scope of the study. And it also shaped the way that his work was received.

The institutional nature of the report makes the harsh critique by Keynes even more noteworthy. Robertson, Haberler, Frisch, and others had all chosen to voice their criticisms internally, but outwardly they promoted the study. Keynes voiced his criticism at least once internally but also did so in a scathing review in his own *The Economic Journal*. The review was aimed at the technical aspects and suggested that no progress in correlation analysis had been made in the past thirty years, when Keynes himself wrote a book about probability.[70] He spoke of the "frightful inadequacy of most of the statistics employed," to conclude that the book "has been a nightmare to live with." But it was also personal when Keynes suggested that "Tinbergen may agree with much of my comment, but ... his reaction will be to engage another ten computers and drown his sorrows in arithmetic." Most striking perhaps was the final sentence aimed at the League as institution: "It is a strange reflection that this book looks likely, as far as 1939 is concerned, to be the principal activity and raison d'être of the League of Nations."[71]

It is hard to not see part of the fierceness of Keynes's reaction as being political.[72] His series of negative reactions, from the Haberler report to the Tinbergen report, can also be read as a response against the type of activity the League of Nations sponsored. Its reliance on technical expertise, he seemed to argue, was misguided. What was needed instead was political intuition and judgment, of the type he possessed, and that was much more likely to inform a particular course of political action. Keynes's own involvement at the postwar negotiations was on the side of British politics, next to the leaders, not as part of an international institution. It was a position he had occupied many times before. By 1939, the League of Nations had become powerless, and it is tempting to interpret Keynes's final sentence as an implicit argument that if anything was to be expected politically at this

[70] Boumans, "Econometrics: The Keynes–Tinbergen Controversy," 2019.
[71] Keynes, "Professor Tinbergen's Method," 1939.
[72] We will not cover separately the points of technical criticism raised by Keynes, since most of them have already been discussed as points of critique raised by others in this chapter and the previous one. For good overviews of the technicalities of the debate, see Patinkin, "Keynes and Econometrics: On the Interaction between the Macroeconomic Revolutions of the Interwar Period," 1976; Louçã, "The Econometric Challenge to Keynes: Arguments and Contradictions in the Early Debates about a Late Issue," 1999; Boumans, "Econometrics: The Keynes–Tinbergen Controversy," 2019.

point it was from the major world powers directly and no longer from the failing League of Nations.

That it was experienced as partly an attack on the institution is also reflected in the urging of Loveday and Koopmans to Tinbergen[73] to formulate a response. Koopmans egged Tinbergen on: "Please make your answer a little more powerful than the letter you wrote to him as a response to his earlier criticism."[74] After Koopmans had read the draft, he praised the – at least by Tinbergen's standards – polemic nature of the reply. But he also went on to point out several passages that could be formulated more directly.[75] Keynes, however, remained unshaken, and with his characteristic wit he responded in print: "There is no one … so far as human qualities go, whom it would be safer to trust with black magic [than Tinbergen]. That there is anyone I would trust with it at the present stage … I am not yet persuaded. But Newton, Boyle and Locke all played with alchemy. So let him continue."[76] He did not conclude with "but let the League put an end to it," but it is not hard to imagine that was the implication.

8.5 A Third Volume on International Economic Order?

The continuation of Tinbergen's own work on the international business cycle, as well as that of the League of Nations more generally, was not in a more technical direction. Instead, it was aimed at, as Clavin has termed it, "securing the world economy." The reality of the 1930s had been that of economic nationalism and the complete breakdown, especially within Europe, of a shared market. This nationalism was widely believed to have been the outcome of a long series of misguided policies undertaken after World War I, including the heavy reparation burden on the losers, most notably, Germany. This had led to a long period of economic instability, which covered nearly the whole interwar period and not just what has gone down in history as the Great Depression. The Great Depression was an economic crisis, but it was believed that the crisis of the 1930s was at least as much a crisis in international cooperation.

---

[73] Koopmans, despite his urgings to Tinbergen, actually agreed with much of Keynes's criticism, which he argued was in part the result of "biting off more than one can chew" and time pressure; Tjalling Koopmans to JT, 11 October 1939, TL.

[74] Tjalling Koopmans to JT, 11 October 1939, TL.

[75] Tjalling Koopmans to JT, 28 November 1939, TL.

[76] Tinbergen and Keynes, "On a Method of Statistical Business-Cycle Research. A Comment," 1940.

Tinbergen described that period in his 1944 book *The Lessons of Thirty Years*,[77] but it was in his *International Economic Co-operation*[78] that he developed the implications from the lessons of the past decades. This book was written in what was supposed to be the final year of the war, 1944, but the Allied progress had halted in the Netherlands, and The Hague remained occupied until May 1945. The book on international cooperation could not be more different from the League of Nations reports. Its explicit aim was the search for a stable international economic order. This was to be achieved through an international currency system and an internationally coordinated business-cycle policy aimed at the largest possible production while ensuring stability. Securing the world economy required institutions: these policies could not be effective without a strong international organization. This international organization should be powerful enough that it was able to limit national sovereignty in certain key areas of economic policy.

The international economy, just like the national economies, needed better economic organization. Tinbergen proposed, before they came into existence, an International Equalization Fund for the settlement of international payments, a Bank for Reconstruction and Development, and a continuation of both the Secretariat of the League of Nations and the International Labor Office (ILO). The latter two were Geneva institutions, and the ILO was the corporatist counterpart to the expertise of the League. As such the proposed international order mirrored the national order he had proposed in the Plan of Labor. "It must be observed that expert knowledge for this work is essential and must not be subordinated to the representation of special interests. Both in the International Labor Office and in the Secretariat of the League of Nations experiences have been gained in this respect which do not call for repetition," Tinbergen continued.[79] It was clear that he was looking for an independent international organization, at least more independent from the Rockefeller Foundation and the Great Powers than the League of Nations had been.

A similar message came from within the EFO at the League of Nations. Its report on the transition from the war to the peace economy sketched a similar line from the poor transition to peace of the 1920s to the crisis of

---

[77] Tinbergen, *De Les van Dertig Jaar: Economische Ervaringen en Mogelijkheden*, 1944.

[78] Tinbergen, *International Economic Co-operation*, 1945. Some years earlier, James Meade, who also worked for the League, published a book with a similar message, which he completed in Geneva; Meade, *The Economic Basis of a Durable Peace*, 1940.

[79] Tinbergen, *International Economic Co-operation*, 170, 1945.

the 1930s, and the resulting breakdown of internationalism. The report was explicit on the link between political and economic organization. Economic security was impossible if there was a lurking threat of war, and military security was intimately linked to a prospering and stable economy.[80] In order to achieve this, not only more coordination but also more international governance was indispensable.

But whereas this first war volume restricted itself mainly to the 1920s program of the League of Nations – currency stabilization and fostering international trade – it is the second war volume that synthesized the outcomes of the Haberler and Tinbergen reports along with additional work on business cycles to argue definitely that business cycles are international phenomena that require international coordination in order to be combatted successfully. "Depressions are international phenomena and no country can hope to pursue its policies in isolation," the report stated openly. And the dangers of national policies were significant: "[T]here is a danger that [national policies] will run counter to each other, that one country will tend to spread depression abroad in order to avoid it at home, and that the world will be divided into a number of autarkic pugnacious national units."[81]

At some points it is hard to identify differences between Tinbergen's book on international cooperation and the League of Nations reports, as if the institutional consensus had become part of Tinbergen's own belief system. The EFO, by then, could speak more openly, because political oversight of the national functionaries had effectively stopped. Tinbergen was no longer restricted by his institutional position as business-cycle expert. Without these constraints it was clear that the real priority was not econometric studies, but questions of economic order, questions of *Ordnung* at the international level.

The one big difference was that the EFO reports were largely silent on the relation between the West and the rest of the world. Tinbergen spoke far more openly than the reports did about underdeveloped regions. The League of Nations has been described as an intercolonial organization, that is, the institutional cooperation of the various colonial powers.[82] Tinbergen, on the other hand, was more outspokenly anticolonial and

---

[80] League of Nations, *The Transition from War to Peace Economy*, 1943.

[81] League of Nations, *Economic Stability in the Post-war World*, 1945.

[82] Akami, "A Quest to Be Global: The League of Nations Health Organization and Inter-colonial Regional Governing Agendas of the Far Eastern Association of Tropical Medicine 1910–25," 2016.

concerned with decolonization. In his book he argued for capital transfers to developing regions, most notably, India and China, both of which he believed had enormous growth potential and whose development was necessary if one wanted to ensure long-term stability in the world. Creating stability for him was directly connected to an even global development. It foreshadowed much of his later work on development economics.

Because he sought a balanced international order, Tinbergen was explicitly skeptical of a renewed Western or European order based on the former Great Powers. He argued that such a collaboration would be purely defensive, "only a substitute for what they really want: an ordered world economy."[83] The "they" here is referring to the Western European countries, but it is safe to say that it really was Tinbergen's hope and wish, his vision for the postwar world. It is the reason that Keynes's critique of Tinbergen as the rational computer, the black magician, is such a poor representation of him. The model he developed was a mere means to study the instability of the 1930s and perhaps to improve potential methods of stabilization, but the goal was a peaceful world economy. Keynes was repeatedly on Tinbergen's mind during these years, but it was the Keynes of the *Economic Consequences of the Peace*,[84] not the Keynes critical of his econometric studies. In that earlier book Keynes had warned of the devastating economic and ultimately political effects that the revengeful treaty of Versailles would have for Europe. Tinbergen's book on international cooperation was a call to heed this warning, and to take the opportunity to build a truly international order this time around. It even included moral and economic arguments about why reparation payments and land confiscation from Germany were a bad idea – arguments that were directly reminiscent of Keynes's own arguments after World War I.

If we read Tinbergen's *International Economic Co-operation* as the third volume, or rather the companion to the statistical studies he produced earlier, our perspective changes in important ways. Much of the discussion over the report has focused on the scientific qualities of the model and the method more generally. But what was equally important to Tinbergen was the position of the League of Nations in world politics, and the position of economic expertise within the League. His legacy in that respect is to be found in the work of Koos Polak at the IMF, and Tinbergen's own

[83] Tinbergen, *International Economic Co-operation*, 181, 1945.
[84] Keynes, *The Economic Consequences of the Peace*, 1920.

work on international order. The League of Nations, as an organization, was for him a stepping-stone toward a stable international order. After the Peace Palace, it was the next important step toward a peaceful and integrated world. And, if anything, the 1930s had proved that economic stability and international peace were even more intimately related than he had previously realized.

9

Fascism at Home

The core of the business cycle policy of the "Third Reich" is undoubtedly
correct and there is no reason to deny that.
—Jan Tinbergen, 1936

9.1 Wartime

Jan Tinbergen has never been very open about his war experiences. In an
interview late in life, he mentioned that he had been in hiding during the
winter of 1944.[1] His daughter remembered how even in these dire circumstances he was writing. There was hardly any food left in the cities, in what
became known in the Netherlands as the "hunger winter," and the house
was unheated. Tinbergen wore a foot muff (*voetenzak*), a kind of sleeping
bag from the waist down to keep warm. The everyday human suffering of
the war spared no one, especially during the later stages of the war. One of
his more fortunate friends described the shock he experienced when he
realized that at lunch, not long after the war, the entire Tinbergen family
even emptied the crumbs off their plates.[2] The remaining letters from that
final winter detail how Tinbergen arranged food to be delivered from
friends in the countryside where there was still some: some potatoes, some
onions and tulip bulbs (for consumption!).[3]

The other side of Tinbergen's involvement in the war is completely
untold.[4] Although he has been criticized for the publication of a theory

---

[1] Magnus and Morgan, "The ET Interview: Professor J. Tinbergen," 1987.
[2] De Wolff in Jolink and Barendrecht-Tinbergen, *Gedeelde Herinneringen*, 41, 1993.
[3] See, for example, Koos Roose to JT, 15 January 1945, and Luuk Tinbergen to JT,
20 January, 1945, TL.
[4] The exception are two notorious articles from 2006 by Jan Pen in *Het Hollands
Maandblad*, which, as far as I have been able to ascertain, are inaccurate with regard to
the war experience of both men. There is, for example, no evidence that either of the two

of economic growth in the German journal *Weltwirtschaftliches Archiv* in 1942, very little is known about his day-to-day activities. And neither to his children nor to his colleagues does he seem to have confided much. The sole exception, to the best of my knowledge, is a long letter from September 1945, four months after the liberation of the Netherlands, to his friend Tjalling Koopmans, by then in the United States.

It has often been observed that those who went through the war remained silent about it. Those who had experienced it knew how bad it had been, and those who had not experienced could never really understand. In that sense his confiding in Koopmans is exceptional, since Koopmans had not experienced the war on the Continent. He had spent most of the war in United States where he had worked on a shipping transportation model for the British War Office that would later help earn him the Nobel Prize. It was clear that he would not return any time soon to a prominent position in the Netherlands. Koopmans had become an intimate friend of Tinbergen through their joint development of econometric modeling techniques, first in the Netherlands and then for the League of Nations. And although Koopmans was more of a pure academic, at least intellectually the two were by now nearly on equal footing – all the more so since Koopmans had joined the prestigious Cowles Commission (a position for which Tinbergen had been considered in the late 1930s).

In the letter,[5] Jan Tinbergen wrote in the crucial passages about Ernst Wagemann, the brilliant statistician and economist from Germany with whom he had been in contact since the early 1930s. The ambitious Wagemann had used the seizure of power by the Nazis to become head of the Institut für Konjunkturforschung (IfK) in Germany.[6] In many of the occupied countries he sought to set up similar institutes or incorporate existing business-cycle institutes. Because of his personal relation to Wagemann, Tinbergen was able to prevent the CBS coming under the direct authority of the IfK. Nonetheless, the employees of the CBS were still officially under the command of the German government, which had occupied the Netherlands in May 1940 (Figure 9.1). But the Bureau retained some of its independence. Much had changed, nonetheless; they were now reporting their economic statistics and findings to the German

has had to testify before the so-called *zuiveringscommissie* (purge committee) after the war. There are no records for both men in the relevant archive, NA: CABR.
[5] JT to Tjalling Koopmans, 1 September 1945, YKC.
[6] Tooze, *Statistics and the German State, 1900–1945: The Making of Modern Economic Knowledge*, 2001.

Figure 9.1 Despite the outbreak of the war the family went on holiday in the summer of 1940. Jan with his daughter Tineke and his bicycle.

authorities. And to the dismay of the employees, the Bureau could no longer publish most of its statistics publicly.[7] As they say, in war, truth is the first casualty.

Tinbergen did not make perfectly clear what the "deal" with Wagemann entailed. He suggested to Koopmans that the Germans never discovered his department, which not only is contradicted later in the letter, but also seems virtually impossible. Wagemann very well aware from the early 1930s onward of the activities of Tinbergen and his team, and Tinbergen was repeatedly visited by Wagemann and his colleague Hoffmann during the war.[8] The letter did reveal some aspects of the deal. It appears that Tinbergen had negotiated with Wagemann a degree of independence for

[7] Van Maarseveen and Schreijnders, *Welgeteld een Eeuw*, 1999.
[8] See letters from Ernst Wagemann and Walther Hoffmann to JT during the period, TL.

the Bureau of Statistics, in return promising not merely to share the statistics and studies of the Dutch economy, but also to maintain "scientific contact." That sounds innocent enough, but during the war Wagemann published a study, the *The Law of Alternation* (*Alternationsgesetz*). The law was a variation on an old Malthusian theme, overpopulation. Wagemann argued that there was no simple linear relationship between population density and prosperity, but rather an alternating relationship: sometimes a growing population and high economic growth levels went hand in hand, at other times population growth would lead to lower growth levels. Tinbergen did not elaborate to Koopmans what the theory was used for, or the conclusion that Wagemann drew from it.

That goal, however, was obvious from the subtitle to Wagemann's study: "A Contribution on the Question of *Lebensraum*" – *Lebensraum* was the concept used by the Nazis for their policy of territorial expansion. The book conveniently justified the policy of expansion, because it demonstrated that in Germany there were too many people (and too much capital) in relation to the available land. And although, because of the alternation, this was not a permanent condition, it did provide a justification for the current expansionary "policies" of the Germans. In his review of the book, Tinbergen suggested that Wagemann offered an interesting hypothesis, but he was not at all convinced of the empirical demonstration of this law. Nonetheless, Tinbergen was attracted to Wagemann's formulation since it allowed for the synthesis of two competing theories: the Malthusian theory according to which population growth will lead to lower prosperity, and the anti-Malthusian one according to which population growth will lead to more prosperity.[9] Even in war, or perhaps especially in war, formulations of a more noble nature were preferable.

Tinbergen's attraction to Wagemann's ideas was certainly not merely rhetorical. Tinbergen was ambiguous about Malthus's theory that population growth will outrun economic growth. He only had two children himself, which he regarded as the proper number so as not to further worsen the overpopulation problem. It was not only a norm he lived by, but also one that he hoped his children would follow (although one of his daughters would later break the "rule"). And in his later development work, he was again particularly outspoken about population policies, when most other economists emphasized only growth.[10]

---

[9] Tinbergen, "Wagemann's 'Alternatiewet,'" 1944.
[10] Tinbergen, "Welfare Economics and Income Distribution," 1957.

In the first half of the twentieth century there was a broader intellectual discussion about the quality and quantity of the population. The racial Nazi theories about superiority are the most notorious and the most widely known. But in progressive circles there was also a widespread belief that the genetic quality of the population could be and had to be improved. The progressive program about the improvement in the social conditions, such as housing and workplace conditions, went hand in hand with ethical and cultural programs of the type we have seen at the AJC, and with demographic programs to improve the genetic quality of the working classes. The latter field was known as eugenics. One might expect that this new science was also attractive to a thinker like Tinbergen. After all, it was so to many progressive scientists of the age in Germany, the United Kingdom, and the United States,[11] not in the least so among statisticians such as Francis Galton and Karl Pearson. One would thus suspect that Tinbergen also had such interests, or at least that those around him did. The director of the Bureau of Statistics and direct superior to Tinbergen, Henri Methorst, did publish a book on the "population question," but his own contributions to it remained restricted to socioeconomic statistics.[12] And although Methorst did publish work in eugenic journals, it appears that the genetic component remained largely absent. Like Tinbergen, he was concerned about population levels and population growth, but he never believed that genetics was an attractive way of dealing with this issue.

The more purely demographic component in the form of population growth levels, and the possible dangers of overpopulation, remained a constant in Tinbergen's work, including his work in development economics. The theme first appeared in his work during the war, even before Wagemann wrote about it. In 1942, the Dutch journal of economics and statistics, *Economische-Statistische Berichten*, which was published by the NEI, published a special issue on the population question. Tinbergen's fellow Rotterdam economist François de Vries argued that the population question was primarily a problem of international organization and the current erection of borders in economic life: if people could migrate freely, overpopulation problems would soon disappear. But Tinbergen, along with the other contributors, was more worried about the recent surge in population

---

[11] Leonard, *Illiberal Reformers: Race, Eugenics and American Economics in the Progressive Era,* 2016.

[12] Mok, "In de Ban van het Ras. Aardrijkskunde tussen Wetenschap en Samenleving 1876–1992," 280, 1999; Noordman, *Om de Kwaliteit van het Nageslacht: Eugenetica in Nederland 1900–1950,* 1989.

(at that moment in time the Dutch population had just reached 9 million, compared with about 5 million in 1900 and the 16 million it would reach in 2000). He argued that the growth of capital had not kept up with the growth of the population, which had led to comparatively slower growth and prosperity in the Netherlands compared with other countries. That same year, Tinbergen published a popular brochure entitled *Is the Netherlands Overpopulated?*[13]

Overpopulation was a theme that also popped up in his most important publication during the war, his theory of long-term economic growth.[14] It was a new theme for Tinbergen, away from the short-run concerns over business cycles and toward the long-term concerns about growth patterns. If anything, one would think that long-term issues were the furthest from anyone's mind in 1942, and that was probably true for Tinbergen as well. But under the Nazi regime, business cycles were declared a thing of the past, a relic of capitalist economies.[15] And hence the focus of the statistical institute both in Germany and in the Netherlands shifted toward the study of two quite different economic themes: the production capacity of the economy and long-term growth trends. In fact, the two often went hand in hand, since what else was economic growth but the long-run development of the production capacity of a given country? The production capacity of the economy was also of direct relevance to the war effort, in which the entire economy was mobilized to produce for the war.

Both themes required a measure of the production capacity or the output of an economy, and it was precisely during these years that crucial breakthroughs were made in the subject of the measurement of national income, for example, by James Meade in Britain, Simon Kuznets in the United States, and Ed van Cleeff and J. B. D. Derksen at the CBS.[16] In 1940, Tinbergen wrote for the first time about national income and national

---

[13] Tinbergen, *Is Nederland Overbevolkt?*, 1942.
[14] Tinbergen, "Zur Theorie der langfristigen Wirtschaftsentwicklung," 1942.
[15] DIW Berlin, *Geschichte Deutsches Institut für Wirtschaftsforschung 1925–2015*, 2015. Tinbergen's paper on economic growth contained an interesting section that asked the question whether the analysis of a long-term trend while neglecting short-term movements is relevant at all. His answer was ambiguous in part because he realized that the trend itself crucially depended on the extent to which the cycle is actively combatted through policy and therefore whether we can assume that the economy operates close to a situation of full employment.
[16] Derksen, "Het Onderzoek van het Nationale Inkomen," 1940; Oomens, "De Ontwikkeling van de Nationale Rekeningen in Nederland," 1985.

production.[17] The context was as painful as understandable: the costs of mobilization for the impending war. In 1941, he estimated the production capacity of Indonesia,[18] the Netherlands' largest colony at the time, at the request of the German occupiers. In 1930 he had already estimated the productive capacity of Indonesia, at the request of his party, the SDAP. Back then, his study was meant to prove that decolonization was a feasible policy for the Netherlands.[19] Now he was forced to calculate how much the colony could contribute to colonial war efforts. To make matters worse, the study, although itself neutral in tone, was published in a volume that celebrated what the Dutch had accomplished overseas; it was called "Something Major was Accomplished There."[20] For Tinbergen, the pacifist and anticolonialist, it was one of the many moral compromises he had to make during the war years at the Bureau of Statistics.

But let us return to his study of long-term growth. His model has often been regarded as one of the major forerunners of Solow's growth model, which became the standard way of thinking about economic growth after 1960.[21] The model is based on what in economics is called a Cobb–Douglas production function, which regards the production in the economy as the simple combination of capital and labor, as if the economy was one big firm. The important economic implication is that production is assumed to be performed with a constant proportion of labor and capital. Elsewhere, Tinbergen repeatedly argued against this simplifying assumption, which failed to differentiate between capital-intensive sectors such as the industrial sector and more labor-intensive sectors such as education or agriculture (at the time).[22] It was certainly at odds with the insights he had gained from the rationalization debate in the early 1930s, which had been all about the effects of industrialization and the replacement of workers by machines in different industries, the conclusions of which he had published only a year before in book form.[23] The long-term growth model explored different

[17] Tinbergen, "Enkele Cijfers en Beschouwingen over de Algemeene Aspecten der Financieele Politiek," 1940.
[18] Tinbergen and Derksen, "Nederlandsch-Indië in Cijfers," 1941.
[19] Stokvis, "Na Utrecht," 1930.
[20] In an interview later in life, Tinbergen called this title "ridiculous"; De Jong, Van Paridon, and Passenier, "Jan Tinbergen over zijn Jaren op het CPB," 657, 1988. But in the correspondence with the editors of the volume there is no evidence Tinbergen suggested changing the title.
[21] Boianovsky and Hoover, "The Neoclassical Growth Model and Twentieth-Century Economics," 2019.
[22] Tinbergen, "Professor Douglas' Production Function," 1942.
[23] Tinbergen, *Technische Ontwikkeling en Werkgelegenheid*, 1941.

possible effects of a growth in population and included scenarios under which population growth would lead to a lower productivity per person,[24] in line with Wagemann's hypothesis. Tinbergen suggested that scenarios with this outcome should be considered the most realistic. The essence of his model, however, was in line with the famous Solow growth model: savings and technology are the main drivers of economic growth.

Many of these themes culminate in what is perhaps Tinbergen's most controversial publication, *Lessons of the Past Thirty Years*. In the final year of the War, known in the Netherlands as the "hunger winter," he was still living in The Hague. Tinbergen and his family had moved house for the second time. The first time had been to relocate from their house at the Kauwlaan in The Hague, where the Germans were building the Atlantic Wall, to the center of The Hague. This time, they had gone into hiding a few streets further away, where they moved in with the Van der Lugt family. The reasons for this are unclear; his daughter remembered him saying that he was on some "blacklist,"[25] and at least once the Germans raided the place looking for men. During the final stages of the war, more and more men were rounded up to fight, and it might have been the case that they were looking for Tinbergen too, although this is doubtful given his position and the strategic importance of the CBS as well as his age (he turned forty-one in 1944, whereas forty was the official maximum age for the final rounds of the draft). It might also have reflected the fundamental uncertainty of everyday life in the final year of the war, in which the Germans attempted to scramble everything together to hold off the Allied forces.

In January 1944, the Bureau of Statistics had to evacuate its headquarters, because the neighborhood it was in was labeled a strategic fighting zone by the Germans. The statistical materials, no less than 1,800 tons, were brought over to a temporary location in the nearby town of Leidschendam, but not long after, all trains and trams were canceled and most work ceased (Figure 9.2). Tinbergen along with some others continued to work in a smaller office at the Bezuidenhout, west of the center of the city. From September 1944 onward, the Germans deployed their new V-2 rockets[26] in a park in The Hague from where they could target English cities. The Allied forces attempted to bomb these rocket installations, but by mistake bombed the Bezuidenhout neighborhood. Afterward, activities

---

[24] Tinbergen, "Zur Theorie der langfristigen Wirtschaftsentwicklung," 538–39, 1942.
[25] Conversations with Els Barendrecht-Tinbergen, Tinbergen's daughter.
[26] Tinbergen referred to the launching of these rockets in his letter to Koopmans.

Figure 9.2 For a trip to the United Nations headquarters in New York in 1947 Tinbergen took the ship from Rotterdam, the Netherlands.

at the CBS came to a definite halt.[27] More generally, all throughout the winter, work was virtually impossible because fuel supplies were exhausted and some of the machines were stripped for valuable resources in a final effort to gather everything for the war effort.

Unfortunately, we do not know much about these final months since the bombing destroyed the materials. What is worth noting is that in August 1944 somebody tipped off the authorities about a conversation his wife had overheard between two CBS employees, in which they discussed secret information. This led to the arrest of eight employees, five of whom died in a concentration camp. This incident coincided roughly with the moment that Tinbergen went into hiding and could thus potentially explain why he felt so insecure that he decided to hide. While in hiding he was still writing; there was no longer any fuel left in the city, houses were stripped of all wood, trees cut down, but work could not stop. He was sitting in the freezing cold with his legs in a sleeping bag, to complete a book that summed up the "lessons of the past thirty years."[28] The book attempted to draw the policy lessons from the experiences of the past decades. Its

---

[27] Van Maarseveen and Schreijnders, *Welgeteld een Eeuw*, 1999.
[28] Tinbergen, *De Les van Dertig Jaar: Economische Ervaringen en Mogelijkheden*, 1944.

introduction is characteristic of his pragmatic attitude, where solving problems was always the priority: "Life demands, every now and then, deeds from the man of learning, even when the theory is not yet finished. In such instances he has to, as so often in life, make do with what is given to him. It is as such that I present you this book."

The book was first published when the Netherlands was still occupied in 1944, which might have meant that Tinbergen also registered for the Kulturkammer (a Nazi organization of which artists and writers had to become members in order to continue publishing their work).[29] The book contained a particularly noteworthy chapter in which Tinbergen discussed the various responses to the Great Depression. As before, Tinbergen was critical of Roosevelt's response to the Depression, which he considered to have been somewhat reluctant and ambivalent, worsened by the fact that entrepreneurs were initially leery of the New Deal arrangements.[30] About Hitler's efforts, Tinbergen wrote much more positively: without a single word about the massive mobilization and war industry of the 1930s, he praised the decisive policies of the Germans and described in detail the various measures undertaken, which resulted in steady recovery.

In another chapter on the consequences of the wars, we see Tinbergen biting his tongue in a rather unique way:

Also, in the cultural [*geistliche*] sphere there was an emancipation after WWI. It strengthened the humanistic and pacifistic tendencies, especially in the countries that emerged as victors out of WWI. In Germany and equally in Italy there were strong reactions against it, which especially after the outbreak of the great crisis of 1929 led to a shift in the development of thought in these countries, which prepared the ground for WWII. It would, however, lead us astray from our concerns, to discuss these matters further.

Tinbergen the pacifist, for whom matters of peace and war and economic development were intimately related, decided to hold back and not discuss any further the currents that led to this war, even though it was perfectly clear to him that nationalism and militarization were the great obstacles to prosperity. It was this very relationship between peace and prosperity that was the big theme of his book *International Economic Co-operation*,[31]

---

[29] The archive of the Kulturkammer, however, contains no entry for Tinbergen, NIOD.

[30] Tinbergen, *De Les van Dertig Jaar: Economische Ervaringen en Mogelijkheden*, 72, 1944.

[31] Tinbergen, *International Economic Co-operation*, 1945. It is more surprising perhaps that the second print of the *Lessons* book from 1946 was completely unchanged. In an interview given in 1982 he repeated the same sentiment: "The Germans did a good job as well. Even before Hitler came to power, plans had been prepared in government bureaus for major public works. Hitler executed those plans, and in doing so he did

published in 1945. That was not a late realization. As early as 1936, he had proposed to publish a pamphlet denouncing war as the greatest threat to economic well-being with his fellow members of the Econometric Society, following the example of some other academic societies.[32] In 1944, however, he decided that this meager statement was the best compromise. In his mind he was looking forward, not backward. He was already thinking about better policies to be pursued after the war, and his book was the programmatic statement of that. Around this time, Tinbergen was also busy working on a memorandum for the economic policy institute he wanted to set up after the war.[33]

Despite the somewhat desperate attempt of Tinbergen to look ahead with hope to better times, the war was an everyday reality. He shifted away from business-cycle research because it was no longer a matter of concern of the current regime, although he did publish a more theoretical book on economic dynamics.[34] Much of his research became concerned with statistical investigations into the production capacity and output level, because these statistics were essential strategic information. This was not merely desk research, but directly confronted him and his assistants at the CBS with the devastation of the war.

In a particularly gripping story, Piet de Wolff recounted how he was sent to Rotterdam in 1940 after the Germans bombed the entire city center to make the Dutch surrender. His mission was to estimate the loss in the housing stock of the city: "I remember well the sinister task to visit Rotterdam just a few days after the bombing to sketch out, with the help of local officials, the borders of the bombed area.[35] Back at the CBS we estimated the number of houses damaged as a result, based on the last data we had on housing in the area. Afterwards it became clear that our estimates had been quite good."[36]

It is clear from his letter to Koopmans that Tinbergen did not want to say too much about these hardships. They were perhaps better left unsaid.

---

exactly what Keynes had proposed. It is true, even though it might not be 'proper' to say so. Germany also implemented import-tariffs, sadly." "Tinbergen: Europa moet Economie Stimuleren," *NRC Handelsblad*, 5 June 1982).

[32] JT to Ragnar Frisch, 20 March 1936, NLN: FC.

[33] Passenier, *Van Planning naar Scanning: Een Halve Eeuw Planbureau in Nederland*, 30–31, 1994.

[34] Tinbergen, *Economische Bewegingsleer*, 1943.

[35] This border is still marked with plaques embedded in the pavement depicting the flames of war.

[36] De Wolff in Jolink and Barendrecht-Tinbergen, *Gedeelde Herinneringen*, 1993.

And indeed, Tinbergen said very little about it afterward to anyone, including his family. This makes it hard to get a full grip on his activities and the extent to which he had to compromise and was perhaps compromised. In the same letter to Koopmans he suggested that he broke off contact with Hoffmann, the editor of the Nazified economics journal, *Weltwirtschaftliches Archiv*, in 1942. But from the letters in his archive it is clear that this correspondence continued well into 1944. In these letters, Hoffmann addressed Tinbergen as Ministerialrat, a term used for high officials in government institutions, and mentions a recent visit to Tinbergen. After June 1944, there are no further letters with his German colleagues, but that could be because there are hardly any letters from the final year of the war in the archive. A book review Hoffmann requested from Tinbergen did appear, but in a Dutch journal, not a German one.

His good relations with the Germans also enabled him to help friends. Pieter Lieftinck was trained in law and economics, and Tinbergen knew him since the mid-1930s when both men worked at the Netherlands School of Economics (NEH). Lieftinck was a progressive politician like Tinbergen and would become treasurer in the first progressive postwar government in the Netherlands. During the war he was interned, initially under very good conditions, in St. Michelsgestel. But later Lieftinck was transferred to prison camps. The wife of Lieftinck and some close friends appealed to Tinbergen to get him released, which Tinbergen attempted.[37] He signed a request to Wagemann to get Lieftinck a position at the IfK in Kiel. In Lieftinck's version of the story he refused the offer for the position, whose origin he did not know, because he did want to give any impression that he had collaborated with the Germans.[38] But only a week after the request to Wagemann was sent, Lieftinck thanked Tinbergen in a letter for the fact that he had received his working papers and mentioned Wagemann, positively.[39]

Tinbergen thus sought to steer through these difficult times without giving up his prominent position at the CBS or his scientific work, unlike, for example, his brother Niko and his sister Mien, who were actively involved in helping Jews. This pragmatic stance stands in rather stark contrast to his principled stance in the lead-up to the Nazi occupation.

---

[37] Unknown to JT, 14 July 1943, archived as NL-RtEUR_TBCOR01_006H007, TL.
[38] Lieftinck, Bakker, and Van Lent, *Pieter Lieftinck, 1902–1989: Een Leven in Vogelvlucht*, 1989. The (late) reminiscences contain various passages in which Tinbergen is repeatedly criticized.
[39] Pieter Lieftinck to JT, 20 July 1943, TL.

9.2 Fascism on the Rise

The Plan of Labor was the main campaign against fascism at a time when it still seemed that an alternative was possible. After Hitler came to power, the Dutch social-democratic party and the associated union had started the Bureau of Action and Propaganda against fascism and communism.[40] After the initial successes of the Dutch national-socialist party, a broader society was founded: Unity through Democracy (*Eenheid door Democratie*), with many of Tinbergen's friends such as Koos Vorrink and Jan Goudriaan in prominent positions. Tinbergen was aware of the looming dangers. When a register of Jewish legal scholars and economists was drawn up in 1936 in Germany, Tinbergen was one of the people who signed the petition to block the development of such a register.[41] It was one of the various petitions and committees he joined during this crucial year. In various countries such as England, France, and Belgium, committees were founded of "vigilant" individuals who warned of the dangers that fascism posed to freedom of expression and inquiry, and Tinbergen was one of the early members of this committee of vigilance in the Netherlands.

Tinbergen also inquired with Frisch whether it would be possible to publish a petition that spoke out against fascism and in favor of peaceful cooperation between nations. Inspired by a similar petition from psychologists, he drafted a petition in which he described econometricians as concerned with "human well-being," and as such they have a special duty to "raise their voices against the tendencies leading to the largest wholesale destruction of human welfare: the war."[42] The petition concluded with the hope that "human Ratio" may solve the problems rather than "the wild instincts."

In 1938, Tinbergen was part of a large group of intellectuals who petitioned for the acceptance of more refugees into the Netherlands. At that point a steady stream of Jewish refugees was trying to leave Germany and enter the Netherlands. From such actions it was clear that Tinbergen did not believe there was a strict line that could be drawn between science and politics. In fact, scientists, in his view, had a special duty as moral

---

[40] De Jong, *Het Koninkrijk der Nederlanden in de Tweede Wereldoorlog 1939–1945, Deel 2: Neutraal,* 1969.
[41] Van Kamp, *Dien Hoetink: "Bij Benadering." Biografie van een Landbouw-Juriste in Crisis en Oorlogstijd,* 2005.
[42] JT to Ragnar Frisch, 20 March 1936, NLN: FC.

leaders. It was this characteristic more than anything that Ehrenfest and Tinbergen had admired in Keynes. The core argument of his *Economic Consequences of the Peace*, which pleaded for an arrangement that was less harsh on Germany, in particular, was a recurring theme in Tinbergen's reflections on the interwar period. This awareness makes it even more curious that in some of his economic writings, the analysis of economic processes and the rest of the world were so completely disconnected. And this was not merely true for his academic articles, where one might expect it, but was equally true of his more popular articles.

One striking example of this disconnect between his economics and his political convictions was in fact published in a magazine dedicated to antifascism. In the article Tinbergen first praised the cycle policies pursued in Italy and Germany, in particular, the public works and the reforms in the financial sector. And although he was critical of some of their industrial policies, he argued that "the core of the business cycle policies of the 'Third Reich' is undoubtedly correct, and there is no use denying it."[43] He even suggested that social democrats should be courageous enough to take credit for these policies, because they were similar to the ones proposed by them. This analysis was followed by a strong condemnation of the direction in which public spending had been done, in uneconomic areas and often for military purposes. But, argued Tinbergen, with this condemnation one is moving beyond the terrain of economics, and entering that of philosophy.

One might argue that Tinbergen was trying to protect his ethos as a scientist. In order to be able to do so, he could have demonstrated the harmful economic consequences of such investments, but he could not condemn them on moral grounds. As such he would be the ideal Weberian scientist, who kept his analysis and personal values completely separated. But we have already seen that Tinbergen did not particularly believe strongly in an autonomous science, independent from politics. And at the very least it is hard to use this type of reasoning to explain a publication in an antifascist publication meant for a wide readership. In such a publication, the moral and the economic critique could easily go hand in hand, even by Weberian standards.

What was in fact happening is something rather more fundamental, and in contradiction to the goal of a synthetic vision on politics and the economy. Tinbergen increasingly started to decouple the economy from

---

[43] Tinbergen, "Fascistische Economie," 2, 1936.

other domains. This is nowhere more evident than in his work on business cycles in which the goal is to find an endogenous theory of the cycle: a self-contained economic mechanism that can explain the cycle. In his most theoretical book on economic dynamics there is an almost desperate attempt to separate the political and societal changes from purely economic dynamics.[44] That such an attempt can indeed border on desperation is clear when we examine what he has to do in order to achieve this.

Tinbergen listed the many social changes of the interwar period: the decline in infant mortality, the decrease in family size, the increase in education levels, the improvement of management techniques, the rise of unions and cooperatives, and the increasing size and role of the government in the economy. It would be hard enough to believe that given all these social changes there would be a stable type of economic dynamics throughout the period that the book covers, 1910–40. But then Tinbergen begins talking about what he considers the "structural breaks" during the period: episodes of war and inflation, episodes of major inflation in peacetime, sudden breaks in economic structure such as the introduction of the New Deal or the economic policies of Hitler, and smaller breaks caused by minor wars or prolonged strikes. It is hard to believe in hindsight that during such a period a new science of business cycles came into being, the hallmark of which was an endogenous theory of the cycle. There was more than enough reason to argue that disruptions in the economic sphere were caused by disruptions either in the political sphere or in society. But instead this is the period that business-cycle theory was decoupled from politics and social change more broadly.

This was not very visible in the Plan of Labor, which was after all the combination of the new science of business cycles and a political campaign. But now that the political situation had changed and Tinbergen could no longer directly engage with policy, this decoupling became clearer. It sounds paradoxical to suggest that precisely during the war period when everything was political, economics and politics became disconnected. But this paradox had been observed before, and it is best understood as the attempt to turn "the economy" into a purely technical domain, quite distinct from other political or ideological domains. As such it is easier to understand why this strategy was attractive to Tinbergen. He already believed that in order to solve the economic and social problems of the day,

[44] Tinbergen, *Economische Bewegingsleer*, 1943.

we had to overcome ideological and political approaches, and focus on what worked.

In an interesting book that does not quite live up to its promise, Timothy Mitchell has suggested that during the crucial years of the 1930s and 1940s, the "economy" was invented.[45] On some level, that claim can only be regarded as historically grotesque. In economics there are well-recognized attempts from the eighteenth century, when Adam Smith and François Quesnay wrote to analyze the economy as an autonomous entity. And it is hard not to regard David Ricardo and Karl Marx as inventors of a separate sphere of economics, with its own set of laws. But Mitchell is correct that a fundamental shift took place during the 1930s, when the economy was increasingly regarded as a controllable separate domain. In this perspective, the economy, in particular, the national economy, is not only governed by particular dynamic economic laws, but can also be controlled. It is this view that underlies Tinbergen's book on economic dynamics from 1943. As Mitchell points out, detailed knowledge in the form of statistics was a requirement, and formed the basis for the most important economic statistic: the GDP. But equally crucial for this invention of the "engineerable" economy was the development of policy instruments in the hands of the national government. They allowed experts to suggest the optimal policies to steer the economy in the desired direction. That this was possible was demonstrated by the economic policies of the Nazis, and so Tinbergen was in some way correct. But that idea of control was true only if one was willing to adopt a rather peculiar perspective as a Dutch economist, namely that of a policymaker in a country like Germany. For Dutch policymakers there had been far less control during this period, when resources had to be directed toward the mobilization, and when later they simply lost control. The period before had not been better. As Koos Polak had demonstrated clearly in his model of the international business cycle, a small open economy like the Netherlands was helpless in the face of a global economic downturn. National economic policy was powerless in such cases.

It has been noted by some scholars that the rise of the idea of a planned economy was closely tied to the planned war economies, first during World War I, and then more comprehensively during World War II. But the rise of the idea that the economy could be governed (by experts) is at least as much the outcome of the political struggle over the economy of this period.

---

[45] Mitchell, *Rule of Experts: Egypt, Techno-Politics, Modernity*, 2002.

This struggle over the economy involved all the major ideologies of the period. Communist Russia adopted methods of central planning that were copied, for example, in Turkey under Atatürk, who drew up five-year modernization plans. The Plans of Labor and the New Deal both came out of a broadly social-democratic tradition, which sought to retain the best features of capitalism, while overcoming some of its (perceived) shortcomings. Meanwhile, the fascists, not just in Germany and Italy but also, for example, in Portugal, sought to govern the economy through a system called corporatism. In this system there would be functional representation along economic lines: both class lines (workers and employers) and occupational lines (industry organizations and cartels). Even the neoliberals such as Friedrich Hayek and Walter Eucken argued that one could plan for competition and that the state could steer the economy by providing a stable legal framework. In other words, the idea of a separate controllable economy was paradoxically developed in a period when the state sought to bring the economy under control.

In each of these proposed economics systems – socialism, fascism, neoliberalism, and social democracy – the economy was presented as a system in which one could intervene, but more importantly as a system that could actively be designed. In fact, the four systems all proposed an institutional reordering of the economy. The economy was no longer a set of natural (or iron) laws which had to be obeyed, as it had been for much of the nineteenth century, or a set of historically determined institutions appropriate for its age, as it had been portrayed in the German historical tradition. Instead, it was a system that could be actively constructed. And despite the deep differences over what that design should be, there was an important role for the economic experts, and economic expertise in all the proposed systems.

Tinbergen's own work and professional activities exemplified this shift. When he first explored business cycles, there was still a sense that economic downturns were natural occurrences, as unavoidable as earthquakes. By the time the war was finished, there was a growing consensus that business cycles were features of imperfect systems that could be overcome through an improved order. The near ban of business-cycle research under fascism is perhaps an extreme example, but signified a broader belief that economic dynamics could be brought under control.[46] From the mid-1950s onward, Tinbergen would be working on the

---

[46] It has also given risen to a periodically recurring claim by economists that the cycle is now finally under control, something that so far has been proven wrong by history.

"planning" of economic growth in the developing world. In the decade between the war and his development work, he would bring the business cycle under control through his work at the Central Planning Bureau in the Netherlands. And as such he came to embody what it meant to be an economic expert, or macroeconomic engineer, if you will.

Much of his work and activity during the war and directly after is concerned with concrete measurements of output, production, and reconstruction, and could hardly be more practical and driven by necessity. But the strictures of the war also led to more reflective work. He drew the lessons of the past thirty years in an extensive volume;[47] wrote the most theoretical book of his career, *Economic Dynamics*;[48] wrote what is perhaps his most significant paper in economic theory on growth;[49] and developed sophisticated reflections on the notion of economic equilibrium.[50] That is to say, particularly if we compare it with the rest of Tinbergen's oeuvre, the war years gave rise to some of his most fundamental work in economics, precisely at a time when he could be of little concrete help in economic policy, and precisely when the economy itself was fully politicized.

Econometrics itself had started as an ambitious program in the early 1930s, not merely to be of assistance to economics, but rather to supersede and ultimately replace economics. It has been noted that this ambition was never fulfilled, and econometrics "just" became a part of the discipline. But econometricians such as Tinbergen and Frisch did manage to achieve something of great significance. The economy was at the end of the war considered the domain of experts, and both Tinbergen and Frisch would go on to head the most important economic policy research centers in their respective countries after the war. Such policy research centers were, and often still are, populated by quantitative economists. In that sense at least, the title of Mitchell's book was spot on: the era of the "rule of experts" had arrived. Tinbergen was very aware of this change; in the *Lessons of the Past 30 Years*, he wrote that economics was becoming a true science and that economists would have more influence in the future: "[T]herefore it is important that they limit themselves to their own area

---

[47] Tinbergen, *De Les van Dertig Jaar: Economische Ervaringen en Mogelijkheden*, 1944.
[48] Tinbergen, *Economische Bewegingsleer*, 1943.
[49] Tinbergen, "Zur Theorie der langfristigen Wirtschaftsentwicklung," 1942.
[50] Tinbergen, "Indifferente en Labiele Evenwichten in Economische Stelsels." Since we will not discuss the work elsewhere, it is worthy of note that Tinbergen also published his only book in microeconomic theory a year after the war; it discussed in particular "imperfect competition." Tinbergen, *Beperkte Concurrentie*, 1946.

of expertise. For that reason, this book has attempted to isolate the economic, wherever possible."[51]

A focus on Tinbergen's involvement in the war, the compromises he was forced to make, and the dubious choices he made quickly loses sight of the bigger story. That bigger story is the fact that the war, if anything, accelerated the development of the state as the active manager of the economy, and the quantitative economist as the ultimate expert. Koopmans, whom Tinbergen had confided in, did his seminal work on the optimal allocation of resources in the service of the British government during World War II. For that work he shared the Nobel Prize in economics with Leonid Kantorovich, a Russian economist who had developed a similar technique for the Soviet authorities. It was that type of technical economic expertise that Tinbergen had in mind. And this apolitical, or at least anti-ideological, stance also became a goal for Tinbergen after the war. In the Netherlands, it would make political history as the Breakthrough (Doorbraak) movement.

9.3 The War and the Breakthrough Movement

In contrast to Tinbergen, many of his political associates spent much of the war in an internment camp. They were put together in the infamous camp Beeckvliet in Sint Michielsgestel, an internment camp for the elite with a mild regime. The conditions in the camp were generally good and the prisoners interned were mostly intellectuals and political figures of Tinbergen's age: too young to have wielded much direct political power or influence before the war, but likely to do so in the near future. The internment camp gave rise to a group known as the Seventeen Gentlemen (Heren Zeventien), many of whom would come to occupy important political positions after the war. They included the first prime minister after the war, Willem Schermerhorn, and his minister of finance, Pieter Lieftinck, who later became executive director at the IMF and the World Bank in 1955.

The Seventeen Gentlemen represented various political parties, mostly of a broadly progressive orientation. Their shared belief was that one of the major political obstacles of the prewar period was the pillarization of the Netherlands along religious lines. This pillarization had prevented cooperation between groups within the various parties that shared a similar

---

[51] Tinbergen, *De Les van Dertig Jaar: Economische Ervaringen en Mogelijkheden*, 264, 1944.

progressive outlook. The Seventeen sought to overcome partisan differences and the traps of party politics more generally. Tinbergen's friend
Marinus van der Goes van Naters, by then a member of parliament, was
convinced that except for the old liberals and conservative Protestants,
everyone could be united in one party.[52]

The Seventeen Gentlemen brainstormed about this future political order
in the rather odd circumstances of the internment camp. But much like the
war provided an opportunity for Tinbergen to write some of his more
reflective books, so the time spent in confinement and away from direct
political concerns provided an opportunity for more reflective politics. The
distance from everyday politics helped to create more unity between these
men, something that was further stimulated, especially in the later war
years, by the unification of the Dutch behind the "orange" banner and the
Queen. The Dutch People's Movement was the concrete result of the
Breakthrough ideal, deliberately not yet a party, but a movement that
aimed to break through traditional party and class lines,[53] and which
hoped to create a more integrated society.

The movement's program was largely based on the personalistic
socialism that had its roots in the AJC movement and the work of
Hendrik de Man, but also in more recent developments in France. Its
socialism was primarily a socialism of the mind whose first goal was
personal betterment and emancipation. From there it developed a political
program often described as democratic socialism. Like De Man's work of
the 1920s, it sought an improvement of working conditions, but especially
emancipation and development through work. For its morality, it sought to
draw on both the Christian tradition and modern forms of humanism. It
thus fitted Tinbergen's outlook very well, and many of those from the AJC
felt attracted to the movement, although loyalty to the old party, the SDAP,
sometimes made it hard for them to join.

We have already discussed the rise of the Volkspartei in the 1930s. The
Breakthrough movement is best understood as the continuation of that
development. It sought to break through class, religious, and ideological
lines to create a united progressive front. Its personalistic focus reflected
the fact that it sought to replace not merely traditional parties but also the
traditional sources of morality, most notably, organized religion. Within
this movement there was no place for older ideologies, and a natural place

---

[52] Bank, *Opkomst en Ondergang van de Nederlandse Volksbeweging*, 1978.
[53] Nederlandse Volksbeweging, *Program en Toelichting van de Nederlandse* Volksbeweging,
1945.

for modern experts with backgrounds in science. The type of expertise that Tinbergen represented, which aimed to stand above the parties, was quite naturally at home in the Breakthrough movement.

Tinbergen was not one of the people directly involved with this movement, but most of his closest associates were and the movement would have a decisive impact on him. He would repeatedly return in his work to a plea for a reduction in the number of political parties, as the Breakthrough movement had suggested.[54] His social-democratic colleagues of the Plan of Labor, such as Hein Vos, believed that the Plan idea would be important for the Breakthrough movement. In the transformation of politics from competing ideologies and underlying world visions into the art of finding the best solution, the pillarization could be broken down and politics could be organized into two major blocs, a conservative and a progressive one.[55]

Tinbergen was also working alongside J. H. W. Verzijl and F. A. Baron van Asbeck on the formulation of an international agenda for the Netherlands. The Breakthrough movement favored an international legal order, and it was this that Verzijl, Van Asbeck, and Tinbergen attempted to develop. The three men wrote a book in 1944 in which they explored the international position of the Netherlands after the war, in relation to Germany and the rest of Europe, in relation to the Atlantic Charter, and in relation to the overseas colonies. Verzijl and Asbeck were both scholars of international law and Van Asbeck was also associated with the Breakthrough movement. Verzijl had in the past written a case-by-case commentary of the cases that had been brought before the International Court of Justice in The Hague. His biographer has suggested that he was the very embodiment of the motto of a generation of Dutch international lawyers: "World peace through world law."[56]

Their joint book was explicitly framed as a continuation of the project that had started with the Hague Peace Conference and was left unfinished at the League of Nations in Geneva. The book ended with a quote from the American Nobel Peace Prize winner Elihu Root, who argued that every one of his students should spend some time in Geneva, for it was there that one could learn how the modern world is to be governed.[57] The book also contained a detailed proposal for a Dutch Center for the Study of

---

[54] Tinbergen, "De Toekomstige Sociale Orde en Onze Beweging," 738–39, 1965; Tinbergen, "Ideologies and Scientific Development," 1965.
[55] Keulen, *Monumenten van Beleid: De Wisselwerking tussen Nederlandse Rijksoverheid, Sociale Wetenschappen en Politieke Cultuur, 1945–2002,* 2014.
[56] Roelofsen, "Jan Hendrik Willem Verzijl," 1995.
[57] Mazower, *Governing the World: The History of an Idea, 1815 to the Present,* 2012.

International Relations, modeled after the British Institute for Foreign
Affairs, an initiative developed after the Paris Peace Conference of 1919.
Nearly all of the practical suggestions from the memorandum of
Tinbergen, Verzijl, and Van Asbeck on the international order ended up
in the Breakthrough movement's program (Figure 9.2).[58]
  One of the other prominent symbols of the Breakthrough movement
was the newspaper *Het Parool*. The newspaper was founded during the
occupation, and many of its editors had been arrested by the Germans. It
became a symbol of resistance on the progressive side and a symbol of the
desired unity that should be achieved after the war. Before the war all
national newspapers had had direct ties to a particular party, and a clear
ideological profile. Tinbergen started consulting with the editors of the
newspaper in the spring of 1945 on economic matters.[59] And briefly after
the liberation of May 1945 Tinbergen also published in the newspaper.[60]
That not everyone was ready for such a nonpartisan newspaper is clear
from the reactions that Tinbergen received. The editor of *Vrije Volk*, the
party newspaper of the SDAP, wrote of his shock and disappointment at
this choice; he felt betrayed. Tjalling Koopmans mildly mocked Tinbergen
for his contributions to the newspaper.[61] It might help explain why
Tinbergen did not fully commit to the Breakthrough movement, nor
indeed to the new paper.
  The Breakthrough movement was only partially successful in breaking
up the existing party system in the Netherlands. Its major result was the
new Labor Party (Partij van de Arbeid, PvdA), which was no longer
committed to Marxism or socialism as the SDAP had been. It was a
broader party that hoped to recruit progressives from all classes, and it
incorporated some smaller progressive Christian and humanist parties.
This new party was hoped to embody the pragmatist spirit in matters of
economic policy that the Plan of Labor had failed to bring about. And it
was based on the personalist socialism that many of the generation of
Tinbergen picked up in the youth movement of the 1920s. But the formation of this Labor Party was much less than the Breakthrough movement
had hoped for. It managed to find unity between just a few parties (the
large SDAP and a few small ones). The progressives in the other major

[58] Van Asbeck, Tinbergen, and Verzijl, *Bouwstof voor de Oplossing van Na-Oorlogsche Vraagstukken*, 1946. The manuscript was prepared and circulated in 1944, NIOD, archive 217b, inv. no 1.
[59] NIOD archive 185c, inv. no. 61.
[60] "Wat zal Amerika doen," *Het Parool*, 16 May 1945.
[61] Tjalling Koopmans to JT, 18 July 1945, TL.

parties, with a few exceptions, stayed where they were, and they failed to convince major blocs of Catholics or Protestants to join the party. The new Labor Party would still find itself in a situation where it was competing with a major Protestant, a major Catholic, and a liberal party. Not surprisingly, some within the Breakthrough movement felt that the founding of the Labor Party came too quick. Perhaps all it managed to achieve was to complete the transformation of the SDAP from an ideological party for the working class to a social-democratic party of the people.

To make matters worse, the immediate electoral success of the new Labor Party was limited. The coalition government that was formed based on these 1946 elections was headed by Willem Drees. But he and his coalition represented a more conservative version of left-wing politics, especially compared with the emergency government that ruled the country leading up the first postwar elections, from June 1945 to July 1946. That interim government was influenced strongly by members of the Seventeen Gentlemen, and appointed as minister of industrial affairs Hein Vos, Tinbergen's close friend and the first openly gay minister of the country.

Although its political success was limited, the movement was more successful in changing the position of science in society.[62] The scientists who felt attracted to the Breakthrough movement shared two basic beliefs: First, that scientists had a moral responsibility toward their fellow men; this could be practical, such as engineering knowledge, but also moral, in the guidance they provided. Second, that science could be of use to improve human beings themselves, in the form of emancipation. This combined vision was present during the early years of the Central Planning Bureau, which Tinbergen headed. Ed van Cleeff, his friend from the 1930s, was put in charge of the second emancipatory goal, which explored how the quality of life could be improved, while Tinbergen focused more on the technology of economic planning.[63]

Although Van Cleeff's program always remained more a hope than a reality,[64] the goal remained on the mind of many of that generation, including Tinbergen. Not long after the Dutch economy was back on track, he shifted his focus back to social, cultural, and spiritual goals, as we will see in later chapters. Behind these ideas was still De Man's insight that the

---

[62] Somsen, "Waardevolle Wetenschap. Bespiegelingen over Natuurwetenschap, Moraal en Samenleving in de Aanloop naar de Doorbraakbeweging," 2001.

[63] Van den Bogaard, "Economie als Wiskundige Abstractie of als Uitdrukking van Zingeving? Strijdende Visies bij het Ontstaan van het Centraal Planbureau," 2001.

[64] In 1973 a Social and Cultural Planning Bureau (SCP) was founded, modeled after the economic Central Planning Bureau.

real threat for the modern worker was not material impoverishment, but moral and cultural impoverishment. In 1945, Tinbergen together with Burgers calculated how many workers would be available for "cultural work"; in their eyes the Reconstruction should be not merely material but also cultural.[65] And at the CPB Ed van Cleeff and Harry de Lange worked on sociocultural subjects, which Tinbergen encouraged.[66] One of the most prominent voices of the Breakthrough movement and a friend of Tinbergen, Harry de Lange, would later write of the period: "Perhaps outsiders believe that calculation – or even just numbers – is your passion. They are mistaken, because you calculate, because you know that the foundations of our society – first nationally and later internationally – are in danger."[67] Another voice of the Breakthrough movement, and former SDAP member, Marinus van der Goes van Naters, suggested in a similar vein that Tinbergen's greatest contribution to economics had been to have made it a moral science again, a science with a sense of responsibility, in the spirit of Adam Smith.[68]

These close friends and acquaintances of Tinbergen were correct. He did share their ideals, and he did personally believe that through his economic work he was contributing to the realization of a set of moral ideals. Tinbergen also shared their idea of moral leadership, and he sought to embody the society he hoped to realize through his lifestyle. But outsiders can be forgiven for failing to notice this most of the time, as the ideals are often well hidden in his technical economic work. What is more, Tinbergen himself often drew a sharp line between economics and morality. To keep the former pure and neutral, it had to stay away from both philosophy and ethics. In that sense Tinbergen actively worked against the synthesis of social, moral, and economic ideals that his close friends sought. That same tension was also visible in the CPB.

The prominent position gained by "neutral" experts in policymaking and policy institutes was indicative of a fundamental change in the way that the modern state was organized, and in the position that science had in modern society. It has therefore been suggested that the Central Planning Bureau, the center of economic expertise, of which Tinbergen

[65] Somsen, "Waardevolle Wetenschap. Bespiegelingen over Natuurwetenschap, Moraal en Samenleving in de Aanloop naar de Doorbraakbeweging," 2001.
[66] Witte-Rang, *Geen Recht de Moed te Verliezen. Leven en Werken van Dr. H. M. de Lange (1919–2001)*, 2008.
[67] De Lange in Jolink and Barendrecht-Tinbergen, *Gedeelde Herinneringen*, 1993.
[68] Van der Goes van Naters in ibid.

became the first director, was a typical Breakthrough institution.[69] We will discuss the Bureau in more detail in the next chapter, but it is important to note that no simple line can be drawn between the CPB and the Breakthrough movement. The expertise of the CPB came to function in service of the state, and never managed to realize the Breakthrough dream of emancipation through knowledge. The way that the Bureau functioned was more instrumental than emancipatory. Tinbergen was open to the possibility of more emancipatory qualities of knowledge, and the development of a cultural agenda within the CPB by his friend Ed van Cleeff. And he recognized this quality in the work of others. To the editors of *Het Parool* he suggested Wilhelm Röpke's book *The Social Crisis of Our Times*.[70] The book was influential in the formation of neoliberalism at the time. But Tinbergen identified a set of qualities in Röpke that he found lacking in men of science such as Tjalling Koopmans: a sense of responsibility, a lack of dogmatism, and a visionary quality.[71] These qualities were necessary for the moral and intellectual leadership the Breakthrough movement aspired to.[72]

The CPB under Tinbergen's directorship never attained such a cultural or emancipatory position in society. Tinbergen's own models were crucially policy models, meant to inform interventions by the state. In the 1930s his inaugural lecture spoke of "mathematics and statistics in service of business-cycle research," but by the mid-1940s it had become "mathematics, statistics and business-cycle research in service of the state." Tinbergen did not succeed in combining that program with the emancipatory goals of his friends in the Breakthrough movement.

9.4 The Reconstruction Years

The diversion of the Breakthrough program was partly caused by the circumstances. The elections of 1946 enforced the start of a new political

---

[69] Van den Bogaard, "Economie als Wiskundige Abstractie of als Uitdrukking van Zingeving? Strijdende Visies bij het Ontstaan van het Centraal Planbureau," 2001; Somsen, "Waardevolle Wetenschap. Bespiegelingen over Natuurwetenschap, Moraal en Samenleving in de Aanloop naar de Doorbraakbeweging," 2001.

[70] Röpke, *The Social Crisis of Our Time*, 1950. The book appeared in German in 1942 as *Gesellschaftskrise der Gegenwart*.

[71] De B. to Sjef and Chiel (full names are not used because the paper was still underground), 15 March 1944, NIOD archive 185c, inv. no. 61.

[72] Tinbergen, "De Plaats van den Econoom in de Maatschappij," 1946; Tinbergen, "De Derde Weg," 1946.

party, and Tinbergen's work, like that of most of his friends, was dictated by necessity, not choice, during the early Reconstruction years. It is easily forgotten that the worst shortages in many Western European countries were in the immediate postwar years, not during the war. And the rationing systems implemented during the war existed, depending on the particular good, for another two to four years; the market for coffee in the Netherlands was finally "liberated" in 1952. Macroeconomically, inflation was a big worry, as was the shortage of dollars to pay for necessary imports.[73] Before dreams of a better society could come to fruition, necessity called.

Much as during the war years, a great deal of Tinbergen's time was spent on practical matters in the Reconstruction years. The Central Planning Bureau, which he now headed, began with great ambitions of creating a more stable economy and the formulation of rational and effective economic policies. Its name reflected the ambition, particularly of Hein Vos, that a new era of the planned economy had arrived. It was therefore more than a little ironic that in these first years Tinbergen's policy assignments were aimed at "unplanning" the economy.[74] The first task after the war was to free up the economy again. Ever the quick writer, Tinbergen already produced a booklet on this challenge in 1945, in which he argued that planning should concern only the broad outlines, a vision that in France and other countries would come to be known as "indicative planning."[75] But particularly in the first years, the major challenge facing the country and its policymakers was how to balance the current needs with those of the future.

There was a shortage of nearly all consumption goods, but there was an equally pressing need for investments in the productive capacity for the future and in the reconstruction of destroyed infrastructure. It is part of Tinbergen's legacy that a radical choice was made in favor of future requirements. He had always favored thrift in his personal life, and the

[73] Tinbergen, "Dollarschaarste en Prijsaanpassing," 1947; Tinbergen, "Some Remarks on the Problem of Dollar Scarcity," 1949.
[74] Tinbergen, "Het Nederlandsche Welvaartplan," 1946; Tinbergen, "Gesteld, dat men Tezijnertijd het Huidige Systeem van Geleide Economie weer Geheel of Gedeeltelijk door een Stelsel van Vrije Economie zal willen Vervangen, welke Voorwaarden moeten dan zijn Vervuld en welke Maatregelen zullen daartoe moeten worden Genomen," 1947.
[75] Tinbergen, *Enkele Problemen van Centrale Planning*, 1945; for a comparative perspective on planning in various European countries, see Desrosières, *The Politics of Large Numbers: A History of Statistical Reasoning*, chapters 5 and 6, 2002.

reconstruction plans of the CPB proposed to put the entire country on a strict diet. It is hard to imagine now, but the precise supply of many goods was determined at a central level in the rationing system of those years. This choice also reflected Tinbergen's belief that it was more important to focus on the structural side, the production capacity, of the economy.

One of his employees at the CPB, Jaap Hartog, described wonderfully how thrift and prudence were both preached and practiced at the new economic planning institution. In 1946, there was an actual list of the precise amount of semi-luxury products, such as new plates or stockings, that would be available in the country that year.[76] The employees of the CPB were also constantly made aware of the costs that they themselves imposed on society; an infamous sign at the office reminded everyone of how much the bureau cost per day.[77]

In 1952, the social-democratic newspaper even half-jokingly wondered whether the country could still afford the St. Nicolas celebration (the Dutch equivalent of Christmas). The spoof article suggested hard numbers were required to make the decision. And so, the spoof suggested, Tinbergen at the CPB had to be asked to explore the different options: no St. Nicolas, St. Nicolas without his horse and scepter, St. Nicolas with scepter but without horse, St. Nicolas only in department stores and not private homes, and so on. For all scenarios, the effects on import, export, employment levels, economic growth, and school grades (there would be less incentive now to be a "good boy") would be calculated. The findings would be reported on 8 December, three days after the celebrations on 5 December.[78] Planning for the future was hard, when so much was happening in the present.

There was one shortage that was plaguing the Netherlands and Europe more generally after the war: a shortage of dollars. Tinbergen wrote often about the subject in these years, even resulting in a formal model that was published in *Econometrica*.[79] This shortage of dollars was directly related to low exports and high imports (because of the shortages), and therefore to the balance of trade. Tinbergen worked briefly but intensely on this subject. In all of his articles, both popular and more scientific, he started

---

[76] Hartog in Jolink and Barendrecht-Tinbergen, *Gedeelde Herinneringen*, 1993.

[77] Glinstra-Bleeker in ibid.

[78] "Het is niet alleen Verantwoord, het is zelfs Onmisbaar," *Het Vrije Volk*, 29 November 1952.

[79] Tinbergen and Van der Werff, "Four Alternative Policies to Restore Balance of Payments Equilibrium: A Comment and an Extension," 1953; Tinbergen, "Some Remarks on the Problem of Dollar Scarcity," 1949.

from the idea that countries should have a "balanced" balance of payments: imports could not exceed exports.[80] This meant that in these difficult years of scarcity and shortages, the Netherlands had to export as much as it could. Only the fact that the Dutch guilder was devalued not long after the war brought some (temporary) relief.

Most economists, then and now, are quick to point out that a balance of payments should never be a goal in itself. The fact that Tinbergen argued for it is another example of how his work was sometimes shaped by political constraints rather than scientific concerns. The requirement of the balanced budget was a political constraint in these years, which he internalized in his writings. When he later worked in developing countries, he was very willing to accept (temporary) shortages on the trade balance.

We have compared Tinbergen and Keynes more often in the previous chapters, but here we hit upon a crucial difference between the two. Part of Keynes's legacy is a focus on the short run ("in the long run we're all dead"). Tinbergen, on the contrary, was always focused on the future and the long run. In the context of the reconstruction, this meant that we could hope for a better future but would have to make sacrifices in the present. Or to express it in economic terms: consumption had to be restricted so that we could save for a better future.[81] It would be a few years before he would write explicitly about the optimal savings rate, expressing his admiration for the level of savings achieved under communism,[82] but it was in these years that he put a similar vision into practice. Later, he himself acknowledged that the rationing regime might have been a little too strict.

The Reconstruction years were one of the interesting instances in which Tinbergen's personal vision of thrift was in near perfect accord with his policy views. His thrift was notorious: he never owned a car, measured the amount of water he took to cook tea, rejected any of the perks that increasingly came with his status as world-renowned professor, and apologized for "indulging" in chocolate milk rather than plain milk with his lunch by suggesting that it contained more calories. This outlook made Tinbergen an unlikely Keynesian, and he never became an enthusiast for the Keynesian recipe of deficit spending. Although he believed that Keynes

---

[80] Tinbergen, "Deense Problemen," 1947; Tinbergen, "Het Evenwicht in de Dollarbalans," 1950; Tinbergen, "Unstable Equilibria in the Balance of Payments," 1946.

[81] Tinbergen, *De Betekenis van het Sparen voor het Herstel van de Volkswelvaart*, 1950.

[82] Tinbergen, "The Optimum Rate of Saving," 1956; Tinbergen, "Optimum Savings and Utility Maximization over Time," 1960.

had done much for business-cycle research, Tinbergen was skeptical of the idea of the multiplier and never an enthusiast for government spending in the abstract.[83] It is more generally true that Tinbergen never became very skeptical of markets. Although he knew the danger of macro-imbalances and the business-cycle mechanism, he remained wedded to a belief in the working of the price system and private initiative.[84] The reconstruction and industrialization were the responsibility of entrepreneurs, not the state, he argued in a prominent newspaper article.[85] And his reports on the (rental) housing market, one of the most problematic markets during the reconstruction years, demonstrate that his main goal was to restore market rates, although he argued that this could be done only incrementally.[86]

Tinbergen's forward-looking attitude, however, had something in common with the younger Keynes. Reconstruction was about building peace, not taking revenge, as Keynes had argued after World War I. After World War II, it was Tinbergen's turn to argue against demands in the Netherlands that were frequently heard: reparations and territory.[87] Such demands were mistaken, he argued; what was required was a spirit of international cooperation and the construction of an international order.

***

What his work in the Reconstruction years demonstrates more than anything is that in these years he was not able to develop his own research agenda. Whereas the war had still left some opportunities for him to work on bigger book projects and more strictly scientific economic themes, this was not true during the first five years after the war. His work during this period responded to whatever current policy challenge he was facing; his research autonomy was more limited than ever. One thing illustrates that perhaps better than anything else. It took until 1952 before the CPB started working with an economic model that approached the sophistication of the 1936 model of the Dutch economy. More than fifteen years had passed before Tinbergen could finally put his model to good use.

---

[83] Tinbergen, "The Significance of Keynes' Theories from the Econometric Point of View," 1947.

[84] Tinbergen, "Gesteld, dat men Tezijnertijd het Huidige Systeem van Geleide Economie weer Geheel of Gedeeltelijk door een Stelsel van Vrije Economie zal willen Vervangen, welke Voorwaarden moeten dan zijn Vervuld en welke Maatregelen zullen Daartoe moeten worden Genomen," 1947.

[85] Tinbergen, "Kern van Industrialisatie dient te Berusten bij Ondernemers," 1948.

[86] Sociaal-Economische Raad, *Advies inzake het Vraagstuk van de Huren*, 1953.

[87] Tinbergen, "Herstelbetalingen," 1946.

During these fifteen years, most of his activities were in his role as civil servant, dominated by political requirements. This was true for his work at the League of Nations; it was true during the war years at the Bureau of Statistics; and it was equally true during the first five years at the Central Planning Bureau. One of the major themes in this biography is how Tinbergen was able to find a place for economic policy expertise. But this chapter has also made clear that there is a story to be told from the other side: how the state was able to mobilize modern economic expertise in its service. Tinbergen was one of their most successful recruits. We have not yet reached the year 1954 in our story, when Tinbergen would bid farewell to his position as a civil servant in the Netherlands. But at least from one perspective, we should call that moment his own "liberation," even if, with his own deep sense of responsibility, he never would have called it that.

10

Tinbergen's Theory of Economic Policymaking

This institute costs 1000 guilders a day. What is your contribution?
—Cardboard sign at the CPB[1]

Between 1945 and 1955 Tinbergen was the director of the Central Planning
Bureau (CPB). It was the period in which he most actively shaped macroeconomic policy in his home country, and the tools he developed during
this period are still in use today. The techniques Tinbergen developed at
the CPB relied crucially on the macro-econometric models of the 1930s.
But we will see that a quite fundamental shift in the modeling techniques
took place during this period. This shift was directly motivated by his
role as policy advisor. The 1930s models were primarily designed to
explain the dynamics of the economy with the hope that this might provide
clues about how to stabilize it. His 1936 model had even contained a
primitive simulation of the likely effects of various proposed policies. But
policy was still believed to be an external influence, an intervention, in the
economy system. The decision models he developed of the 1950s put
the policymaker, and thus implicitly the economic expert, into the model.
The policymaker became an economic decisionmaker just like the producers and consumers. If the intended audience of the 1930s was economic
theorists, those of the 1950s were designed for policymakers. For
Tinbergen the change marked his new position, as the premier economic
policy expert of the period. In economics it marked the age of macroeconomic management, sometimes known as the era of Keynesianism.

If there was any doubt that Tinbergen would be primarily a policy
economist, rather than an academic economist, that doubt was squashed
in this period. In hindsight that might seem obvious. But some of the more

---

[1] Glinstra Blinker in Jolink and Barendrecht, *Gedeelde Herinneringen*, 81, 1993.

important students and peers of Tinbergen and Ragnar Frisch chose the latter path and continued to contribute at a fundamental level to the development of econometrics and economic theory more broadly, most notably Tjalling Koopmans and Trygve Haavelmo at the Cowles Commission. Tinbergen and Frisch instead sought to formulate simpler models that could be used in policy. Their decision models with target and instrument variables turned the traditional logic of econometric modeling upside down. The goal for Tinbergen was not to identify fundamental economic relationships, but instead to analyze as simply as possible what was most likely to influence different policy decisions.

In the war years, Tinbergen worked extensively on the nature of equilibria inspired by Goudriaan.[2] But it was a remark by Goudriaan that Tinbergen kept returning to: "It is of no use to study an essentially indeterminate system,"[3] a remark that was both simple and deep at the same time. This was a radical version of the critique that both his Dutch and League of Nations model had received. Nearly all commentators had worried about the stability of particular relationships Tinbergen identified, and this prompted Frisch and Haavelmo to investigate their "autonomy," their relative stability. Tinbergen himself became convinced that the problem was not merely methodological but represented a more fundamental problem in the study of the economy.

The relevant question was not whether the identified relationship was stable, but whether the economic system as a whole was stable. If it was not, then any scientific investigations of it were bound to fail, since after all science requires some degree of stability. The problem was not the incompleteness of the model, but the indeterminate underlying structure of the economy. Goudriaan frequently used the metaphor of the collapsing bridge to contrast his vision with that of the cyclical movement typical of business-cycle theories.[4] The system might not even tend to equilibrium in the absence of certain preconditions.[5] While Haavelmo and Koopmans were perfecting a methodology to model the macro-economy, Tinbergen

---

[2] Tinbergen, "Over Verschillende Soorten Evenwicht en de Conjunctuurbeweging," 1943.

[3] The note occurs repeatedly in Tinbergen's archive. For a direct quote, see Tinbergen, *Shaping the World Economy*, 188–89, 1962; and for a more general appreciation, Tinbergen, "Goudriaans Analystische Economie," 1952.

[4] Rodenburg, "The Goudriaan–Tinbergen Debate on Dynamics and Equilibrium: 1931–1952," 2010.

[5] This idea was also explored by others; see, for example, Dimand, "Fisher, Keynes, and the Corridor of Stability," 2005; Assous and Carret, "(In)Stability at the Cowles Commission," 2020.

had slowly moved on to something much more ambitious: reforming the economy so that it would become a determinate and predictable *system*.

This had two components. First, there was the institutional component of making sure that there was a stable framework in which the economy could function; that framework was the appropriate *Ordnung* of the economy. Second, there was the more practical economic planning of investments and more generally the targeting of certain outcomes. The combination of both could set the economy on a determinate path, but stability should never be taken for granted. Therefore, he called the main task of the Central Planning Bureau task-setting, and throughout his career he remained dismissive of attempts to predict the course of the economy. This development led to his seminal books, which are the core of his oeuvre, on economic policy and the optimal level of decision-making.[6]

At the institutional level many of the changes proposed in the Plan of Labor came to fruition. The most important of these were the CPB and the Socio-Economic Council (SER). The former was a bureau of planning and modeling expertise, while the latter was a forum for the discussion of socioeconomic policy between experts, employers, and employees. The SER soon became known in the Netherlands as the second parliament. It was this institution that was crucial in creating acceptance for the new type of economic expertise. The postwar decade was thus crucial for finding a place for modern economic expertise within the nation-state and the development of tools for the pursuit of particular policy goals.

10.1 Economic Dynamics without Policy

During World War II, Tinbergen published a textbook on economic dynamics.[7] It was the first of his books that contained the extremely clear expository style that would come to characterize most of his works. In the first half of the book, different types of economic movements were introduced to the reader. Systematic movements were differentiated from random movements, and trend movements were distinguished from cyclical. The cyclical movements were subdivided into damped, undamped, and anti-damped (explosive) movements. This approach reflected Tinbergen's style: systematic, clear, and always with practical illustrations. Perhaps it was the influence of his parents that Tinbergen always wrote as

[6] Tinbergen, "On the Theory of Economic Integration," 1952; Tinbergen, *Centralization and Decentralization in Economic Policy*, 1954.
[7] Tinbergen, *Economische Bewegingsleer*, 1943.

if he were teaching: his books are those of a schoolmaster laying out the field. Setting out theoretical frameworks in their most basic and simplest way would remain his biggest strength and would be one of the reasons why he had such a long-lasting influence over the way in which economics was taught in the Netherlands.[8] But the book was also interesting for how it laid out Tinbergen's conception of economics: "[T]he subject matter of economic science is the process of the satisfaction of human needs. This process takes place within the framework of natural, technical, and institutional conditions that may be considered as given."[9] This represented the standard view of the 1930s, which took as exogenous to the model not merely the technical conditions of production but also the institutional decision structure of the economy. By the 1950s Tinbergen has endogenized this decision structure. After the 1950s his central question became that of the optimal decision-making structure, or what he called the optimal (institutional) order, rather than the study of economic dynamics within a given structure.

Tinbergen's book on economic dynamics hinted only in a few places that the real goal of all this inquiry into the nature and causes of the business cycle was to be able to control the cycle. The strictures of the war meant that he could not develop his work in the direction of policy, but in the concluding chapter Tinbergen cautiously suggested that "the task of business cycle policy is to indicate how the structure of a system should be changed in order to arrive at the most stable growth trend. The possibility exists that stable growth can only be achieved at the cost of a lower growth rate."[10] It already clearly hinted at what he had in mind for the postwar economic order. Fundamental changes had to make the economy more stable, and that would probably come at the cost of some of the dynamism in the economy.

But what these fundamental changes would be was still mostly unclear. The planning debates of the 1930s had not led to very clear results, and the meaning of planning was still contested. Tinbergen had expressed admiration for public works, and particularly the investment in public works when the economy was undergoing a downturn. But on a more structural level, it was not yet clear what modern economic policy could be. In the

---

[8] Dalen and Klamer, *Telgen van Tinbergen: Het Verhaal van de Nederlandse Economen*, 1996.

[9] Tinbergen, *Economische Bewegingsleer*, 109, 1943; translated as Tinbergen and Polak, *The Dynamics of Business Cycles: A Study in Economic Fluctuations*, 1950.

[10] Tinbergen, *Economische Bewegingsleer*, 268, 1943.

League of Nations study, he had distinguished between three types of policy: (1) changes in the coefficients or lags, (2) shocks, and (3) changes in the average level of some variable.[11] For (3), he provided the example of minimum-wage legislation, which he considered of very limited relevance for business-cycle policy. As far as shocks were concerned, it was clear that they could also be used to correct the course of the economy. An external shock would then be countered with a "policy shock" in the opposite direction. Public works were an example, but they were reactive at best. And they left the underlying system untouched.

What a change in the coefficients or lags would entail was hard to grasp, even for those familiar with his formal modeling theory. There was no reason to assume that the estimated lags and coefficients in his models were amenable to policy, and even if they were, his model provided no sense of how they could be altered.[12] It showed how particular variables such as investment changed when other variables such as the interest rate changed. The coefficient reflected the relative strength of this relationship. But the model did not provide guidance about the meaning of these coefficients, or what determined them in turn. In fact, much of the criticism directed at his modeling approach was aimed at those coefficients: Were they stable over time, between countries, and did they reflect under-lying economic realities? Or were they primarily statistical artifacts? In Frisch's terms, how autonomous were they?

In his League of Nations report, Tinbergen did provide a practical example of a tax on consumption, which would lower the propensity to consume, but, as he admitted, it was unclear how this would impact the rest of the system. How one could get rid of lags in the system was even less clear. A lagged reaction occurs primarily because of long production times or a belated response caused by some other factors such as ignorance, and it was unclear how this could be prevented. What is more, most types of stabilization policies proposed would make the economy more rigid, not more flexible, and hence increase the importance of lags. Hence to suggest that policy could alter these coefficients was little more than hand-waving at the time. It did suggest that Tinbergen was already thinking about changing the structure of the economy, rather than fixing certain variables. It was structural change that he was after, and not the correction of preexisting movements. In that sense Tinbergen's program was a lot more

---

[11] Tinbergen, *Statistical Testing of Business-Cycle Theories: II Business Cycles in the United States of America 1919–1932*, 166, 1939.
[12] Orcutt, "Toward the Partial Redirection of Econometrics," 1952.

ambitious than the famous regime of anticyclical Keynesian policies, which is a purely reactive regime.

10.2 Not Prediction, Task-Setting

In 1945, Tinbergen was called upon to become the director of the Central Planning Bureau by Hein Vos, his great ally in the socialist Plan movement of the 1930s. In the government of national unity, Hein Vos had become Minister of Trade and Industry. It was in many ways a crucial moment in Tinbergen's career. As one of the pioneers in econometrics and the first one to build a macro-econometric model, as well as former head economist of the League of Nations, Tinbergen was on the path to become one of the most prominent economists of the world. But in order to realize that, he would have had to leave the Netherlands and move to one of the burgeoning centers of economic research in the United States, or perhaps Cambridge or Oxford in the United Kingdom. Tjalling Koopmans, who had worked with him closely in Geneva, joined the Cowles Commission in Chicago in 1944. There he joined the cream of the crop of professional economists and mathematical social scientists, who in 1947 included Jacob Marschak, Kenneth Arrow, Evsey Domar, Lawrence Klein, Don Patinkin, Trygve Haavelmo, Leonid Hurwicz, and Herbert Simon (six of whom would later win a Nobel Prize).

Tinbergen, however, opted for a political advisory position, where he was able to surround himself with some of his friends from the 1930s who shared his vision of transforming the structure of the economy: Ed van Cleeff, H. Stuvel, Johannes Petrus Verdoorn,[13] and Johan Witteveen, most of whom he had trained. It was a setting full of bustling enthusiasm, with a group hand-picked by Tinbergen that largely shared a common perspective. These young men were all part of a new generation of social scientists who sought to improve society through rational means. When the Bureau officially opened, the average age of its employees was only thirty-one.[14] But despite all the enthusiasm and shared spirit, the CPB remained a policy institute; it was not an academic center. And his colleagues were promising Dutch economists, but not a selection of the best migrants from all over Europe as could be found at the Cowles Commission or at Oxford. As Tinbergen would put it later: "[W]e studied not primarily in order to

---

[13] Verdoorn is famous for the so-called Verdoorn's law, which states that long-run productivity generally grows proportionally to the square root of output.
[14] Passenier, *Van Planning naar Scanning: Een Halve Eeuw Planbureau in Nederland*, 1994.

develop theory, instead our concern was to solve the problems of the day, and to provide policy advice."[15]

Tinbergen himself was important in the founding of this new institute through a memorandum he had circulated in 1943, in which he argued in favor of a deliberate business-cycle policy (*Conjunctuurpolitiek*) in the broadest sense of that term, including the maintenance of a high level of economic activity. In order to do this, Tinbergen favored planning the broad outlines of the economy with as much space left for individual economic activity as possible. The government ought to provide a broad framework that included structural policies aimed at the control of global wage development and tax policies. In order to realize these types of policies, he proposed a new institute that would function as the fourth section of the Central Bureau of Statistics, where he still worked at the time.

By 1945, the plan had become more ambitious and the idea now was that it should be an independent institute. This reflected the increased importance that Hein Vos gave to the institute, but also the fact that planning was quite different from statistical work. The CBS was ultimately an accounting organization, taking stock of what had happened, studying trends of the past. The CPB was fundamentally different: it was forward-looking and sought to shape the course of the economy.

But the precise position and purpose of the CPB was anything but clear. Not only did it take a full two years before the legal basis of the new institute was fully approved in parliament; it was also unclear what the status of its recommendations would be. The first postwar government, which was shaped so heavily by the progressive Breakthrough movement, believed that an integrated plan could form the basis for nearly all economic policy of the government. Vos and Tinbergen believed that the development of the plan would be the primary responsibility of the Bureau. But it soon became clear that the responsible ministers in the second postwar government had no intention at all to outsource policymaking to the new institute.[16]

To complicate matters further, the institutional position of the CPB was unclear. At this early stage the CPB was strongly dependent on the good will of the current government. This had advantages. Tinbergen was also a member of the small committee of ministers in which the Plan for 1946 was discussed. But it also had clear downsides: whereas Vos and Tinbergen believed that the (draft) Plan could be published in order to gain

---

[15] Tinbergen quoted in ibid., 58.
[16] Don, "The Influence of Jan Tinbergen on Dutch Economic Policy," 2019.

support for the policies, the other members of the cabinet insisted that this could be done only when the Plan had become official policy, which meant that a public version would represent not the expert consensus, nor the vision of the CPB, but instead the vision of the government.

At stake was also the relevant notion of planning. While Tinbergen had already come around to the idea that the main role of the government in the economy was to provide stability, others still clung to a 1930s notion of planning, in which the planning of production was key. The latter obviously entailed a deeper change in the decision structure of the economy. This older (and more socialist) understanding of planning was also frequently used to make Tinbergen's own version of planning politically suspicious.[17] The following years were characterized by a struggle to figure out the precise position and role of the institute. On the one hand, there was a desire for direct influence on policymaking, in which the yearly Plan developed by the CPB would be the direct basis for socioeconomic policy decisions. On the other hand, Tinbergen and others at the institute believed it was important that they could independently develop Plans and projections. That was impossible if they worked in the service of various ministries, because the CPB would soon become a party in the various internal debates. During the late 1940s, Tinbergen kept hoping that the yearly Plans of the CPB would provide the basis for a discussion in the small council of relevant ministers, but these remained reluctant to join him on his territory, and instead treated the Plans as one input for the formulation of their own policies.

Publication of the Plans, which sometimes contained criticism of government policies, was repeatedly refused. Tinbergen slowly but surely came to accept that his institute would function best as an advisory body. The economic experts remained advisors; they did not become lawmakers. This was certainly also due to the personal qualities, or perhaps the lack of political savvy, of Tinbergen. He himself recognized this well: "In America that was quite different; there they had the Council of Economic Advisors, and they forced themselves into politics, they played a much bigger role. The chairman was an ambitious man, he even tried to sell his ideas to the president, and he tried to tell him what to do. That is absolutely not in my nature. But he was someone of a quite different caliber, a smart politician."[18]

---

[17] De Jong, Van Paridon, and Passenier, "Jan Tinbergen over zijn Jaren op het CPB," 1988.
[18] Tinbergen cited in ibid. The chairman Tinbergen referred to was Edwin Nourse, who served under President Truman.

While Tinbergen might have dreamt of more direct influence on politics, the long-term outcome of the distance from the CPB to politics worked to its advantage, or at the very least contributed to its reputation. The institute came to represent a more anonymous type of expertise that depended not on the personal political and economic qualities of the head of the bureau, but rather on the methods employed by the CPB.

The founding of the CPB was part of a bigger overhaul of the structure of decision-making in the economy of the Netherlands, and Tinbergen was at the very heart of it. Part of the institutional design of the Plan of Labor had been a central economic committee. It was to provide the bridge between the political sphere and the economic sphere. In the early 1950s, two organizations were founded that closely resembled such a central committee. One was the SER; in this council, employers, employees, and expert members (officially called crown members) were represented in equal numbers, reflecting the idea that interests had to be represented equally and that joint-decision making was the new normal.[19] Tinbergen was one of the crown members and smartly used his dual role as director of the CPB and crown member to garner support for his economic plans.[20] Here, open discussion was much more acceptable since none of the members was politically tied, although of course the representatives of labor and capital were expected to represent their groups' interests.

The other crucial organization during this period was the Central Economic Council (CEC). In some ways it was a continuation of the small committee of involved ministers, but it was placed at some distance from the cabinet. In practice, it was the domain of senior civil servants as well as the head of the Central Bank, and Jan Tinbergen as director of the CPB. The advice by the CEC was much more likely to gain the support of the cabinet members because of the way it was institutionally embedded. On paper the institutional design of the Dutch political economy now strongly resembled that of the Plan of Labor (Figure 5.2). But that was on the surface; something quite important had changed since the 1930s. In the 1930s it was still believed that an institution like the SER or the CEC could coordinate policy and formulate an overall Plan for the next year, largely independent of government. The way it worked out institutionally was that in order to function as institutes of depoliticized expertise, the institutions had to function at some distance from politics. And the way these

---

[19] A somewhat similar institution was the Labor Council, which dealt with labor conditions, but which was organized similarly with representatives of labor, employers, and experts.
[20] Don, "The Influence of Jan Tinbergen on Dutch Economic Policy," 2019.

institutions found their place and purpose had as much to do with a process of trial and error as it had to do with design. The different institutions slowly found their place in the decision-making process, a place, moreover, that was not fixed in some design but was the outcome of the contestation between different institutions.

What Tinbergen discovered in his decade as director of the CPB was that institutions such as the CEC and the SER were crucial for the creation of widespread support for economic expertise. Models or Plans, however technically sophisticated, were unable to do this, and in fact might even generate resistance. Political support required bodies, committees, and organizations where the experts and the politicians and their senior advisors met. Therefore, the SER and the CEC were of great importance for the success of the technical advice of the CPB.

Tinbergen was well aware of these fundamental changes between the 1930s and the 1950s. He reflected on the modern form of policymaking in a brochure written in a Dutch neoliberal series. In that booklet he argued that the free market failed to order economic activity well. Prices and particularly wages adjusted slowly, and they therefore did a poor job at generating the appropriate adjustments. Tinbergen argued: "It is therefore curious, that it is more and more common, that conscious intervention (through *Ordnung*) is attempting to achieve that which theory has always suggested were the great merits of the system of free competition."[21] In other words, since the actual market failed to live up to the theoretical efficiency of markets, institutional design should be aimed at making actual markets resemble more those from ideal theory. This is not central planning of the Soviet type, and not even a central direction of investments, but much closer to the modern idea of correcting market failures. But whereas market failures are now believed to be particularly micro-phenomena, for example, negative externalities generated in the form of noise and air pollution by the flight industry, they were by and large macro-phenomena for Tinbergen. The biggest market failure of them all was the fact that markets did not generate stability, and hence it was up to the economists to suggest institutional improvements to economy to make it more stable.

In the free market economy, the dominant ordering principle is that of price, while in the postwar Dutch economy we see a mixture of at least three different ordering principles: price, expertise, and cooperation. Tinbergen's later quest for an optimal economic order should be regarded

[21] Tinbergen, *De Grenzen der Ordening*, 8–9, 1949.

as his attempt to find the right balance between these three ordering principles; he never argued that one could suffice or was superior in all respects. The SER was an example of cooperation, a platform where the different interests of labor and capital met. The CPB was an example of an expertise organization, which helped inform centralized decisions in the economy. And these institutions created a framework, or "ordered," the market that operated based on prices.

This institutional discovery process was important in another way. The new institutions such as the nationalized Central Bank, the SER, and the CEC were in control of crucial "levers" of policy. Key economic variables now came "under control of the government," and from the perspective of a policy expert like Tinbergen were thus no longer the background; rather, they became the foreground. An example of such a lever was the determination of wages. The central wage policy of the postwar years in the Netherlands meant effectively that wage development was agreed on collectively in the SER. That was one instrument available at the central level, and it coexisted with more commonly recognized instruments of the government: monetary and fiscal policy. Much of the postwar debate in macroeconomics was shaped by a controversy over the relative importance and effectiveness of monetary and fiscal policies, with the Keynesians favoring fiscal policies, while monetarists suggested that monetary policy should be primary. Tinbergen has hardly contributed to that debate, and yet the debate took place largely within his intellectual framework, because it was in his work that economic policy came to be understood as the pursuit of certain targets, with a set of instruments. Others fought over the most appropriate and effective instruments, but they were all working within Tinbergen's broader perspective on economic policymaking. This perspective resulted from his focus on the decision-making structure in the economy. After the founding of new institutions such as the CPB, the nationalized Central Bank, and the SER, crucial economic decisions were now "set" or "controlled" by policymakers.[22]

Within this changed decision structure, the advice that the CPB could offer was different from that offered by business-cycle institutes in the 1930s. In those days, the institutes offered statistical overviews and

---

[22] We will not explore it here, but the struggle over the control of monetary policy and the use of econometric modeling techniques within the Dutch Central Bank represent an exemplary case study of this change; see Den Butter and Maas, "From Expert Judgment to Model Based Monetary Analysis: The Case of the Dutch Central Bank in the Post-war Period," 2011.

forecasts of particular markets, as well as some macroeconomic indicators. The CPB had a completely different position. It did not publish statistics at all; that was left to the CBS. Instead, it created projections about the requirements of the coming year, and suggested policy changes and limitations. It was Tinbergen's contribution, based on an idea by Ragnar Frisch (again), that it could do something more ambitious. It could suggest the "correct" values of key economic policy variables to achieve policy goals. Under his leadership, the institute's primary purpose was not to predict the course of the economy, as if it were a natural system; instead, its purpose was to demonstrate what needed to be done in order to achieve certain (realistic) policy goals.

Although deeply caught up in the shortage planning of the immediate postwar years, Tinbergen in 1947 already had developed a set of interesting reflections on planning and its functions. In front of a Danish crowd he explained what he believed to be the function of the new planning bureau he headed. The goal, he argued, was not to provide forecasts in the way that business-cycle institutes had done up to that point, but instead its advice "should contain an element of task-setting." The function was not merely to provide the best estimate of what would happen if the current tendencies continued, but more to improve those tendencies. He was still cautious at this point: "[I]t goes without saying that the task-setting element must always remain realistic."[23] It was a caution that perhaps reflected the political struggle over the precise status of the CPB and its plans. While still in Copenhagen, Tinbergen received a telegram that the law establishing the CPB had finally passed, that the Central Planning Bureau was now officially open, and that he was officially its first director.[24]

One might argue that all policy has this element of task-setting; we desire a certain growth rate or a certain level of unemployment. But this is not quite what Tinbergen had in mind. He continued: "[O]ne of the objectives of central planning, as distinct from individual and decentralized planning, is to reduce as much as possible the differences between what the Swedish economists would call ex ante and ex post values."[25] This difference between ex ante and ex post was important in many theories of the cycle, including not just the Swedish theory but also the Austrian variant. According to these theories, fluctuations in part arose because there were diverging expectations among producers about key economic variables

---

[23] Tinbergen, "Problems of Central Economic Planning in the Netherlands," 99, 1947.
[24] Passenier, *Van Planning naar Scanning: Een Halve Eeuw Planbureau in Nederland*, 1994.
[25] Tinbergen, "Problems of Central Economic Planning in the Netherlands," 100, 1947.

(ex ante), which diverged in important ways from the realized values (ex post). Tinbergen argued that providing a stable framework made it possible to coordinate the expectations of different individuals, firms, and government organizations, so that one of the fundamental causes of economic discoordination could be eliminated.[26] The ideas of planning that were implemented by Tinbergen and his colleagues at the CPB had much in common with business plans, in that they set targets that then had to be met and that coordinated activity within the firm. Except that now the country was the firm, and the targets were framed in terms of macro-economic variables.

National income accounts were therefore indispensable. Ed van Cleeff and J. B. D. Derksen, the latter had remained at the CBS, had done pioneering work on those during the war years. These income accounts provided a measuring rod for the policy targets. And this combination of targets and measurements of the macro-economy was far more essential than (dynamic) econometric models in the early years of the CPB.

It is important here to realize how far removed we already are from the 1930s attempt to smooth out the business cycle. Instead, Tinbergen was now thinking about institutional order and how this shaped economic activity and economic stability. For this, some econometric tools were necessary, but the extent to which certain parameters were stable in the econometric model was not merely a matter of methodology – did we estimate them correctly? – but also a matter of institutional stability. For many, the lesson of his League of Nations study was that we should improve our estimates of the relationships between key economic variables. For Tinbergen the lesson was rather different: How can we reform the structure of the economy so that some of these relationships become more stable? The content of economic policy was a key element in that project, but so was the institutional framework in which economic policy was shaped.

10.3 The Theory of Economic Policy

In the early years at the Central Planning Bureau, econometric models remained a distant dream. Tinbergen and his colleagues were trying to make do with the limited data that were available, which were often of a fragmentary nature. The time series they dealt with were very short or incomplete because of the war. And the data from the time before were

---

[26] Passenier, *Van Planning naar Scanning: Een Halve Eeuw Planbureau in Nederland*, 1994.

believed to be of limited value; after all, the economy was now differently organized.[27] What further complicated matters was that in the shortage years just after the war, almost the entire economy was planned; many consumption goods were still rationed, and important prices were still fixed; housing rents would remain price-controlled until 1953.[28] The status of the different reports of the CPB remained contested, despite Tinbergen's attempt to make them more binding and more explicit about the course of action to be followed.[29] But that did not prevent him from developing a framework of economic policymaking. This framework idealized away the messy process of getting the results discussed every year, but certainly did not become pure or abstract theory (ideal theory, as the philosophers call it). It took important political and scientific constraints into account. For example, it included a way to model political constraints, if certain policy options were simply not acceptable. And it did not aim for some optimal policy that would have been scientifically satisfactory but opted for an approach that focused on the feasibility of particular goals.

Much of the groundwork for his book on economic policy was contained in an addition to his book on economic dynamics published as part three in the third print of 1946. There Tinbergen laid out the goals of economic policy. Business-cycle policy, now aptly renamed structural policy, should aim to alter the functioning of the economy. Structural policies should aim to dampen or get rid of the endogenous cyclical movement within the economy.[30] So the real investigation of the economy should try to look for *preconditions* that limit the possibility of (strong) cyclical movements: "[O]ne cannot attain movements as stable as possible by leaving the reactions within the system as they are – after all that is why the empirical cyclical movement occurs – instead we should alter one or more of them."[31]

However, it took the contribution of Frisch to generate the breakthrough. As he later explained, the models of the 1930s represented the perspective of the onlooker, and the models of the 1950s placed the policymaker inside the model and were crucially "decision models," that

---

[27] De Jong, Van Paridon, and Passenier, "Jan Tinbergen over zijn Jaren op het CPB," 1988.
[28] Sociaal-Economische Raad, *Advies inzake het Vraagstuk van de Huren*, 1953.
[29] Passenier, *Van Planning naar Scanning: Een Halve Eeuw Planbureau in Nederland*, 1994. Passenier traced the mostly frustrated attempts by Tinbergen to set goals and frameworks for government policy. This meant that Tinbergen's direct influence on policy remained limited, but his indirect influence increased through the development of his theory of economic policy.
[30] Tinbergen, *Conjunctuurpolitiek*, 4–6, 1946.   [31] Ibid., 87.

is, models "where the possible decisions are built in *explicitly* as essential variables."[32] The first model of this kind was presented by Frisch for a UN committee in 1949.[33] Tinbergen immediately recognized the significance of this model, and within a year he was developing such decision models for the Netherlands.[34]

In his 1952 book *On the Theory of Economic Policy*, Tinbergen presented an integrated account of decision models. The decision models relied on the type of models of the economy Tinbergen had pioneered in the 1930s. But in those models, policy was considered an exogenous variable, which meant that policy was relevant but outside the domain of economic analysis. This is the reason why Frisch termed it the "onlooker approach." But by 1950 Tinbergen the economist no longer was an onlooker but was directly advising those in charge of policy. From the perspective of the policymaker, certain key economic variables were determined by their decisions, and hence were called decision variables in the model. It reversed the logic of economic modeling, because these models did not take policy as given (exogenous) and the behavioral coefficients as variable (endogenous). Instead, the decision models took the policy variables as amenable to change (endogenous), and they took the behavioral coefficients as given (exogenous) to the degree they could not be altered by policy.

Tinbergen's theory of economic policy was based around five elements: (1) the collective preference function, (2) the targets as deduced from this function, (3) the choice of instruments, (4) the determination of the quantitative values of these instruments, and (5) the model describing the relation of these instruments to the rest of the economy. Variables were the changing quantities in the economy that could be explained or chosen, while data were those factors external to the economy that were simply taken as given. Using this distinction, Tinbergen argued that "for economic analysis the policy is data, for economic policy the structure of the economy is data."[35]

Now that Tinbergen was in the driver's seat, or at least directly advising those who were, he developed models with the purpose of steering the economy. The idea that policy was that part of the economy that could be

[32] Frisch, "Preface to the Oslo Channel Model," 1962.
[33] Frisch, "Memorandum on Price-Wage-Tax Subsidy Policy as Instruments in Maintaining Optimal Employment," 1949.
[34] JT to Ragnar Frisch, 21 March 1950, NLN: FC.
[35] Tinbergen, "On the Theory of Economic Integration," 1952.

decided on might sound obvious, but it was a fundamental break with traditional economic models. Ever since the mathematical economists of the first generations such as Leon Walras had studied the economic system, the perspective had been one from outside the economic system. The economy was believed to be a natural system, which could be studied the same way that the natural scientist studied nature, as an outside observer. The 1930s saw various modifications to that view: government was increasingly seen as an active economic agent whose policies could change, and the dynamic models of that period sought to give more agency to planning firms and to consumers and their expectations about the future. Theorists of the time, most notably, Oskar Morgenstern, realized that this meant that economic predictions and policy would no longer be neutral descriptions from the outside, but that these would impact the plans of producers and consumers. Keynes had suggested how fear and panic, as well as exuberance, could impact the economy. Tinbergen had also acknowledged that the success of the New Deal policies in part depended on whether they had been supported and recognized by the entrepreneurs. But nobody had yet suggested that the economic expert as policy advisor had a position inside the economic model. But that is precisely what Frisch and Tinbergen's model of the early 1950s suggested.

The reversal of the 1930s logic was also visible in the way Tinbergen talked about completeness. Completeness in the 1930s models was the condition that the number of unknowns (variables) should not exceed the amount of structural equations. If this was the case, then there was a definite solution to the model. In the 1950s a model's completeness was defined as the relation between the number of policy instruments and targets. If the latter was equal or smaller than the former, the goals could be achieved, otherwise not. This latter condition is in policymaking circles still known as the Tinbergen rule.

The fact that certain key economic variables were now under the control of the Dutch "policymaker" was a consequence of the changing decision structure in the economy. Tinbergen was fully aware of this, as his discussion of the relation between instrument variables and targets demonstrated. He made it clear that the number of instruments could be larger or smaller depending on the institutional structure of the economy. The control over the wage level in the Netherlands, for example, was an instrument not available to policymakers in most other countries. On the other hand, for the Dutch policymakers, there were certain international policy variables that had to be taken as given, over which governments of bigger countries had more control. The structure of the economy had thus become the decision-making structure of the economy. This meant that institutional stability had, in the models, replaced the stability of behavioral relations in the economy.

Tinbergen was deeply aware of the fundamental shift this entailed.[36] His work on decision models can be understood as an admission that the 1930s problem of identifying a fundamental economic structure was not feasible. There was no fixed structure independent of the institutional organization of the economy. But he turned those limitations into new possibilities by arguing that policy could provide the necessary stability. Or perhaps, he made the most of his position as policy advisor by suggesting that steering the economy was more important than explaining its fundamental dynamics. In any case, he suggested that, in this new approach, knowing the underlying structure of the economy was not necessary for economic policymaking. A mere knowledge of the effect of certain interventions would suffice. In a historical sketch he suggested:

Originally the idea behind them [decomposition of unemployment figures into cyclical and structural components] was to distinguish cycles of different length, such as seasonal movements and shorter and longer cyclical movements; and the techniques used were devised according to this objective. A first shift intervened when gradually the empiristic viewpoint of business cycle research developed into a need for causal explanation. The techniques used were supposed to reveal, at the same time, movements due to different causes.[37]

Tinbergen clearly detailed the shift from the 1920s work on business-cycle statistics, which merely tracked economic movements, to the modeling approach he pioneered, and which was perfected at the Cowles Commission. But, he argued, many factors impact various types of unemployment, and so a simple decomposition into causal factors will not work. Therefore, a second shift was required, argued Tinbergen, one that moved away from causal factors and sought to analyze unemployment from the perspective of policymakers. From their perspective, what is to be addressed is not the causes of unemployment but what can be done to

---

[36] Tinbergen certainly did not hide this shift, but the secondary literature has given relatively little attention to it. One exception is Andvig, "From Macrodynamics to Macroeconomic Planning: A Basic Shift in Ragnar Frisch's Thinking?," 1988. Andvig was convinced that this amounted not merely to an evolution but to a revolution. He described the shift as an "ambitious all-embracing research programme that in reality had implications for most fields of economics, a program that in many ways collided head-on with the econometric revolution Frisch had once led."

[37] Tinbergen, "The Analysis of Unemployment Figures and the Alleged Correspondence between Causes and Cures," 43, 1953.

lower unemployment. Employment policy, he argued, is often undertaken with instruments that do not directly combat the causes of unemployment. Sometimes this is not possible; if the causes are international, say, resulting from tariffs, then they cannot be combatted on the national level. At other times it is undesirable or too costly to fight the underlying causes of a problem. But more generally, a policymaker is interested not so much in causes but rather in effective instruments, in solutions that work.

Tinbergen suggested that the 1930s program had been informative at best: "It seems useful, for a well-designed policy, not to ask for the historical causes of a given state of unemployment, but to ask for the optimum situation that the policy will be able to create."[38] The structure of the economy is given; we can change only the instruments; and hence we should study the effects of change in our instruments, not the causes of unemployment.[39] This was a quite fundamental break with the economic theoreticians of his age, who were still primarily interested in the causal structure of the economy. But for Tinbergen personally there was considerable consistency with his position from the 1930s. Even back then he had not been interested in theories of underlying causes. Now the focus on what worked had been given a more definite form.

Pragmatism was, however, far from the only motivation. Tinbergen was also attempting to change our perspective on society, to make us think like the economic expert, if you will. What makes Tinbergen's argument more fascinating and challenging is that he suggested that we should change the way we think about unemployment. Decomposition along causal lines is not the one that makes the most economic sense; instead, it is the decomposition along policy lines that is the most relevant. And that is what he provided.

He proposed the following decomposition. There is the minimum level of unemployment we find acceptable or that is too costly to fight (economists tend to call this the natural rate of employment). Then there is the part of total unemployment that can be effectively combatted with the use of policy instruments. And finally, there is that part of total unemployment

---

[38] Ibid., 44.
[39] This view has roots in the 1930s. In a comparison between Schumpeter's work on the business cycle and that of himself and Frisch, Tinbergen already made clear that while Schumpeter was interested in the true cause of the cycle (the shock), Frisch and he were more interested in the mechanism (how the shock propagated through the system). Tinbergen, "Schumpeter and Quantitative Research in Economics," 1951.

that cannot be eliminated with the current set of instruments. The decrease in unemployment reached through our instruments can then be further subdivided into two parts, one part that has been eliminated by fighting the cause and one part that has been eliminated otherwise.

This decomposition by cures makes sense only if, like Tinbergen, we conceive of the economist as engineer of the economy in control of a number of instruments. It does not make much sense if we think of the economist as the natural scientist who seeks to study the dynamics of the economy. It was this latter perspective that marked his work in the 1930s and that was summed up in his *Economic Dynamics.* Tinbergen made it abundantly clear that he favored the perspective of the economic engineer, and that was the major achievement of his postwar work.

If one follows his reasoning about unemployment, it is not difficult to make a similar argument about the business cycle. We can subdivide the cycle into the minimum level of fluctuations we are willing to accept, the part of the cycle that can be eliminated by policy instruments, and possibly the residual undesired movement. Analogous to what Tinbergen suggested for unemployment, the reduction in the cycle through instruments can then be further subdivided into those instruments that fight the causes and those that merely fight the effects.

What is taken as given in this new approach becomes entirely dependent on the perspective one takes, or, as Tinbergen would put it, the problem at hand. For him that is typically the perspective of the national policymaker. But nothing prevents one from applying those insights to that of the business owner, the regional planner, or the international policymaker. The economy is literally "made" by such decisions. The question of perspective is thus a direct outcome of institutional changes in the economy. In the classic economic model of perfect competition, the perspective of every decision-maker in the economy is identical: they are all small units whose decisions have only very limited effects on overall outcomes. Now that the economy is reordered, the perspective of different (institutional) actors in the economy is no longer identical. Major firms, like monopolies, shape markets; union leaders have direct influence on the overall wage development in the economy; and policymakers have certain policy instruments at their disposal that affect the other decision-makers quite directly. The development of economic expertise in the form of macroeconomic statistics, of policy institutes such as the CPB, and of economic modeling techniques such as the decision models have thus gone hand in hand to create a modern notion of economic policymaking.

There was, however, a quite serious tension left in the view he presented in his early 1950s work on economic policy.[40] It was a tension that, although Tinbergen seemed to be aware of, never quite came to occupy the central position it demands. In Tinbergen's engineering view, it was no longer clear what the fundamental structure of the economy was. Many other econometricians were looking for the underlying causal structure of the economy on which policy instruments operate. Their contention would be that this underlying structure was stable and that good policies depend precisely on accurate knowledge of this underlying causal structure of the economy. In Tinbergen's engineering view, the structure of the economy was merely a methodological decision, depending on one's perspective. If only monetary and fiscal policies were taken as instruments, then the occupational and regional structure of the economy could be taken for granted. But if one was interested in altering the regional structure of the economy or the occupational structure through education policies, as Tinbergen would be later, then these factors were not given as data, but were dependent on decision variables (instruments). This demonstrates well how constructivist Tinbergen was in his thinking about the economy. Nothing, or so it seems, was in principle completely given; everything could be influenced through structural policy.

But even if one is interested only in policy and the effectiveness of instruments, one does need some understanding of what structure the instruments are "operating" on. And, more importantly, we would like to know whether the effect of a particular instrument is (relatively) stable or, to complicate matters slightly, whether instruments do not negatively affect one another. To make decisions regarding policy requires the assumption that one can be relatively certain that the use of the instruments will have the desired effects. And hence the stability question rears its head again.

Part of the reason that Tinbergen did not pay as much attention to the question as one might expect was his deep sense of responsibility. In later interviews, he spoke of a "categorical imperative" for governments to take responsibility and to act.[41] And if one failed, one simply had to try again. Knowing about the underlying structure was helpful in figuring out what

---

[40] For a contemporary discussion over the exogenous and endogenous variables and the use of econometric models to policymakers, see Orcutt, "Toward the Partial Redirection of Econometrics," 1952, and responses by Koopmans et al., "Toward Partial Redirection of Econometrics: Comments," 1952.

[41] De Jong, Van Paridon, and Passenier, "Jan Tinbergen over zijn Jaren op het CPB," 653, 1988.

could work, but finding something that worked was even more important. "Making it work" was not merely a moral imperative; it was turned into a methodology. The ultimate goal of the 1930s program had been the prediction of the course of the economy, but Tinbergen had expressed serious reservations about prediction as a possibility from his earliest writings.[42] If the economy was itself not a stable system, or if indeed the structure of the economy was not stable over time, prediction was beyond the reach of the economist. The alternative for Tinbergen was what he called task-setting, the setting of particular targets that could be achieved in the next period.[43] If stability was something to be achieved, rather than a property of the system, then pursuing clear targets could contribute to stability. More importantly, the decision models were not merely descriptive; they were explorations of the possible. They allowed the economist to explore the full consequences of particular decisions, and hence demonstrate what *could* be achieved. But such explorations were futile if it was not clear which targets were desirable.

Which targets were desirable is a normative question, a question typically resolved within politics. And Tinbergen indeed suggested that the targets should be derived from the values in society or, alternatively, from those held by the government in power. Strictly speaking, they should be derived from a social preference function. The theoretical idea of a social preference function in economics is used for a hypothetical preference function of all citizens in society. The major problem in the definition of such a function is how preferences of individuals are supposed to be aggregated, and whether this is possible at all. Frisch would spend much of his later work seeking to define such a preference function.[44] And although Tinbergen had sympathy for that endeavor, he typically opted for a far more pragmatic method. He suggested that targets could be set in consultation with the government. The aim in this process was not to arrive at some optimal policy, but rather to set feasible targets that were supported by the current government.[45] In fact, the way he used the models was twofold. On the one hand, the decision models showed what was possible and so it was constructive. But at the same time, the decision

[42] An early example from 1932 is Tinbergen, "Is het Einde van de Crisis in Zicht?," 1932.
[43] Tinbergen, "Problems of Central Economic Planning in the Netherlands," 1947; Tinbergen, *Government Budget and Central Economic Plan*, 1949.
[44] Johansen, "Establishing Preference Function for Macroeconomic Decision Models: Some Observations on Ragnar Frisch's Contributions," 1974.
[45] Herbert Simon later recognized Tinbergen's decision models as an early example of the satisficing approach; see Simon, "From Substantive to Procedural Rationality," 75, 1976.

models also allowed the economist to demonstrate that a desired set of targets was in fact unfeasible (given the current set of instruments). As such the model was a check on overambitious politicians and, possibly, on their empty promises. In Dutch politics, it was this insight that is understood as the Tinbergen rule: the number of achievable targets is limited by the number of available instruments. One cannot kill two birds with one stone.

No matter where the targets came from precisely, it was clear that for Frisch and Tinbergen the scientific and the political were blending into one another. Econometrics had the potential to become a prescriptive science, and they both hoped it could become this. Many other economists were far less attracted to that ideal. Their contemporary, Maurice Allais, was worried that too much subjectivity would be introduced this way: "In itself, [econometrics] cannot determine what economic policy should be, but only analyze observations and derive, in a rigorous way, the consequences of specified hypotheses.... In Frisch's sense there are in reality at least two, three or maybe ten econometrics of the future; the Stone future, the Wold future, the Allais future, and so on."[46]

Allais's framing of the objective and the subjective is a natural way for scientists to contrast the political and the scientific. The political is the world of beliefs and values, the scientific is the world of facts and theories. But that frame largely misunderstands the goal of Frisch and Tinbergen. They sought to make the political more scientific, by making science more useful. That had an impact on science, and Allais was right to worry about the likely effects of that, but Tinbergen primarily sought to have an impact on politics or, more precisely, on the design of economic policy. After all, he developed a theory of economic policymaking, not a theory of the economy.

10.4 Who Does the Planning? Centralization and Decentralization

The constructivist perspective that Tinbergen developed easily could come across as hubris, based on the belief that the economic system can be simply controlled. Such a dismissal might be too easy; in fact, there is a significant nuance in Tinbergen's beliefs about what policy can and cannot achieve. He thought in terms of practical problems and how these could be solved. To define the problem – and this is something one finds him doing

[46] Allais quoted in Andvig, "From Macrodynamics to Macroeconomic Planning: A Basic Shift in Ragnar Frisch's Thinking?," 501, 1988.

again and again in many fields – means figuring out what instruments are at our disposal, and what the structural features are that cannot be changed from the *perspective* of the person who is making the decisions. This perspectivist stance came out very clearly in the second edition of his book on economic policy, when he considered the issue of centralization and decentralization.

In a famous critique of central planning in 1945, Hayek had argued that it made no sense to deny the importance of planning in the economy; the relevant question was, who does the planning? "This is not a dispute about whether planning is to be done or not. It is a dispute as to whether planning is to be done centrally, by one authority for the whole economic system, or is to be divided among many individuals."[47] Tinbergen explicitly took up this point in his book on centralization and decentralization when he argued: "One could indeed state that by increasing the number of policymakers we gradually transform our decentralized policy problem into the ordinary problem of analysis."[48] In other words, his new perspective could be used to analyze planning at any level. In a fully decentralized system, the "policymakers" were small individual producers and consumers. In the modern, partly centralized economy, the policymakers were more varied. But for everyone the decision problem had a similar structure: there was a structure that was beyond their control and a set of decision variables that were under their control.

This new perspective allowed Tinbergen to capture the fact that within one government there were often multiple decision centers, something he knew well from his own practical policy work in the Netherlands.[49] Different ministers might have different responsibilities and hence different targets. Or one could think of the central bank whose institutional setup in most countries today is to pursue its own set of targets with its own set of instruments, independent from the more short-term goals of economic policy. The economy in this perspective becomes a complex system of multiple, interdependent decision centers.

To that extent Tinbergen agreed with Hayek's way of framing the problem. But beyond that point their views began to diverge. Hayek argued that the coordination of all these smaller and bigger plans required

---

[47] Hayek, "The Use of Knowledge in Society," 1945.
[48] Tinbergen, *Centralization and Decentralization in Economic Policy*, 21, 1954.
[49] It is worth noting that this approach was later also used to analyze decision-making within an officially fully centralized economy, that of the USSR; see Laqueur and Labedz, *Polycentrism: The New Factor in International Communism*, 1962. Tinbergen would similarly use this perspective as an argument in his convergence thesis; see Chapter 15.

extensive communication and mutual adjustment, which he argued could best be achieved through the (decentralized) price system. Tinbergen, on the other hand, sought coordination of the different plans through the establishment of a hierarchy of plans, in which coordination was sequential. First, the framework and policy were to be decided on at the highest level, and then slowly lower level planning would commence. The question, however, remained similar: What planning should be done at which level of (de)centralization?

The answer to the question of the optimal level of (de)centralization relied on the idea that some decisions have important effects for others. If such spillover effects are potentially significant *and* negative for others, then there is a reason to move the decision one level up. Take the example of policymakers in the Netherlands and its neighboring country Germany deciding on the level of import tariffs. When Germany, in order to reach its targets, imposes a tariff that significantly obstructs the plans of the Netherlands, there is a prima facie reason to move this decision one level up. The decision could then be better made at a higher level in which the goals of both countries are taken into account, or rather where a joint welfare function is drawn up, and the respective targets could be reached in a consistent manner. No complete centralization of policies is necessary, suggested Tinbergen. A customs union that would fix only some parts of the tariff framework could suffice to prevent a conflict of interests, while still leaving significant policy freedom at the national level.

Deciding on the optimum degree of centralization, however, required more than just knowing the benefits of centralization. It also required knowing its costs. Tinbergen recognized that decentralization was the status quo and that more generally there was a preference for decentralization and freedom for individuals; it was therefore preferable to centralize only when such harmful effects were likely to be significant in size. And although he never included it in his models, he noted that centralization involved additional costs in the form of "administrative machinery."[50] Many political theorists and economists of the age worried much more deeply about the rise of the administrative state and its limits. Tinbergen recognized the issue, and always reminded his own employees at the CPB of the costs of the bureau, but he never paid serious attention to the costs of the institutional organization of the state, and the economy more broadly.

---

[50] Tinbergen, *Centralization and Decentralization in Economic Policy*, 59, 1954.

Tinbergen thus provided not merely a model of decision-making for policymaking, but also a framework for thinking about the appropriate level of decision-making. Although he worked at the national level as director of the CPB, he made it clear that it would be desirable and necessary to centralize certain decisions even more, to the international or global level. Hayek's own answer to the question of the right degree of (de)centralization crucially depended on the necessary knowledge for decision-making, which he argued was mostly decentralized. Tinbergen, on the other hand, argued that the relevant knowledge to take decisions impacting others was available only at higher levels, where the impacts on different parties could be balanced against each other. To do so, the decision models he had developed were crucial.

Tinbergen realized clearly that this meant a fundamentally different view of economics as a science. In the 1930s, the implicit understanding among business-cycle theorists was that they were studying, as onlookers, a natural system that underwent shocks and whose dynamics should be analyzed as well as possible. In the 1950s he concluded: "The problem of comparing alternatives forms of organization of economic life constitutes the problem *par excellence* of economic science; its real raison d'être."[51] Economics had now become a science that studied alternative forms of decision-making structures in the economy and alternative institutional arrangements. And the normative counterpart of that was the study of the optimal decision-making structure and institutional organization of the economy.[52]

What has been missed in most of the scholarship on Tinbergen is how deeply he thought in terms of the organization of the economy, of the order in an economy.[53] And, in his perspective, that order is malleable, not given. The big flaw in the econometric work of the 1930s was that it sought to study the structure of the economy as if that was a given, as if the econometric studies could get at the fundamental behavioral equations of the economy. What Tinbergen did explicitly in his work on centralization and decentralization was to make the behavioral equations flexible: they depended on the organizational form of the economy, the decision

[51] Ibid., 47.   [52] Tinbergen, "The Theory of the Optimum Regime," 1959.
[53] This can be called surprising because when he was asked to write about testing business-cycle theories by the NBER, Tinbergen made it very clear that the mere understanding of the business cycle was not the *purpose* of this testing; rather, the purpose was policy-making: "It is of some use to state this ultimate purpose, since theoretical investigations seem hardly germane to it." Tinbergen, "Reformulation of Current Business Cycle Theories as Refutable Hypotheses," 131, 1951.

structure, and the structural policies. Econometric work was still an important input, especially for the way in which instruments could be used by policymakers to reach targets, but they were no longer the primary way forward for economics, certainly not economics as he practiced it.

One interpretation of this shift is that Tinbergen simply developed an approach that was more appropriate for policymaking. It is hard to dispute this, given Tinbergen's concern with practical results and his position as director of the CPB. And there is no direct evidence that he accepted the harsh critiques of his League of Nations model, but his repeated references to Goudriaan's suggestion that the economic system itself was unstable do suggest as much. In 1962, in his seminal book *Shaping the World Economy*, he quoted Goudriaan again: "[W]e do not need to know the dynamics of the present unstable equilibrium just as an engineer does not need to know the dynamics of a collapsing bridge. What we need to know is the statics of a stable equilibrium, just as an engineer must know the statics of a bridge that will not collapse." And then concluded: "Let us therefore look for a stable equilibrium, or at least for a more stable one."[54] His close collaborator Frisch explicitly believed the decision models represented a next step in econometric modeling, not merely a complement.[55] In a retrospective book, Tinbergen made the same point. The study of business cycles was discussed in a chapter entitled "Lessons from the Past," whereas the later decision models and task-setting were discussed under the heading "Planning for the Future."[56] From this perspective, the decision models were the next step in the development of a useful economics. Usefulness was the ultimate criterion for Tinbergen. Measurement was important, even fundamental; without it, any econometric approach was impossible. But econometrics became useful when its findings could be used to improve the world.

***

From the early 1930s onward, Tinbergen was in frequent contact with Goudriaan, with whom he had a long exchange on the nature of equilibria in the economy and the extent to which the system itself needed to be reformed. Goudriaan argued that the monetary system was fundamentally unstable, that it was not a self-equilibrating system giving rise to merely

[54] Tinbergen, *Shaping the World Economy*, 188–89, 1962.
[55] Frisch, "Preface to the Oslo Channel Model," 1962.
[56] Tinbergen, *Lessons from the Past*, 1963.

cyclical movements, but rather a bridge in danger of collapsing. Initially, Tinbergen sought to integrate this criticism into a special case of the more general dynamics of the economy.[57]

But in the longer run, Tinbergen provided a more substantial answer to Goudriaan and many other critics of the 1930s econometrics program. The goal was to find an optimal economic order, most importantly one that was stable. The question was no longer what the dynamics of the existing system were, but rather whether we could formulate a set of institutional preconditions for a stable system, and realize these preconditions through structural policy. That question was so difficult that in practice Tinbergen opted for a middle ground. Rather than seeking to predict the course of the economy, or even the outcomes of various policy interventions, he suggested that policymakers should seek to steer the economy in the desired direction. In order to do this, they had to make well-informed choices about the best use of the instruments at their disposal.

In the 1930s there had been a distant desire to "rationalize" the state and to engage in economic planning, in the same way that modern firms had rationalized their management and planning techniques. In the early 1950s Tinbergen came close to realizing that dream. In important ways Tinbergen understood the problem of national economic planning to be like that of planning within the firm. The senior management set broad targets and defined an overall strategy. The lower departments worked within this broad framework to reach their own targets, all the way down to the individual employee – except that now senior management was the national policymaker, and the sub-departments were various industries (or firms), all the way down to the consumer, or citizen.

The reality, of course, was messier. There was not one policymaker, and the policymakers who existed were anything but willing to give up their discretionary power by adopting Tinbergen's decision models. Nonetheless, his approach provided a rationalization of the way economic expertise could contribute to policy, not merely in scientific terms – in fact, it partly moved away from those – but particularly in practical terms. His theory demonstrated how econometric models could contribute to political decision-making, and it legitimized centralized decision-making on several key economic issues.

---

[57] Rodenburg, "The Goudriaan–Tinbergen Debate on Dynamics and Equilibrium: 1931–1952," 2010.

11

The Expert *in* the Model, the Economist *outside* the Model

The Lucas critique is one of the landmarks in modern econometrics. Its main target was the theory of economic policymaking. Robert Lucas, writing in 1976, suggested that virtually all macroeconomic policy discussions were conducted within the theoretical framework for policymaking that Tinbergen developed. But those models were all flawed in a similar manner, argued Lucas: they assumed that citizens would passively accept policy decisions made by the policymakers (or experts) within the models. Or to put that more precisely, it was assumed that the behavior of economic agents would not change when a new set of policies was introduced. Lucas concluded his classic paper: "In short, it appears that policy makers, if they wish to forecast the response of citizens, must take the latter into their confidence. This conclusion, if ill-suited to current econometric practice, seems to accord well with a preference for democratic decision making."[1]

There are narrow interpretations of the Lucas critique, which turn it into essentially a point about the right way to do econometric modeling. But there is a more interesting and deeper philosophical point in his critique, one that hits at the heart of the relationship between expert and citizens, and Tinbergen's program of steering the economy.

Whether the government decides to pursue a strategy of austerity or an expansionary policy during an economic downturn will not itself affect the behavior of firms and consumers. That kind of passive response to government policy by economic actors is of course unlikely. Tinbergen himself had acknowledged that the efficacy of Roosevelt's New Deal had crucially depended on the response of American entrepreneurs to the

---

[1] Lucas, "Econometric Policy Evaluation: A Critique," 42, 1976.

policies. The fact that firms and consumers had not been convinced of the efficacy of the New Deal measures meant that they were reluctant to start investing and spending again. And hence the famous Keynesian multiplier, which suggested that government expenditure would kick-start the economy, never fully materialized.

What is interesting about the Lucas critique is that Lucas argued completely on Tinbergen's own terms. In the conclusion, he argued that "given that the structure of an econometric model consists of optimal decision rules of economic agents, and that optimal decision rules vary systematically with changes in the structure of the series relevant to the decision maker, it follows that any policy change will systematically alter the structure of econometric models."[2] This was the precise view that Tinbergen had developed in his theory of economic policymaking. The structure of the economy should be understood not as an invariant underlying economic system but rather as the outcome of the structure of decision-making within an economy.

Lucas argued that Tinbergen, and those using his framework, had smuggled in a simplifying assumption that could not be justified. They had assumed that economic agents did not alter their behavior based on the policy decisions in the period under consideration. In other words, Tinbergen had imagined the public as a relatively passive recipient of policy decisions, and thus in a very real way the transformation of the 1950s had been incomplete. Its goal had been to endogenize policy, to put the policymaker into the model. But the model assumed that policy decisions did not impact the model itself, that they left the structure untouched. And hence policy was still mostly an external "intervention" into the economy, rather than an integral part of it.

The Lucas critique took Tinbergen right back to the 1930s. In the papers on expectations from that period, Tinbergen had taken inspiration from the work of Oskar Morgenstern, the Austrian mathematical economist. Morgenstern had argued that economic prediction was impossible, because the moment that predictions would become part of the economic system, they would impact the course of the economy.[3] A credible prediction of an upcoming downturn in a year from now would have a direct impact on entrepreneurial decisions. Depending on the circumstances, the prediction might prevent the downturn, or it might bring it forward, because

[2] Ibid.
[3] Morgenstern, *Wirtschaftsprognose: Eine Untersuchung ihrer Voraussetzungen und Möglichkeiten*, 1928.

investments would drop in anticipation of the downturn. Economic predictions thus bore a strong resemblance to self-fulfilling and self-defeating prophecies.[4]

Lucas suggested that this was not merely true of predictions, but equally true of (unexpected) changes in policies. The policies would alter the structure of the economy, and thus the decisions of economic agents. That critique could also be made in the conceptual language of Morgenstern; the newly announced policy would send a strong new signal about the current state of the economy, and thus merely through its signaling function alter the behavior of economic agents.

What is even more interesting is that Lucas's constructive suggestions further developed the knowledge critique of Morgenstern. Tinbergen had been interested in creating a stable framework in which expectations of economic agents would converge. By creating the preconditions for a stable economy, the ex ante expectations and the ex post realizations of individuals in the economy would come close to each other. This meant that the plans that economic agents had for the next period would be realized as expected. Lucas suggested that unanticipated policies would upset the plans of economic agents: they could cause discoordination, and at the very least would require adjustments.

Lucas, who in his critique was as policy-oriented as Tinbergen, suggested that the only real solution to this problem was to develop policies based on clear, transparent, and stable rules. This would limit the possibilities of surprise and discoordination. In important ways it was a suggestion in line with Tinbergen's own way of thinking. As we have seen, Tinbergen was interested in economic order, and only secondarily in questions of direct economic policy. He was at least as interested in the creation of a stable institutional framework as he was in specific policies. But it could not be denied that Tinbergen's applied theory of economic policymaking was based on discretionary decisions that were not anticipated by firms and consumers.

What Lucas crucially argued was that policies, in order to be effective – that is, produce the desired effects – had to be public knowledge. Thus, if the government announced that it would engage in a certain type of policy response if the unemployment rate rose above 4 percent, then all economic agents could take this into account in their plans, and differences between ex ante plans and ex post realizations would be minimized. It was

---

[4] Merton, "The Unanticipated Consequences of Purposive Social Action," 1936.

this type of transparency that Lucas called democratic: the public would know policies in advance. In Lucas's words, policymakers would have to take the citizens "into their confidence." In Tinbergen's theory of economic policy, it was merely the targets that were open to public debate and that were public knowledge. The way in which instruments would be manipulated to reach those targets would be under the control of the economic experts. It was somewhat reminiscent of Goudriaan's metaphor of the night train. The public knew where it was going but did not how it would arrive there. The Lucas critique questioned whether the type of manipulation of levers to arrive at desired economic results was compatible with democratic decision-making, and suggested it was not.

The practical political import of the Lucas critique was that he wished to severely limit the discretion of the policymaker. If structural policies and rules had to be announced far in advance, this would mean that both policymakers and economic experts had to give up most of their policy discretion. In that sense it was a reversal of the transformation that Tinbergen had proposed. Tinbergen proposed that major decision makers in the economy could control key policy variables and that the economy could be steered this way. Lucas proposed that a structural framework be put in place, so that decentralized economic agents were free to make up their own plans. In that sense the discussion was also quite directly about the best mixture between centralization and decentralization.

Probably the most interesting implication of the Lucas critique was about the position of the economic expert and the policymaker in the model. As we have seen, Tinbergen put the policymaker into the model as a well-intentioned and (very) well-informed decision maker able to manipulate key economic variables, the so-called instrument variables. The most common response to the Lucas critique was based on the idea that it was wrong to assume that policymakers could make decisions that would be a (major) surprise to economic decision makers. These economists, including Lucas himself, suggested that we should model the economic agents as "more rational." This became known as the "rational expectations" revolution in macroeconomics, which gave rise to a set of models that suggested that economic agents formed rational expectations not merely about the likely course of the economy (as Tinbergen had already suggested in the 1930s), but also about the likely policy responses of the government. This effectively meant that implemented policies no longer impacted the behavior of economic agents, but also that policies were very unlikely to be effective. Some of the models, for example, assumed that if a tax cut was implemented, economic agents would realize that taxes would have to be raised in the future and would thus start saving more now. This would effectively cancel the desired effects of the policy. It was epistemically a highly interesting modeling strategy, since it essentially assumed that economic agents had access to the same type of economic models that were at the disposal of the economic experts. All economic agents became fully rational planners, as well informed as the imagined ideal policymaker in Tinbergen's models. Lucas's connection to democratic decision-making was soon forgotten. The rational expectations assumption was solely justified on the capabilities of the individuals, and not on the fact that policy responses could be anticipated because they had been made public knowledge.

But the relevance of the Lucas critique in part derived from the fact that Keynesian policy responses were increasingly expected and anticipated. Throughout the 1950s and 1960s Western governments had used monetary policy to boost the economy, and by the 1970s inflationary policies no longer appeared to boost the economy. Not long after the econometric models became the basis for policymaking in Dutch politics, both unions and other interest groups became interested in using the models for their own purposes. They started developing or hiring the necessary expertise and proposed policies in such a way that the model gave results they desired or justified higher nominal wage increases. In Chapter 14 we will find the Turkish government manipulating one of the development models to demand more development aid. In present-day Dutch politics the CPB helps different political parties to fine-tune their policy proposals to generate the desired policy outcomes from the model. In this way the model used to make policy is made transparent to the different political parties, so that the calculations of the CPB, which occupy a crucial position in the public debate surrounding upcoming elections, do not take them by surprise. Most parties are even advised by the CPB experts as to how they can tweak their proposals to lead to optimal outcomes in the model.

A similar phenomenon is visible in modern monetary policy. The announcement of the interest rate by central banks, for instance, the Federal Reserve or the European Central Bank, is a major public event. The lowering of the interest rate is typically meant to boost economic activity. But as Roger Koppl has demonstrated, if big players such as the central bank control important economic levers, then a great deal of attention will be paid to their most likely behavior.[5] This consequently

---

[5] Koppl, *Big Players and the Economic Theory of Expectations*, 2002.

means that it is highly unlikely that the central bank can unexpectedly lower interest rates. In fact, not infrequently, a lowering of the interest rates, when announced, disappoints investors. The announced rate cut was already anticipated, and investors had perhaps hoped for a larger cut. In that case the immediate effect is the opposite of the desired effect: investment plans are adjusted not upward but downward (since they had already been adjusted upward in anticipation of the announcement).

The extreme versions of the rational expectations hypothesis in economics are easily ridiculed since they turn every economic agent into a version of the master econometrician. But that does not invalidate the broader point that citizens will adapt their behavior to expected changes in policy. This also means that it is likely that the effectiveness of certain instruments will decrease over time, since their usage has already been anticipated.

Tinbergen had put the policymaker inside the model, but without fully exploring the implications of this modification. He had implicitly assumed that the reactions of the public were stable and predictable, and somewhat naïve. The implication of the Lucas critique was that the reactions of the public were not as stable and predictable, and certainly not naïve. The distance between the policymaker and the economic expert, on the one hand, and economic actors, on the other hand, was diminished by the Lucas critique. Lucas did so based on a behavioral argument that economic agents will adapt their behavior in the light of (structural) policy changes. But it should be clear that the distance in knowledge between the expert and the public was also diminished: the people could be fooled some of the time, but not all the time.

The charge of opacity had haunted Tinbergen ever since he first presented his model of the Dutch economy in 1936 before his fellow Dutch economists. It pointed to a deeper tension in his work and life project. In 1934 a member of the Vienna circle of logical positivists, Otto Neurath, had settled down in The Hague. Neurath was one of the premier proponents of economic planning and had been one of the leading intellectuals at the major Planning Conference in Amsterdam in the early 1930s. Tinbergen had favorably reviewed Neurath's book on rational planning. One would expect that a quite natural collaboration would start between the two planning enthusiasts who now lived in the same city. And Neurath was certainly eager to start one.

One of Neurath's main projects at the time was a method of visually representing social, technological, biological, and historical changes through visual statistics called Isotype (from the acronym for the International

System of Typographic Picture Education). These early infographics sought to educate the public and raise awareness about social and economic conditions in the modern world. Neurath had organized public exhibitions in progressive Vienna in the 1920s and sought to start a social museum along these lines in the Netherlands. Eager for any application of Isotype he could find, Neurath offered to Tinbergen to develop Isotype graphics for the Plan of Labor in 1936 and sought to come into contact with other statisticians at the Bureau of Statistics via Tinbergen. But Tinbergen appeared not very eager to develop his work in the direction of Neurath,[6] even though the two men shared political goals and a social vision. Coincidentally, Neurath also believed that his visual statistics could be appealing to Montessori schools, the type of school that Tinbergen's daughter would start attending only a few years later.

The program of public education and making the world visible to as large an audience as possible was central to Neurath's intellectual work. Tinbergen instead developed his own program in the direction of expert education and steering the world in what he believed to be the desired direction. If one would frame it as starkly as possible, Neurath's was a program of emancipation, Tinbergen's was a program of control. Neurath's program was aimed at society, Tinbergen's program was aimed at the state. Although his youth in the AJC had instilled in him that change had to come from within society, his economic and broader intellectual program was aimed at steering society from above. The set of ideals that the AJC had instilled in him never left him, but the argument that these goals could be achieved only through the emancipation of the working classes through education and cultural and moral improvement faded more and more into the background.

It was for this reason that his critics could accuse him of a lack of democratic sensibility. The consequence of the theory of policymaking, whether intended or unintended, was that it put experts and policymakers in control of the economy. The Lucas critique was all the more effective because it came after two decades of fairly stable growth, when the experts appeared to lose that control: in the early 1970 the oil crisis had disrupted economies everywhere, and there was the problem of stagflation, the combination of high inflation and high unemployment. But even without that economic crisis, Lucas's critique of Tinbergen's project touched an open nerve. Although Tinbergen's intentions were to make economic

---

[6] Their correspondence between 1934 and 1936 is available in TL. I have drawn on these letters for this section.

policy work for everyone in society, he did so without involving society. Even though he had put the policymaker, himself, into the model with his decision models, he had still elevated the expert far above the rest of society.

Robert Lucas forced economists to reconsider the appropriate position of the economist in a democratic society. It was a question that occupied other economists as well. James Buchanan repeatedly criticized the position of the economist as policy expert working in service of the state.[7] The problem was not that some economists worked in government service, but rather that the explicit audience of economics had become the state. It became a tradition in the postwar period to end economic papers with a section entitled "policy implications." Buchanan suggested that the proper audience of economists was their fellow citizens, and it was only through public debate and democratic decision-making that economic policy could be legitimized.[8] But Buchanan, too, made a knowledge argument. It was ultimately the individuals themselves who knew best what was good for them.

No matter from which side the argument was made, the underlying point was the same. The knowledge of the policymaker was more limited than the decision models of Tinbergen suggested, and the citizens who made up society possessed more relevant knowledge than the models assumed. It was a lesson in humility for the type of economic expertise that Tinbergen represented.

But, interestingly, the work of Buchanan also provided a possible way out of the Lucas critique. In Tinbergen's own work there was a difference between quantitative policy, that is, the manipulation of certain key variables such as the interest rate, and the institutional order of the economy. Buchanan made a similar argument about the structure of the economy. He argued that economists should differentiate between the constitutional level, at which the rules of the game were determined, and the postconstitutional level, or, in simpler terms, the game itself. The critique of Lucas made the world flat; he presented every change in policy as a change in the structure of the economy. Tinbergen had always argued that the structure of the economy was determined by the decision-making structure in the economy, in Buchanan's terms the rules of the game. He had never

[7] Buchanan, "Positive Economics, Welfare Economics, and Political Economy," 1959; Buchanan, "What Should Economists Do?," 1979.

[8] It was a vision rooted in the views of his mentor Frank H. Knight; see, for example, Knight, *Intelligence and Democratic Action*, 1960.

suggested that a simple policy change, such as a change in the interest rate, would change the structure of the economy. And rightly so: the behavioral equations in the model were precisely meant to be stable or accurate for relatively small changes in policy. Tinbergen had always acknowledged that the structural equations in his model would have to be adjusted if the institutional structure of the economy was altered.

What Buchanan's work thus suggested for Tinbergen's project is that a clearer distinction was required between the policymaker inside the game and the economist as institutional analyst outside the game. The policymaker was fully part of the economic system, and other agents would form expectations about the most likely actions of the policymaker. But there was also a role for the economist outside the model: in this role they were actively making suggestions for a better institutional order in society. Tinbergen's search for the optimal economic order is best understood as such. As he concluded himself: "[C]omparing alternative forms of organization of economic life constitutes the problem *par excellence* of economic science; its real raison d'être." His departure from the CPB, his departure from his function inside the model, would be marked by increased interest in the search for the optimal form of organization of the economy, from outside the model.

This reading of Tinbergen's work through Buchanan's lens makes sense for one more reason. Buchanan argued that the constitutional level was all about finding peaceful arrangements between the different groups and individuals in society. Tinbergen understood that the precondition for the type of economic expertise he desired was this kind of social peace and stability. The rise of the Volkspartei was intimately tied up with the rejection of confrontational politics and the search for cooperative arrangements with other groups in society. The Breakthrough movement sought to complete this development by integrating Dutch society further and diminishing differences between different religious and ideological groups. In Buchanan's terms, these were developments at the constitutional level. The post-constitutional stage was relevant only when such rules were agreed on by the different groups in society. When Tinbergen turned to the exploration of an international economic order, he was again confronted with problems at the constitutional level. The capitalist West and the communist East were headed for direct confrontation, so the first challenge was to establish the right terms of coexistence. That was the constitutional stage in which the rules could be developed for stable and peaceful arrangements of living together. Only afterward was there a possibility to search for optimal international economic policies. The first stage was about institutional order and qualitative arrangements; the second stage was about optimal policies and quantitative measures. In the first stage, the economist needed to address society and think outside the current institutional arrangements. At that level the Lucas critique was correct, but also largely beside the point. Tinbergen had never believed that behavioral equations would be stable across different institutional orders. In the second stage, the expert accepted the current institutional arrangements – he was inside the model. At that level the Lucas critique lost some of its force: with an institutional order there were good reasons to believe that behavior was stable. But his epistemological point was still relevant. There was no reason to believe that at this second stage the economic expert could consistently outsmart the other economic actors.

PART III

GLOBAL EXPERTISE

12

Opening up Vistas

India and the World

Vasudhaiva kutumbakam. (The world is one family.)
—Old Sanskrit phrase, popularized by Mahatma Gandhi

After his time in Geneva for his League of Nations study, Tinbergen was tied up for a long time in the Netherlands. First, because the war made it hard to leave his position, and later, because his close friend Hein Vos asked him to become the head of the new Planning Bureau. He worked through the difficult war years, as well as the meager reconstruction years, but then made a radical career move. That change was not at all obvious from his professional position in 1951. Next to his directorship of the CPB, he was involved in at least five different committees about the economic future of the Netherlands: its investment strategy, the development of a pension system, the position of the Netherlands in the European Coal and Steel Community, the future of the construction sector, and the design of unemployment insurance. In 1952, he headed the study of the fishing industry of the Netherlands, was appointed to a committee on full employment, concerned himself with the position of the Netherlands in NATO, published a report on housing rents, and was rumored to become treasurer in the newly formed government.[1]

It seemed certain that Tinbergen was destined for a future at the very top of Dutch economic policymaking, the policy expert par excellence. After all, his book on economic policymaking had just come out, and with his mixture of social-democratic ideals, Protestant background, and appreciation for markets, he was an acceptable expert to at least three of the four of the major political parties. But then he was invited to a conference of the

---

[1] "Kabinetsformatie tijdens het Weekeind weinig verder Gekomen," *Algemeen Handelsblad*, 14 July 1952, p. 1.

International Statistical Institute in New Delhi, in December of that year. It was his first trip to Asia, and it moved him so deeply that he fell physically ill afterward; he was that moved by what he had seen.

That moment, and more broadly the early 1950s, was a pivotal moment in his career. He received offers to spend the rest of his academic career in the United States, where the cutting-edge economists were located by now. But what Tinbergen had seen in India proved decisive and would shape the rest of his career. Policymaking remained at the heart of his approach, but his working field became more international and less and less concerned with academic economics. His encounter with India also meant that he left behind the further perfection of domestic economic policy and the welfare state, in favor of a new start in development economics. It allowed Tinbergen to develop his views on the international economic order more fully. But most importantly, the period marked an important return to a more idealistic agenda. As functionary of the Dutch government he was constrained in the extent to which he could develop his own research agenda, but also in the freedom he had in the public expression of his more idealistic and ideological views. The moment he left the CPB he took this liberty to attempt to renew the agenda of international social democracy.

12.1 Stuck at Home?

An internal document from the CPB listed the various functions of its personnel in 1953. The entry for "Tinbergen, J." included no fewer than twenty-two government functions, besides his main function as director of the CPB. About half of these entries listed him as chair or deputy chair. They ranged from the Bank Council of the Dutch Central Bank to a committee on price and wage control at the ministry of social affairs, council member of the KLM (the national airline), council member on various committees about European integration, and a host of advisory committees to three different ministries.[2] The list left out his academic position at the Netherlands School of Economics (NEH) and his activities at the Netherlands Economics Institute, and it did not speak of his active role in the social-democratic party. It is hard to think of somebody more influential in Dutch society at that point in time. What it also demonstrates is how well positioned Tinbergen was at that point in time, and therefore

---

[2] NA: CPB, folder 23.

how likely it would be that he would continue his career within the Netherlands, and with a primarily Dutch policy focus.

Another part of his rising stature was that many of his (former) students did well. Crucial in the development of many of them was their work at the NEI. It kick-started many careers, and the institute increasingly developed into a commercial economic research institute. In the initial years after 1929, much of the income came from donations and the Rockefeller Foundation. But since the outbreak of World War II, the institute increasingly focused on business economics and market analysis at the request of larger firms, industry organizations, and local and national governments. In 1949, the institute employed thirty-three people, of whom nineteen were academic research staff.[3] The institute was important for the applied nature of its work, but even more so because it created a set of professional opportunities for doctoral students and recent graduates. It meant that Tinbergen was surrounded by talented economists of his own making, who would later be labeled the Sprigs (Telgen) van Tinbergen.[4]

At the NEI, Tinbergen had worked closely with Jacob van der Wijk, who specialized in statistical studies of income distribution and was a committed socialist who died during the war. H. J. Witteveen worked on the relation between wages and employment and would later serve twice as treasurer during the 1960s, becoming president of the IMF in 1973. He was also someone who combined religious idealism with his scientific career, much like Tinbergen. Henk Bos started in 1951 and developed mathematical models of economic growth with Tinbergen.[5] Bos joined the NEI in 1951 and would later become one of the heads of research there. Two professors at the Netherlands School of Economics (NEH) in Rotterdam were also leading researchers at the NEI, Leo Klaassen and Henk Lambers. The latter was a specialist on competition policy and served no fewer than four terms as president (rector magnificus) of the NEH. The former was an applied (spatial) economist whose areas of work greatly overlapped with Tinbergen, and like him he often worked for international organizations. The NEI was one important center; the CBS and the CPB were two others.

In 1953, the CPB staff consisted of various talented economists. Ed van Cleeff pioneered national income accounts and worked closely on the theme of economic order with Tinbergen. F. L. Polak (not to be confused

[3] Tinbergen, "Het Nederlandsch Economisch Instituut in 1949," 1949.
[4] Dalen and Klamer, *Telgen van Tinbergen: Het Verhaal van de Nederlandse Economen*, 1996.
[5] Tinbergen and Bos, *Mathematical Models of Economic Growth*, 1962.

with J. J. Polak, his colleague at the League of Nations and then at the IMF) worked extensively on the concept of economic planning in its various forms, and would become known as a pioneer in futurology. D. B. J. Schouten was a talented recent graduate who would go on to make important contributions in the field of public finance. Schouten would become the longest serving member of the corporatist Socio-Economic Council (which at that time was headed by Tinbergen). Verdoorn, already a professor, was an engineering-oriented specialist in market and efficiency analysis who had the Verdoorn law in econometrics named after him. Tik (M. H.) Ekker was another talented quantitative economist, who worked at the CPB but pursued an international career and, during the 1940s and 1950s, was an important connection at the United Nations for Tinbergen.[6] Sam (C. A.) Oomens was another pioneer in the field on national income accounts in the Netherlands, but stayed behind at the CBS after Tinbergen left for the CPB.

Although not directly his colleague, perhaps one of the most important other figures in the Netherlands for Tinbergen was Henri Theil. As Tinbergen was occupied more and more in policy work, he looked for someone to take over his more technical courses at the NEH (Figure 12.1). Theil was a technical econometrician; his work was more oriented toward the formal econometric models developed at the Cowles Commission and the RAND Corporation in the United States than with the applied models of Tinbergen. In April 1953, Tinbergen asked him whether he was interested in teaching these more technical subjects at the NEH and combining this with work at the CPB, just as Verdoorn, Polak, and he himself were doing: "[W]e hope to keep you in our midst a little longer, this way."[7] Tinbergen was actively creating an environment in which he could pursue his policy work alongside the more academic work, and could keep some of the greatest talents around him, before they would take up positions in the United States. Theil left for the University of Chicago in 1966 where he became director of the Center for Mathematical Studies in Business and Economics.

Tinbergen had great admiration for the technical work of Theil and nominated him for the Nobel Prize later in his life.[8] But the two men

---

[6] See the correspondence between the CPB and Ekker in NA: CPB, folder 557.

[7] JT to Henri Theil, 15 April 1953, TL.

[8] Tinbergen wrote: "I want to repeat my suggestion of several years ago to consider as a candidate for the prize in economic sciences in memory of Alfred Nobel Professor Henri Theil." JT to Karl-Göran Mäler, 8 May 1989, JTC.

Figure 12.1 Group picture of professors at the NEH in 1958 in Maarsbergen, the Netherlands. Standing, from left to right: H. Drion, B. Pruijt, H. J. Witteveen, J. H. van Stuyvenberg, T. J. Bezemer. Sitting, from left to right: J. Wisselink, B. Schendstok, Tinbergen, Ch. Glasz, H. W. Lambers, N. E. H. van Esveld.

represented quite different approaches to econometrics. Whereas econometrics was instrumental for Tinbergen, it was a science in and of itself for Henri Theil. He was responsible for the fact that econometrics literally became a separate field of study, independent of economics, at Dutch universities. This historical curiosity, unique in the world, persists to this day. When choosing a major, students in the Netherlands must choose either economics or econometrics.

A symbolic high point in Tinbergen's position as premier policy advisor and applied economist in the Netherlands was his cost–benefit analysis of the Deltaworks (Figure 12.2). In 1953, a major flood hit the southwest of the country and the Delta Plan was developed to prevent a similar flood in the future. The resulting Deltaworks remain one of the crowning achievements of Dutch engineering and a symbol of national unity in the fight against the sea. The report, written in preparation for the construction of these Deltaworks, covered many technical areas, and Tinbergen was commissioned to write the economic paragraph of the report. The works were first discussed in 1954, but the report did not come out until 1961. The calculation posed formidable challenges. The material costs of the

Economic Account of the Dike Raising Plan and Deltplan (I and II), both excluding the works north of the
Rotterdamse Waterweg and the Lek and south of the Westerschelde
Amounts in Millions of Guilders (price-level 1955)

Costs			Benefits		
A. Works and Costs to increase the security	I	II	*A. Primary Gains*	I	II
1. Works according to Dike Raising Plan	1500		5. Decrease in Maintenance Costs	15	85
2. Works according to Delta Law art. 1-3		1650	*Closing Item:*		
3. Higher Costs from Dike Raising Plan in neighboring areas	50		6. Primary amount for the increased security and other imponderable advantages		
4. Interest losses, insurance costs, unforeseen expenses	50	150		1585	1715
Total A	1600	1800	Total A	1600	1800
B. Additional Works			B. Additional Advantages		
1. Land gains, roads, bridges and drainage works and harbors, etc.	30	150	2. Land Gains	20	125
Advantageous Balance	20	300	3. Traffic	20	125
			4. Prevention Salinization Water	—	160
			5. Public Goods, Fresh Water Fishery, and unforeseen	10	40
Total B	50	450	Total B	50	450
A + B. Works and Expenses	1630	1950	A + B. Advantages	65	535
			C. Net-gains from 1. prevention of desiccation and 2. recreation	—	300*
			D. *Closing Item* for the increased security and other imponderables	1565	1100*
Total General	1630	1950	Total General	1630	1950

* Estimates

Figure 12.2 Overview of the costs and benefits of the Deltaplan intended to secure the Netherlands from future floods.

1953 flood could be estimated, as well as some of the more direct effects on the fishing and agricultural industry in the area. But what was one to do with the lost lives and the suffering? And what about the positive effects it would have on engineering knowledge and the added recreational areas in the west of the country? These were factors that Tinbergen considered "imponderables," factors that could not be expressed in monetary terms.

His calculations considered two different scenarios: the more extensive version of the project and a more limited one. But the results were clear-cut: no matter which option was chosen, the project was not even close to being profitable. Of the projected 1.6 billion guilders in costs with the more limited option, only 15 million, less than 1 percent of the costs, could be covered by measurable benefits. The rest was an entry intended to create balance in the balance sheet, a so-called closing entry, that considered the various imponderables. When secondary effects were considered for the more extensive option, a total of 535 million guilders, or a little more than 25 percent of the total costs, would be recouped in measurable benefits. When Tinbergen also included the possible but uncertain benefits in terms of better agricultural conditions and recreational opportunities, there was still a deficit of 1.1 billion guilders left.

The numbers could not convince Tinbergen that the Deltaplan should not be undertaken. He struggled to justify it on purely economic grounds, but suggested considering the material and immaterial costs if another flood would happen:

The Deltaplan has functions, to which absolutely no economic significance, let alone value, can be assigned, but for which every country would be willing to pay a hefty price. The reputation and the goodwill of the Netherlands in the world will increase through the closure of these waters, and the national pride will also be satisfied by this new exhibit of how a small country achieve something major.[9]

He thought the Deltaworks would be an important project for the Netherlands, but to argue for it, Tinbergen had to rely on arguments normally foreign to his thinking. But with the example of the leading Leiden physicist Lorentz, who had advised on a similarly prestigious water engineering project to close off the Zuiderzee, in the back of his mind, he strongly argued in favor of the project. He emphasized the prestige gained by the project, and especially the boost the project would bring to Dutch water engineering, a sector that to this day has an export value of about 6–7 billion euros a year. It was a nice symbolic end to his role as national calculator, as the CPB is still colloquially known.

12.2 To India?

In 1951 Tinbergen was invited to join a conference of the International Statistical Institute in New Delhi, India. The meetings were co-sponsored by the Econometric Society and took place in early December. Other notable economists present were the statistical economists R. G. D. Allen and Simon Kuznets. Toward the end of the month there were also the annual meetings of the Indian Economics Society. Tinbergen later recalled that he was invited by Professor Prasanta Chandra Mahalanobis to these meetings. Mahalanobis, a brilliant Indian statistician, presided over the meetings. Both the Indian president, Rajendra Prasad, and the prime minister, Jawaharlal Nehru, gave opening speeches. Tinbergen was

---

[9] Tinbergen, "Sociaal-Economische Aspecten van het Deltaplan," 1961.

particularly impressed by the vision that the latter presented. Nehru spoke
of the combination of intellect and statistics through which one comes to
know about unemployment, poverty, and the lack of primary necessities, as
well as the importance of emotional awareness of these problems: "so that
Statistics in my mind were at no time a dry subject of long figures in
columns but of human beings."[10] It was a combination of feeling and
intellect that instantly appealed to Tinbergen.

Statistics for Nehru ought to be an input into the development of
national economic plans. The planning he had in mind was of the coord-
inative kind: "[O]f course, no plan can have finality in a moving and
changing world, but anyhow one must have some ground to stand and
to work upon and we hope that that plan will give us that standing room or
jumping off place."[11] Like many early development economists, Nehru
believed that the main problem was in production, and hence any plan
should be aimed at the expansion of production. It was a pragmatic
approach to planning similar in character to Tinbergen's, who would also
have been happy to hear that Nehru believed that statistical and economic
experts should occupy an important position in the government of India.

A similar vision was presented by Mahalanobis, at that moment vice
president of the International Statistical Institute and head of the Indian
Statistical Institute. For the 1951 meeting, Tinbergen was also in contact
with N. S. R. Sastry, the organizer of the economics meetings, as well as
various people at the Indian Planning Commission in New Delhi. Over the
summer, K. N. Raj forwarded him a draft of the first five-year plan that the
Commission had drawn up. Statistics and econometrics at the conferences
in India were directly connected to matters of policy and planning.

It is beyond doubt that this first visit to India made a tremendous
impression on Tinbergen. The absolute poverty he witnessed there made
him realize in the most direct way that his priority should be in helping
the poor in India, not to perfect the welfare state in the West. Tinbergen
later suggested that he gave up what he was doing at the same moment to
focus on problems of economic development. But there is little evidence
that the change was that quick. It took about six months before he resumed
contact with the people he met in India,[12] and from those initial contacts it
was not at all clear that he would soon return or that his work was already
moving in a different direction. In fact, it was not before 1953 that he

---

[10] Nehru, "Address," 1952.   [11] Ibid.

[12] There is no earlier correspondence in his archive, which for this period is fairly complete.

inquired with the Dutch government whether he could perhaps be relieved of his post at the CPB.

That does not mean that there was absolutely no change in his work after his visit to India. In January 1952, on his return, he reported on the present economic problems of India. He demonstrated detailed knowledge of the production circumstances in Indian agriculture as well as the ongoing land reforms taking place at the state level. He described a Malthusian economy in which population growth tended to outpace growth in agricultural output, and hence that "family planning" was of great importance. Tinbergen concluded that aid from capital-exporting countries would be essential.[13] In an Indonesian journal, *Berita Mapie*, he reported on the first Indian five-year plan, in the hope that it might inspire the Indonesian government to develop something similar.[14] In a different article, Tinbergen reported on the living conditions in India based on the research of Mahalanobis. And although the report was nowhere as emotional as Tinbergen's youthful reports of poverty in the slums of Leiden, it was perhaps the closest he ever came to it in his later career. It is one of the very few instances in which he used vivid descriptions to make his point clear: "a family of 5 persons uses two liters of milk . . . a month."[15] And after a later visit: "overcrowded trains, limited infrastructure, stores of two by two meters with primitive equipment, no roof over their heads for hundreds of thousands, so that they sleep, cook their meal, and run their household on the street."[16] In that same year he was requested to write an article for the newly established *Journal of Indian Economics*. It was Tinbergen's first systematic article on development economics and connected his work on long-term growth during the war with the new field of development. The major problem for developing economies, Tinbergen argued, was the lack of (physical) capital, and hence the strategy for development should be to develop more capital-intensive industries.

In the early 1950s, Tinbergen was thus engaged with the socioeconomic situation in India but remained an onlooker. This did not change much, especially when he received an invitation to spend the fall semester of 1953 in the United States. It was to be expected that such invitations would come after his groundbreaking work in econometrics and his new work on

[13] Tinbergen, "Actuele Economische Problemen van India," 1952.
[14] Tinbergen, "India's Five Year Plan," 1952.
[15] Tinbergen, "De Levensomstandigheden in India," 494, 1953.
[16] "Prof. J. Tinbergen: Wij zijn nog niet te Laat," *Het Vrije Volk*, 7 March 1956, p. 3.

economic policy, but the invitation came from an unlikely place – not Harvard, but Haverford, a small, intimate, all-male college of no more than 300 students at that time, which was founded on Quaker principles. The irony was that Tinbergen did receive an offer for a professorship in statistics around the same time from the department of economics at Harvard. Arthur Smithies offered him the position of chair, but Tinbergen kindly declined because he had no interest in a professorship in statistics.[17]

It is one of the many remarkable choices he made at this juncture of his career. He could have lived the life of a celebrated professor of economics for the rest of his life, and he could have done so in one of the more intellectually stimulating academic environments in the world for an economist at that point in time. But Tinbergen had already, in his mind, started to move away from academic economics. As he made clear to Smithies in his response, he was more interested in questions of economic policy. At Haverford, he formally taught Economics 71: "Problems of Domestic Stability and Growth," but more important was the informal seminar he ran for interested economists from nearby institutions on development planning.[18] At age fifty, many perhaps would have chosen to build further on what was already an impressive career. But Tinbergen instead switched fields, or rather decided to help build the new burgeoning field of development economics.

Haverford provided a place to combine his idealism with his science. Tinbergen, who never really enjoyed spending longer periods away from home, felt at home in the Quaker environment. The emphasis on simplicity and thrift fitted well with the lifestyle and outlook of Tinbergen, who had been in contact with a Dutch variant of them in the 1930s, the Woodbrookers. The Quakers shared an internationalist and pacifist outlook; they are known as one of the "Churches of Peace" alongside the Remonstrants (of which Tinbergen was a lifelong member). One of the professors described Jan and his wife Tine as "natural-born Quakers."[19] The president of Haverford College, Gilbert White, took an active interest in the development problems in India.[20] Tinbergen did take the opportunity to visit various universities in the United States, among them, Princeton where he met with Morgenstern, and Harvard where he was impressed by

---

[17] Arthur Smithies to JT, 17 December 1952, TL; JT to Arthur Smithies, 23 January 1953, TL. Tinbergen would spend time at Harvard in 1956 as a Fulbright scholar.
[18] Hunter in Jolink and Barendrecht-Tinbergen, *Gedeelde Herinneringen*, 1993.   [19] Ibid.
[20] Gilbert White to JT, 5 February 1954, TL.

the work that Wassily Leontieff and Paul Rosenstein-Rodan were doing. At his departure, Tinbergen remarked that the task of eliminating poverty could be achieved with a combination of "the technical skill of the Western world with the simplicity of the Quakers and the patience of the East."[21]

But something at home happened that was of equal importance. In the early 1950s, the Dutch government decided that it needed a knowledge institute fit for the postcolonial world. The various universities in the Netherlands joined forces and the outcome was the start of a new institute in The Hague. This institute was to be devoted to the study of development problems, although it went under the more neutral name of International Institute of Social Studies. Tinbergen was involved from the start when the institute was in the Royal Palace Noordeinde, right in the center of his hometown. The royal family was an early supporter of the efforts directed at the developing countries, in particular, Queen Juliana and her husband Prince Bernhard.

From the very start, the institute attracted many Indian students who worked on problems in development. C. M. Palvia was one of the early graduates who formally obtained his PhD through the Netherlands School of Economics but was a student at the ISS.[22] His dissertation, "An Econometric Model for Development Planning: With Special Reference to India," was quickly published and represented one of the early cross-overs between Tinbergen's approach and planning in India. Another early example of such an exchange was A. Mitra, who developed a complete model of the Indian economy inspired by Tinbergen's macroeconomic models.

Although the ISS was still getting started in these early years – its first rector, Egbert de Vries, would not be formally appointed until 1956 – it already provided a place where Tinbergen could develop his expertise and approach to development economics. The other institution that proved important was a new subdivision at the NEI, Balanced International Growth (BIG). In the first years of its existence, the subdivision published on balance-of-trade issues and capital–labor ratios in various industries for developing countries, but also on a range of more practical problems such as the productivity of mills and handlooms in the weaving industry in India, the provision of nitrogen fertilizer around the world, and the possibilities of reusing machines in the developing world. Its specialty soon

---

[21] Holland Hunter in Jolink and Barendrecht-Tinbergen, *Gedeelde Herinneringen*, 1993.
[22] "Bijzondere Promotie aan de Economische Hogeschool," *Het Vrije Volk*, 10 July 1953, p. 3.

Figure 12.3 Group picture from his visit to India in 1954. From left to right: Oskar Lange, Mrs. Lange, Mrs. Podea, Paul Baran, Mrs. Galbraith, Titus Podea, Mrs. Bettelheim, Charles Bettelheim, Mrs. Mahalanobis, Prasanta Chandra Mahalonobis, John Kenneth Galbraith, Jan Tinbergen, Mr. Links, and Margaret Engemann (identified as Mrs. Norbert Wiener).

became a particular type of investigation: the appraisal of investment projects.[23]

In January 1956, Tinbergen finally, after repeated failed attempts and cancellations, did manage to go to India for a longer period. He was invited by Mahalanobis to spend six weeks in the country, to help develop the second five-year plan (Figure 12.3). By then he was part of a growing trend of Dutch and, more broadly, Western experts traveling the world to aid governments in former colonies. When Tinbergen left, a Dutch newspaper reported that no fewer than eleven Dutch experts were heading out into the world: to India, Sudan, Israel, Pakistan, and Burma.[24] Most of the others were engineers and technicians; Tinbergen was one of the few "social engineers." The trip was the symbolic start of his development career.

---

[23] Netherlands Economic Institute, Division of Balanced International Growth, "Economic Development, Transportation and the National Income Test," 1957.

[24] "Elf deskundigen naar Buitenland," *De Volkskrant*, 19 January 1956, p. 9.

With that new career came an expanded internationalist vision. It was not one that was alien to his early pacifism or the internationalist outlook of the League of Nations, but it was one that now had found a goal, development planning, to which he could contribute.

12.3 Imagining the World Economy

In 1949, President Truman announced in his inaugural speech: "We must embark on a bold new program for making the benefits of our scientific advances and industrial progress available for the improvement and growth of underdeveloped areas." He hoped it would be the start of a great new project that would lead not merely to economic benefits: "Greater production is the key to prosperity and peace. And the key to greater production is a wider and more vigorous application of modern scientific and technical knowledge." It was also a new type of project: not confined to the national political imagination, it was an international agenda for a postcolonial world.

In 1949, the Netherlands had not quite left that colonial mindset. In fact, during the 1940s Tinbergen had contributed chapters to two volumes that praised the colonial heritage of the Netherlands. The title of the first volume referred to the seventeenth-century colonial phrase, "Something great was achieved over there."[25] Although his contributions were mere statistical overviews, it was curious for the committed pacifist Tinbergen to publish in these volumes, which sought to defend the colonial activities of the Dutch. After all, anticolonialism had been one of the rallying causes of the pacifist movement in the Netherlands. But his position so close to the Dutch government and its official line might explain why Tinbergen, as *the* national statistical economist, had to contribute to these volumes. It was a consequence of being so close to positions of power that ideological convictions sometimes had to take a back seat. The social-democratic prime minister Willem Drees, the leader of the newly formed Labor Party, which grew out of the anticolonial SDAP, lead a colonial war in Indonesia not long after he came into power. During this period, the Netherlands was engaged in a strenuous process to "let go" of Indonesia, which involved a bloody war between 1945 and 1949 and ultimately required the intervention of the Security Council to force the Netherlands to give up its colonial territory in the East (with the exception

---

[25] Tinbergen and Derksen, "Nederlandsch-Indië in Cijfers," 1941; Tinbergen, "Nederland in de Twintigste Eeuw," 1946.

of New Guinea). That being said, as early as 1946, Tinbergen expounded a vision of the international economy that would remain mostly unchanged: "[A] healthy international socio-economic policy will consist of: a world production as stable and large as possible, an income distribution as just as possible, the fewest possible conflicts, and as much freedom as possible for individuals."[26]

Another economist, Colin Clark, who was similarly entangled in the colonial history of his country, would greatly inspire Tinbergen's vision for economic development. Clark was one of the pioneers of national income accounts in Britain, alongside James Meade. And as early as the 1930s, he had attempted to estimate the national income of India. But it was his book *The Economics of 1960*, written during the war, that became a near obsession of Tinbergen. In a review from 1944, he wrote that it was "a bold and most important, new contribution to econometrics."[27] In the book Clark estimated the productivity of agriculture in different countries in order to arrive at an estimate of world economic output in 1960. Tinbergen praised not only the ingenious estimation methods in the book, but also the way in which Clark combined his model with special provisions for various countries: "[T]he above scheme has not been applied mechanically." But what was most remarkable about Clark's work was that it covered the entire globe, which had been subdivided into thirty-four regions. Clark had imagined and conceptualized an integrated "world economy."

The primary value for Tinbergen did not lie in the fact that Clark provided completely reliable figures; in fact, he pointed out that some of Clark's estimates of the war damage had already been falsified. Instead, its great value was in the way that Clark had organized the data and had provided a common framework that could be updated, adjusted, and used in further work. As such he regarded it as a direct continuation of the work that was done by the Economic Intelligence Service of the League of Nations: "Mr. Clark's step is the counterpart, in the realm of statistical analysis, to what Wagemann's work is in statistical information: the integration to a world system of equations. This marks its very importance."[28] But it was not just the integration; it was also the comparison that was enabled by Clark's work. His work for the first time demonstrated the magnitude of international inequalities.[29]

---

[26] Tinbergen cited in De Ruijter, "Inleidingen op ons Congres," 2, 1946.
[27] Tinbergen, "Colin Clark's *Economics of 1960*," 1, 1944.   [28] Ibid., 3.
[29] Arndt, *Economic Development: The History of an Idea*, 51, 1987.

In a second review of the book, from 1951, Tinbergen praised Clark for the way in which he connected the growth in productivity to integrated world markets,[30] a connection that he himself had already explored in his book on international economic cooperation.[31] This was an important step because just as national economic planning required the imagination of the national economy, for which national income accounts were indispensable, so international economic planning required the imagination of a global economy: "It is the beginning of a new period in market analysis and international planning and it is to be hoped that the continuation and improvement of this work will give us a basis for the activity of the newly created international agencies."[32] When he was asked to write another pre-advice in 1949, he again referenced Clark's work.[33] The question at hand was how the balance of payments problem of the Netherlands could be resolved, for which the various elasticities of import and export that Clark developed were useful.[34]

In 1954, an updated version of Tinbergen's 1945 *International Economic Co-operation* came out, now redubbed *International Economic Integration*.[35] The book incorporated his new vision on policy and centralization and decentralization. But it also sought to advance economic integration beyond the postwar Bretton Woods institutions. More clearly than ever, he came out in favor of an integrated world market. That same year his good friend Polak, who had stayed at the League of Nations and was now head of research at the IMF, published an econometric study that did his teacher proud: his macro-econometric model of the international economy included no fewer than twenty-five countries. The book was appropriately dedicated to Jan Tinbergen. Its goal was literally to show that the economy was not a national but an international system: "It aims at showing how certain elementary relationships, the significance of which in national economies is already well-known, can be transferred to the field of international trade."[36] Clark in the meantime was engaged in a study

---

[30] Tinbergen, "Boekbespreking van C. Clark's *The Conditions of Economic Progress*," 1951.

[31] Tinbergen, *International Economic Co-operation*, 1945.

[32] Tinbergen, "Review of C. Clark's *Economics of 1960*," 1947.

[33] Tinbergen, "Welke Mogelijkheden en Middelen Bestaan er tot het in Evenwicht Brengen van de Betalingsbalans van Nederland na Afloop van de Marshall-Hulp onder Gelijktijdig Streven naar een Overwegend Vrijer Internationaal Handels- en Betalingsverkeer?," 1949.

[34] Tinbergen, "Long-Term Foreign Trade Elasticities," 1949.

[35] Tinbergen, *International Economic Integration*, 1954.

[36] Polak, *An International Economic System*, 1954.

regarding full-employment policies for the UN, on a world scale.[37] To solve economic problems, the nation-state was not enough. This was not a completely new vision; after all, it had been present at the League of Nations, at which, for example, efforts were made to harmonize international statistics. But in the 1930s, the imagination was typically that of a set of national economies, or rather a set of colonial economies. In the postwar period there was for the first time a global imagination.[38] Bretton Woods still represented an ultimately Atlantic vision of economic integration; therefore, Tinbergen put more faith in the United Nations to help bring about a truly integrated global economy.

Tinbergen's international vision, based on the imagination of a world economy and the institutional framework of the United Nations, was complemented by a moral vision. He increasingly started to develop into an advocate for the developing countries. Sometimes this was mostly to raise awareness about the economic and living conditions in countries such as India. In 1959, for example, the ISS hosted a photo exhibition on the Second Five-Year Plan in India, which was opened by Tinbergen.[39] But there was a far more activist side to his development work, which was perhaps comparable only to the propaganda campaign that accompanied the Plan of Labor in 1935.

12.4 Imagining World Development

The extension of the scientific imagination to the global scale had to be accompanied by an extension of moral imagination to a global scale. The primary way in which Tinbergen did this was through his activism for development aid. He was involved with the founding of the NOVIB, the Dutch Organization for International Aid (later part of Oxfam-Novib). In 1949, the Netherlands had reluctantly started with development aid, aimed at its former colonies. It was part of a more general change in outlook during the period, away from the official neutrality stance that had characterized the country until it was invaded by Germany during World War II. It started orienting itself toward Atlantic and European cooperation, which resulted in a reorganization of the ministry of Foreign Affairs, where Jan Meijer, a student of Tinbergen and fellow Breakthrough member, was hired at the ministry to manage relations with the United Nations. Meijer's career quickly took off within the ministry, and he soon became director of the International Organizations Service, where he was a strong proponent

---

[37] United Nations, *Maintenance of Full Employment*, 1949.
[38] Slobodian, *Globalists: The End of Empire and the Birth of Neoliberalism*, 2018.
[39] "Tweede Vijfjarenplan India," *Algemeen Handelsblad*, 20 June 1959, p. 5.

Figure 12.4 Father Simon Jelsma during one of his Plein-speeches for international aid and justice in The Hague.

of plan-based development aid. His mark on the development strategy for 1956 was clear. The strategy presented development as a new area of policy, a new function for the Dutch government. Planning for development would help create a balanced international economic structure.[40]

Meanwhile, out on the streets of The Hague, pressure for structural development aid was building. Simon Jelsma, a Catholic pastor who was widely regarded as a breakthrough figure because of his connections to the Labor Party and his ecumenical work, started what became known as the "Square Sermons." In these sermons, he preached in favor of peace and justice, and was highly critical of the complacent and inward-looking political parties (see Figure 12.4). In 1945, he argued, the world seemed open and hopeful, but nine years later, little was left of that spirit. His Protestant counterpart was the minister J. B. Th. Hugenholtz. The movement embodied the Breakthrough ideals of breaking down the walls between the different religious groups. The Netherlands had received much international aid after the major flood in 1953 (which gave rise to the

---

[40] Keulen, *Monumenten van Beleid: De Wisselwerking tussen Nederlandse Rijksoverheid, Sociale Wetenschappen en Politieke Cultuur, 1945–2002*, 88, 2014.

Deltaworks), and Hugenholtz argued that the time had come to recipro-
cate. Churches across the country, at his initiative, started collecting money
for the underdeveloped world at the one-year commemoration of the 1953
flood. Underlying the campaign was a growing awareness that the world
was becoming smaller: the support was directed at "a distant neighbor."

Together these two religious leaders, with the help of others, among
them Jan Tinbergen, formed the Square movement. In many ways they saw
it as a continuation of the Breakthrough movement. The Square movement
gave rise to a campaign for Asia (Square Asia),[41] and later NOVIB. It was
supposed to be a broad social progressive movement that went beyond the
different parties. Tinbergen was one of the original board members, although
he was not very active,[42] along with Jelsma, who at the first meeting described
what he hoped to achieve: "Our goal is certainly not merely to organize
social actions and to raise funds. We wish to inform, educate, awaken the
conscience of the people, raise awareness of the needs, awaken a sense of
solidarity. In short, create a climate in which the idea of international aid can
grow. Therefore we have a spiritual (*geistlich*) goal."[43] Tinbergen was not
averse to such goals, but his contribution was more to direct the movement
to institutional goals; the 1958 declaration, in which his influence was most
clearly visible, suggested that we should strive for world peace, a world legal
order, and a world economy realized through the United Nations.[44]

If ever there was a moment that Tinbergen was close to the idealism of his
youth, it was at this moment. The goal of NOVIB, much like that of the AJC
in the 1920s, was cultural and spiritual, driven by a mixture of religious and
socialist ideals and rooted in a social movement. But now the former AJC
member was no longer young and poorly connected; instead, he and many
of his friends were now well established in society and could draw on a
broad network of contacts. From the very start, the charismatic Prince
Bernhard, husband of the queen, was involved with NOVIB. He made clear
that this organization was not an old-fashioned charity, but a modern
organization aimed at a more balanced world order. Bernhard wanted to
dispel the idea that the movement was naïve; he emphasized that such an

---

[41] See the brief history in their brochure: NOVIB, *Nederlandse Organisatie Voor
Internationale Bijstand*, 1958.

[42] The first president of the organization was E. de Vries, who was also rector of the ISS,
The Hague.

[43] Jelsma cited in Keulen, *Monumenten van Beleid: De Wisselwerking tussen Nederlandse
Rijksoverheid, Sociale Wetenschappen en Politieke Cultuur, 1945–2002*, 2014.

[44] Pleingroep, "Verklaring," 1958. See also the other articles in the issue on "Oorlog en
Vrede" (War and Peace) in this magazine.

order was in the self-interest of the Western world.[45] This appeal to an enlightened self-interest became the dominant theme of Tinbergen's internationalist writings of the second half of his career. In a retrospective, one of the authors even suggested that much like the AJC, NOVIB was to be an avant-garde movement: raising awareness and showing the path forward. This avant-garde movement should demonstrate to the masses, according to Tinbergen, "that it is also in their interest to strengthen our development policies."[46] But there was also a clear difference: NOVIB, for all its idealism, was an establishment organization. For much of its early existence, its goal was to promote the activities of the United Nations, and in its proposed policies it was closely aligned with official international bodies.

During the first decade, the NOVIB raised 11 million guilders, which they spent in forty-six countries, predominantly in Africa and Asia. Little more than a drop in the ocean, as Tinbergen suggested: "not even a tenth of a thousandth of what has to happen." The "Tinbergen norm" was that 1 percent of GDP should be set aside for development aid; according to his own estimates, that would amount to a transfer of 50 billion guilders per year from the rich to the poor countries (the total yearly transfer in 1963 was about 8 billion).[47] It was a norm that was first proposed as a personal goal in one of the Square-related campaigns for "genuine justice." Supporters of the movement were urged to put 1 percent of their income aside and donate it to Asia; Tinbergen promoted it as a norm at the national level, as well.

One of the more remarkable parts of Tinbergen's perspective on the global economy and international economic order was that his imagination was crucially shaped by the national economy. Tinbergen compared the current relation of the rich to the poor countries to that of the workers and the capitalists in the West. He argued that in the West, since the nineteenth century, the position of workers in society gradually improved, resulting in a harmonious and balanced society. A similar development should take place internationally. This would require supporting the emancipation of the poorer countries and strengthening their relative power position. One way of doing so was by supporting the regional organizations and negotiation blocs formed within the United Nations' world trade conference.[48] Whereas Tinbergen was critical of regional integration of the West, he supported it

---

[45] Prince Bernhard cited in "Installatie Organisatie voor Internationale Bijstand. Geen Liefdadigheid maar Plicht," *Leeuwarder Courant*, 24 March 1956, p. 5.

[46] Tinbergen, "Ontwikkelingshulp in Wereldperspectief," 1966.

[47] NOVIB, *Nederlandse Organisatie Voor Internationale Bijstand*, 1958; NOVIB, *1% Aktie: Daadwerkelijke Gerechtigheid*, 1961.

[48] Tinbergen, "Ontwikkelingshulp in Wereldperspectief," 1966.

for the developing world. Such regional blocs of underdeveloped countries could have a function like the one that unions had had on the national level. They could strengthen the relative position of the disadvantaged group.

The structural global changes should include not merely new institutional and political arrangements, but also a willingness of the West to open its markets, in particular, its agricultural markets. Global free trade was one of Tinbergen's main themes; in fact, his internationalism was marked by a continued commitment to world free trade, as well as an opposition to regional trading blocs, which he believed would hinder further international integration. Jelsma internalized this view, later recounting that "while we currently spend 0.8% of government spending on development aid, we take with our other hand five times as much back through tariffs and agricultural subsidies."[49] As early as 1945, Tinbergen warned that regional integration in the West might merely be a defensive move, preventing the West from reaching the real goal of "an ordered world economy."[50] Such a goal was explicitly part of the constitutional amendment of 1953 in the Netherlands. The new Article 58.2 stated that "the government promotes the development of an international order." Perhaps unexpectedly for somebody on the left, Tinbergen was a staunch defender of international free trade. In many respects he was even pro-business, whose internationalism he often contrasted favorably with the nationalism of politics.

Within the postwar order, free trade was anything but a given. Not only was the setup of Bretton Woods primarily a Western affair, so were many of the other institutions founded around this period. Clearly, NATO was that, and the predecessors of the European Union, as well as the OECD, were all Western economic organizations, not international ones. Tinbergen was openly critical of European integration, which he feared would lead to free trade within the region, but also to tariffs around the region, a warning that proved prescient. In papers he started exploring the effects of economic integration on what he called "third countries." But it was very clear that his models were designed to assess the effects of European integration on countries such as Brazil and India.[51]

---

[49] "Interview: Pleinpreker en Mister Postcode Simon Jelsma: Ik heb vaak zwaar de pest in," *De Groene Amsterdammer*, 29 May 2004, no. 22.

[50] Tinbergen, *International Economic Co-operation*, 1945.

[51] Tinbergen, "The Impact of the European Economic Community on Third Countries," 1960.

The support for this new orientation was not limited to Prince Bernhard; his wife, the queen, also promoted the internationalist agenda of Tinbergen. Juliana was only a few years younger than Tinbergen and leaned toward pacifism after her student years in Leiden.[52] In the longest speech that she delivered, entire passages appear to have been written by Jan Tinbergen, who was known to visit her for afternoon tea. This speech contained unusually specific empirical figures about the economic and demographic conditions in the world for a royal speech ("The technically highly developed countries, which currently make up one-third of the world population, produce, according to the most advanced statistical data, more than 80 percent of the world income"). And in the middle of her speech she argued for a World Welfare Plan:

> A careful jointly prepared plan, something like an advisory plan bureau on a world scale, would be best positioned, in light of various plans and actions, to coordinate and harmonize these, and it could provide an administrative and visionary leadership for the total world production. This would promote an international equilibrium . . . the goal of foreign aid should be that it would make itself superfluous. . . . This development should take place in a balanced and sustainable manner.[53]

The language of the middle part and the overall spirit of the entire speech was clearly inspired, if not directly written, by Tinbergen.[54] Responsibility was the central moral concept of the speech, which accorded with Tinbergen's idea that development aid was a moral responsibility of the West. But this responsibility had to be accompanied by a moral vision, as well as a plan, or, as the queen argued, "pre-vision" was required. And just like Tinbergen, she believed that the change required to make this happen was primarily a moral and spiritual one, in which educators played a central role. It was up to the moral avant-garde to expand the moral imagination and demonstrate that nobody in their right mind could seriously object to aid for the developing countries.

The conclusion of her speech was more explicitly Christian than Tinbergen ever was in his own work. But her Protestant outlook, with emphasis on responsibility and duty, resonated well with Tinbergen's 1 percent norm and his personal ethic. What was even more striking was that a theme that would only five years later become central in Tinbergen's work – the resolution of the East–West conflict through convergence – was

---

[52] Withuis, *Juliana: Vorstin in een Mannenwereld*, 2016.
[53] Juliana, *De Welvaart der Wereld als Gemeenschappelijke Verantwoordelijkheid*, 1955.
[54] Schenk and Van Herk, *Juliana: Vorstin naast de Rode Loper*, 1980.

already very explicit in her speech. But most of all, the two shared the idea that they were part of a moral elite that should guide society into the future, and both saw the Netherlands explicitly as a "guiding country."

This vision has sometimes been called naïve, much like the ideals behind the Peace Palace. But it is important to realize that given its small size, the Netherlands had little more than moral persuasion to draw on. Moreover, as a small open economy, located on the sea and locked between the great powers of Germany, France, and Great Britain, it had much to gain from international integration. It could have opted for an alliance with one of them, but it was much safer as part of a larger, international, integrated society.

Tinbergen's influence was clear not only in the queen's vision but also in the official foreign policy of the Netherlands. Since 1950, development aid was an official policy goal, but it took until the second policy memorandum in 1956 for a real vision to be developed.[55] That vision, formulated by his former student and Breakthrough compatriot Jan Meijer, was in line with Tinbergen's vision. The memorandum suggested that the positive reception of the queen's speech was proof that the responsibility toward the rest of the world was widely felt in Dutch society. It then laid out the problem of developing countries, by comparing the situation in India with that in the Netherlands. The section that suggested the path forward used the word "plan" no fewer than thirty-five times in the span of some seven pages. The problem facing the developing countries is portrayed as primarily "a technical" problem due to the lack of capital. And the policy aim should be the creation of a "balanced" structure.

Even in the means, through the International Bank for Reconstruction and Development (IBRD) and the newly started UN project of SUNFED, the memorandum mirrored the vision of Tinbergen. SUNFED was the Special United Nations Fund for Economic Development and was headed by the German pioneer of development economics Hans Singer. Just as did the queen and Tinbergen, the memorandum spoke of a new "task" for the West. Two years earlier, in 1954, Tinbergen wrote to one of his international contacts: "I got two jobs in this connection, namely to participate sometime around February [1955] in a working group headed by Mr. Scheyven, in order to make some draft rules and regulations for SUNFED, and, second, to advise the IBRD on their methods to determine

---

[55] Keulen, *Monumenten van Beleid: De Wisselwerking tussen Nederlandse Rijksoverheid, Sociale Wetenschappen en Politieke Cultuur, 1945–2002*, chapter 2, 2014.

priorities."[56] His national and international work were quickly reinforcing one another.

The founding of SUNFED was a contested affair, much opposed by the United States. In a memorandum Tinbergen wrote for the Dutch government in 1955, it was clear that initial support for SUNFED, which would provide aid, rather than loans, was limited to some smaller European countries. Tinbergen and the head of the initial committee, Scheyven, were the most ardent supporters of an organization like SUNFED, and they got their way. Tinbergen would remain the official Dutch government representative within SUNFED.

Domestically, he continued to build support for this internationalist approach with the help of civil servants in the ministry of Foreign Affairs. Civil servants, at the advice of Tinbergen, would invite members of parliament along on their trips to UN meetings.[57] There they would encounter external advisors like Tinbergen and representatives from the Socio-Economic Council. It was a strategy that secured domestic support for the internationalist agenda, which accorded well with the new, more outward-looking self-image of the Netherlands. But not all was self-reinforcing. NOVIB was to some extent perceived as a threat to official state development policies. In 1962, it was described negatively as a pressure group seeking to capture government policy. It was a role that the minister considered unworthy of an organization associated with Prince Bernhard. The compromise reached within this conflict, however, put Tinbergen even more solidly in the driver's seat. It was agreed that a new official think tank for development policy should be established with representatives from civil society organizations and the government. Not unsurprisingly, the think tank was chaired by Jan Tinbergen.[58]

Such influence did not remain domestic. When the first development decade from 1960 to 1969 was drawing to a close, Tinbergen succeeded in persuading the Dutch minister of foreign affairs to propose a second development decade (DD2). This proposal was eventually accepted, and Tinbergen quickly developed a draft strategy for DD2 that could be proposed by the new minister of development aid (now a separate post). The minister of foreign affairs reflected: "[O]ur national program has become a kind of testing ground for what the international program should

[56] JT to Hal B. Lary, 29 December 1954, TL.
[57] Keulen, *Monumenten van Beleid: De Wisselwerking tussen Nederlandse Rijksoverheid, Sociale Wetenschappen en Politieke Cultuur, 1945–2002*, 2014.
[58] Ibid.

become. We can be proud, that one currently finds elements at the international level which were developed in the Netherlands."[59]

In conversation, Jan Pronk, perhaps Tinbergen's most famous student as later High Commissioner of Refugees at the United Nations as well as minister of development cooperation, suggested that Tinbergen was more diplomatic than political. There is much truth in that statement, but it is primarily true as an observation about Tinbergen's means. His high-minded idealism and internationalist outlook, which always emphasized peaceful, friendly, and cooperative relationships, was well received in diplomatic circles. He was also at his best when he could chair a committee and bring diverging perspectives together, through his integrative moral leadership. It was also for this reason that he thought so highly of the Socio-Economic Council and what he achieved there. The Council embodied Tinbergen's ideal way of achieving a consensus: through conversation between experts representing various groups in society, assisted by a group of "neutral experts," after which a synthesis could be reached between the various groups. He was particularly proud of the way in which he managed to convince the labor unions of wage moderation. The unions, who had reacted with such hostility to Tinbergen's approach in the 1930s, accepted that it was also in their interest to improve the competitive position of the Netherlands through wage moderation.

But those diplomatic qualities should not blind us from the obvious fact that Tinbergen's goals were political. They were political in the sense that he sought to reorder priorities within his own social-democratic party. He kindly reminded his readers of the original international agenda of socialism.[60] Domestically, he argued, the most important goals had been achieved – there was even some danger of decadence. He urged his fellow democrats to develop a new international agenda, an agenda of international solidarity. This meant a radical expansion of the imagined community of which one is part: "The world is our home."[61] It was a phrase inspired by his visits to India where that idea was known in the old Sanskrit saying "Vasudhaiva kutumbakam." But it was also political in the sense that Tinbergen made smart use of his unique position in the Netherlands in the early 1950s. He utilized his connections with the highest political circles in the country to develop a new area of policy:

[59] Udink cited in ibid., 107.
[60] Tinbergen, "Internationale Socialistische Politiek," 1957; Tinbergen, "De Internationale Taak van de Sociaal-Democratie," 1957.
[61] Tinbergen, *Lessons from the Past*, 114, 1963.

development aid and cooperation. If theoretical work on economic policy had been a perfect justification for the activities undertaken by the CPB, now he was arguing that the state should extend its responsibilities across the border. In that sense he created a new policy field in which he would soon develop into one of the most influential thinkers.

And it was also political because Tinbergen ultimately helped define the new relationship between the postcolonial West and the newly independent nations. The war for independence had proven how hard it was for the Netherlands, and many other colonial powers, to let go of their colonies. The new agenda of development provided a justification for renewed or, rather, continued involvement in the former colonies. It was significant that one of the early iconic posters of NOVIB contained a picture of the Netherlands; the poster stated that it "could achieve something great" (see Figure 12.5). The words were eerily familiar: the phrase had been used before to describe what had been achieved in colonial Indonesia.

At the NEH that transition was symbolically marked when Tinbergen was appointed to his new chair. George Gonggrijp retired from his chair in "colonial economics" and Tinbergen took up the new chair in "development planning." Economics and politics were now closer to one another than ever before: "I feel strongly that it is the economist's responsibility to indicate the most appropriate organization of international economic policy and not the politician's – at least not that of the politician with a vested interest in existing institutions."[62] Tinbergen had found a new purpose.

That new purpose also meant a new mission. His work in development would send him on many so-called development missions. Those missions were missionary in the sense that they were purpose-driven: to bring development to the underdeveloped countries. But the missions were also missionary in the older Christian sense of that word. Development planning was the new gospel that had to be spread, and NOVIB was the new church organization that collected donations that could finance these missions. From 1954 onward, it was no exaggeration to call Tinbergen a missionary for development. The word "mission," however, also had another connotation less congenial to the pacifist Tinbergen. It could be thought of as a new kind of military mission meant to expand the power of

[62] Tinbergen, "International Co-ordination of Stabilization and Development Policies," 290, 1959.

Figure 12.5 Iconic early poster from 1958 of the NOVIB: "2/3rds of the world is in need / the Netherlands could achieve something great / let your heart speak / support the campaign of the NOVIB." The phrase "something great could be achieved" had in the past also been used to describe the achievements of the colonial government of the Netherlands in Indonesia.

the West, now that colonization was no longer acceptable. His view that development could contribute to peace between the Global North and South, makes clear that Tinbergen was aware of this military or strategic dimension of his work. But perhaps he did not yet sufficiently realize how deeply he would become entangled in international power politics.

13

Development Planning on Paper

Economic development was considered to be a problem of imbalances in the 1950s, a mismatch between the amount of capital and the number of workers in a particular region. The perspective was reminiscent of Wagemann's tainted theory of the optimal relation between the different production factors. The imbalance, it was believed, would without intervention only worsen. Underdeveloped countries lacked capital, and the population was growing too rapidly. If there was some economic growth, it was not enough to compensate for the growing amount of mouths to feed; they were stuck in a so-called Malthusian trap – a trap because more growth would merely lead to more population growth, not to higher living standards. It was named after the British economist Thomas Malthus, who had predicted that economies in the long run would stagnate because food production could not keep up with population growth. Tinbergen's description of the problem was no different; poor countries needed additional capital to get out of this condition of underdevelopment.

Development economists like Tinbergen argued that capital transfers needed to take place from the developed world to the underdeveloped world. In fact, many of the early models sought to estimate the capital requirements for the underdeveloped world; the 1951 United Nations (UN) report concluded, based on an early model by Hans Singer, that $20 billion annually was needed to raise GDP per capita by 2 percent annually in the developing world.[1] Not much later, an introductory book to development economics could state: "The first question in development planning is: 'How much total investment is needed to produce target

---

[1] United Nations, "Measures for the Economic Development of Under-Developed Countries," chapter 11, 1951.

increases in per capita income?"[2] But if one side of the imbalance was the lack of capital, the other one was population growth. And although most development economists emphasized the need for capital, some, like Tinbergen, also asked for attention for the "problem" of overpopulation.

And yet there was something unique to Tinbergen's approach to development. Whereas many of the other "pioneers of development"[3] were concerned with theories of economic growth and development, those issues are peripheral in Tinbergen's writings. His most famous model, planning in three stages, was a model of policymaking. And hence its origins and purpose should be understood as continuous with his policy planning work in the Netherlands. Tinbergen built decision models and institutional models of how to plan. This makes his connection to international organizations, most importantly the UN, easy and natural. But it also created a curious emptiness at the core of his development work. If Tinbergen did not develop or rely on a particular model of economic development, how could he arrive at a methodology for planning for development?

The transformation we analyzed in Chapter 10 finds its full completion in his development work. What Tinbergen offered was a framework for policymaking for developing countries. This framework was still rooted in economics, in the sense that the models were geared to socioeconomic problems. But the approach was not committed to a particular theory of economic growth or to a particular theory of business cycles (which increasingly faded into the background, anyhow), and it was not even strongly committed to a particular theory of how markets functioned. One might therefore be tempted to think of it as only a framework rather than a fully developed theory, but that would be a serious misunderstanding.

The framework was committed to certain institutions that it regarded as essential for development planning. Much like his work on economic policy on a domestic level, his development planning worked from the idea that certain key policymaking institutions (as well as relevant statistical material) were in place. In the next chapter, we will investigate what such institutional design looked like through a case study of his work in Turkey. In this chapter, we will analyze his more theoretical work on development planning. That theoretical work consisted of the theory of

[2] Arndt, *Economic Development: The History of an Idea*, 55, 1987.
[3] Meier, *Pioneers of Development*, 1984.

planning in stages, with, on the one hand, extensions into the area of educational and regional planning. On the other hand, reflections on the institutions that made development planning possible domestically and, more importantly, how an international economic order could be designed that facilitated the integration of the developing countries into the world economy.

Tinbergen's development planning work rested on a new economic consensus that made his institutional contributions possible. That consensus suggested that development could not be left to spontaneous market forces and, more strongly, that development required state planning. Colonial rule was no longer possible, but neither could a return to laissez-faire be accepted. Within such a paradigm of state-led growth, there was ample opportunity for Tinbergen to expand his work on economic policymaking beyond the domestic level.

13.1 Procedural Excellence

The dual nature of his work, institutional and policy-oriented, was well reflected in his first systematic treatment of the subject. It was a manual on development planning that he was requested to write by the International Bank for Reconstruction and Development (IBRD). Its title is telling for its "noneconomic" nature: *Design of Development*.[4] The booklet from 1958 is a relatively slim manual, totaling little more than seventy pages. The economic problem of development was glossed over in fewer than seven pages. There was a quick acknowledgment of the need for basic investments in infrastructure and the need for stimulating private entrepreneurial activity, but Tinbergen did not provide a theory of how development takes place, or what the economic and social preconditions of development were. Development as a goal was also left unexplored; it was equated with an increase in the productive capacity of a country. The manual was, instead, about the need for a "coordinated and coherent plan." Consequently, it outlined the requirements for the development of such a plan.

Tinbergen was unique among the early contributors to development economics for his near-singular focus on decision models. The other early development economists were more occupied with an economic theory of development. These are nicely summarized by Hans Singer in his

---

[4] Tinbergen, *The Design of Development*, 1958.

Economic Progress in Underdeveloped Countries.[5] The basic idea underlying most of the theories was that underdeveloped countries were stuck in
a vicious circle, and to break this circle a so-called Big Push was required.
This Big Push would enable them to exploit economies of scale, since the
economy was currently stuck at a level of low productivity. The most
common explanation of this low productivity was that there was underemployment in the agricultural sector of the economy.[6] Many of the early
development economists were hopeful than once such a "take-off" had
taken place, the countries would reach a stage of self-sustained growth.
This meant that the country itself would be able to save enough to increase
the capital stock at a rate sufficient to continue to grow their economy.

In Tinbergen's organizational logic, the main obstacles are not of an
economic but of an administrative nature. He wrote that there was need for
"a harmonious program" and the "avoidance of international duplication."
In other words, coordination between the different planning departments
within a country and between the various international development
organizations was necessary. The central problem in this logic of organization is to find a means of combining the private and the public sector in
developing economies. As early as this first major publication, Tinbergen
made clear that the means for doing this might be provided by what he
called public management. This should lead to finding "the optimum
pattern of organization." This might be a mixed form since "mixed ownership may sometimes afford a means of combining private efficiency with
a desirable direct public control."[7] The developing countries' economies, or
rather the administrative machinery, had to be remade according to the
model of mixed economies, which were common at that point in
Western Europe.

One might argue that in a manual written for the IBRD one should not
expect to find a discussion of economic theory. As its director explained,
the Economic Development Institute (part of the IBRD) existed to enable
administrators from member countries of the Bank "engaged with a
development plan, to convene for discussion and instruction on drawing
up and implementing such plans."[8] But we will see that the emphasis on
the organizational aspects will, if anything, only become stronger in

[5] Singer, "Economic Progress in Underdeveloped Countries," 1949.
[6] Hirschman, "The Rise and Decline of Development Economics," 2013.
[7] Tinbergen, *The Design of Development*, 66, 1958.
[8] De Marchi, "Models and Misperceptions: Chenery, Hirschman and Tinbergen on
Development Planning," 93, 2016.

Tinbergen's writings on the subject. His way of thinking had, by then, become that of the economic planner or expert who sought to form rational policies, and the tools he would develop in his development economics work were thus either tools to arrive at such rational policies or institutional concerns of how to organize planning. And that is also how he increasingly trained his students, as policy experts, not as econometricians or economic theorists. After their training they were expected to work in a planning institute in a developing country.

This distinguished his approach from that of many of the other famous names associated with early development economics. It is common to think of debates in development planning as debates about the causes of economic growth or development.[9] There are those who have drawn on classical economic theory such as Arthur Lewis,[10] while others drew on neoclassical growth theory, pioneered by Harrod and Domar and given its definite form by Robert Solow. The classical approach was more focused on structural factors in the economy (population and production capacity), while the neoclassical approach treated growth as mostly a technological issue. For the neoclassical growth theorists, the goal was to remove the obstacles that prevented underdeveloped countries from fully utilizing the latest technology. But much of Tinbergen's approach was eclectic and pragmatic; he was not particularly wedded to one type of economic theory. He had never had a direct stake in the debate over business-cycle theories but instead had been looking for a synthesis of the different theories. After World War II, even the goal of a synthesis faded into the background, in favor of the investigation of which policies worked. This time the goal was to make the economy grow, and any theory that could contribute to that goal was a useful input, certainly not an article of faith.

Tinbergen was engaged in a debate about how to implement such policies, and about that he had a very definite idea: "[G]eneral programming has to supply a bird's-eye view of the pattern of future development of the country ... the aim is to arrive at a framework of figures for the possible development of an economy."[11] This entailed not merely a vision of how this should be done but also a vision of who should do it. In the Netherlands, he had successfully wrested economic policy away from parliament and into the hands of expert institutions. Now economic policy

[9] Meier, *Pioneers of Development*, 1984.
[10] Boianovsky, "Arthur Lewis and the Classical Foundations of Development Economics," 2019.
[11] Tinbergen, *The Design of Development*, 6, 1958.

in developing countries had to become the domain of experts. That vision complemented the more theoretical visions of economic development, but historically it was much more of a break. The theories of economic growth of the early development economists had important links with the work of the classical economists like Adam Smith and Karl Marx. But these theories tended to be structural: they focused on underlying changes in technology, population levels, and trade regimes. There was a smaller, but not insignificant tradition, with roots in the work of the German economist Friedrich List, that argued that the state had a more active role to play in steering economic development. Curiously, by the late 1950s it was virtually uncontested that the state should play a leading role in economic development.

Tinbergen's contribution to development economics was therefore not a theory of take-off growth (Walt Rostow), linkages (Raul Prebisch, Albert Hirschman, and others), or dependency of the South on the North (Henrique Cardoso); rather, he created legitimacy and space for economic development experts. In his own reflections on these efforts he made this fairly clear: "In *The Design of Development* I discussed some of the techniques available and used for setting realistic targets and deriving appropriate policy instruments."[12] It was the same logic of economic policymaking he had developed domestically, but now applied to the problem of development. The emphasis was on *techniques* not theories. And the employment of these techniques required able experts in appropriate institutions.

These experts were modeled after Tinbergen. They were to be modest and diplomatic, and crucially depended on the cooperation of local entrepreneurs and policymakers. He tellingly described this to an audience of ambassadors:

The success of planning partly depends therefore on the personal attitudes of the planners. The examples are many where planning agencies were staffed with enthusiastic young people who thought that they would tell the whole population, business men included, what to do: what had been done before was just only playing; now the real thing had to commence. If they start planning with this attitude, I need not tell you that they won't have great success.[13]

Instead, he continued, planners needed to be able to listen, be tolerant, and be humorous (not his own strength) when necessary. What Tinbergen

[12] Tinbergen, "Development Cooperation as a Learning Process," 319, 1984.
[13] Tinbergen, "Economic Planning for Development," 8, 1963.

projected was not an ideal of top-down planning. His favored approach was a mixture of private initiative and government planning.

This approach was solidified in his book *Development Planning*.[14] The book does not stand out for its originality in his oeuvre; all the elements discussed can be found in the writings of the early 1960s. But the book is the epitome of Tinbergen's organized way of writing and presenting a subject. And it demonstrates his two-fold contributions to this field. The book described planning as a three-stage process consisting of a macro phase, in the which the general plan for the coming period for a particular country is developed; a regional phase, in which the plan is specified for various regions and industries of the country; and a micro or project phase in which projects are chosen through which the regional plans are executed. The planning-in-stages methodology focused on the *consistency* between these various stages. It is a methodology for the development and execution of plans, a bit like a sophisticated checklist.

The only section that discussed "factors conducive to economic development" in the book was devoted to a very brief overview of some cultural or psychological factors that hamper economic development. Tinbergen's views on this subject are not original or different from that of others, but in hindsight they seem to be based on a very naïve view of modernization, which is slowed down by "an indifference towards the betterment of one's material condition, an aversion to complicated techniques and an inclination to routine habits, shortsightedness and a fear of uncertainty, lack of energy, and individualism."[15] The other part of his contribution was to provide an institutional analysis of how development planning could be executed in a country. This included a discussion of Tinbergen's theory of instrument and target variables, but most importantly a discussion of the procedure of national planning and the type of planning organization required at the national level. The model he had in mind was clearly the CPB in the Netherlands. To this he added an emphasis on international coordination, which should prevent conflicting plans across countries.

The development planning techniques he developed were useful tools, but also disciplinary instruments. Tinbergen's planning methodology of instruments and targets had already been understood that way. The primary lesson for policymakers was that the number of targets could not exceed the number of instruments. The development planning techniques were understood and used in a similar manner. One of his students

---

[14] Tinbergen, *Development Planning*, 1967. [15] Ibid., 26–28.

remembered how he used Tinbergen's models to check the various import and export plans of the OECD countries to conclude that the sum of all the (planned) exports was twice as high as the sum of all planned imports. Proudly, he remembered that he could explain to the others in the room that "a 'plan' is not a simple addition of all our wishes."[16]

The planning-in-stages model had a similar disciplinary force. The macro plan was used as a check on the various industrial plans. Did the industrial plans jointly achieve the targets? And, more importantly, were there sufficient resources available in the overall plan to finance the various industrial plans? And would they not be competing for skilled manpower? Or to take another example, were the expected returns and the estimates used by the various committees consistent? It was all too easy to base plans on too optimistic predictions about future returns.

What stands out most in retrospect is Tinbergen's confidence in his approach and the *technique* of development planning. The new applied science of development planning was explicitly presented as the outcome of a long process of scientific progress in the West. The final chapter of *Development Planning* discussed how the rise of mathematical economics and mathematical statistics gave rise to econometrics. When econometrics was combined with rational policy design, the result was the development of long-run and short-run planning models. It was now time to apply these models all around the world and make the world modern. The chapter was a somewhat unusual excursion into historical analysis for Tinbergen. He positioned his own work as the culmination of a long tradition of scientific progress and the rise of rational policy making. It is a sign of the fact that he was riding a wave of recognition, renown, and success that gave rise to seemingly ever-growing confidence and ambitions.

13.2 Shaping the World Economy

The manual Tinbergen was asked to write for IBRD was not the only such request he received from the major international organizations concerned with development in the late fifties and early sixties.[17] His writing output, consistently high throughout his career, took a new flight, but no longer in scientific journals and party publications. Instead, it now appeared

---

[16] Barend Buys in Jolink and Barendrecht, *Gedeelde Herinneringen*, 30, 1993.
[17] He also coauthored a more technical manual on programming techniques for development planning five years later. Group of Experts, *Programming Techniques for Economic Development with Special Reference to Asia and the Far East*, 1960.

increasingly in magazines and journals of international development organizations, in reports for governments around the world, and in requested articles from professional and more popular magazines. One of the larger requests came from the Inter-University Committee on Comparative Economics, supported by the Ford Foundation. Tinbergen was commissioned to write a comparative study of planning methods in various countries. It resulted in the book *Central Planning*,[18] based on a set of surveys sent out to the various planning agencies around the world (fifty-one in total) to assess the various approaches to planning. But the book itself was more an introduction to Tinbergen's mature views on planning. Perhaps most noticeably, these did not include an explicit defense of planning vis-à-vis markets or laissez-faire, but rather presented planning as the modern form of policymaking that had a natural place in both Eastern and Western economies. The book failed to satisfy most reviewers, who found it shallow and questioned the extent to which Tinbergen had drawn the full benefits from a comparative study.[19] His own student, Hans Linneman, who worked on the surveys later, even wondered whether Tinbergen in fact did not prepare the text for the book without waiting for the results of the survey.[20]

Economic planning had become an article of faith in international policy circles, a surprising fact given the wider context. In 1964, with the Cold War in full effect, he could publish an international book called *Central Planning* for an American organization. A decade earlier, the IBRD had still refused to include the word "planning" in the title of his manual, which consequently was called the *Design of Development*.[21]

An even more ambitious book was a study written at the request of the Twentieth Century Fund, *Shaping the World Economy*.[22] It was explicitly commissioned to sketch a vision of how the economy of the West could better cooperate with the developing world. Several of his students at the NEI were involved in the preparation of the study, including two Japanese researchers temporarily at the NEI, as well as two economists from the Dutch companies Philips and Shell. The research team reflected the international outlook and the belief that the cooperation of the private and the public sector was the future.

---

[18] Tinbergen, *Central Planning*, 1964.
[19] Ames, "Review of *Central Planning* by Jan Tinbergen," 1965; Wiles, "Review of *Central Planning* by Jan Tinbergen," 1965; Ennerfelt, "Review of *Central Planning* by Jan Tinbergen," 1965.
[20] Linneman in Jolink and Barendrecht-Tinbergen, *Gedeelde Herinneringen*, 1993.
[21] De Vries in ibid.   [22] Tinbergen, *Shaping the World Economy*, 1962.

The study was again meant to be empirically grounded like the one on planning. But rather than planning techniques, this book was to be based on experiences around the world with trade and production agreements. The appendices to this book are testimony to the scope of this study, but just as in *Central Planning*, the book is best read as Tinbergen's own vision and reflection on his own experiences. Linneman later wrote the following to Tinbergen:

> The travels of Leida van Oven, Hartog, Rijken van Olst and me took place in the summer of 1961. In September you returned from your holidays on De Veluwe. Who can describe our amazement when you took the draft-text out of your briefcase! Ten chapters, neat, in your clear handwriting on office sheets. I had gotten used to quite a bit over the years, but now I really had to bat my eyelashes. The others were completely taken aback: how was this possible? What task was left for them? Well that became crystal clear: some sections had to be worked out a bit more or filled in, we would jointly discuss the text, and then the book would be finished. The travel reports became appendices, with a summary of barely four pages in the main text. The empirical research would be reported by me in three more technical appendices. When you later read them, you expressed your positive surprise over the great amount of work that had gone into them.... Three years later the Dutch translation appeared, done by our colleague Hartog, this time the title page mentioned five authors, but whether that was really justified?[23]

What was equally surprising is that Linneman nonetheless thought of *Shaping the World Economy* as the epitome of their work at the Balanced International Growth Division of the NEI. On the one hand, this was because the empirical work contained an analysis of trade flows in the world based on a so-called gravity equation. This equation, which suggested that trade partners closer to one another were more attracted to each other, would prove empirically fruitful and is used to this day.[24] And on the other hand, it was because it contained a coherent vision and provided guidance for the work done by him and others at the division. Tinbergen at this point in his career had not only mostly left the empirical handiwork behind to be done by his many students and coworkers, but he also increasingly focused on providing a vision and direction for others to work along. Ehrenfest had early on suggested that what was needed more

---

[23] Linneman in Jolink and Barendrecht-Tinbergen, *Gedeelde Herinneringen*, 1993.
[24] Bergstrand and Egger, "Gravity Equations and Economic Frictions in the World Economy," 2013; Linneman, *An Econometric Study of International Trade Flows*, 1966. The gravity model of international trade explained frictions in world trade by suggesting that closer countries are more attracted (or likely) to trade with each. More precisely, trade between two countries is inversely proportional to the distance between them.

than scientifically trained economists were those who could combine it with vision; Tinbergen indeed increasingly took up that latter role.

Shaping the World Economy is thus best read as a visionary document of where the world should go, rather than an empirical inquiry into how the economy is currently shaped. This optimistic and visionary character was even highlighted in the cautious preface by August Heckser (himself a famous trade economist), who expressed some skepticism of the vision Tinbergen presented. The book's tone was set in the introduction, which sketched the threats the world was facing, from the rise of communism to nuclear weapons, as well as the opportunities that emerged with the newly gained freedom in many countries now that colonialism was over: "[T]he world, characterized by a vast gap between technical ability and moral power, is in desperate need of a policy – a policy which will give it shape, and create a framework for the solution of its most urgent problems."[25]

Tinbergen positioned himself as a moral guide, not an engineer providing more technical skills. This moral guiding role, he argued, was even more necessary for the nonaligned countries: those who had not yet chosen between capitalism and communism. Nehru, the leader of India, had started the movement of nonaligned countries in 1955. Development, Tinbergen argued, was possible only when there was an interest in material well-being, a willingness to look ahead and take risks, an interest in technology, a willingness to cooperate, a certain degree of persistence, and a willingness to accept the rules of the game.[26]

A central part of that vision was Tinbergen's plea for free international trade facilitated through multilateral trade agreements. In 1958 Tinbergen had reunited with Haberler and James Meade, with whom he had worked in Geneva to write a report for the General Agreement for Tariffs and Trade (GATT).[27] The GATT, he argued, was an important stepping-stone, but the next step should be the International Trade Organization (ITO), which would further develop a global regime of free trade. There were obstacles on the road, the most important of which was a lack of vision and a narrow concern with national or private interests. The development of an international business cycle policy was held back by what he called, in German, "Kleinstaaterei": thinking small, in national terms, where thinking big, in global terms, was required. He understood well that his plea for international integration and more power vested with global organizations

---

[25] Tinbergen, *Shaping the World Economy*, 3–4, 1962. [26] Ibid., 12.
[27] Haberler et al., *Trends in International Trade*, 1958.

would sound awfully utopian in the era of the Cold War, where a new global conflict seemed far more likely than a new global order. Yet: "It is the task of the economist to make clear what is the best technical solution to an urgent problem, even if that solution seems at the time 'politically impossible.'" The rhetorical switch back to his role as a technical economist was noteworthy, but from a reference in the book to Arnold J. Toynbee, the British historian and philosopher of history, it is clear that he was after something far more ambitious than technical advice, namely, to "make the benefits of civilization available for the whole human race."[28]

The second half of the book made clear what this new world order should consist of. It would be a world order of international solidarity that would be brought about by the UN, which, like national governments, had to develop clear goals and instruments to achieve those goals: "[W]e can no longer afford the luxury of national autonomy." At this point in his career, for Tinbergen the UN was the only viable option for this world order, since it was the only institution that at least on paper included both the capitalist and the communist countries. He hoped that the regional units such as Benelux (BElgium, NEtherlands, and LUXemburg), the OECD, and the European Economic Community (EEC) would all become superfluous. That same optimism about a global order was reflected in his suggestion that developed countries should donate 1 percent of their GDP to underdeveloped countries.

The international optimism of the 1960s was built on confidence and stability at home. The 1950s and early 1960s were remarkably stable years in which there was growing confidence that the business cycle was a thing of the past and that a mixed economy with an important role for economic expertise represented a mature version of capitalism (or a mature socialism, as Tinbergen suggested). This confidence allowed Tinbergen and many others of his age to export this model, not only to developing countries but also to the international level. *Shaping the World Economy* repeatedly drew analogies between the national and the international level.

On the national level, the fundamental conflict of the nineteenth century and the first decades of the twentieth was between the working class and the capitalists. Tinbergen suggested that this conflict had been overcome in the postwar national order, and now the most important (lurking) conflict was that between the underdeveloped countries (the Global South) and the

---

[28] Tinbergen, *Shaping the World Economy*, 92, 1962.

developed countries (the Global North). Finding a solution to this would require an international order that would give the underdeveloped countries a similar seat at the table and redraw the power balance in their favor. This should also include significant income transfers.

Some of the initial mistakes that were made at the national level should be avoided at the international level. So, international parliaments or governing bodies should be supplemented from the start with experts, who preferably also had voting rights. This would lead – and here he was once again drawing from his experience in the Netherlands – to the construction of a more stable order.[29] That stable international order ought to include new international institutions such as a world treasury and a world central bank. The ordering project that he had completed at the national level now had to be continued at the international level.

The book generated an enormous response. At least twelve professional reviews appeared, but most were quite a bit more skeptical than an early one in the Netherlands entitled: "The Plan of a Grand Master."[30] The general tone of the reviews is well captured by the following passage from one of them:

Fifty years ago few would have believed that the U.S. Government could have achieved the degree of economic powers it now has. Thirty years ago, many people would have labeled as Utopian the idea that a multinational army would be fighting for an internationally directed solution to the internal problems of one nation in the heart of Africa. And but ten years ago a host of experts labeled the idea of a united Europe as starry eyed dreaming.... So it is not at all impossible that by 1980 many of his [Tinbergen's] ideas will have come to fruition.[31]

A somewhat more cautious lesson was drawn by another reviewer: "The fact that Professor Tinbergen's proposals may be currently impracticable, and that by some they may even be considered politically naïve, ought not to diminish the merits of the study. If there is anybody to be blamed in this context, it is the author least of all."[32] At face value these were compliments, but virtually all reviewers expressed skepticism toward the radically globalist vision and hopes that Tinbergen had laid out.

A recurring complaint in the reception of the book was that while Tinbergen sketched a vision and a way forward, he was hardly concerned with diagnosis. Leibenstein made the point concisely: "The orientation is a

[29] Ibid., 188–92.   [30] Hagen, "Het Plan van een Grootmeester," 1963.
[31] From an anonymous review in *The International Executive*, "Review of *Shaping the World Economy* by Jan Tinbergen," 1963.
[32] Vanek, "Review of *Shaping the World Economy* by Jan Tinbergen," 101, 1964.

direct relation between objectives, instruments, plans and results. What seems to be missing is an interest in diagnosis. To use a medical analogy, the underlying belief seems to be that one could prescribe for the health of a nation without understanding its ills."[33] It would be a damning criticism from the perspective of economic theory. But it in fact captured the distinct character of Tinbergen's approach quite well. It indeed did not excel in diagnosis, nor in a theory of economic development, but it excelled in showing how we could get from A to B, and how policy could help in that respect. It is therefore even more significant, or perhaps surprising, that the means of getting from A to B, through development *planning*, was hardly criticized in the discourse of the 1960s.

13.3 Planning in Space and Time

Tinbergen's development planning work was so expansive that we cannot do full justice to it, but it is helpful to distinguish between two directions in which Tinbergen developed his work with the help of many colleagues and students around him. The first direction was that of applied planning models, the most noticeable being regional planning and education planning. The second direction was that of measurement. Tinbergen was convinced that economic development could be measured in various ways and sought to expand more traditional yardsticks, most importantly GDP.

The topic of regional development was briefly touched in Tinbergen's *Design for Development*. Here, national examples from the Netherlands were often held up as models to follow more generally. In the late 1950s, he was working on regional development in the north of the Netherlands – a region that was still predominantly agricultural. In his report he argued that the problem of underdevelopment of a region could be solved by either trying to develop the area or moving the people to more economically developed areas. He expressed a clear preference for the development of various regions, in part because he feared overurbanization might strengthen tendencies toward a mass society.

His model on regional planning developed out of an article originally written for the Venezuelan government.[34] In the model, the relevant data were the mobility of production factors (how easily capital and labor "migrate"), the geographical differences between regions (resulting in

---

[33] Leibenstein, "Review of *Shaping the World Economy* by Jan Tinbergen," 94, 1966.
[34] Tinbergen, *Regional Planning: Some Principles*, 1960; for the original publication, see Tinbergen, "Algunas Técnicas de Planeación del Desarrollo," 1955.

different costs of production), and the relevance of agriculture (the most space-consuming type of production), as well as indivisibilities. Indivisibilities were industries that needed a certain scale to be profit-making and were therefore by their very nature centralized in terms of production: steel factories were the prototypical example of an industry that benefited from scale. The main variable to be explained in the regional planning models was the degree of centralization of production within a country. The instruments available to the government to influence the regional pattern of production were direct investments in infrastructure or certain industries, as well as subsidies and taxes. The regional planning model was thus again a decision model with instrument variables and policy targets.

There was another similarity with his national policy models, and that was the crucial emphasis on the level of decision-making. In his models, there were regional, national, and international industries.[35] In order to make informed policy decisions, the issue of the scale of decision-making that he explored in his policy work was of crucial relevance. One did not want all regions to specialize in a particular industry, because this would lead to vast overproduction at the national level. And one did not want all developing countries to specialize in similar types of industries because this would lead to overproduction and low prices at the international level. An integrated development plan, therefore, by necessity required international coordination according to Tinbergen. The logic of planning went hand in hand with the logic of centralization.

The idea of regional development became ever more prominent throughout the period. As we will also see in our detailed case study of his development work in Turkey, one of the major problems that developing countries faced was the great disparity between the urban centers and the countryside. By the late 1960s, Tinbergen often presented the regional phase of planning and the project phase side by side, turning his three-stage planning model into a kind of four-stage model. These models became the gold standard at the NEI where a special division, Balanced International Growth, was founded to advise both international agencies and national governments on development planning. The refinements included the consideration of local circumstances and constraints, but Tinbergen himself remained mostly concerned with the national level. Regional development and the underlying causes of regional disparities never became central to his work.

---

[35] Tinbergen, "International, National, Regional and Local Industries," 1965.

More interesting in that respect was Tinbergen's work on educational planning. There was a danger that at this point a new area of planning simply meant a new opportunity to apply similar models, and that was to some extent true. If regional planning meant planning in terms of space, then education planning was planning in terms of time. The central problem was the speed at which developing countries could educate their (future) workforce, so that the benefits of new technologies and planning techniques could be fully utilized.

Initial development aid projects were often ineffective, and it was believed that this failure was closely related to the fact that local skills were absent, which meant that simple "technology transfers" were not sufficient. But there was a more pressing reason why education and training were so high on the agenda of development economists. The early development experts were all flown in from the West, and this generated significant tensions. As we will also see in the case study of Turkey in the next chapter, there was limited willingness in the developing countries to accept foreign expertise. This was even more so the case in the newly independent states, which had just ousted their colonial oppressors.

Tinbergen described the problem as follows: "Former colonies usually start their independent life as a nation with considerable numbers of foreigners in their leading circles. For understandable reasons these countries want to replace these foreigners by citizens of their own nation. This gives rise to a problem of Indianization in India, of Egyptianization in Egypt, of Africanization in Africa and so on."[36] The problem was indeed known at the time as the "-ization problem." One would perhaps expect that Tinbergen would engage in a discussion of cultural differences and colonial and postcolonial relations after he had introduced the problem. And Tinbergen did briefly acknowledge that the problem was wider than education and had "many other aspects." But then he went on to present his model, in which cultural factors were completely absent, and the problem was transformed into a purely quantitative problem about the length of time that was required to train qualified personnel. The problem was consequently reduced to the development of "an optimum program" of additional students and temporary foreign experts necessary for training, without interrupting the current production patterns too much.

In doing so Tinbergen had reduced the problem of "-ization" to a problem of linear programming in which, given a number of side

---

[36] Tinbergen, "Introductory Remarks on the 'Ization Problem,'" 328, 1963.

constraints (the amount of initial foreign experts available, the amount of trained personnel required in production sectors), one could calculate the time it would take before foreign experts were no longer required. This method was characteristic of his solution-oriented approach and his ability to bring a problem back to its "essentials." But for somebody who had been involved within the movement of cultural socialism in the Netherlands, and later was involved with the progressive Breakthrough movement, it also seems curiously naïve to believe that merely increasing the *years* of schooling would really alter much in the economy. He briefly alluded to "differing circumstances and habits taken over from the past," but never specified what those might be. Even the so-called essential notion of education was not discussed at all; instead, we were left with a purely quantitative measure of education, whose only "quality" was whether it was primary, secondary, or tertiary education.

In the 1920s, the AJC had shown a clear awareness that part of the challenge was the emancipation of workers both culturally and morally. In fact, the movement prioritized such issues over more access to education. Awareness of their own condition, possibilities, and a better lifestyle was prioritized over more access to (public) education. Ultimately, it was a movement of self-help for the workers. In the development economics project of the 1960s, very little was left of such emancipatory goals, and instead the focus was purely on skills in an instrumental sense. Even economic expertise no longer required the combination of skills Ehrenfest and Tinbergen had admired in Keynes; it had become a matter of technical skills obtained through training.

Although the education planning models found quite widespread adoption, there were also contemporaries critical of his approach. One of the other early development economists, Thomas Balogh, was asked to comment on the paper during an OECD symposium on the so-called residual factor in the theory of economic growth. Balogh's opening remark could hardly have been less critical: "I fear that I felt somewhat embarrassed when I received Professor Tinbergen's paper for comment. I was quite uncertain of its real intent. Was it a huge joke? Or was it an attempt to reduce econometrics *ad absurdum:* a model, so to speak, to end all models? Or, least plausibly, did it really set out to do what it said?"[37]

The critique Balogh offered was in some ways reminiscent of that offered by Keynes. He questioned the linearity assumption Tinbergen

---

[37] Balogh, "Education and Economic Growth: Comments on Professor Tinbergen's Planning 'Model,'" 261, 1964.

made between economic growth and the amount of education. Such a relationship was highly dependent on contextual factors, and certainly we should not expect that by simply increasing the amount of educated people we might expect economic growth, he argued. Balogh even suggested that in some very underdeveloped areas, increasing the level of education would actually lead to more unemployment since the jobs that required qualifications were simply not available: "[A]n education in the feudal-aristocratic countries of South America, the colonial-aristocratic areas of British Africa, and the litterateur-colonial areas of French Africa would produce not merely no growth, but possible refusal to work on farms, an increase in urban employment, subversion and collapse."[38] But his more general point was that Tinbergen never bothered to analyze the difficulties associated with implementing a new educational system, and the associated social consequences.

Balogh's response was fierce, but it also reflected his broader discomfort with what are currently called neoclassical growth models, which treat knowledge (education) and technology as exogenous factors that cannot themselves be explained or analyzed. As an alternative, Balogh proposed a more historical and locally informed approach that paid attention to local conditions and comparative advantages. Tinbergen was little impressed with the criticism; he emphasized that he in fact had good data to support the linearity assumption and that any starting model had to be simple. Models will "have to be made more complicated for practical purposes."[39] However, what was at stake was not merely simplicity, but also the starting point. For Balogh, this had to be the historical conditions and circumstances of a country (what Leibenstien in his review called the diagnosis). Tinbergen instead proposed a simple policy model that allowed one to plan, without inquiring into what type of education was necessary or what local difficulties such an educational program might run into.

And there was another issue at stake. Tinbergen's approach to development planning became popular because it provided definite answers based on a relatively limited amount of data. Moreover, it provided a "tool" that could be applied in many different settings. In a follow-up publication on educational planning, he wrote:

As in so many walks of life, there is an optimum solution in the form of a compromise between the degree of precision and the manageability of a model or method.... Manageability in this context implies not only how the model

---

[38] Ibid., 266.   [39] Tinbergen, "Education and Economic Growth: A Reply," 1964.

should be used but also how it should be explained to policymakers. This problem of communication is very important in planning.[40]

Tinbergen's models, which had always tended toward the practical and the simple, were now used in a wide variety of contexts and not merely in the relatively confined context of the League of Nations or the Dutch CPB where he himself was present. Instead, the models now became part of planning manuals for development specialists all around the world. Although the models required some basic mathematical knowledge, they relied on relatively little data and provided definite answers based on which planning could take place. In addition, they created a shared set of international knowledge among development experts, which was congenial to the international approach taken by the major organizations such as the OECD, the UN, and the IBRD.

These organizations were not local development organizations or governments, but international bodies that naturally sought to formulate a coherent policy that could be applied in a larger number of countries. As such, the "-ization" problem reared its head here in a serious manner. Whereas Balogh implicitly made the argument that the "-ization" problem was in part a problem of local knowledge and historical specificity, a problem that made the development challenge different in every country, Tinbergen presented a universalist approach. Tinbergen's approach was internationalist in outlook and treated national economies as variants of a common underlying structure. Specific features could be added on with local parameters or by extending the model for specific problem settings. But the models were designed as universal tools.

A rather extreme example of the universalistic approach was that his regional planning started from a uniform square on which the optimal locations of various industries could be determined. The abstraction involved was not primarily a consequence of some scientific desirability for generality or universality; Tinbergen was not directly concerned with such scientific "virtues" at this point in his career. Rather, the abstraction was a result of the *institutional* fact that these models were developed as regional development tools to be applied all across the world, whether the region was flat or mountainous, fertile or dry as a desert, rich in natural resources or devoid of these, or whether the population was evenly spread or concentrated at a coast. Similarly, education became a kind of abstraction that referred only to years of training – not what was being taught, by

---

[40] Tinbergen and Bos, "Appraisal of the Model and Results of Its Application," 1965.

whom, or in what type of educational system. In Chapter 15, we will see that his own daughter would recognize the dangers of this way of thinking. It was only a model, but when a model is used often and repeatedly, there is always a danger it might be mistaken for reality.

13.4 Development Economics without Culture and Morality?

What went missing in the development planning of Tinbergen was any emphasis on the emancipatory process that had to take place in these countries. He still highlighted some psychological or cultural factors that hampered the development process, but these were mere obstacles to be overcome. That was radically different from the cultural socialism of his youth, which argued that socialism was first and foremost a personal change and a cultural shift in the attitudes of the workers. It was also quite different from the ideals of the breakthrough movement, which had sought a more meaningful version of progress. Hendrik de Man had worried about cultural degeneration precisely during the process of economic development and industrialization.

The situation in the developing countries was clearly different than in the Netherlands of the 1920s. Tinbergen might have believed that material needs were simply more important than cultural and spiritual needs at this stage of development. But it was precisely the AJC of his youth that had criticized the one-sided, Marxist focus on material conditions. De Man's foremost worry was that the working classes were materially enriched but culturally impoverished during the process of industrialization. And something else was quite radically different now. The AJC and the Breakthrough movement were both civil society organizations that involved the very people that the movements were supposed to help. Development planning, on the other hand, was a purely technocratic project for Tinbergen. The means for bringing about change was no longer civil society, but the state.

In fact, Balogh's criticism in some sense did not go far enough. He shared Tinbergen's treatment of education as one among many factors of production: capital, land, and education (or human capital, as it would later be called). Tinbergen never abandoned this way of thinking afterward; in his reflective piece on his development work he called education "the longest production process." That was not merely a metaphor; it had become the dominant way of thinking about education in his development work. This was odd, to say the least, for a man whose own personal philosophy was deeply shaped by moral concerns, someone who believed and embodied the idea that knowing what was important in life was much more important than material riches or skills. In his own family, it had been very clear that education entailed more than acquiring skills. His father as well as his mentor, Ehrenfest, had both been part of a generation of progressive educators who sought to develop the youth into complete human beings. The love for languages fostered by his parents, the trips outdoors meant to stimulate curiosity in the natural world, the empathy and solidarity he preached for the poor everywhere and that was widely shared in his social circles all suggested that most of the progress could in fact be made through cultural, not economic, change; cultural change often preceded economic change, or at the very least the two had to accompany one another. His personal abstinence and thrift were a clear symbol of this: the moral was more important than the material. To this day it is tradition in the Tinbergen family line to send one's kids to Montessori schools, primary schools that work from the assumption that children have an innate desire for self-development, often summed up in Maria Monetessori's adage: "Help me do it by myself." Yet one searches in vain for acknowledgments of these aspects of education in his development planning. Tinbergen repeatedly objected to cultural relativist charges against development aid: "Not all cultural features are sacrosanct." But there is much middle ground between becoming culturally relativist and considering existing cultural habits *only* as barriers to economic development.

The sole exception to this overly technocratic perspective was the issue of population growth. In 1960 he argued: "The only way, then, to avoid a further stagnation in the development of regions concerned consists in putting a check on population increase."[41] And some years earlier he had already called it his professional duty to point out the relevance of population policy in the process of development, something he suggested not all his colleagues were willing to do.[42] But rather than developing planning models for population growth or being attracted to eugenicist types of ideas, as, for example, his fellow development economist Gunnar Myrdal was,[43] Tinbergen never felt that this was an area of direct government intervention.[44] Instead, he argued that the choice of having children was a

[41] Tinbergen, "Europe and the World," 380–81, 1960.
[42] Tinbergen, "Welfare Economics and Income Distribution," 498, 1957.
[43] Leonard, "'More Merciful and Not Less Effective': Eugenics and American Economics in the Progressive Era," 2003.
[44] This might have changed after environmental concerns became more prominent, such as in the report on population growth in the Netherlands in which Tinbergen participated; see Staatscommissie Bevolkingsvraagstuk Muntendam, "Bevolking en Welzijn in Nederland," 1976.

personal choice that could be influenced only by spiritual and social leaders.[45] Promoting awareness of the overpopulation problem was acceptable, but direct intervention was not. It was a principle he not merely preached but also practiced. He had only two children (and adopted two more) and even attempted to convince his daughter to not have more than two children.

His theoretical work on development economics might be one of those instances where Tinbergen the scientist was disconnected from Tinbergen the man, just as we saw earlier in his paradoxical attempts to provide a scientific analysis of fascist economics. It is hard not to think that his emphasis on the production process and quantitative targets of economic policy contributed to the materialism he denounced so strongly elsewhere. In order to make sense of the contradiction, one might alternatively suggest that for Tinbergen there was a strict separation between public policy and personal choices. After all, his views on population policies pointed in that direction. But such a separation is hard to maintain when analyzing and promoting a disruptive process such as "development." As Tinbergen himself acknowledged, economic development cannot take place without cultural change. And in a field like education, it seems impossible to maintain a separation between public policy and personal choices; education shapes what individuals become. In this sense, development economist Myrdal, whom Tinbergen admired, realized much better that the goal of economic development required more than raising living standards; it required "new men, modern men."[46]

---

[45] In this he followed in the footsteps of Robert Malthus, who had first theorized the problem of overpopulation. He too believed that only morality could provide a true solution to the problem.

[46] Myrdal cited in Arndt, *Economic Development: The History of an Idea*, 53, 1987.

14

Development Planning on the Ground

Tinbergen in Turkey

14.1 The Prehistory

Tinbergen worked as a development expert in many countries in Asia, South America, and Africa, but he was nowhere involved for as long as in Turkey. There he designed a planning organization and was involved with the preparation of two consecutive five-year plans. In this chapter we will analyze how development planning worked or failed to work "on the ground."

In the spring of 1960, Jan Tinbergen was invited to Turkey to help plan the economic development of the country, he brought along Joop Koopman as his man on the ground. Their initial reception was lukewarm, to say the least. The Turkish government, headed by the Democratic Party, was forced to accept foreign expertise by the OECD. A year earlier the same government had been forced to implement a reform package of the IMF. It was a reform program of the kind that is still associated with the IMF: devaluation of the currency, reform of public finance, and privatization of state firms. But soon internal pressures within the Democratic Party forced it back into expansionary policies, which led to renewed inflation and the continuation of the foreign currency crisis.

The Democratic Party, which found most of its support in the countryside from independent farmers, had liberalized the Turkish economy with considerable success in the early 1950s. Turkey had successfully applied for Marshall Aid early on and afterward pursued a policy geared toward the West and, in particular, toward the United States. It had generously supported the Korean War in the early 1950s, opened some of its important military bases to the United States, and joined NATO. Along with this orientation came "American-style" economic reforms, which meant opening the economy and encouraging private initiative rather than state bureaucratic control over the economy. State growth and bureaucratic growth in Turkey had been smaller than elsewhere during World War II, because the country remained neutral during the war – that is, until the very late stages when American aid was on the horizon for Allied countries. But one of the legacies of Mustafa Kemal Atatürk's interwar regime was a strong bureaucracy, in part developed to enable the Turkish experiment with five-year industrialization plans under his leadership.[1]

The liberalization of the economy in the 1950s was a great success. It led to increased exports of agricultural products, as well as technological improvements in that sector, which increased prosperity in the countryside. But fortunes reversed after the end of the Korean War when world agricultural prices dropped and bad harvests plagued Turkey. The Democratic Party, whose base was mostly in the countryside, responded with the expansionary policies that would lay the foundation for the economic crisis of the late 1950s. And although attempts were made to openup the State Economic Enterprises (SEEs), an important industrial structure inherited from the 1930s, to competition with the private sector, they were not privatized.[2] These state-owned firms formed about half of the industrial sector and included most of the financial infrastructure of the country. So, while Turkey in the 1950s became far more integrated into the world economy, internally it remained a mixed economy with extensive state involvement.[3]

When the IMF and the OECD pushed for reforms after Turkey requested yet more foreign aid and extension of its debts in the late 1950s, the international discourse surrounding development had significantly changed. The American aversion to planning of the immediate postwar period was fading and giving way to a belief that economic development could be managed and planned, much like the economies in Western Europe were at the time. The early 1950s reports on Turkey by the International Bank for Reconstruction and Development (IBRD) and the OECD, the latter written by Hollis Chenery, did not yet push for development planning. They cautioned against overreliance on the SEEs and pushed for a balanced government budget and trade balance.[4] By the late 1950s the reports of the international organizations all favored some

---

[1] Cooper, "The Legacy of Atatürk: Turkish Political Structures and Policymaking," 2000.
[2] Övgün, *Türkiye'de Kamu İktisadi Teşebbüsü Olgusu*, 66–67, 2009.
[3] Keyder, "Economic Development and Crisis: 1950–1980," 1987; Kesik, "Development Planning in Turkey: An Assessment," 2015.
[4] Sönmez, "The Re-emergence of the Idea of Planning," 31, 1967.

form of development planning. The development planning experiments in India were widely admired. The same type of planning was suggested for Turkey, although the change should not be overstated. The hope in the early 1950s was still that a more rational economic policy would lead to a balanced government budget and trade balance. That is, underlying the international perspective was still a firm belief that sound economic policies would be enough to generate development. The instruments of what was considered rational economic policy had altered, but not the belief that economic policies by themselves could spur development.

The Democratic Party, however, had a hard time accepting this new consensus since its early policies and successes had been based on a policy of liberalization and because it depended for its electoral support on small farmers and artisans who clearly stood to lose the most from planned development with a focus on industrialization. The president at the time even called planning "totalitarian."[5] Pressure on Turkey further mounted when German Chancellor Ludwig Erhard visited the country. A hasty memorandum on planning was drawn up and shown to him, but he was not impressed and suggested that the Turkish government first needed to bring in somebody with knowledge about planning.[6] Until they had done so, Germany would withhold most of its financial aid to Turkey.[7] An investment committee was drawn together to prepare a kind of plan, but it completely lacked the expertise or authority for this, and when they sent their report to Erhard, he was again dismissive: "This document is not a plan but a list of projects." A little later, the Ministry of Foreign Affairs announced, unexpectedly to the members of the investment committee, that Tinbergen would come as planning expert in March 1960.[8] Word soon spread among Turkish bureaucrats that his total salary would be a mere $800, and it was expected that this would be little more than a PR effort to suggest that development planning would be adopted.

It was an impression that was not too far off the mark. When Tinbergen and his assistant Koopman arrived in the country, the government sought to hide the "foreign" planning experts from the public eye to save their own face. According to one account, Tinbergen and Koopman were first located at the Electrical Affairs Administration, only to be moved to the State

[5] Mıhçıoğlu, "Devlet Planlama Örgütünün Kuruluş Günleri," 230, 1983.
[6] Erder, *Plânlı Kalkınma Serüveni: 1960'larda Türkiye'de Plânlama Deneyimi (Panel Discussion)*, 22–25, 2003.
[7] Kansu, *Planli Yillar: Anilarla DPT'nin Öyküsü*, 42, 2004.
[8] Mıhçıoğlu, "Yi ne Devlet Planlama Örgütünün Kuruluşu Üzeri ne," 1988.

Water Administration and later to an office at the Middle East Technical University.[9] One newspaper at the time described their situation pitifully:

> The (ex-)government's imprisonment of invaluable planning experts like Prof. Tinbergen in a tiny room at the Middle East Technical University represents a deliberate and unfortunate attempt to isolate them from Turkish experts who are holding the pulse of the national economy. How could Tinbergen prepare a development plan when the accuracy of information given to him is in serious doubt?[10]

The resistance of the Turkish government to the demanded reforms of the international community was clear to all interested parties. In fact, Turkey had put off foreign experts for as long as it could. When Gunnar Myrdal was suggested, they declined because of his socialist convictions.[11] When Hollis Chenery was recommended, he was rejected because he had suggested in his 1953 report that the Turkish lira was overvalued. And now they clearly obstructed attempts from Tinbergen and Koopman to start their work. In a letter written at the end of May, Tinbergen complained that promised data were never provided and that his assistant Koopman had not been paid his promised salary. In fact, Koopman was under such supervision that the government "helped" him in his interviews with the foreign press so that they could ensure these obstructions would not become known to the public.[12] The only positive aspect of these first months was that Koopman, precisely because he was moved around so much, managed to meet quite a few capable technicians who were eager to engage in efforts at planning.

14.2 A Fresh Start

The political reality in Turkey, however, completely changed within a matter of months. On 27 May 1960, the army intervened in the political

---

[9] Ünay, *The Political Economy of Development Planning in Turkey: Neoliberal Globalization and Institutional Reform*, 95, n. 42, 2006; Erder, *Plânlı Kalkınma Serüveni: 1960'larda Türkiye'de Plânlama Deneyimi (Panel Discussion)*, 2003.

[10] Ünay, *The Political Economy of Development Planning in Turkey: Neoliberal Globalization and Institutional Reform*, 95, 2006.

[11] Whether it was Myrdal is not completely certain since the sources mention only a Norwegian Marxist; see Türkcan, Attila Sönmez'e Armağan: Türkiye'de Planlamanın Yükselişi ve Çöküşü 1960–1980, 2010, 320; Emre, The Emergence of Social Democracy in Turkey: The Left and the Transformation of the Republican People's Party, 201, 2014. Myrdal was Swedish. Frisch is another possible candidate, but he was certainly not Marxist, but social democratic.

[12] Milor, "The Genesis of Planning in Turkey," 12, 1990.

crisis and took over the government in a coup. The economic crisis had led to firm opposition of various parties, which had joined forces to attempt to enforce new elections. In response, the Democratic Party had attempted to shut down the opposition through detainment and investigations into the various parties. Turkey was in danger of reverting back to a one-party state at that point, which Western powers used as justification for the coup, which they (unofficially) supported.[13] But more important was the fact that the current government was unwilling to cooperate with Western powers and the associated international organizations.

The interim military government was much more favorable to the idea of planning. And it was clear it hoped that the Republican People's Party (RPP), the party of Atatürk, at that point headed by İsmet İnönü, would win the next elections. The RPP sought to continue the modernization set in motion by Atatürk, although the more conservative side of the party was not convinced of the need for economic planning to achieve this. It was within this context that Tinbergen and Koopman could really start their work. Tinbergen drafted two memoranda in June on a new organization that would eventually become the Devlet Plânlama Teşkilâtı (DPT), the State Planning Organization (SPO).

Some histories of the period suggest that it was at the initiative of the interim military government that Tinbergen was asked to write his memoranda. But there is important evidence suggesting that Koopman actively lobbied for the creation of a planning agency. In his reminiscences of this period, economist Cemal Mıhçıoğlu described that on the day after the coup, Koopman went to the Office of Foreign Trade. He met with trade minister Cihat İren and suggested that Turkey needed a central planning agency. İren said that his government was temporary and that the creation of a new agency was a task for a future civilian government. Koopman replied that "civilian politicians might not want to create such a planning organization. Because you want to restore the national unity, I think that you are best equipped/capable of executing such a creation."[14] On 4 June, İren and Koopman met again, this time for a two-hour conversation conducted in German, in which Koopman managed to convince İren of the need for a planning agency. İren promised to take it up with the Council of Ministers. The council accepted and state minister Şefik İnan was asked to oversee the creation of a central planning agency.

[13] Eroğul, "The Establishment of Multiparty Rule: 1945–1971," 1987.
[14] Mıhçıoğlu, "Devlet Planlama Örgütünün Kuruluş Günleri," 1983.

Tinbergen produced a memorandum in June 1960 for the design of a planning agency. The proposal contained three principal organizations: the Advisory Planning Board, the Central Planning Commission, and the Central Planning Bureau. The latter was to become the technical heart of development planning in Turkey and was to be organized along the lines he knew from the Netherlands and his work in India. It would be responsible for the development of long-term and annual plans and the coordination of the economic policies of the various ministries. The only new element in its tasks was that the planning bureau would also be in charge of developing regional plans, in line with Tinbergen's idea of planning in stages.

The Central Planning Commission was a higher decision-making body that would meet under the chairmanship of the director of the Central Planning Bureau and would include key representatives of the various ministries and economic experts. It would formulate and decide on the overall goals and principles of the plan, which would then be worked out within the bureau. Finally, the Advisory Planning Board would provide a consultation function for the bureau without explicit responsibilities or authority.

Tinbergen was not quite sure whether the necessary expertise and political will was present to set up a complete planning bureau. In fact, he explicitly suggested to keep the planning bureau relatively small in the first years and to make use of foreign expertise where necessary.[15] And in character with his approach, he suggested that the bureau might gain much by exchange trips with planning bureaus in other countries. Once the work was underway and some framework had been developed, the Central Planning Bureau could then grow into maturity, with one administrative and four technical sections: (1) long-term planning, (2) annual planning, (3) sectoral studies, and (4) regional planning. The role of the Advisory Planning Board was similarly conceived to provide additional expertise lacking from the bureau. That ambition was soon fulfilled: by 1964 the Planning Bureau consisted of a staff of about 130 people, about double the original size of the Central Planning Bureau in the Netherlands.[16] Turkey is a much bigger country than the Netherlands, but given the relatively short period of time that had passed since the Planning Bureau's founding, the organization's growth was impressive.

[15] Kansu, *Planli Yillar: Anilarla DPT'nin Öyküsü*, 48, 2004.
[16] Tinbergen, "Probleme der modernen Türkei," 25, 1964.

His memoranda were the basis for two different draft bills, which both dealt in different ways with the integration of his proposal into the bureaucratic structure of the Turkish state. The first draft came from the hand of the liberal minister İnan, who oversaw the setting up of a planning agency. His draft proposed an extensive General Planning Council to which appointments would be made by the prime minister. And he suggested that the Economic Planning Office should be placed within the first ministry and headed by a state minister. In other words, the technical Planning Bureau would be placed under direct political control and would be further checked by a council consisting of about thirty politicians and leading industrialists. Additionally, the planning experts were expected to work closely with, and would in fact be outnumbered by, practitioners from the various economic sectors within the bureau. The purpose of İnan's draft was clearly to minimize the impact of the new agency.

The Türkeş draft, also known as the Orel draft after the chairman of the committee, Colonel Şinasi Orel, was much closer to Tinbergen's original memoranda and respected the idea of an internally autonomous central planning bureau.[17] But it too involved the prime minister quite directly by placing the office within the first ministry and by proposing a High Planning Council, which was chaired by the prime minister. In the draft bill, this High Council was to have fifteen members, eight of whom were technical experts. In the final bill, this was reduced to eight members, four of whom were technical experts, and with the power of the prime minister to decide when the vote was split. This draft also proposed an Economic Council whose general assembly consisted of high functionaries drawn from the elite of society and representatives of universities, chambers of commerce, industry, and civil or religious organizations, totaling about seventy people. From this Economic Council, four representatives would be in the permanent council. This was meant to represent the different groups in society and to build support among those groups for the plan. The idea that the Planning Bureau would be supplemented by an Economic Council to create support for the plan resembled the role of the Socio-Economic Council (SER) in the Netherlands, which consisted of ten members representing labor, ten representing capital, and ten "crown" experts. This makes it likely that Tinbergen and Koopman were actively involved in the drafting of this bill.[18]

---

[17] Yılmaz, "Türkiye'de Planlama Politikası ve Yönetimi," 190–91, 2012.
[18] Torun, "The Establishment and Structure of the State Planning Organization," 59, 1967; Milor, "The Genesis of Planning in Turkey," 1990.

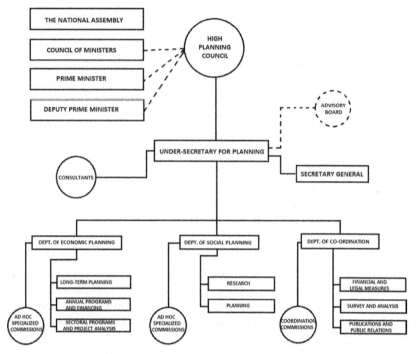

Figure 14.1 Organizational chart of the SPO and its relation to the Turkish government. Adapted from Torun, 1967

A modified version of the Türkeş draft was accepted. Nothing, however, came of the proposed Economic Council, which was scrapped in the revision process. The final name of the Central Planning Bureau became the State Planning Organization (see Figure 14.1). All of this took place within the first four months of the interim regime, and the law formalizing the new organization was passed on 30 September 1960. Tinbergen was so eager to start that, despite this speed, he complained afterward that the perfectionism of the Turkish bureaucrats had led to a lengthy process in formulating the law.[19] Perhaps Tinbergen had little patience for the political discussions about the precise status and nature of the new organization. But more likely is that he was in a hurry to establish the SPO while the military was still in power. Two years later, in the fall of 1962, the SPO presented its first five-year plan.

[19] Tinbergen, "Probleme der modernen Türkei," 25, 1964.

The radical wing of the interim government had wanted to go much further in their plans for the SPO. It had wanted to declare the superiority of socialism over capitalism, and place economic policy completely in the hands of the SPO.[20] But a more moderate version of planning carried the day, which was based on the idea of rational economic management and indicative planning. Tinbergen made it abundantly clear in his original memoranda that the SPO should not oversee the execution of the plan. That was to be left to the politicians and other parts of the bureaucracy. As in the Netherlands, he never desired an executive role for the planning bureau.

Tinbergen and Koopman, however, also faced opposition from groups far less supportive of planning, such as business owners who had their own ideas about the purpose of planning. They had understood at this point that development could well mean the protection of certain industries from imports through a policy regime that became known as import substitution. Tinbergen and Koopman sought to resist this. Koopman argued that "protectionism is not a healthy method" and attempted to convince them that planning should create an environment conducive to the flourishing of private business. And Tinbergen had made clear in his original memorandum that "the type of planning it seems appropriate to apply in this country is not the interference, in considerable detail, of government agencies with the economic activities of the private sector ... accordingly there seems to be a need of long-term plans, mainly meant as a *guide* to both government and business."[21]

But it was precisely this latter conviction that also made the position of the new planning organization vulnerable. Tinbergen's idea to engage only in indicative planning meant that they relied on the consent and cooperation of private sector entrepreneurs as well as the government. Koopman initially was optimistic that much could be achieved on this front, but it became clear to him in a meeting with the Chamber of Commerce in Istanbul that businessmen were reluctant to hand over strategic information about their investments and were certainly not willing to adjust their investment plans in line with the plan. And although the SPO would

[20] Emre, *The Emergence of Social Democracy in Turkey: The Left and the Transformation of the Republican People's Party*, 2014.
[21] Tinbergen cited in ibid. As such it was in line with the Turkish Forum movement of the 1950s, which had argued for planning as "an instrument of prudent and effect macroeconomic management in a free-market environment." Ünay, *The Political Economy of Development Planning in Turkey: Neoliberal Globalization and Institutional Reform*, 85–86, 2006.

have lots of power over the investments in the state-owned economic enterprises, it had to rely on the cooperation of the private sector for both the level and direction of overall investments.[22]

The interim military government had its own set of objectives, which were at odds with those of the planners. First, the military budget made up no less than 30 percent of the government budget, but any discussion to lower this amount was soon terminated. Second, there was an older, conservative tradition in the Turkish state, which was strengthened by Atatürk in various ways. The state in this tradition made sure food prices would not rise too much and generally favored social stability over economic growth. The industrial projects favored by the planners did not sit well with this conservative group, and the interim military government worried about the possible (temporary) unemployment resulting from it, as well as the extent to which the development strategies would further widen the gap between the eastern regions and the major cities.[23]

In the larger scheme of things, however, these were minor issues. Overall, a great optimism about the prospects of development planning and the new SPO prevailed in the first year of its existence. Matters started deteriorating after the elections of October 1961. The period in which the first five-year plan was developed was politically turbulent. A new constitution was drafted with a special article related to socioeconomic development, Article 129, entitled "Development": "Development Projects and the State Planning Organization: Economic, social and cultural development is based on a plan. Development is carried out according to this plan." The military organized new elections in which the major competitor of the RPP) was the newly formed Justice Party (*Adalet Partisi*). This Justice Party was in many ways the continuation of the older Democratic Party that had been ousted by the army a year before. The electoral campaign was a continuation of the unfinished bitter conflict of the 1950s. The interim government demanded that the Justice Party would express its support of the new constitution, which it did officially, but unofficially it continued to voice its discontent. At the same time, the trials against Menderes, the prime minister for the Democratic Party before the coup, and a few other high officials came to an end. They received the death sentence and were executed during the electoral campaign in the fall of 1961. The leader of the RPP, İnönü, attempted to prevent these executions but to no avail. While the military succeeded in stepping back and

---

[22] Milor, "The Genesis of Planning in Turkey," 17–18, 1990.   [23] Ibid., 19.

organizing new multiparty elections (two smaller parties also won seats), it also left behind a polarized political environment, so much so that even though the RPP had enjoyed a number of benefits during the campaign, and its party members had helped draft the new constitution, to its own surprise, it failed to win a majority in parliament. As a consequence, there would be three different, never quite stable, coalition governments, all headed by Inönü of the RPP.[24]

The RPP was thus weaker when it entered government than it had hoped to be, and this put immediate pressure on the first five-year plan. The left-leaning side of the party, which was well represented among the planners at the SPO, favored the development plan along with a number of quite radical reforms. They hoped to reorganize the state enterprises and implement a tax reform that would put a heavier burden on agricultural production (the electoral base of the rival Justice Party). These issues dominated discussions over the first five-year plan, and would frustrate development planning before it had started properly.

14.3 The Process of Planning

The first head of the SPO – his official title was undersecretary – was Osman Nuri Torun. Torun was not yet forty when he took up the position, but had already worked at the Ministry of Finance, as well as at the Industrial Bank of Turkey. Tinbergen had no formal position inside the organization but kept advising it over the years, and paid repeated short visits to the country, typically about four per year.[25] The organization bore his stamp all the way through: the way planning was done was completely in line with his notion of planning in stages. First, a national plan was drawn up, then a sectoral plan; the sectoral plans were then combined to check for consistency, and the same step was repeated for the project stage in which appropriate investment projects were selected.[26]

The first of the three stages was the macro stage, in which the overall goals were formulated. For this purpose, a twenty-sector input–output model was developed. Tinbergen thus did not work with a full macro-econometric model of the Turkish economy, but instead worked with a sectoral input–output model, which was combined with a Harrod–Domar-type growth model in order to determine the level of savings and

---

[24] Eroğul, "The Establishment of Multiparty Rule: 1945–1971," 1987.
[25] Milor, "The Genesis of Planning in Turkey," 25, 1990.
[26] Tinbergen, "Planning in Stages," 1962.

investments necessary to realize the desired growth rate.[27] That approach required the setting of targets, and it was decided that raising the national income would be the overriding goal of development planning in Turkey. It was assumed, or hoped, that high employment rates and a fair distribution of income would follow naturally.[28]

The desired growth rate was set at 7 percent. Theory demanded a full social-welfare function from which targets could be derived. And the political reality required attention to a somewhat even distribution of the development investments, in particular, between the agricultural and the industrial sectors. But the planners and Tinbergen argued that setting a growth target not only was simpler, but also reflected the development needs of the Turkish economy. The 7 percent target was as much a desideratum as it was a realistic goal. As Tinbergen had argued before about such targets, they were not to be regarded primarily as predictions, but rather as statements of the desirable.

From this target the level of required savings was calculated. The total savings consisted of private savings, public savings, and foreign savings, which are best thought of as the development aid Turkey received at that point. But even such rudimentary macroeconomic data were not available in reliable form to the planners. Although they could gather data about public savings, mainly at the SEEs, and knew how much foreign investment was coming into the country, they could only estimate private savings as a residual between the overall level of investment and the public and foreign savings. It was a highly imperfect method, not in the least because it forced them to equate investments with savings.

The model assumed a balanced government budget, and an aggregate marginal capital–output ratio was estimated for the Turkish economy between 1950 and 1960. A capital–output ratio reflects the amount of capital necessary to produce an additional unit of output. The estimates suggested that the ratio was 3.5, that is, for every 3.5 liras saved and invested, one additional lira would be earned. This would have implied that to achieve the 7 percent yearly growth, 18 percent of GDP would have to be "saved," that is, made available for investment. The actual planning went ahead based on a ratio of 2.6 (or, in other words, new investments were believed to be 25 percent more productive than the investments made in the previous decade). The planners were optimistic that this was possible since they believed that previous investments had been suboptimal.

[27] Hershlag, *Economic Planning in Turkey*, 1968.
[28] Küçük, "The Macro-Model of the Plan," 1967.

The SPO highlighted the investments in luxury housing as being relatively unproductive.[29] But to make that assessment properly, it would have been preferable to know what the capital–output ratio was for specific sectors. It was plausible that there was underutilization in some sectors, but there was no clear economic reason why this should have been true across the entire economy.

The choice for the lower capital–output ratio, and thus the higher expected returns, reflected the planners' belief that they could transform a sluggish industrial sector in a relatively short period of time. Küçük, a planner closely involved with these matters, soberly concluded a couple of years later that "in underdeveloped countries such as Turkey, where powerful planning instruments have not been developed, such expectations are rather optimistic."[30] The one area about which the planners were not optimistic was that of private investment. And consequently, the projected boost in the rate of growth had to come nearly completely from public sector investments. The state did not merely develop a plan for development; it was now also expected to be the economic motor of the country. This was part ideology, and part practical constraint, since little cooperation was forthcoming from the private sector.

Once the national plan was developed, the second stage, the sectoral stage, could get underway. It consisted of three elements: the construction of an input–output table for the year 1959, the preparation of sectoral programs, and the activities of ad hoc committees.[31] While the macro phase had been based on a clear and standard model, the sectoral planning was already a lot more pragmatic and ad hoc, based on whatever material and expertise was available.

The input–output model was certainly the most advanced tool they used, and a popular one at that moment in time. The American development economist Hollis Chenery had done much to promote it, and international organizations provided handbooks and brochures about its use. Nonetheless, the construction of one required technical expertise and a quite sophisticated statistical apparatus. And although Turkey had a State Statistical Office, such data were not available, in part because the statistical office felt that the SPO threatened its existence. So, the SPO had to rely, for

[29] Given the political nature of investment decisions then and before, it could well have been the case that investments were channeled to sectors that favored the government parties, and the low capital–output ratio was thus in fact an outcome of political bargaining and not of economic structure.
[30] Küçük, "The Macro-Model of the Plan," 1967.
[31] Küçük, "Sectoral Progamming in the Plan," 97, 1967.

the construction of the input–output model, on data it gathered itself.[32] Another obstacle they faced was picking an appropriate base year that could be used as a reference point for planning. They settled on 1959, the most "normal" recent year, since 1958 had been the year of the economic crisis, and 1960 the year of the coup.

The input–output table itself, or rather a memorandum on it, had been drawn up by Tinbergen. He at the time had been thinking about how to simplify the input–output model, most notably in the form of the semi input–output model. An input–output model is based on the idea of interdependence of different sectors. If an investment is undertaken in the manufacturing sector, this would also require growth in related sectors. After all, in order to grow, the manufacturing sector requires inputs. The table demonstrated the particular interdependence between sectors and could thus be of help in creating a viable growth plan consistent with these interdependencies.[33] Tinbergen's simplification, in the semi input–output model, was to differentiate between domestic and international sectors. If investments were undertaken in a domestic sector such as manufacturing, the country would still require related domestic investments such as those in infrastructure, but it could rely on imports for the inputs from international sectors, say, raw materials.[34] This simplified the number of interdependencies within the model, and thus allowed one to leave certain parts of the table empty, something that not only made the evaluation of new investments easier, but also required less data as input. The downside of it was that lots of foreign currency was needed in order to buy these resources, and Turkey had very little of those at the time. The only alternative in that instance was more foreign aid.

Although not made explicit in the table, it appears that about half of the sectors were judged to be international sectors, which reduced the total number of interdependencies in the table by about 75 percent,[35] and

[32] Ibid., 99.
[33] This idea is the complete opposite of the Keynesian way of thinking, which Tinbergen repeatedly criticized during this period. Whereas the Keynesian multiplier idea suggested that some initial investments would lead to multiplier effects in other industries, the input–output method, on the other hand, suggests that isolated investments are unlikely to be successful, for they create imbalances between sectors or, in other words, overcapacity.
[34] Tinbergen, "The Appraisal of Investment Projects," 1963.
[35] Denoting one sector as a national sector removes a great number of dependencies; in a four-sector model, if one sector is removed, the amount of interdependencies is reduced from $4 \times 3 = 12$ to $3 \times 2 = 6$, where the first number is the number of sectors and the second number is that of the sectors on which it is dependent.

therefore radically simplified the associated matrix algebra. This semi input–output model was again used in the construction of the second five-year plan.[36]

Even so, the construction of the table was far from easy, since there was no systematic data source. Most of the data came from ad hoc committees that often could provide only rough estimates. This meant data for prices were sketchy at best, and in many cases absent. Therefore, the planners often had to rely on so-called shadow prices. Shadow prices are prices based on costs and other estimates rather than market prices. In some cases, this was the preferred method of the planners since market prices were heavily distorted by subsidies, more so because much of the produc-tion took place in the inefficient and state-supported SEEs. But the usage of shadow prices also made it tempting to work with idealized, low cost levels, while the reality was that production of goods in the Turkish economy was not very efficient. One could not simply wish the SEEs away.

In an ideal scenario, such shadow prices could be calculated from the input–output table itself, but that was certainly not the case in Turkey.[37] The draft of the 1959 input–output table consisted of twenty sectors, but in the end only fifteen were included because data for the other five were completely missing. These varied in size between the large sectors, "Cereals and Pulses" and "Fruits and Vegetables," which each made up about 8 percent of the Turkish economy, and smaller sectors, such as "transpor-tation" and "electricity and water," which made up between 1 and 2 percent of the Turkish economy. The table reflected well the degree to which the Turkish economy was still predominantly agricultural. Of the remaining five sectors, some aggregate data were included for two, but three were left out altogether, rendering the model incomplete and necessarily inconsistent.

If only the extent of the information and knowledge problems ended there. This input–output table, however, was only the baseline, the struc-ture of the economy in 1959; it was not yet a plan for development in the different sectors. In order to formulate those, it was necessary to estimate how much capital would be necessary to raise output by a certain amount in each sector. It was the same basic issue as that of the marginal capital-output ratio discussed above, but now per sector. Not much is known about the details of this process, and quite a lot of variety existed in the

---

[36] Cornelisse and Tilanus, "The Semi-Input–Output Method: With an Application to Turkish Data," 1966.
[37] Küçük, "Sectoral Progamming in the Plan," 99, 1967.

methods employed because the personnel of the SPO were given a free hand in trying to make as good an estimation as possible given the limited data.[38]

What was more interesting in terms of technique was the use of ad hoc committees.[39] During the preparation of the first five-year plan, Tinbergen arranged for some of the employees of the SPO to travel to India for a study trip in development planning. India, where Tinbergen had worked before, was at that point in time considered the premier example of successful development planning, or at the very least the developing country with the most advanced planning apparatus.[40] Prime Minister Nehru gave them realistic advice: "Don't be too ambitious."[41] The sectoral committees, consisting of key economic actors within the sector, were considered a key to the success of planning in India. They supplied much of the industry-level data and provided important qualitative context to the figures. Another potential benefit of such committees was that some understanding and support for the plan could be fostered, although it remains unclear to what extent such potential benefits materialized in Turkey.[42]

The sectoral phase was crucial in determining where the development should come from in Turkey. Whereas much of the economic growth of the early 1950s had originated in the modernization of agriculture and the resulting exports, it was clear that this time around the growth was expected from the industrial sector. Politically, this was desirable for RPP because its main support came from the urban areas, but it was also a dangerous strategy that could widen already existing disparities and political divisions. The projected growth of the industrial sector was 11.4 percent, compared with just under 5 percent for the agricultural sector (see Table 14.1). One might wonder why such divergent growth rates were projected. In the evaluation of the first five-year plan, this issue was also crucially raised by Küçük, former head of long-term planning within the SPO. In fact, he went so far as to argue that the projected growth rates suggested that ultimately the planners resorted to partial sector analysis, precisely the partial analysis that the input–output technique was supposed to prevent. It was unclear to him how the rest of the Turkish economy

[38] Ibid., 100.   [39] In Turkish, the Özel İhtisas Komisyonları.

[40] Boumans and De Marchi, "Models, Measurement, and 'Universal Patterns': Jan Tinbergen and Development Planning without Theory," 2018.

[41] Ünay, *The Political Economy of Development Planning in Turkey: Neoliberal Globalization and Institutional Reform*, 97, 2006.

[42] Küçük, "Sectoral Progamming in the Plan," 101–2, 1967.

Table 14.1 *Overview of the targets and results of the first five-year plan in Turkey (adapted from Küçük, 1967)*
OUTPUT FORECASTS AND REALIZED GROWTH RATES

Sector	Input-output (1962–1967)	Plan (1962–1966)	Realization (1962–1967)
Agriculture	5.8	4.7	3.0
Industry	8.5	11.4	8.8
Construction	10.3	10.5	8.0
Transportation	7.7	9.6	7.5

could support such rapid growth of the industrial sector. He argued that although the official plan suggested this was not the case, his conversations with the original planners confirmed that this indeed was what had happened.[43] If so, it was a typical flaw of early development planning, which was later accused of being unbalanced, as opposed to a balanced growth path in which the interdependencies of different sectors were considered. But it reflected an issue not merely of technique, but also of the pressure for high growth rates and the lack of control over and cooperation of the agricultural sector.

This lack of support for planning was, as Küçük suggested, most visible in the fact that the third, project stage failed. Not only did the private sector not put forward any proposed investments, but also from the SEEs only a limited number of proposed projects came through. This meant that planning effectively stopped at the sectoral level, and a quite intense battle broke out over how the investments would be allocated within these sectors. The project stage, in Küçük's understated words, was replaced with a fourth and totally independent stage. What happened was not an orderly planning stage, but a highly political and politicized bargaining process over the allocation of investment funds with the organizations representing the various sectors and the SEEs. Küçük euphemistically described it: "Here, there has been a clash between the efforts of the officials to secure as large investment possibilities for their organizations as possible, and the planners' desire to channel investments into productive fields."[44] Pressure from powerful businesses thus trumped economic planning, and it was hard not to see the different projected growth rates for agriculture and industry as the outcome of the successful lobbying of

---

[43] Ibid., 104.   [44] Ibid.; Hershlag, *Economic Planning in Turkey*, 1968.

budding industrialists, rather than an outcome of the planning models. And at that point the real political battle, and the execution of the plan, had yet to start.

14.4 The Great Resignation

In 1962, the draft plan was finished and submitted to the government. It contained optimistic estimates and a sizable reliance on further amounts of foreign development aid, which Tinbergen in Turkish newspapers suggested would be provided through NATO as part of their anticommunist efforts.[45] If these funds would come through, the plan would be consistent in the sense that it would entail a balanced budget for the Turkish government. In order to achieve this, however, the plan included a major tax reform, for which the advice of Nicholas Kaldor had been requested.[46] Like Tinbergen, Kaldor had worked for the Indian government before, where he had also provided advice on tax reform.[47] In that proposal, as in this one, he proposed direct taxation as a means of furthering the cause of development, for which, in his view, public investments in education and infrastructure were necessary.[48] More reliance on direct taxes, such as income and corporate taxes, would increase the tax base of the state. The SPO was a major proponent of this plan, which was called the resource view, and would make planning of new investments much easier. This was opposed to the incentive view, in which the government would provide tax incentives to stimulate private investment. It was thus another step in the direction of the state as driver of economic development.

The choice of Kaldor, who had given similar advice in India, and believed that the resource approach generally was the best approach in developing countries, was a strategic one by the SPO. When the British conservative government showed reluctance to send Kaldor, who was believed to have socialist sympathies, the SPO doubled down; when asked for three alternative names, they suggested Kaldor, Kaldor, and Kaldor.[49]

[45] Yılmaz, "Türkiye'de Planlama Politikası ve Yönetimi," 186–206, 2012.
[46] Bulutoğlu, "Financing Turkey's Development," 1967.
[47] Around the same time, Kaldor and Tinbergen, along with Albert Hart, worked on a report for an international commodity reserve currency. Hart, Kaldor, and Tinbergen, *The Case for an International Commodity Reserve Currency*, 1964.
[48] Chakravarty, "Nicholas Kaldor on Indian Economic Problems," 1989.
[49] Emre, *The Emergence of Social Democracy in Turkey: The Left and the Transformation of the Republican People's Party*, 2014.

His proposal suggested that taxes had to be imposed on the agricultural sector. This sector had enjoyed very low taxes as a result of a happy coalition between the rhetoric of liberalization and laissez-faire and agricultural interests, which formed the foundation for the governments of the Democratic Party during the 1950s.

The Plan also included a proposal for land reform that was likely to further upset the agricultural sector. The land reform had two goals. On the one hand, it sought to encourage a more active use of land by imposing a tax on the hypothetical yield of the plot (varying by region), which was meant to make large landholdings less attractive. On the other hand, it sought to impose a minimum size of plots so that the agricultural sector could benefit from economies of scale and modern methods of production. This process had to take place by joining different existing plots together. It was a recurring theme in Turkish politics and had been on the political agenda ever since the modernization in the 1930s under Atatürk, but the Turkish state never achieved much on this front.[50]

But it was not just the agricultural sector that had to be modernized according to the first five-year plan; this was also true for the industrial sector. The original plan sought to modernize the organization of the SEEs through a variety of measures, which ultimately sought to make them function more like private enterprises and move them further away from the state bureaucracy. State influence had traditionally been large and had extended to pricing policies as well as the internal management of the firm. The SEEs had always had an easy line of credit with the Turkish central bank. Most of them therefore operated at significant losses. The reforms, among other things, involved making managers accountable for the losses and removing price distortions so that the inputs provided by SEEs to private firms would have to be sold at market rates.[51]

In the later literature, the planners were sometimes criticized for failing to deal with the more structural issues of the Turkish economy, but it was clear from this original plan that they sought to deal with precisely these. And initially, this seemed to ultimately get the approval of the politicians, even though they all had reservations about particular reforms. In June 1961, the council of ministers approved the strategy document that contained the reform package, but this was before the disappointing elections

[50] Ünay, *The Political Economy of Development Planning in Turkey: Neoliberal Globalization and Institutional Reform*, 42, 2006.
[51] Milor, "The Genesis of Planning in Turkey," 1990; Sönmez, "The Re-emergence of the Idea of Planning and the Scope and Targets of the 1963–1967 Plan," 1967.

in the fall of that same year. The strategy document, after being approved by the High Planning Council, now had to be worked out into a more detailed plan by the SPO.

When the final plan came up for discussion in the High Planning Council in 1962, the new coalition government headed by İnönü of the RPP had taken office and many of the central reforms of the plan were opposed. The land reform was not even put on the agenda; it was simply removed from the plan. The proposed reforms to the SEEs fared no better and were "refused by the High Planning Council and deleted from the text."[52] The third area of dispute was the financing of the plan. First, the Kaldor proposals for a new system of direct taxes were refused, and then new disagreements broke out over the extent to which indirect taxes could be increased. The government agreed to a modest increase of indirect taxes of 800 million liras (1 percent of GDP), which would leave a deficit in the financing of the plan of a relatively small sum of 400 million liras (0.5 percent of GDP). But the relation between the planners and the new government was deteriorating quickly. Prime Minister İnönü was not the problem; he visited the SPO often and favored the idea of development planning. But since his party had not won a majority in the elections, he had to negotiate with other parties less favorable to planning. And the more conservative wing in his party was still skeptical of the technocratic SPO and did not want to further alienate the rural voters from the party.

As a result, a conflict broke out over the consequences of the deficit. The planners insisted that this meant that some investment projects could not be undertaken and therefore the growth prediction had to be lowered to 6.5 percent. This also meant that the original strategy document approved a year earlier had to be revised, so that the planners could claim consistency. Instead, the ministers in the government doubled down and demanded that the planners promise a growth rate of 7.6 percent for the first year of the plan, 1963. At this point the situation came to a head, and the planners decided to stand their ground.[53] The new logic of expertise clashed vehemently with the logic of politics, and the result was the resignation of the four planners who were members of the High Planning Council: the undersecretary and the three department heads of the SPO.

Prime Minister İnönü was now trapped between the planners and the institution of the SPO, in the founding of which he had been instrumental, and the political demands of his coalition government. He attempted to

[52] Sönmez, "The Re-emergence of the Idea of Planning," 41, 1967.
[53] Sur, *Prof. Dr. Fadıl H. Sur'un Anısına Armağan*, 278–85, 1983.

function as a negotiator between the parties, but to no avail. He then called on Jan Tinbergen to intervene in the situation. Tinbergen, however, stood up for the same principles that had led to the resignation of the planners. In a memorandum of November of the next year, Tinbergen was still arguing for tax reforms and the redirection of investments away from low-productivity luxury construction and toward the industries suggested by the SPO.[54] But unlike the other planners, Tinbergen stayed on and remained attached to the SPO until 1966. Some of his students would continue to work within the organization for much longer.

It is tempting to read this episode only, or primarily, as a clash between technical expertise and politics, or, to put a slightly different emphasis, as a clash between an older form of "Etatism" (perhaps best described as Bismarckian) and a modern form of bureaucratic expertise. But that is to miss two important dimensions of the episode. There was also an important ideological dimension. The early planners were young, well-educated men between twenty-eight and thirty-eight years of age, with strong socialist convictions. They embraced Tinbergen and Kaldor not merely as technical experts but also as socialist economists. After they resigned, they joined the Socialist Culture Association; the former undersecretary of the SPO, Osman Nuri Torun, even became its president. Erder and Karaosmanoğlu, two former department heads, also occupied important functions within this organization. This ideological factor played an important role in these years, when the SPO was frequently depicted as a socialist organization, a charge that become stronger after its support for land reform.[55]

And there was an important international dimension of development planning. We saw at the start of this chapter how first the IMF and then the OECD forced foreign expertise upon the Turkish government. That same international community tacitly approved the military coup and supported the planning efforts of Tinbergen and the new government. But not only that; the resigned planners were afterward given jobs in the international economic organizations that orchestrated development planning during the period. Karaosmanoğlu became vice chairman of the World Bank and Atilla Sönmez became the lead economist of the World Bank for several

---

[54] Milor, "The Genesis of Planning in Turkey," 25, 1990.
[55] Emre, *The Emergence of Social Democracy in Turkey: The Left and the Transformation of the Republican People's Party*, 2014.

countries in Africa and East Asia.[56] The great irony was that later these same individuals were brought back into Turkey as technocratic experts to advise the government on its economic policies.

Tinbergen was also caught up in this international web. His own embassy was keeping a constant check on his work and the extent to which national and international (Western) interests were represented. When he gave an interview to the socialist magazine *Yön*, for example, there was some worry that he had become too leftist to still act as state functionary of the Netherlands.[57] He was in Turkey as an official representative of the country, not simply as an economist, and he also reported back regularly. Within the SPO it was well known that the information that was collected and produced was reported back to interested states such as Germany and the United States. This created further tensions between the Dutch experts working in the SPO and the domestic functionaries.

The aid that was of crucial importance for the financing of the plan was extended in part by the United States in the context of NATO. The planners were part of the political struggle over economic policy within Turkey. They were part of the international economic regime dominated by the United States and Europe, which argued for and financially supported development policies. And they were part of the international struggle between the West and the USSR, which soon would become more actively involved.

14.5 The Second Five-Year Plan and Tinbergen's Departure

Although Tinbergen had agreed with the resigned planners, he did not give up his position as chief advisor to the SPO. In fact, he seemed to have started with renewed energy on the second five-year plan. In a letter from May 1964, he suggested that the second plan should not seek to incorporate the latest techniques in development planning, such as those of education planning. Rather, it should stick to basic methods that both fitted the skills of the people at the SPO and could be readily understood by the relevant ministers in the High Planning Council. Furthermore, he suggested that a new look should be had at the capital–output ratio, which had been chosen too optimistically in the first plan. He suggested gathering more, and more accurate, information for the project stage. But most

[56] Ünay, *The Political Economy of Development Planning in Turkey: Neoliberal Globalization and Institutional Reform*, n. 53, 2006.
[57] NA: TE, folder 70, file 246/73, dated 26 January 1962.

noticeable was Tinbergen's idea that Turkey should join the European Economic Community soon, and that it should adjust its economic development with an eye to this common market.[58] He also had his own international political agenda, which pursued the integration of developing countries into the global (Western) economic market. In August 1964, he again reported on his progress. It was clear by then that 1964 looked to be another disappointing year, but Tinbergen seemed little deterred by it. He paid scant attention to short-term issues and suggested they take the long view, in terms of both goals and development strategy. Although he still suggested that knowledge about projects was important, it seems he was suggesting that the development strategy should select particular industries and prepare them for export.[59]

Turkey by then had become an international development "project." Not only was Tinbergen involved, but the Swedish economist Bent Hansen had prepared a flow-of-funds model of the Turkish economy, and the Indian economist Jagdish Bhagwati had helped with the determination of both export and import requirements. In 1964, there was an international meeting in Paris to discuss the economic development of Turkey, and in November 1966 there was a major meeting in Ankara to discuss the draft of the second five-year plan. Not only was the Turkish presence strong – it included then president Süleyman Demirel as well as some of the resigned planners – but so was the international presence. There were representatives from no fewer than twenty-two foreign countries, mostly European, including experts and representatives of international organizations such as the IMF, the IBRD, and the UN's Food and Agricultural Organization (FAO).

The conference was marked by several tensions. The official goal of the development strategy was to make Turkey able to stand on its own feet without the requirement of development aid, but it was announced that the date would be pushed another five years into the future, to 1977. The dynamic around this date was interesting. The stated hope of the international community was that Turkey would grow as fast as possible. But if the planned growth rate was again set at 7 percent (with a more realistic capital–output ratio of 3.15, compared with 2.6 for the first plan, and the "real" ratio of 3.5), Turkey would require extensive foreign aid to finance the investments. Turkey therefore pushed for a high growth rate, which

---

[58] Letter reprinted in Milor, "The Genesis of Planning in Turkey," 1990.   [59] Ibid.

given the models used at the SPO, *justified* a high level of foreign aid for the near future. The other card the Turkish government held in their hands was that in case the West did not support them, they might turn to the Soviet Union for help, a strategy Pakistan was also employing at that point in time.[60]

The political status of the plan was also contested at the conference. Prime Minister Demirel of the Justice Party, which was back in power after the RPP lost in the last elections, made it clear that he was going to play hardball. In his opening speech he expressed that planning was only secondary; first was "the right to property, free life, democratic life, and free enterprise." Tinbergen in his own speech remained diplomatic and argued: "By planning I mean an activity with mainly three characteristics: looking ahead, setting certain targets and the coordination of the execution of the Plan, all this in an advisory capacity."[61] Demirel was gaining the upper hand over the SPO, and the second five-year plan was in danger of becoming little more than an advisory report. This was also the impression Tinbergen gave in a letter to the Dutch government. The language was diplomatic, but the underlying message clear:

To this report may be added some remarks about the status of the SPO. A lot of attention has been given by the press to the changes in this status, real or apparent, as a consequence of the conduct of the current government, which is supported by a majority in parliament of the Justice Party, as opposed to previous governments. A prominent part of the press has been critical toward the first minister and a part of the criticism entails that he wishes to sideline the SPO. Moreover, a number of important people from the top of the SPO have resigned, in part due to this change in status [this referred to a second round of resignations]. The internal shifts within the SPO afterwards, have delayed the work. Moreover, only an interim under-secretary has been appointed, one who would like to be relieved of his duties as soon as possible because of health problems. So far no permanent under-secretary has been found. Mister Demirel is a very active engineer who has the tendency to make decisions on his own; he has expressed himself in favor of rationally planned politics of strong development, but it appears that his views on this way of planning differ significantly from those of the SPO and that of the opposition.[62]

[60] C. G. Verdonck Huffnagel to Ministry of Economic Affairs, 26 March 1965, National Archives Netherlands, Archiefbloknr. Z178, inv. no. 71.
[61] Opening Statement by the Prime Minister at the International Colloquium on the Technical Aspects of the Second Five Year Plan organized by the SPO, in JTC.
[62] Short report (Kort Verslag) of the "International Colloquium on the Technical Aspects of Turkey's Second Year Plan," JTC.

If one reads beyond the euphemisms of Tinbergen, it was evident that the prospects for the SPO were bleak, very bleak.

Tinbergen, however, remained committed to Turkey, much longer than was perhaps to be expected. In a speech delivered to various interested parties in Europe in 1964, he argued that Turkey should become part of the European bloc, not the Arabic or the communist bloc. And he faulted those in the audience for not being more committed in their financial support for Turkey,[63] which came with too many conditions and lacked long-term guarantees. The speech showed that for all his reported political naïvete, Tinbergen did know how to talk the language of power politics and regional interests,[64] although he opted for the language of ideals more often. His criticism was also reflective of a tension in the West's and Europe's relation to Turkey that is evident to this day: the West likes its development, but not a Turkey that is too strong or independent.

In December 1966, Tinbergen did finally resign his post as primary adviser to the SPO. At that point the second five-year plan was nearly completed, and Tinbergen in his farewell letter suggested that the expertise at the SPO on the technical front was enough to carry out the second plan. His farewell letter contained some strong recommendations, or perhaps warnings. He believed the SPO was too hierarchically organized and left too little space for initiative from lower-ranked officials. More generally, he feared for the independence of both the institution and the staff working there.[65] But he was silent about the underlying problems of the Turkish economy; perhaps he felt that he had emphasized them enough. His departure was a surprise to those working at the SPO,[66] but fit within the pattern of his career: he set up something and then left it to others to develop the project or institution further.

The question is whether he left behind enough to rest assured. As far as the SPO was concerned, it has proven a strong technocratic institution, which has provided a steady stream of future leaders in Turkish politics and the bureaucracy. The institutional setup of the organization has proven strong enough to stand the test of time, although its precise status was often altered. Its original status as an institute of expertise did not

---

[63] For an overview of the financial support to Turkey during this period, see Eralp, "Turkey in Changing Postwar World Order Strategies of Development and Westernization," 1994.

[64] Tinbergen, "Probleme der modernen Türkei," 1964.

[65] Letter from September 1966 is reprinted in Kansu, *Planli Yillar: Anilarla DPT'nin Öyküsü*, 2004.

[66] Private conversations with Tinbergen's student Peter Cornelisse, who worked at the SPO during this period.

survive; instead, the SPO was "promoted" into a ministry. This meant that it became a "normal" element in Turkish politics, and not the elite institution above politics that it was designed to be. Well into the 1980s, the SPO would produce five-year plans, although planning never became as prominent in Turkish politics as in the early 1960s. The retrospective volume *Planning in Turkey* from 1967, which collected the views of many of the early (resigned) planners, was dedicated to "all frustrated planners in the world." But Tinbergen did not seem to share most of their frustration. In his farewell letter, he suggested that plans were ultimately indications and that governments should oversee the setting of targets as well as the implementation. As such, his time spent in Turkey should be considered a success. The plans themselves may have failed, but economic expertise had gained a permanent seat at the table in Turkish politics.

But as in so many development programs of the time, the real problem was with the smothered attempts at structural change. The SPO failed in its goal of land reform, as well as in its goal to disentangle the state and the private sector. Ünay in his study of the period suggests that the problem may have been quite fundamental to the project of development through the state. Planning through the state entailed two important dangers: the purported apolitical nature could easily lead to antidemocratic and authoritarian tendencies, and institutionalized state businesses were likely to develop or strengthen clientele relations with the planners.[67]

The authoritarian tendency was most visible in the military coup that made possible the founding of the SPO and therefore development planning, but had also been evident in the authoritarian tendencies under Atatürk's original industrialization plans. The danger of corruption and clientelism is most easily recognized in the unchanged position of the SEEs, whose dependence on the state grew stronger through the industrialization policies. It was not that Tinbergen was completely blind to these dangers. In his most systematic discussion of the conditions in Turkey he highlighted the weak position of the agricultural sector and the countryside. Outside the urban centers, illiteracy was still widespread, and the agricultural sector was too weak to be an active counterweight to the state.[68] But Tinbergen did not believe that this posed fundamental problems to economic development through the state. He expressed his hope that the West would support the reform-minded youth, foster education, and seek to

[67] Ünay, *The Political Economy of Development Planning in Turkey: Neoliberal Globalization and Institutional Reform*, 22, 2006.
[68] Tinbergen, "Probleme der modernen Türkei," 1964.

strengthen private initiative. In other words, the state could help strengthen both society and the economy at the same time. It is striking that Tinbergen, the man who started out in the cultural socialism of the AJC, and who was part of the big social movement for social democracy that sought to build on existing trends in society, in his development work believed that the state would be able to bring about such changes on its own.

He hoped that the symbolic value of the SPO, as a pioneering rational institution, would count for something. It was a message that resonated with the socialist movement in Turkey. In their magazine *Yön* they urged the planners of the SPO to act on behalf of the people, free from the will of politicians and the state more generally. They did so in an article appropriately titled: "Tinbergen's Advice." It was extremely ambitious to believe that the state could transform both society and the economy at the same time, but Tinbergen's hopes were about as grand. He hoped that an institution like the SPO could help rationalize the economy, as well as the state – in stark contrast to the Netherlands, where the state had in many ways followed the lead of modern business.

Albert Hirschman, one of the early development economists, later reflected that it was particularly odd for a group of economists who had just lived through the turmoil of the 1930s and 1940s to believe that economic development would take place without major social and political upheaval, that a rise in economic prosperity and the satisfaction of material needs would simply lead to more social cohesion and political stability. In that sense the development economics of Tinbergen mirrored the paradoxical origins of business-cycle theory in the 1930s. The cycle theory was meant to be a purely endogenous mechanism within an autonomous economy, separated from political and social contexts. Development was imagined to be an endogenous mechanism within the state-led economy, separated from the political and social contexts. As Hirschman concluded: "We have learned otherwise."[69]

[69] Hirschman, "The Rise and Decline of Development Economics," 70, 2013.

15

Sometime the Twain Shall Meet: The
Optimal Order

The present structure of Western societies may be given various names, but "capitalist" suggests an identity with nineteenth century conditions. For lack of a better name we may chose the adjective "mixed"; even better, perhaps, would be "on its way to democratic socialism," or "on its way to optimality."
—Jan Tinbergen, 1979[1]

In 1964 Peter Cornelisse published an article in which he used the international trade patterns between Western countries to compare actual trade between the West and the East with the values one might expect if trade was free or optimal. The article was published in a new magazine, *Coexistence*, dedicated to mutual understanding of the East and the West.[2] The calculations were an elaboration of the gravity model of international trade developed in Tinbergen's book *Shaping the World Economy*.[3] In the model, trade patterns were explained by the distance between countries. The results of calculations demonstrated an enormous gap in trade volumes between the East and the West. Exports from the West to communist countries were just 21 percent of the value that the model predicted. Imports from communist countries into the West were no more than 19 percent of what the model suggested. The one exception was Yugoslavia, whose trade patterns were very close to what one would expect from the model. Cornelisse, a student of Tinbergen who also worked at the SPO in Turkey, remembered being thanked by Polish economists afterward for his calculations, for they had provided a strong argument in debates within the Soviet Union for more openness in trade.

---

[1] Tinbergen, "Recollections of Professional Experiences," 351, 1979.
[2] Cornelisse, "The Volume of East-West Trade," 1964.
[3] Tinbergen, *Shaping the World Economy*, 1962.

That same year, Boris N. Mikhalevsky, a young econometrician in the Soviet Union, was creatively using the official statistics to estimate the country's real economic performance. He was summoned to the KGB headquarters after a group of critical Marxist reformers pointed to him as the source of the figures. Mikhalevsky was charged with leaking official figures by the KGB. But Mikhalevsky made clear that he had no access to such figures and instead offered to demonstrate how he could construct the figures from inconsistencies in the officially published data, which he obtained from the public library. Consequently, the KGB agents tore up the arrest warrants.[4]

Some years earlier, Warren G. Nutter, a right-leaning economist, had published estimates of economic growth figures of the Soviet Union, and contrasted them with those during the Tsarist era. He demonstrated that the USSR was doing far worse than was often believed. The figures were met with disbelief, if not outright rejection; the academic establishment was not ready to believe the corrections that Nutter had made to the official figures.[5] Tinbergen was not among those who dismissed them; instead, he faulted a recent collection of writings on the Soviet economy for failing to include authors from the right such as Nutter.[6]

These small episodes were encouraging signs that something could be learned from an exchange of ideas and information between the Soviet Union and the West. Tinbergen sought to promote this convergence and stimulate conversations between the opposing powers of the Cold War. This brought him in contact with many of the world political leaders of the period, but it also created several difficult dilemmas. Was it morally acceptable to remain in contact with evil communist leaders? What about the fascist regimes of Southern Europe? Could he remain credible to his home base? And what was precisely the role of an economic scientist in the hot years of the Cold War?

At home his attempts to "reach out" were regarded with suspicion, while at least officially, the communists could never accept Tinbergen's bourgeois ideas. But when Stalin passed away in 1953 and his successor Khrushchev officially distanced himself from Stalin's rule in 1956, there

---

[4] Alexeyeva and Goldberg, *The Thaw Generation: Coming of Age in the Post-Stalin Era*, 1993.

[5] Balabkins, "Measuring Soviet Economic Growth: Old Problems and New Complications. A Comment," 1992.

[6] Tinbergen, "Boekbespreking van M. Bornstein en D. R. Fusfeld's *The Soviet Economy: A Book of Readings* & F. D. Holzman's *Readings on the Soviet Economy*," 1964.

was hope that change was on the horizon. And Tinbergen hoped to be part of that change.

15.1 Coexistence

In the 1930s, Tinbergen had sought a practical socialism free from dogmatism. In his reflections on America at the time, he was equally critical of an impractical capitalism with dogmas. The laissez-faire attitude among the Americans, and to a lesser extent the British, reeked to him of the same dogmatism he knew from the socialist movements he had been part of. The Breakthrough movement, with which he was involved around 1950, was an explicit attempt to move beyond party politics. But Tinbergen's anti-dogmatism was most visible in his convergence theory. His most famous statement on the matter, "Do Communist and Free Societies Show a Converging Pattern?,"[7] was from 1961, but the basic idea emerged early in the 1950s when he started touching on the subject in various talks about the communist bloc.

The source of the convergence thesis, however, should be sought on a more basic level. Ever since the 1920s, Tinbergen had been looking for peaceful change. His rejection of revolutionary socialism, and the embrace of a theory of gradual change toward a socialist society, was the clearest sign of it. His pacifist convictions had always made him favor nonviolent solutions. That sentiment was not just in the background for him – an Indian student of his from the early 1950s recollected: "Through my interaction with Professor Tinbergen I was attracted to the studies of peace and nonviolence. This influence led me to discard pure economics and [pure] sociology and take up the study of philosophy and sociology of non-violence and peace and particularly the contributions of Mahatma Gandhi."[8]

It was precisely violence at an unprecedented scale that was the big threat of the Cold War in the early 1950s. The Soviet Union and the United States were engaged in the first arms race, which included nuclear weapons. In Hungary, the first major opposition to Soviet domination had been crushed. And America was under the spell of McCarthyism. The priority was therefore to avoid confrontation between the two major powers. In order to avoid open conflict, a few intellectuals started promoting the ideal of coexistence. Tinbergen suggested that the only way forward

---

[7] Tinbergen, "Do Communist and Free Economies Show a Converging Pattern?," 1961.
[8] T. K. N. Unnithan in Jolink and Barendrecht-Tinbergen, *Gedeelde Herinneringen*, 1993.

was that of "organized co-existence of communists and non-communists." This was different from the convergence (and cooperation) he later theorized, but it was a definite step in that direction. Coexistence was the acceptance that both parties had a legitimate position in (world) society. In Tinbergen's reading of social history, this had been the first step in the process of convergence between capitalist and labor. It came when the socialists accepted the existence of capitalists as a legitimate part of society, a step that Marxists had never been willing to make. The challenge was now to achieve this on the global level.

He did so first in the context of debates within the Dutch Labor Party over the most desirable foreign policy. He urged his fellow social-democrats, however much they despised communism, to come to grips with the basic fact that the communist bloc could not be defeated. Once this was accepted, they could start to think about the appropriate attitude toward the communist bloc, and to make sure that they at the very least developed a viable alternative for the new independent nations in the development world. He started these debates in 1956 not long after he had left the CPB, and around the time that the reality of the bipolar world was setting in. The acceptance of bipolarity was a step back in Tinbergen's own worldview. Ever since the building of the Peace Palace he had hoped for an integrated world order of equally powerful units. Both the League of Nations and the United Nations pursued that type of integration, but by the mid-1950s it appeared as if the world was heading in the opposite direction. In 1957, it even appeared to some as if the Soviets were winning the arms and space race. It was the year they launched an intercontinental ballistic missile, then the *Sputnik* satellite, soon followed up by *Sputnik 2*, which sent stray dog Laika into space.

It was not just Tinbergen who argued for a new position vis-à-vis the Russians. Just after the publication of his articles, the Dutch communist newspaper ran an interesting piece in which it compared Tinbergen's argument for coexistence with that of the most prominent American columnist of his age, Walter Lippmann.[9] Both men agreed on the fundamental point that the United States could not defeat both the Soviet Union and China. Therefore, they should develop an alternative strategy, and both Lippmann and Tinbergen believed they had to lead by example. This should take the form of substantial support to underdeveloped countries, starting in Asia. Since the arms race between the United States and the

---

[9] Goodwin, *Walter Lippmann: Public Economist*, 2014.

USSR was leading nowhere, there should be a new race for the hearts and minds of the people in Asia. And given the enormous prestige the Soviet Union enjoyed at that moment, this would require a new constructive program for the future.[10] The challenge posed by the USSR was, for both Lippmann and Tinbergen, not merely a security threat but also a threat to the values they held dear.

And although Tinbergen found a prominent ally in Lippmann, most of the responses to their arguments were negative. This was true in the United States as well as in the Soviet Union, where ideological hardliners were not ready to accept coexistence. Tinbergen's article drew critical responses from two "official" Soviet authors, A. Nikonov and J. Arbatov.[11] Their responses were in equal measure critical and appreciative. Tinbergen was praised for attempting to open a dialogue and for being critical of the general trends within Western social-democratic parties. After all, Tinbergen was voicing similar criticisms of the social democrats as the communists had done for a long time. But Tinbergen's status was also called into question: Was he not a bourgeois economist operating under bourgeois illusions? Was the Dutch Labor Party truly socialist and committed to internationalism? Tinbergen's fear of communism was hypocritical at best, Arbatov argued, for, after all, the real threat to peace came from capitalism and the NATO. But Arbatov ultimately saw the article as a hopeful sign that the social-democratic parties were realizing the need for a united workers' front.

The response by Nikonov brought out a more interesting dimension of the differences. Tinbergen sought to engage the communists on the level of practical aims and policies. But Nikonov rejected those terms, stating that a debate could start only from a proper perspective on the world, in other words, from socialist ideology. Tinbergen strongly rejected such grounds; ever since his cultural socialism of the 1930s, he had rejected them. And in his follow-up article published in the fall of 1957, he expanded on this idea through a discussion of the relation between the practical aims of political parties and their "foundational programs."[12] What Tinbergen aimed to do in his essay was to nudge people away from the foundational programs to what he called, following his policy work, the practical instruments used to achieve political and economic goals. It was much easier to find mutual understanding there, he argued.

[10] "Zij die het Anders Willen," *De Waarheid*, 4 September 1957, p. 3.
[11] "Een Discussie met Professor dr. J. Tinbergen," *De Waarheid*, 18 May 1957, p. 2.
[12] Tinbergen, "Internationale Socialistische Politiek," 1957.

While the West often thought of itself as fully democratic as opposed to the dictatorships associated with the East, there were numerous exceptions to this reliance on democracy: "We provide executive power to governments; we demand qualified majorities; . . . [and] we remember the lack of power of parliaments to combat the Great Depression." The purportedly centralized production structure of the communist countries, he argued, was equally impure. It contained pockets of decentralization and could take the form of firms with mixed control and ownership. Pure systems, he concluded, do not exist anywhere in reality, and would be highly inefficient in practice. Therefore, we must look at what works best and not what is in line with some ideological preconceptions. Once this was recognized, a sober look at the societies in question would lead us to the realization that "the differences between communists and non-communists are less significant than the popular propaganda suggests."[13]

Despite his continued effort to reach out to the communists, he did feel the need to distance himself from some readings of his original essay, and in particular the suggestion made by the two Soviet authors that he was making an argument for cooperation between the East and the West. Before cooperation was possible, argued Tinbergen, the two parties first needed to show willingness to revise their own "foundational programs." Without such internal change, there was no possibility of cooperation, only of coexistence. And quite critically, he concluded that the two pieces by the Soviet authors demonstrated that the division was still very deep; he even felt the need to criticize their "way of doing science," a euphemism for their Marxism.

15.2 Socialism at Home

One might therefore wonder why Tinbergen ended up with a theory of convergence. Despite the "thaw" under Khrushchev, it remained difficult to engage in a real conversation with those behind the Iron Curtain. The answer to that question should, perhaps, not be sought abroad, in an international discussion,[14] but rather at home. The motivation for Tinbergen was as much domestic as it was international.[15] He certainly

---

[13] Ibid., 669.

[14] Lauterbach, "The 'Convergence' Controversy Revisited," 1976; Van den Doel, "Konvergentie en Evolutie: De Konvergentietheorie van Tinbergen en de Evolutie van Ekonomische Ordes in Oost en West," 1971.

[15] Kuitenbrouwer, *De Ontdekking van de Derde Wereld*, 1994.

hoped to contribute to peaceful coexistence, but his contributions to the debate were deeply shaped by his vision of the future of social democracy in the West.

The thesis that the East and West were converging was often made on materialist grounds. Many economists and sociologists of the age argued that both capitalism and socialism would have to adapt to various developments, especially technological ones, and hence would out of necessity converge.[16] Other variations of the convergence thesis suggested, following Max Weber, that the two systems would develop similar bureaucratic tendencies, and over time, the state and large firms in both countries would be virtually indistinguishable. Both would be ruled by bureaucratic hierarchies. It was this political-economic version, with a little bit of technology mixed in, that became the popular version of the thesis. In the work of the popular American economist John Kenneth Galbraith, for example, the United States and the Soviet Union were both instances of *The New Industrial State*.[17] Galbraith became the public face of the view that, official ideology notwithstanding, the East and the West were more alike than the officials on either side were willing to admit. In the *New York Times* in 1966, he suggested that "there are strong convergent tendencies between industrial societies ... despite their very different billing as capitalist or socialist or communist."[18]

Tinbergen's convergence thesis differed significantly from these economic, technological, and political theories. His convergence thesis was an argument that was rooted in a new understanding of the role of social democracy in the Netherlands and Europe. He wanted to argue, much in line with his turn to development, that social-democratic parties in Europe should formulate a more international agenda. There were good reasons why Tinbergen was looking for a new cause for social democracy. Social democrats occupied an uncomfortable position in an age of extremes. They were literally caught between the opposing camps of the Cold War. The heated atmosphere of the Cold War was not particularly suitable for a rational discussion of pragmatic reforms. And many of the valuable resources that the social democrats would have liked to dedicate to the building of a modern welfare state, or, in Tinbergen's case, the

---

[16] Prybyla, "The Convergence of Western and Communist Economic Systems: A Critical Estimate," 1964; Meyer, "Theories of Convergence," 1970.

[17] Galbraith, *The New Industrial State*, 1967.

[18] Galbraith quoted in Balabkins, "Soviet-American Convergence by A.D. 2000? An Analysis of the Trends of Two Social Orders," 1968.

economic development of Asia, were being eaten up by ever-increasing defense budgets.[19]

These general factors were relevant, but there was something quite distinct about Tinbergen's motivation. It was remarkable how quickly Tinbergen became critical of developments within Dutch social democracy. During the Reconstruction years he had been responsible as head of the CPB for putting the entire population on a strict consumption diet, something that even he later admitted might have been too harsh. After these meager Reconstruction years, the 1950s were a flourishing decade when the Dutch economy grew considerably, not in the least because its neighboring German economy was enjoying its *Wirtschaftswunder* (economic miracle). Most of his fellow social democrats were busy with the further architecture of the welfare state, enabled by this new prosperity: in 1956, a universal pension for those who reached the age of sixty-five was introduced; a few years earlier, a law that protected unemployed workers had been introduced. A law protecting workers disabled from work was introduced in 1966; many other elements of the modern welfare state were still under construction. But already in the mid-1950s, Tinbergen started to worry about the dangers of decadence.

In his articles on the development of an international program, he still channeled that discomfort into a constructive suggestion: it was now time to broaden our focus. By the early 1960s, he was openly critical of what he perceived as the dangers of materialism within the social-democratic movement. It was as if after a period of only economic concerns, Tinbergen returned to the critique of Hendrik de Man on the socialism of his day: it was too materialistic and culturally impoverished. In 1965, Tinbergen wrote about the three major problems facing social democracy. Two were international: the danger of a nuclear confrontation between the East and the West and the growing disparity between the North and the South. The third one was domestic: the petering out of the social and cultural development of the West.

He critiqued the "wage explosion" of 1963, a sign that the social-democratic movement had become obsessed with material gain and indifferent about cultural matters. Tinbergen's concerns sound culturally conservative to the modern ear: he called Western culture "empty" and was worried about the cultural degeneration in films produced for commercial reasons only. He worried about moral decay and excess displays of

---

[19] Ellman, "Against Convergence," 1980.

opulence. But it was no simple cultural conservatism; it was much more a return to the socialist idealism of his youth, as he argued: "Formulated more constructively, there is a need for a conscious formation of an elite as an element of the coming social structure, also in the moral and cultural domain. This was precisely what the AJC represented in the 1920s, a youth elite group which would point to the way forward to the *lifestyle* of the future."[20] This elitism became more pronounced, and he now drew explicit comparisons between the political-economic realm and the cultural realm. The economy had been successfully ordered; it was now time to think about the right cultural order.

One such example was that of the Film Classification Board (Filmkeuring). It was a committee consisting of no fewer than sixty members of the different pillars (Protestant, Catholic, Socialist, and Liberal) in Dutch society. Tinbergen's wife Tine was part of this committee for several years. It banned about 5 percent of films from cinemas because they contained pornography, excessive violence, or other content not in line with the requirements of "public order." It was this model that was held up by Tinbergen as an example of what could be done in various other media such as magazines and books.[21] Tinbergen, like some of the religious Protestants he was close to, was a moral puritan and absolutely opposed to pornography. Just as alcoholism and tobacco were leading the youth astray, so could certain elements of popular culture, he believed. In some ways it was the continuation of the AJC aesthetic, where only "proper" films were shown, and only "proper" dances and plays were performed.

But also, the more positive sides of the 1920s program gained renewed attention. In an article on the future of work, he referred to the writings of Hendrik de Man on the importance of joy in work. His son-in-law, Adriaan van Peski, inspired by Tinbergen, completed a book on Hendrik de Man in 1963 urging for a reevaluation of De Man, whose reputation had suffered enormously after his collaboration with the Nazis. It was the first book after the war that seriously attempted to rehabilitate de Man. Both Tinbergen and his son-in-law praised de Man for his emphasis on psychological factors in well-being, and the moral and spiritual dimensions of life more generally.[22] The future of work should not be a better paid job, but a more fulfilling job.

---

[20] Tinbergen, "De Toekomstige Sociale Orde en Onze Beweging," 1965.
[21] Pen, "Tussen Elitisme en Egalitarisme," 1988.
[22] See the contributions of Tinbergen and Van Peski to Publikaties van de Stadsbibliotheek en het Archief en Museum voor het Vlaamse Cultuurleven, *Hendrik de Man: Een Portret, 1885–1953,* 1985.

Just as important as work was education. The most visible way in which Tinbergen promoted education was in his work on income distribution. Equality for Tinbergen was not primarily about redistribution but about (personal) development. Egalitarians have often been critiqued for wanting to "level down" inequalities; in the end, it was more important for them to eliminate inequalities than it was to make people better off. Tinbergen saw education as the most important policy instrument with which to fight inequalities; it was through education that people could develop themselves and earn more. He was therefore critical of simple redistribution schemes to fight inequality.

It was for these reasons that Tinbergen had little sympathy for the libertine revolutions of 1968. His socialism was one that combined bourgeois values (he and Ehrenfest admired Bach above all else) with progressive socioeconomic goals. In the late 1960s, the socialists and social democrats in Western Europe and the United States desired more democracy: democracy on the work floor, democracy in the university, and democracy in church. But also on the cultural front, they revolted against old hierarchies and the establishment. The Beatles and Bach could stand next to one another for the youth of 1968. Tinbergen did not often respond to the movement directly, and typically bit his tongue about these developments.[23] But it was perfectly clear that he found these demands misguided. Instead, he warned about the limits of democracy. In the firm, it was limited by the extent to which workers really wanted to carry responsibility. In politics it had to be limited to avoid group interests becoming too strong. His solution to the problem was telling: we needed more experts – in this instance, independent "general" experts, who were skilled at weighing group interests and pursuing the general interest. Experts like him, although he left that unsaid.

It was perhaps good that Tinbergen did not often directly debate the revolutionaries of 1968. An important exception was an article in which he called for ordering in the cultural sphere analogous to the socioeconomic sphere.[24] He started from the premise that since it was now widely accepted that absolute freedom in the socioeconomic sphere was undesirable, we should attempt to contain or, rather, organize the freedom in the spiritual and cultural domain (Tinbergen used the adjective *geestelijke*,

---

[23] One issue that he could not avoid was debates about neocolonialism in development studies. In the Netherlands he was criticized by his fellow development economist W. F. Wertheim, see Chapter 16.

[24] Tinbergen "Ook Geestelijke Vrijheid vraagt Ordening," *Het Vrije Volk*, 8 February 1968, p. 2.

similar to the German *geistliche*). But the proposed ordering for the cultural domain, for the protection of shared values, was less institutional than in his economic work. He proposed the formation of a broad cultural board whose authority to ban cultural goods would extend well beyond the formalistic constraints of the "laws and disturbance of the peace." This was necessary for a broad range of problems that Tinbergen identified: too much openness about sexuality, a crude egoism, and too much emphasis on novelty in books, films, magazines, and TV shows. Months before, a Dutch TV show had caused a sensation when Phil Bloom was shown fully naked on national television, the first time this was done anywhere in the world. These developments undermined a sense of responsibility, compassion, solidarity, and the value of moral education. Later he would also add to this list the lax way in which laws were applied, and the soft punishments for violent crimes.[25] Although he was aware that what he in practice promoted was a type of censorship, he tried to defend such measures by relying on examples in which we had restricted economic freedom: the eight-hour workday, the ban on child labor, building and safety regulations, and regulations about education. As he argued: "Unrestricted freedom is never the solution: a dedicated and well-executed policy is one to which the best in society have contributed, from all strata of society." Later he would even draw comparisons between this newly proposed cultural council and the Socio-Economic Council he had helped to establish in the Netherlands.[26]

Tinbergen's argument received considerable support in Dutch media, at a time when they were still strongly linked to the various (Christian Democratic) parties. But the more progressive and liberal outlets were strongly critical and did not fail to point out that given Tinbergen's socialist convictions he was treading dangerous ground when he argued for limits on cultural expression. Most of them did not even have to mention the USSR explicitly. But it was from his old friend Willem Banning that he received the most relevant pushback. Banning, a fellow Breakthrough activist, wondered whether Tinbergen was not losing faith in inner freedoms, and the power of individuals to learn to make responsible choices. Was he not mistaken in his means, by relying on an expert body and rules from above?[27]

[25] "Professor doctor Jan Tinbergen nam Afscheid als Hoogleraar," *Het Vrije Volk*, 8 November 1973.

[26] Tinbergen, "Om de Kwaliteit van onze Beschaving," *Het Vrije Volk*, 7 March 1968, p. 2. See also "Professor Tinbergen en zijn Culturele SER," *De Waarheid*, 16 March 1968, p. 3.

[27] "Banning: Begrip – en toch oneens met Tinbergen," *Het Vrije Volk*, 16 February 1968, p. 2. See also "Prof. Tinbergen en de Media," *De Volkskrant*, 9 March 1968, p. 10.

15.3 What Is Optimal about the Optimal Order?

Tinbergen's motivation was thus deeply shaped by domestic concerns. But there was an important international dimension to the convergence debate. And in Tinbergen's case, there was also an important scientific component. In an article in *Soviet Studies*, Tinbergen attempted to demonstrate that the economic systems of the East and West were converging. He listed several trends in the USSR that had made it move toward the capitalist system: the reintroduction of managers, the reintroduction of a differentiated wage system, the reintroduction of monetary calculation, free consumption choices, and the use of mathematical planning methods. The West, meanwhile, had experienced a growth of the public sector, higher taxes, the introduction of antitrust laws, more public education, and planning methods in agricultural markets and economic development. Tinbergen acknowledged that the two economic systems were still very different, but he argued that they were also showing hopeful signs of convergence.[28]

The debate, for Tinbergen, was not primarily about the USSR and the West, but more about the so-called nonaligned countries. India and Turkey, the two countries where he worked extensively as a development economist, were examples of countries that were emerging out of feudalism and were facing the choice between socialism and capitalism: "The communist example impresses them greatly. Planning is in high esteem. State initiative does take up part of the tasks neglected by private initiative." In the context of the Cold War it was important to demonstrate to the nonaligned countries that "capitalism or communism" was a false dichotomy. Instead, these countries should be stimulated to try to combine "the best elements from communism and free enterprise."[29] He regarded it as the task of European social democrats to establish a reputable alternative to these two extremes. The elements of such a combination were the basis for his work about the optimal order.

Tinbergen believed that by laying out an optimal order, his ideas could be a *guide* toward a better organized society. Thus, an essential part of his convergence thesis was the development of the theory of the optimal order, which he sometimes called "mature socialism."[30] Looking back on his work on the optimal order, Tinbergen wrote:

My feeling was that welfare economics could teach us much about [the optimal socioeconomic order] and that the true unknowns of welfare economics are not the

---

[28] Tinbergen, "Do Communist and Free Economies Show a Converging Pattern?," 1961.
[29] Ibid., 341.   [30] Tinbergen, "Some Thoughts on Mature Socialism," 1973.

quantities of goods and services consumed in an optimum situation, but the fact that one could dig more deeply and consider as the ultimate unknowns a number of institutions together constituting the socio-economic order and that along that line a synthesis between market economies and centrally planned economies could be found.[31]

The optimal order[32] was Tinbergen's contribution to welfare economics. This is easily missed because welfare economics after Arrow was all about the optimal allocation of resources and the constrained optimization of a given social welfare function. Tinbergen's work fitted poorly in this tradition.[33]

When the Russian economist Leonid Kantorovich and Tjalling Koopmans shared the Nobel Prize in economics for their discovery of linear programming in economics, it was held up as the ultimate example that science could unite the East and West. Ever since the socialist calculation debate of the 1920s and 1930s, it had been recognized that for the optimal allocation of resources, capitalism and socialism faced a similar problem. This (formal) similarity was accepted by economists on both the left and the right. It was what Hayek called "the pure logic of choice" and what for Koopmans and Kantorovich was "pure decision theory." The basic premise of the underlying (pure) economics was that the technologically optimal way of production was similar to – or, rather, independent of – political institutions. When the two men shared the Nobel Prize in 1975, Yale economist Scarf wrote:

The techniques of activity analysis [perfected by Kantorovich and Koopmans] exemplify the pure theory of decision-making, and, as such, are remarkably indifferent to economic institutions and organizational forms ... one of the great

[31] Tinbergen, "My Life Philosophy," 7, 1984.
[32] Tinbergen, "The Theory of the Optimum Regime," 1959. The first essay, on the optimal order, which appeared as the conclusion to his collected papers from 1959, contained a characteristic Tinbergen footnote: "Although the precise influence exerted on him by the various authors on welfare economics cannot be easily traced, the author wants to express his gratitude to William J. Baumol, Abram Bergson, Gerard Debreu, J. Marcus Fleming, Ragnar Frisch, J. de Villiers de Graaff, Harold Hotelling, Nicholas Kaldor, Tjalling C. Koopmans, Oskar Lange, Abba P. Lerner, James E. Meade, Nancy Ruggles, Paul A. Samuelson, Tibor de Scitovsky, and Robert H. Strotz, for the contributions they made to his understanding, if any, of the subject matter." Except for Frisch none of them got a direct citation in the article, and Tinbergen proceeded in a very different direction than they did.
[33] Till Düppe has suggested that Koopmans might have been inspired by Tinbergen in his symmetrical analysis of communism and capitalism. Düppe, "Koopmans in the Soviet Union: A Travel Report of the Summer of 1965," 2016.

achievements of this methodological revolution [is that] economists of the East and West [could enjoy] continued dialogue – free of ideological overtones.[34]

It seemed like precisely the type of dialogue that Tinbergen favored. But Tinbergen was a much more institutional thinker than most of his neo-classical peers, and his contribution to welfare economics bore this deep institutional mark. Although his theory of the optimal order built on the idea of a social welfare function (an aggregation of the preferences of individuals in a society), the real essence of his theory was the set of institutions by which the economy and the state were organized. His optimal order specified the decision structure that could lead to optimality, while most other welfare economists were focused on the search for the optimal decisions.

The central choices in the design of the decision structure were the degree of centralization in government and the degree of centralization in production. Where Koopmans wanted to talk about allocation independent from institutions, Tinbergen wanted to talk primarily about institutions that ensured a good allocation. By formalizing the problem in this way, Tinbergen hoped to find neutral ground on which the issues could be objectively discussed. But unlike Koopmans's explicitly apolitical neutral ground, Tinbergen sought a neutral scientific ground on which to discuss political matters. It was for this reason that the final section of his first contribution on the optimal order was called "Is There a Basis for Discussion?"

The ideal of an undogmatic dialogue free of ideological overtones was a recurring one. It was shared by some across the Iron Curtain, prominently by Sakharov, also a natural scientist, as Tinbergen was quick to highlight.[35] But more common were responses such as the one by Wassily Leontieff, a prominent Russian mathematical economist who had migrated to the United States. He was dismissive of both the empirical support for Tinbergen's convergence theory and the theory itself. Leontieff argued that capitalism and communism were incompatible in their essence, and he called the optimal order proposed by Tinbergen "hybrid, just as unnatural as a horse-cow."[36] Other responses from the United States were similar; it was widely believed that their capitalist system was fundamentally

---

[34] Düppe; Bockman, and Bernstein, *Scientific Community in a Divided World: Economists, Planning, and Research Priority during the Cold War*, 582, 2008.

[35] Kelley, "The Soviet Debate on the Convergence of the American and Soviet Systems," 1973; Tinbergen, "De Convergentietheorie: Antikritiek," 1972.

[36] Leontieff quoted in Tinbergen, "On the Optimal Social Order and a World Economic Policy: A Discussion with Professor Lev Leontiev," 1966.

incompatible with that of the communists. To argue for this incompatibility, they all sought to capture something that was qualitatively and fundamentally different about "their" system.[37]

An example of what Tinbergen called the dogmatic approach was the reply by Tchernikov, who attempted to show in *Pravda* that the convergence theory was just anticommunist propaganda. Tinbergen resisted such attempts vehemently. In his strongest reply, he objected to theorists who thought qualitatively and wrote that they "are always speaking of things, which are according to them, 'fundamentally different', about principles and such ... even worse than the qualitative approach of a subject is the dogmatic approach."[38] For Tinbergen the goal instead was to measure the *degree* of convergence. As he had done so often, Tinbergen tried to make the debate quantitative. One of his students, Van den Doel, completed a dissertation on the empirical verification of the theory along such quantitative lines.[39]

Tinbergen made clear that his notion of the optimal order was not a compromise between the East and West (a kind of horse-trading); rather, it was an optimum, "a synthesis."[40] This synthesis, he argued, was not yet discovered and might require completely new elements that were not contained in capitalism or communism. And, indeed, over time Tinbergen kept working on his theory of the optimal order and included other elements, such as the environment and international security.[41] His own inclinations had always been in the direction of a synthesis of different systems. Even in his purely scientific efforts, the goal was often to reach a synthesis between different theories, rather than to prove one correct and the other wrong. The notion of the optimal order provided a lens through which the convergence thesis could be made tangible and, as he repeatedly urged, to which others could add.

Meyer[42] has suggested that the convergence controversy was a debate with three different positions. The first position was that of "a doctrine of salvation and damnation stressing the irreconcilable hostility between the two systems." The second position was "a pragmatic, instrumental

---

[37] Meyer, "Theories of Convergence," 1970.
[38] Tinbergen, "De Convergentietheorie: Antikritiek," 1972.
[39] Van den Doel, "Konvergentie en Evolutie: De Konvergentietheorie van Tinbergen en de Evolutie van Ekonomische Ordes in Oost en West," 1971.
[40] Tinbergen, "De Convergentietheorie: Antikritiek," 1972.
[41] Tinbergen and Fischer, *Warfare and Welfare: Integrating Security into Socio-economic Policy*, 1987.
[42] Meyer, "Theories of Convergence," 1970.

orientation seeking to free itself from ideological ties and believing itself to be non-ideological." The debate between the first two positions was straightforward. There are convinced capitalists and socialists who believe there is one clearly superior system, and the other system is doomed. The convinced socialists predicted that a socialist revolution would sooner or later happen in the West, while the convinced capitalists predicted the imminent collapse of the socialist system. The pragmatists, on the other hand, refused to see fundamental differences and instead argued that both systems were adapting to the times, and argued that for pragmatic reasons they would find similar responses. If one looked well, they said, it was clear that they had never been pure anyhow.

Prima facie, Tinbergen was a pragmatist. But it was the third position that Meyer identified that was much closer to his true intentions: "a humanist alternative to the establishment way of life." For Tinbergen, the goal was not mere pragmatic compromise, as was clear from his emphasis on synthesis. The precise contents of this synthesis, called the optimal order, kept changing, as other problems became more salient (redistribution, the environment, and international safety). But what was consistent was that Tinbergen sought to function as a guide. His notion of the optimal order was to provide a point on the horizon to which countries, governments, and political movements could aspire. There was nothing pragmatic about that; it was deeply idealistic. As he framed it in the most comprehensive paper on the convergence thesis: "[W]e must do our utmost to analyze these differences in the hope of finding a way to cooperation."[43]

It was also in his work on the convergence thesis that Tinbergen for the first time expressed, albeit in cautious terms, his pessimism. Characteristically, he avoided using the term directly, but rather suggested that one did not need to be optimistic to consider it one's task to strive for a common conversation and rapprochement.[44] He put his hopes in science as a means for creating a basis for discussion, but he recognized that it also required shared institutions. This was the reason he was critical of NATO; it was a divisive institution. And the danger was that the European Union would be equally so. To enable a shared conversation, and ultimately convergence, truly inclusive organizations such as the United Nations were required.

---

[43] Tinbergen, Linneman, and Pronk, "The Meeting of the Twain," 1966.
[44] Tinbergen, "Meer Economisch Begrip tussen Oost en West," 1958.

Over time, however, he did develop an appreciation for the moral ideal that Europe might embody. Although he remained skeptical of Europe as a regional power, he grew increasingly convinced that Europe might have a positive role to play in the world.[45] It could embody a third way as an alternative to the extremes of the United States and the USSR. But here again, it was the idealistic side, the moral leadership, that was crucial for him. It was easy to mistake the convergence debate as a materialistic debate about the underlying structural forces that steered both systems into a kind of convergence. For Tinbergen, any simple materialism was much more likely to lead to violent conflict than to convergence. To improve the world required hard work, ideals, and a plan to move in the desired direction.

To see whether his pessimism or his earlier hopes were at all justified, we must return to the question of whether a conversation between the East and West, across or perhaps above ideological lines was ever possible. Tinbergen himself was aware that it was a Herculean undertaking: "[I]t presupposes a truly scientific attitude on both sides, that is a willing- ness to accept the evidence of empirical facts and true curiosity."[46] Sakharov, the natural scientist who had proposed something similar in the Soviet Union, was fiercely criticized for naïve hopes in scientific persuasion. Estonian dissidents argued: "The fact that Sakharov belongs to the world of science has a great influence on his line of thought. He places too much hope on scientific-technical means, on economic meas- ures, on the goodwill of the leaders of our society."[47] The same could be said of Tinbergen: Did he not also trust too much in the fact that good scientific arguments would carry the day? And was this not hopelessly naïve, given that even among social scientists his arguments often failed to convince?

15.4 Above the Parties, or, Head in the Clouds

In the Dutch political-religious journal *Wending*, a curious article appeared. To my knowledge it is the only joint article of Jan Tinbergen's daughter Tineke and her husband Adriaan van Peski, the latter a Remonstrant minister, a path he pursued at the encouragement of Jan

---

[45] Dekker, "Jan Tinbergen and the Construction of an International Economic Order," 2021.
[46] Tinbergen, "Alternative Optimal Social Orders," 1984.
[47] Kelley, "The Soviet Debate on the Convergence of the American and Soviet Systems," 190, 1973.

Tinbergen, and the former a promising physicist. The two were living in Germany at a Remonstrant seminary in Friedrichstadt. The article detailed the way in which the socialist youth of the GDR were raised, and it did not paint a pretty picture. According to the couple, the situation was appalling: intellectual freedom and all creativity were denied to these youths. One of the concluding paragraphs of the article stood out:

> It is for this reason that we simply cannot stand the slogan of the two materialisms, of the "theoretical materialism of the East" and the "practical materialism of the West," any longer. There is truly something different going on in the East; and he who believes that he can nonetheless start a conversation between the two after a confession that the West, in its own way, is equally concerned with its pocketbook and its stuff, makes a terrible mistake.[48]

They also mocked those who still believed in the idea of a dialogue. It was impossible to have a dialogue with "functionaries of the system," in whom all critical capacity had been systematically erased.

Five issues later, Tineke's father would write in the same journal about the need for more (economic) understanding between the East and the West. In the article, he laid out the ideas of convergence both empirically and deductively, and although he did not directly quote his daughter and son-in-law, it was not hard to see that the conclusion directly addressed their concerns: "Will it not lead to the greater glory of dictatorships and is all of this not one great naïve mistake?"[49] Tinbergen admitted the danger but suggested that there was another danger – that of a large international conflict – and so we had to walk on a dangerous cliff and attempt to avoid both dangers: "He who in every domain of life thinks in polar terms . . . helps to make the conflict inevitable. . . . One does not have to be an optimist to try."[50]

His own daughter and son-in-law were not the only ones who accused Tinbergen of naïvete and complicity with communism. Jacques de Kadt, the representative of the party on foreign affairs and, like Tinbergen, a convinced anticolonialist, denounced his plea as "socialism of the Tinbergen–Khrushchev variety." That might sound harsh, but the direction promoted in foreign affairs by Tinbergen was indeed quite radical. Building on an idea from his friend, pastor J. J. Buskes, he suggested in response to the newly formed NATO alliance that the Netherlands should

---

[48] Van Peski-Tinbergen and Van Peski, "Communistische Opvoeding en Gedachtenvorming bij de Jeugd in de D.D.R.," 1958.
[49] Tinbergen, "Meer Economisch Begrip tussen Oost en West," 530, 1958.   [50] Ibid., 531.

strive for a third way that did not choose sides in the cold war, but instead started from the idea that freedom required "eternal vigilance to both sides."[51]

When Tinbergen joined a discussion in the spring of 1961 with Soviet delegates, he was again faced with the objection that he was merely a figurehead in Soviet propaganda. Tinbergen did not seek to deny that such propaganda existed and that it was one of the main reasons for the organization of such conferences.[52] But he repeated that this was no reason not to attend them. It was important to sustain a joint conversation and to seek mutual understanding, especially between scientists. The complaint kept recurring in Tinbergen's career. It perhaps never became more heated than when he accepted an honorary doctorate at the University of Bilbao in 1970, a year after he won the Nobel Prize. In 1970, Spain was still under the military dictatorship of General Franco, and the choice of Bilbao to confer the doctorate was a strategic one made by the Spanish authorities.

The American Socialist Party, which was involved in the opposition, explained the significance of the location: "Bilbao [was the] one-time center of socialist strength and of uninterrupted and vigorous opposition to the Franco dictatorship, where literally hundreds have been imprisoned for their fight for freedom and democracy.... The Socialist Party USA believes that acceptance of an honorary degree from Franco is in discordance with the highly valued solidarity of all people fighting dictatorship."[53] In Dutch newspapers, similar voices were heard: one simply should not talk to fascists. There was even some (ironic) pity, for Tinbergen, the "victim of an illusion."[54]

Also, within Spain, Tinbergen was repeatedly urged to refuse the doctorate by local students who offered him a petition about the position of intellectuals in Spain. The same group of students occupied the economics faculty and interrupted one of the lectures he gave. Tinbergen's response was calm, at least on the surface. He again explained his belief that science was an international endeavor, which transcended political differences. But even if this were not so, it was important to always seek some common

---

[51] Schenk and Van Herk, *Juliana: Vorstin naast de Rode Loper*, 1980.
[52] Henk Bos has suggested that such events were also used for espionage by the Russians; in particular, he recounted a conference in Antananarivo in Madagascar, with suspicious Russian activity. See Henk Bos in Jolink and Barendrecht-Tinbergen, *Gedeelde Herinneringen*, 68, 1993.
[53] Undated letter from Socialist Party USA, probably from June 1970, JTC.
[54] "Met Fascisten valt niet te Praten, Prof. Tinbergen!," *Het Vrije Volk*, 7 April 1970.

ground and to resist thinking in terms of absolutes. The best system was to be found somewhere in the middle, and one should offer constructive proposals to help bring about such a system. An honorary doctorate made clear that the people were interested in his ideas, and it was important to keep discussing them, he argued.[55] As if to add fuel to the fire, Tinbergen suggested that if the students had listened to him, they might have discovered that his scientific arguments could provide ammunition to them in their struggle for more freedom. What he failed to mention was that in Bilbao his speech was about a "Framework for Regional Planning,"[56] hardly a revolutionary subject.

In that same year, Tinbergen led a petition for a more constructive and positive attitude of the West toward Cuba.[57] Ever since 1964 Tinbergen had also repeatedly visited Indonesia, initially governed by Sukarno. The Indonesian leader was struggling throughout the period to remain in power. After a failed coup in which several army generals were killed, his position weakened further. The army distanced themselves increasingly from Sukarno and sought revenge for their losses. With the help of the West, which had come into conflict with Sukarno, the army killed between 500,000 and 1,000,000 people, supposedly communist enemies. When Tinbergen left for one of his advisory missions to Indonesia, it was unclear whether Sukarno was still in power, and students were protesting in the streets against the government. Yet Tinbergen remained committed to helping the regime fix the economic situation in Indonesia, which was close to bankruptcy and in the midst of corruption scandals against various senior members in government and the army. Like in Turkey, his position was not affected by political changes. He continued his advisory work in 1967 when Suharto had replaced Sukarno. At the time, it attracted little explicit criticism; the Dutch communist newspaper was one of the few to call the whole endeavor "neocolonialist." Tinbergen remained committed to the idea that as a scientist it was his duty to engage in conversations with everyone.

Looking back, it is easy to call all of it incredibly naïve and misguided. Various economists have recently come under attack for their association with "bad regimes": Hayek and a number of Chicago economists for their

<hr/>

[55] Tinbergen, "Prof. Tinbergen: Begrip voor Kritiek," *Het Vrije Volk*, 1 April 1970.
[56] Part of the manuscripts in JTC.
[57] Jan Tinbergen, "Tinbergen Pleit met 62 Anderen voor Positieve Cuba-Houding," *Het Vrije Volk*, 9 February 1970.

association with Pinochet in Chile, or Joseph Stiglitz for his involvement with Nicholas Maduro in Venezuela. If we were trying to make Tinbergen guilty by association, he would have a bad track record: contacts with officials of the Nazi regime, whose economic policies he (conditionally) praised; various visits to the USSR under Brezhnev, after he had earlier praised the impressive savings rate under Stalin; advice to the Indonesian government during what is now called the Indonesian genocide; and, if all that were not enough, publishing in an official state journal in Romania while it was ruled by Ceausescu.[58] He did not associate out of ignorance with these regimes; he was aware of (most of) their wrongdoings but argued that it was important to maintain the peace, to keep talking.

What in hindsight is even more disturbing is that during this period he started to develop explicit criticisms of democracy. His "constitutional" design of the Plan of Labor was meant to restrict the absolute power of parliament. So, while he had never been a great enthusiast of too much democracy, beginning in 1962, he also starting expressing skepticism about the capabilities of citizens: "The indecision and the conservatism of public opinion is a consequence of a lack of knowledge and of interested propaganda."[59] In a 1964 booklet on central planning, democracy was presented mostly as an obstacle.[60] And it turned into a central element of Tinbergen's theory of the optimal order a year later:

Experience has shown that for most if not all developing countries parliamentary democracy does not work as a system of governing a country. In the few cases where so far such a system did work, more or less, it was due to exceptional men or circumstances. But even in some developed countries, including such an important country as France, the system did not work very well. In the history of the West, on numerous occasions, dictatorial powers were given, but only temporarily, to overcome emergencies. One of the main reasons behind all this is the narrow-mindedness of the average citizen, who cannot help to let short-term or small-group interests prevail while determining his vote in any election. Most character-istic of the limits of democracy is perhaps the opinion in circles of proponents of parliamentary democracy that the referendum has to be rejected as an instrument of collective decision making. All this shows that for a good form of government, a number of decisions must be left to elites.[61]

---

[58] Editor *Viata Economica* to JT, 5 January 1968, JTC. The article is on a "world economic policy"; a copy of the article is included "Este Necesară o Politică Mondială Pentru Dezvoltare," JTC.
[59] Tinbergen, *Lessons from the Past*, 125, 1963.
[60] Tinbergen, *Central Planning*, 16, 1964.
[61] Tinbergen, "Ideologies and Scientific Development," 6, 1965.

Without seeking to acquit Tinbergen, we should observe that these observations match a longtime consistent pattern in his thought. His theory of decision-making had sought the optimal mixture of centralization and decentralization, and now he was drawing the practical consequences of that theory in relation to democracy. The rejection of referendums, but also the acceptance of representative democracy and constitutional constraints were all exceptions to a pure democracy, so Tinbergen in his characteristic way could suggest that some optimum had to be found between pure direct democracy and rule by a small elite or one dictator.

If we leave aside the moral question about whether what he did was wrong or not, it is worth observing that despite all the claims of naïvete against him, Tinbergen was frequently quite successful in generating a dialogue. This was not always direct, or in the way he had intended. The anecdote at the start of this chapter about the study in East–West trade by his student Cornelisse was such an example of unintended outcomes. And in Indonesia, one of Tinbergen's early students who pursued studies in development economics, Sumitro Djojohadikusumo, was at the foundation of the modernization of economic policy along Tinbergen lines. He was able to pursue a modernization that indeed took place after the demise of Sukarno. Later, Djojohadikusumo was a minister in government no fewer than five times and was important in shaping the economic plans during the twenty-five years since 1968.[62] In 1961, Tinbergen reported on a joint meeting with the Soviets about convergence, which was sparked by his own article from that year.[63] And in 1967, there was even a symposium among Soviet scientists about the subject of convergence, although more from a sociological angle.[64] These meetings were not always fully open – sometimes they did not even involve the West – but they were clear signs that subjects put on the agenda in the West could have an impact behind the Iron Curtain.

The impact of such discussions and visits is not easy to assess. In an official letter of gratitude after a visit of Tinbergen to the USSR in 1966, which had included a discussion of the optimal order, his critique of capitalism was embraced. But in that same letter the Soviets distanced themselves from his critique of socialism. It was moreover naïve, the letter argued, to believe that economists or politicians could exert (much) influence on the economy. After all, as Marx had argued, the economy was

[62] "Prof. Sumitro Djojohadikusumo over het Indonesische Economische Wonder," 15 May 1993, *NRC Handelsblad*, p. 3 (Zaterdags Bijvoegsel).
[63] Tinbergen, "Oost-West-Gesprekken," 1961.
[64] Sarlemijn, "Konvergenz in Bezug auf Planung der Forschung?," 1987.

governed by objective forces: "Where we observe the dialectics of objective development, the dynamics of movement, you observe the rejection of dogmas.... And whether you like it or not, capitalism will be followed by the 'highest' form of socialism and not by some mythical optimal order."[65] Officially, Tinbergen's idea of convergence remained anathema in Soviet Russia. But he was invited, and within the USSR his ideas were discussed among top intellectuals.

If his real goal was to act as a guide, if his optimal order was mostly an aspirational model for leaders to pursue, then it should be judged as a great success of his convergence theory that it inspired Mikhail Gorbachev. Tinbergen was quick to realize that Gorbachev's leadership might provide new opportunities for a conversation, and he attempted to blow new life into his convergence theory. Or in his understated manner of speaking: "[I]rritation has made way for curiosity: What can we learn from each other's experiences and what are the characteristics of the optimal social order?"[66] Meanwhile, the United States under Reagan was drifting further away from this optimal order, so he was also working on articles about a new socialism for the United States.[67] Even more encouraging was the fact that in 1987, John Kenneth Galbraith published a debate with Stanislav Menchikov, member of the central committee of the Soviet Communist Party, entitled *Capitalism, Communism and Coexistence*.[68] The book contained a serious and open debate in which the idea of convergence was prominent.

In 1993, Gorbachev paid a personal visit to thank Tinbergen for the inspiration he drew from his work (Figure 15.1). In 1989, the Berlin Wall came down; it was a milestone in the history of the East and West, and, therefore, also for the work of Tinbergen, although it was hard to argue that the conflict had been resolved through a process of convergence. Instead, it was the heightened conflict of the 1980s that is now widely believed to have contributed to the collapse of the Soviet Union. But Gorbachev indicated that he had benefited from Tinbergen's convergence theory as well as the framework of targets and instruments for economic policy. Gorbachev suggested that his ideas of perestroika (reforms) had been inspired by Tinbergen's work. The admiration was mutual; Tinbergen had already praised Gorbachev's

---

[65] 1966 letter with Dutch translation, JTC.
[66] Tinbergen, "Ideologische Harmonisatie tussen Oost en West?," 1989.
[67] Tinbergen, "A Socialism for the USA?," 1989.
[68] Tinbergen reviewed the book for a Dutch newspaper: "Dialoog op Wereldniveau," *NRC Handelsblad*, 12 January 1989, p. 2.

Figure 15.1 Gorbachev paid Tinbergen a personal visit at his home on the Haviklaan, The Hague, in May 1993.

courage some years earlier.[69] It was the end of a long attempt to establish a meaningful dialogue between the East and West, which came only a year before Tinbergen's death in 1994. It had been a struggle that often ran into ideological walls, and one that even in the end was far from fully satisfying, because the direction taken in many former countries of the East was that of shock therapy, not of gradual convergence to some ideal order. And as Tinbergen's critics pointed out, despite Gorbachev's good intentions, he never succeeded in reform; instead, the system collapsed.

In the years since, the world has moved further from the optimal order as envisaged by Tinbergen. Beneath his idea of an optimal order was a universalism that suggested that the world was ultimately one and that cultural differences, like economic differences, could be overcome. It was an idea that was in no small part inspired by Gandhi. In his Nehru Memorial lecture in India on "mature socialism," Tinbergen reminded his audience that Rudyard Kipling's famous poem "The Ballad of East and West" continued in a quite different vein after the first famous line:[70]

[69] Tinbergen, "Gorbatsjov's Moed," *Het Parool*, 20 December 1989, p. 7.
[70] Tinbergen, "Some Thoughts on Mature Socialism," 24, 1973.

> Oh, East is East, and West is West, and never the twain shall meet,
> Till Earth and Sky stand presently at God's great Judgment Seat;
> But there is neither East nor West, Border, nor Breed, nor Birth,
> When two strong men stand face to face, though they come from the
> ends of the earth!

***

There is a recurring pattern in Tinbergen's engagement with bad regimes. He consistently seeks to be the peacekeeper, much in the same way that the UN would later describe its own missions. When matters were in danger of escalating, after the invasion of Hungary and the development of the *Sputnik* rockets, Tinbergen warned of the dangers of polarization that would only escalate matters further. At the height of the Cold War, during the Cuban Crisis, Tinbergen wrote extensively on the idea of convergence. When his fellow social democrats became complacent, he urged them to think more internationally. When Reagan moved back in the direction of pure capitalism, he started urging for more social democracy in the United States. If his models were primarily attempts to guide us to a world that could be, this was never more urgent than when the world was in danger of losing sight of these long-term goals, and that was when Tinbergen felt most called upon. If convergence was out of sight, then at least coexistence was required. Naïvete is not the right word to describe that pattern. It was a pattern of looking for potential sources of conflict and then minimizing them or warning of the dangers of further escalation and attempting to contribute to deescalation. He was appalled by the confrontational strategy of Reagan during the 1980s and was a great admirer of the policy of Ostpolitik, which sought to reach out to Russia, by the German leader Willy Brandt. In that sense, it was only natural that in the 1980s he sought to incorporate the dimension of security into his optimal order. For more than anything, the security situation was the real danger of the ongoing Cold War. When communism had lost most of its intellectual appeal, the danger of a violent conflict between the East and the West persisted and had to be prevented at all costs. It was fear coupled with a deep-seated longing for harmony that best describes his feelings during the Cold War. If the United Nations was his most favored institution, then peacekeeping was its most essential role.

That combination put him at odds with others, including those in science. This is perhaps nowhere better illustrated than in an exchange with Oskar Morgenstern, whom he knew from his work on the business cycle in the 1930s. Some years before he formulated the convergence thesis in 1954, Tinbergen had inquired: "My question to you is whether the US

government which evidently spends quite some money for research projects in connection with defense also has tried to get the co-operation of
the best experts in analyzing the diplomatic side and the juridical side
of the world conflict."[71] The question was anything but innocent, since
Morgenstern was at that point in time working at the RAND Corporation,
the big government-funded military think tank that was at the heart of the
Cold War mentality.[72] (The RAND Corporation was notoriously spoofed as
the Bland Corporation in *Dr. Strangelove* by Stanley Kubrick.)

Morgenstern's response was supportive of the question, which he had
"discussed with friends." But "the difficulty lies, of course, in the fact that it
is much easier to use exact and rigorous thinking in military strategy than
in political strategy . . . This is a great difficulty which nobody knows really
how to overcome. Therefore, I am somewhat skeptical about the possibility
of applying rigorous methods when the general situation is not very
suitable for them." Morgenstern concluded that the chief problem in
politics was that "nobody has really as vivid an imagination as is necessary."[73] If Tinbergen would have written that sentence, he would have
thought that imagination was best applied to the development of a new
shared vocabulary or a clearer way of showing how coexistence and
peaceful solutions could be achieved. Morgenstern, however, thought
completely in terms of the deterrence effect that atomic weapons might
have, so the problem was that nobody could "imagine" how destructive
their actual use would be. What was required for Morgenstern was a
dystopian imagination that would make people and politicians aware
how grave the danger was. What was required for Tinbergen was a utopian
imagination of what the world could be. His theory of the optimal order
was the furthest he ever reached in that direction.

There was another difference between Morgenstern and Tinbergen.
Whereas Tinbergen strongly believed that mutual understanding would
lead to more peaceful relations, Morgenstern was working on a rather
different project. As one of the originators of game theory, he was exploring strategic interactions between individuals or countries, and how this
depended on knowledge and rationality. Tinbergen believed that an
enlightened rationality would lead to peaceful relationships among nations.
One of the major outcomes of game theory as developed during this period

---

[71] JT to Oskar Morgenstern, 20 August 1954, TL.
[72] Erickson et al., *How Reason Almost Lost Its Mind: The Strange Career of Cold War Rationality*, 2015.
[73] Oskar Morgenstern to JT, 23 December 1954, TL.

was that it is rational to deliver the first strike in a nuclear war.[74] If that result was not quite universally accepted, then at least the major symbolic impact for game theory was made through the game known as the prisoner's dilemma, which demonstrated that it was the rational strategy to not cooperate with one's "fellow" player.

Tinbergen hoped that an exploration of possible outcomes would lead to more cooperative outcomes. He made the point explicitly when he reflected on the coexistence idea in 1984:

> In principle there are two ways of dealing with the future. One is to speculate about the most likely future, the other to discuss the most desirable future. The former is more difficult than the latter. In order to arrive at a picture of the most likely future one has to know the most likely unforeseen events. An example is the escalation of one of the existing military conflicts to a nuclear war; another is that the use of nuclear weapons is triggered off by coincidence. Such forecasts are not only difficult to make but many of them are of little use also. They offer little help to the construction of an optimal world order.... So I propose to discuss the most desirable social order.[75]

Morgenstern planned for the worst; Tinbergen hoped for the best.

---

[74] Erickson et al., *How Reason Almost Lost Its Mind: The Strange Career of Cold War Rationality*, 2015; Morgan, *The World in a Model: How Economists Work and Think*, 2012.

[75] Tinbergen, "Coexistence: From the Past to the Future," 1984.

16

Expertise Far from Home

In 1966 Gunnar Myrdal published *The Asian Drama: An Inquiry into the Poverty of Nations*.[1] In his magnum opus of nearly 2,200 pages, Myrdal argued that nearly all development aid since World War II had been wasted. He was critical of both Western and Asian elites. The book had a big impact in the world of development economics and the way in which the West thought about its own role in the formerly colonized world. It fitted in with a growing criticism of the development policies, which fostered relationships of dependence between the West and the developing world.[2] In the Netherlands, Tinbergen was harshly criticized by Willem Frederik Wertheim, who argued that development aid was a form of neocolonialism.[3]

The critique of Myrdal was part of a radicalization in the discourse on the left in Western Europe and the United States, which became increasingly critical of capitalism and colonialism. After years of peaceful reformism promoted by the social democrats, a new type of critical theory was developed that sought to reconnect with the revolutionary spirit of Marx. This new critical theory was widely popular among the student movement and the activists of 1968. Tinbergen's rival on development economics, Wertheim, openly supported the regime of Mao in China. Myrdal was not quite as radical, and worried about the rise of communism in Asia. But as observers at the time noted, his rhetoric bore resemblance to the messages coming from Peking and Havana.[4] But for all its radicalism, the criticism

---

[1] Myrdal, *Asian Drama: An Inquiry into the Poverty of Nations*, 1968.
[2] Frank, *Capitalism and Underdevelopment in Latin America*, 1967.
[3] Wertheim, *Tien Jaar Onrecht in Indonesië: Militaire Dictatuur en Internationale Steun*, 1976.
[4] Busch, "Book Review of Gunnar Myrdal's *Asian Drama: An Inquiry into the Poverty of Nations*," 1968.

of development economics by Myrdal, Wertheim, and others had something crucial in common with the development economics of Tinbergen, Rostow, and others: a belief in universalism and modernization. Both the Marxist left and the mainstream proponents of development economics believed that economic modernization was a universal process that would lead to the kind of modern societies familiar from the West. The countries in Asia were not different, merely underdeveloped.

Tinbergen had repeatedly been charged with a lack of diagnosis and sole focus on the cure. Clifford Geertz, the renowned anthropologist, charged Myrdal, despite all his criticism of the hypocrisy of the West, with doing the same:

It would seem impossible to write nearly a million words on a country [India] with so rich a history, so profound a culture, and so complex a social system and fail to convey the force of its originality and the vitality of its spirit somewhere; but Professor Myrdal has accomplished it. There is no passage to India here, but only to some off-shore elevation from which its bolder features can be dimly and uncertainly seen.[5]

In the bird's-eye view of Myrdal, India was a country troubled by social and political stagnation in which superstitious beliefs dominated. When he referred to local culture, it was invariably as a hindrance to economic development.

If Myrdal and Tinbergen were prone to complain about the lack of relevant data, Geertz reversed their perspective: "Meaningful aggregates are impossible to calculate. Financial magnitudes are severed from physical realities. Statistics are fantasy quantified. Critical variables are beyond practical measurement."[6] For Geertz, the reliance on aggregate data that had been so crucial in the development of economic expertise in the West was not simply more difficult in the developing world, but a form of willful ignorance. It was a form of hiding behind abstractions, generalizations, and categories that were often crucially shaped in the West.

He took unemployment as an example; it was a phenomenon that in its normal guise of involuntary joblessness was virtually nonexistent in India. The development economists consequently redefined it as underemployment, that is, labor employed below its capacity. But such a perspective, argued Geertz, did not do justice to the complex social system of India in which many were active in spiritual pursuits, such as Brahmins, and in other social functions that were not obviously economically productive to the development expert. To argue that these individuals could be more

---

[5] Geertz, "Myrdal's Mythology: 'Modernism' and the Third World," 31, 1969.   [6] Ibid.

usefully employed in industry or agriculture was to misunderstand crucially their social role, position, and function, as well as the way in which such careers provided alternative career paths for those not attracted to or capable of physical labor. Geertz's critique highlighted, most of all, that a policy of industrial development as suggested by the development planners of the 1950s, and a policy of agricultural development as suggested by Myrdal, would radically upset social relations in India, would be opposed by most in society, and would almost certainly fail.

Geertz suggested that even as a description of Western development the picture of Myrdal, and by implication Tinbergen, was one-sided. They presented economic and social development as it had happened in England and Sweden, rather than Germany or Italy. It was a poignant observation in relation to Tinbergen's work. From the way he thought about (regional) planning to how he thought about the proper place of expertise in politics and how he conceptualized the international order, it was all based on his work in the Netherlands. His own vision of development economics was in crucial ways Dutch – it was homegrown.

The fact that Tinbergen drew so much from his Dutch experience in many ways should have made him wary of the whole project of development planning by experts. After all, the establishment of economic expertise in the Netherlands, which functioned, more or less, successfully above the parties, had been the outcome of long historical development, a development that involved the transformation of the social-democratic party in the broad labor party, the transformation from socialist ideology to pragmatic social democracy, and the establishment of new institutions: first the CBS, then the CPB, and, most importantly, the intermediary agencies such as the SER, which facilitated the interaction between experts and the government.

Most of all the functioning of neutral expertise depended, as Tinbergen frequently acknowledged, on the gradual integration of different groups into a coherent and stable society. He had pursued the integration of the working class, but it was equally important that the different religious groups, most prominently the Catholics and Protestants, accepted each other as legitimate partners in Dutch society. The "pacification" of Dutch society achieved in 1917 was crucial for creating social peace and a society in which the different groups all accepted each other as legitimate members of Dutch society.[7] The Breakthrough movement, for which Tinbergen had

---

[7] Lijphart, *The Politics of Accomodation: Pluralism and Democracy in the Netherlands*, 1968.

so much sympathy, sought to complete this integration by further breaking down barriers between different socioeconomic and religious groups.

These preconditions and the institutional setting provided the context in which economic policymaking as Tinbergen envisioned it could function. But it was precisely this set of preconditions and institutional setting that was absent in the countries where Tinbergen worked as development expert. That was only to be expected; many of these countries had only recently gained their independence and there was often open social and political conflict between different groups. Frequently such conflicts were a direct consequence of colonization. The British had done much to preserve the Indian caste system. And the Dutch had used existing conflicts within Indonesia to mobilize certain groups against the Indonesian independence movement in their attempts to regain control over the country after World War II. When Tinbergen advised Sukarno in Indonesia in February 1966, the country was in a state of civil war. In 1965 there had been a failed coup that was blamed on the communists. With support from the United States and other European countries the Indonesian army undertook a purge of everyone suspected of communist sympathies. Ethnic Chinese and Javanese groups were specifically targeted. Estimates suggest that between half a million and a million people were killed. Pressure mounted on Sukarno, who had historically depended on support from the communists and who around this period was also internationally seeking more support from the communists.[8] He famously proclaimed to the West: "Go to hell with your aid" and withdrew his country from the United Nations. In March 1966 he had to hand over power to Suharto, the general leading the army, who would formally become president in 1967 and rule the country until 1998.

We have seen that in Turkey, despite Atatürk's efforts to unite the country, there was still great social conflict by the early 1960s. Parties did not accept each other's existence and attempted to dominate their opponents rather than to work with them. There were great disparities and seeds for serious conflict between the urban centers and the more traditional countryside. To this day the Kurds who live in the southeastern part of the country are not accepted as a legitimate part of Turkish society. Within such a context it is anything but clear what working in the national or general interest means. A 7 perrcent growth rate, even if achieved, might equally well lead to more conflict if it appears to benefit some group in

---

[8] De Jong, "De Nederlands-Indonesische Betrekkingen 1963–1985," 1986.

society more than the others. We have seen how the more structural reforms proposed by the SPO were immediately interpreted in these terms, as attempts to redistribute power and resources from one group in society to another.

These problems were exacerbated because the development experts who came in from outside such as Tinbergen did not have the institutional setting and independence that were required. We have seen how important it was for the CPB to find the right place within Dutch politics: not too close to the government because it would lose its independence, and not too far from government, because it would lose its influence. An intermediary institution like the SER could be crucial as an entry point for the type of advice and knowledge produced at the CPB. Tinbergen attempted to develop something like the CPB in Turkey, with the SPO. But it is important to recognize how different its setting was. It directly advised the government, and after only a few years an open political conflict had broken out between the planners and government. The SPO was in constant danger of coming under more direct political control. But more importantly the institution was implemented by the military interim government after the coup of 1960 and had little independent standing or authority in society independent of government.

Tinbergen knew that institutions mattered. More than most economists he was aware of the political structure that facilitated economic stability and growth. In the Netherlands he had demonstrated a keen awareness of social differences and how more social integration might be achieved. Social integration was crucial for the creation of widespread support and legitimacy for the economic system, including the position of neutral experts working in the general interest. But when he was away from home, he lacked both the institutional awareness and the intimate knowledge of social relations that were natural to him in the Netherlands. When devoid of the knowledge of time and place, his expertise quickly lost most of its power and relevance.

It did not help that Tinbergen had little of the anthropologist in him. He moved in government circles and among the high bureaucracy of the countries his visited but never spent longer periods in development countries. Home was too dear to him. When he visited Turkey, one of his students who was working for a longer period at the SPO took him to the Turkish bazaar. Tinbergen grew uncomfortable quickly. It did not take long before his student realized that it was better to take him back to his hotel. Tinbergen helped plan the Turkish economy, but when faced with its most characteristic market, he turned away.

The danger of expertise far from home is a two-way street. The advice he and his fellow development economists of the first generation gave was generic, universalist, and narrowly economic. And their theories have been criticized from nearly every angle for being so. For Tinbergen his work in development economics was primarily an extension of his theory of economic policymaking. Although he did not take strong positions in the more theoretical debates about the correct development strategies – industrialization or modernization of agriculture, big push or focus on interdependencies – his work was broadly in line with the mainstream views about these subjects in the 1960s. It resulted in many efforts that misfired, and the development of a type of expertise that often poorly fitted the needs of local industries and communities. But there was an equally serious danger that his type of expertise was politically abused, by domestic or international powers. To function well expertise does not merely require a degree of influence, but also a degree of independence. And it was precisely this independence that was lacking.

In both Turkey and Indonesia, a coup took place around the time of Tinbergen's involvement. In Turkey we witnessed how the international planning expertise Tinbergen represented was perceived as a direct threat to the existing regime. Within months after his first visit, the Turkish army, with the help of Western powers, had taken power with a coup. In such a situation Tinbergen's position was anything but independent, he was directly involved with the international power struggle over the future of Turkey. The type of expertise he represented was used to foster and legitimize political change and the geopolitical interests of Germany and United States. In Indonesia the pattern recurred. Again, his first visit came during the final stages of the Sukarno regime. The new Suharto regime, described at the time as the regime of generals, directly enlisted Tinbergen as one of its advisors. Again, the danger lurked large that he was there mainly to create legitimacy for the new regime.

Tinbergen was not merely a hapless victim in these developments, although he certainly lacked some political intuition. Nonetheless, he attempted to develop his own position. He shared some of the criticism of the hypocrisy of the West, which Myrdal expressed, and worried repeatedly about the economic and political conditions attached to development aid. He criticized the protectionist policies of the West. He sought to strengthen the position of the United Nations in the development process, since he understood that it was more likely that development experts could achieve some degree of independence under this banner. In Turkey he had attempted to design a relatively independent institution with the SPO. But good intentions did not guarantee good outcomes. And within the context of his work in both Turkey and Indonesia it is all the more troubling that within his writing he openly started questioning the value of democracy in developing countries. He expressed clear criticism of the narrow-mindedness of the citizens and the dominance of small group interests, but failed to acknowledge the problem that many of the governments he advised ignored the rights and interests of other groups in society.

The most surprising blind spot in Tinbergen's development economics, however, did not lie in the way he thought of planning as mostly a technical exercise or in his lack of political tact. These dangers had been highlighted by his critics in the Netherlands, although they had been less visible in his home country. The more surprising blind spot was well captured by Geertz in his critique of Myrdal: "Institutional modernization in India cannot be simply a matter of 'wiping out' archaic customs and unpleasant attitudes. It must be a matter of directing a process of social and cultural change already in motion in the appropriate directions.... It is a struggle which consists in shaping patterns of change already in motion, not in creating a nation out of nothing."[9] It was as if Geertz was reading a page from Hendrik de Man's cultural socialism. In his youthful critiques of Marx, Tinbergen had been clear enough: revolution was a dangerous idea. If a better society could emerge, it had to grow out of the current society. The logical consequence of that insight was a development planning that sought to develop what was already present in a country such as India, a development economics that sought to recognize internal forces for change, and foster these, much as the AJC had tried to steer the direction of the labor movement.

The development of civil society was not mere idealism. In recent work on economic development, Daron Acemoglu and James Robinson have demonstrated that success is dependent on the co-evolution of the state and civil society.[10] They used the metaphor of a "narrow corridor" to describe the delicate balance between state and civil society, where there is a constant danger that one will overpower the other.

Tinbergen was not completely blind to these requirements. In his reflections on Turkey he sought to identify such positive internal forces. And in India he recognized cultural and moral elements that he valued

---

[9] Geertz, "Myrdal's Mythology: 'Modernism' and the Third World," 1969.
[10] Acemoglu and Robinson, *The Narrow Corridor: States, Societies, and the Fate of Liberty*, 2019.

highly himself. But he was never able to connect this recognition on a personal level with his own theories of economic development. The theories remained purely technical and economistic. As Balogh pointed out, his education planning thought of knowledge as purely instrumental, as a set of technical skills, completely disconnected from local cultural traditions of knowledge. When Tinbergen was faced with the "-ization" problem, he managed to turn it into a technical problem in no time. If India or Turkey wanted to plan their own development, this was merely a matter of training enough technical experts, so that foreign expertise was no longer necessary.

His self-proclaimed desire to solve "the most urgent problems first" made him travel far beyond his original area of expertise. It took him to fields and countries with which he had relatively little acquaintance, but his deep sense of responsibility and idealism never let him give up. The severity of the problems required him to keep working at them, even if they were beyond his (direct) field of competence. But responsibility and will were no replacement for knowledge and expertise. In a telling interview, Tinbergen suggested: "My friends the sociologists believe that it is required to spend at least three years in a country to understand it. In my field that is, I believe, not necessary."[11]

Tinbergen's universalism made him a truly global thinker, who more than most of his contemporaries sought to create a truly international economic order, with an associated global idea of economic and social justice. In that worldview there was no place for the idea that Turkish development would be a quite different process with a quite different outcome than Indian development. For all the connection he felt to the poor in India when he first visited the country, and his desire to develop a more humane economy, he never came to grips with human, social, and cultural diversity in his economic work.

That universalism had and has many attractive features. Without it, the idea of universal human rights would probably be unthinkable, nor would we ever have arrived at a global standard of poverty: those living on less than $2 per day. But that same universalism, which many, including Tinbergen, found so attractive in the moral domain, was not guaranteed to work in economic science and policy. It favored the general over the specific, the technical and universal, over the cultural and local. It made Tinbergen forget that what was achieved in the Netherlands and other Western European

[11] "Ontwikkelingslanden op de Been Helpen," *Het Parool*, 27 June 1964, p. 7.

countries was the outcome of a contingent and painful historical process, not the result of development planning and economic management. Rather, it was the other way around: the historical development of national unification, social integration, and the growth of the welfare state in Western Europe had made economic expertise of the Tinbergen type possible.

PART IV

THE LIMITS OF EXPERTISE

17

Measuring the Unmeasurable

Welfare and Justice

Much do I know – but to know all is my ambition.
—Goethe[1]

It is sometimes suggested that we learn more from failure than from success. Following this idea, this chapter traces Tinbergen's attempts to develop a scientific theory of justice. He never satisfactorily developed that theory, but he returned to it repeatedly over his career, most famously in the 1970s, around the time of his retirement. But he started early in his career, when he wrote an article entitled "Mathematical Psychology" in the social-democratic party magazine.[2] Read from the perspective of today, the article is prescient: among other things, it argued for the introduction of experiments into economics, something that would not find wide acceptance in that field before the 1980s.[3] Tinbergen proposed to do experiments in a tradition that went back to the pioneering mathematical economists Francis Y. Edgeworth and William Stanley Jevons, who were interested in the scientific measurement of utility.[4] Utility is the elusive concept that economists use to describe the "amount of pleasure" derived from the consumption of a good, and more generally for welfare. It is a term that is meant to capture all the subjective pleasures derived from goods. Jeremy Bentham, the early nineteenth-century utilitarian philosopher (society should pursue the greatest utility for the greatest amount of

---

[1] In German: "Zwar weiß ich viel, doch möcht' ich alles wissen." Tinbergen, Cited in "Desiderata op het Punt van de Conjunctuurstatistiek," 1935.
[2] Tinbergen, "Mathematiese Psychologie," 1930.
[3] Svorenčík, "The Experimental Turn in Economics: A History of Experimental Economics," 2015.
[4] Maas, *William Stanley Jevons and the Making of Modern Economics*, 2005; Moscati, *Measuring Utility: From the Marginal Revolution to Behavioral Economics*, 2018.

people), described utility as the calculation of pleasure and pain. And for a wide range of economists, this calculation was the holy grail of economics.

This was no different for Jan Tinbergen; he too believed that one of the ultimate goals of economics as a science was to develop a way to measure utility. He did so during a period when many economists were abandoning the goal: they considered the comparison of subjective states of mind of different individuals unscientific. Especially after Lionel Robbins's classic statement to that effect in 1932, most economists left the (direct) measurement of utility behind in the realm of (distant) scientific dreams.[5]

Measurement of welfare would not have been so important to Tinbergen if it did not have profound moral and political implications. The measurement of welfare was crucial to discussions about justice and equality. This was well recognized even by the economists who decided to abandon the project of direct measurement of welfare. Without the comparison of utility between different individuals, it was impossible to say who was better off: those with lots of money or those with a little. If, however, economists would succeed in measuring utility directly, they could say something meaningful and important about inequality between different individuals, families, and nations. The measurement of utility thus presented a dilemma to economists, believed Tinbergen. Would they go ahead and measure it, however imperfectly, or would they admit that on purely scientific grounds measurement was not (yet) possible? Tinbergen, after repeated failures, decided to go ahead. If meaningful work could be done only by admitting moral and political values into science, then that was a price worth paying.

His work on utility measurement also brought out a feature of his work that is not as visible in other projects. Measurement was central for Tinbergen. In the Leiden laboratory where he received his training in physics, the major figure next to Paul Ehrenfest was Heike Kamerlingh Onnes. In his inaugural lecture, Kamerlingh Onnes had pleaded for a physics in which measurement of quantitative relationships was central. In the Leiden laboratory there was a banner that read "From Measurement to Knowledge" (*Van Meten tot Weten*). In Tinbergen's own work the reliance on data is often so natural that it appears as if matters had never been different. But they had been. None of the major economic statistics, from unemployment rates to GDP, had existed before the twentieth century. Tinbergen was instrumental in developing them and promoting their usage, so it is even more informative to study how he sought to develop a

[5] Robbins, *An Essay on the Nature and Significance of Economic Science*, 1932.

measure of welfare, despite the fact that this measure never found widespread acceptance.

17.1 Ehrenfest's Intuition and Frisch's Explorations

Tinbergen's mentor Ehrenfest had suggested that an income distribution is just when two individuals did not want to trade places. Let us imagine that one person is working in a demanding management job at a pay of $150,000 per year and the other is an office clerk with a pay of $80,000 per year.[6] This distribution is fair, according to Ehrenfest, if the office clerk is willing to accept the lower pay given that the work is less demanding and requires fewer skills (and hence less training). From Tinbergen's description of his mentor's views, it seems that Ehrenfest broadly believed that people in society were paid a just wage. It reflected his beliefs that there was a kind of natural hierarchy that was reflected in the jobs that people held, a hierarchy from which both the more gifted and the less gifted did not want to deviate (much).

Tinbergen, on the other hand, was willing to go much further based on the same basic notion of justice. In the press, around 1930, he suggested that the pay of professors ought to be lowered in order to make the income distribution more just. After all, professors enjoyed a safe job that involved little physical strain and that allowed them to engage in activities they liked anyhow.[7] To ensure that lower-paid workers would not want to trade jobs with them, a serious pay cut was required.[8]

The moral intuition about trading places underlies Tinbergen's work on utility, but the measurement component was suggested by Ragnar Frisch.[9] Frisch had attempted to measure the marginal utility of money based on

---

[6] Ehrenfest's idea is somewhat of a historical curiosity, and his thought experiment is somewhat problematic – after all, what if the other person is simply not fit for the job? But like the most famous welfare criterion in economics, the Pareto criterion, it is based on the idea of hypothetical exchanges. According to the Pareto criterion, a given distribution is efficient if no more trades can be made that would make anyone better off without making somebody else worse off. Although Ehrenfest's intuition is less demanding – only one side must agree to the exchange rather than both sides as in the Pareto criterion – the underlying idea to base normative principles on hypothetical exchanges is similar.

[7] Tinbergen, "Socialisten en Hoge Inkomens," 1930.

[8] It is interesting that Jan Pen would later claim that he had the same dispute with Tinbergen, except that now Tinbergen occupied Ehrenfest's position, and Jan Pen that of the younger Tinbergen. See Pen, *Vandaag Staat Niet Alleen: Essays en Memoires*, 2006. Elsewhere Pen's reminiscences have not always proven to be accurate.

[9] It is highly probable that the issue of utility measurement first came to Tinbergen's attention in a 1928 article in *De Economist* that makes reference to both Fisher's and

detailed statistics about the consumption of sugar. From his work he concluded that there was a decreasing marginal utility of money. In other words, as income grows, utility grows less than proportional with it. Similar attempts were undertaken at the time by Irving Fisher, who suggested an approach much like that of Frisch. The use of budget statistics was believed to be key to the measurement of utility. The reception of Frisch's work, and of his later book, *New Methods of Measuring Marginal Utility*,[10] however, was not very positive. The critics were unsure about the stringent assumptions he had to make. Frisch had to assume that utility functions were the same for groups of people,[11] and he had to assume that the marginal utility of a particular good, such as sugar, depended only on the amount of sugar already bought (and not also on the amount of other goods such as complements like flour, coffee, or substitutes). Tinbergen relied on a similar methodology to that of Frisch.[12] But unlike Frisch, he was primarily interested not in the measurement of utility of consumption, but rather in the fairness of the distribution of incomes. Tinbergen's starting point was the idea that similar work done by two workers should result in equal rewards. If so, the system would automatically lead to a just distribution of income. If not, then there were factors outside the control of the individual that influenced their earnings. Such "unearned" differences should be compensated.[13] Although Tinbergen thus made an interesting addition to the problem of the question of a just distribution, he did not manage to take concrete steps in the direction of the measurement of utility.

17.2 Work Classification and Appropriate Wages

The initial attempt to arrive at an economic theory of justice was put on hold, because no satisfactory method for the measurement of utility came about. And it was not until the 1950s that the theme returned in Tinbergen's work. In the 1950s, the Netherlands had a wage policy that is now hard to even imagine. Wages in most Dutch industries were

Frisch's attempts to measure marginal utility; see Valk, "Een Poging, om het Grensnut te Meten," 1928.

[10] Frisch, *New Methods of Measuring Marginal Utility*, 1932.

[11] Budget statistics allowed one to compare the consumption patterns of different individuals and hence the change in behavior resulting from different levels of income, but this meant that the conclusions drawn were based on behavior of different individuals, not of one individual.

[12] Tinbergen, "Mathematiese Psychologie," 1930.		[13] Ibid., 350–51.

centrally determined, not directly by government or in parliament, but rather by the Labor Council, which consisted of representatives of workers and employers. This policy posed quite formidable challenges; first and foremost the difficult political negotiation process between workers and employers. In order to facilitate this process, a work classification scheme was developed.

This system was meant to indicate how much every type of function should be rewarded in the different sectors of the Dutch economy. This central wage policy has long been discarded in the Netherlands.[14] But one particular remnant of it is present to this day in many Dutch industries: a system of wage scales and "levels" within those scales. And although there is now room for negotiation about which scale is appropriate for an individual, it is still true that for a significant number of jobs, its classification and hence the pay is fixed. This system of scales and levels that typically indicate years of experience reflects the idea that work can be classified in an organized system and that there is a just or correct wage associated with that job. It represents one of the more grandiose schemes to rationalize and plan the economy.

Tinbergen's advice was sought for the determination of the "correct" pay for every job during the 1950s. There was already a classification system in place, but the Labor Council was looking for an improved system. Tinbergen worked on a highly sophisticated system that was meant to determine the correct pay for each job, based on nine characteristics of the job. Each job description received a score for each of the characteristics, and the total score would determine the "correct" pay. Such a methodology would later become known as the system of shadow-pricing; in this approach, a job or good is split up into various components and a price or reward is calculated for these separate components.[15]

Let us look at the item *knowledge* as an example of how such scoring took place (Table 17.1). Knowledge was described as consisting of both theoretical and practical knowledge, as well as a kind of general education.

[14] Tinbergen remained in support of a central-wage policy; an article he coauthored started a lengthy debate in the late 1970s on the reintroduction of this system. It was written in the context of the runaway inflation of the time; see Van den Doel, De Galan, and Tinbergen, "Pleidooi voor een Geleide Loonpolitiek," 1976.

[15] James Heckman has recently demonstrated that Tinbergen based this system on the "shadow prices" of these characteristics, and thus was an early pioneer of this approach, which is typically credited to Lancaster, who worked on the subject in the early 1970s. See Heckman, "The Race between Demand and Supply: Tinbergen's Pioneering Studies of Earnings Inequality," 2019.

Table 17.1 *Scoring table for the item knowledge from the report on work classification*

	Knowledge					
			Nature of knowledge			
Relation with other knowledge	Some	Average	Significant	Fairly deep	Deep	Very deep
Very simple	0,5	1	1	2	3	4,5
Simple	1,5	2	3	4,5	6	8
Les simple	3	4,5	6	8	10	12
Complicated	6	8	10	12	15	18
Very complicated	10	12	15	18	21	25
Extremely complicated	15	18	21	25	29	34

Adapted from Deskundigencommissie voor Werkclassificatie, *Ontwerp Genormaliseerde Methode voor Werklclassificatie*, 1956, JTC.

But it explicitly did not include the ability to apply this knowledge and make decisions based on various alternatives, a skill that was part of other items. The information that ought to be collected to "score" a job was the "nature of the required knowledge" (wide or narrow) and the "relation with other knowledge." The instructional guide cautioned users of the system not to rely on approximations of the level of knowledge required, such as the years of experience of a typical worker, or the educational requirements. The rest of the descriptive guide seemed likely to confuse any user: it attempted to restrict the meaning of knowledge to the more theoretical side of it, at the exclusion of the application of knowledge. But a little later the guide instructed that this item *knowledge* certainly does go beyond knowledge of facts and procedures. Then another eight items still had to be scored; it was a difficult process.

In the history of utility theory in economics, there is a gradual evolution from the idea that utility can be measured as a unit (say, distance) to the notion that utility is only an ordinal variable. In the latter view, saying that good A has more utility to an individual than good B means nothing more than saying that good A is preferred to B, without any notion of how much more A is preferred to B. To use the example of distance, with cardinal data one would be able to say that city A is twenty-five kilometers away, while city B is ten kilometers away. But if one has only ordinal data, we could say only that city A is farther away than city B. In the report on work classification, the instructions specify that if job function A is given a higher value on one scale (say, riskiness), this merely means that it is riskier than job function B (but it is unclear how much riskier). In other words, a modern ordinal scale was adopted. Yet at the same time, that ordinal assumption had to be dropped when the overall score on all different aspects was translated into an appropriate wage. Then a decision had to be made how much each additional "point" was worth. The report acknowledged that "this transformation is a difficult point in the technique of work-classification."[16]

This problem of translating work scores into wages was eerily reminiscent of the problem with utility measurement in the 1930s: How were monetary values to be translated into utility levels? Tinbergen and his assistant, J. Sandee, wrote a separate note on the interdependence of items in which the problem was recognized and illustrated with some numerical examples, but the note was mainly an attempt to suggest that the problem was not too serious.[17] They argued that it was best to devise a different relationship for each of the nine items and the wage; this relationship could be made linear, but if it proved harder to find sufficient individuals for the more exceptional jobs, one could make the relationship nonlinear and reward relatively exceptional characteristics proportionally more. But Tinbergen and Sandee had to admit that by devising separate relationships for each of the items, the problem of the interdependence of the items reared its head again.[18]

The problems did not stop there. A system of correct wages based on the objective scores of the difficulties of the jobs could well lead to a highly distorted labor market. The value of a worker, after all, depends not merely on the type of job performed but also on the availability of workers who could and were willing to perform that task.[19] As economics teaches us, the value of a good (or worker) is determined by both the demand and the supply of the good (or worker).

That realization stimulated Tinbergen to develop a general framework for thinking about the labor market. In a seminal article published in the *Weltwirtschaftliches Archiv* in 1956, he developed a full model of the labor market, which was far ahead of its time.[20] The model considered not

---

[16] Stichting van den Arbeid, *Werkclassificatie als Hulpmiddel bij de Loonpolitiek*, 1952.
[17] J. Sandee to Jhr. Mr. R. A. Th. Gevers Deynoot, 16 May 1956, JTC.
[18] Tinbergen, *Verband tussen Puntenaantal en Beloning*, JTC.
[19] Report Deskundigencommissie voor Werkclassificatie (Herzieningsvoorstel 1956), *Ontwerp Genormaliseerde Methode voor Werkclassificatie*, 1 July 1956, JTC.
[20] Tinbergen, "On the Theory of Income Distribution," 1956; Heckman, "The Race between Demand and Supply: Tinbergen's Pioneering Studies of Earnings Inequality," 2019.

merely the characteristics of the jobs available, the subject of the work-classification project, but also the characteristics of the people. This turned the labor market into a matching market between a set of skills bundled in individuals and a set of skills bundled in job functions. The problem of the work-classification report was thus now theorized as the (mis)match between the available skills (among the workers) and the required skills (among the required jobs). And hence the crucial problem was the pricing of skills, or in the world of work-classification, the relationship between points given for skills and monetary remuneration. If skills were rewarded in the right way, then workers would have incentives of their own to develop these skills.

This meant that the question posed by the ministry about the proper relationship between the points and the monetary wage, according to Tinbergen, could not be answered on the basis of counting skills only: "[T]here is *no pre-ordained wage ratio* between skilled and unskilled workers or any other type of labor."[21] This ratio was the outcome of a process of supply and demand. If there was a short-term oversupply of highly educated workers, then their relative wage would drop. For most economists, this amounted to a quite devastating critique of the central wage policy. Was it not unreasonable to expect that a centrally governed point-reward system could get the wages right? And was it not easier to rely on the market to figure out the correct wages, and let the supply of skills adjust that way?

Tinbergen, however, did not draw this conclusion. He regarded it as a reason to do better planning. The underlying reason went all the way back to his first work on the cyclical nature of production in markets with a long production process such as the pig and shipbuilding cycles. Education, he argued, was the ultimate long production process. And in such markets, one should not expect markets to adjust of their own accord. He argued that it would be impossible for a young person at fifteen or eighteen to make the correct decision about the right type of education to take up, since they would not know the future conditions of the labor market.

This highlighted an even more difficult part of the problem of the labor market. The requirements of skills changed over time, and workers would attempt to train themselves in those fields where there was scarcity. The labor market was a dynamic process in which having more or different

Heckman correctly observed that Tinbergen's model can be used for both the labor market and goods markets.

[21] Tinbergen, *Income Distribution: Analysis and Policies*, 1975.

skills than others was rewarded, but only until others caught up. Or, as Tinbergen was quick to add, before technology caught up. He spoke often about a race between technology and education. This dynamic process meant that redistribution of income was dangerous, because it might slow down the investment in relevant skills.

His political goal was the reduction of inequality. At first sight, it seems that this can easily be achieved through redistribution. On the campus of the Erasmus University in Rotterdam that idea is represented in shiny letters, "Redistribution generates gain," a quote attributed to Tinbergen. And it was indeed the title of a very early prize-winning paper of his from 1930.[22] But his later explorations make him unsure of the virtues of redistribution. It takes away incentives to work and, even more important, to invest more in education. In his theory of economic policy, he made that explicit:

> Various well-known theories have been put forward to prove that the distribution of income was largely a question of power and that once power was attained by the suppressed groups, incomes could be made more equal, so to speak, "by decree."... Income distribution cannot easily be detached from a complicated and refined system of stimuli to production which are vital to present-day economies.[23]

Achieving a just income distribution could not simply be willed or implemented but had to be broadly consistent with the way in which the labor market functioned.[24]

The most effective way to create a better match between the skills required and the skills available was through training. Tinbergen took the demand side of the labor market more or less for granted, so a better match had to be generated by adjustments on the supply side, in the skills of the workers. The model could help evaluate which skills were in short supply and which skills would have to be developed. But even the ambitious planner Tinbergen had to admit that there were limits to the development of skills. Some skills were innate and could not really be taught; the acquisition of other types of skills could be too costly.

---

[22] The essay itself is lost, and all that is left are some newspaper reports that contain the jury's verdict. Those and the question itself strongly suggest that Tinbergen had used the idea of diminishing marginal utility of money to argue for redistribution from those with high money incomes (or wealth) to those with low money incomes (or without monetary wealth); see *Leidsch Dagblad*, 17 June 1930, p. 1.

[23] Tinbergen, *Economic Policy: Principles and Design*, 1956.

[24] Tinbergen early on considered the notion of a (universal) basic income; see Chapter 5, n. 52.

But for the other skills, he suggested that education was the most effective way to reduce inequalities in income. From the distinction between innate and acquired skills, he developed another important policy recommendation. In welfare economics, it is a long-standing question what the least disruptive taxes are. Economists, including Tinbergen, are worried that taxes on work, wealth, or consumption will have disruptive effects and hence lead to less efficiency and output in the economy. Tinbergen suggested that taxes on innate skills would hardly have disruptive effects since they did not affect incentives to work or acquire new skills. What these innate skills were was an (unresolved) empirical question, but Tinbergen suggested that factors like IQ and conscientiousness might be of this kind.[25] On these skills, we should charge a "talent tax," he argued.[26] It was an idea perfectly in line with his interpretation of the biblical parable of the talents: those who were given more had a duty to contribute more. Or as the Dutch are fond of saying, "The broadest shoulders should carry the heaviest load."

His work on income distribution contained more of his own early convictions. In contrast to most economists, Tinbergen emphasized that work was not merely a cost that workers incurred to earn an income. He returned to the work of Hendrik de Man, on the psychology and joy of work, to argue that work could also provide joy, a sense of dignity, and a place to build relationships. There were also traces of Ehrenfest's conviction that jobs could be too demanding. One source of costs in Tinbergen's model of the labor market was the "tension" that resulted from the mismatch between the requirements of the particular job and the skills of the particular individual. This tension[27] could be negative (in the case of underqualification for the job) or positive (in the case of overqualification for the job), and Tinbergen assumed that both situations would lead to some dissatisfaction. Given somebody's skill level there was thus a correct kind of job for them, a correct position in society, if you will. Once individuals had completed the education process, there was a proper position for them. In that sense mentor and student were not that far apart; after all, Ehrenfest and his family were passionate educators who strongly believed in the benefits of self-development.

---

[25] Tinbergen, *Income Distribution: Analysis and Policies*, 1975.

[26] The idea of taxing what is given by nature has various other proponents in economics; famous is Henry George's proposal to tax land and only land, because it is given by nature. It also has an intuitive resonance with ideas of justice that claim one only deserves what one has "earned."

[27] Tinbergen, "The Tension Theory of Welfare," 1987.

In that spirit Anna Galinka Ehrenfest, Paul's daughter, developed a plea for what she called the "stork arrangement" for mothers.[28] She made the argument in the middle of the heated debates about equality of man and woman during the second feminist wave around 1970. Especially during the period around the birth of a child, the mother had more needs than others and therefore required compensation, she argued. Although she did not use the notions of utility or welfare, and instead framed the whole problem in terms of the emancipation of women, it was clear that she was thinking along the same lines that her father and Tinbergen developed. The idea was picked up in one of the feminist organizations of the time in the Netherlands, Man-Woman-Society (Man-Vrouw-Maatschappij), where a work group started to calculate the costs of the stork arrangement. As someone in that work group remembered: "Anna Galinka came to have dinner with us each Friday, afterwards we had a meeting in Rijswijk, and then I brought her to Jan Tinbergen and his wife, with whom she had been friends since her childhood .... Jan Tinbergen gave his approval of the calculations we prepared."[29] But Anna Galinka's efforts to make Jan Tinbergen and Jan Pen, who around the time were writing about inequality together, to promote the plans came to nothing.[30] Tinbergen's own writings about inequality always remained restricted to households and never ventured into the relationships within the household, as Ehrenfest's daughter wanted to do.

But for all the progress he made in modeling the labor market, there was little progress on the normative front. Tinbergen was frank about the fact that the utility-based approach that he pursued contained both contestable philosophical and moral choices.[31] The usage of a uniform utility function entailed "some sort of *equivalence* of all human beings"; this was the best baseline, argued Tinbergen. The just income distribution, for Tinbergen, was the distribution that gave to everyone what they deserved, based on skills but also on the (special) needs they had. But that conclusion was primarily derived from his own moral vision, not from his models of the labor market. In the introduction to his major book on the subject, he expressed the expectation that the reviews of the book would mostly contest these normative assumptions.

---

[28] Ehrenfest, "De Ooievaarsregeling (Contra Mina)," 1972.
[29] Remembrances of Hieke Snijders-Borst, www.haagseherinneringen.nl/pagina/274/man vrouwmaatschappij.
[30] Anna Galinka Ehrenfest to JT, 8 February 1977, JTC.
[31] Tinbergen, *Income Distribution: Analysis and Policies*, 1975.

He had hoped that he could arrive at a clearly quantifiable notion of justice, but he could do so only by making crucial moral assumptions. Around the same time John Rawls's *Theory of Justice* came out. It was equally rooted in economic concerns about efficiency and fairness but contained a much more elaborate philosophical and moral justification for the pursuit of equality. Tinbergen was gifted Rawls's book by his students not long after it came out in 1973, and a few of his students attempted to connect the two complementing theories of (economic) justice.[32] Tinbergen himself made it clear that he found Rawls's approach insufficiently quantifiable. Indeed, Rawls's difference principle, which suggested that inequality in society could increase only if the absolute level of income of the worst-off would improve, was notoriously hard to use in practice. But Rawls's theory nonetheless became a cornerstone of modern political thought, precisely because of the extensive moral justification he provided for his egalitarianism.

17.3 The Leiden Approach

To realize his dream of a quantitative scientific theory of justice, Tinbergen was still in search of the holy grail: the direct measurement of utility. His estimations, based on work and income decisions, were a definite improvement over the estimations of Frisch based on consumption choices, but they still had to assume the very thing that the critics of the measurement of utility found most objectionable: the idea that human beings and their preferences were basically the same. It was around the time that Tinbergen completed his studies of income distribution that some bold young economists in Leiden sought to measure utility directly. The existing approaches for utility measurement had typically relied on observed choices; economists to this day study what people *do* rather than what they *say* they are going to do. Two economists in Leiden, Bernard van Praag and Arie Kapteyn, were undeterred by such concerns and developed a method for the measurement of utility based on surveys. The basic question that Van Praag and Kapteyn asked of people was how they evaluated different levels of income, including their current level of income. The possible

---

[32] For an example of Tinbergen's critique of Rawls' theory, see *Naar een Rechtvaardiger Inkomensverdeling*, 1977. For Tinbergen's more general perspective on the relation between law and economics, see Tinbergen, "Kan de Economische Wetenschap Bijdragen tot de Ontwikkeling van het Recht?," 1982.

answers ranged from excellent to sufficient to very bad, on a nine-point scale. From these answers, the two Leiden economists derived two important parameters: the want parameter and welfare-sensitivity. The want parameter measured the level of income that was deemed sufficient by an individual (in Tinbergen's terms, this parameter reflected the needs of the person).[33] Welfare-sensitivity measured the extent to which one's utility depended on one's monetary income. The great advantage of the Leiden approach was the possibility to estimate individual welfare functions based on individual preferences regarding monetary income (versus alternatives such as joy in work or a preference for more leisure time). One of the first important findings of Van Praag was that preferences drift as one moves up the income scale. Individuals believed they would become much happier when they had more income, but once they had obtained more income their happiness had increased far less than they had expected (or hoped). The Leiden group suggested that this was probably caused by the fact that as one moved up the income scale, one's reference group changes. The person now earned more than their old friends, but colleagues at their new job, and the friends at their new sports club, all earned more too.

Tinbergen, it appears, was not directly drawn to the survey method (Ragnar Frisch, on the other hand, repeatedly relied on it). But what he was certainly drawn to was that many of the primary findings of the team from Leiden were in line with his own. Although the Leiden methodology allowed for the estimation of parameters of every individual, the parameters they found proved to be stable between individuals, and the results comparable between countries. In other words, Tinbergen had not been so far off the mark when he assumed a similar preference function for all individuals.

This removed, for him, the most important objection to his own approach. His own measurements might have been imperfect, but if another imperfect method arrived at similar results, the trustworthiness of both was enhanced. Tinbergen made that point explicit when he compared the recent developments in utility measurement to the late nineteenth-century developments in the measurement of temperature: economics was in the situation that researchers of heat were in before the discovery of the measurement of temperature.

There was a time that people stuck their hand in a bath to find out whether the water was cold, cool, tepid, warm or hot. An ordinal classification, and one that

---

[33] Like Tinbergen, Van Praag emphasized family size as one of the main determinants.

was subjective.... Physicists discovered that most substances, when heat is added, will expand in a linear fashion. That way they developed instruments, filled with mercury or alcohol, which pretended to measure the degree of warmth or temperature.... And so, temperature became an example of a subjective measurement on an ordinal scale which became a measurable unit, amenable to cardinal, objective measurement.[34]

Soon after, Van Praag sent him a letter in which he applauded his analogy.[35] It seemed as if there would be a great convergence of the two approaches. Much like Tinbergen, Van Praag and Kapteyn also examined variables such as family size and education level as main determinants of the preferences of different families.[36] And both Tinbergen and the Leiden researchers were explicitly driven by a normative agenda that aimed at the measurement of utility to make the discussion about inequality more scientific.[37] Tinbergen relied on his theory of desert, based on skills and needs, to determine the answer. Van Praag relied on surveys, to determine how much inequality individuals were willing to accept in society.[38]

After his retirement in Rotterdam in 1973, Tinbergen was offered the Cleveringa chair in Leiden, which he occupied from 1973 to 1975. It was not only a return to his alma mater at the very end of his academic career but also a great opportunity to further collaborate with the local research team on utility measurement. But despite repeated calls by Tinbergen to integrate the research programs, it did not attract many followers.[39] The research program was, however, not completely marginalized. It found supporters in the editors of the newly founded journal, the *European Economic Review*, as well as encouragement from Amartya Sen, the Indian economist famous for his capabilities approach. Sen's own approach measured the preconditions for human flourishing rather than well-being, but he too sought to move beyond merely monetary measures of welfare.

---

[34] Tinbergen, *Meten in de Menswetenschappen*, 1971.
[35] Bernard van Praag to Tinbergen, 30 March 1973, JTC.
[36] Bouma, Van Praag, and Tinbergen, "Testing and Applying a Theory of Utility: An Attempt to Decompose Income in Compensatory and Scarcity Rents," 1976.
[37] Tinbergen outlined the areas of convergence between the two approaches. Both approaches are based on the measurability of utility, both agree that it depends on the same set of independent variables (income, education, profession, family size), and both suggested how the other elements could be integrated; see Tinbergen to Bernard van Praag, 15 June 1973, JTC.
[38] Goedhart et al., "The Poverty Line: Concept and Measurement," 1977.
[39] Tinbergen, "Measurability of Utility (or Welfare)," 1985.

Sen's capability approach has since attracted many followers, not in the least in the field of development economics. For example, it was a major inspiration for the United Nations–led Human Development Index.[40] The project to move beyond monetary measures of welfare is also enjoying a resurgence under the banner of happiness studies. In this new approach, it is no longer monetary income that is the primary measure, but rather happiness as reported by individuals in surveys. This project, in important ways, builds on the approach developed by Van Praag.[41] Such projects all continue the search that Tinbergen undertook, to combine scientific measurement with the concept of justice.

17.4 Measuring Sustainability

The search for a connection between scientific measurement and political ideals was not restricted to justice. Another example was his work sustainability. Since the late 1960s, Tinbergen was increasingly worried about the environmental impact of economic activities. And one of the questions that quite naturally arose was how we might measure the environmental impact of economic activity. The first Club of Rome report, which came out in 1972, emphasized the limits to growth both in terms of population and in terms of resource use. It caused a great sense of alarm about the viability of continued growth. A natural response to this line of thinking was to attempt to limit population growth as well as the use of resources. But the "how much" question loomed large over the debate, and in many ways still does today. How much should we limit economic production in order to protect the environment? To answer the "how much" question, it was important to develop a good measure. What such a measure might be was suggested in 1968 by the Dutch statistical economist Roefie Hueting.[42] Although Tinbergen's involvement in the alternative measurement was relatively limited, it was clear that he was aware of the problem. In an article he coauthored late in life with Roefie Hueting, he sought to provide a scientific measure of the concept of sustainability.[43]

[40] The 2010 report contained data going back to 1980 for this index; Human Development Report Team, *Human Development Report 2010. The Real Wealth of Nations: Pathways to Human Development*, 2010.
[41] Van Praag and Ferrer-i-Carbonell, *Happiness Quantified: A Satisfaction Calculus Approach*, 2004.
[42] Hueting, "Welvaartsparadoxen," 1968.
[43] Tinbergen and Hueting, "GNP and Market Prices: Wrong Signals for Sustainable Economic Success That Mask Environmental Destruction," 1992.

Hueting, a researcher at the Central Bureau of Statistics, where Tinbergen had also started his career, did not seek to estimate optimal levels of population growth or economic growth. Rather, he sought to correct how we measured economic growth, and hence provide a clear signal about the sustainability of our current economic growth. The approach was based on the idea that all economic activity was dependent on environmental functions. A sustainable level of economic growth or development of the economy would keep these environmental functions intact. But the approach did not suggest that we should leave nature untouched or unused, but rather that we should seek to maintain the current level of environmental functions. This would require compensation for the extent to which economic activities used up the environmental functions.

Hueting and Tinbergen sought not to replace GDP, but rather to provide a secondary measure that indicated the level of compensation required. The environmentally sustainable national income (eSNI) was calculated by subtracting the costs for renewing the environmental functions. The proposed method to calculate the costs of compensation, as Tinbergen and Hueting acknowledged, was laborious but essential. It involved a cost–benefit analysis of (long-term) projects that would restore environmental functions. For some environmental functions, say, the maintenance of the amount of forest that absorbed CO_2 emissions, the method was straightforward. For other resources such as oil or coal, the issue was not as clear, for there was no known method to reproduce oil. Tinbergen proposed that our usage of such resources should be in line with the rate of efficiency growth in their usage. He calculated that the efficiency growth in the use of energy was about 1.67 percent per year, which would mean that we could use 1.67 percent of the existing resources and leave as much available energy to future generations as we currently had.[44]

17.5 Measurement and the Normative

Tinbergen was mostly silent on philosophical matters, and when he discussed them, he preferred to be matter-of-fact about them: scientists prefer deterministic theories. That's that. So, it is only on rare occasions that we

---

[44] Jan Tinbergen, "Levenspeil van Komende Generaties zijn ons een Zorg; Zuinigaan met Energie," *NRC Handelsblad*, 22 June 1990. This back-of-the-envelope calculation ignored the famous Jevons paradox, which states that as the efficiency in production goes up, the use of the resource tends to go up (rather than down).

find him reflecting on his own research practice. One of the very few exceptions are his reflections on "measurement in the human sciences." In this article he argued for the key role of measurement in modern science. Not only was measurement how we could test theories, but more importantly through measurement we can "influence the course of nature and society for the improvement of human welfare."[45] In fact, the two were so intimately intertwined for Tinbergen that it becomes hard to separate the purely scientific measurement and the normative purpose of his scientific project: "[O]ne of the most important purposes of measuring in the human sciences is finding the optimal social order. This requires finding an answer to the question, whether we can hope that we at some point are able to measure the welfare of individuals and of groups of people."[46]

It is fair to say that Tinbergen consciously abandoned the purely scientific and did so knowingly. He argued, in rather stark contrast to his earlier work, that it no longer mattered whether one looked at the problem from the perspective of an economist or an ethicist, or even from a subjective personal viewpoint. The improvement of welfare and the pursuit of justice were simply too important to be ignored. Political and social decisions depended crucially on the "measurement" of the welfare. And, therefore, imperfect measurement was better than none: "The development of the understanding of temperature can be a model for the development of science as a whole: the reduction of the subjective in favor of the objective; this is her calling."[47]

This quote also contains an insight that Tinbergen never explicitly developed, but which is very evident from the way he used measurement. The measurement of welfare, inequality, and sustainability, and also of unemployment, the business cycle, and growth, informs his normative concepts. Tinbergen's conception of justice was not a fixed value that he sought to realize. Justice was not a value judgment that was plugged into his analysis at some point to arrive at a policy conclusion. Rather, his inquiries into the measurement of welfare informed his idea of justice. His criticism of Rawls's theory of justice was that the concept of justice itself was not developed enough.

In the standard positivist view of science, the scientist seeks to keep value judgments out of science. That same view accepts that the domain of ethics and ideals is beyond the reach of science. Tinbergen was not content

---

[45] Tinbergen, *Meten in de Menswetenschappen*, 1971.
[46] Tinbergen, "De Convergentietheorie: Antikritiek," 1972.
[47] Tinbergen, *Meten in de Menswetenschappen*, 1971.

with that view. He sought to discover objective elements in our normative concepts.[48] It was in this sense that the measurement of welfare could improve our notion of justice, or that the measurement of the environmental impact of economic activity could help illuminate our understanding of sustainability.

It was this conception of ideals that was already present in the cultural socialism of the 1920s. Hendrik de Man and Jan Goudriaan attempted to decouple the idea of justice from the socialist organization of society. They were striving for ideals, but they openly acknowledged that they did not know in detail how these could be realized. For Tinbergen, socialism was in part a feeling and in part a direction; perhaps we should say it was a sensibility. It was, most definitely, not an end point that could be reached. Instead, captured in the concept of synthesis, so central in his work, was an idea that values were discovered in the process of their realization. Science was of crucial importance in that process; not because the technologies developed in science improved the world, but because scientific inquiries could improve our understanding of the content of our ideals.

The interaction between science and values also worked the other way around for Tinbergen. In order to be helpful, science needed a purpose, a direction. It was his socialism that gave Tinbergen his direction, and he used science to explore the meaning of socialism and the content of justice. Science was thus an integral part of the socialist ideal. The entanglement between the normative and the scientific was not always obvious in his work. But his work on the measurement of welfare, justice, and sustainability is a clear instance of this entanglement. For many, that entanglement is a clear sign that these projects are unscientific. They can accuse Tinbergen of wanting to extend science to domains where it simply cannot go. For Tinbergen himself, it was the way to reconcile his socialism and his science – it was his form of scientific socialism.

---

[48] It would be even more precise, and general, to say "objective elements in our *subjective* concepts." Before a measurement method was developed, temperature was a subjective concept.

18

Governing the Ungovernable

Can We Govern the Planet?

All humans are sinners, that is what makes them equal; what makes them different is their ability to lead.
—Father of Gereon Rath in *Babylon Berlin*[1]

In his book *Seeing like a State*[2] James C. Scott sought to understand why the grand projects of state reform of the twentieth century had failed, or worse yet why they had led to catastrophes such as in Cambodia under the Khmer Rouge. Scott's analysis is challenging because he argued that these failures and catastrophes are distinctly modern. They arose from a combination of the administrative ordering of nature and society and the ideology of high modernism. The first, he argued, is little more than an unremarkable tool of modern statecraft; it is the use of statistics and tools of standardization to facilitate efficient governance. In Tinbergen's career it is best reflected in his early work at the Bureau of Statistics.

The second element, high modernism, is more complex. It is a strong self-confidence in scientific and technological progress, and the belief that these can be used to create a rational and well-ordered society. The combination of administrative statistical tools and high modernism is potentially dangerous. They represented, to use Tinbergen's language, the instruments and the goals of state policy, respectively. Catastrophe, argued Scott, was likely to be the outcome when there was an authoritarian government and a weak civil society. Scott, interestingly, uses not merely the term "confidence" but "self-confidence," to emphasize that this belief originated in the

---

[1] In German: "Alle Menschen sind Sünder, darin sind sie gleich und sie unterscheiden sich in ihrem Führungspotenzial"; father of Gereon Rath in the TV series *Babylon Berlin*, season 2, episode 3.
[2] Scott, *Seeing like a State: How Certain Schemes to Improve the Human Condition Have Failed*, 1998.

West from where it was used, for example, in development economics, to modernize the rest of the world. But the emphasis on self-confidence had other connotations, since it was often scientists themselves, as well as modern industrialists, who expressed this faith.

In the case of Tinbergen, this self-confidence was most visible in the work of the 1960s. Books such as *Shaping the World Economy* expressed an almost limitless ambition and faith in his own ability to build a better world. Faith seems to be the appropriate word, since the book, as we have seen, was primarily his visionary document; the empirical studies had become an afterthought. Such hopes and convictions, as well as the underlying assumptions, have roots. This book has analyzed those roots in the progressive scientific milieu around Ehrenfest, the cultural socialism of the AJC, and the outlook of someone growing up in The Hague in the first decades of the twentieth century. But what was equally important was Tinbergen's own trajectory. In his lifetime Western states had modernized, and the 1950s had given rise to the belief not merely that destructive business cycles were a thing of the past, but more generally that a stable and just economy could be "constructed." Expertise had become firmly embedded within the modern state, and society was stable and prosperous during the first two decades after World War II. Scott acknowledged the great degree of progress in science and industry that gave rise to the confidence of the high modernists. Be he appears to have overlooked how much the state itself had changed. And Tinbergen had witnessed and contributed to that firsthand. His confidence was not merely ideological; it was also experiential.

His journey from an early expert institution, the bureau of statistics, via the planning bureau and on to international organizations wonderfully exemplifies the rise of the expert. But it was at the international level that the rise of experts, technical knowledge, and rational management slowly but surely ran into its limits. The crisis was not merely international. In the late 1960s environmental problems grew more visible and were put on the political agenda by the first report of the Club of Rome.[3] The turbulent economic decade of the 1970s plagued by international oil crises and rising inflation and unemployment at home caused doubts about the extent to which the economy could be controlled.

Scott suggested that when the plans of the high modernists miscarried or were thwarted, they tended toward miniaturization: planning on a smaller

---

[3] Meadows, *The Limits to Growth: A Report for the Club of Rome's Project on the Predicament of Mankind*, 1972.

scale. We will see that Tinbergen responded quite differently. We should think bigger, not smaller, he argued. But the cracks in his self-confidence became more visible.

18.1 Planning for Peace and Prosperity

Let us start at the very end. In the final decade of his life Tinbergen spent much time thinking about conflict and peace, and, in particular, about the organization of peace. In his work on the economics of warfare, or as he preferred to call it, the economics of peace, Tinbergen tried to make some fundamental contributions to this alternative perspective. As he put it, "institutions and policies" should replace military activity.[4] Tinbergen's model for international relations was based on an economic analogy. He argued that there were two roads toward a world without war. The first one relied on spontaneous historical developments that have tended toward integration, albeit with serious setbacks. The other road was the deliberate construction of an international order, as was tried at the League of Nations, and which could be attempted again with an improved version of the United Nations. It was the approach of laissez-faire versus that of planning and – no surprise here – Tinbergen favored a planning approach to international integration.

An international order had to include, in his vision, basic economic institutions such as a world treasury, a world central bank, and a set of expert institutions along the lines of what most Western national economies had developed. But his hopes extended to turning the FAO into the World Ministry of Agriculture, the United Nations Industrial Development Organization (UNIDO) into the World Ministry of Industry, and the ILO into the World Ministry of Social Affairs.[5] In fact, Tinbergen was thinking so much along the lines of the way in which the "national order" had developed to get out of the 1970s crisis that he, alongside his fellow Labor Party front men Jan Pronk, former Dutch prime minister Joop den Uyl, and future prime minister Wim Kok, proposed an international Plan of Labor under the name, A New World Employment Plan (Figure 18.1).[6]

---

[4] Tinbergen, "Conventional and New Thinking in Defence Economics," 1990. The article was published in the second issue of the newly founded journal *Defence Economics*; much in line with Tinbergen's argument, the journal would later be renamed *Defence and Peace Economics*.

[5] United Nations Development Programme, *Human Development Report 1994*, 88, 1994.

[6] Tinbergen et al., "A New World Employment Plan," 1981.

Figure 18.1 Tinbergen at the presentation of the World Employment Plan in 1981. Left to right: Wim Kok (prime minister from 1994 to 2002), Joop den Uyl (prime minister from 1973 to 1977), Tinbergen, and Jan Pronk (a student of Tinbergen and influential politician for the Dutch Labor Party).

Like the creation of economic order, the creation of an international order required expertise. This was best done through expert committees, which had played a key role in the not-so-distant past, for example: the Brandt Commission (1980), chaired by former German chancellor Willy Brandt, which had formulated a blueprint for a global economy for the twenty-first century and primarily sought to overcome the North–South divide; the Palme Commission (1982), headed by Olof Palme, former Prime Minister of Sweden, which had formulated a blueprint for common security in a report on disarmament, and sought to overcome the East–West divide; and the Brundtland Commission, headed by Gro Harlem Brundtland (1983), former prime minister of Norway, which produced a report entitled *Our Common Future*, which formulated a strategy to tackle the environmental problems on a worldwide scale.

National sovereignty was, just as in economic policy, one of the major threats to stability in Tinbergen's vision. He argued for an international police force to make permanent and stable what had been the ad hoc intervention forces of the United Nations. This police force – he consciously avoided the word "army" – would maintain law and order around the world. It was one of the few areas where Tinbergen changed his mind over time; the former pacifist now argued that violence was sometimes legitimate and necessary.

But not that much had changed. At the very base of his thinking about society was the peaceful coexistence of different groups. Within nations, these could be classes or groups of different ethnicities. Internationally, these were the different nations and regions. Peaceful coexistence depended first and foremost on the acceptance of difference and the way tolerance was practiced in daily life. But understanding and trust between different groups could also be facilitated through rational discourse, free from dogma and ideology. His attempts to promote the optimal order were a way to overcome both dogma and ideology, and to foster this mutual understanding. If that succeeded, convergence was the goal. His argument was a stylized characterization of the developments he had sought to bring about at the national level: the transformation of socialism into a broad people's movement, the promotion of peaceful gradual change, and finally the Breakthrough movement, which sought to complete the convergence between different groups in Dutch society.

At the international level, however, few of the preconditions for convergence or the development of an international order were present. In fact, he feared that war was on the horizon in the 1980s. To prevent this, he helped found the initiative Economists against the Arms Race (ECAAR). It was an organization that also boasted Wassily Leontief, Franco Modigliani, James Tobin, Kenneth Arrow, and Lawrence R. Klein (all Nobel Prize winners) among its first group of trustees, and lives on today as Economists for Peace and Security. The goal of securing peace reflected Tinbergen's belief that only after international peace was secured would economic stability be possible. It was peace that was fundamental: social peace at the domestic level, and peace between nations at the international level.

Many economic thinkers have suggested that trade is a facilitator of peace and that integrated markets help create a shared interest in peace and economic prosperity. But Tinbergen was not convinced by such natural harmony theories. Perhaps they reeked too much of "laissez-faire" dogmas to him. He believed that the preconditions for peace and trade were not natural but had to be created. His vision, which was fundamentally shaped in the 1930s, was that neither peace nor international trade was natural or self-reinforcing. Both must be actively pursued, specifically through international ordering (Figure 18.2). In this sense, his international vision was a direct continuation of the project started by the

Figure 18.2 Tinbergen kicking in a tariff wall, late 1970s.

Peace Palace. The integrated vision that Tinbergen presented toward the end of his life argued that international legal order and international economic order were intimately connected and part of the same project of peace and prosperity.[7]

This vision received an important impetus during the 1970s when for the first time since World War II, there was again a worldwide sense of crisis. During this period, there appeared to be a kind of obsession with the long-term future, which was mainly sparked by the debate about the first report of the Club of Rome, *Limits to Growth*. Various commentators provided alternative predictions for what the world would be like in the year 2000. Tinbergen was critical of such attempts; he still believed that prediction was rather pointless. After all, predictions were based on models with given institutional constraints, which themselves were liable to change over time. The alternative for Tinbergen was planning, that is, seeking consciously to direct the path of institutional development. When faced with the threat of disorder, he sought control.

---

[7] Dekker, "Jan Tinbergen and the Construction of an International Economic Order," 2021.

But to generate control, the problem had to be made technical. Or at least that was Tinbergen's idea. The threats to the environment and the pursuit of sustainability was, after all, "a technical problem." The Economic and Financial Section at the League of Nations had focused on the "technical" aspects of the problem of the business cycle and economic instability, attempting to turn contested political and scientific problems into an area of technical expertise: "It appears that one can only reach acceptable proposals when one takes into account the experiential fact that close cooperation succeeds best when the aim is very precisely described and is of a technical nature."[8]

18.2 Hubris

The reforms that had worked at home, and internationally in the first decades since World War II, had run out of steam. Tinbergen reflected: "Until today none of the proposals [for a world government] has had any influence on the course of events. The proposed solutions are disqualified as unrealistic by the most prominent politicians. On existing governments, they fail to make an impression. But that does not mean that these governments themselves are realistic. They are myopic." And their myopia was reinforced by the way democracies were designed: "A dogmatic belief in parliamentary democracy and four-yearly election cycles furthers the election of short-sighted politicians."[9] The self-confidence of the 1950s and the early development economics gave way to frustration.

In one of his final major books, coauthored with Dietrich Fischer, he drew a parallel between the myopia of individuals and that of governments. Just as we corrected for myopic preferences through, for example, mandatory schooling or excise taxes on addictive or harmful goods, so we should attempt to find ways to correct the myopic preferences of governments: "In that situation the International Court of Justice might be the appropriate institution to correct preferences. In other cases, a non-government organization such as a peace movement, or scientists such as peace researchers may make the correction."[10] He was unwilling to accept the limitations of expertise in politics. Instead, in the conflict between politics and rational

---

[8] Tinbergen, "How Should the Future Be Studied?," 1972.
[9] Tinbergen, *Hoe Kunnen wij Machtsstructuren Veranderen?*, 24, 1974.
[10] Tinbergen and Fischer, *Warfare and Welfare: Integrating Security into Socio-economic Policy*, 1987.

science he kept urging for more power in the hands of the latter. His ambitions grew with his frustrations.

Tinbergen, whose oeuvre contains titles such as *Reshaping the International Order, Shaping the World Economy, Central Planning, A New World Employment Program,* and *Can we Manage the Earth?,* has repeatedly been charged with naïvete. Jan Pronk, one of his most prominent political students, emphasized that Tinbergen never developed much of a political intuition.[11] And in hindsight it is easy to dismiss as naïve Tinbergen's visions of a world government. The World Federalist Movement, of which he was an active member, sought a world government, a goal that seems further away at this moment than at any time in recent history. But the more relevant danger of his work might lie in the fact that his proposals were so grandiose that their very implementation would require a type of authority that would be considered undesirable and dangerous by democratic societies. And when political forces opposed his proposals, he grew increasingly critical of the existing political system.

It is therefore puzzling that Tinbergen's work remained imprecise as to how his proposals could be implemented. He acknowledged some role for social action, such as in the case of the peace movement. And it could also take the form of raising awareness for a problem by scientists, as the Club of Rome sought to do. But it appears that Tinbergen's ambition often reached considerably further than petitioning. The correction of individual preferences is regarded with suspicion by many economists precisely because it easily becomes a slippery slope, but also for the simple reason that it is likely to introduce personal values into science. It appears sensible to have a similar worry when Tinbergen proposes that expert authorities should have the power to correct the preferences of governments.

In his discussions of democracy, he pointed repeatedly to well-recognized exceptions to the principle of simple majority rule, such as qualified majorities, constitutional rules, and systems of representation. Democracy was never absolute, he argued. In his later years, however, he suggested that it might be desirable to limit the number of political parties, and to further limit democracy. In the convergence debate he even started comparing political systems on a purely quantitative scale. Despite his awareness of the importance of institutions, he hardly paid attention to the limits of the power of (political) institutions. There are clear instances in which it is acceptable to limit what parliaments or politicians can decide.

[11] Pronk, "Tinbergen, Idealist and Inspirer," 2019.

Most constitutions protect minorities against certain majority decisions. And most constitutions explicitly define limits to what state actors or organizations can do. These are well-recognized, and justified, exceptions to majority rule in most democratic states. Tinbergen can, legitimately, reason by analogy to suggest that some of these principles should be extended to the international level. That was how the international organizations in The Hague were typically constructed.

But many of his proposals for international organization go much further. They give far more power to expert bodies than had ever been the case at the national level. This was similar to how the SPO in Turkey was meant to have a lot more power than the CPB ever had in the Netherlands. He proposed to put the IMF and the World Bank in charge of important elements of international economic policy. But he never seriously discussed the dangers of them overstepping their spheres of authority. Tinbergen hardly made distinctions about the types of institutions and the way they themselves should be "constitutionally" constrained in their operation. It seemed that Tinbergen was increasingly seeking to promote particular policy outcomes, such as international integration, rather than the means through which this was achieved.

The central challenge in the later decades of his career was of a new kind. If we can describe the 1930s and 1940s as a period when an intellectual framework to improve government policies was developed, and the 1950s and 1960s as a period in which Tinbergen was shaping government policies, both nationally and internationally, then the 1970s and 1980s were a period when he no longer directly held this power. It coincided with a time when the political will to implement the kind of policies he favored was fading. The reasons for this were multiple: the world was slowly moving away from the Keynesian consensus in which the government had a dominant steering role (through experts) in the economy. On top of that, the Cold War dichotomies were hardening. And the first development decade of the United Nations was widely considered a failure.

In such a period it might be tempting to give in to a call for more expertise, and expert authority, and become more critical of democracy. This certainly happened to Tinbergen. However, he did not allow himself to become bitter. Instead, he again started to identify with the underdogs in international society and became more critical of existing power structures. In some sense, this meant a return to the days before the Plan of Labor, the days of cultural socialism. The interviews he gave during this period were becoming distinctly more radical; one even depicted him as the new

"Marx."[12] Surprisingly, given his early antipathy, Tinbergen himself also referred more and more to Marx and his theories of social change. And although he consistently rejected the violent and revolutionary methods associated with Marx, Tinbergen became markedly more interested in the origins of major social change.[13]

After his retirement in Rotterdam, he occupied the Cleveringa chair in Leiden from 1973 to 1975. In his inaugural lecture, he addressed the center–periphery theory of international relations, which held that there was a fundamental power asymmetry between the developed world and the developing countries. Its proponents argued that because of this power asymmetry, it was best for the developing world to cut off relations with the imperial developed world. Tinbergen was unwilling to accept that conclusion because it implied international conflict. But he expressed his agreement with the diagnosis. Around that time, he started to support the G-77 and other initiatives that sought to empower the developing countries vis-à-vis the established powers. He even pointed to the OPEC cartel as an example of how non-Western countries could use their power.

He was aware that such support could easily lead to more tensions. In the hope to prevent this, he suggested that the West no longer thought narrowly about its own self-interest. He pointed to the fact that many countries now devoted some part of their own national income to development aid. He hoped that the moral power of arguments and an appeal to (enlightened) self-interest could convince the West to change its ways:

Idealistic movements are often told they cherish illusions, which are impossible to realize. But fundamentally they are forms of politics. Politics is the "art of the possible" and the domain of the possible is constrained by human egoism, habit and limited capabilities. These constraints are more important in the short run than for changes in the long run. It happens so often that things, which until recently were considered impossible – apparently for good reasons – happen nonetheless.[14]

Tinbergen understood that his idealism was a political strategy. It was the political strategy for somebody from a relatively insignificant country in global politics such as the Netherlands. It was the political strategy of an intellectual who knew that military and political power was in the hands of others, and he therefore had to try to win the political game otherwise. His idealism, however paradoxical this may sound, was his own way of

---

[12] "Tinbergen is de Niewe Marx," *HP de Tijd*, 12 July 1985.
[13] Tinbergen, *Entering the Third Millennium*, 1991.
[14] Tinbergen, *Kunnen wij de Aarde Beheren?*, 1987.

practicing politics as "the art of the possible" – not by staying within the realm of what was currently politically feasible, but rather by broadening the imagination of what could be achieved in the first place.

In his Cleveringa departure lecture, he addressed the way in which public opinion was formed as one instance of how structural change in society could be brought about. The discussion of public opinion was in many ways a return to the early work he did within the AJC, where discussion evenings and self-education were central. This is perhaps why his valedictory lecture started off reluctantly. He first discussed the many ways in which public opinion was misguided. It suffered from "fads"; children were no longer raised properly; and nationalism and other sentiments often infected public opinion. But then he reached the more constructive proposals about how public opinion could develop and how collective learning could take place. In one of the few instances in which he engaged with the work of his brother, biologist Niko Tinbergen, Jan distinguished between four stages of personal development: "automatic adjustment" to changing circumstances, following orders, imitation of others, and the use of experience of one's actions and those of others. Above these four more primitive stages was the fifth and highest stage: the ability to develop new concepts and see new relationships.

Tinbergen was not convinced that the public could by itself reach the fifth and highest stage. In order to be able to be informed, they required the leadership of gifted intellectuals who possessed moral leadership: "From Christ to Marx, from Buddha to Mao, from Plato to Jean Monnet."[15] The learning process would take place top-down, but only when it was facilitated by major organizations and, in particular, transnational organizations, of course. For somebody who had been active in the AJC, had helped set up NOVIB, and donated generously to various civil society organizations, it was a remarkable conclusion. Typically, such organizations were characterized as bottom-up or even grassroots organizations. Tinbergen, on the contrary, regarded as crucial the vision that the leaders of such movements laid out. Such leadership was a rare quality. He emphasized his disappointment that the labor parties had never managed to transcend national boundaries, and he expressed his doubts about whether churches had proven themselves to be up for the task.

As if to complete his return to the 1920s when he had praised the rational management of modern firms and their enlightened way of

---

[15] Tinbergen, *Het Leerproces der Openbare Mening*, 1975.

creating better working and living conditions for workers, he pointed to
the positive example set by business. He praised the way that international
firms had invested in the developing world and created jobs: "In matters of
supra-national management, business leaders have been more advanced
than public authorities."[16] National and even regional governments had
often been more of a hindrance than a facilitator of this process: "[T]he
European Union and other trading blocs still protected their agricultural
markets and the GATT has also recently allowed quotas."[17]

What Tinbergen's explorations also revealed was how much he
remained committed to his model of elite leadership. This was the essential
model of the AJC that proposed to educate and socialize an elite within the
worker community that would lead by example. It was also the way that
Ehrenfest thought about the role of the scientist in modern society, and
also the perspective that the Remonstrant Brotherhood held about its role
in society. It would lead not by converting others and expanding its
numbers – the brotherhood remained small by choice – but rather through
intellectual and moral leadership. As Heering, the Remonstrant minister
Tinbergen knew best, wrote: "[I]n our Brotherhood we are strongly reliant
on *personal* convictions, on the *personal* responsibility [of our
members]."[18] Individuals who could combine vision with scientific insight
and were able to generate social change remained the role models
for Tinbergen.

It was clear that Tinbergen hoped he could be a moral leader himself; to
do so, he mirrored himself in others he admired. The first honorary
doctorate he gave out went to K. P. van der Mandele, who had been
important in the founding of the Netherlands School of Economics:
"Already in 1929 you saw the significance for economic science of work
within a group, to do what the individual is unable to do, and where the
necessary integration of theory and observation and theory and practice
can be realized."[19] But the distinguishing feature of Van der Mandele had
been his entrepreneurial quality in using his knowledge to facilitate the
reconstruction of Rotterdam after the war, his role in the founding of the

[16] Tinbergen and Fischer, *Warfare and Welfare: Integrating Security into Socio-economic Policy*, 1987.
[17] "Interview met Tinbergen," *De Nederlandse Onderneming*, 1970.
[18] Heering, Tjalsma, and De Heer-Cremer, *De Remonstrantse Broederschap: Wat zij is en wat zij Wil*, 16, 1948.
[19] Tinbergen and Van der Mandele, *Redevoeringen Uitgesproken ter Gelegenheid van de Ere-Promotie van Mr. K. P. van Der Mandele*, 9, 1958.

Boijmans art museum, and his role in the establishment of the Rotterdam School of Economics.

In a review of the way that the social question had been dealt with in the Netherlands, the conclusion praised the efforts of Charles Stork over a host of Dutch economists. Stork was an industrial entrepreneur famous for the technical innovation his company brought about in the production of machines, but also for the way his company was concerned with the living conditions and wages of workers. It was Stork, as a Dutch incarnation of Henry Ford, who was singled out as having contributed more to an improvement in social conditions than the economics profession.[20]

It was for this reason that Tinbergen reserved the very highest praise for Jean Monnet, whom he, curiously, called the greatest economist of the twentieth century.[21] Although Monnet was trained in economics, he was much better known as the "father of Europe." He was intellectually gifted, but it was his ability to bring about positive social change and inspire others that stood out for Tinbergen. He reserved the most praise for individuals who had furthered the cause of the integration of disadvantaged groups in (international) society. When he praised Keynes, it was the Keynes of *The Economic Consequences of the Peace* and not the Keynes of the *General Theory*.

And Tinbergen, although he was always praised for his modesty, did not shy away from talking about himself in these terms. When he wrote about the optimal order, he confessed: "This is a very ambitious project and we are aware that most readers and fellow economists will consider it to be over-ambitious." But, if anything, such ambition was called for since "an overwhelming majority of our colleagues, of policymakers and of world citizens are suffering from the opposite attitude: setting too modest tasks." Who was to blame them, since, after all, "they are deeply impressed by the complex picture, by the innumerable forces at work, by the myriad of conflicts threatening the world. Aware of the limitations of what conscious action can do they are forced into modest endeavors." Thus, there was the need for a more ambitious and forward-looking elite: "It is this state of affairs that creates the need for a small number of both professions – scientists and politicians – who dare to stick out their necks and speculate

---

[20] Tinbergen, "De Economist en het Sociale Vraagstuk," 1952.
[21] Ibid.; Tinbergen, and Fischer, *Warfare and Welfare: Integrating Security into Socioeconomic Policy*, 1987.

from a 'helicopter view,' from which inspiration may be gained for our common tasks."[22]

In the follow-up to his book *Warfare and Welfare*, Tinbergen developed such a perspective: "[W]e believe that our analyses help to develop what has been called a 'helicopter view,' which is considered an important characteristic for managers of large – mostly transnational – enterprises. It should also be a characteristic of statesmen: that is, great politicians."[23] The book developed global decision models with two (East and West), three (East, West, and South), or four (East, West, South, and China) decision-making centers. It was based on the premise that we should attempt to maximize the welfare of the world population. In the 1920s Tinbergen addressed himself to the socialist youth, in the 1930s to his fellow social democrats, in the 1950s to Dutch policymakers, and by the end of his career to world leaders. But behind these global ambitions, there were also doubts and fears.

18.3 Can We Manage the Earth?

These doubts and fears were nowhere more evident than in a short book Tinbergen published in 1987 and which reads as a kind of intellectual testament, even though he would keep on publishing until the very end of his life in 1994. The book was entitled *Can We Manage the Earth? (Kunnen we de Aarde Beheren?).*[24] The Dutch "beheren" can be translated as both "manage" and "steward." It was particularly the latter religious connotation that Tinbergen exploited, in this book with strong Christian undertones. Although the style was still mostly factual and business-like, the purpose of the book was much higher, and its tone at times apocalyptic: nothing less was at stake than the survival of humanity. And more than once Tinbergen appealed to our shared humanity and the *belief* in a better future.[25]

The structure of the book is modeled after the Bible. The book opens with two chapters that mirror Genesis: "The Planet without People" and "The Arrival of Man and Human Culture." The third chapter is a description of the economy before the Fall; man is depicted as primitive and primarily in need of food, which is still in plentiful supply in the form of

---

[22] Tinbergen and Fischer, *Warfare and Welfare: Integrating Security into Socio-economic Policy*, 1987.
[23] Tinbergen, *World Security and Equity*, 81–82, 1990.
[24] Tinbergen, *Kunnen wij de Aarde Beheren?*, 1987.
[25] See ibid., epilogue, for this appeal.

"free goods": "There was much more pure air, pure water, and natural soil than man needed ... there was no environmental question yet."[26] But then man moved into cities, under the (false) impression that *Stadtluft macht frei* (City air makes free) and the need for a division of labor and governance structures emerged.

After this Fall, new goals emerged. "Not by Bread Alone"[27] is the title of the chapter introducing the needs of humans beyond the material. They ranged from a notion of justice to religion and ethics, as well as education and science. It was culture that made up the highest goals of humanity: the collection of the cultural achievements made up a civilization.[28] But the virtuous side of human life was accompanied by its counterpart of vice and conflict. And the further we advanced technologically, the greater became the problems that humanity faced. For Tinbergen, this was most evident in our security situation, complicated beyond imagination by the development of nuclear weapons. But this dynamic was equally visible in the environmental sphere. Pollution of the atmosphere and a lack of clean water and fertile soil were bigger problems than humanity had ever faced before. Inequality, initially a local or at best national issue, was now a global issue, with possibly global repercussions in the form of mass migration and violent conflict. Increased material prosperity had not satisfied man but had given rise to an enormous growth in population and materialism. These developments necessitated governance and authority, to make possible living together peacefully.

The first part of the book concluded with the enormous challenges that humanity and the planet were facing. This half was the story of becoming; the second half of the book was the hopeful promise of the future. If the first part was the world that humans inhabited after the Fall, then the second part was the world that humans could create. Tinbergen's promise was that a better world could be constructed. It was a promise of equality and prosperity, but the leading metaphor was that of peace. Liberal theorists such as Isaiah Berlin have theorized negative and positive freedom. Negative freedom is the absence of constraints, and positive freedom the ability to reach one's potential. For Tinbergen, the distinction was between negative peace and positive peace. Negative peace was the absence of violent conflict, of war. Positive peace was the harmony between humans,

---

[26] Tinbergen, *Kunnen wij de Aarde Beheren?*, 1987.
[27] The phrase originates from the title of a novel published during the thaw in the Soviet Union.
[28] Tinbergen, "Will Western Civilization Survive?," 1981.

as well as humans and nature. It consisted of the peaceful use of the oceans as governed by the law of the seas, pioneered by Grotius. It consisted of the peaceful use of land and air, as governed by the law of the atmosphere (to control pollution). It consisted of the peaceful use of the earth, as governed by the way we managed natural resources, but also the way we maintained forestry on the planet. And finally, it consisted of peaceful coexistence, which covered the entire range of governance structures between humans: from trade to criminal and international law. The next ten short chapters covered the various instruments of governance that were available to humans, both domestically and internationally. No fewer than half of these chapters were explicitly dedicated to peace policies, covering existing and future treatises, the current structure of the United Nations and its desired expansion, as well international integration from the "bottom-up," such as in the European Union.

In 1970, Tinbergen had written a book that covered the same themes, but it had still been confidently called *A Viable Earth* (*Een Leefbare Aarde*).[29] His later book had a question mark in the title: *Can We Manage the Earth?*. "The question, now, is whether there are individuals of sufficient distinction in our midst for the bigger task ahead of us, that of world integration. Perhaps the threat of the alternative, mass extinction, will help us take up the task."[30] Harry de Lange, a former student of Tinbergen, who was also member of the Remonstrant Brotherhood, described Tinbergen as perhaps not religious, but deeply ethical. Tinbergen never wanted to call himself religious, but De Lange recognized well the moral motivation and themes in his work, and the way in which Tinbergen constantly saw threats to the organization of society, threats that could be countered only from a moral starting point of responsibility and a desire for justice.[31]

Tinbergen's doubts also had a markedly religious character. Since man is flawed, it is unclear whether the forces of evil or good would win out and whether the forces of peace would beat those of. Order was required not merely because the economic system and the political system were unstable, but also because man himself could not be trusted. "Can we manage the earth?" was the title of his book, and the answer was uncertain, not because we lacked the knowledge or the techniques to do so, but because we might be incapable of doing the right thing: "[M]ost human

---

[29] Tinbergen, *Een Leefbare Aarde*, 1970.
[30] Tinbergen, *Kunnen wij de Aarde Beheren?*, 1987.
[31] H. M. de Lange in Jolink and Barendrecht-Tinbergen, *Gedeelde Herinneringen*, 1993.

Figure 18.3 Tinbergen in conversation with the next generation about the third millennium, early 1990s.

beings tend to be shortsighted, which may have disastrous consequences."[32] Tinbergen's plea for long-term enlightened self-interest was
increasingly tainted by the worry that enlightened self-interest would not
win out (Figure 18.3).

18.4 Stability, Harmony, and Balance

In one of the very few instances in which Tinbergen wrote about family
life, it was harmonious relations that he emphasized.[33] It is telling for the
way in which stability occupied a central place in his work. The theme
recurred time and again in his work: in the search for equilibrium in
economic models in his dissertation, in the search for stability in the
1930s and the overcoming of the business cycle in the middle of the
century. But it was also clearly on display in his approach to the Soviet
Union and his convergence theory. Another version of this search for
harmony was the ideal of synthesis. In his valedictory lecture at the
Netherlands School of Economics, he compared the optimistic visions of
the future, those that believed we would soon reach a posteconomic era

[32] Tinbergen, *Entering the Third Millennium*, 1991.   [33] Ibid.

dominated by leisure, with the pessimistic visions about the future ranging from Malthus to the then recent Club of Rome Report, *Limits to Growth*: "The only correct behavior for economists is to build a theory which unites the thesis and the antithesis into a synthesis – in other words, a theory which tells us under which circumstances the optimists, and under which conditions the pessimists, are correct."[34] The good and bad were both part of this world, but even in scientific theories, Tinbergen preferred to think not of conflict, but rather of complementary theories that might be joined. His League of Nations model was explicitly an attempt to synthesize the various business cycle theories, although it was not perceived by his contemporaries as such.

Synthesis also carried a more transcendental meaning for the (natural) scientists of the interwar period who trained Tinbergen.[35] One of Tinbergen's more prominent students, Johan Witteveen, head of the IMF from 1973 to 1978, was a longtime proponent of the universal Sufism movement that sought to bridge religion in the East and West. Another one of his later students, Piet Terhal, explored the connections between Tinbergen's work and that of Pierre Teilhard de Chardin, who attempted to bridge modern science and Catholicism.[36] Synthesis was the search for integration and wholeness in the world.

In his late work such as *Can We Govern the Planet?* the theme of harmony was explicitly connected to the theme of peace. Tinbergen spoke about the harmonious relations or peaceful relations between human beings, and about the harmony and peace between man and his environment. Synthesis, harmony, and peace have romantic connotations, and that is what attracted idealists to Tinbergen's work. It would be wrong to ignore those connotations and how they gave direction to his work. After the Club of Rome report, Tinbergen quickly incorporated a concern with the environment into his thinking. In fact, already in 1971, a year before the report came out, he had given a speech on how to approach the future in which the environmental challenge would be central. In the speech, he sketched out three scenarios for the future. In the first scenario, by far the most preferable, all negative effects of pollution would be overcome

---

[34] Tinbergen, *Komt er Wel een Post-Economisch Tijdperk*, 4–5, 1973.

[35] *Synthetisch Denken: Natuurwetenschappers over hun Rol in een Moderne Maatschappij 1900–1940*, 2008.

[36] Terhal, *Wegen naar een Menswaardige Toekomst*. Marinus van der Goes van Naters suggested that Tinbergen was inspired by Teilhard de Chardin's work on convergence from the interwar period onward; see Jolink and Barendrecht-Tinbergen, *Gedeelde Herinneringen*, 135–39.

through technological innovation. It was a hopeful scenario that is still relatively prominent among economists who expect that the true solution to climate change will come from innovation, not limits to growth. In the second scenario, we would have to adapt our lifestyle, live simpler, and discard imaginary wants, and rich groups and countries would have to return to consumption patterns much below their current level. He suggested that our style of living would have to change from "a culture of cars" to "a culture of domesticity," something that he personally favored anyway. In the third scenario, the impending environmental disaster would lead to rationing and an economy run like a fully planned war economy. Consumption levels would have to be largely equalized, and various products would have to be banned.[37]

The existence of positive and the negative (as tendencies) necessitated "conscious planning" and organization. They were his two primary ways to create stability and harmony, and they often went together. They also betrayed, if that is the right word, the ultimate core of his thinking: harmony was not natural and had to be consciously pursued through rational organization. That belief was fundamentally at odds with perhaps the central idea in economics: spontaneous order, or what is known as Adam Smith's "invisible hand." For Tinbergen, there was no invisible hand that guided the world toward progress or harmony, no natural process that led to peace. Instead, progress, stability, and peace necessarily had to be organized, and his intellectual effort is best understood as an attempt to bring that about.

At times it succeeded. He regarded it as one of his major achievements in his long career that he was able to bring employers and employees together in the Socio-Economic Council (SER). What the SER represented as an institution, with its makeup of equal parts workers, employers, and experts, was the ultimate embodiment of "social peace." It was the organization of harmonious relationships between social groups (capital and labor) and science (experts) that was previously believed to be in a perpetual state of conflict. After all, Marx had theorized the conflict between labor and capital as the fundamental characteristic of capitalism. The SER represented a synthesis of different interests and a way to find harmony facilitated by rational discussion under the guidance of science.[38]

---

[37] Tinbergen, "How Should the Future Be Studied?," 1972.
[38] Tinbergen, "Inflatie, Integratie en Maatschappelijke Orde: Antwoord aan Professor Witteveen," 1959.

But his own perspective of peaceful change, and the problems he had dealing with the more violent and barbaric elements of Nazism, communism, and the dictators in the Third World, also revealed the limits of his own project. We have already seen that his work on "the economy" in the 1930s and 1940s involved a heroic effort to insulate the economy from political and social developments so that we could analyze its endogenous dynamics. It was economics as if politics and society did not matter. But more generally, Tinbergen's work and vision provided a picture of peaceful change that was of limited use to understand the twentieth century. The Russian revolution and its violent aftermath, including the mass starvation, did not fit into his perspective. Neither did the fact that the origins of the planned economy in Germany were so intimately connected with the rise of fascism. Nor could it make sense of the often-violent decolonization process that finally gave the new nations some power to develop their own economic policies. The one partial exception was the downfall of communism, which involved relatively little bloodshed. But as Tinbergen's contemporaries pointed out, it was hardly apt to describe it as a process of convergence, as Tinbergen attempted to do. The Peace Palace existed, but so did war.

Nonetheless, Tinbergen stuck to his attempts to reconcile fundamental differences. This was even true when it came to intellectual disagreements. When Keynes attacked him violently and personally, Tinbergen sought to reconcile the differences between them, and correct some misunderstandings on the side of his opponent. When Balogh ridiculed his approach to educational planning, Tinbergen kindly and patiently replied that many of the issues Balogh raised could be fruitfully incorporated into his model.

***

The history of Dutch political commentary is a longing for more serious ideological debate, without much success. Pragmatism typically prevails, and conflicts are mostly contained. It was perhaps for this reason that Tinbergen had such an aversion against philosophy, the most qualitative discipline of them all. It would create only discord, discord that could be resolved much better on pragmatic levels where different solutions to practical problems could be made compatible. But as philosophers will tell you, simply ignoring philosophical work does not mean one's own work is suddenly devoid of a philosophical perspective.

The philosophy of Tinbergen's thought was part of the high modernism that James Scott has described, the combination of administrative machinery and state control by rational means. But that does not exhaust Tinbergen's perspective. The first nuance is that James Scott suggested that the high modernists sought to improve the world. Tinbergen certainly had that goal, but just as much did he seek to avoid conflict, and disaster. His experience was crucially shaped by the disasters of the first half of the twentieth century. He had a constant awareness, which became crucially visible in the final decades, of the possibility of regress. Many economic theorists, including the greats of the twentieth century – John Maynard Keynes, Friedrich Hayek, and Frank Knight – have pointed to the fundamentally uncertain nature of the future, and Tinbergen agreed with them. He remained forever skeptical of prediction. But rather than theorizing what it meant to live in an uncertain world, as they did, he sought control over the future. Even if one could not predict it, one should at least attempt to plan it. Fear of uncertainty, of conflict and war, drove him to planning, to a philosophy of control.

If there was fear, on the one hand, then there was the deep sense of responsibility, on the other. It was not just that things had to be brought under control, but also that he was one of the individuals who carried a special responsibility to gain that control. That perhaps explains the self-confidence that his work sometimes exuded, but its roots are deeper. Both the AJC ethos and the ethos of the Remonstrant Brotherhood emphasized the personal responsibility (especially) of those to whom a lot was given (in talents), as he himself frequently recounted. His book titles suggested that we can *shape* the international order, but can we also *govern* the planet? In a very real sense, we ought to read these questions not merely as intellectual, but also as personal questions. It was a similar sentiment that was beneath Ehrenfest's doubts: Could *he* contribute enough? It is in this sense that Tinbergen's later work also revealed his personal doubts about whether he had done enough. His intellectual effort came to an end with his death in 1994. That year, his publications included *The Future of Social-Democracy, What Is Peace Economics?*, and *Global Governance for the 21st Century*. Tinbergen was not one to let go, or to forsake the responsibility he felt he had. Some things might be beyond our control, but as it is written in Luke 12:48, "To whom much is given, much will be required."

19

Expert or Idealist?

Ah, if only humans were wise/ And they meant well / The earth would be a paradise / Now she often resembles hell.[1]

Economics is known as the dismal science,[2] infamous for its gloomy predictions and its focus on trade-offs: the inescapability of hard choices and the inevitability of inequality. Yet it has also given rise to utopian visions, from socialism to the idea of eternal and stable growth, or the promise that development is possible for every country. The economist Joseph Schumpeter famously argued that every major economist has a distinct vision that shaped their perspective on economics, that reflected their hopes and fears about what could be realized in the world.[3] The purpose of a biography could be to examine this vision, to uncover it, if you will. But Schumpeter's perspective is unnecessarily static.

Jan Tinbergen's vision was shaped by developments within science. Therefore, we should seek not just to uncover some underlying (ideological) vision that shaped his scientific work but also to uncover how Tinbergen's science shaped his vision on life and the world. His perspective on equality, for example, was fundamentally shaped by his theoretical and empirical work in economics. His perspective on politics was informed by the way in which Ehrenfest sought to overcome disputes in physics. Tinbergen's idea of mature socialism and the associated optimal order

[1] In Dutch: "Ach! waren alle mensen wijs / En wilden daarbij wel / De aard' waar haar een paradijs / Nu is ze meest een hel." Final lines of the poem "Maysche Morgenstond" ("Morning in May") by Dirck Rafaëlsz (1586–1627).
[2] Levy, How the Dismal Science Got Its Name: Classical Economics and the Ur-Text of Racial Politics, 2002.
[3] Schumpeter, "Science and Ideology," 1949.

Expert or Idealist? 415

arose out of his scientific work and understanding of economics.[4] The relationship between scientific work and vision is a two-way street.

19.1 Vision and Synthesis

A striking characteristic of Tinbergen's work is his hostility toward methodological and philosophical reflection. But there was one philosophical economic essay to which he referred repeatedly: Werner Sombart's *Three Types of Economics*.[5] Sombart was one of the final representatives of the German historical school. His work studied the evolution of capitalism with ample attention to the cultural aspects of economies; he was not particularly an economist akin to Tinbergen. Nonetheless, Tinbergen returned several times to Sombart's distinction between three types of economics: *ordnend* (analytical and empirical), *verstehend* (based on subjective understanding), and *richtend* (normative). One might expect Tinbergen to side strongly with the economics of the *ordnende* type, even more so since Sombart aligned it with the work of Pareto and other mathematical economists in whose tradition Tinbergen worked.

But Tinbergen did nothing of the sort. Instead, he argued that a good economist needed empathy and subjective understanding, *verstehen*. His attempt not merely to be a socialist for the people but also to understand poverty and the lack of opportunities from up close was his attempt at *verstehen*. Except for the very early newspaper writings, one will search in vain for evidence of this in his work, but even so it was deeply important to him. And it was not merely important as motivation, but also to arrive at a good measure of welfare, he suggested.

Yet despite the importance of the *ordnende* and the *verstehende* type of economics, the highest form of economics was *richtend* (direction-giving). It is easy to mistake the man who received a Nobel Prize for turning economics into a quantitative science for a hard-nosed scientist. But Tinbergen was no positivist who believed that science should restrict itself to empirically verifiable statements, not even close to it. For Tinbergen, the normative was always the most important, and it was science's ultimate purpose to inform our normative ideas, our conceptions of the good life and the good society.

His mentor Ehrenfest believed that physics should be *anschaulich*. When we discussed this idea earlier, we noted that it referred to qualities

[4] Tinbergen, "Some Thoughts on Mature Socialism," 1973.
[5] Sombart, *Die drei Nationalökonomien*, 1930.

like intuitiveness and vividness. But the concept had a broader connotation in the interwar period, which Tinbergen realized all too well. When the idea of *anschauliche* theory in economics was developed by Edgar Salin, it was used for a type of economics that was able to incorporate scientific elements into a coherent worldview. An *anschauliche* theory explained the world but could also help to make sense of the world and give direction and perspective. Salin contrasted the purely scientific economists from those who were able to combine this with a synthesis, who succeeded in making their theories *anschaulich*.[6] Economics had known both. Adam Smith, Friedrich List, and Karl Marx were those who had arrived at *anschauliche* theories, whereas William Stanley Jevons, David Ricardo, and Alfred Marshall had remained more pure scientists. This was not to say that the pure scientists had no political views; of course they did. But they had not been able to integrate them into a synthesis with their scientific theories.

Tinbergen admired economists who combined a deep knowledge of their subject with vision. He judged Floor Wibaut the superior economist to Nicolaas Pierson. The latter was widely recognized as the premier economic theorist within the Netherlands, whereas Wibaut never wrote anything systematic on economics. But it was the way in which Wibaut combined economic knowledge with vision and social action that he admired. Even when he did not agree with their views, he preferred those with a vision and a sense of moral responsibility and commitment to pure scientists. For example, he favored the work of Wilhelm Röpke, a conservative liberal and member of the German Ordoliberals, over that of his close friend and colleague, the pure scientist Tjalling Koopmans.

What such men were able to accomplish was to sketch a unified vision. They could create a comprehensive perspective of the subject, with one stroke, as Salin suggested. For Tinbergen, synthesis was not merely a quality of their work, but also a personal quality: one's vision should converge with one's life, just as in the AJC, where socialism had become a way of life, not merely a theory or a set of ideals. Those who should be truly admired in the world were those who combined moral *character* with vision.[7] Knowledge therefore extended beyond scientific theories and was

---

[6] Salin, "Geschichte der Volkswirtschaftslehre," 1929; and, in particular, the excellent review essay by Neisser, "Der Gegensatz von 'anschaulich' und 'rational' in der Geschichte der Volkswirtschaftslehre," 1931.

[7] Salin, "Walter Eucken: In Memoriam," 1950.

also found in the vision and lifestyle of intellectual leaders; truly great individuals *embodied* what they knew.

19.2 The Wrong Nobel

That poses the question: What did Tinbergen embody? Most visible was his strict observance of certain rules, such as being a teetotaler and a principled user of public transport. It was also reflected in certain norms that became associated with his work, most famously the 1 percent of GDP norm for development aid from the North to the South. In the Netherlands, his name also became attached to a norm about the relation between wages at the top of an organization and the shop floor – that it should never exceed 1:10 (or 1:5 in some versions).[8] Although Tinbergen never proposed such a norm, it is telling that this way of thinking was so easily associated with this vision. He was a rule-follower, a man of principles. The anecdotes about him, recounted by his students and friends, inevitably involved the breaking of these rules. He did so in particular to have something sweet, preferably a cake, dessert, or some chocolate milk. But the fact that these anecdotes are worth telling demonstrates how important these life rules were to Tinbergen.

There was also an interesting convergence between Tinbergen's way of living and some of the central ideas in economics. The idea that we live in a world of scarcity with limited means for competing ends was matched by his own frugality and obsession with time. When he was young, he had built a mechanical clock, and the library stamp he had designed for his books read "Every hour counts." His meetings with others would characteristically start with the announcement that he did not have much time, a potentially harmless remark, except that Tinbergen would then put his watch on the table and say to his visitor that they had about seven and a half minutes, or fifteen if they were lucky. His motto, that we should tackle "the most urgent problems first," is a good illustration of the thinking ascribed to rational economic man. And indeed, one of his former employees described him as a true *homo economicus.*[9]

However, these are at best interesting convergences. Those who knew him also observed something deeper that he embodied. As Solomon Cohen, one of his students, suggested: "Through the years he developed

---

[8] Akkerboom, "De Tinbergennorm bestaat Niet," 2015.
[9] Rijco J. P. Glinstra Bleeker in Jolink and Barendrecht-Tinbergen, *Gedeelde Herinneringen*, 79, 1993.

a kind of personal code of conduct which is based on a sort of socio-economic theory of optimal action. In this manner his way of thinking and his conduct formed into a consistent whole." The peace he pursued in the world was also something that he embodied. One of his friends with a Christian background said that Tinbergen reminded him of the early Christians, "who through their everyday attitude and behavior of uncon-ditional charity inspired each other and others." Or take one of his Indian students, Unnithan: "[I]t is his compassionate and gentle considerations for other human beings and his commitments to the values of peace and non-violence [which made me turn to the study of Gandhi]."[10] It is hard to capture that quality, and it easily becomes a kind of exaggeration. One commemorative volume, for example, is subtitled: *The Economist as Noble Saint*.[11] The economist who won the Nobel Prize right after Tinbergen and Frisch, Paul Samuelson, called Tinbergen a "humanist saint."[12]

To understand the way Tinbergen inspired those around him, we must capture and understand this quality, or perhaps the dual, but irreconciled, qualities of his scientific work and his personal life. When I started reading the retrospective work on Tinbergen, I was soon struck by a strong divergence. There was one group of people for whom Tinbergen was first and foremost one of the greatest economists of the twentieth century, not one with the allure of Keynes, but one whose less visible technical contri-butions had had more impact in the long run. His contributions became standard tools, which economists and policymakers used without even associating them with Tinbergen. This group of scientific followers saw Tinbergen's great strength in his amazing ability to boil down economic problems to their essence and capture this essence in simple models, which his students could then develop for whatever purpose they had. As such, he influenced at least two generations of economists: first, a generation who built macroeconomic models that in many countries became a backbone of economic policymaking; second, a generation of development economists who sought to spread the rational economic policies from the West to less developed parts of the world, so that they could be integrated into the world economy and share in the prosperity it brought along. For this group, it was clear that he was fully deserving of his Nobel Prize in economics (see Figure 19.1).

[10] All taken from reminiscences collected in ibid.
[11] Puttaswamaiah, *Tinbergen and Modern Economics: The Noble Economist Saint*, 1996.
[12] Samuelson, "Homage to Jan Tinbergen," 2004.

Figure 19.1 Jan Tinbergen receiving the first Nobel Prize in economics in 1969; behind him, his wife Tine is proudly observing the proceedings.

The other group recognized the technical brilliance of Tinbergen, but quickly noted that they themselves were not able to do this type of work. They praised his humanity and his idealism. They expressed how they felt inspired by him to devote themselves to improving the lives of others and

Figure 19.2 At the reception of the Erasmus Prize in 1967. Left to right: Prince Claus and Princess Beatrix (heir), Queen Juliana, Jan and Tine Tinbergen, Prince Bernhard (Juliana's husband), and Princess Margriet (third daughter of Juliana and Bernhard).

to promote peace. They praised Tinbergen as somebody who lived his ideals, somebody who was modest and never felt himself to be above anyone else. Most of all, they tended to admire the way in which he stuck to his ideals, despite many disappointments, and most importantly despite the cynicism all around him. For this group his effect was mostly personal: "around him everyone become a bit nobler." This group thought he rightfully won the Erasmus Prize, the prize for scholars whose work exhibited a great humanistic spirit (see Figure 19.2). And they will, only half in jest, suggest that he really should have won the Nobel Peace Prize, not the one in economics.

As remarkable as this dual set of qualities is the fact that there was limited connection between the two legacies. It was telling that after Tinbergen's retirement in Rotterdam, the Center for Development Planning split between the idealists and the technical economists. As we have seen in his own work, Tinbergen also struggled to integrate them. He was fiercely opposed to fascism but attempted to analyze its economic system on purely technical grounds. He deeply believed in the transformative and emancipatory qualities of education, but modeled education in terms of years of schooling. He believed that economics had to be a quantitative science, devoid as much as possible of ideology and qualitative discussion, but it was vision and perspective that he hoped to generate in his economics.

The Swedish economist Bent Hansen wrote one of the best appreciations of the work of Frisch and Tinbergen just after they shared the first Nobel Prize in economics, but his final lines were unexpected:

It remains only to be said, that the humanitarian idealism which Nobel wanted to reward has no representative in our profession so fine and noble as Jan Tinbergen. As much as he is respected in the privileged world, he is beloved by the underprivileged, the underdogs. Always at their service, always on their side, always working on improving their conditions, Tinbergen would be an equally worthy candidate for the Nobel Peace Prize.[13]

Perhaps it was an innocent remark. After all, appreciations can be a little grandiloquent. But Hansen was not the only one. In his reminiscences to Tinbergen, his student George Waardenburg made the same suggestion: "You would be equally deserving the Nobel Prize for Peace."[14] And in the many congratulatory notes that he received, the same remark kept recurring.

It stung for more than one reason. Tinbergen had consciously decided to leave econometrics behind in the 1950s to focus on the problem of development. Yet the Nobel was awarded for his work in econometrics in the 1930s. Not that he wanted to dissociate himself from his work in econometrics, but in 1969 he was in the middle of preparations for Development Decade II for the United Nations and wanted all the attention to be focused on the problem of development. The prestigious Erasmus Prize, of which he was the first Dutch winner, and which he received from Prince Bernhard – husband to the Queen – had in that sense been more meaningful, for it explicitly cited his compassion and projects for the developing world. It also placed him in line with winners like Robert Schumann, Martin Buber, and the Union Académique Internationale, an organization that stimulated international scientific exchange.

His book *Welfare and Warfare* was his final attempt to connect economics and peace. He wrote: "'Die Waffen nieder' (Down with weapons) wrote Bertha von Suttner. [She] showed her abhorrence and acted accordingly. Then politicians began to act, in the Peace Conferences of 1899 and

[13] Hansen, "Jan Tinbergen: An Appraisal of His Contributions to Economics," 336, 1969.
[14] Jolink and Barendrecht-Tinbergen, *Gedeelde Herinneringen*, 1993.

1907 in The Hague, leading to the building of the Peace Palace in that same city, now the seat of the International Court of Justice."[15] It was this project that had started in The Hague that Tinbergen had sought to continue. At its core was the vision to build international institutions that would make integration possible. He wanted to fulfill the promise of the Peace Palace and the League of Nations. It was still an unfinished project when he died in 1994, but as the brochure for the Peace Palace suggested, "This is not a Palace *of* the Peace, ready to provide a home for it, it is a palace *for* the Peace." This was true for the work of Tinbergen as well, or so he hoped. His oeuvre was not a place *of* peace, it was a place *for* peace, something on which we he hoped others would continue to build. The driving force behind his work had been simple: it was created *for* peace.

His friend Van der Goes van Naters praised him for turning economics into a moral science again, in the spirit of Adam Smith. But Tinbergen's moral convictions existed next to his economics. His economics and policy models were meant to remove ideology, vision, and morality out of science and politics. His fate was more reminiscent of that of Max Weber, who vehemently argued for a value-free science, but believed that this pursuit entailed a deep moral responsibility for the individual scientist. Tinbergen the idealist and Tinbergen the economist could not be fully integrated; they coexisted.

Such tensions were also personal. One of the most important personal decisions was the choice by Jan and Tine to adopt two orphaned German girls after World War II, Hanneke and Marian. In doing so, Tinbergen followed an example his parents had set by providing a home to Austrian refugees after World War I. One of them, Tilde, ended up marrying his brother Niko. Hanneke and Marian were old at the time of adoption, and it was certainly a struggle to integrate them into the family. But the adoption was his attempt to do on the personal level what he sought to promote on the societal level. It is tempting to psychologize whether the adoption was motivated by the fact that he in hindsight felt that he did not oppose the German occupiers sufficiently. Perhaps it was simply his own attempt at forgiveness, and his search for peace. He promoted a similar forgiveness in the new political-economic relations with Germany after World War II, by arguing against financial and territorial reparations.[16] His moral idealism and consistency were an

<hr/>

[15] Tinbergen and Fischer, *Warfare and Welfare: Integrating Security into Socio-economic Policy*, 117, 1987.
[16] Tinbergen, "Herstelbetalingen," 1946.

inspiration to many, but also a high bar to live up to for those around him. The way that Tinbergen sought to embody his ideals could be suffocating; it was hard to do enough, to live up to the standards he set.

The goal of peace in the world, paradoxically, left little room for inner peace. There was a restlessness about Tinbergen's search for peace in the world. There were always new tasks awaiting and new burdens to shoulder. We saw how Paul Ehrenfest took his own life when he felt that he could no longer accomplish the standards he had set for himself. In his close environment, such feelings were anything but unique. Tinbergen's youngest biological daughter Tineke was diagnosed with cancer at a relatively young age. She told nearly nobody about the bad news and kept giving all her energies to her work in physics until she passed away, unexpectedly to many who were close to her. Tinbergen's youngest brother, Luuk, was already a successful biologist and ornithologist when he committed suicide at the age of forty. Tinbergen himself suffered from what he called "somber periods," or depressions.

It is impossible to establish a definite link between these tragic events and his deep sense of duty. Suicides are, ultimately, not rational choices. And depressions are clinical phenomena, not simply the result of the severe standards people set themselves. But it was, without a doubt, a demanding environment, one in which excellence in intellectual pursuits as well as exemplary moral behavior were expected.

And yet it was precisely at home that Tinbergen found some peace. In his youthful travel diaries, we came across a longing for home, if not a certain home sickness. A tribute to his wife, written in 1962, is evidence that this never really changed. In the tribute, Jan detailed how during his travels he would calculate every evening in his hotel bed what percentage of the trip was already completed. He longed for the moment to return home:

Finally, there is the KLM-plane, already a piece of home, and the opportunity of just sitting alone reading or writing without having to talk is a relief.... And then finally the moment when the many ditches and neat houses of the Netherlands appear underneath us. All the famous buildings, the Fokker factory, the contours of Schiphol Airport. Through passport control ... and then I find out, who will be there. Is anybody ill? Sometimes two pairs of very young eyes are awaiting grandpa. For a moment my breath halts, how delightful to see them again. Sometimes there are some daughters present, it is a privilege to have them, especially when they are happy. But the center of the family that is clear.... When you [Tine, his wife] are there, then my happiness is complete. Even when you have been together for over thirty years, the reunion is a fulfillment, a fulfillment like in our younger years. Traveling is really a way to remain young. The parting is like the parting during our engagement, on Sunday nights: *mourir un peu.*... At home there is the reward of our own colors. Your atmosphere, and all my stress disappears. With some satisfaction you take everything out of the suitcase and put it back in its place.[17]

When Tinbergen was looking for peace, he went home, or even better to the family holiday cottage, the Hulshorst, which even today occupies a special place in the family. Home was peace in the sense of rest, but his idealist search for peace was restless.

His students praised him for always focusing on constructive trends and positive examples. But such an atmosphere of constant optimism could also be disconcerting, as if negative experiences and even failures did not have any impact on Tinbergen and his approach. Similarly, there is something unsettling about the constant pacifism in Tinbergen's thought and attitude, as if conflict could be willed away if we just focused on what united us. His engagements with Keynes and his other critics were telling for the way that Tinbergen avoided conflicts, a method he formalized in a strategy he ascribed to Ehrenfest: there is always a nobler way to describe a scientific disagreement than in terms of conflict. Even in science, he favored the integration of theories. The philosopher of science Karl Popper argued that all progress in human knowledge happened through disagreement; the (imagined) philosopher of science, Jan Tinbergen, would argue that all progress in human knowledge happens through integration and synthesis.

The other side of making peace, and seeking for integration, was the avoidance of conflict and his own fear of conflict. The purpose of the Breakthrough movement was to integrate the progressive parties in the Netherlands into one progressive front; the Socio-Economic Council, which he so hoped to establish at the international level as well, integrated social classes; the United Nations was a step toward the integration of the world; and Jean Monnet had helped to integrate Europe.

And where there was integration, the chances of conflict radically diminished. Tinbergen was therefore deeply fearful of the polarized world of the Cold War. And he was both overwhelmed and fearful of the deep cleavages between the rich and the poor. It was again this combination of empathy and fear that deeply touched him when he first saw the poverty in India; he became physically sick afterward.

Despite all his desires to overcome dogmatism, his own search for peace and avoidance of conflict hardened into dogma. It led him to approach

---

[17] From the family album dated 27 October 1962, "Snippers opgedragen aan een Vrouw, Moeder, Oma."

anyone with the assumption that they, like him, had good intentions. Even Nazism was not purely evil. Condemning communism in strong (ideological) terms would be harmful to the goal of convergence and, ultimately, integration. And it made him stay in advisory positions to some of the dictatorial leaders in the developing world, such as Indonesia, for too long. We saw in Chapter 15 that even when he was offered an honorary doctorate in Spain, under the Franco regime, this was not an opportunity for a public boycott, but rather an opportunity to talk. It was therefore the United Nations that was his most favored institution, because its aspiration was to be a political organization in which every nation was represented. His business-cycle model at the League of Nations had sought to find a place for all of the different explanations of the business-cycle mechanism. The optimal socioeconomic order had to be a synthesis of the systems of the East and the West. If the world disagreed, it had to be brought together. That was Tinbergen's way of making peace, even though he himself never really found it.

19.3 Tinbergen and Expertise

The final remaining question is whether economic policy could be the bridge between his moral ideals and scientific knowledge. This book has suggested that his most important contribution was the development of modern economic expertise. A recent commemorative series of interviews highlights precisely that legacy. It consists of a set of interviews between Nobel Prize-winning economists and national and international policymakers of the first order.[18] The themes are wide-ranging, but the underlying message is clear: Tinbergen's contribution is that he made this conversation possible, that he found a way to make economic knowledge relevant for policy.

He did so through the development of new techniques and models, and the application of these to the problems of the day. But his role as policy expert was anything but passive. What Tinbergen did throughout his career is better understood as putting a series of economic problems on the political agenda. He literally made those problems urgent. He did so not merely by drawing attention to the severity of the problems but also by demonstrating that something could be done about them. Nobody doubted the severity of the Great Depression in 1933, but it was anything but clear that something could be done about it. The Plan of Labor suggested that a

---

[18] Sent and Bartelsman, *Conversations between Nobel Laureates and Policymakers*, 2019.

remedy could be found. There was a widespread sense in Europe after the war that the economy had to be made more stable, but it took the imagination of Tinbergen and others to show how this could be done. The poverty in the developing world was simply not part of the moral and political imagination of the Netherlands when Tinbergen started working on the problem. He was responsible, of course alongside others, for moving it up the political agenda. The same was true when he started working on the environmental challenges around 1970.

In fact, a closer reading of Tinbergen's own theory of economic policy reveals that political targets were derived from the realm of values. The expert accepted these values, handed down by society as input to the decision models. But Tinbergen often operated at this level of values. There were limited periods, such as when he was director of the CPB or advisor to the League of Nations, during which he acted primarily as economic expert, the expert who in service of the government figured out the most effective way of reaching pre-determined targets. More frequently in his career he was trying to influence the values in society and shaping the perspective on the world's most urgent problems.

The economist Frank Knight wrote critically about those who believed that life was about maximizing welfare or utility, as Tinbergen's decision models suggested. He argued that "life is at bottom an exploration in the field of values, an attempt to discover values, rather than on the basis of knowledge of them to produce and enjoy them to the greatest possible extent."[19] The tension between these two goals marked the work of Tinbergen. It had been present ever since his youth, when he was striving in the AJC for emancipation of the working classes and the promotion of socialism and justice, and in his studies in science where he was from the very start interested in the measurement and improvement of (material) welfare. That tension was also present in his image of humankind.

In 1978, the newly formed Christian Democratic Party published their vision on economic order and the responsibility of citizens.[20] In their report, they argued for the improvement of the moral fabric of society, to which Tinbergen responded critically.[21] Although he agreed that in the long run there had been moral progress, he was worried that there had been serious lapses in recent history. Tinbergen contrasted the idea of the

---

[19] Knight, *The Ethics of Competition and Other Essays*, 101, 1935.
[20] Steenkamp, "Gespreide Verantwoordelijk. Een Christen-Democratische Bijdrage aan de Discussie over de Economische Orde," 1978.
[21] Tinbergen, "De Beste Sociale Orde," 1978.

moral individual with the idea of the individual in economics: *homo economicus*. Homo economicus, according to Tinbergen, strove to maximize his own welfare in the broadest sense of the word: "the utility derived through the use of goods and services, the satisfaction derived from work and the relationships to others." But, however broad the conception of welfare was, it was self-directed, egoistic, if you like, because "economic science is skeptical about the reliance on neighborly love." Tinbergen argued that economists were correct in their skepticism; not too much should be expected from altruism. "The Christian call upon neighborly love, in personal behavior or in politics, is a call upon a rare quality; a quality which deserves high praise, but which is in short supply."

Yet Tinbergen had not abandoned the project of moral improvement. He was skeptical that it could be achieved through the promotion of altruism but believed that a call on the sense of responsibility of individuals might have better results. He praised markets as institutions, because they called on this sense of responsibility. And what was more, the pursuit of self-interest was not static. People could come to value immaterial goods more and become less materialistic. People could come to value the future more and become less short-sighted. They could learn to consume better, by cutting out smoking and drinking, for example, or by consuming more cultural goods. But such improvements were more likely to come from a different perception of self-interest than a call for altruism.

This moral strategy is visible in several places in his work. He typically argued for development aid not by relying on a call for solidarity with the poor, or a sense of duty to help the least well-off, even though he himself believed that this duty existed.[22] Instead, he appealed to the (enlightened) self-interest of the West, which should seek to avoid harmful and violent conflicts in the future. And by helping the poor, and poor nations, the likelihood of such conflicts was diminished. We saw in previous chapters that he did not argue for the redistribution of income but preferred to argue for better opportunities for every individual to develop their own skills. Again, not solidarity, but responsibility was the answer. His pleas for better care of the environment and for disarmament (of nuclear weapons) followed a similar strategy. He hoped that he could change how others perceived their self-interest.

Human beings were imperfect; they could never live up to the Christian ideal. And, therefore, not too much should be expected from moral

---

[22] In his essay on mature socialism, he did suggest that the spread of solidarity should be the ultimate goal; Tinbergen, "Some Thoughts on Mature Socialism," 1973.

improvement itself. Tinbergen was part of a long Protestant tradition that considered it necessary to restrict individual actions through rules and institutions. Society needed to be ordered because man was imperfect. What was distinct about Tinbergen's perspective, however, was that he was convinced that some individuals were better equipped to make good decisions than others. Even if he was skeptical about the moral improvement of all in society, he was hopeful that visionary leaders, and experts more generally, could make decisions that were at the very least not too rooted in short-term concerns. This elite had a duty of moral leadership, but that could never replace the need for ordering institutions.

As such, the expert could embody the combination of vision and knowledge that Tinbergen aspired to. His central contribution was a theory of economic policymaking, and an institutional theory of how economic policymaking should be positioned in relation to government and parliament. In the Netherlands that legacy is well recognized: the CPB still occupies a prominent place in the political arena. In Turkey, the SPO survived much political turmoil and regime changes, to be finally incorporated into the ministry of development in 2011. But the indirect influence of the institutionalization of economic expertise reached much further. Economic experts play a key role in international organizations such as the IMF and the World Bank, and at central banks economic experts have long replaced legal and narrow monetary experts. Many such institutions developed quite independently of Tinbergen, and many of them do not neatly fit into Tinbergen's vision of the role and position of economic expertise. Yet the idea that economic policy is primarily the domain of experts, rather than politicians, ideology, or democratic deliberation has become firmly ingrained. Tinbergen did not merely help turn economics into a quantitative empirical science through his work in econometrics. He helped turn economic policymaking into a quantitative domain in which instruments are manipulated to achieve policy goals.

That institutional legacy – his contribution to the rise of economic expertise – was not in perfect harmony with some of the other aspects of his work and personality. He created a place for social and cultural issues at the CPB, but its institutional legacy was purely in terms of technical economic expertise. As a committed pacifist he was opposed to colonialism and violent regimes but offered technical advice to all regimes that requested it. His elevation of the economic expert above the public, and frequently imposed from above on the regimes of developing countries, clashed with his ideal of internal peaceful change generated through self-help. And after the 1970s when the broad Keynesian consensus in economics began to crumble, economic expertise was employed for a set of economic and social goals, sometimes labeled neoliberalism, for which Tinbergen had little sympathy. Neoliberalism is often associated with a top-down economic regime of experts as embodied in the Washington consensus, as well as the depoliticization of economic policy. But it was Tinbergen who, from the left, did much to develop the techniques of economic policymaking and the institutionalization of expertise. What happened in the 1980s was not that experts took over control of the economy; they had done so much earlier. Instead, the expert consensus changed, but the idea that economic policy could be used to steer the economy in the desired direction remained.

If there is a synthesis to be found in his work, it lies in his role as economic expert. It was there that his personal desire for stability and orderliness could be combined with his aspirations for a better world. It was there, also, that his somewhat fearful outlook on the future could be turned into a positive force. It was through his work as policy advisor that he could attempt to control and improve the future. From the way he rationally planned his own days to how he hoped to achieve economic and social development in Turkey, and from his policy models that stipulated how to get from A to B in the most efficient manner to his planning approach for the future, the underlying desire was to brings matters under control. He simply could not let go, and neither could the economy be left to its own devices.

For an economist, that is rather atypical. Whether it was Adam Smith's invisible hand or Marx's belief in the inevitable collapse of capitalism, economists tended to believe that economic forces are too powerful to control. The silent revolution of economic expertise was how that universally shared belief in the economy as a natural and self-governing system was given up for the idea that the economy had to be ordered, steered, controlled, and planned.

That program was uniquely attractive to someone like Tinbergen, not even primarily because it provided an opportunity to attempt to bring the future under control, to make it stable and predictable. But more so, because it provided an opportunity to pursue social goals in service of the state and international organizations. The philosopher Michel Foucault has done much to uncover the rise and means of state power over the subjects of the state. He used the term "governmentality" to refer the rationalities and techniques by which the state governs. And it was to this governmentality that Tinbergen made crucial contributions through his theory of economic policymaking and his efforts in the institutionalization of economic expertise. The research on business cycles was crucial because it fostered the belief that the economy could be controlled, that it could be made stable. But that was purely a technical achievement. It was the fact that the economy was governed in the pursuit of social goals, such as justice, freedom, and equality, that made it especially attractive to idealists like Tinbergen. Economists are often, rightly, faulted for a singular focus on economic growth and GDP figures. But it was the promise that modern economic policy could be used to achieve social goals beyond these that attracted so many idealists to the field of economics.

The self-restraint that his role as economic expert and government advisor, in practice, often demanded was in tension with his high-minded social goals. And his own moral idealism and cultural aspirations never found a place in his economic models. Policy models, and economic experts themselves, could often be effective only by being emptied of most of their moral content. States often acted against the well-meaning advice of the idealistic experts such as Tinbergen or, worse yet, used them to justify harmful policies. Even if implemented, expert policies often did not have the desired effects. And yet it was the promise that economics could serve society that attracted Tinbergen to the role of economic expert.

The twentieth-century program in which the steering of the economy by economic experts was combined with the belief that economic policy could improve society is still with us today. It is reflected in the idea, more current than ever, that the main *responsibility* of the state is to stabilize and steer the economy in the socially desired direction. Tinbergen embodied that responsibility. He was fearful of international conflicts, economic instability, and environmental destruction, and moved by social injustice. He believed it was his personal duty to do something about these problems. Perhaps it was for that reason that Tinbergen himself never found peace. He kept writing, warning, and most of all, he kept on attempting to plan and control. For the expert the hardest thing to do is to let go.

Bibliography

ARCHIVES

Delpher, archive of Dutch newspapers, www.delpher.nl.
International Institute for Social History (IISG), Amsterdam.
Jan Tinbergen Collection at the Erasmus University Rotterdam, www.eur.nl/en/library/
collections/jan-tinbergen-collection (JTC).
League of Nations Archive, Geneva (LoN), section 10B, R4539-R4540/10B/12653.
Museum Boerhaave Archive, Ehrenfest Collection (BA: EC), Leiden.
National Library of Norway, Frisch Correspondence (NLN: FC).
NIOD, Institute for War, Holocaust and Genocide Studies, Amsterdam (NIOD).
Tinbergen Letters, online archive, https://tinbergenletters.eur.nl/ (TL).
Nationaal Archief, The Hague.
    Archive of the Centraal Planbureau (NA:CPB, Central Planning Bureau) Centraal
    Archief Bijzondere Rechtpleging (NA:CABR, Central Archive Special Justice).
    Ministerie van Buitenlandse Zaken, Ambassade en Consulaat-Generaal Turkije
    1955–1984 (NA:TE, Ministry of Foreign Affairs, Turkish Embassy and
    Consulate-General).
Yale Archives, Tjalling Koopmans Collection, New Haven, CT (YKC), MS 1439,
    Series I.

Publications

Abma, R. 1977. "Het Plan van de Arbeid en de SDAP." *Bijdragen en Mededelingen
    Betreffende de Geschiedenis der Nederlanden* 92: 37–68.
Acemoglu, Daron, and James A. Robinson. 2019. *The Narrow Corridor: States, Societies,
    and the Fate of Liberty.* New York: Penguin.
Akami, Tomoko. 2016. "A Quest to Be Global: The League of Nations Health
    Organization and Inter-Colonial Regional Governing Agendas of the Far
    Eastern Association of Tropical Medicine 1910–25." *International History
    Review* 38 (1): 1–23.
Akkerboom, Broer. 2015. "De Tinbergennorm Bestaat Niet." *MeJudice,* 2015. www
    .mejudice.nl/artikelen/detail/de-tinbergennorm-bestaat-niet.

431

Alberts, Gerard. 1994. "On Connecting Socialism and Mathematics: Dirk Struik, Jan Burgers, and Jan Tinbergen." *Historia Mathematica* 21 (3): 280–305.

Alberts, Gerard, and Pieter Weeder. 1988. *Distantie en Engagement: Jan Tinbergen Autobiografisch.* Eindhoven: Technische Universiteit Eindhoven.

Alexeyeva, Ludmilla, and Paul Goldberg. 1993. *The Thaw Generation: Coming of Age in the Post-Stalin Era.* Pittsburgh, PA: University of Pittsburgh Press.

Algemeene Nederlandsche Bond "Vrede door Recht." 1913. *Het Vredespaleis: Gedenkboek: Ten Dage van de Plechtige Opening op 28 Augustus 1913.* 's-Gravenhage: Belinfante.

Ames, Edward. 1965. "Review of *Central Planning* by Jan Tinbergen." *The Annals of the American Academy of Political and Social Science* 361: 167–68.

Andvig, Jens Christopher. 1988. "From Macrodynamics to Macroeconomic Planning: A Basic Shift in Ragnar Frisch's Thinking?" *European Economic Review* 32: 495–502.

Anonymous. "Review of Shaping the World Economy by Jan Tinbergen." 1963. *The International Executive* 5 (1): 27–30.

Anonymous. 1927. A "Een Gesprek met Hendrik de Man, de Eerste Sekretaris Der Sosialistiese Jeugdinternationale." 1927. *Het Jonge Volk* 14: 194.

Arndt, H. W. 1987. *Economic Development: The History of an Idea.* Chicago, IL: University of Chicago Press.

Asbeck, F. M. Baron van, Jan Tinbergen, and J. H. W. Verzijl. 1946. *Bouwstof Voor de Oplossing van Na-Oorlogsche Vraagstukken.* 's-Gravenhage: Martinus Nijhoff.

Assous, Michaël, and Vincent Carret. 2020. "(In)Stability at the Cowles Commission." *European Journal of the History of Economic Thought* 27: 1–39.

Backhouse, Roger E., and Bradley W. Bateman. 2011. *Capitalist Revolutionary: John Maynard Keynes.* Cambridge, MA: Harvard University Press.

Backhouse, Roger E., and Yann Giraud. 2010. "Circular Flow Diagrams." In *Famous Figures and Diagrams in Economics*, edited by Mark Blaug and Peter Lloyd, 221–29. Northhampton: Edward Elgar.

Balabkins, Nicholas. 1968. "Soviet-American Convergence by A.D. 2000? An Analysis of the Trends of Two Social Orders." *Canadian Slavonic Papers* 10: 133–47.

1992. "Measuring Soviet Economic Growth: Old Problems and New Complications. A Comment." *Journal of Institutional and Theoretical Economics* 148 (1): 93–97.

Balisciano, Márcia L. 1998. "Hope for America: American Notions of Economic Planning between Pluralism and Neoclassicism, 1930–1950." *History of Political Economy* 30 (Annual Supplement): 153–78.

Balogh, T. 1964. "Education and Economic Growth: Comments on Professor Tinbergen's Planning 'Model.'" *Kyklos* 17: 261–74.

Baneke, David Maarten. 2008. *Synthetisch Denken: Natuurwetenschappers over hun Rol in een Moderne Maatschappij 1900-1940.* Hilversum: Verloren.

Bank, Jan. 1978. *Opkomst en Ondergang van de Nederlandse Volksbeweging.* Deventer: Kluwer.

Batenburg, Paul van, and Jan Tinbergen. 1984. "Income Distribution: A Correction and a Generalization." *Weltwirtschaftliches Archiv* 120 (2): 361–65.

Bauer, Otto. 1931. *Kapitalismus und Sozialismus nach dem Weltkrieg.* Wien: Wiener Volksbuchhandlung.

Bergstrand, J. H., and P. Egger. 2013. "Gravity Equations and Economic Frictions in the World Economy." In *Palgrave Handbook of International Trade*, edited by D. Bernhofen, R. Falvey, D. Greenaway, and U. Kreickemeier, 532–70. London: Palgrave Macmillan.

Bijnsdorp, Ine, Ria Ermers, and Hennie Kenkhuis. 1985. *De Wapens Neder 1*. Nijmegen: De Haktol.

Bjerkholt, Olav. 1995. *Foundations of Econometrics: The Selected Essays of Ragnar Frisch*. London: Edward Elgar.

Bockman, Johanna, and Michael A. Bernstein. 2008. "Scientific Community in a Divided World: Economists, Planning, and Research Priority during the Cold War." *Comparative Studies in Society and History* 50 (3): 581–613.

Bogaard, Adrienne van den. 1999. "Past Measurements and Future Prediction." In *Models as Mediators: Perspectives on Natural and Social Science*, edited by Mary S. Morgan and Margaret Morison, 282–326. Cambridge: Cambridge University Press.

2001. "Economie als Wiskundige Abstractie of als Uitdrukking van Zingeving? Strijdende Visies bij het Ontstaan van het Centraal Planbureau." *Gewina* 24: 225–41.

Böhm-Bawerk, Eugen von. 1924. "Macht oder ökonomisch Gesetz." In *Gesammelte Schriften von Eugen von Böhm Bawerk*, edited by Franz X. Weiss, 230–300. Wien: Hölder-Pichler-Tempsky.

Boianovsky, Mauro. 2019. "Arthur Lewis and the Classical Foundations of Development Economics." *Research in the History and Methodology of Economic Thought* 37 (A): 103–43.

Boianovsky, Mauro, and Kevin D. Hoover. 20019. "The Neoclassical Growth Model and Twentieth-Century Economics." *History of Political Economy* 41 (Annual Supplement): 1–23.

Boianovsky, Mauro, and Hans-Michael Trautwein. 2006. "Haberler, the League of Nations, and the Quest for Consensus in Business Cycle Theory in the 1930s." *History of Political Economy* 38 (1): 45–89.

Boomen, Gerard van den. 1983. *Honderd Jaar Vredesbeweging in Nederland*. Amstelveen: Uitgeverij Luyten.

Bouma, Nienke, Bernard M. S. van Praag, and Jan Tinbergen. 1976. "Testing and Applying a Theory of Utility: An Attempt to Decompose Income in Compensatory and Scarcity Rents." *European Economic Review* 8: 181–91.

Boumans, Marcel. 1992. *A Case of Limited Physics Transfer: Jan Tinbergen's Resources for Re-shaping Economics*. Amsterdam: Tinbergen Institute.

2003. "Jan Tinbergen." In *Biografisch Woordenboek van Het Socialisme en de Arbeidersbeweging in Nederland*, 8: 296–301. Amsterdam: IISG. https://socialhistory .org/bwsa/biografie/tinbergen.

2019. "Econometrics: The Keynes–Tinbergen Controversy." In *The Elgar Companion to John Maynard Keynes*, edited by Robert W. Dimand and Harald Hagemann, 283–89. Cheltenham: Edward Elgar.

Boumans, Marcel, and Ariane Dupont-Kieffer. 2011. "A History of the Histories of Econometrics." *History of Political Economy* 43 (Annual Supplement): 5–31.

Boumans, Marcel, and Neil De Marchi. 2018. "Models, Measurement, and 'Universal Patterns': Jan Tinbergen and Development Planning without Theory." *History of Political Economy* 50 (S1): 231–48.

Brandsma, Margriet. 1996. *Jan Pronk: Rebel Met Een Missie*. Amsterdam: Scheffers.

Brolsma, Marjet. 2015. "'Het Humanitaire Moment.' Nederlandse Intellectuelen, de Eerste Wereldoorlog En de Crisis van de Europese Beschaving (1914–1930).'" Dissertation, University of Amsterdam. https://hdl.handle.net/11245/1.477826.

Buchanan, James M. 1959. "Positive Economics, Welfare Economics, and Political Economy." *The Journal of Law and Economics* 2: 124–38.

———. 1979. "What Should Economists Do?" *Southern Economic Journal* 30: 213–22.

Bulutoğlu, K. 1967. "Financing Turkey's Development." In *Planning in Turkey*, edited by S. İlkin and E. İnanç, 181–214. Ankara: Faculty of Administrative Sciences.

Busch, Joel H. 1968. "Book Review of Gunnar Myrdal's *Asian Drama: An Inquiry into the Poverty of Nations*." *The Australian Quarterly* 40 (4): 118–21.

Butter, Frank A. G. den, and Harro Maas. 2011. "From Expert Judgment to Model Based Monetary Analysis: The Case of the Dutch Central Bank in the Postwar Period." Tinbergen Institute Discussion Paper, no. 11-161/3.

Casimir, Hendrik B. G. 1983. *Haphazard Reality: Half a Century of Science*. New York: Harper & Row.

Centraal Bureau voor Statistiek. 2001. *Tweehonderd Jaar Statistiek in Tijdreeksen 1800–1999*. Amsterdam: IISG.

Chakravarty, Sukhamoy. 1989. "Nicholas Kaldor on Indian Economic Problems." *Cambridge Journal of Economics* 13: 237–44.

Clavin, Patricia. 2015. *Securing the World Economy: The Reinvention of the League of Nations, 1920–1946*. Oxford: Oxford University Press.

Clavin, Patricia, and Jens Wilhelm Wessels. 2005. "Transnationalism and the League of Nations: Understanding the Work of Its Economic and Financial Organisation." *Contemporary European History* 14 (4): 465–92.

Cleeff, Ed van. 1929. "Hendrik de Man's *Die Intellektuellen und der Sozialismus*." *Regeneratie: Maandschrift Voor Praktisch-Idealisme* 10 (10): 294–300.

———. 1931. "Het Sociaal-Ekonomies Wereldkongres." *Regeneratie: Maandschrift voor Praktisch-Idealisme* 12 (10): 306–9.

Commissie uit N.V.V. en S.D.A.P. 1936. "Het Plan van de Arbeid." Amsterdam.

Cooper, Malcolm. 2000. "The Legacy of Atatürk: Turkish Political Structures and Policy-Making." *International Affairs* 78 (1): 115–28.

Cornelisse, Peter A. 1964. "The Volume of East-West Trade." *Co-Existence* 1: 99–106.

Cornelisse, Peter A., and C. B. Tilanus. 1966. "The Semi-Input-Output Method: With an Application to Turkish Data." *De Economist* 114: 521–33.

Craver, Earlene. 1986. "Patronage and the Directions of Research in Economics: The Rockefeller Foundation in Europe, 1924–1938." *Minerva* 24 (2): 205–22.

Dalen, Harry van, and Arjo Klamer. 1996. *Telgen van Tinbergen: Het Verhaal van de Nederlandse Economen*. Amsterdam: Balans.

Dekker, Erwin. 2019. "Parallel Lives: Jan Tinbergen and Ragnar Frisch." *Erasmus Journal for Philosophy and Economics* 12 (2): 65–85.

———. 2021. "Jan Tinbergen and the Construction of an International Economic Order." In *Political Economy and International Order in Interwar Europe*, edited by Alexandre Mendes de Cunha and Carlos Eduardo Suprinyak, 117–37. New York: Palgrave Macmillan.

Derksen, J. B. D. 1940. "Het Onderzoek van het Nationale Inkomen." *De Economist* 89: 571–94.

Desrosières, Alain. 2002. *The Politics of Large Numbers: A History of Statistical Reasoning.* Cambridge, MA: Harvard University Press.

Dimand, Robert W. 2005. "Fisher, Keynes, and the Corridor of Stability." *American Journal of Economics and Sociology* 64: 185–99.

Dimand, Robert W., and Bradley W. Bateman. 2016. "John Maynard Keynes Narrates the Great Depression: His Reports to the Philips Electronics Firm." Charles Gide Conference, Strassbourg.

Dimand, Robert W., and William Veloce. 2007. "Charles F. Roos, Harold T. Davis and the Quantitative Approach to Business Cycle Analysis at the Cowles Commission in the 1930s and Early 1940s." *The European Journal of the History of Economic Thought* 14: 519–42.

DIW Berlin. 2015. *Geschichte Deutsches Institut für Wirtschaftsforschung 1925–2015.* Berlin: DIW.

Dodge, Peter. 1979. *Hendrik de Man, Socialist Critic of Marxism.* Princeton, NJ: Princeton University Press.

Doel, J. C. van den. 1971. "Konvergentie en Evolutie: De Konvergentietheorie van Tinbergen en de Evolutie van Ekonomische Ordes in Oost en West." Dissertation, Nederlandse Economische Hogeschool.

Doel, J. C. van den, C. de Galan, and Jan Tinbergen. 1976. "Pleidooi voor een Geleide Loonpolitiek." *Economisch-Statistische Berichten* 61 (3044): 264–68.

Don, F. J. H. 2019. "The Influence of Jan Tinbergen on Dutch Economic Policy." *De Economist* 167 (3): 259–82.

Düppe, Till. 2016. "Koopmans in the Soviet Union: A Travel Report of the Summer of 1965." *Journal of the History of Economic Thought* 38 (1): 81–104.

Ehrenfest, Anna Galinka. 1972. "De Ooievaarsregeling (Contra Mina)." *Hollands Maandblad* 13 (298): 13–16.

Ehrenfest-Afanassjewa, Tatjana. 1924. *Wat Kan en Moet het Meetkunde-Onderwijs aan een Niet-Wiskundige Geven?* Groningen: Wolters.

1960. *Didactische Opstellen Wiskunde.* Zutphen: N. V. W. J. Thieme.

Ehrenfest-Afanassjewa, Tatjana, and Hans Freudenthal. 1951. *Kan het Wiskundeonderwijs tot Opvoeding van het Denkvermogen Bijdragen?* Purmerend: Muuses.

Ehrenfreund, Max. 2019. "The World Economy as Scientific Object, 1930–1939." HSS Meetings 2019 Utrecht. Harvard.

Ellman, Michael. 1980. "Against Convergence." *Cambridge Journal of Economics* 4: 199–210.

Emre, Yunus. 2014. *The Emergence of Social Democracy in Turkey: The Left and the Transformation of the Republican People's Party.* London: I. B. Tauris.

Ennerfelt, P. Göran. 1965. "Review of *Central Planning* by Jan Tinbergen." *The Swedish Journal of Economics* 67 (3): 258–60.

Eralp, Atila. 1994. "Turkey in Changing Postwar World Order Strategies of Development and Westernization." In *Developmentalism and Beyond: Society and Politics in Egypt and Turkey*, edited by Ayşe Öncü, Çağlar Keyder, and Saad Eddin Ibrahim, 204–29. Cairo: American University Press.

Erder, Necat. 2003. *Plânlı Kalkınma Serüveni: 1960'larda Türkiye'de Plânlama Deneyimi (Panel Discussion).* Istanbul: İstanbul Bilgi Üniversitesi Yayınları.

Erickson, Paul, Judy L. Klein, Lorraine Daston, Rebecca Lemov, Thomas Sturm, and Michael D. Gordin. 2015. *How Reason Almost Lost Its Mind: The Strange Career of Cold War Rationality.* Chicago: University of Chicago Press.

Eroğul, Cem. 1987. "The Establishment of Multiparty Rule: 1945–1971." In *Turkey in Transition*, edited by Irvin C. Schick and Ertuğrul Ahmet Tonak, 101–43. New York: Oxford University Press.

Eyffinger, Arthur, and Jan den Hengst. 1988. *Het Vredespaleis*. Amsterdam: Sijthoff.

Fleddérus, Mary L., and Mary van Kleeck. 1931. *World Social Economic Planning: The Necessity for Planned Adjustment of Productive Capacity and Standards of Living*. The Hague: International Industrial Relations Institute.

Frank, Andre Gunder. 1967. *Capitalism and Underdevelopment in Latin America*. New York: Monthly Review Press.

Frank, Leonhard. 1925. *De Burger*. Amsterdam: N. V. Ontwikkeling.

Friedman, Walter. 2013. *Fortune Tellers: The Story of America's First Economic Forecasters*. Princeton, NJ: Princeton University Press.

Frisch, Ragnar. 1931. "Plan eller Kaos." *Tidens Tegn*, November 1931.

———. 1932. *New Methods of Measuring Marginal Utility*. Tübingen: J. C. B. Mohr.

———. 1934. *Statistical Confluence Analysis by Means of Complete Regression Systems*. Oslo: Universitetets økonomiske Institut.

———. 1949. "Memorandum on Price-Wage-Tax Subsidy Policy as Instruments in Maintaining Optimal Employment." United Nations Sub-commission on Employment and Economic Stability, 18 April. New York. Reprinted at www.maggs.com/departments/modern_books_and_manuscripts/all_categories/234346/.

———. 1962. "Preface to the Oslo Channel Model." In *Europe's Future in Figures*, edited by R. C. Geary, 248–86. Amsterdam: North Holland.

———. 1995. "Autonomy of Economic Relations: Statistical versus Theoretical Relations in Economic Macrodynamics." In *The Foundations of Econometric Analysis*, edited by David F. Hendry and Mary S. Morgan, 407–19. Cambridge: Cambridge University Press.

Galbraith, John Kenneth. 1967. *The New Industrial State*. Boston: Houghton Mifflin.

Geertz, Clifford. 1969. "Myrdal's Mythology: 'Modernism' and the Third World." *Encounter* 33 (July): 26–34.

Ginneken, Jac van. 1917. *De Roman van een Kleuter*. Nijmegen: Malmberg.

Goedhart, Theo, Victor Halberstadt, Arie Kapteyn, and Bernard M. S. van Praag. 1977. "The Poverty Line: Concept and Measurement." *The Journal of Human Resources* 12: 503–20.

Goodwin, Crauford D. 2014. *Walter Lippmann: Public Economist*. Cambridge, MA: Harvard University Press.

Goudriaan, J. 1933. *Socialisme zonder Dogma's*. Haarlem: H. D. Tjeenk Willink & Zoon.

Group of Experts. 1960. *Programming Techniques for Economic Development with Special Reference to Asia and the Far East*. Bangkok: United Nations Economic Commission for Asia and the Far East.

Haberler, Gottfried. 1937. *Prosperity and Depression: A Theoretical Analysis of Cyclical Movements*. Geneva: League of Nations: Economic Intelligence Service.

Haberler, Gottfried, James E. Meade, Roberto Oliveira de Campos, and Jan Tinbergen. 1958. *Trends in International Trade*. Geneva: GATT.

Hagen, T. J. 1963. "Het Plan van een Grootmeester." *Paraat* 18: 311–12.

Hahn, Hans, Otto Neurath, and Rudolf Carnap. 1979. "Wissenschaftliche Weltauffassung: Der Wiener Kreis." In *Otto Neurath: Wissenschaftliche Weltauffassung, Sozialismus und logischer Empirismus*, edited by Rainer Hegelsmann, 79–101. Frankfurt am Main: Suhrkamp Verlag.

Hakker, W., and B. van Tijn. 1924. "Kentering." *Kentering* 1 (1): 1–5.

Hamburger, L. 1929. "Boekbespreking van J. Tinbergen's *Minimumproblemen in de Natuurkunde en de Economie*." *De Economist* 78: 623–25.

Hanau, Arthur. 1928. "Die Prognose der Schweinepreise." *Vierteljahreshefte zur Konjunkturforschung*, Sonderheft no. 7.

Hansen, Bent. 1969. "Jan Tinbergen: An Appraisal of His Contributions to Economics." *The Swedish Journal of Economics* 71 (4): 325–36.

Harrod, R. F. 1970. "Harrod after Twenty-One Years: A Comment." *The Economic Journal* 80 (319): 737–41.

Hart, Albert G., Nicholas Kaldor, and Jan Tinbergen. 1964. *The Case for an International Commodity Reserve Currency*. Geneva: United Nations Conference on Trade and Development.

Hartmans, Rob. 1991. "Van 'wetenschappelijk Socialisme' naar Wetenschap en Socialisme. De Ideologische Heroriëntering van de SDAP in de Jaren Dertig." In *Het Twaalfde Jaarboek voor het Democratisch Socialisme*, edited by Marnix Krop, Martin Ros, Saskia Stuiveling, and Bart Tromp, 17–46. Amsterdam: De Arbeiderspers.

Heckman, James J. 2019. "The Race between Demand and Supply: Tinbergen's Pioneering Studies of Earnings Inequality." *De Economist* 167.

Heering, G. J., P. D. Tjalsma, and A. L. de Heer-Cremer. 1948. *De Remonstrantste Broederschap: Wat zij is en Wat zij Wil*. Lochem: De Tijdstroom.

Hendry, David F., and Mary S. Morgan. 1995. *The Foundations of Econometric Analysis*. Cambridge: Cambridge University Press.

Hershlag, Zvi Yehuda. 1968. *Economic Planning in Turkey*. Istanbul: Economic Research Foundation.

Hirschman, Albert O. 2013. "The Rise and Decline of Development Economics." In *The Essential Hirschman*, edited by Jeremy Adelman, 49–73. Princeton, NJ: Princeton University Press.

Hollestelle, Marijn. 2011. *Paul Ehrenfest: Worstelingen met de Moderne Wetenschap, 1912–1933*. Leiden: Leiden University Press.

Hoover, Kevin D. 2004. "Lost Causes." *Journal of the History of Economic Thought* 26 (2): 149–64.

Horn, Gerd-Rainer. 1996. *European Socialists Respond to Fascism: Ideology, Activism and Contingency in the 1930s*. Oxford: Oxford University Press.

Hueting, Roefie. 1968. "Welvaartsparadoxen." *Economisch-Statistische Berichten* 53 (2636): 263–64.

Human Development Report Team. 2010. *Human Development Report 2010. The Real Wealth of Nations: Pathways to Human Development. Population and Development Review*. Vol. 21. New York: Palgrave Macmillan.

Jansen van Galen, John. 1985. "Doorbraak: Het Plan in de Herinnering van Tijdgenoten." In *Het Moet, het Kan! Op voor het Plan!*, 156–93. Amsterdam: Bert Bakker.

Johansen, Leif. 1974. "Establishing Preference Function for Macroeconomic Decision Models: Some Observations on Ragnar Frisch's Contributions." *European Economic Review* 5: 41–66.

Jolink, Albert, and Els Barendrecht-Tinbergen. 1993. *Gedeelde Herinneringen*. Rotterdam: Erasmus Universiteit Rotterdam.

Jong, A. H. M. de, C. W. A. M. van Paridon, and J. Passenier. 1988. "Jan Tinbergen over zijn Jaren op het CPB." *Economisch-Statistische Berichten* 73 (3664): 653–62.

Jong, Fr. de. 1961. "Naar een Socialistisch Plan." *Socialisme en Democratie* 18 (1): 3–12.

Jong, J. J. P. de. 1986. "De Nederlands-Indonesische Betrekkingen 1963–1985." *Internationale Spectator* 40 (2): 129–38.

Jong, Loe de. 1969. *Het Koninkrijk der Nederlanden in de Tweede Wereldoorlog 1939–1945, Deel 2: Neutraal*. 's-Gravenhage: Martinus Nijhoff.

Joor, Johan. 2013. "The Way of the Law above the Way of Violence." In *The Building of Peace: A Hundred Years of Work on Peace through Law*, edited by Bob Duynstee, Daan Meijer, and Floris Tilanus, 15–285. Den Haag: Carnegie Foundation.

Juliana, Hare Majesteit Koninging. 1955. *De Welvaart der Wereld als Gemeenschappelijke Verantwoordelijkheid*. Amsterdam: De Nederlandse Jeugd Gemeenschap.

Kamp, J. E. van. 2005. *Dien Hoetink: "Bij Benadering." Biografie van een Landbouw-Juriste in Crisis en Oorlogstijd*. Groningen: Nederlands Agronomisch Historisch Instituut.

Kansu, Günal. 2004. *Planli Yillar: Anilarla DPT'nin Öyküsü*. Istanbul: Türkiye Iş Bankasi.

Kayzel, Tom. 2019. "A Night Train in Broad Daylight: Changing Economic Expertise at the Dutch Central Planning Bureau 1945–1977." *Oeconomia* 9 (2): 337–70.

Kelley, Donald R. 1973. "The Soviet Debate on the Convergence of the American & Soviet Systems." *Polity* 6: 174–96.

Kesik, Ahmet. 2015. "Development Planning in Turkey: An Assessment." In *Economic Planning and Industrial Policy in the Globalizing Economy*, edited by Murat Yülek, 77–113. New York: Springer.

Keulen, Sjoerd J. 2014. *Monumenten van Beleid: De Wisselwerking tussen Nederlandse Rijksoverheid, Sociale Wetenschappen en Politieke Cultuur, 1945–2002*. Hilversum: Verloren.

Keuzenkamp, Hugo A. 1991. "A Precursor to Muth: Tinbergen's 1932 Model of Rational Expectations." *The Economic Journal* 101 (408): 1245–53.

Keyder, Çağlar. 1987. "Economic Development and Crisis: 1950–1980." In *Turkey in Transition*, edited by Irvin C. Schick and Ertuğrul Ahmet Tonak, 293–308. New York: Oxford University Press.

Keynes, John Maynard. 1920. *The Economic Consequences of the Peace*. New York: Harcourt, Brace & Howe.

1939. "Professor Tinbergen's Method." *The Economic Journal* 49 (195): 558–77.

1963. *Essays in Persuasion*. London: W. W. Norton.

Klein, Martin J. 1958. "Ehrenfest Comes to Leiden." *Delta* 5 (4): 5–14.

1981. "Not by Discoveries Alone: The Centennial of Paul Ehrenfest." *Physica A: Statistical Mechanics and Its Applications* 106 (1–2): 3–14.

1985. *Paul Ehrenfest: The Making of a Theoretical Physicist*. Amsterdam: North Holland.

1989. "Physics in the Making in Leiden: Paul Ehrenfest as Teacher." In *Physics in the Making: Essays on Developments in 20th Century Physics*, edited by A. Sarlemijn and M. J. Sparnaay, 29–44. Amsterdam: North Holland.

Klomp, H. A. 1997. *De Relativiteitstheorie in Nederland: Breekijzer voor Democratisering in het Interbellum*. Amsterdam: Epsilon.

Knegtmans, Peter Jan. 2008. "Voor Wetenschap en Maatschappij. Het Zelfbeeld van Studenten in de Sociaal-Democratische Studentenclubs." In *Keurige Wereldbestormers*, edited by L. J. Dorsman and Peter Jan Knegtmans, 39–52. Hilversum: Verloren.

Knight, Frank H. 1935. *The Ethics of Competition and Other Essays*. New York: Freeport.

1960. *Intelligence and Democratic Action*. Cambridge, MA: Harvard University Press.

Koopmans, J. G. 1932. "De Mogelijkheid van een Meervoudig Economisch Evenwicht I." *De Economist* 81: 679–702.

1932. "De Mogelijkheid van een Meervoudig Economisch Evenwicht II." *De Economist* 81: 766–85.

1932. "De Mogelijkheid van een Meervoudig Economisch Evenwicht III." *De Economist* 81: 841–56.

Koopmans, Tjalling C. 1937. *Linear Regression Analysis of Economic Time Series*. Haarlem: Bohn.

1947. "Measurement without Theory." *The Review of Economics and Statistics* 29 (3): 161–72.

Koopmans, Tjalling C., Jan Tinbergen, Nicholas Georgescu-Roegen, and Guy H. Orcutt. 1952. "Toward Partial Redirection of Econometrics: Comments." *The Review of Economics and Statistics* 34 (3): 200–213.

Koppl, Roger. 2002. *Big Players and the Economic Theory of Expectations*. New York: Palgrave Macmillan.

Kröger, Marianne. 1999. "Vervolging, Verbanning en het Nazi-Regime in het Tijdschrift 'Het Fundament.'" *Tijdschrift voor Tijdschriftstudies* 3 (5): 26–35.

Kruuk, Hans. 2003. *Niko's Nature*. Oxford: Oxford University Press.

Küçük, Y. 1967. "Sectoral Programming in the Plan." In *Planning in Turkey*, edited by S. Ilkin and E. Inanç, 96–113. Ankara: Faculty of Administrative Sciences.

196b. "The Macro-Model of the Plan." In *Planning in Turkey*, edited by S. Ilkin and E. Inanç, 78–95. Ankara: Faculty of Administrative Sciences.

Kuitenbrouwer, Maarten. 1994. *De Ontdekking van de Derde Wereld*. Den Haag: SDU Uitgevers.

Laqueur, Walter, and Leopold Labedz. 1962. *Polycentrism: The New Factor in International Communism*. New York: Frederick A. Praeger.

Lauterbach, Albert. 1976. "The 'Convergence' Controversy Revisited." *Kyklos* 29: 733–54.

League of Nations. 1943. *The Transition from War to Peace Economy*. Geneva: League of Nations.

1945. *Economic Stability in the Post-war World*. Geneva: League of Nations.

Leibenstein, Harvey. 1966. "Review of *Shaping the World Economy* by Jan Tinbergen." *The Economic Journal* 76 (301): 92–95.

Leijonhufvud, Axel. 1967. "Keynes and the Keynesians: A Suggested Interpretation." *The American Economic Review* 57 (2): 401–10.

Leonard, Thomas C. 2003. "'More Merciful and Not Less Effective': Eugenics and American Economics in the Progressive Era." *History of Political Economy* 35 (4): 687–712.

———. 2016. *Illiberal Reformers: Race, Eugenics and American Economics in the Progressive Era*. Princeton, NJ: Princeton University Press.

Levy, David M. 2002. *How the Dismal Science Got Its Name: Classical Economics and the Ur-Text of Racial Politics*. Ann Arbor, MI: University of Michigan Press.

Lieftinck, Pieter, Adri Bakker, and M. M. P. van Lent. 1989. *Pieter Lieftinck, 1902–1989: Een Leven in Vogelvlucht*. Utrecht: Veen.

Lijphart, Arend. 1968. *The Politics of Accommodation: Pluralism and Democracy. in the Netherlands*. Berkeley, CA: University of California Press.

Linneman, Hans. 1966. *An Econometric Study of International Trade Flows*. Amsterdam: North Holland.

Louçã, Francisco. 1999. "The Econometric Challenge to Keynes: Arguments and Contradictions in the Early Debates about a Late Issue." *The European Journal of the History of Economic Thought* 6 (3): 404–38.

———. 2007. *The Years of High Econometrics: A Short History of the Generation That Reinvented Economics*. New York: Routledge.

Louw, Andre Van der. 1974. *Rood als je Hart: Geschiedenis van de AJC*. Amsterdam: Arbeiderspers.

Lucas, Robert E. 1976. "Econometric Policy Evaluation: A Critique." *Carnegie-Rochester Conference Series on Public Policy* 1 (1): 19–46.

Lunteren, Frans H. van. 2006. "Wissenschaft internationalisieren: Hendrik Antoon Lorentz, Paul Ehrenfest und ihre Arbeit für die internationale Wissenschafts-Community." In *Einstein und Europa – Dimensionen moderner Forschung*, edited by A. Claussen, 25–35. Düsseldorf: Wissenschaftszentrum NRW.

Lunteren, Frans H. van, and Marijn J. Hollestelle. 2013. "Paul Ehrenfest and the Dilemmas of Modernity." *Isis* 104: 504–36.

Luytelaer, Th. van, and Jan Tinbergen. 1932. "De Koffievalorisaties: Geschiedenis en Resultaten." *De Economist* 81: 517–38.

Maarseveen, J. G. S. J. van, and R. Schreijnders. 1999. *Welgeteld Een Eeuw*. Zeist: CBS/IISG.

Maas, Harro. 2005. *William Stanley Jevons and the Making of Modern Economics*. Historical Perspectives on Modern Economics. Cambridge: Cambridge University Press.

———. 2014. *Economic Methodology: A Historical Introduction*. London: Routledge.

Magnus, Jan R., and Mary S. Morgan. 1987. "The ET Interview: Professor J. Tinbergen." *Econometric Theory* 3: 117–42.

Maier, Charles S. 1970. "Between Taylorism and Technocracy: European Ideologies and the Vision of Industrial Productivity in the 1920s." *Journal of Contemporary History* 5 (2): 27–61.

Malinvaud, Edmond. 2007. "About the Role, in Older Days, of Econometrics in Quantitative Economics." *The European Journal of the History of Economic Thought* 14 (3): 423–48.

Man, Hendrik de. 1927. *Die Kampf um die Arbeitsfreude*. Jena: Eugen Diederichs.

———. 1927. *Zur Pscyhologie des Sozialismus*. Jena: Eugen Diederichs.

———. 1932. *Massen und Führer*. Potsdam: Protte.

1934. *Voor een Plan van Actie*. Amsterdam: Contact.

Marchi, Neil De. 1991. "League of Nations Economists and the Ideal of Peaceful Change in the Decade of the Thirties." In *Economics and National Security*, edited by Crauford D. Goodwin, 143–78. Durham, NC: Duke University Press.

2016. "Models and Misperceptions: Chenery, Hirschman and Tinbergen on Development Planning." *Research in the History and Methodology of Economic Thought* 34B: 91–99.

Mazower, Mark. 2012. *Governing the World: The History of an Idea, 1815 to the Present*. New York: Penguin Books.

Meade, James E. 1940. *The Economic Basis of a Durable Peace*. London: George Allen & Unwin.

Meadows, Donella H. 1972. *The Limits to Growth: A Report for the Club of Rome's Project on the Predicament of Mankind*. New York: Universe Books.

Meier, Gerald M. 1984. *Pioneers of Development*. Oxford: Oxford University Press.

Merton, Robert K. 1936. "The Unanticipated Consequences of Purposive Social Action." *American Sociological Review* 1 (6): 894–904.

Meyer, Alfred G. 1970. "Theories of Convergence." In *Change in Communist Systems*, edited by Chalmers Johnson, 313–41. Stanford, CA: Stanford University Press.

Mıhçıoğlu, Cemal. 1983. "Devlet Planlama Örgütünün Kuruluş Günleri." In *Prof. Dr. Fadıl H. Sur'un Anısına Armağan*, 229–57. Ankara: Ankara Üniversitesi Siyasal Bilgiler Fakültesi Yayınları.

1988. "Yi ne Devlet Planlama Örgütünün Kuruluşu Üzeri ne." *Ankara Üniversitesi SBF Dergisi* 43 (1): 113–46.

Milor, Vedat. 1990. "The Genesis of Planning in Turkey." *New Perspectives on Turkey* 4: 1–30.

Mintzel, Alf. 1983. *Die Volkspartei: Typus und Wirklichkeit*. Wiesbaden: Springer Fachmedien.

Mitchell, Timothy. 2002. *Rule of Experts: Egypt, Techno-Politics, Modernity*. Los Angeles, CA: University of California Press.

Mizen, Paul, Don Moggridge, and John Presley. 1998. "The Papers of Dennis Robertson: The Discovery of Unexpected Riches." *History of Political Economy* 29 (4): 573–82.

Mok, R. J. M. 1999. "In de Ban van het Ras. Aardrijkskunde tussen Wetenschap en Samenleving 1876–1992." University of Amsterdam. http://dare.uva.nl/document/2/34891.

Mok, S. 1927. "Slechte Voorlichting." *Kentering* 4 (2): 27–29.

Morgan, Mary S. 1990. *History of Econometric Ideas*. Cambridge: Cambridge University Press.

1991. "The Stamping out of Process Analysis in Econometrics." In *Appraising Economic Theories: Studies in the Methodology of Research Programs*, edited by Neil de Marchi and Mark Blaug, 237–63. Brookfield: Aldershot.

2012. *The World in a Model: How Economists Work and Think*. Cambridge: Cambridge University Press.

Morgenstern, Oskar. 1928. *Wirtschaftsprognose: Eine Untersuchung ihrer Voraussetzungen und Möglichkeiten*. Wien: Julius Fischer Verlag.

1935. "Vollkommene Voraussicht und wirtschaftliches Gleichgewicht." *Zeitschrift für Nationalökonomie* 6 (3): 337–57.

Moscati, Ivan. 2018. *Measuring Utility: From the Marginal Revolution to Behavioral Economics*. Oxford: Oxford University Press.

Mrijen, Anne-Marie. 2015. *De Rode Jonker: De Eeuw van Marinus van Goes van Naters (1900–2005)*. Amsterdam: Boom.

Myrdal, Gunnar. 1968. *Asian Drama: An Inquiry into the Poverty of Nations*. New York: Twentieth Century Fund.

Nagel, Thomas. 1986. *The View from Nowhere*. Oxford: Oxford University Press.

Nederhorst, G. 1936. "Vooruitzichten der Internationale Productie Ordening." *Fundament* 3 (12): 30–46.

Nederlandse Volksbeweging. 1945. *Program en Toelichting van de Nederlandse Volksbeweging*. Amsterdam: Anderson.

Nehru, Jawaharlal. 1952. "Address." In *International Statistical Conferences: December 1951 India*, 12–18. Calcutta: EKA Press.

Neisser, Hans. 1931. "Der Gegensatz von 'anschaulich' und 'rational' in der Geschichte der Volkswirtschaftslehre." *Archiv für Sozialwissenschaften und Sozialpolitik* 65 (2): 225–50.

Nekkers, Jan. 1985a. "Een Ingenieur in de Politiek: Hein Vos. En het Plan van de Arbeid." In *Het Moet, het Kan! Op voor het Plan!*, edited by John Jansen van Galen, Jan Nekkers, Dick Pels, and Jan P. Pronk, 101–23. Amsterdam: Bert Bakker.

        1985b. "Sentiment en Program." In *Het Moet, het Kan! Op voor het Plan!*, edited by John Jansen van Galen, Jan Nekkers, Dick Pels, and Jan P. Pronk, 11–100. Amsterdam: Bert Bakker.

Netherlands Economic Institute, Division of Balanced International Growth. 1957. "Economic Development, Transportation and the National Income Test." Rotterdam: Netherlands Economics Institute.

Neurath, Otto. 1935. *Was bedeutet rationale Wirtschaftsbetrachtung*. Wien: Gerold.

Noble, David F. 1977. *America by Design: Science, Technology and the Rise of Corporate Capitalism*. Oxford: Oxford University Press.

Noordergraaf, Herman. 1994. *Niet met de Wapenen der Barbaren: Het Christen-Socialisme van Bart de Ligt*. Baarn: Ten Haave.

Noordman, Jan. 1989. *Om de Kwaliteit van het Nageslacht: Eugenetica in Nederland 1900–1950*. Nijmegen: Sun.

NOVIB. 1958. *Nederlandse Organisatie voor Internationale Bijstand*. Den Haag: NOVIB.

        1961. *1% Aktie: Daadwerkelijke Gerechtigheid*. Den Haag: NOVIB.

Oomens, C. A. 1985. "De Ontwikkeling van de Nationale Rekeningen in Nederland." In *Voor Praktijk of Wetenschap*, edited by W. Begeer, C. A. Oomens, and W. F. M. De Vries, 23–46. Den Haag: Centraal Bureau voor de Statistiek.

Orcutt, Guy H. 1952. "Toward the Partial Redirection of Econometrics." *The Review of Economics and Statistics* 34 (3): 195–200.

Övgün, Barış. 2009. *Türkiye'de Kamu İktisadi Teşebbüsü Olgusu*. Ankara: Mülkiyeliler Birliği Vakıf Yayınları.

Passenier, Jacques. 1994. *Van Planning naar Scanning: Een Halve Eeuw Planbureau in Nederland*. Groningen: Wolters-Noordhoff.

Patinkin, Don. 1976. "Keynes and Econometrics: On the Interaction between the Macroeconomic Revolutions of the Interwar Period." *Econometrica* 44 (6): 1091–1123.

Pauly, Louis W. 1996. *The League of Nations and the Foreshadowing of the International Monetary Fund*. Princeton, NJ: Princeton University Press.

Pels, Dick. 1985. "Hendrik de Man en de Ideologie van het Planisme." In *Het Moet, het Kan! Op voor het Plan!*, edited by John Jansen van Galen, Jan Nekkers, Dick Pels, and Jan P. Pronk, 124–55. Amsterdam: Bert Bakker.

Pen, Jan. 1988. "Tussen Elitisme En Egalitarisme." In *Distantie En Engagement*, edited by Gerard Alberts and P. Weeder, 55–64. Eindhoven: Technische Universiteit Eindhoven.

2006. *Vandaag Staat Niet Alleen: Essays and Memoires*. Amsterdam: Nieuwe Amsterdam.

Pen, Jan, and Jan Tinbergen. 1977. *Naar een Rechtvaardiger Inkomensverdeling*. Amsterdam: Elsevier.

Peski, Adriaan M. van. 1969. *Hendrik de Man*. Brugge: Desclée de Brouwer.

Peski-Tinbergen, Tineke van, and Adriaan M. van Peski. 1958. "Communistische Opvoeding en Gedachtenvorming bij de Jeugd in de D.D.R." *Wending* 13 (3): 149–172.

Pleingroep. 1958. "Verklaring." *Plein* 5 (July): 2–3.

Polak, Fred L. 1948. "De Problematiek der Welvaartsplanning en haar Ontwikkeling in de Buitenlandse Litteratuur." *De Economist* 96 (1): 161–92.

Polak, Jacques J. 1937. "Publieke Werken als Vorm van Conjunctuurpolitiek." Dissertation, University of Amsterdam.

1939. "International Propagation of Business Cycles." *The Review of Economic Studies* 6 (2): 79–99.

1954. *An International Economic System*. London: George Allen & Unwin.

1997. "The Contribution of the International Monetary Fund." *History of Political Economy* 28 (Annual Supplement): 211–24.

Praag, Bernard M. S. van, and Ada Ferrer-i-Carbonell. 2004. *Happiness Quantified: A Satisfaction Calculus Approach*. Oxford: Oxford University Press.

Pronk, Jan P. 2019. "Tinbergen, Idealist and Inspirer." Tinbergen Today. 2019. www .janpronk.nl/essays/english-and-german/tinbergen-idealist-and-inspirer-by-jan-pronk-article.html.

Prybyla, Jan S. 1964. "The Convergence of Western and Communist Economic Systems: A Critical Estimate." *The Russian Review* 23 (1): 3–17.

Publikaties van de Stadsbibliotheek en het Archief en Museum voor het Vlaamse Cultuurleven. 1985. *Hendrik de Man: Een Portret, 1885–1953*. Antwerpen: Archief en Museum voor het Vlaamse Cultuurleven.

Puttaswamaiah, K. 1996. *Tinbergen and Modern Economics: The Noble Economist Saint*. New Delhi: Indus Publishing.

Reinders, J. S. 1987. "Macht in Dienst van Recht. Gereformeerden over Oorlog en Vrede in de Periode 1918–1940." In *Een Land nog Niet in Kaart Gebracht*, 241–58. Amsterdam: J. de Bruijn.

Reindersma, W., and Teunis van Lohuizen. 1930. *Nieuw Leerboek der Natuurkunde: Voor Hoogere Burgerscholen met 5-Jarigen Cursus, Lycea en Gymnasia*. Groningen: Wolters.

Robbins, Lionel R. 1932. *An Essay on the Nature and Significance of Economic Science*. Macmillan.

Rodenburg, Peter. 2010. "The Goudriaan–Tinbergen Debate on Dynamics and Equilibrium: 1931–1952." http://dx.doi.org/10.2139/ssrn.1615458.

Roelofsen, C. G. 1995. "Jan Hendrik Willem Verzijl." In *The Moulding of International Law: Ten Dutch Proponents*, edited by Gerard J. Tanja, 335–66. The Hague: Asser Instituut.

Roos, Charles Frederick. 1948. *Charting the Course of Your Business: Measuring the Effects of External Influences*. New York: Funk & Wagnalls.

Röpke, Wilhelm. 1950. *The Social Crisis of Our Time*. Chicago: University of Chicago Press.

Rugina, Anghel N. 1988. "The Unending Search for Universal and Lasting Peace, from Leon Walras to Jan Tinbergen and Beyond." *Review of Social Economy* 46 (3): 283–306.

Ruijter, A. de. 1946. "Inleidingen op ons Congres." *De Vakbeweging* 2 (25): 2.

Salin, Edgar. 1923. *Geschichte der Volkswirtschaftslehre*. Berlin: Springer.

1950. "Walter Eucken: In Memoriam." *Kyklos* 4: 1–4.

Samuelson, Paul A. 2004. "Homage to Jan Tinbergen." *De Economist* 152 (2): 152–53.

Sarlemijn, Andries. 1987. "Konvergenz in Bezug auf Planung der Forschung?" In *Wissenschaftsforschung Im Internationalen Vergleich*, edited by Clemens Burrichter and G. Lauterbach, 227–81. Nuernberg: Erlangen.

Scheall, Scott, and Reinhard Schumacher. 2018. "Karl Menger as Son of Carl Menger." *History of Political Economy* 50: 649–78.

Schenk, M. G., and Magdaleen Van Herk. 1980. *Juliana: Vorstin naast de Rode Loper*. Amsterdam: De Boekerij.

Schils, René. 2012. "Hendrik Antoon Lorentz." In *How James Watt Invented the Copier: Forgotten Inventions of Our Great Scientists*, 95–101. New York: Springer New York.

Schmoller, Gustav. 1897. "Wechselnde Theorien und feststehende Wahrheiten im Gebiete der Staats- und Socialwissenschaften und die heutige Deutsche Volkswirtschaftslehre." *Jahrbuch für Gesetzgebung, Verwaltung und Volkswirtschaft im Deutschen Reich* 21 (4): 243–64.

Schöll, Guus van. 1981. *Dienstweigering in Nederland voor de Tweede Wereldoorlog*. Zwolle: Stichting Voorlichting Aktieve Geweldloosheid.

Schumpeter, Joseph A. 1926. "Gustav v. Schmoller und die Probleme von Heute." *Schmollers Jahrbuch* 50 (3): 337–88.

1949. "Science and Ideology." *The American Economic Review* 39 (2): 346–59.

Scott, James C. 1998. *Seeing like a State: How Certain Schemes to Improve the Human Condition Have Failed*. New Haven, CT: Yale University Press.

SDAP. 1931. "Nieuwe Organen." Amsterdam.

Sent, Esther-Mirjam, and Eric Bartelsman. 2019. *Conversations between Nobel Laureates and Policymakers*. Den Haag: KVS.

Shapin, Steven. 2008. *The Scientific Life: A Moral History of a Late Modern Vocation*. Chicago: University of Chicago Press.

Simon, Herbert A. 1976. "From Substantive to Procedural Rationality." In *25 Years of Economic Theory*, edited by T. J. Kastelein, Simon K. Kuipers, W. A. Nijenhuis, and R. G. Wagenaar, 65–86. Boston: Springer.

Singer, H. W. 1949. "Economic Progress in Underdeveloped Countries." *Social Research* 16 (1): 1–11.

Slobodian, Quinn. 2018. *Globalists: The End of Empire and the Birth of Neoliberalism*. Cambridge, MA: Harvard University Press.

Sluga, Glenda. 2013. *Internationalism in the Age of Nationalism*. Philadelphia: University of Pennsylvania Press.

Sluyser, M. 1934. *Planmatige Socialistische Politiek*. Amsterdam: De Arbeiderspers.

Sociaal-Economische Raad. 1953. *Advies inzake het Vraagstuk van de Huren*. Den Haag: Sociaal-Economische Raad.

Sombart, Werner. 1930. *Die Drei Nationalökonomien*. Munich: Duncker & Humblot.

Somsen, Geert. 2001. "Waardevolle Wetenschap. Bespiegelingen over Natuurwetenschap, Moraal en Samenleving in de Aanloop naar de Doorbraakbeweging." *Gewina* 24: 207–24.

Sönmez, A. 1967. "The Re-Emergence of the Idea of Planning and the Scope and Targets of the 1963–1967 Plan." In *Planning in Turkey*, edited by S. Ilkin and E. Inanç, 28–43. Ankara: Faculty of Administrative Sciences.

Staatscommissie Bevolkingsvraagstuk Muntendam. 1976. "Bevolking en Welzijn in Nederland." 's-Gravenhage.

Steenkamp, P. J. A. M. 1978. "Gespreide Verantwoordelijk. Een Christen-Democratische Bijdrage aan de Discussie over de Economische Orde." Den Haag. https://d2vry01uvf8h31.cloudfront.net/Organisaties/WI/1978%20-%20Gespreide%20ver antwoordelijkheid%20deel%201.pdf.

Sterk, H. 1937. "Van Jeugdbeweging naar Socialisme." *Het Fundament* 4 (11): 1–12.

Steur, J. A. G. van der. 1914. *Beschrijving, behoorende bij het Vredespaleis*. Rotterdam: Nijgh & Van Ditmar.

Stichting van den Arbeid. 1952. *Werkclassificatie als Hulpmiddel bij de Loonpolitiek*. 's-Gravenhage: Stichting van den Arbeid.

Stokvis, J.E. 1930. "Na Utrecht." *De Socialistische Gids* 15 (3): 198–205.

Sur, Fadil H. 1983. *Prof. Dr. Fadıl H. Sur'un Anısına Armağan*. Ankara: A. Ü. S. B. F. ve Basın-Yayın Yüksek Okulu Basımevi.

Svorenčík, Andrej. 2015. "The Experimental Turn in Economics: A History of Experimental Economics." PhD dissertation, University of Amsterdam. https://papers.ssrn.com/sol3/papers.cfm?abstract_id=2560026.

Terhal, Piet. 2015. *Wegen naar een Menswaardige Toekomst*. Soesterberg: Aspekt.

Tinbergen, Dirk Cornelis. 1919. "Kinderpraat." *De Nieuwe Taalgids* 13: 1–16, 65–86.

Tinbergen, Jan. 1924. "Verstand of Gevoel?" *Kentering* 1: 24–25.

1925. "Buitenland. Zweden." *Kentering* 1: 7–8.

1925. "Faze- en Energieverandering van een Slinger en een Snaar gedurende hun Brown'se Beweging." *Physica: Nederlandsch Tijdschrift voor Natuurkunde* 5 (11–12): 361–63.

1925. "Opmerkingen over de Arbeidswaardeleer." *Kentering* 2 (2): 25–28.

1925. "Wiskunde – Grenswaarde – Marx." *Kentering* 1 (5): 65–68.

1925. "Het Leven van Werklozen: Onze Plicht." *Het Volk*, 28 November.

1925. "Het Leven van Werklozen: Gruwelike Armoe." *Het Volk*, 8 December.

1925. "Het Leven van Werklozen: De 'Zegen' van een Groot Gezin." *Het Volk*, 17 December.

1925. "Het Leven van Werklozen: Van een die Rust Nodig heeft." *Het Volk*, 24 December.

1926. "Boekbespreking van H. Ford's *Productie en Welvaart*." *Kentering* 2 (3): 45–47.

1926. "Boekbespreking van R. Hilferding's *Das Finanzkapital*." *Kentering* 2 (7): 83–85.

1926. "Boekbespreking van L. Frank's *De Burger.*" *Kentering* 2 (4): 92–93.

1926. "Uit een Andere Wereld." *Kentering* 2 (4): 57–58.

1926. "Wat we Doen Moeten." *Kentering* 2 (8): 117–19.

1926. "Het Leven van Werklozen: 'De Luxe S.D.A.P.-er te Zijn.'" *Het Volk*, 7 January.

1926. "Het Leven van Werklozen: Schande!" *Het Volk*, 15 January.

1926. "Het Leven van Werklozen: Een 'Gewoon' Geval." *Het Volk*, 12 February.

1927. "Gewonnen." *Het Jonge Volk* 14 (26).

1927. "Over de Mathematies-Statistiese Methoden voor Konjunktuuronderzoek." *De Economist* 76: 711–23.

1927. "Wetenschappelijk Sosialisties Werk." *Kentering* 4 (1): 5–9.

1927. "Tewerkstelling-Premie." *Het Volk*, 15 July.

1927. "Werkloosheidsproblemen." *Het Volk*, 22 August.

1928. "A.J.C.-er en Student." *Het Jonge Volk* 15: 76.

1928. "In der Steden Donk're Stegen is een Lichte Roep Ontwaakt …" *Het Jonge Volk* 15 (6): 99.

1928. "Macht en Ekonomiese Wet." *Kentering* 4 (4): 57–60.

1928. "Opmerkingen over Ruiltheorie." *De Socialistische Gids* 13 (5–6): 431–45, 539–48.

1928. "Opmerkingen over Ruiltheorie II." *De Socialistische Gids* 13 (6): 539–48.

1928. "Werktijdverkorting een Middel tegen Werkloosheid." *Het Volk*, 15 September.

1928. "Eenmanswagens." *Het Volk*, 18 October.

1929. "Boekbespreking van O. Morgenstern's *Wirtschaftsprognose.*" *De Economist* 78: 141–43.

1929. "Konjunkturforschung und Variationsrechnung." *Archiv für Sozialwissenschaften und Sozialpolitik* 61 (3): 533–41.

1929. "Minimumproblemen in de Natuurkunde en de Ekonomie." Dissertation, University of Leiden.

1929. "Vraagstukken van Socialistiese Ekonomie." *De Socialistische Gids* 14 (6): 528–40.

1930. "Bestimmung und Deutung von Angebotskurven: Ein Beispiel." *Zeitschrift für Nationalökonomie* 1 (5): 669–79.

1930. "De Werkloosheid." *De Socialistische Gids* 15 (12): 817–23.

1930. "Mathematiese Psychologie." *Mensch en Maatschappij* 6: 342–52.

1930. "Review of R. Wedemeyer's *Konjunkturverslechterung durch Lohnerhöhungen.*" *Zeitschrift für Nationalökonomie* 1: 481–85.

1930e. "Socialisten en Hoge Inkomens." *Het Volk*, 20 May.

1930. "Socialisten en Hoge Inkomens: Een Antwoord." *Het Volk*, 28 July.

1930. "Vóór-Marxistisch?" *Het Volk*, 25 August.

1931. "De Landbouwkrisis: Praeadvies Uitgebracht voor de Socialistiese Vereniging ter Bevordering van de Studie van Maatschappelike Vraagstukken." *De Socialistische Gids* 16 (4–5): 300–13, 384–93.

1931. "Ein Schiffbauzyklus?" *Weltwirtschaftliches Archiv* 34: 152–64.

1931. "Oorzaken en Bestrijding der Werkloosheid." *De Socialistische Gids* 16 (3): 169–80.

1931. "Review of J. Marschak's *Die Lohndiskussion.*" *Zeitschrift für Nationalökonomie* 2: 820.

1932. "Ein Problem der Dynamik." *Zeitschrift für Nationalökonomie* 3 (2): 169–84.

1932. "In Hoeverre kan het Regelen van den Omvang der Voortbrenging of van het Aanbod van Bepaalde Goederen door Producenten, al dan Niet met Medewerking van de Overheid, Bevorderlijk worden Geacht voor de Volkswelvaart?" In *Prae-Adviezen voor de Vereeniging voor de Staatshuishoudkunde en de Statistiek*, 48–78.

1932. "Is het Einde van de Crisis in Zicht?" *De Sociaal-Democraat* 10 (September): 2.

1932. "Kapitaalvorming en Conjunctuur in Nederland 1880–1930." *De Nederlandsche Conjunctuur* 3 (1): 8–16.

1932. "Prijsvorming op de Aandelenmarkt." *De Nederlandsche Conjunctuur* 3 (3): 12–23.

1932. "Review of A. Ammon's *Das Lohnproblem*." *Zeitschrift für Nationalökonomie* 3: 123–24.

1933. "De Invloed van de Werkloosheid op het Loonpeil." *De Nederlandsche Conjunctuur* 4 (2): 10–13.

1933. *De Konjunktuur*. Amsterdam: Arbeiderspers.

1933. "L'Utilisation des Équations fonctionnelles et des Nombres complexes dans les Recherches économiques." *Econometrica* 1 (1): 36–51.

1933. *Statistiek en Wiskunde in Dienst van het Konjunktuuronderzoek*. Amsterdam: Arbeiderspers.

1933. "The Notions of Horizon and Expectancy in Dynamic Economics." *Econometrica* 1 (3): 247–64.

1934. "De Politiek van Roosevelt." *Kentering* 9 (7): 99–100.

1934. "Der Einfluß der Kaufkraftregulierung auf den Konjunkturverlauf." *Zeitschrift für Nationalökonomie* 5 (3): 289–319.

1934. *Praeadvies Nationale Vereeniging tegen de Werkloosheid: Is te Verwachten dat de Maatregelen van President Roosevelt zullen Bijdragen, en zo Ja in welke Mate, tot een Blijvende Vermindering der Werkloosheid in de Verenigde Staten van Noord-Amerika*.

1935. "Annual Survey: Suggestions on Quantitative Business Cycle Theory." *Econometrica* 3 (3): 241–308.

1935. "De Economische Zijde van het Ordeningsvraagstuk." In *Ordening*, 17–29. Delft: Delftsch Hogeschoolfonds.

1935. "De Politiek van Roosevelt." *De Socialistische Gids* 20 (2): 87–97.

1935. "Desiderata op het Punt van de Conjunctuurstatistiek." *Economisch-Statistische Berichten* 20 (1000): 199.

1935. "La Politique des Salaires, les Cycles économiques et les mathématiques." *Revue des Sciences économiques* 9 (1): 17–29.

1935. "Ordening: Een Arbeidersbelang." *De Groene Amsterdammer*, no. 3012: 4.

1936. "Conjunctuurpolitiek en Prijsstabilisatie." *De Economist* 85: 443–56.

1936. "De Conjunctuurpolitiek in Zweden." *Hollandsche Revue* 41 (8): 351–53.

1936. "De Positie van het Plan van de Arbeid." *Fundament* 3 (5): 3–6.

1936. "Fascistische Economie." *Anti-Fascistische Stemmen* 1 (2): 2–3.

1936. "Kan hier te Lande, al dan Niet na Overheidsingrijpen, een Verbetering van de Binnenlandse Conjunctuur Intreden, ook zonder Verbetering van onze Exportpositie?" In *Prae-Adviezen voor de Vereeniging voor de Staatshuishoudkunde en de Statistiek*, 62–108. Den Haag: Nijhoff.

1936. "Review of Otto Neurath's *Was Bedeutet Rationale Wirtschaftsbetragtung.*" *Erkenntnis* 7: 70–71.

1936. "Sur la Détermination statistique de la Position d'équilibre cyclique." *Revue de l'Institut international de Statistique* 4 (2): 173–88.

1937. "Review of R. F. Harrod's *The Trade Cycle.*" *Weltwirtschaftliches Archiv* 51: 89–91.

1939. *Statistical Testing of Business Cycle Theories: I. A Method and Its Application to Investment Activity.* Geneva: League of Nations Economic Intelligence Service.

1939. *Statistical Testing of Business-Cycle Theories: II. Business Cycles in the United States. of America 1919–1932.* Geneva: League of Nations Economic Intelligence Service.

1940. "Enkele Cijfers en Beschouwingen over de Algemeene Aspecten der Financieele Politiek." *Economisch-Statistische Berichten* 25 (1262): 174–76.

1940. "On a Method of Statistical Business-Cycle Research. A Comment." *The Economic Journal* 50 (197): 154–56.

1941. "Indifferente en Labiele Evenwichten in Economische Stelsels." *De Economist* 90: 561–84.

1941. *Technische Ontwikkeling en Werkgelegenheid.* Amsterdam: N. V. Noord-Hollandsche Uitgevers Maatschappij.

1942. "Critical Remarks on Some Business-Cycle Theories." *Econometrica* 10: 129–46.

1942. *Is Nederland Overbevolkt?* Leiden: Stenfert Kroese.

1942. "Professor Douglas' Production Function." *Revue de l'Institut international de Statistique* 10: 37–48.

1942. "Zur Theorie der langfristigen Wirtschaftsentwicklung." *Weltwirtschaftliches Archiv* 55: 511–49.

1943. *Economische Bewegingsleer.* Amsterdam: N. V. Noord-Hollandsche Uitgevers Maatschappij.

1943. "Over Verschillende Soorten Evenwicht en de Conjunctuurbeweging." *De Economist* 92 (1943): 129–47.

1944. "Colin Clark's 'Economics of 1960.'" *Revue de l'Institut international de Statistique* 12: 1–4.

1944. *De Les van Dertig Jaar: Economische Ervaringen en Mogelijkheden.* Amsterdam: Elsevier.

1944. "Wagemann's 'Alternatiewet.'" *Economisch-Statistische Berichten* 29 (1443): 86–87.

1945. *Enkele Problemen van Centrale Planning.* 's-Gravenhage: Nederlandsch Instituut voor Efficiency.

1945. *International Economic Co-operation.* Amsterdam: Elsevier.

1946. *Beperkte Concurrentie.* Leiden: H. E. Stenfert Kroese.

1946. *Conjunctuurpolitiek.* Amsterdam: Noord-Hollandse Uitgevers Maatschappij.

1946. "De Derde Weg." *Socialisme en Democratie* 3: 369–72.

1946. "De Plaats van den Econoom in de Maatschappij." *Wording* 2: 189–91.

1946. "Herstelbetalingen." In *Bouwstof voor de Oplossing van Na-Oorlogsche Vraagstukken*, 44–53. Den Haag: Martinus Nijhoff.

1946. "Het Nederlandsche Welvaartplan." *De Ingenieur* 58 (31): A297–A305.

1946. "Nederland in de Twintigste Eeuw." In *Hecht Verbonden in Lief en Leed*, 1–44. Amsterdam: Elsevier.

1946. "Some Measurements of Elasticities of Substitution." *The Review of Economics and Statistics* 28 (3): 109–16.

1946. "Unstable Equilibria in the Balance of Payments." In *Economic Research and the Development of Economic Science and Public Policy*, 133–42. New York: NBER.

1947. "Deense Problemen." *Economisch-Statistische Berichten* 32 (1564): 352–53.

1947. "Dollarschaarste en Prijsaanpassing." *Economisch-Statistische Berichten* 32 (1588): 816.

1947. "Gesteld, dat men Tezijnertijd het Huidige Systeem van Geleide Economie weer Geheel of Gedeeltelijk door een Stelsel van Vrije Economie zal Willen Vervangen, welke Voorwaarden moeten dan zijn Vervuld en welke Maatregelen zullen daartoe moeten worden Genomen." In *Prae-Adviezen voor de Vereeniging voor de Staatshuishoudkunde en de Statistiek*, 101–19. 's-Gravenhage: Martinus Nijhoff.

1947. "Problems of Central Economic Planning in the Netherlands." *Nationaløkonomisk Tidsskrift* 85: 96–104.

1947. "Review of C. Clark's *Economics of 1960*." *Erasmus Speculum Scientiarum* 1 (1): 54.

1947. "The Significance of Keynes' Theories from the Econometric Point of View." In *The New Economics: Keynes' Influence on Theory and Public Policy*, edited by Seymour E. Harris, 208–18. New York: Alfred A Knopf.

1948. "Kern van Industrialisatie dient te Berusten bij Ondernemers." *Trouw*, December 9, 1948.

1949. *De Grenzen der Ordening*. Voorburg: Comité ter Bestudering van Ordeningsvraagstukken.

1949. *Government Budget and Central Economic Plan*. Reprinted by CPB. The Hague: Centraal Planbureau.

1949. "Het Nederlandsch Economisch Instituut in 1949." *Economisch-Statistische Berichten* 34 (1680): 576–77.

1949. "Long-Term Foreign Trade Elasticities." *Metroeconomica* 1: 174–85.

1949. "Some Remarks on the Problem of Dollar Scarcity." *Econometrica* 17 (Supplement): 73–97.

1949. "Welke Mogelijkheden en Middelen Bestaan er tot het in Evenwicht Brengen van de Betalingsbalans van Nederland na Afloop van de Marshall-Hulp onder Gelijktijdig Streven naar een Overwegend Vrijer Internationaal Handels- en Betalingsverkeer?" In *Prae-Adviezen voor de Vereeniging voor de Staatshuishoudkunde en de Statistiek*, 1–53. 's-Gravenhage: Martinus Nijhoff.

1950. *De Betekenis van het Sparen voor het Herstel van de Volkswelvaart*. Amersfoort: Nederlandse Spaarbankbond.

1950. "Het Evenwicht in de Dollarbalans." *Internationale Spectator* 4 (17): 1–4.

1951. "Boekbespreking van C. Clark's *The Conditions of Economic Progress*." *De Economist* 99: 540–41.

1951. *Business Cycles in the United Kingdom 1870–1914*. Amsterdam: North Holland.

1951. "De Centrale Gedachte van de Correlatierekening." *Statistica Neerlandica* 5: 3–6.

1951. *Econometrics.* London: Allen & Unwin.

1951. "Reformulation of Current Business Cycle Theories as Refutable Hypotheses." In *Conference on Business Cycles NBER,* 131–48.

1951. "Schumpeter and Quantitative Research in Economics." *The Review of Economics and Statistics* 33 (2): 109–11.

1952. "Actuele Economische Problemen van India." *Economisch-Statistische Berichten* 37 (1808): 41–43.

1952. "De Economist En Het Sociale Vraagstuk." *De Economist* 100: 1011–24.

1952. "Goudriaans Analystische Economie." *De Economist* 100: 401–10.

1952. "India's Five Year Plan." *Berita Mapie* 2 (10): 8–10.

1952. "On the Theory of Economic Integration." *Les Cahiers de Bruges* 2 (4): 292–309.

1953. "De Levensomstandigheden in India." *Economisch-Statistische Berichten* 38 (1882): 494–95.

1953. "The Analysis of Unemployment Figures and the Alleged Correspondence between Causes and Cures." *Metroeconomica* 5 (2): 43–49.

1954. "Antwoord Prof. Tinbergen op Erepromotie." *Folia Civitatis* 8 (2): 1–2.

1954. *Centralization and Decentralization in Economic Policy.* Amsterdam: North Holland.

1954. "De Voorspelling en de Beïnvloeding van de Conjunctuur." *Socialisme en Democratie* 11 (3): 169–77.

1954. "Het Economisch Aspect." In *Het Deltaplan, Afdamming Zee-Armen: Prae-Adviezen voor de Jaarlijkse Algemene Vergadering te Maastricht op 17 Juni 1954,* 29–54. Haarlem: Nederlandsche Maatschappij voor Nijverheid en Handel.

1954. *International Economic Integration.* Amsterdam: Elsevier.

1955. "Algunas Técnicas de Planeación del Desarrollo." *El Trimestre Económico* 22: 401–20.

1956. *Economic Policy: Principles and Design.* Amsterdam: North Holland.

1956. "On the Theory of Income Distribution." *Weltwirtschaftliches Archiv* 77 (2): 155–75.

1956. "The Optimum Rate of Saving." *The Economic Journal* 66 (264): 603–9.

1957. "De Internationale Taak van de Sociaal-Democratie." *Socialisme en Democratie* 14 (2): 84–89.

1957. "Internationale Socialistische Politiek." *Socialisme en Democratie* 14 (11): 666–71.

1957. "Welfare Economics and Income Distribution." *The American Economic Review: Papers and Proceedings* 47 (2): 490–503.

1958. "Meer Economisch Begrip tussen Oost en West." *Wending* 13 (8): 523–31.

1958. *The Design of Development.* Baltimore, MD: Johns Hopkins University Press.

1959. "Inflatie, Integratie en Maatschappelijke Orde: Antwoord aan Professor Witteveen." *Economisch-Statistische Berichten* 44 (2188): 476–77.

1959. "International Co-ordination of Stabilizaiton and Development Policies." *Kyklos* 12 (3): 283–89.

1959. "The Theory of the Optimum Regime." In *Selected Papers,* edited by L. H. Klaassen, L. M. Koyck, and H. J. Witteveen, 264–304. Amsterdam: North Holland.

1960. "Europe and the World." In *Sciences humaines et Intégration Européene,* edited by H. Brugmans, L. Cerych, and M. J. Lory, 379–85. Leiden: A. W. Sythoff.

1960. "Optimum Savings and Utility Maximization over Time." *Econometrica* 28 (2): 481–89.

1960. *Regional Planning: Some Principles.* Rotterdam: Netherlands Economic Institute.

1960. "The Impact of the European Economic Community on Third Countries." In *Sciences humaines et Intégration Européene,* edited by H. Brugmans, L. Cerych, and M. J. Lory, 386–98. Leiden: A. W. Sythoff.

1961. "Do Communist and Free Economies Show a Converging Pattern?" *Soviet Studies* 12 (4): 333–41.

1961. "Oost-West-Gesprekken." *Economisch-Statistische Berichten* 46 (2279): 323.

1961. "Sociaal-Economische Aspecten van het Deltaplan." In *Rapport Deltacommissie, Dl. 6,* 61–74. Den Haag: Staatsdrukkerij.

1962. "Planning in Stages." *Statsøkonomisk Tidsskrift* 76 (1): 1–20.

1962. *Shaping the World Economy.* New York: Twentieth Century Fund.

1962. "Voorspellingen in Politiek, Economie en Sociologie." *Nederlandsch Tijdschrift voor de Psychologie* 17 (3): 193–97.

1963. "Economic Planning for Development." In *Ambassadors Days at the Netherlands Trade Promotion Centre,* edited by S. J. van den Bergh, 8–12. The Hague: Netherlands Trade Promotion Centre.

1963. "Introductory Remarks on the 'Ization Problem.'" *Zeitschrift für die gesamte Staatswissenschaft* 119 (2): 328–33.

1963. *Lessons from the Past.* Amsterdam: Elsevier.

1963. "The Appraisal of Investment Projects." Rotterdam: Netherlands Economic Institute.

1964. "Boekbespreking van M. Bornstein En D. R. Fusfeld's *The Soviet Economy: A Book of Readings* & F. D. Holzman's *Readings on the Soviet Economy.*" *De Economist* 112: 58–60.

1964. *Central Planning.* New Haven, CT: Yale University Press.

1964. "Education and Economic Growth: A Reply." *Kyklos* 17 (2): 274–75.

1964. "Probleme der modernen Türkei." *Bustan* 5 (4): 24–31.

1965. "De Toekomstige Sociale Orde en onze Beweging." *Socialisme en Democratie* 22 (11): 728–43.

1965. "Ideologies and Scientific Development." *Review of International Affairs* 16 (372): 6–7.

1965. "International, National, Regional and Local Industries." In *Trade, Growth, and the Balance of Payments: Essays in Honor of Gottfried Haberler,* edited by Richard E. Caves, Harry G. Johnson, and Peter B. Kenen, 116–25. Chicago: Rand McNally.

1966. "On the Optimal Social Order and a World Economic Policy: A Discussion with Professor Lev Leontiev." *Oost-West* 5 (10): 242–44.

1966. "Ontwikkelingshulp in Wereldperspectief." In *10 Jaar Novib. 10 Jaar Ontwikkelingshulp,* 52–55. 's-Gravenhage: NOVIB.

1967. *Development Planning.* London: World University Library.

1970. *Een Leefbare Aarde.* Amsterdam: Agon Elsevier.

1971. *Meten in de Menswetenschappen.* Assen: Van Gorcum.

1972. "De Convergentietheorie: Antikritiek." In *Mens en Keuze,* edited by H. de Haan, S. K. Kuipers, and J. K. T. Postma, 1–12. Amsterdam: Noord-Hollandse Uitgevers Maatschappij.

1972. "How Should the Future Be Studied?" In *Possible Futures of European Education*, edited by Stefan Jensen, 109–33. The Hague: Martinus Nijhoff.

1973. *Komt er wel een Post-Economisch Tijdperk*. Amsterdam: Agon Elsevier.

1973. "Some Thoughts on Mature Socialism." In *Studies in Economic Planning over Space and Time*, edited by George G. Judge and Takashi Takayama, 9–25. Amsterdam: North Holland.

1974. *Hoe kunnen wij Machtsstructuren Veranderen?* Zwolle: W. E. J. Tjeenk Willink.

1975. *Het Leerproces der Openbare Mening*. Groningen: H. D. Tjeenk Willink.

1975. *Income Distribution: Analysis and Policies*. New York: North Holland.

1976. *Reshaping the International Order: A Report to the Club of Rome*. New York: New American Library.

1978. "De Beste Sociale Orde." *AR Staatkunde* 48 (12): 469–75.

1981. "Will Western Civilization Survive?" *Coexistence* 18 (1): 1–4.

1982. "Kan de Economische Wetenschap Bijdragen tot de Ontwikkeling van het Recht?" In *In Orde: Liber Amicorum Pieter Verloren van Themaat*, 295–300. Deventer: Kluwer.

1984. "Alternative Optimal Social Orders." *The Pakistan Development Review* 23: 1–7.

1984. "Coexistence: From the Past to the Future." *Coexistence* 21: 3–6.

1984. "Development Cooperation as a Learning Process." In *Pioneers of Development*, edited by Gerald M. Meier, 315–34. Oxford: Oxford University Press.

1984. "Ik Heb Geluk Gehad . . ." In *Dienstweigeraars: Over Dienstweigering en Verzet tegen het Militarisme vanaf de Eeuwwisseling Tot Nu*, edited by Guus Termeer, 74–79. Amsterdam: LINK.

1984. "My Life Philosophy." *The American Economist* 28 (2): 5–8.

1985. "Measurability of Utility (or Welfare)." *De Economist* 133: 411–14.

1987. "Het Getal Twee is van Keynes." *Economisch-Statistische Berichten* 72 (3632): 1092.

1987. *Kunnen Wij de Aarde Beheren?* Kampen: Kok Agora.

1987. "Over Modellen." In *Lessen uit het Verleden: 125 Jaar Vereniging voor de Staathuishoudkunde*, edited by A. Knoester, 99–112. 's-Gravenhage: Vereniging voor de Staathuishoudkunde.

1987. "The Tension Theory of Welfare." In *Arrow and the Foundations of the Theory of Economic Policy*, edited by George R. Feiwel, 410–20. New York: Macmillan.

1989. "A Socialism for the USA?" *Coexistence* 26 (2): 213–17.

1989. "Ideologische Harmonisatie tussen Oost en West?" *Economisch-Statistische Berichten* 74 (3736): 1203.

1990. "Conventional and New Thinking in Defence Economics." *Defence Economics* 1 (2): 121–28.

1990. *World Security and Equity*. Aldershot: Edward Elgar.

1991. *Entering the Third Millennium*. Rotterdam: P. J. Fijan Publications.

1992. "Solving the Most Urgent Problems First." In *Eminent Economists: Their Life Philosophies*, edited by Michael Szenberg, 275–82. Cambridge: Cambridge University Press.

Tinbergen, Jan, and Hendricus C. Bos. 1962. *Mathematical Models of Economic Growth*. New York: McGraw-Hill.

1965. "Appraisal of the Model and Results of Its Application." In *Econometric Models of Education: Some Applications*, 95–99. Paris: OECD.

Tinbergen, Jan, and J. B. D. Derksen. 1941. "Nederlandsch-Indië in Cijfers." In *Daar wèrd wat Groots Verricht . . .*, edited by W. H. van Helsdingen and H. Hoogenberk, 495–512. Amsterdam: Elsevier.

Tinbergen, Jan, and Dietrich Fischer. 1987. *Warfare and Welfare: Integrating Security into Socio-economic Policy*. Sussex: Wheatsheaf Books.

Tinbergen, Jan, and Roefie Hueting. 1992. "GNP and Market Prices: Wrong Signals for Sustainable Economic Success That Mask Environmental Destruction." In *Population, Technology and Lifestyle: The Transition to Sustainability*, edited by Robert Goodland, Herman E. Daly, and Salah El Serafy, 52–62. Washington, DC: Island Press.

Tinbergen, Jan, and K. P. van der Mandele. 1958. *Redevoeringen Uitgesproken ter Gelegenheid van de Ere-Promotie van Mr. K. P. van der Mandele*. Rotterdam: Nederlandse Economische Hoogeschool.

Tinbergen, Jan, and Jacques J. Polak. 1950. *The Dynamics of Business Cycles: A Study in Economic Fluctuations*. Chicago: University of Chicago Press.

Tinbergen, Jan, and H. M. A. van der Werff. 1953. "Four Alternative Policies to Restore Balance of Payments Equilibrium: A Comment and an Extension." *Econometrica* 21 (2): 332–35.

Tinbergen, Jan, Henk Linneman, and Jan P. Pronk. 1966. "The Meeting of the Twain." *The Columbia Journal of World Business* 2 (1): 139–49.

Tinbergen, Jan, J. M. den Uyl, Jan P. Pronk, and Wim Kok. 1981. "A New World Employment Plan." *Peace & Development* 2: 10–20.

Tompitak, Marco, and Danny Beckers. 2015. "Solide en Gedegen Onderwijs. Wiskunde en Natuurkunde Onderwijsdiscussies in de Jaren 1920 als Monitor voor Disciplinevorming." *Studium: Tijdschrift voor Wetenschaps- en Universiteitsgeschiedenis* 8 (2): 84–100.

Tooze, Adam J. 2001. *Statistics and the German. State, 1900–1945: The Making of Modern Economic Knowledge*. Cambridge: Cambridge University Press.

Toporowski, Jan. 2013. *Michał Kalecki: An Intellectual Biography*. London: Palgrave Macmillan.

Torun, O. N. 1967. "The Establishment and Structure of the State Planning Organization." In *Planning in Turkey*, edited by S. Ilkin and E. Inanç, 44–70. Ankara: Faculty of Administrative Sciences.

Türkcan, Ergun. 2010. *Attila Sönmez'e Armağan: Türkiye'de Planlamanın Yükselişi ve Çöküşü 1960–1980*. Istanbul: İstanbul Bilgi Üniversitesi.

Tworek, Heidi J. S. 2019. "Communicable Disease: Information, Health, and Globalization in the Interwar Period." *The American Historical Review* 124 (3): 813–42.

Ünay, Sadik. 2006. *The Political Economy of Development Planning in Turkey: Neoliberal Globalization and Institutional Reform*. New York: Nova Science Publishers.

United Nations. 1949. *Maintenance of Full Employment*. Publication no. 1949.II.A.2. New York: United Nations.

1951. "Measures for the Economic Development of Under-developed Countries." New York.

United Nations Development Programme. 1994. *Human Development Report 1994*. New York: Oxford University Press.

Valk, W. L. 1928. "Een Poging, om het Grensnut te Meten." *De Economist* 77: 202–7.

Vanek, Jaroslav. 1964. "Review of *Shaping the World Economy* by Jan Tinbergen." *The Review of Economics and Statistics* 46 (1): 99–101.

Verwey-Jonker, Hilda. 1936. "Plan en Internationalisme." In *Handboek voor het Plan van de Arbeid*, edited by Floor Wibaut, 135–42. Amsterdam: Arbeiderspers.

   1938. "Vijf en Twintig Jaar Socialistische Theorie." In *Ir. J. W. Albarda: Een Kwart Eeuw Parlementaire Werkzaamheid in Dienst van de Bevrijding der Nederlandse Arbeidersklasse: Een Beeld van de Groei der Nederlandse Volksgemeenschap*, edited by E. Boekman, 330–48. Amsterdam: Arbeiderspers.

Vooys, C. G. N. de. 1916. "Iets over Woordvorming en Woordbetekenis in Kindertaal." *De Nieuwe Taalgids* 10: 93–100.

Vooys, C. G. N. de, J. H. van den Bosch, and Dirk Cornelis Tinbergen. 1919. *Letterkundig Leesboek Voor Hoogere Burgerscholen, Gymnasia En Kweekscholen.* Groningen: Wolters.

Vos, Hein. 1936. *Waar het op Staat: Het Plan van de Arbeid Verdedigd.* Amsterdam: De Arbeiderspers.

   1938. "Recente Literatuur over Openbare Werken en Conjunctuur." *De Economist* 87: 290–315.

   1961. "Naar een Structuurplan." *Socialisme En Democratie* 18 (1): 43–55.

Weintraub, E. Roy. 1991. *Stabilizing Dynamics: Constructing Economic Knowledge.* Cambridge: Cambridge University Press.

   2005. "Roy F. Harrod and the Interwar Years." *History of Political Economy* 37 (1): 133–55.

Wertheim, W. F. 1976. *Tien Jaar Onrecht in Indonesië: Militaire Dictatuur en Internationale Steun.* Amsterdam: Van Gennep.

Wigbold, Herman. 1955. "Alles is maar Betrekkelijk!" *Het Vrije Volk*, 11 June, p. 5.

Wijk, Hein van. 1935. "Plan-Politiek en Plan-Socialisme." *Fundament* 2 (12): 22.

Wiles, Peter. 1965. "Review of *Central Planning* by Jan Tinbergen." *The American Economic Review* 55 (4): 909–10.

Withuis, Jolande. 2016. *Juliana: Vorstin in een Mannenwereld.* Amsterdam: Bezige Bij.

Witte-Rang, M. E. 2008. *Geen Recht de Moed te Verliezen. Leven en Werken van Dr. H.M. de Lange (1919–2001).* Utrecht: Boekencentrum.

Yılmaz, Aslı. 2012. "Türkiye'de Planlama Politikası ve Yönetimi." PhD dissertation, Ankara University.

Zamora, Daniel, and Anton Jager. 2020. "Free from Our Labors and Joined Back to Nature: Basic Income and the Politics of Post-Work in France and the Low Countries." In *Basic Income: An Intellectual History.*

Ziliak, Steve T., and Deirdre N. McCloskey. 2008. *The Cult of Statistical Significance.* Ann Arbor, MI: University of Michigan Press.

Index

Index   457

Dupriez, Leon, 171
Dutch Royal Society of Economics (KVS), 129, 141, 146
Dutch Youth League for the Study of Nature (NJN), 25–26
dynamic economic theory, 76, 86, 132–35, 137, 139–40, 150–51, 207, 234, 237

econometric models, 143, 150, 154, 164, 223, 232, 247–48
Econometric Society, 61, 85, 90, 93, 134, 141, 202, 267
econometrics, 57, 61, 86, 95, 125–26, 143, 145, 150–51, 181, 209, 223, 227, 243, 247–48, 264–65, 268–69, 274
economic expertise, 43, 95, 115, 190, 208, 210, 215, 221, 224, 231, 240, 248
Economists against the Arms Race (ECAAR), 397
Edgeworth, Francis Y., 70
education planning, 300–3, 370
education reform, 64, 82
Eek, Jeanette van, 17, 23
Ehrenfest, Anna Galinka, 91, 385
Ehrenfest, Paul, 29, 41, 43, 57, 60–71, 73, 75–85, 87–92, 103–6, 126, 135, 148, 153, 164, 205, 345, 377, 385, 413
Ehrenfest Colloquium, 64–65, 67, 332
Einstein, Albert, 60–62, 68, 75, 77, 85, 88
elasticity, 151, 275
emancipation, 89–90, 103, 201, 211, 214, 216, 279
enlightened self-interest, 278
environmentalism, 307
equality, 92, 100
equilibrium (in economics), 129, 131–33, 136, 139–40, 146, 148, 150, 173, 209, 223, 247, 281
Erasmus, Desiderius, 53
Erasmus Prize, 420–21
Erhard, Ludwig, 311
ethology, 26–28
Eucken, Walter, 208, 416
eugenics, 196
European Economic Community., 280
European Union, 55, 280, 351
ex-ante and ex-post values, 233
expectations (in economics), 33, 132–33, 135, 138, 233, 237

fascism, 95–96, 104–5, 107, 111–12, 120–24, 132, 138, 204–5, 208, 337, 354
federalism, 10, 400

Film Classification Board, 344
Fisher, Irving, 223, 377
Fleddérus, Mary L., 107, 110
Food and Agricultural Organization (FAO), 331
Ford, Henry, 71, 82, 106, 118
Ford Foundation, 295
Foucault, Michel, 429
France, 85, 114, 169, 174, 204, 211, 217, 282, 356
Franco, Francisco, 354
Frank, Leonhard, 33–35
free enterprise, 138, 347
free trade, 280
Frisch, Ragnar, 77, 85, 111, 125, 133–34, 140, 143–44, 157, 164, 173, 175–76, 178–81, 184, 186, 202, 204, 209, 223, 226, 233, 235, 237–39, 242–43, 247, 312, 348, 378

Galbraith, John Kenneth, 342, 358
Gandhi, Mahatma, 261, 338, 359
Geertz, Clifford, 364, 369
General Agreement for Tariffs and Trade (GATT), 297, 404
general interest, 112, 345
Geneva, 149, 154, 166, 171, 173, 185, 188, 212, 227, 261
Germany, 15, 33, 45, 53, 68, 71–72, 78–79, 85, 97, 104, 109, 115, 124, 130–31, 138, 142, 165, 169, 171, 174, 187, 190, 193, 195–98, 201, 203–4, 207–8, 212, 216, 245, 276, 282, 343, 346, 353, 360, 375, 393
Gini, Corrado, 72
global south, 14, 298
God, 88, 360
Goes van Naters, Marinus van der, 38, 42, 50, 120, 211, 215, 410
Gorbachev, Michael, 358
Goudriaan, Jan, 78–79, 104–7, 148, 204, 223, 247–48, 252
Great Britain, 170–71, 282
Great Depression, 41, 78–79, 94, 109, 111, 130, 137–38, 140, 152, 169, 187, 201, 341
Grotius (Hugo de Groot), 10, 408
Group of 77 (G-77), 402

Haavelmo, Trygve, 175, 180, 223, 227
Haberler, Gustav, 169–73, 175–82, 185–86, 189, 297
Hanau, Arthur, 125, 128, 135, 140
Hansen, Bent, 171, 421

Other Books in the Series (*continued from page ii*)

Samuel Hollander, *The Economics of Karl Marx: Analysis and Applications* (2008)

Donald Moggridge, *Harry Johnson: A Life in Economics* (2008)

Filippo Cesarano, *Monetary Theory and Bretton Woods: The Construction of an International Monetary Order* (2006)

Timothy Davis, *Ricardo's Macroeconomics: Money, Trade Cycles, and Growth* (2005)

Jerry Evensky, *Adam Smith's Moral Philosophy: A Historical and Contemporary Perspective on Markets, Law, Ethics, and Culture* (2005)

Harro Maas, *William Stanley Jevons and the Making of Modern Economics (2005)*

Anthony M. Endres, Grant A. Fleming, *International Organizations and the Analysis of Economic Policy, 1919–1950* (2002)

David Laidler, *Fabricating the Keynesian Revolution: Studies of the Inter-War Literature on Money, the Cycle, and Unemployment* (1999)

Esther-Mirjam Sent, *The Evolving Rationality of Rational Expectations: An Assessment of Thomas Sargent's Achievements* (1998)

Heath Pearson, *Origins of Law and Economics: The Economists' New Science of Law, 1830–1930* (1997)

Odd Langholm, *The Legacy of Scholasticism in Economic Thought: Antecedents of Choice and Power* (1998)

Yuichi Shionoya, *Schumpeter and the Idea of Social Science* (1997)

J. Daniel Hammond, *Theory and Measurement: Causality Issues in Milton Friedman's Monetary Economics* (1996)

William J. Barber, *Designs within Disorder: Franklin D. Roosevelt, the Economists, and the Shaping of American Economic Policy, 1933–1945* (1996)

Juan Gabriel Valdes, *Pinochet's Economists: The Chicago School of Economics in Chile* (1995)

Philip Mirowski (ed.), *Natural Images in Economic Thought: "Markets Read in Tooth and Claw"* (1994)

Malcolm Rutherford, *Institutions in Economics: The Old and the New Institutionalism* (1994)

Karen I. Vaughn, *Austrian Economics in America: The Migration of a Tradition* (1994)

Lars Jonung (ed.), *The Stockholm School of Economics Revisited* (1991)

E. Roy Weintraub, *Stabilizing Dynamics: Constructing Economic Knowledge* (1991)

M. June Flanders, *International Monetary Economics, 1870–1960: Between the Classical and the New Classical* (1990)

Philip Mirowski, *More Heat Than Light: Economics as Social Physics, Physics as Nature's Economics* (1990)

Mary S. Morgan, *The History of Econometric Ideas* (1990)

Gerald M. Koot, *English Historical Economics, 1870–1926: The Rise of Economic History and Mercantilism* (1988)

Kim Kyun, *Equilibrium Business Cycle Theory in Historical Perspective* (1988)

From New Era to New Deal: Herbert Hoover, the Economists, and American Economic Policy, 1921–1933 (1985)

Takashi Negishi, *Economic Theories in a Non-Walrasian Tradition* (1985)